C000009346

HARDPRESS.NET
HOME OF HARD-TO-FIND BOOKS

Belgravia
by Mary Elizabeth Braddon

Copyright © 2019 by HardPress

Address:
HardPress
8345 NW 66TH ST #2561
MIAMI FL 33166-2626
USA
Email: info@hardpress.net

Belgravia

Mary Elizabeth Braddon

26.2

.54

Harvard College Library

FROM

Charles Boucher

BELGRAVIA

AN

Illustrated London Magazine

Lol 3o

VOL. XXX.

JULY to OCTOBER 1876

London

CHATTO AND WINDUS, PICCADILLY

1876

[*All rights reserved*]

HARVARD COLLEGE LIBRARY
MAR 5 1903
CAMBRIDGE, MASS.

Charles Roucher,
N. Y. City.

LONDON : PRINTED BY
SPOTTISWOODE AND CO., NEW-STREET SQUARE
AND PARLIAMENT STREET

CONTENTS OF VOL. XXX.

iv

LIST OF ILLUSTRATIONS.

PRICE ONE SHILLING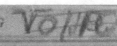

Vol. XXX.

No. 117.

BELGRAVIA

A LONDON MAGAZINE

JULY
1876

CHATTO & WINDUS, PICCADILLY, LONDON, W.

J. & P. COATS'
BEST SOFT 6-CORD
SEWING COTTON.
SUITABLE FOR
ALL SEWING MACHINES.

SEWING
EXTRA GLACÉ COTTON.
This Cotton being greatly improved in
quality and finish, will be found unsurpassed for
Machine or Hand Sewing.
On Reels, 100, 200, or 500 Yards.

COTTON
CROCHET OR
TATTING COTTON,
Unsurpassed in Quality.

To be had of all Wholesale & Retail Drapers throughout the United Kingdom.

Johnston's

'Quite free from Adulteration.'
—*Lancet.*

Corn Flour

Is the Best.

'Is decidedly superior.'
—*Lancet.*

LADIES TRAVELLING,
Exposed to the hot sun and dust,
will find

ROWLANDS'
KALYDOR

Most cooling and refreshing for the face
and hands; it eradicates Sunburn, Tan,
Freckles, &c.
4s. 6d. and 8s. 6d. per bottle.

THE HOT SUN
Has a very injurious effect on the hair,
but

ROWLANDS'
MACASSAR OIL

Prevents it falling off or becoming dry.
Price 3s. 6d., 7s., 10s. 6d. (equal to four
small bottles), and 21s.

ASK ANY CHEMIST, PERFUMER, OR HAIRDRESSER FOR ROWLANDS' ARTICLES, AND AVOID IMITATIONS.

KINAHAN'S L.L. WHISKY

the most delicious and mellow spirit is the very
CREAM OF IRISH
In quality unrivalled, perfectly pure and more
than finest Cognac Brandy. None

KINAHAN'S L.L. WHISKY

On Seal, Label, and Cork. Wholesale Depot,
20 GREAT TITCHFIELD STREET, OXFORD STREET, W.

'THE WINDOW WAS LIKE A PICTURE-FRAME.'

BELGRAVIA.

JULY 1876.

GOOD STORIES OF MAN AND OTHER ANIMALS.

BY CHARLES READE.

2. A Special Constable.

TWO women, sisters, kept the toll-bar at a village in Yorkshire. It stood apart from the village, and they often felt uneasy at night, being lone women.

One day they received a considerable sum of money, bequeathed them by a relative, and that set the simple souls all in a flutter.

They had a friend in the village, the blacksmith's wife; so they went and told her their fears. She admitted that theirs was a lonesome place, and she would not live there, for one—without a man. Her discourse sent them home downright miserable.

The blacksmith's wife told her husband all about it, when he came in for his dinner. 'The fools!' said he: 'how is anybody to know they have got brass in the house?'

'Well,' said the wife, 'they make no secret of it to me; but you need not go for to tell it to all the town—poor souls.'

'Not I,' said the man: 'but they will publish it, never fear; leave women-folk alone for making their own trouble with their tongues.'

There the subject dropped, as man and wife have things to talk about besides their neighbours.

The old women at the toll-bar, what with their own fears, and their Job's comforter, began to shiver with apprehension as night came on. However, at sunset the carrier passed through the gate; and at sight of his friendly face they brightened up. They told him their care, and begged him to sleep in the house that night. 'Why, how can I?' said he. 'I'm due at *; but I will leave you my dog.' The dog was a powerful mastiff.

The women looked at each other expressively. 'He won't hurt us, will he?' sighed one of them, faintly. 'Not he,' said the carrier cheerfully. Then he called the dog into the house, and told them to lock the door; and went away whistling.

The women were left contemplating the dog with that tender interest apprehension is sure to excite. At first he seemed staggered at this off-hand proceeding of his master; it confused him; then he snuffed at the door; then, as the wheels retreated, he began to see plainly he was an abandoned dog; he delivered a fearful howl, and flew at the door, scratching and barking furiously.

The old women fled the apartment, and were next seen at an upper window, screaming to the carrier. 'Come back!—come back, John! He is tearing the house down.'

'Drat the varmint!' said John; and came back. On the road he thought what was best to be done. The good-natured fellow took his great coat out of the cart, and laid it down on the floor. The mastiff instantly laid himself on it. 'Now,' said John, sternly, 'let us have no more nonsense; you take charge of that till I come back, and don't ye let nobody steal that there, nor yet t' wives' brass. There now,' said he, kindly, to the women, 'I shall be back this way breakfast time, and he won't budge till then.'

'And he won't hurt *us*, John?'

'Lord, no. Bless your heart, he is as sensible as any Christian; only, Lordsake, woman, don't ye go to take the coat from him; or you'll be wanting a new gown yourself, and maybe, a petticoat and all.'

He retired, and the old women kept at a respectful distance from their protector. He never molested them; and, indeed, when they spoke cajolingly to him, he even wagged his tail in a dubious way; but still, as they moved about, he squinted at them out of his blood-shot eye in a way that checked all desire, on their parts, to try on the carrier's coat.

Thus protected, they went to bed earlier than usual; but they did not undress, they were too much afraid of everything, especially their protector. The night wore on, and presently their sharpened senses let them know that the dog was getting restless: he snuffed, and then he growled, and then he got up and pattered about, muttering to himself. Straightway, with furniture, they barricaded the door, through which their protector must pass to devour them.

But by and by, listening acutely, they heard a scraping and a grating outside the window of the room where the dog was; and he continued growling low. This was enough; they slipped out at the back door, and left their money to save their lives: they got into the village. It was pitch dark, and all the houses black but two: one was the public-house, casting a triangular gleam across the road a long way off, and the other was the blacksmith's house. Here was a piece of fortune for the terrified women. They burst into their friend's house. 'Oh Jane! the thieves are come!' and they told her in a few words all that had happened.

'La!' said she; 'how timoursome you are: ten to one he was only growling at some one that passed by.'

'Nay, Jane, we heard the scraping outside the window; oh, woman, call your man, and let him go with us.'

'My man—he is not here.'

'Where is he, then?'

'I suppose he is where other working women's husbands are — at the public-house,' said she rather bitterly, for she had her experience.

The old women wanted to go to the public-house for him, but the blacksmith's wife was a courageous woman, and, besides, she thought it was most likely a false alarm. 'Nay, nay,' said she, 'last time I went for him there, I got a fine affront. I'll come with you,' said she. 'I'll take the poker, and we have got our tongues to raise the town with, I suppose.' So they marched to the toll-bar. When they got near it, they saw something that staggered this heroine. There was actually a man half in and half out of the window. This brought the blacksmith's wife to a stand-still, and the timid pair implored her to go back to the village. 'Nay,' said she, 'what for? I see but one—and—hark! it is my belief the dog is holding of him.' However, she thought it safest to be on the same side with the dog, lest the man might turn on her. So she made her way into the kitchen, followed by the other two; and there a sight met their eyes that changed all their feelings, both towards the robber and towards each other. The great mastiff had pinned a man by the throat, and was pulling at him, to draw him through the window, with fierce but muffled snarls. The man's weight alone prevented it. The window was like a picture frame, and in that frame there glared, with lolling tongue and starting eyes, the white face of the blacksmith, their courageous friend's villanous husband. She uttered an appalling scream, and flew upon the dog and choked him with her two hands. He held, and growled, and tore, till he was all but throttled himself; then he let go, and the man fell. But what struck the ground outside, like a lump of lead, was, in truth, a lump of clay; the man was quite dead, and fearfully torn about the throat. So did a comedy end in an appalling and most piteous tragedy; not that the scoundrel himself deserved any pity, but his poor brave honest

wife, to whom he had not dared confide the villany he meditated.

The outlines of this true story were in several journals. I have
put the disjointed particulars together as well as I could. I have
tried to learn the name of the village, and what became of this
poor widow, but have failed hitherto. Should these lines meet
the eye of anyone who can tell me, I hope he will, and without
delay.

A Song in Season.

BY ALGERNON CHARLES SWINBURNE.

I.

Thou whose beauty
Knows no duty
Due to love that moves thee never,
Thou whose mercies
Are men's curses,
And thy smile a scourge for ever,

II.

Thou that givest
Death and livest
On the death of thy sweet giving,
Thou that sparest
Not nor carest
Though thy scorn leave no love living,

III.

Thou whose rootless
Flower is fruitless
As the pride its heart encloses,
But thine eyes are
As May skies are,
And thy words like spoken roses,

IV.

Thou whose grace is
In men's faces
Fierce and wayward as thy will is,
Thou whose peerless
Eyes are tearless,
And thy thoughts as cold sweet lilies,

A SONG IN SEASON.

V.

Thou that takest
Hearts and makest
Wrecks of loves to strew behind thee,
Whom the swallow
Sure should follow,
Finding summer where we find thee,

VI.

Thou that wakest
Hearts and breakest,
And thy broken hearts forgive thee,
That wilt make no
Pause and take no
Gift that love for love might give thee,

VII.

Thou that bindest
Eyes and blindest,
Serving worst who served thee longest ;
Thou that speakest,
And the weakest
Heart is his that was the strongest ;

VIII.

Take in season
Thought with reason ;
Think what gifts are ours for giving ;
Hear what beauty
Owes of duty
To the love that keeps it living.

IX.

Dust that covers
Long dead lovers
Song blows off with breath that brightens ;
At its flashes
Their white ashes
Burst in bloom that lives and lightens.

x.

Had they bent not
Head or lent not
Ear to love and amorous duties,
Song had never
Saved for ever
Love, the least of all their beauties.

xi.

All the golden
Names of olden
Women yet by men's love cherished,
All our dearest
Thoughts hold nearest,
Had they loved not, all had perished.

xii.

If no fruit is
Of thy beauties,
Tell me yet, since none may win them,
What and wherefore
Love should care for
Of all good things hidden in them ?

xiii.

Pain for profit
Comes but of it,
If the lips that lure their lover's
Hold no treasure
Past the measure
Of the lightest hour that hovers.

xiv.

If they give not
Or forgive not
Gifts or thefts for grace or guerdon,
Love that misses
Fruit of kisses
Long will bear no thankless burden.

A SONG IN SEASON.

XV.

If they care not
Though love were not,
If no breath of his burn through them,
Joy must borrow
Song from sorrow,
Fear teach hope the way to woo them.

XVI.

Grief has measures
Soft as pleasure's,
Fear has moods that hope lies deep in,
Songs to sing him,
Dreams to bring him,
And a red-rose bed to sleep in.

XVII.

Hope with fearless
Looks and tearless
Lies and laughs too near the thunder;
Fear hath sweeter
Speech and meeter
For heart's love to hide him under.

XVIII.

Joy by daytime
Fills his playtime
Full of songs loud mirth takes pride in;
Night and morrow
Weave round sorrow
Thoughts as soft as sleep to hide in.

XIX.

Graceless faces,
Loveless graces
Are but motes in light that quicken,
Sands that run down
Ere the sundown,
Rose-leaves dead ere autumn sicken.

XX.

Fair and fruitless
Charms are bootless
Spells to ward off age's peril :
Lips that give not
Love shall live not,
Eyes that meet not eyes are sterile.

XXI.

But the beauty
Bound in duty
Fast to love that falls off never,
Love shall cherish
Lest it perish,
And its root bears fruit for ever.

Joshua Haggard's Daughter.

BY THE AUTHOR OF 'LADY AUDLEY'S SECRET.'

CHAPTER XIX.

'TWO SOULS MAY SLEEP AND WAKE UP ONE.'

IT was about a week after Mr. Pentreath had begun Werther, and he was now approaching the end of the story, when he came to the minister's house at his usual hour, and found Cynthia sitting alone in the parlour. Naomi had a headache, and had gone upstairs to lie down. It was not often that Joshua Haggard's daughter gave way to any such feminine ailment, and it was a surprise to Oswald to find her absent. He had been riding among his farms all the morning, looking at ancient tiled roofs that had a tendency to subside in the middle; at barns and cart-sheds, with mouldering thatches and worm-eaten timbers; at enclosures of meadow-land, where primroses, cowslips, and wild hyacinths grew abundantly, but where the grass was sour for lack of draining.

'I wanted her to rest on the sofa here,' said Cynthia, 'but she fancied she would be better in a darkened room. She has been looking ill for the last few days. I am sometimes afraid '—timidly, and with hesitation—'that she is not quite happy.'

'I am afraid we are none of us quite happy,' answered Oswald, with an undisguised sigh.

Cynthia's needle travelled to and fro with the usual rhythm. It seemed to Oswald as if it were some weary tune to which he was forced to listen.

'Shall I go on with Werther?' he asked presently, after he had looked at the stocks and carnations, and over them at the sleepy old Inn, where the landlord stood in his porch and contemplated his neighbours, like an image of immutability. People who could remember Combhollow twenty years ago, remembered just the same figure in the porch. It had grown a trifle more obese in the twenty years, that was all.

'I would rather you waited till Naomi was well enough to hear the end,' said Cynthia.

'But are not you anxious to know what becomes of that unhappy wretch? Have you no pity for him?' asked Oswald, almost angrily.

'I pity him for being so wretched,' answered Cynthia; 'but I think if he had been good, and wise, and brave, he would have gone far away where he would never have seen Charlotte any more. Instead of writing unhappy letters to his friend he would have prayed to God to help him, and fled from temptation.'

'You will see that in the end he did go away—very far from Charlotte and temptation. But you have seen him in the heat of the battle: you will see him by and by a conqueror—or conquered —whichever you like to call it.'

'Will you let me read the end for myself? You can read it aloud to us both when Naomi is better.'

'No; you shall hear the end, as you have heard the rest—from my lips.'

'But Naomi—' expostulated Cynthia.

'I will read it again to Naomi. Why should I not read it to you this afternoon? You have been more interested in the story than Naomi.'

Cynthia made no further objection, but went on with her work silently. Oswald took his favourite seat by the open window, in the shadow of the chintz curtain, with the spicy odours of stocks and carnations floating in upon the sultry air. They had the room almost entirely to themselves. Aunt Judith came in and out two or three times in the afternoon on some small errand, and looked at the two with a curious expression in her sharp black eyes —a look which might have set Oswald thinking had he been observant enough to notice it. But he was deep in the sorrows of Werther, who was fast approaching his final agony, and Cynthia was listening as she had listened that other day in the wood, with her hands lying idle in her lap, and the glossy white linen she had been working upon crumpled in a heap under those idle hands.

'Very nicely Joshua's new shirts will get on at that rate, and she so eager to set about them,' mused Judith as she went back to the shop, with close-locked lips. 'To think that novel-reading and such abominations should flourish in my brother's house! But what else could be expected of such a marriage? Lucky for Joshua if nothing worse comes of it.'

Oswald read on, in nowise disturbed by Miss Haggard's entrance to look for an account-book in the bureau, or to get her thimble from the chimney-piece. He had come to that scene of abject passion—of self-abandonment and despair—when Werther, having resolved to put an end to his misery, comes in the winter evening to see his idol for the last time. Forgetful of herself for the moment, Charlotte reproaches him for coming. She shrinks from the idea of being alone with him, and recovers her self-possession with an effort. She seats herself at her harpsichord, and begins a minuet ; then asks Werther to read to her his own translation of a part of Ossian, which he brought her a few days ago. Perhaps no scene in the wide range of sentimental fiction surpasses this in restrained power, in suppressed passion. Not a whisper, not a thought of impurity sullies the picture from the first line to the last : there is only a fatal, irresistible love.

'She tore herself from him, and in hopeless bewilderment, trembling between love and anger, she cried : " This is the last time, Werther ! You must see me no more." And casting a look full of love upon the wretched one, she fled into the adjoining room, and shut the door behind her. ' Werther stretched out his arms after her, but dared not detain her. He lay upon the ground, his head on the sofa, and remained in this position for half an hour, until a sudden noise recalled him to himself. It was the servant, who came to lay the table. He walked up and down the room, and when he found himself alone again, went to Charlotte's door, and called in a low voice : " Lotte, Lotte ! only one word—one farewell ! " There was no answer. He waited, and knocked, and waited again—then tore himself away, crying, " Farewell, Lotte ! Farewell, for ever ! "

Cynthia sat listening with dilated eyes and hands tightly clasped, as if the whole scene were reality—as if she could see Werther there, at her feet, grovelling on the ground. There stood the open harpsichord at which Charlotte had been playing. The vivid picture shaped itself before her eyes : the winter evening and home-like fire-lit room ; the hopeless sinner lying there unpitied and alone, the suicide's dark resolve in his mind. And Charlotte knew not his fatal intention. She refused him the poor comfort of a last farewell. No hand was stretched out to save him. It was too awful a picture.

Cynthia clasped her hands before her face, and burst into tears. In the next moment Oswald was on his knees beside her, trying to unclasp those small nervous hands.

'You pity *him*,' he cried, passionately ; ' pity me, then, for I suffer as he suffered ; I love as he loved, and yet have courage to live, and to go on fighting with an invincible passion—though I feel the struggle is vain—and to try to be happy with another—yes, to hold firmly to the tie which once promised happiness, and which now means only bondage. Pity me, Cynthia, pity *me*—not that poor shadow in the book, who lived and suffered, and is dead

'IT IS MY OWN STORY.'

and at rest—for there was such a man. Pity me, Cynthia, for I have loved you and have been fighting against that love ever since that sweet time before my father's death, when you came to his sick-bed as an angel of mercy, and brought woe unutterable to me.'

He had poured forth his confession in a torrent of words not to be arrested by Cynthia's choked sobs or look of horror, or the pleading gesture of her tremulous hands.

'Oswald, how can you be so cruel?'

'Cruel! Is it cruel to suffer, to be miserable, to know myself the worst and weakest of men, and to hate myself—as I do, Cynthia, from my soul? Do you think I have not struggled? Yes, and conquered myself, after a fashion. I am going to marry Naomi, and we are to be a happy couple, as married couples go nowadays—happier than nine out of ten, perhaps, for at least I can admire and respect my wife, and I once believed I loved her, before I knew you and the hidden depths of my own heart, and the meaning of that word "love." Yes, we are going to be vastly happy. The builders are doing wonders for our house, and we shall be thought much of, and looked up to by the neighbourhood. I may keep a pack of hounds, very likely, by and by, and teach my wife to ride across country. I am not going to shoot myself as Werther did.'

'Why did you read that book to me?' asked Cynthia, with a piteous accent that thrilled him. It sounded like an admission of weakness—a faint cry of despair.

'Why?' he cried, trying to take her hands in both his own. 'Can't you understand why? Because it is my own story; because it was my only way of telling you my love; and I burned to tell you. It was an irresistible longing. I could not keep silence any longer: somehow—in some language, if not in plainest speech—I must tell you. And now bid me die, my Charlotte, and I will slay myself like Werther. Only say to me, Life would be easier for all of us if thou wert dead, and I will not live another day to disturb your placid existence. I am your slave, dearest—your abject obedient slave.'

'If you are,' said Cynthia, trembling violently, and paler than the wood anemones she had gathered to deck the old Squire's sick room,—' if you are, you will obey me. Never speak to me again as you have spoken to-day—forget that you have ever been so wicked. Ask your Saviour to give you a better heart, and respect my dear husband and his daughter.'

Before Oswald could answer, honest Sally entered with the big mahogany tea-tray, knowing no more of the thundercloud of passion in the atmosphere than the maid who laid the supper in the story of Werther. Mr. Pentreath had risen from his knees to pace the room after that last speech of his, and there was no extraordinary picture offered to the eye of the hand-maiden. Cynthia folded her work even more carefully than usual, but with hands that trembled sorely. She smoothed the white linen garment which had progressed so slightly towards completion this afternoon, and laid it in its allotted place, and took her stand by the window, watching for her husband's return. She tried to seem at her ease, but not the faintest tinge of colour relieved the absolute pallor of her face. Strangely was that face changed from the radiant countenance that had welcomed Joshua Haggard at Penmoyle, one little year ago.

Oswald walked up and down the parlour while Sally set out the homely feast—a big loaf in an iron tray, a brown butter-pot of Wedgwood ware, a dish of lettuce and overgrown radishes. Anon appeared Miss Haggard; and had either Oswald or Cynthia been in an observant mood, they might have remarked that the industrious Judith had not paid as much attention as usual to her afternoon toilet. The corkscrew curls were somewhat roughened, the large mosaic brooch, which she was wont to put on by way of evening dress, was missing.

'I think I'll go and have a look at the builders,' said Oswald, taking up his hat. 'I'll come round again in the evening, perhaps, and see how Naomi is.'

No one attempted to hinder his going; so, after a brief adieu to the two ladies, he departed, leaving Werther lying on the little round table by the window. Cynthia took up the volume, and turned eagerly to the page at which he had left off reading.

'Ah!' sighed Miss Haggard, 'that's the worst of novel reading. It grows upon people.'

Cynthia neither heeded nor heard. Her thoughts were with the suicide who was roaming bareheaded in the winter night, outside the gates of the little town, not knowing whither or how long he wandered.

Joshua came in while his wife was standing with the open book in her hand, absorbed, unconscious of his entrance.

'Why, little one, how pale you are,' he said, in that gentler tone which his voice assumed unwittingly whenever he spoke to his wife. 'I missed your welcoming look as I came across the street.'

'There's too much novel-reading in this family,' snapped Judith. 'You mustn't expect things to go on as they ought, if you let the young squire bring bad books into your house.'

'This is not a bad book,' cried Cynthia, indignantly. 'It is a beautiful book.'

'I say that it is a bad book,' answered Judith, fiercely. 'And I've good reason to know it—a book that puts bad thoughts into people's heads. Gainsay me if you dare, Mrs. Haggard.'

Cynthia's white face turned from her dumbly. What did she guess—what had she overheard? Something, assuredly. Deepest shame took possession of Joshua's wife. She felt the burden of unspeakable guilt—she who was only the passive object of an unauthorised passion.

'Why, Judith, Cynthia, what is this! Who would dare to bring a wicked book into my house; my son that soon is to be, above all? And if he were capable of doing such a shameful thing, would my wife read the book?'

'It is not wicked,' said Cynthia, handing him the offending Werther. 'It is a story of sorrow—not wickedness. If stories are to be written at all, they must tell of sorrow—and human weakness, and sinfulness. Even the Bible tells us that life is made up of these.'

'Very much so,' remarked Judith. 'There's nothing the Bible says about human nature's wickedness that human nature doesn't faithfully carry out.'

Joshua took the book and glanced at it helplessly. He was not able to take a bird's eye view of plot and style, swoop upon a catchword here and there; and straightway make up his mind that the book was altogether vile, after the manner of certain modern critics. He turned the leaves thoughtfully, saw a story told in a series of letters, much talk of the beauties of nature, a little philosophy, some mention of a country pastor, and children—their innocent gambols in rustic gardens, their affection for a kind elder sister, bread and butter, village life, a pastoral air altogether: not a bad book assuredly, decided Joshua.

'I do not think, my dear Judith, that you are a very acute judge of literature,' he said, mildly.

'Perhaps not,' assented Miss Haggard, with a faint moan. 'But I hope I am a tolerable judge of human nature.'

'I can trust my future son's honour for not bringing any ill-chosen book into my house; and I can trust my wife's purity well enough to know that it would revolt against anything evil.'

'Nothing like trustfulness in this life,' remarked Judith, sententiously, as she took up the teapot.

Now a general proposition—indisputable in its nature though vague in its drift—flung out in this way, has a tendency to instil disquiet into the most tranquil mind. There was not much in the words, but the tone meant a great deal; most of all, a kind of scornful pity. It was like that remark of Iago's anent Michael Cassio's honesty. The plainest, most straightforward observation; yet dropping the poison seed of doubt into the heart of the listener.

Joshua Haggard looked at his sister's pursed-up lips wonderingly, and then at his wife's pale face, in which there was an expression that was new to him.

Great heavens! what did it mean? Not guilt; not the lightest taint of evil? No; he could never believe the faintest shadow of evil of his beloved—not even the most venial deceit, the smallest double-dealing. She was the purest of the pure; pure as the saintly damsels of old—the women who ministered to the apostles in the sweet early dawn of Christianity. He could admit her to be no less pure than these—as white a soul—unsullied by human frailty. He had preached the sinfulness of the human heart—it was the very key-stone of his creed—a sinful humanity in need of being called and regenerated, chosen and purified, redeemed by a vicarious sacrifice. But here he was false to his own theology—he would not admit of original sin in this one pure soul. Love had issued his imperious edict, like a papal bull, and this one woman was to be without sin.

'My love, you are trembling,' said Joshua, taking his wife's cold hand, after a long and earnest scrutiny of the pale sad face. 'There must be something amiss in the book if it has agitated you so.'

'It is a very sorrowful story,' she faltered; 'I could not help crying—at the end.'

'Oswald must bring you no more books to make you unhappy. I heard you all laughing pleasantly one afternoon when he was reading some Scotch book, about an old gentleman and a dog. He must bring you only pleasant books. In a world where there is so much real sorrow, it is foolish and even wrong to waste our tears upon story-books. That is one reason why I have always tried to keep such books out of my house.'

'I will never read such stories again,' said Cynthia earnestly. 'Only tell me how to please you, and I will be obedient in all things.'

Judith sighed audibly. It was a way she had at times, and always exercised a depressing influence upon her family circle.

'Is there anything wrong, Judith?' enquired the minister.

'No, brother; it's only my chest.'

This was her invariable answer; but as medical science had never yet discovered anything amiss in this region—not so much as a brief attack of indigestion—the reply was generally accepted as a sort of formula, and her sighing was taken to mean something which Miss Haggard did not choose to communicate.

'My dearest, you have always been obedient,' said Joshua, pressing his wife's little hand. 'I have never been dissatisfied with you. But I do not like to see you low-spirited about a foolish book, written by some weak-minded German,' said Joshua, with a sublime ignorance as to the pretentions of the great Wolfgang.

'Try me with some hard thing,' exclaimed Cynthia with increasing earnestness; 'put my gratitude and affection to the proof. Do I forget what you have done for me—how you saved me from heathen ignorance? how I owe you all that I am and all that I hope to be? *Could* I be ungrateful to you, my benefactor and my deliverer?'

Had Judith Haggard been a student of Shakespeare, she would have here quoted Ophelia's remark upon the player-queen, inwardly or audibly—

'Methinks the lady doth protest too much!'

But, as her sole notion of the poet was that he had been rather a low and loose-lived person who wrote plays, and glorified much drinking of sack and canary as a cardinal virtue, she relieved her feelings with another sigh, deeper than the last.

'Don't mind me, brother,' she said, 'it's only my chest.'

Joshua neither heard the sigh nor the excuse; his eyes were fixed upon his wife's white face, down which the gathering tears rolled slowly.

'Ungrateful, my love!' he cried; 'have I ever claimed gratitude from you? My part has been to thank God for having given me so dear a companion. Only be happy, my darling; that is the sole obedience I ask from you. Let no foolish fancies out of books disturb your peace of mind. God has given us real happiness, dear; let us be thankful for it and value it, lest the cloud should come upon us because we have made light of the sunshine.'

He drew her to him and kissed her tenderly; and in that hour at least there was no shadow of distrust in his mind.

CHAPTER XX.

'AND ALL IS DROSS THAT IS NOT HELENA.'

IT was some time before Oswald saw his betrothed after that last reading of Werther; and the book remained a broken story for Naomi, who knew not the issue of Werther's fatal love. Cynthia carried the volume up to her own room, and read it, and wept over it in secret, and then hid it under the little stock of ribbons and collars and feminine prettinesses—all of the simplest, most puritanical kind—which she had acquired since she had been Joshua Haggard's wife. She put the book away out of sight, as if it were a guilty thing, feeling that it had brought her face to face with a guilty secret. But for the book, those wicked words of Oswald's might never have been spoken. The sad—the awful, inexpiable guilt would have existed, all the same, in the depths of two erring hearts; but it might never have found a voice. Werther had given form and language to that mysterious and sinful passion—bitterest proof of poor humanity's ingrained iniquity.

'Not by ourselves can we escape sin,' she cried, on her knees, in abject self-abasement. 'We are nothing of ourselves: not even faithful to the most sacred ties—not even true to our own affections—not even pure or constant. Only by Thee, O Redeemer!—only by Thee can we escape the snares our erring hearts set for us; only through Thee can we break loose from the bondage of original sin. Oh, pity him, spotless Saviour—pity this helpless sinner; pity me, for I love him.' She was not afraid to carry this secret sorrow, sinful as it was, to the foot of the cross. Her husband's theology had taught her that Calvary was the sinner's altar—his temple of expiation; the threshold of Heaven, on which all guilty hearts could lay their burdens down, and pass, purified from earthly stain, and liberated from earthly chains, through the golden gate beyond it. The deeper the guilt, the surer welcome for the penitent.

Cynthia's guilt was but a thought—a fond, weak yielding to a dream of impossible happiness; a sinful regret for the things that might have been. She had not stood firmly against the insidious approach of the tempter; she had suffered him to steal upon her footsteps unawares; she had not shut her eyes and refused to see the dangerous, dazzling vision. Passion was an unknown element in this purely sentimental and poetic nature. Love, for Cynthia, could never mean storm and fever, guilt and ruin; but it might mean corroding remorse, a slow and silent despair.

When had she first discovered that something amiss in her placid life—that little rift in the lute which made life's music dumb? Closest self-examination would have scarcely enabled her to answer that question. It might be, perhaps, that on the morning when Oswald parted from her at her husband's door—in the blank sorrow of his face, with its look of mute appeal, in the tears he shed upon her hand as he clasped it in his own—she had faintly understood a secret which was to become plainer to her by and by. The thought, vague though it was at first, had brought sorrow.

She had felt a restraint in the presence of Naomi's lover, and had striven to avoid him. But the days in which she did not see him seemed desolate and empty; and then, not weighing the consequences or meaning of her acts, she weakly yielded to the desire to be in his company, and allowed herself to be the companion of Naomi's walks, the sharer of her lover's attentions. This was the sin she now looked back upon as the black spot in her life—this was when she had suffered the tempter to overtake her steps, to walk by her side.

O happy fatal afternoons in wood or wilderness—on the hills—by the malachite and purple sea! She could see the bright face looking up at her; she could hear the low thrilling voice reading sweet sad verse that seemed to speak straight to her heart—to have been written and meant only for her: she could see and hear the earthly tempter even now, in this hour of penitence and grief.

'Oh! if I had never seen you, if I had never known you, I should have been innocent and true all the days of my life; worthy of Joshua's noble heart.'

She could pray no more. She sat upon the ground, lost in foolish memories, recalling her first days at Combhollow, and all the peaceful time, before she had given up her soul to this guilty dream. She remembered that autumn afternoon, the first time she saw Oswald—she standing by the hearth, with her bonnet in her hand; he coming in at the door.

'And he was nothing to me,' she thought, wonderingly. 'If he had died that night, I should only have been sorry for Naomi's sake.'

She had thought him handsome—different in every way from all other men she had ever seen—a new creature. He was like a picture that Joshua had shown her in an old country-house they went to see in their brief honeymoon—the portrait of a young man in dark-green velvet clothes of a curious fashion, with fair hair falling on his shoulders, and a melancholy look in his eyes. How often she had seen that melancholy look in Oswald's eyes, after the Squire's death, and had known only too well that it was not grief for his father that made him sad!

How gradually it had crept into her heart, this weak, wicked love! Had it come like a bold assailant, she could have repulsed it; but sweetly, slowly, gently, like the tender dawn of a summer morning, this new light had overspread the sky of life. How should she bear her life without it!

'Duty, duty,' she cried, wresting herself from this web of foolish memories. 'Oh, let me remember all I owe my husband; let me remember how I worshipped him one little year ago: what a grace and honour I counted it to be chosen by him. I loved him, because he was the best and wisest of men. He *is* best and wisest—kindest, truest. Whom have I ever known equal to him?'

When Naomi went down to the parlour, a little later than usual, on the morning after that last reading of Werther—languid still from yesterday's headache—she found a letter from Oswald on the chimney-piece. Cynthia was sitting at work by the window—just where *he* had sat yesterday. Judith was washing the breakfast cups and saucers in a little crockery pan which she was accustomed to bring into the parlour for that purpose.

Dearest,—I have made up my mind quite suddenly to go to London, and enquire about Arnold's ship. It seems such a strange thing that I have had no answer to my letters, and I am getting really uneasy. I shall go to Lloyd's —or whatever the right place may be to obtain information about a ship in the merchant-service. Forgive me for going away so suddenly and without waiting to say good-bye. An irresistible impulse took hold of me. I shall only stay long enough to make all needful enquiries and to take a hasty look at the city; and I shall write to tell you how I get on.

God bless you, dear, and goodbye.

Your always affectionate

OSWALD.

Naomi read the letter twice over, surprised at this sudden impulse in Oswald, who was not subject to impulses, or at least not subject to carrying out their promptings when they prompted immediate action. He was rather of a dreamy temperament, never doing anything to-day which he could possibly put off till to-morrow.

She read the letter a third time aloud to Cynthia.

'Did he say anything about this yesterday?' she asked. 'Had he any idea of going to London?'

'I think not,' answered Cynthia, working steadily. Oh, blessed mechanical click-click of the needle, which went on with its measured paces while the pulses of the heart throbbed so stormily! Naomi gave a little sigh as she folded the letter. It was hard to lose him for an indefinite time, were it ever so short. And her wedding-day seemed so far off now. The neglected old Grange no longer awaited her with its sober old-world look—the look it had worn since her infancy. Confusion had fallen upon the old house, and Naomi felt as if she could have no part in the new house which was to arise from this chaos. Money was being spent recklessly to make the grave old mansion fit for a fine lady; and Naomi knew that it was not in her to become a fine lady. All the money in the world would never make her like Mrs. Carew of the Knoll, who wore rouge, and drove a curricle; or like Miss Donnisthorpe, the daughter of the master of the hounds, who hunted the innocent red deer, in a short green habit, with a gold band round her velvet hunting-cap.

'If he would only keep to the old simple ways,' she thought, looking back at the departed Squire's miserly plainness of living with a touch of regret, 'I am sure we should be much happier; he would spend his money in doing good.'

She knew, by the experience of one who had succoured and cared for the poor, all the sad details of that dark picture which lies behind the fair outside of country life. That lovely landscape, rich in its variety of colour as the Queen's regalia, is the theatre in which many a drama of sin and suffering, guiltless poverty and unmerited woe, has to be acted. Yonder cottage, whose thatched roof makes so pretty a feature in the view, shelters starvation: a mother toiling to feed her children, while their father lies in gaol for—a rabbit. Pinched faces, untimely wrinkles, meet the traveller in those delightful lanes where the wild apple and the clustering elder suggest to the poetic mind a land of milk and honey and pome-granates—faces marked with the brand of premature care, defiled by the cunning that is engendered of childish struggles with tyrants and taskmasters, and a hard, inexorable fate. Not in fetid alleys and festering London back slums only is man's fight with diffi-culty a bitter and crushing battle; but here even, where earth is a paradise, and the untainted sky an Italian blue, man starves and perishes, and learns to curse the unequal destiny that gives his master all, and him nothing.

Naomi knew what poverty meant in a rural district; and she longed for the power to help and improve, and to use the knowledge which experience had given her. She had talked to Oswald of the labourers' homes on his estate—hovels rather than houses—and had gently urged the need for improvement. He had put her off lightly, in his pleasant yielding way: so full of grace and beauty in her sight, that she forgot the weakness it indicated.

'It shall be done, dear: "The sooner, sweet, for you," as Othello says. We will do wonders for the poor things. The Exeter archi-tect shall make a plan—after we are married. You must let me finish the Grange first, and then I will do anything you like; but I can't take the builder off that till his work is done.' As if there were no other builder in the world!

Oswald was in London, trying to find his Lethe in the somewhat prosaic distractions of that capital;—not the London of to-day, with its Viaduct and Embankment, and houses as tall as those of old Edinburgh and Paris; its innumerable railway-stations, and theatres, and restaurants, and music-halls; but a city of narrower streets and more jovial manners. He knew no one, and put up at the busy commercial hotel at which the Western coach deposited him; taking no trouble to seek a more refined habitation. He made his enquiries about his brother's ship, and, after some trouble, found out the last port she had touched at in the China seas. Yet this was not much: for Arnold might have exchanged to another ship for anything Oswald knew to the contrary. But to gain intelligence about his absent brother had not been Mr. Pentreath's only business in London, or even his chief reason for going there. He went thither in quest of forgetfulness—to cure himself, were it curable, of a passion that threatened to be fatal at once to peace of mind and honour. He had torn himself away from Penmoyle with a wrench, thinking that to turn his back upon Cynthia might be to forget her; but, alas for youth's constancy to a forbidden dream! the sweet face followed him to the crowded city, and harassed him by day, and held him awake at night; the soft blue eyes betrayed love's sad secret; the tremulous lips seemed to him to murmur: ' Yes, dearest, I love and pity you; though it can never be—though we are parted in life and eternity, I love—I pity—I deplore.'

Not quite in vain had he loved her if she but loved him in return; though all hopes, dreams, delights that love could give— were it ever so erring—must be here laid down: a solemn sacrifice to duty and honour. Yes, there was much comfort—nay, more than comfort, a rapture that thrilled him—in knowing that he was loved. And he did most assuredly know it, though no admission had fallen from Cynthia's lips. Their spirits had touched, as flame touches flame, but a moment—swift as the quivering arrows of fire that flash and fade in the instant; yet the touch was a revelation. He did not doubt that she loved him.

He had never meant to speak of his love. This he repeated to himself deprecatingly in his hours of remorse. Passion had forced his secret from him, and he despised himself for the confession that had dishonoured him. He had meant to speak only through Werther; finding a morbid delight in dwelling upon the record of sufferings so like his own, half assured that Cynthia understood and recognised his passion veiled in the words of another; and then impulse and emotion had been too strong for him, and he had given loose to the desire of his heart, and disgraced himself for ever in his own eyes, and in the sight of the woman he loved.

' She could not look upon me without loathing after that wretched scene,' he told himself. Yet the vision of Cynthia which he carried with him everywhere did not regard him with loathing, but with a tender pity, a sad, immeasurable love.

He tried to steep himself in London dissipations, knowing about as much of them as a baby. If he could have fallen in with the mohawks of the day—the gentlemen who went to Epsom races in a hearse, and wrenched off harmless citizens' knockers, or plucked out their bell-wires; who drank porter with Hackney coachmen and their watermen, and made bosom friends of prize-fighters—he would perchance have enrolled himself in that band of choice spirits, and tried to discover a new Lethe in the porter-pot, wherein the Corinthian Tom of the period was generally so fortunate as speedily to find that oblivion which goes by the name of Death. But Oswald Pentreath had no introduction to this patrician set, and was fain to seek for distraction in such simple pleasures as Vauxhall and the theatres, where he found something at every turn which reminded him of himself and of Cynthia.

Sometimes, a face that had been sweet and fair flashed past him under the coloured lamps in the Vauxhall groves—bright with artificial hues—in its venal smile dimly recalling Cynthia's innocent beauty; sometimes a face upon the stage reminded him of hers, or a tone of voice in some young actress thrilled him like hers. Forget her! Everything in life was associated with her. He could not even remember what life had been like before he loved her.

He saw all that London could show him—parks, streets, theatres, gambling-houses, race-courses, folly, extravagance, vacuity—but found no forgetfulness. Nay, his passion grew and strengthened in absence. The aching void in his heart went with him everywhere. At the play, when the house was roaring at Tom and Jerry, and the charlies were being carried off bodily in their ricketty old watch-boxes, Oswald sat staring blankly. His thoughts were in the parlour at Combhollow, acting that foolish scene over again—living again in the light of Cynthia's eyes—draining deep delight from every look—however sad, however reproachful—which told him he was beloved.

He did not yield himself up to despair without a struggle—which was a manly struggle for one whom Nature had made of no heroic mould. He wrestled with himself, and tried to make a stand against the tempter, and had it in his mind to thrust Joshua's wife out of his heart, and to be faithful to Joshua's daughter. He would go back to Combhollow in a month or so, regenerated; and would hurry on his marriage, and begin a new life as a useful and worthy member of society.

'Arnold may be home by that time,' he thought; 'and the delight of seeing him again will make me forget everything.'

In the meanwhile, he wrote twice a week to Naomi, decorous and amiable letters, describing all he saw, and telling nothing of his feelings or impressions—hardly one word of himself from beginning to end. Poor Naomi read and re-read the letters, and puzzled herself sorely about them. He seemed to be enjoying himself, for he was always going to theatres, and operas, and races; and he was staying in London longer than he had intended, which proved that he was pleased with what he saw. Naomi was contented to bear the pain of severance, for the sake of his pleasure; but to be parted from him was a sharper pain than she could have thought possible before he went. Life was so empty without him! She had her father—always the first in her esteem, she had told herself; she had all her old home duties and home ties; but Oswald's absence took the sunshine and colour out of everything.

Chapter XXI.

' IT WAS THY LOVE PROVED FALSE AND FRAIL.'

A cloud had fallen upon that quiet household at Combhollow. A sharper pain than Naomi's sense of loss had crept into the breast of Naomi's father, and gnawed it in secret, while the strong man kept silence, ashamed of his suffering—nay, angry at the human weakness which made it possible for him so to suffer.

That little scene with Cynthia—that unexplained mystery about the book called Werther—had not been without its influence upon Joshua Haggard's mind. He might have forgotten it, and gone on trusting implicitly—as it was his nature to trust where he confided at all—had he been true to his own instincts; but this privilege—the melancholy privilege of being happy and deceived—had not been allowed him. Judith had hinted, and whispered, and looked, and insinuated, and, without committing herself to any direct statement, had contrived to poison her brother's mind with a shapeless suspicion of his wife's purity.

Cynthia had drooped somewhat after that evening on which she sobbed out her despair upon her husband's breast. The pale cheek had not regained its wild-rose bloom; the sweet blue eyes had grown dull and languid. The young wife looked like one who sickened under the burden of some secret sorrow. She was not strong enough to suppress the outward signs of a heart ill at ease.

Joshua saw the change; at first wondered at it, and then, enlightened by Judith's hints, began to suspect.

Cynthia was not happy. It was no bodily sickness which oppressed her, but a secret grief.

Was it that she regretted her marriage with him—that she had chosen him hastily, mistaking religious fervour for love? This seemed likely enough.

'How should she love me,' he asked himself; 'a man more than twice her age; grave—full of cares for serious things? Is it natural that she should find happiness in my society or in the life she leads here? Naomi is different; she has been brought up to this quiet life—to see all things in the same sober light. Cynthia was a wanderer, used to motion and variety—to crowds and noise. How can she help it if the longing for the old gipsy life comes back to her? How can I blame her if she wearies of my dull home?'

This is how he would have explained the change to himself; but Judith's oracular sentences hinted at something darker.

'What is it that you mean, Judith?' he asked one day, with a burst of anger; 'you and my wife speak fairly enough to each other's faces, and seem to live peacefully together; but there is something lurking in your mind—there is something underneath all this smoothness. Is it Christianlike to deal in hints and dark looks?'

'I should think it was Christianlike to stand by my brother,' answered Judith, with her injured air, 'and to consider him before everybody.'

'Is it a sign of consideration for me to speak unkindly of my wife?'

'What have I said that is unkind? Perhaps it might be kindness to say more. There's things that can't go on without bringing misery to more than you, brother; but it isn't my business to talk about 'em if you've no eyes to see 'em for yourself.'

'What do you mean, woman?'

'Yes; things must have come to a pretty pass when my only brother, that I've toiled for and served faithfully all my life, calls me names. A minister, too, who preaches against bad language. But I knew what it would be when that young woman crossed this threshold. Goodbye family affection! The man who is led away by a pretty face turns his back upon blood-relations. He's bound to follow where his new fancy leads him.'

With these random arrows of speech did Miss Haggard harass her victim and relieve her own feelings.

'Judith, do you want to drive me mad?' he cried with exasperation, 'or to make me think that you are fit for a mad-house yourself? How has my wife offended you? What evil have you ever seen in her?'

He stood with his back against the parlour-door, facing his sister, with a resolute look in his dark eyes—resolute even to fierceness, which told her that a crisis had come. She would be obliged to speak out; and to speak out was the very last thing she desired. Never before had she seen that sombre fire in Joshua's dark eyes. She quailed before the unknown demon she had raised.

' What is amiss ? ' he demanded savagely ; ' how has my wife sinned against purity, or against me ? '

' I am not accusing her of sin,' faltered Judith. ' You shouldn't be so hot-tempered, brother ; it isn't becoming in a Christian minister. I do not accuse her of sin ; but there's foolishness which brings young women to the threshold of sin ; and, once there, it is easy to cross over to fire and brimstone. I say that a girl of nineteen is no wife for a man of your age ; that Providence must have meant her for a trial of your patience : that's what I've always thought and shall always say, as willingly before her face as behind her back.'

' Is this all you have to say ? You might have said as much the night I brought my wife home. Is this the upshot of all your dark looks and insinuations ? You have kept me on thorns for the last three weeks ; and, driven into a corner, you can only beat about the bush like this.'

His scornful tone stung her. To be ridiculed—to be made of no account in her brother's household—was more than Judith Haggard could bear. Whatever wealth of affection there was in her nature had been given to Joshua. He was the one man she believed in and honoured, even when least respectful in her attitude towards him. She could not tamely see him wronged ; and her jealousy of Cynthia was quick to suspect and imagine wrong. She had seen and heard enough to give force and meaning to her suspicions ; and her bosom had been labouring with the weight of that secret knowledge. She wanted to tell Joshua—she wanted not to tell him. The secret gave her a sense of power. It was as if she held a thunderbolt which she might launch at any moment on the heads of the household ; but the bolt once launched, and the domestic sky darkened, her power would be gone. Pity for Joshua she had none, although she loved him. He had wronged her love too deeply in marrying a nameless girl. It would do her good to see him suffer through his wife. She would stand by him afterwards--stand by him and console him, comfort him with her love, instead of Cynthia's. But Providence—and Judith as an instrument of Providence—meant him to suffer this ordeal.

' You've no call to make light of me,' she said ; ' I'm not one to speak without authority. I can hold my tongue as I've held it for the last twelvemonth. Do you want me to speak plainly ? Do you want me to say all I know ? '

' All—to the last word,' said Joshua, white with rage.

' Don't turn round upon me afterwards and say it would have been better if I'd kept my counsel.'

' Say your say, woman, and make an end of it.'

'Well, brother, I've seen a change in Mr. Pentreath ever since his father's death : absent looks—and smothered sighs—and restlessness—and no pleasure in life. Grief for his father, you'll say, perhaps ; but is it likely he'd give way like that for an old man, that kept him short of money, and hadn't anybody's good word? It isn't in nature.'

'Who made you a judge of nature? But go on.'

'Well, brother, I had my own ideas, and I kept 'em to myself, and should have so kept 'em as long as I lived, if I'd had no stronger cause for suspicion. But when I see a young man on his knees at a young woman's feet, and hear him asking her to pity him because he's miserable for love of her, and threatening to shoot himself, and the young woman sobbing as if her heart would break all the time—and that young woman my brother's wife—when things came to such a pass as this, I think it's my duty to speak.'

'Lies !—lies !' gasped Joshua. 'You see my happiness, and envy me ! You hate my wife because she is lovely, as you never were ; passionately loved, as you never were.'

Judith laughed hysterically.

'I don't know about beauty,' she said ; 'but I had a high colour and jet black hair, with a natural curl, when I was a young woman—and that used to be thought good looks enough for any girl in my time—and I might have married a hundred and fifty acres of land and a flour-mill. But I'm sorry to see you so beside yourself with passion, Joshua, because I speak plainly for your own good.'

'Is it for my good to tell me lies? My wife listening to Oswald Pentreath's wicked love ! No—I'll never believe it.'

'Turn it over in your own mind a little more before you call your only sister a liar. Have you forgotten the last afternoon Mr. Pentreath was here—when Naomi was lying down with a sick headache, and those two—Mrs. Haggard ' and the young squire—were alone together from dinner till tea ; and you came home and found your wife all in a flutter, and as white as a sheet of paper ; and I accused her to her face of reading a wicked book ; and you turned against me to take her part ; and she burst into tears in the middle of tea, and told you she was grateful to you, and would do her duty by you ? What was that but a guilty conscience ? Why, a mole could have seen through it ! But a man of your age, who marries a young woman for the sake of her pretty face, is blinder than the blindest mole. He has no eyes to see anything but the prettiness.'

Joshua wiped the sweat-drops from his forehead with a broad muscular hand, that shook like a leaf. Never had his manhood

been so shaken—never in all the trials of his early life, when to
hold fast by his thorny path had cost him many a struggle, had
he felt the hot blood surging in his brain as it surged to-day.
There was a fiery cloud before his eyes.   He could scarcely see his
sister's face, looking at him full of angry eagerness, intent to prove
her own case, to assert her own dignity—and with but little consideration for his anguish.

'Judith,' he said, falteringly—and that strong voice of his so
rarely faltered that its weakness had a touch of deepest pathos—
'you are my own and only sister.   I cannot think you would tell
me lies on purpose to make me miserable.   Forgive me for what I
said just now.   No; I cannot believe my sister a liar.   I will not
believe my wife unfaithful to me, by so much as a thought.   But
this young man is a weak vessel.   Tell me—plainly—all you saw
and heard.'

'That's easily told.   He had been reading that book to her—
what's his name?—Werther.   I went in and out to fetch my thimble,
and such like; and whenever I went in it was the same story:
"Didst thou but know how I love thee," and "Charlotte, it is
decided—I must die," and such rubbish; and there sat your wife,
with her work crumpled up in her lap, staring straight at him with
tears in her eyes.   It was close upon tea-time, and I was going in
again when I heard something that stopped me.   The door stood a
little way ajar—it's an old box-lock, and the catch is always giving
way, as you know, Joshua—and I waited outside just to find out
what it all meant, for I felt that I was bound to do that much
by my duty to you.   I could just see into the room.   He was on
his knees, holding her hands, and she sobbing as if her heart would
break.   He told her how he loved her, and asked her to pity him;
and she never said him nay, only went on crying, and presently told
him he was cruel; and oh, why did he read such a book to her!
Because it was his own story, he said, and the only way he could
find of telling her his love.'

'And she did not cry out against such iniquity?' cried Joshua;
'she did not reprove him for such wickedness—rise up before him in
her dignity as an offended woman, and my true and loyal wife?'

'I heard myself called in the shop just at that moment, and I
was obliged to go,' answered Judith.   'When I came back to the
parlour, Sally was laying the tea-things.'

'I will answer for my wife's truth and honour,' said Joshua
firmly.   'I will pledge myself that she repulsed and upbraided this
guilty young man as he deserved—that she looks upon his wicked
passion with abhorrence.   That was why she looked so pale—
shocked to the heart, my gentle one—that was why she clung to me

so piteously, seeking sanctuary in my affection. My lily—no villain shall sully thy purity while I am near to shield thee. My dearest! has the tempter assailed thee so soon—sin's poisoned breath so soon tarnished thy soul's whiteness? I will love thee all the more—guard thee more closely, honour thee more deeply—because thou hast been in danger.'

Judith stared at her brother in dumb amazement. Against such infatuation as this the voice of reason was powerless. It almost tempted her to believe in witchcraft—a superstition by no means extinct in this Western world. Judith had put the thought behind her hitherto, as a delusion of the dark ages unworthy of a strong-minded woman. But here, surely, was a case of demoniac possession—an example of something more foolish than mortal folly.

'But as for him,' continued Joshua, with clenched fist, ' for the tempter—the would-be seducer—he shall never cross this threshold again; and let him beware how he crosses my path, lest I should slay him in my righteous rage, as Moses slew the Egyptian.'

'And Naomi's engagement?' suggested Judith, timidly. There was a power in her brother's look which awed her.

'Naomi's engagement is cancelled from this hour. My daughter shall marry no double-dealer—swearing to be true to her at God's altar with lips that are defiled by the avowal of love for another man's wife. My daughter shall go unmarried to her grave rather than be the wife of such a man, were his place the highest in the land.'

'It was a very grand match for her,' said Judith, with a propitiating air; ' but for my part I never saw happiness come from an unequal marriage, and I've seen many such in my time. But I'm afraid Naomi will take it to heart.'

'Poor child!' sighed the father. 'Is it my sin that I have brought this sorrow upon her? How could I know that her lover would prove so base? Poor child! She must bear her burden—she must carry her cross.'

He was deadly pale; and, now that the angry light had gone out of his eyes, his face had a faded look, as if the anguish of many years had aged him within the last half-hour.

'I can't but remember what Jabez Long said the day the 'Dolphin' went down: "No good ever came of saving a drowning man; he's bound to do you wrong afterwards." It's come true, you see,' said Judith.

'Do you think I believe that heathen superstition any more because Oswald Pentreath has proved a villain? I thought you had more sense, Judith.'

'Well, I don't say I believe it; but, to say the least, it's curious. However, I never did think much of young Mr. Pentreath, or of the stock he comes from.   But it seems hard upon Naomi.   Shall you tell her the reason?'

'Tell her that a villain has insulted my wife! No, Judith.   My daughter will obey me, though I bid her sacrifice her heart's desire ; as Jephthah's daughter obeyed when she laid down her life in fulfilment of her father's promise.'

'Ah,' sighed Judith, with suppressed gusto, 'it's a world of trouble.'

She felt more in her element now that things were going wrong, and that she was at the helm once more, in a manner.   Her little world had been given over to two girls, and she had felt herself, in her own language, a cipher.

It was hardly in Joshua's nature to be slow to act, however painful the business which duty imposed upon him.   On that very evening he found Naomi alone in the wilderness, on her knees before a craggy bank, planting some wild flowers which she had discovered in her afternoon rambles.

She looked up from her clustering ferns and humble way-side blossoms with a smile as her father approached ; but the troubled expression of his face alarmed her, and she rose quickly and came to him.

'Dear father, is anything wrong?'

She had not seen him since his interview with Judith, and that aged and altered look in his face, which had struck the sister, alarmed the daughter.

'Yes, my dear, there is something very wrong.   Providence bids me inflict pain upon one I fondly love—upon you, my Naomi.'

He drew her towards him, looking down at her with tender pity.   It seemed very hard that she should suffer—that this young life was so soon to be clouded.

'Dear father! what has happened?' cried Naomi, tremulous in her agitation.   'It is about Oswald.   The evening post has just come—you have had a letter—is he ill?   Yes, yes, I can see that it is about him.'

'He is well enough, my love ;   I have heard nothing to the contrary.   I am very sorry that he is so dear to you.'

'Why, dear father?'

'Because I have learned lately that he is unworthy of your affection ; and I must desire you, as you are my true and obedient daughter, to give up all thought of marrying him.'

The girl's face blanched, her eyelids closed for a moment, and the slender figure swayed against Joshua's arm as if it would have fallen.   But only for a moment ; Naomi was not made of feeble stuff, nor prone to fainting.   She lifted her eyelids, and looked at her father steadily, holding his arm with fingers that tightened upon it almost convulsively in that moment of pain.

'What have you heard against him, father, and from whom?' she asked resolutely. 'You are bound to tell me that, in common justice. It is my duty to obey you, but not blindly. I am not a child—I can bear to know the worst. What has he done, my love, my dearest—too gentle to hurt a worm—what evil thing has he done, that you should turn against him?'

'That I cannot tell you, Naomi; and in this matter you must obey me blindly as a child. He has sinned; and his sin proves him alike false and feeble—a broken reed—a man not to be relied on— unworthy of a woman's trust. Naomi, believe me, your father, who never deceived you, that if I inflict pain upon you to-day, in forbidding this marriage, I spare you ten-thousand-fold of misery in days to come. It is not possible that you could be happy as Oswald's wife!'

'Let me be the judge of that. It is my venture—it is my happiness that is at stake. Let me be the judge. What is his sin?'

'Again I say I cannot tell you. You must trust me and obey me, Naomi, or you cease to be my daughter. Oswald Pentreath will never cross my threshold again with my sanction. I shall never more speak to him in friendship.'

'Father, is this Christian-like?'

'It is my duty to myself as a man.'

'How has he offended you?'

'By his sin.'

'But he has not sinned against me,' said Naomi piteously. 'Why am I to renounce him?'

'He has sinned against you and against God.'

'If he has sinned, he has so much the more need of my love. Am I to forsake him in his sorrow—I, who would die for him?'

'He does not need your love, Naomi, or desire it. It is for the happiness of both that you should be parted.'

'For his happiness?' faltered Naomi, with a look of acute pain.

It was as if all her vague doubts of the past few months were suddenly condensed into a horrible certainty.

'Do you mean that Oswald has ceased to love me?'

'Yes, Naomi. At the beginning I was doubtful of his sta- bility. I feared that his was a character in which impressions are quick to come and go. I stipulated for delay, in order that your lover's constancy might be tested. The event has proved my doubts but too well grounded.'

'I offered to release him only a little while ago,' said Naomi, 'and he would not be set free. He assured me of his unchanging love.'

'He was a liar!' cried Joshua fiercely; and his daughter recoiled before the fury in that dark face. Never had she seen such anger there till to-day—never had she believed him capable of such passion. The revelation shocked her; the father whom she so tenderly loved was degraded in her eyes by this un-Christian-like resentment.

'Why are you so angry, father?' she asked, pleadingly.

'Because I hate falsehood—treachery—double-dealing— a fair face and a foul heart. I can say no more, Naomi. I have said enough to warn you; it is for you to accept or reject my warning. Marry Oswald Pentreath if you choose; but remember that from the hour of your marriage you cease to be my daughter. I will never acknowledge that man as my son. I will never acknowledge that man's wife as my flesh and blood. It is for you to choose between us.'

'Father, you know I have no choice; you know that you are first—have always held the first place in my heart. There is no one else whose love I could weigh against yours—not even Oswald, though I love him dearly, must love him to the end, love him all the more for his weakness—for his sorrow. I am your true and loyal daughter, dearest; and I give you up my heart, as I would give up my life—yes, dear father, freely, gladly, for your sake.'

'That's my own brave Naomi. It is for your own welfare, believe me, dearest, however hard the trial may be to bear just now. The man is not true; there could be no happiness for you with him.'

'Do not say anything more against him, father,' pleaded Naomi, gently. 'I give him up; but let me honour him as much as I can—let him hold a high place in my thoughts. It is easier to bear the pain of parting from him if I can keep his image in my heart undefiled.'

'I will say no more, Naomi. You will write to him, and tell him your engagement is ended, at my desire. A few decided words will say all that is needful. His own heart will tell him the reason. I do not think that he will question or plead against your decision.'

'I will write, father.'

Joshua folded her in his arms, and kissed the pale sad brow, drawn with pain.

'May God bless and comfort you, dearest, and give you joy in this sacrifice,' he said solemnly. 'On my honour, as your father and your pastor, it is for the best.'

And so he left her, standing in her desolated wilderness, from which the beauty had gone forth for ever. Her ferns and hedge-row blossoms smiled at her in the rosy evening light—feathery mosses, trailing periwinkle, opalescent dog-roses, steeped in golden glory; purple fox-gloves towering from a sea of fern—all the sweet wild things she had gathered together looked at her, and gave her no comfort in this hour of bitter agony. She cast herself, face downward, on the grassy path, and gave herself up, body and soul, to despair.

Yes, she had known it, long ago; he loved her no more. She had tried to put away the thought. She had made her direct appeal to him, and been reassured by his loving reply. But the aching pain had lingered at the bottom of her heart. She had not been happy.

Better so—better, as her father said, to renounce him alto-gether—to give him back his freedom—than to let him chain himself in a loveless wedlock. Better anything than the humi-liation of an unloved wife.

But this sin which her father spoke of with such deep resent-ment—this offence which had kindled such unseemly anger in a Christian's breast : what was this deadly and desperate error? Herein lay the bitterest trial of all—to be kept in the dark, not to be able to comfort or succour the sinner.

CHAPTER XXII.
'THE DEEP OF NIGHT IS CREPT UPON OUR TALK.'

JOSHUA proved a true prophet in so far as related to Oswald Pentreath's line of conduct on receipt of his betrothed's letter. To Naomi's sad epistle, renouncing all claim upon him at her father's desire, he answered briefly :

Your letter has taken me by surprise, dearest; but harsh and sudden as your decision seems, I acquiesce. I know not how your father may have arrived at his estimate of my character, or what has influenced him to desire that our engagement shall be cancelled; but I am willing to abide his sentence. He may be right, perhaps. I am by nature unstable. I am not worthy of so noble a heart as yours. Yet be assured, Naomi, that, although unworthy, I am at least capable of appreciating and admiring your character as well as a better man. To the end of my life I shall honour and esteem you. To the end of my life I shall deem you the purest and noblest of women, and think those days of my life happiest in which I loved you best, and when there was no shadow of mistrust between us.

God bless you, dearest, and farewell! It may be long before I revisit Comb-hollow—and this may be a life-long farewell.

> Your friend, your servant always,
> OSWALD PENTREATH.

'He is grateful to me for letting him go,' thought Naomi, with a touch of bitterness. She could read gratitude for his release between the lines of this letter. It confirmed all her sad doubts.

' He might have spared me much pain if he had been more candid,' she told herself—' if he had confessed the truth that day I told him of the change I had seen in him.'

She opened the drawer where her wedding-dress lay on the day she received this final letter—the last she could ever expect from Oswald Pentreath. She looked at the pale silken gown with such sorrowful eyes as look upon a corpse. Was it not the dead corpse of her lost happiness which lay there, with sprigs of rosemary among the folds of its shroud ?

' Poor wedding-gown ! ' she said to herself; ' I shall give it to Lucy Simmonds. Why should it lie and fade in a drawer when it would make her happy ? Would it be any comfort to me to look at it in years to come, and remember that I was once young, and very happy, fancying myself beloved ? '

Lucy Simmonds had been Naomi's favourite pupil in the Sunday school of Little Bethel—an intelligent biblical student, who knew ' Kings ' and ' Chronicles ' as well as a bishop, and had never been known to confound the miracles of Elijah and Elisha. She had blossomed into womanhood, and was about to unite her fate with that of a promising young butcher—a staunch member of Joshua's congregation.

Naomi folded the dress carefully, and packed it in a large sheet of white paper. The skirts of those days were scanty, and the silk dress did not make a large parcel. She wrote a loving letter to her old pupil, and sent the parcel to the widow Simmonds's house that afternoon. The dress might be too good for Lucy's present station, but not for her future position as the wife of an aspiring butcher. The young matron would wear that pretty grey silk at friendly tea-parties and Christmas gatherings for years to come, and would think affectionately of the donor. It seemed a small thing, this giving away of her wedding-gown, but to Naomi it meant the total surrender of hope. There was nothing left for her in life but duty, and her love for her father.

She bore her cross meekly. None could have told how withering a sorrow had passed over her young life. There was a curious compound of pride and humbleness in her nature. She accepted her lot humbly, as a trial which was but her portion of humanity's common burden ; but she was too proud to let others see how deeply she had been wounded. She put on a brave front, and her father gave her credit for stoicism, in no wise suspecting that the weight of her secret grief was almost intolerable.

Very little was said in the small household about this change in Naomi's fortunes.   The cancelment of her engagement was accepted as an act of Joshua's.   He had forbidden the marriage for some good reason of his own.   No one dared ask him why—his wife least of all.   She could not have spoken Oswald's name to him.   Her heart was full of fear, sorrow, and deepest pity for Naomi.   Yet she dared not offer her sympathy.   There was a look in Naomi's face that forbade all approach—every offer of love. Cynthia felt that there was a gulf between them.   Naomi tacitly avoided her.   She was not unkind, but she shrank from all companionship with her father's wife; and henceforward Cynthia's life became very lonely.   Her husband's hours were closely occupied and spent for the most part away from her.   Naomi lived her own life as much as possible apart from her step-mother, and Judith was harsh and unfriendly.   Jim was always Cynthia's friend and champion; but his busy life did not admit of much companionship. The small household met at meals at the same hours, with the same regulations and ceremonies; but these family assemblies were silent and gloomy.

‘ Our dinner-time is getting uncommonly like a quakers' meeting,' observed the audacious Jim at one of these dreary gatherings ; ‘ I wish the spirit would move some of us to be lively,'

‘ When you've as much trouble on your mind as your father has, you won't be quite so active with your tongue,' retorted Aunt Judith.

The works at the Grange had undergone a sudden check. Oswald had written peremptory orders to his architect.   The contract was to be carried out only so far as concerned the substantial repairs of the house.   There was to be no rotunda, and the end of the drawing-room was to be walled up again.

‘ I am going abroad,' he wrote ; ‘ make as good a job as you can of the place, and write to me at the subjoined address for cheques as you want them.'

The subjoined address was that of a London solicitor, a man who had done business for the old Squire occasionally.

The architect wondered and talked ; and before many days everybody in Combhollow knew that Mr. Pentreath's engagement to Joshua Haggard's daughter was broken off.   There was a great deal of talk, and much discussion and disputation about details, but a wonderful unanimity of opinion.   The match would have been most unsuitable.   Naomi Haggard was much too serious for a Squire's lady.   The Grange could never have held up its head properly under such a mistress ; and a glass rotunda would have been absurdly out of keeping.   ‘ He ought to marry Mr. Pinkley's only daughter,' said Combhollow, deciding for him offhand.   ‘ There's only an accommodation road between Pinkley's land and his.'

The builders finished their work; the end of the long drawing-room was walled up again; and there was no more talk of palms, or fountains, or an Italian garden. The Grange resumed its air of gloom and emptiness, and looked almost as dismal as in the life-time of the old Squire.

So the summer ripened and grew more glorious, bringing no delight of heart to the minister's small household. The colours of the sea took a more vivid lustre from the fullness of the sun, like jewels in an Indian temple shining in the glare of many torches. There came over the land the sultry hush of the days before har-vest. Very little doing in those rich fields, where the corn was gently stirred by the hot south wind, like the waves of a golden sea; very little doing in the big farmyards, where the cattle stood knee-deep in the tawny gorse-litter, and contemplated the outer world listlessly, with dreamy brown eyes, and a general air of bene-volence—stillness and repose on all things. Cynthia Haggard looked at this lovely external universe languidly, with eyes that saw its beauty dimly, as in a dream in which one absorbing sense of overwhelming trouble makes all things faint and blurred. Her husband had spoken no unkind word to her since that scene with Oswald; yet she felt that he was estranged. He read more; he shut himself up in his own thoughts, gave himself up more completely to his contemplative and subjective religion, and that religion seemed to take a more gloomy and inexorable character. In his sermons he dwelt less on the divine love and charity, and harped on a harsher string—the doom of sinners destined to perdition—wretches on whom the divine light had never shone, for whom that all-saving faith, which could lift the sinner out of the mire by one upward impulse of an awakened soul, was a dead letter.

Cynthia shuddered as she listened. Was Oswald Pentreath one of these lost spirits?

She could see that her husband was unhappy; yet had no power to comfort him. That weighed upon her heavily. She dared not complain to him of this disunion, lest she should be drawn into a confession of her sinful weakness, and constrained to admit her guilty love for the sinner. She could not have stood up before that righteous man, and spoken falsely.

He never questioned her about Oswald Pentreath; yet she felt that there must be some strong suspicion of evil in his mind, and at the root of his arbitrary conduct in cancelling his daughter's engagement. It never occurred to her that Oswald's wild talk that afternoon had been overheard, and told to Joshua. She looked upon his knowledge rather as the result of some occult power of his own. His wisdom had penetrated the guilty secret.

One night, a little while after Naomi had given up her lover, Joshua came up to his bed-chamber somewhat later than usual. He had stayed in the parlour after supper, writing or reading. Cynthia was lying awake, full of sad thoughts, vague forebodings of evil, aching pity for that weak sinner wandering she knew not where. Joshua walked up and down the room in silence for some minutes, and then stopped suddenly beside the bed, and looked down at the small pale face on the pillow, the sad blue eyes glancing up at him timidly, deprecating blame.

'I am glad you are not asleep,' he said; 'I want that book— "The Sorrows of Werther." I have been thinking of what my sister said about it. I want to judge for myself. I looked at it too hurriedly last time. I want to see what kind of book it was that made you unhappy.'

'You can't read it to-night, Joshua, surely? It's so late, and you must be tired.'

'I am tired, but not able to sleep. I would rather read than lie awake. My thoughts have been a burden to me of late. There was a time when my wakeful hours were full of sweetness, when I could lose myself in communion with my Redeemer. That time is past. Human trouble has made a wall between this poor clay and the spirit world.'

This was a reproach which smote the erring wife to the heart.

'Joshua, it is my fault,' she faltered; 'you were happier before you married me.'

'Happier!' he cried bitterly; 'I never knew the extremes of human joy or human pain till I knew you. Well, the pain has been immeasurable as the joy. If I erred, I have paid the penalty. Give me that book, Cynthia!'

Cynthia rose without another word, went to the drawer where she had hidden that fatal romance of real life, and brought the book to her husband with a meek obedience that moved him deeply. Even in his doubt and distrust of her—for he did doubt her, despite his brave words to Judith—there was an abiding love for her in his soul—a yearning to take her to his heart and forgive her, and comfort her, and offer her deeper love than was ever given to woman—the wide, strong love of a heart that had only awakened to passion in the maturity of its force and power. Could the love of youth, in all its glow of romance and poetry, be in any wise equal to this?

Cynthia put the book into his hand, and then remonstrated gently against the folly of midnight studies. 'Read it to-morrow, dear Joshua. You look tired and ill. Hark! it is striking eleven.'

'Go to bed and sleep,' he said sternly; 'I cannot. I want to read the book that melted you—and Oswald Pentreath. I wonder whether it will move me to tears.'

He set the candle on the old mahogany escritoire at which he wrote sometimes, and seated himself in the wide horsehair-covered arm-chair, edged with brass nails, like an old-fashioned coffin. He opened the book with a resolute air, as a man who meant to plod through it, whatever stuff it might be. He read, and read on with an intent face, turning leaf after leaf at measured intervals; Cynthia lying with her face turned towards that gloomy figure, watching him as if he were reading in the book of doom. To her mind that book held the confession of Oswald's weakness and of hers. Joshua would know all when he had read that. Had it been an acknowledgment of sin written with her own hand, signed and attested, she could not have thought it more complete or final.

He read on deep into the night, Cynthia dozing a little now and then, but for the most part watching him. The small hours struck, one after another, on the solemn old church bell; a faint chillness crept into the summer air; then slowly, softly, mysteriously, like a dream, came the gray dawn; first with a glimmer at the window, then with a broad cold light that filled the room and made the flame of the candle pale and ghost-like; then with gleams of saffron and rose, and dim morning sunbeams like an infant's vague sweet smile. Still Joshua sat reading, in the same fixed attitude; reading on with indomitable resolve, bent on knowing the utmost and the worst. For him, too, the book was a confession and a revelation. Werther was Oswald Pentreath; Charlotte was Cynthia; and they loved each other; their young hearts yearned to each other, overflowing with tenderest sympathies, with unspeakable affection; and fate, duty, religion, and honour, stood between them in the person of the unloved husband, separating them for ever.

The room was flooded with sunlight when he closed the book, with one long sigh. He could not refuse the sinner that one expression of pity—so lost, so given over to an unconquerable passion, and yet with so much in him that was gentle, and true, and worthy.

Cynthia had fallen asleep at last. Joshua looked down at the sweet face on the pillow, full of compassion, pitying her, pitying himself. 'Those two lived happily together when Werther was dead,' he said to himself, thinking of Albert and Charlotte; 'but then Albert did not know that his wife's heart had gone from him.'

He washed and dressed himself, and went down to his daily round of labour, and said no word to Cynthia about the fatal book.

(*To be continued.*)

Among the Sea-trout.

And here and there a lusty trout.—TENNYSON.

'COME up the Saguenay with me next summer, and have a try at the sea-trout,' said my hospitable friend S——, as we were sitting over our claret one bleak night in January, 187–. Now, I have always made it a rule to accept invitations of all kinds, whether they be to partake of simoom cutlets in the Sahara Desert, or of icebergs *au naturel* in the pastures of Nova Zembla; so I said, 'Delighted to come; what fun we shall have!' with a faint feeling of hypocrisy at not disclosing my ignorance of the Saguenay and its productions; for I was fresh to the Dominion, and had never even heard of the Saguenay; in fact, the hint at ascension in my friend's remark inclined me to the idea that it was a kind of Canadian Matterhorn, only sea-trout do not grow on the top of Matterhorns. So I went back to my work in the eastern townships very full of our proposed expedition, and, Englishmanlike, very precise in the phonetic pronunciation of the word Sah-gwen-ay; and was rather shocked at the off-hand and indecently glib manner in which my friends dealt with the mystic syllables. 'Oh, going up the Sagny, are you?' Well, the long Canadian winter wore itself away; spring came at last; the crow carolled his lay from the pine-tree and the bull-frog chanted his matins from the swamp. Summer succeeded, hot and sultry; the cat-bird wailed from the forest by day and the mosquito hummed and feasted merrily by night. At last came August, bringing holidays in its train, and S—— and I met once more on the deck of the good steamer *St. Lawrence*, bound for what the time-tables grandly described as 'Tadousac and the far-famed Saguenay.' The city of Quebec has one of the most picturesque situations in the world, and on that lovely August morning the old city looked indeed splendid; the lower or business part of the town and the black walls of Cape Diamond (where the ill-fated Montgomery met his end) in deep shadow, and the battlements of the citadel lighted up in the glorious sun, with the flag of old England floating, as it ever should, from the topmost tower.

On goes the good steamer, casting on each side the waters of its namesake the river, like a great man waving off a poor relation. Past the beautiful Island of Orleans (called by the old French voyagers ' Île de Bacchus,' from the abundance of its vines), studded with picturesque French farm-houses ; past the fleecy torrents of the Falls of Montmorenci, their look of exquisite coolness on this broiling day making one dive below in search of sherry-cobblers. Sixty miles below Quebec we reach Baie St. Paul, where the first genuine whiff of sea-salt air reaches us, and we first see those harbingers of ocean, great white porpoises, rolling about singly or in schools. Of course an immediate rush was made for rifles and revolvers, and an incessant but fruitless popping (for who ever yet managed to hit a porpoise?) was kept up for the rest of the day. Dinner, however, intervened, and the porpoises had rest for a season. Among other delicacies for which a Canadian table is famous, we revelled in an abundance of beautiful wild strawberries, larger than their Alpine cousins, and to the full as toothsome. ' Say,' said an American gentleman opposite me, ' real smart chance for berries around here.' And à *propos* of Americans, why do our own country-women never appear to advantage when travelling? Why do they look as if they had on their Sunday best or their seediest scrub dresses? Why can they not hit the happy medium and imitate the picturesque *costumes de voyage* of their less refined but certainly more artistic cousins?

Still on glides the good ship, the great river widening every hour, till the watering-places of Murray Bay, Cacouna, Rivière du Loup (anglicised into River d'Loo), appear mere rows of faint white dots on each bank. At last our boat leaves the *via media* to which she has kept all the forenoon, and swings easily round towards a dark opening in the bank, blowing off her superfluous steam with a hoarse roar like Andromeda's monster. The engines slacken to half-speed, then stop, and, heralded by the report of an apoplectic little cannon from the front of the hotel, we glide gently up to the wharf, and the predictions of the time-table are fulfilled.

One's first idea at sight of Tadousac is, How on earth did it get there? The little white village lies nestled in a dimple of the great hills forming the entrance to the river Saguenay, protected from the keen sea-winds by a great shoulder of maple-crested hills, which seems to cuddle it—if I may use that unpoetical but most expressive word—in its embrace. Tadousac does not boast many lions. There is a quaint little wooden church, the oldest in Canada, built some three hundred years ago, of which Canadians are very proud one monster hotel, wooden, white-painted, many-windowed, an exact reproduction of what you see by thousands in the United States ; a couple of stores ; twenty or thirty pretty villa-like cottages, for the resort of summer visitors, each surrounded by the invariable verandah ; and a few score of rude log cabins, inhabited by fishermen and Indians, degenerate scions of the grand old Huron tribe, who have utterly abandoned the war-path, and only retain an ignoble yearning for fire-water. A little apart from the village Lord Dufferin, the Governor-General, has built himself a very handsome house, with broad spacious galleries running round it, facing the lake-like St. Lawrence.

Owing to Lord Dufferin's making Tadousac his summer residence, the little village was full almost to overflowing with Canadian and American holiday-makers, and gaiety was in abundance ; but we came neither to dance nor to flirt, but to catch sea-trout ; so, after spending a night at the caravanserai-like hotel, and making a few needful purchases—as pork, potatoes, &c.—we took advantage of the tide, and set sail up the broad Saguenay, with a fair breeze aft. We had chartered 'L'Espérance,' a small cutter of about fifteen tons, of the kind used on the St. Lawrence as pilot boats, and with her a couple of French Canadians, a man and a boy, to look after the boat, 'and do the chores' generally. Our own party consisted of S——, H—— and C——, his son and nephew respectively, both capital specimens of the hardy sun-burnt Canadian school-boy, and myself.

Our sailing-master rejoiced in the high-sounding name of Alexandre Hippolyte de St. Croix, which we promptly abbreviated to Alec, and his understrapper or cabin-boy owned to no other name than Fabien, which our school-boys in time anglicised to 'Johnny.' Our costumes were varied. S——, who had visited the same 'happy hunting-grounds' for nine consecutive years, was beyond any fanciful efflorescence of costume, and was clad in a suit of simple hodden-grey tweed, a wide-awake to match well garnished with flies, and long waterproof fishing boots. I, who, from a youthful course of reading in the pages of Mayne Reid, had ever a leaning towards the wildly picturesque, could only be content with a scarlet flannel shirt, girt with a leathern belt, with multitudinous straps and loops to carry pipe, fly-book, knife, &c. (and this I can confidently recommend to my brother sportsmen as a most invaluable desideratum for fishing, quite doing away with the necessity for a coat, with its attendant pockets, in hot weather) ; grey trowsers, the bonnet-rouge of the country, and porpoise skin brogues, completed my costume. H—— and C—— were attired somewhat similarly, except that they were innocent of shoes or stockings. Alec had a kind of amphibious costume, which he wore indifferently on dry land or in the water, and, I believe, never took off ; while Fabien's dress resembled that of the mud-larks who congregate under

London Bridge at low water, and was only kept from falling off him piecemeal by fragments of string, and failing them with thorns. Thus equipped, then, we started with a fair, but, alas! too soon deceptive breeze; and grander scenery it would be hard to conceive, the black cliffs rising sheer up from the water's edge to a height of 800 or 1,000 feet, fringed and crested with gaunt ragged pines, while, now and again, an opening in their sides gave a view of the luxuriant maple forest beyond; the sombre waters of the Saguenay rolling majestically down to join the mightier St. Lawrence, and the plaintive gulls screaming overhead.

Before we had gone a mile, however, the breeze dropped to a dead calm, and there we lay,

> As idle as a painted ship
> Upon a painted ocean.

And, to make matters worse, the rain fell in torrents. So we got out our sweeps, and, as the Yankees would say, 'kinder rowed some;' and alternate spells of rowing and occasional puffs of wind brought us to L'Aure de Petite Île, where, as Alec informed us, there was 'good water for drink,' and where S——, our skipper, determined to pass the night. As we were to go on early the next morning, we burdened ourselves with as little baggage as possible, anchored the boat, and landed; the rain still pouring in torrents, and the mosquitos hospitable and jubilant. Fabien, after the manner of French Canadians, wandered off in quest of blue-berries, and Alec sat patiently down on a damp rock to smoke until such time as the eatables appeared, when he began to bestir himself with an alacrity that savoured of the sycophant.

We pitched our tent—originally intended to hold two, but for that night destined to hold four mortals—in the least damp spot, built a fire, dismissed our crew to sleep on board the cutter, made a hearty though frugal meal of dry bread and sugar-less, milk-less tea, and wedged ourselves in with a view to sleep. Vain thought! The mosquitos had not seen a human face before that summer, and they wanted to talk to us and see what we were like. So we sat up, lighted our pipes, and killed time and mosquitos as best we could, with an occasional snooze, till morning.

With morning, however, came a welcome change. The rain had ceased, and the sun shone out again with true Canadian splendour, never to be clouded again for the rest of our trip. But before weighing anchor we had a swim, and such a swim : water fifty feet deep and clear as crystal, and, moreover, of a delicious temperature, far different from the icy St. Lawrence.

Before long we were under weigh and running by easy tacks

up the broad river. An idea of the uniform depth of the river
may easily be gained by the fact that, when changing our tack,
we ran so close to the shore that our bowsprit brushed the rock in
wearing round. By noon we had reached our second camping-
ground, L'Aure St. Étienne : there we landed all our cargo and
pitched our three tents, one each for S—— and myself, and one for
the two boys ; the provisions (consisting of pork, potatoes, biscuit,
tea, sugar, condensed milk, preserved meat, rice, golden syrup, &c.)
and utensils being apportioned among us.

By evening the tide was right for fishing, and though the
season was rather late, still we took a fair quantity of good- sized
fish. Sea-trout are a very greedy fish, and will take almost anything with the semblance of wings, but I found a red or brown
hackle a very safe fly to use. The fish themselves are most
beautiful creatures, long and elegant in shape, of a pure silver hue,
with exquisite rock-coloured flesh. Four days passed at L'Aure
St. Étienne without any more remarkable episode than that poor
little H—— cut his leg severely in chopping wood for the morning
fire ; but a plentiful supply of cold water, and the healing properties of youth and spirits, soon set our little fellow-voyager up
again.

On a bright Sunday morning we sailed for the mouth of the river
St. Marguerite, our last resting-place, eighteen miles from Tadousac.
Any scenery we had come across in the former part of our trip
fell far behind this last spot in beauty. We were encamped about
a mile from the mouth of the river, and a mile still further up
lay a tiny French village, the first human habitation we had seen
for a week, a mere dozen of little wooden houses, dotted about
among the maples. Across the river rose a huge conical hill, some
2,000 feet high, perfectly covered with maple, birch, tamarach,
and ash, a regular pyramid of vegetation. On our side of the
river, a few yards from the water's edge, rose a little bluff, some
ten feet high, leading to a plateau of emerald turf, some two acres
in extent, relieved by our three white tents ; beyond this was a
thick belt of dark spruce firs, and beyond that again rose dark
limestone crags, beetling up for 1,000 feet and perfectly barren,
save for a scanty fringe of ragged pines at intervals.

One day at the St. Marguerite was very like another, and,
alas ! the time passed only too quickly. We rose at five, and
chopped fire-wood, &c., breakfasted at seven, and started fishing
about eight. Our usual plan was to row out to certain trout-
haunted rocks at the turn of the tide, and wade in waist-deep ; by
three or four o'clock the tide had generally run out, and our creels
were full, so we would pull home with light hearts and a heavy

load to dinner. Fortunately, Alec, though a perfect paragon of laziness (not even mosquitos could rouse him to action), was an admirable cook, and S—— himself was an old shikaree in the way of sea-trout, and quite *au fait* in the many ways of cooking those delicate fish. After dinner we would loaf about the camp with that delicious sense of fatigue without pain which generally accompanies such expeditions as ours, or take unavailing shots at stray porpoises, or H—— and C—— would make excursions to the French village in quest of bread, butter, or eggs. One of the inhabitants of this little hamlet visited us the day we landed with a view to tobacco. I was just then being informed most emphatically of the existence of other insects besides mosquitos, viz., horrible little black flies, which busy themselves in your skin and drive you half mad with irritation. I addressed him in French more voluble than grammatical (for my French knowledge is like that of Chaucer's lady—

> Frenche she spake ful fayre and fetisly,
> After the scole of Stratford atte Bowe,
> For Frenche of Paris was to hire unknowe)—

' Je dis, Johnny, vous avez beaucoup de mouches ici, trop beaucoup, je pense!' ' Oui, m'sieu,' replied the urbane Gaul (whose name, curiously enough, happened to be McLean), with a gently indicative wave of the hand, as of one pointing out some great local lion—' Oui, m'sieu, nous sommes fameux pour nos mouches noires ici.'

About seven we took our supper, and finished the day with a yarn or a song, and the invariable pipe of peace, qualified with a very slight modicum of fire-water, round the camp-fire. How delicious was that short hour before turning in ; the great fire sending up tall pillars of flame, and throwing the little white tents into relief, while the surrounding forest lay in black shade : the bright sun-burnt face of good old S—— seen dimly through the smoke-wrack, his favourite G.B.D. pipe between his lips, raising his tin pannikin to drink ' wæs-hæl ; ' the ceaseless plash of the tide ; the rising moon casting her silvery path across the river ; the bright lights from the French village, with an occasional monotonous, yet not untuneful, song from the same, in which Alec and Fabien would join vociferously, utterly regardless of time and tune ; and the numberless mysterious voices of the forest—the hoot of the great horned owl, the chant of the whip-poor-will, or the wailing cry of the poor Kennedy, with occasionally the plaintive howl of some belated bear scared out of his seven senses by the apparition of our camp-fire, or the short sharp bark of a fox. Our sleeping-arrangements were primitive but sufficient: two red Hudson Bay blankets, a strip of sail-cloth, and a piece of mackintosh, formed our properties, which we might vary *à discrétion.* For myself, I placed everything on the bare ground, the mackintosh underneath, rolled myself up in one of the blankets, pillowed my head on a carpet-bag, and slept. The others used to make elaborate preparations, in the way of amateur bedsteads, &c., but they generally came to grief; in fact, H—— and C—— were invariably discovered in the morning in a chaotic condition, looking as if they had passed the night wrestling with some hideous nightmare—a confused mass of limbs, blankets, pine-logs and spruce-boughs. Only once was I disturbed by nocturnal invaders. I had just turned in, and was almost in my first sleep, when I heard a heavy, not human tread in the camp, accompanied by an awful blowing noise, like the escape of steam from an engine. I lay and quaked. I had never seen a bear in his untrammelled state, for they were so shy that we could never get a sight of them. Still I knew a good deal about bears. I knew that bears had a heavy tread, and made noises like steam-engines, and our visitor was an indubitable ursa major. Our only weapon of defence, a small rifle, was kept in S——'s tent, at the extreme end of the camp from me. Moreover, said rifle was always taken carefully to pieces and packed away, making it practically useless in all cases of midnight assault. I lay and quaked: I more than quaked; I positively wobbled. I thought of the grislies of the Mayne Reid of my infancy; I thought of Beauty and the Beast. Closer and closer came the footsteps, louder and louder sounded the blowing; when suddenly, to my intense relief, my bear gave vent to an unmistakable 'moo.' Being pot-valiant, I rushed from my tent, seized an axe-handle, and belaboured the unfortunate 'coo' till she bellowed with terror and fled shuddering to the woods. Curiously enough, this disturbance had not aroused any of my companions, and when, in the morning, I recounted my midnight alarm, I was greeted with a chorus of, 'Why didn't you milk her? But you Englishmen never know anything.'

The curious French-Canadian *patois* of Alec used to tickle me not a little; *par exemple*, at our first dinner I addressed him: " Alec, pommes de terre, s'il vous plaît.' 'M'sieu?' with that admirable look of semi-idiotcy which only a ' Canuck ' can assume. ' Pommes de terre, you loon.' 'M'sieu?' 'Ah,' said S——, ' if you want to get potatoes out of Alec, you must say " potattes." ' That produced the magic effect, and I got my potatoes.

On another occasion : ' Alec, où est bonne pour pêcher?' 'Par lô, m'sieu,' indicating the water generally (as I thought). ' Yes, you mutton-head,' quoth I, waxing English in my wrath, ' of course you will find fish in the water.' After much recrimination it was discovered that what I took for Alec's *l'eau* was his pronunciation of *là*, and that he was pointing out some particular ' bonne place ' for me to try.

The latter part of our stay was enlivened by the arrival of a party of fellow piscators from Quebec, and the little camp looked very pretty at night, with its two fires. One of the new party was of a vocal turn (H—— not inaptly called him the ' Luck of Roaring Camp ') and delighted to roar out a festive chorus, the burthen of which was—

> On the banks of the Yang, Yang, Yang-tse-kiang,
> On the banks of the Yang-tse-kiang.

But all pleasant things must have an end; and after a fortnight's pure unadulterated enjoyment, we ' up stick ' and departed, having given a good account of some forty dozen trout. The perfectly unalloyed happiness of our camp-life, which seemed to culminate in our last stopping-place, I can never forget. The early hours, the healthful and not excessive day's work, the ever-varying grandeur of the scenery, the exhilarating delight of landing a fine three-pound trout, the capacious appetite with which we always attacked our meals, the calm pleasant hours of rest and repose, and last, but by no means least, the great charm of the company of a cheerful and equable friend, threw a halo of sweet recollection over that summer which can never be effaced. I can only say to those who have health, strength, average means, good digestions, and an appreciation of beautiful scenery, let them take rod and knapsack, and explore the Saguenay, or any other of the score of beautiful rivers which lie in the neighbourhood of the Gulf of the St. Lawrence, and they will never regret it.

Regarding the ' poor Kennedy ' to which I alluded, there is a pretty but wholly apocryphal legend. Some years ago a young English officer, Kennedy by name, was hunting in the woods near Quebec, and was entirely lost; not a trace of him was ever found again. But ever since, say the Indian hunters, a bird, whose note was never heard before, perpetually utters plaintive notes resembling the syllables ' Oh, poor Kennedy, Kennedy ; ' of which, as Charles Kingsley says, ' let every man believe as much as he list.'

I conclude with a ' bear story,' which obtained some notoriety in the township of Compton, province of Quebec. A young English farmer, noted alike for his convivial habits and his great personal strength, was returning from the village to his farm in that state commonly known among sailors as ' three sheets in the wind.' On his way home he met a bear, with whom he alleged himself to have had the following rencontre : — 'About a mile from here last night, gentlemen, I met a big slouching-looking fellow, *in a buffalo coat,* who refused to let me pass him, so of course I took off my coat and closed with him at once. I never wrestled with such a rum customer before. He did not use his legs at all, but seemed as if he *wanted to hug me with his arms.* At last, however, I tripped him up, and down he went in the snow. But, gentlemen, you take my advice—unless you are good wrestlers, as I pride myself on being, when you meet a big man in a fur coat who wants to try a fall with you, *let him go by.*'

A. WENTWORTH POWELL.

The New Republic;

OR, CULTURE, FAITH, AND PHILOSOPHY IN AN ENGLISH
COUNTRY HOUSE.

BOOK I. (*continued*).—CHAPTER IV.

IT was a calm, lovely evening. The moon was rising over the
sea, and the sea was slowly silvering under it. A soft breeze
breathed gently, full of the scents of flowers ; and in the low sky
of the west there yet lingered a tender peach-colour.

The ladies were sitting about on chairs, grouped together, but
with several little groups within the group : and amongst them all
was Dr. Jenkinson, making himself particularly agreeable to Mrs.
Sinclair. When the gentlemen emerged there was a general stir.

'Well, Mr. Laurence,' said Lady Ambrose, shutting up a volume
of St. Simon's Memoirs, 'we have been talking most industriously
about the future.'

Laurence was standing with Mr. Luke on the step of the dining-
room window, and both were looking out gravely on the tranquil
scene.

'Do you remember,' said Laurence, 'that it was here, three
years ago, that you composed the lines that stand last in your
published volumes ?'

'I remember,' said Mr. Luke dreamily. 'What an evening that
was !'

'I wish you would repeat them,' said Laurence.

'What is the good ?' said Mr. Luke, 'why rouse again the voices
that haunt
>About the mouldered lodges of the past?'

'Is Mr. Luke going to recite poetry ? How delicious !' said
Mrs. Sinclair, coming languidly up to them. She was looking
lovely in the dim light, with a diamond star shining in her dark
hair.

'Mr. Luke, do !' said Lady Ambrose appealingly.

Mr. Luke, with a silent composure, pressed his hands for a
moment against his forehead ; gave one hem ; and in a clear melodious voice began.

Softly the evening descends,
Violet and soft. The sea
Adds to the silence, below
Pleasant and cool on the beach
Breaking ; yes, and a breeze
Calm as the twilight itself
Furtively sighs through the dusk,
Listlessly lifting my hair,
Fanning my thought-wearied brow.
  Thus I stand in the gloom
Watching the moon-track begin
Quivering to die like a dream
Over the far sea-line
To the unknown region beyond.

  So for ages hath man
Gazed on the ocean of time
From the shores of his birth, and, turning
His eyes from the quays, the thronged
Marts, the noise and the din
To the far horizon, hath dreamed
Of a timeless country beyond.
  Vainly—for how should he pass,
Being on foot, o'er the wet
Ways of the unplumbed waves ?
How, without ship, should he pass
Over the shipless sea
To the timeless country beyond ?

  Ah, but once—once long ago,
Came there a ship white-sailed
From the country beyond, with bright
Oarsmen, and men that sang
Came to Humanity's coasts,
Called to the men on the shore,
Joyously touched at the port.
  Then did time-weary man
Climb the bulwarks, the decks
Eagerly crowding. Anon
With jubilant voices raised,
And singing, ' When Israel came
Out of Egypt,' and whatso else
In the psalm is written, they passed
Out of the ken of the land,
Over the far sea-line,
To the unknown region beyond.

  Where are they now, then—they
That were borne out of sight by the ship—
Our brothers, of times gone by ?
Why have they left us here
Solemn, dejected, alone,
Gathered in groups on the shore ?
Why ? For we, too, have gazed

O'er the waste of waters, and watched
For a sail as keenly as they.
Ah, wretched men that we are !
On our haggard faces, and brows
Aching, a wild breeze fawns
Full of the scents of the sea,
Redolent of regions beyond.
Why, then, tarries the ship ?
When will her white sail rise
Like a star on the sea-line ? When ?

When ?—And the answer comes
From the sailless face of the sea,
' Ah vain watchers, what boots
The calm of the evening ?
Have ye not watched through the day
Turbulent waves, the expanse
Endless, shaken with storm ?
And ask ye where is the ship ?
Deeper than plummet can dive
She is bedded deep in the ooze,
And over her tall mast floats
The purple plain of the calm.'

Yes—and never a ship
Since this is sunken, will come
Ever again o'er the waves—
Nay, not even the craft with the fierce
Steersman, him of the marsh
Livid, with wheels of flame
Circling his eyes, to smite
The lingering soul with his oar.
—Not that even.   But we
Drop where we stand one by one
On the shingles and sands of time,
And cover in taciturn gloom,
With only perhaps some tear,
Each for his brother the hushed
Heart and the limitless dreams
With a little gift of sand.

'Thank you, Mr. Luke, so much,' said Lady Ambrose.   'How charming !   I am always so fond of poems about the sea.'

'Ah,' said Mr. Luke, turning to Mrs. Sinclair, 'these are emotions scarcely worth describing.'

'Certainly not,' muttered Mr. Storks, half aloud, as he moved off to discover Lady Grace.

Mr. Luke stood apart, and surveyed the party with a look of pensive pity.   On Mr. Storks, however, whose last remark he had overheard, his eyes rested with an expression somewhat more contemptuous.   The brightening moonlight fell softly on the group before him, giving it a particularly picturesque effect, touching as it did the many colours and folds of the ladies' dresses, and striking here and there a furtive flash from a gem on wrist or throat. The tranquil hour seemed to have a tranquillizing effect on nearly everyone; and the conversation reached Mr. Luke's ears as a low murmur, broken only by the deep sound of Mr. Storks's voice, and the occasional high notes of Mr. Saunders, who seemed to Mr. Luke, in his present frame of mind, to be like a shrill cock, crowing to the world before the sunrise of universal philistinism.

Laurence had caught Miss Merton's eyes, looking at him with a grave regard; and this had brought him instantly to her side, when Mr. Luke had ended his recital.

'We didn't spare the times we live in, to-night, did we?' he said slowly, in a low voice. 'Well, well—I wonder what it is all coming to—we and our times together! We are a curious medley here, all of us. I suppose no age but ours could have produced one like it—at least, let us hope so, for the credit of the ages in general.'

'I must say,' said Miss Merton, smiling, 'that you seem to take to the age very kindly, and to be very happy amongst your friends. But you did not tell us very much of what you thought yourself.'

'I don't often say what I think,' said Laurence, 'because I don't often know what I think; but I know a great many things that I don't think; and I confess I take a pleasure in saying these, and in hearing others say them; so the society that I choose as a rule represents not the things I think I approve, but the things I am sure I repudiate.'

'I confess,' said Miss Merton, 'I don't quite understand that.'

'Shall I tell you,' said Laurence, 'why I live so much in society—amongst my friends, as you call them? Simply because I feel, in my life, as a child does in a dark room; and I must have some one to talk to, or else I think I should go mad. What one says is little matter, so long as one makes a noise of some sort, and forgets the ghosts that in one's heart one is shuddering at.'

Miss Merton was silent for a moment, and looked up into the sky in which the stars were now one by one appearing.

'I suppose,' she said presently, 'you think that it is a very poor affair—life's whole business? And yet I don't see why you should.'

'Not see why I should!' repeated Laurence; 'that shows how little you, from your position, can sympathize with ours. How, indeed, could you? You, happy in some sustaining faith, can see a meaning in all life, and in all life's affections. You can endure

—you can even welcome its sorrows. For your religion is a kind
of philosopher's stone, turning whatever it touches into gold. But
we—we can only remember that things, for us too, once had a
meaning, but have it no longer. Life stares blankly at us like
the face of a dear friend who has turned an idiot. Perhaps you
never read Clough's Poems, did you? Scarcely a day passes in
which I do not echo to myself his words :—

> Ah well-a-day, for we are souls bereaved !
> Of all the creatures under heaven's wide cope,
> We are most hopeless who had once most hope,
> And most beliefless who had once believed.'

'And do you think that belief in these days brings no painful
perplexities too?' said Miss Merton, in a very low tone. 'Do you
think that we can look out on the state of the world now, and
think about its future, without anxiety? But really,' she went on,
raising her voice, 'if I, like you, thought that Christianity was not
true, I should not waste my time in lamenting over it. I should
rather be glad that I had got free from a gigantic and awful im-
position.'

'What!' exclaimed Laurence, 'should we rejoice at our old
guide dropping dead amongst the mountains, even though he had
lost his way, if so we are left helpless, and without any guide at
all?'

'You have your consciences,' said Miss Merton, with some
decision in her voice; 'you surely don't mean to say that you have
lost them?'

'As for our consciences,' said Leslie, who was standing close by,
'we revere them so much that we fancy they possess some power.
But conscience, in most souls, is like an English Sovereign—it
reigns, but it does not govern. Its function is merely to give a
formal assent to the bills passed by the passions; and it knows, if it
opposes what those are really bent upon, that ten to one it will be
obliged to abdicate.'

'Let us hope that the constitutions of most souls are more
stable than that,' said Miss Merton. 'As far as morality goes, I
expect you have quite enough to guide you; and if you think
religion false, I don't see why its loss should trouble you. And
life itself has plenty of pleasures. It is full of things worth living
for.'

'Is it?' exclaimed Leslie, with an emphasis that made Miss
Merton look up, and she almost started at the worn and haggard expression his face had in the moonlight. 'Is there anything in it that
is worth living for? It seems to me that we are only cursed with
the power of imagining that there might be, and with the know-

ledge that there never is. How happy the blue sea in the sunshine might make us, or this lovely water before us, with its floods of moonlight. Might—but they never do. They only madden us with a vague sorrow, like the memory of a friend for ever taken away from us.'

'Still,' said Miss Merton, 'life is not all moonlight. Surely friendship and affection are worth having.'

'I don't mean,' said Leslie, 'that I am always pining and bemoaning myself. Fortunately, the deeper part of one's nature will often go to sleep, and then the surface can enjoy itself. We can even laugh with our lips at the very things that our hearts in silence are breaking for. But as for happiness, that is always like prophecy, it is only fulfilled in the future ; or else it is a miracle —it only exists in the past. The actual things we wish for we may very likely get, but they always come too late or too soon. When the boy is in love, he tries to feel like a man ; when the man is in love, he tries to feel like a boy ; and both, in vain.'

'I don't exactly feel that,' said Laurence ; 'I think I might be happy, if I had not so much to make me miserable.'

'Might you ?' said Leslie. 'When I look at what we are and what the world is, I can fancy no more melancholy spectacle than a happy man ; though I admit that there is none more amusing than a man who tries to be melancholy.'

As he said this, Leslie moved slowly away.

'I don't know what has happened to Leslie,' said Laurence to Miss Merton ; 'there is a curious bitterness about the things he says sometimes, that there did not use to be. And yet I envy him his temperament. He never lets any melancholy subdue him. He can always laugh it down in a moment ; and he will trample bravely on any of his sentiments if he is on the road to anything he is proud of aiming at.'

Laurence was silent for a moment, and then said abruptly,

'I dare say you think me very morbid ; but perhaps you can hardly realize the intense restless misery that a man endures who can find nothing to do which he really feels worth doing. Could I only find some one thing—one great cause to labour for—one great idea—I could devote my whole self to it, and be happy : for labour, after all, is the only thing that never palls on a man. But such a cause, such an idea—I can find it nowhere. Politics have turned into a petty, weary game ; religion is dead. Our new prophets only offer us Humanity, in place of the God of which they have deprived us. And Humanity makes a very poor Deity, since it is every day disgracing itself, and is never of the same mind from one week's end to another. And so here I am utterly alone—friendless; feeling that, were it not for the petty contemptible interests I manufacture for myself from day to day, life would be quite unbearable.'

'And yet,' said Miss Merton, 'you have much to make you happy—much that you would be sorry to lose.'

'I have a certain position,' said Laurence, 'and a certain amount of wealth, and I would not willingly lose a particle of either of these; but that is not because, in my heart, I value them; but because, if I lost them, I might in my heart cease to despise them.'

'Surely,' said Miss Merton, 'there is a better way of looking at the matter. You came into the world with all your lower ambitions satisfied for you. The ground therefore is quite clear for the higher ambitions. That is why I think an aristocracy, as a rule, must always be the best governors of men, for their ambitions, as a rule, are the only genuine ones. Think, too, what an advantage mere wealth is. The highest labour will never produce money, but generally requires it.'

'That is just the difficulty,' said Laurence. 'What shall I labour for? I am almost maddened sometimes, as I sit all the day idle, and seem to hear the hateful wasted moments slipping away from me. And I *could* do something, I am sure. I feel I have powers.'

'I think,' said Miss Merton, 'that all I should say to you is, find something to do. The power to find or make an object is, I think, a great part of genius. However,' she said, with some sympathy in her voice, 'if you are in difficulties, I am sure I wish I could help you.'

'I beg your pardon for my egoism,' said Laurence, looking at her gratefully. 'I never talked so long about myself in my whole life-time, and I promise never to do so again.'

Leslie meanwhile had moved away towards Mrs. Sinclair, who, looking particularly fascinating, was still commanding the attentions of Dr. Jenkinson. The Doctor was standing by her, all nods and becks and wreathed smiles, and, to Leslie's surprise, was saying something to her about Sappho.

'And now,' said Mrs. Sinclair, with a little dainty smile, 'I want to ask you something about the Greek Anthology too. I can't read much Greek myself; but a gentleman who used to be rather kind to me, translated me a good deal of Greek poetry, once upon a time—when my husband,' she said, with a little shrug of the shoulders, 'used to go to sleep after his dinner.'

Dr. Jenkinson here glanced suspiciously at Mrs. Sinclair.

'Now what I want you to tell me,' she said, 'is something about some little—ahem—love-songs, I think they were.'

The doctor started.

'And please not to think me a terrible blue-stocking,' Mrs. Sinclair went on with an appealing smile, 'for I really hardly know any Greek myself.'

'Nor I either,' the doctor exclaimed suddenly, with an icy brusqueness, the sudden birth of a rapidly matured confusion. This reply completely took aback not only Mrs. Sinclair, but Dr. Jenkinson himself as well, who before the words were out of his mouth had not the remotest notion what he was going to say. However, he felt he had gained the victory, and with an expression on his face of austere gravity, he moved a pace away, and sat down on a chair close to Miss Merton.

Mrs. Sinclair turned to Leslie with a flash of suppressed laughter in her eyes.

'How lovely the evening is!' said Leslie softly, responding to the smile.

'It almost realises one's idea of perfect beauty,' said Mrs. Sinclair, looking out dreamily over the sea.

'You are certainly most Hellenic,' said Leslie. 'First you talk of Sappho, now of Ideas of Beauty. Are you a Platonist?'

'Mr. Leslie, of course I am,' said Mrs. Sinclair, somewhat misapprehending his meaning. 'I never heard such an impertinent question. Platonism, however, is a very rare philosophy in these days, I'm afraid.'

'And so you think we are all of us very bad, do you?' said Leslie. 'Well, I know we men are often apt to think so. And yet we generalise very hastily, and often very wrongly, I am sure. How often, for instance, do we say that all wives nowadays are inconstant, simply because such are the only ones we remember, not because they are the only ones we know.'

This speech was quite in Mrs. Sinclair's own manner, and she looked at Leslie with a smile of appreciation that was half sentimental, half humorous, and had just a touch of sadness in it as well.

'Ah,' she began to say, ' if we could all of us love only when and where we ought——' But here she paused; her voice died away, and she leaned her head upon her hand in silence.

Leslie was going to have spoken; but he was suddenly arrested by the sound of Dr. Jenkinson, close beside him, talking to Miss Merton in a tone of unusual earnestness.

'I don't wonder you should be in perplexity,' he said. 'Whichever way we look at things, there will be perplexities. But there is a God—there is such a thing as goodness: and so, in this large faith let us rest.'

'Ah,' said Donald Gordon to Miss Merton, in his soft deferential voice, which always sounded as if he was saying something deeply devotional, 'don't you think it is a higher thing to be good for good's own sake than for God's? Don't you think morality is its own reward?'

'But what of those poor people,' said Miss Merton, 'who cannot be moral—whom circumstances have kept from being ever anything but brutalised? I dare say,' she said, turning to the Doctor, quite forgetting his sacred character, 'that I shall not be able to commend to you such a notion as that of living for God's glory; but still, if God be not a Person for whose glory we can live—who can exercise mercy on us—who does not leave us all to ourselves, think what difficulties we have to face. Think what a place we make of this world, if the millions of wretched people in it have no one to care for them, and no hope at all anywhere. Think of those who, in spite of hard surroundings, have just had strength enough to struggle to be good, but to struggle only,—whose whole moral being has been left writhing in the road of life, like an animal that a cart-wheel has gone over, just looking up with a piteous appeal at us who will not help it——.'

Miss Merton looked at Dr. Jenkinson and paused. The moon shone tenderly on his silver hair, and his keen eyes had something very like moisture in them.

'There are great difficulties in life,' he said, 'but there is another life in store for us—another life, and a God. And don't think that the world is growing to disbelieve in these. Remember how many intelligent laymen count themselves members of the Church of England, simply because they believe in these two doctrines.'

'It has always been inexplicable to me,' said Mr. Storks, who had been attracted by the sound of the Doctor's voice, 'whence this longing for a future life could have arisen. I suppose there are few things the very possibility of which science so conclusively disproves.'

'And yet,' said Laurence, who had been speaking for a moment to Mrs. Sinclair, 'I can't help thinking, at certain moments, that there may be a whole world of things undreamed of by our scientific philosophy. Such a feeling is touched by the sight of an " ora pro animâ meâ," or a " resurgam," on a quiet tombstone, or the sign of the cross made by a mother in hope and in sorrow on the forehead of her dead child.'

Miss Merton looked at Laurence with some wonder in her large expressive eyes. Mr. Storks snorted, and Dr. Jenkinson blinked.

'See,' said Donald Gordon, 'the moonlight grows brighter and brighter every moment. It is almost bewildering in its dazzling paleness.'

'And there,' said Laurence, 'do you catch it?—that is the light-ship on the horizon, like a large low star.'

Laurence seated himself on the balustrade, and leaning on his elbow, looked up into the clear hollow skies.

'World upon world,' he exclaimed at last, 'and each one crowded, very likely, with beings like ourselves, wondering what this whole great universe is!'

'And the vast majority of them believing in a wise and just God,' said Leslie, 'for I see no reason why ours should be the stupidest world in all creation.'

'Yes,' said Laurence, 'and in each world a small select band, that has pierced through such a husk of lies, and has discovered the all-golden truth, that the universe is aimless, and that for good and evil, the end is all one.'

Dr. Jenkinson had a sensible horror of the stars : and as soon as they were mentioned he turned round in his chair, giving his back to the group, Miss Merton included, whilst Mr. Storks walked away, not without dignity.

'Mrs. Sinclair is going to sing in a moment,' said Laurence, 'some one is gone to fetch her guitar.'

'Hush !' exclaimed Miss Merton, 'do just listen to this.'

'Good gracious !' said Laurence in a whisper, 'Mr. Storks is at my aunt at last.'

Mr. Storks had been watching ever since dinner for an opportunity of discussing with Lady Grace the true position of woman, as settled by modern science. He was peculiarly full of this subject just now, having received only that morning a letter from a celebrated American physician, who stated very strongly as his opinion, that the strain of what is called the higher education was most prejudicial to the functions of maternity, and that the rights of woman might very probably be fatal to the existence of man. As soon as he got hold of Lady Grace, he led up to this point with startling rapidity ; having been perfectly charmed at starting to find that she fully agreed with him that the prejudices of the present day were doing more harm to woman's true interests than anything else.

'It is a pleasure,' said Mr. Storks, 'to discuss these matters with a person so thoroughly enlightened as yourself. You will of course see from what Dr. Boston says how entirely suicidal is the scheme of turning woman into a female man. Nature has marked out her mission for her plainly enough : and so our old friend

Milton was right in his meaning, after all, when he says that man is made for God, and woman for God through him, though of course the expression is antiquated.'

'Surely,' said Lady Grace with animation, ' not only the expression is antiquated, but the meaning also is contrary to all true fairness and enlightenment.'

'I confess, I don't see that,' said Mr. Storks with a look of smiling deference.

'What!' said Lady Grace, ' is it not contrary to reason—let me put it to your own candour—for a man who knows that his wife, ages hence, will be a seraph singing before the throne of God, to consider her only made for God through him—to consider her, indeed, as a thing made for his exclusive use?'

This answer of Lady Grace's took Mr. Storks quite aback. His jaw fell—he stared—he said nothing. He knew not how to comport himself. He felt as though he had been assassinated. But luckily at this very moment, liquid and clear and exquisitely modulated, were heard the sounds of Mrs. Sinclair's voice, singing the following song—

> Darling, can you endure the liquid weather,
>   The jasmine-scented twilights, oh my dear?
> Or do you still remember how together
>   We read the sad sweet Idyll 'Guinevere,'
>   Love, in one last year's twilight?
> *Galeotto fu il libro, e chi lo scrisse.*[1]
>
> Ah, the flowers smelt sweet, and all unheeding
>   Did I read to you that tender tale,
> Oh my love, until my voice, in reading
>   How those lovers 'greeted passion-pale,'
>   Trembled in the soft twilight.
> *Galeotto fu il libro, e chi lo scrisse.*
>
> Then our eyes met, and then all was over—
>   All the world receded cold and far;
> And your lips were on my lips, my lover;
>   And above us shook a silver star,
>   Through depths of melting twilight.
> *Galeotto fu il libro, e chi lo scrisse.*
>
> Darling, no July will ever find us
>   On this earth, together, more. Our fates
> Were but a moment cheated. Then, behind us
>   Shrilled his voice for whom Caïna[2] waits,
>   Shattering our one sweet twilight.
> *Galeotto fu il libro, e chi lo scrisse.*

[1] Dante. Inferno v. 137.   [2] Ibid. v. 107.

I shall know no more of summer weather,
Nought will be for me of glad or fair,
Till I join my darling, and together
We go for ever on the accursed air,[1]
There in the dawnless twilight.
Galeotto fu il libro, e chi lo scrisse.

'What a lovely voice!' said Laurence to Miss Merton. 'I wonder how she will sound singing before the throne.'

'She will be obliged to take lessons in a rather different style,' said Miss Merton, unable to suppress a smile; and then she suddenly checked herself, and looked grave. 'Mrs. Sinclair has always interested me,' she said. 'I often come across her in London, but I hardly know her.'

'Mr. Laurence,' said Mrs. Sinclair, 'you must now make Mr. Leslie sing, for I discover that he can play the guitar too.'

Leslie was of course pressed, and with some reluctance consented to sing.

'I suppose,' he said, 'we are all of us more or less moonstruck to-night, so I had best sing the silliest thing I know; and as I don't think anyone ever wrote a sillier thing than a song I once wrote myself, I will sing that.'

He touched a few chords carelessly, and yet with the manner of a practised player, paused for a moment, and then again striking the instrument began to sing. He was watched at first with merely a languid curiosity; and Miss Prattle said in a whisper that he looked very affected; but curiosity and criticism were both lost in surprise at the first sound of his rich and flexible voice, and still more so at the real and reckless passion which he seemed to breathe into the words of the following song, rude and artless as they were.

Oh, her cheek, her cheek was pale,
Her voice was hardly musical;
But your proud grey eyes grew tender,
Child, when mine they met,
With a piteous self-surrender,
Margaret.

Child, what have I done to thee?
Child, what hast thou done to me?
How you froze me with your tone
That last day we met!
Your sad eyes then were cold as stone,
Margaret.

Oh, it all now seems to me
A far-off weary mystery!

[1] Ibid. v. 31.

> Yet—and yet, her last sad frown
> Awes me still, and yet—
> In vain I laugh your memory down,
> Margaret.

Leslie received loud thanks from many voices. Lady Ambrose was especially delighted, but some were almost silent from surprise at the manner of the singer and the feeling he had shown, for which no one had given him credit. Mrs. Sinclair held out her hand to him, when no one was looking, and said quietly, 'Thank you so much, I can't tell you how I liked your song.'

'Well,' said Laurence, as the party moved indoors into the lighted drawing-room, 'we have been all of us very sentimental to-night, and if we can't get better now, I hope we shall sleep it off, and wake up well and sane to-morrow morning.'

The following day was Sunday, and as the nearest church was some miles distant, it was rumoured amongst the guests that Dr. Jenkinson would perform the service and preach a sermon in the private chapel.

BOOK II.—CHAPTER I.

ON the following morning Lady Ambrose awoke somewhat out of spirits. Last night, whilst her maid was brushing her hair, she had pondered deeply over much that she had heard during the evening ; and her thoughts having been once started in such a direction, the conviction quickly dawned upon her that the world was indeed becoming very bad, and that society was on the point of dissolution. This was quite a new view of things to her, and it had all the charm of novelty. She would yet perhaps have successfully slept it off by the morning, had not the post failed to bring her an invitation to a ball at —— House, which she was anxiously looking out for. Her spirits therefore failed to recover themselves, and whilst she was being dressed her thoughts wandered wistfully away to the promised morning service in the chapel. At breakfast, however, another blow awaited her. How a private chapel had come to be mentioned last evening was not clear. Certainly there was no such appendage to Laurence's villa, and the susceptibilities of Lady Ambrose received a severe shock, as she learnt that the ministrations of Dr. Jenkinson, the comfort of which she was looking forward to, were to take place in the theatre which adjoined the house. She bore up, however, like a brave woman, and resolving that nothing, on her part at least, should be wanting, she appeared shortly before eleven o'clock, in full Sunday costume, with her bonnet, and her books of devotion.

Mrs. Sinclair looked at her in dismay. ' I had thought,' she said plaintively to Laurence, ' that, as this was only a morning performance, I need not make a toilette. And as for a prayer-book, why, dear Mr. Laurence, I have not had one since I was confirmed.'

' Not when you were married ? ' said Leslie.

' Perhaps,' said Mrs. Sinclair pensively, ' but I have forgotten all about that——now.'

At this moment the gong sounded, and the whole party, Lady Ambrose and her bonnet amongst then, adjourned to the place of worship, which was connected with the house by a long corridor.

When the party entered they found themselves in a complete miniature theatre, with the gas, as there were no windows, fully burning. It had been arranged beforehand that the guests should occupy the boxes, the gallery being appropriated to the servants, whilst the stalls were to remain completely empty. The congregation entered with great decorum, and gradually settled themselves in their places with a subdued whispering. Lady Ambrose buried her face in her hands for a few moments, and several of the younger ladies followed her example. Everyone then looked about them silently, in suspense and expectation. The scene that met their eyes was certainly not devotional. The whole little semicircle glittered with heavy gilding and with hangings of crimson satin, and against these the stucco limbs of a number of gods and goddesses gleamed pale and prominent. The gallery rested on the heads of nine scantily-draped Muses, who, had they been two less in number, might have passed for the seven deadly sins ; round the frieze, in high relief, reeled a long procession of Fauns and Bacchanals ; and half the harem of Olympus sprawled and floated on the azure ceiling. Nor was this all. The curtain was down ; and, brilliantly illuminated as it was, displayed before the eyes of the congregation Faust on the Brocken, with a long plume, dancing with the young witch, who could boast of no costume at all. The scene was so strange that everyone forgot to whisper or even to smile. There was a complete silence, and the eyes of all were soon fixed upon the curtain in wonder and expectation.

Presently a sound was heard. A door opened, and Dr. Jenkinson, in his ordinary dress, entered the stalls. He looked deliberately round him for a moment, as though he were taking stock of those present ; then, selecting the central stall as a kind of *prie-Dieu,* he knelt down facing his congregation, and after a moment's pause began to read the service in a simple, earnest voice. Lady Ambrose, however, though she knew her prayer-book as well as most women, could not for the life of her find the place. The reason was not

far to seek. The Doctor had begun with the following passage
from the Koran, which he had once designed to use in Westminster Abbey as the text of a missionary sermon.

' Be constant in prayer,' he began, in a voice tremulous with
emotion, ' and give alms : and what good ye have sent before for
your souls, ye shall find it with God. Surely God seeth that
which ye do. They say, Verily none shall see Paradise except they
be Jews or Christians. This is their wish. Say ye, Produce your
proof of this if ye speak truth. Nay, but he who resigneth himself to God, and doeth that which is right, he shall have his reward
with his Lord ; there shall come no fear on them, neither shall they
be grieved.'

Dr. Jenkinson then went on with the Confession, the Absolution, and a number of other selections from the English morning
service, omitting, however, the creed, and concluded the whole with
a short prayer of St. Francis Xavier's.

But it was discovered that his voice, unless he made an
effort, was unhappily only partly audible from the position which
he occupied ; and Laurence, as soon as the Liturgy was over, went
softly up to him to apprise him of the fact. Dr. Jenkinson was
very grateful for being thus told in time. It was fortunate, he
said, that the prayers only had been missed ; the question was,
where should he go for the sermon. Laurence in a diffident
manner proposed the stage ; but the Doctor accepted the proposal
with great alacrity, and Laurence went immediately out with him
to conduct him to his new pulpit. In a few moments the curtain
was observed to twitch and tremble ; two or three abortive pulls
were evidently being made ; and at last Faust and the young witch
rapidly rolled up, and discovered first the feet and legs, and then
the entire person of Dr. Jenkinson, standing in the middle of a
gorge in the Indian Caucasus—the remains of a presentation of
Prometheus Bound which had taken place last February.

The Doctor was not a man to be abashed by incongruities.
He looked about him for a moment : he slightly raised his eyebrows, and then, without the least discomposure, and in a clear
incisive voice, began :

' In the tenth verse of the hundred and eleventh Psalm, it is
said, ' The fear of the Lord is the beginning of wisdom.' ' The fear
of the Lord,' he again repeated, more slowly, and with more emphasis, looking round the theatre as he spoke, ' is the beginning of
wisdom.'

He then made a long pause, looking down at his feet, as if,
although he held his sermon-book in his hand, he were considering
how to begin. As he stood there silent, the footlights shining

brightly on his silver hair, Lady Ambrose had full time to verify the text in her prayer book. At last the Doctor suddenly raised his head, and with a gentle smile of benignity playing on his lips, shook open his manuscript, and thus proceeded :—

'The main difficulty that occupied the early Greek Philosophers, as soon as philosophy in its proper sense can be said to have begun, was the great dualism that seemed to run through all things. Matter and mind, the presence of imperfection, and the idea of perfection, or the unity and plurality of being, were amongst the various forms in which the two contradictory elements of things were presented to them, as demanding reconcilement or explanation. This manner of viewing things comes to a head, so to speak, amongst the ancients, in the system of Plato. With him the sensible and the intelligible worlds stand separated by a great gulf, the one containing all good, the other of itself only evil, until we recognise its relation to the good, and see that it is only a shadow and a type of it. The world of real existence is something outside, and virtually unconnected with, this world of mere phenomena ; and the Platonic prayer is that we should be taken out of the world, rather than, as Christ says, with a fuller wisdom, that we should be delivered from the evil.

'Plato had, however, by thus dwelling on this antagonism in things, paved the way for a reconciliation—some say he even himself began it. At any rate, it was through him that it was nearly, if not quite, accomplished by his disciple Aristotle. Aristotle first systematized the great principle of evolution, and transformed what had appeared to former thinkers as the dualism of mind and matter into a single scale of ascending existences. Thus what Plato had conceived of as two worlds, were now presented as opposite poles of the same. The $\pi\rho\omega\tau\eta$ $\upsilon\lambda\eta$, the world 'without form and void,' receiving form, at length culminated in the soul of man ; and in the soul of man sensation at length culminated in pure thought.' A slight cough here escaped from Mrs. Sinclair. 'You will perhaps think,' the doctor went on, 'that a sermon is not the place in which to discuss such differences of secular opinion ; or you will perhaps think that such differences are of no very great moment. But if you look under the surface, and at the inner meaning of them, you will find that they bear upon questions which are, or ought to be, of the very highest moment to each of us—questions indeed,' the doctor added, suddenly lowering his manuscript for a moment, and looking sharply round at his audience, ' which we all of us here have very lately—very lately indeed—either discussed ourselves, or heard discussed by others.' This produced an immediate sensation, especially amongst the feminine part of the listeners, to whom the discourse thus far had seemed strange, rather than significant. ' The question,' the doctor continued, ' is one of the relations of the spiritual to the natural ; and the opposition between the views of these two ancient philosophers is by no means obsolete in our own century. There is even now far too prevalent a tendency to look upon the spiritual as something transcending and completely separate from the natural ; and there is in the minds of many well-meaning and earnest persons a sort of alarm felt at any attempt to bring the two into connection. This feeling is experienced not by Christians only, but by a large number of their opponents. There is, for instance, no doctrine more often selected for attack by those who oppose Christianity upon moral grounds, than that of which my text is an expression, I mean the doctrine of a morality enforced by rewards and punishments. Such morality, we hear it continually urged by men who set themselves up as advanced thinkers, is no morality at all. No action can be good, they tell us, that does not spring from the love of good. Virtue is no longer virtue if it springs from fear. The very essence of it is to spring from freedom. Now, these arguments, though specious at the first blush of the thing, are really, if we look them honestly in the face, to the utmost shallow and unphilosophical. They are really but so many denials of the great doctrine of evolution—so many attempts to set up again that absolute antagonism between good and evil which it has been the aim of all the higher thinkers, and of Christ himself, to do away with. If, then, these modern critics of Christianity come to us with such objections, let us not try to disguise the truth that the morality of our religion is based on fear. Let us rather boldly avow this, and try to point out to them that it is they, and not the Psalmist, that are out of harmony with modern thought. For, what is it that the sacred Scripture says ? " The fear of the Lord is the beginning of wisdom." *The beginning,* you will please to observe—the beginning only. It is not perfect wisdom, it is not perfect virtue ; but it is the beginning of both of these. It is, if I may be allowed the expression, the moral protoplasm—it is that out of which they are both evolved. It is, as Aristotle would call it, their potentiality. The actuality is different from the potentiality ; for " perfect love," as St. John says, " casteth out fear." Putting together, then, the ideas of these two good men, St. John and Aristotle, we may say that the love of God—that is, true wisdom—is the actuality of the fear of Him.

' This account of the origin of the true wisdom may not, indeed, be applicable to each individual case. Some persons '—the doctor's voice here grew very soft, and seemed as though it would almost break with feeling—' some persons may have been so fortunate as to have received the truest wisdom into their hearts by education, almost with their mother's milk. But there are those not so fortunate, who may have needed the discipline of a godly fear to lead them upwards from a " wallowing in the sensual sty," towards the higher life. And just as this is true of many of us individually, so is it still more deeply true of the human race as a whole. All study of history, and of social science, and of philosophy, is teaching this to us every day with increasing clearness. The human race, as soon as it became human, feared God before it loved Him. Its fear, as the Scripture puts it, was the beginning of its wisdom ; or, as modern thought has put it, in slightly different words, the love of justice sprang out of the fear of suffering injustice. Thus the end is different from the beginning, and yet springs out of it. Ethics, as it has been well said, are the finest fruits of humanity, but they are not its roots. Our reverence for truth, all our sacred family ties, and the purest and most exalted forms of matrimonial attachment, have each their respective origins in self-interest, self-preservation, and animal appetite.

'There is, I admit, in this truth something that may at first sight repel us, and perhaps even prompt some of us to deny indignantly that it is a truth at all. But this is really a cowardly and unworthy feeling, fatal to any true comprehension of God's dealings with man, and arising from a quite mistaken conception of our own dignity, and our own connection with God. It is some such mistaken conception as this that sets so many of us against the discoveries of modern science as to the origin of our own species, and, what is far worse, prompts us to oppose such discoveries with dishonest objections. How is it possible, some of us ask, that man, with his sublime conceptions of duty and of God, and his fine apparatus of reason, and so forth, should be produced by any process of evolution from a beastly and irrational ape ? But to ask such questions as these is really to call in question the power of God, and so to do Him dishonour. It is true that we cannot trace out, as yet, all the steps of this wonderful evolution ; but let us not be found, like doubting Thomas, resolved not to believe until we have actually seen. And yet, if our faith does indeed require strengthening, we have only to look a little more attentively at the commonest facts before us. For is it not, let me ask you—to take, for instance, a man's sublime faculty of reasoning and logical comprehension—far more wonderful that a reasoning man should have the same parents as a woman, than that they both should have the same parents as a monkey ? Science and religion both alike teach us that with God all things are possible.

'I just touch in passing upon this doctrine that we popularly call Darwinism, because it is the most familiar example to us of the doctrine of evolution. But the point which I am wishing to emphasize is not the outward evolution of man, but the inward, of which, however, the former is an image and a likeness. This theory of moral evolution I wish to point out to you, is alike the Christian and the scientific theory; and I thus wish you to see that the very points in which science seems most opposed to Christianity are really those in which it most fundamentally agrees with it. I will therefore just ask you to notice how foolish and short-sighted those persons are who think that a great result is lessened if it can be proved to have had small beginnings. Is a state less truly a state because we know that it has sprung out of the germ of the family? Surely not. Neither is man less truly man if he have sprung from an ape; nor is love less truly love if it has sprung from fear. Can anything be more irrational than the vulgar instinct to fancy that man has descended from his present dignity, if it can be proved he has ascended to it, or than the desire to prove that the savages of our own day are degradations of what was once good, rather than germs of what one day may be good? Whenever we meet with persons of such views as these, let us always answer them in Christ's words, and remind them that it is not by the roots that we are to judge the tree, but by the fruits of it.

'And now, since we have seen how science and Christianity are at one as to the rise of the moral sentiments, I will pass on to a wider point, the character and the history of Christianity itself, both of which have been misunderstood and misinterpreted for at least eighteen hundred years; and when I have pointed out how this great subject is being now explained by the methods of modern science, I will pass on to an issue that is wider yet.

'The world has hitherto failed to understand Christianity, because it studied it upon a false method—a method based upon that old dualistic theory of things of which I have already spoken. Just as Plato looked upon mind as entirely distinct from matter, so used Christians to look upon things sacred as entirely distinct from things secular. But now this middle wall of partition is being broken down by science, and by scientific criticism, and by a wider view of things in general. The primary way in which all this has affected Christianity, is by the new spirit in which it has led us to study the Bible. We used to look upon the Bible as a book standing apart by itself, and to be interpreted by a peculiar canon of criticism. But we have now learnt that it is to be studied just like all other books: and we are now for the first time coming to understand what, in its true grandeur, a real revelation is. We are learning, in fact, that just as no single scripture " is of any private interpretation ; " still less is the entire body of the Scriptures. They, too, must be interpreted by their context. We must enquire into their origin ; we must ask diligently under what circumstances they were written and edited, and for what ends. To understand the meaning of any text, we must try to see what, from his position and education, the writer could have meant by it ; not what this or that Father, living long afterwards, fancied that he meant. Our motto in religion, as in science, should be, " Vere scire est per causas scire."

' If we study Christianity reverently and carefully, upon these principles, we shall see that it was not a thing that sprang up, as we used to fancy, without any human antecedents, but that its roots reach back with many ramifications into the western and oriental thought of preceding centuries. We shall see how it absorbed into itself all that was highest in Hebraistic Theism and in Hellenic thought—something too, let us admit, of the failings of both. I cannot here enter into any of the details of this, what may be truly termed pre-Christian Christianity. I can only briefly point out its existence, and its double origin, commenting on these by the following few lines from a great German writer. " The yearning after a higher revelation," he tells us, " was the universal characteristic of the last centuries of the ancient world. This was in the first place but a consciousness of the decline of the classical nations and their culture, and the presentiment of the approach of a new era ; and it called into life not only Christianity, but also, and before it, Pagan and Jewish Alexandrianism, and other related developments."

' This, then, is the great point to be borne in mind—viz. that God had been preparing the way for the coming of Christ long before he sent " Elias, which was for to be." Neither John Baptist, no, nor One greater than John, was left by God (as the children of Israel were left by Pharaoh) to gather straw for himself to make bricks. The materials were all prepared ready to their hands by their Heavenly Father. And so, let us be especially and prayerfully on our guard against considering Christianity as having come into the world at once, ready-made, so to speak, by our Saviour, as a body of theological doctrines. Any honest study of history will show us that the Apostles received no such system ; that our Lord Himself never made any claim to the various characters with which subsequent thought invested Him ; and that to attribute such claims to Him would be an anachronism, of which He would Himself have scarcely understood the meaning. If we only clear our eyes of any false theological glamour, a very slight study of the sacred writers will at once show us this. We shall see how uncertain and shifting at first everything was. We shall see what a variety of conflicting opinions the early Church entertained even upon the most fundamental subjects—such, for instance, as the identity of the God of the Old Testament with the God of the New, which was denied by a large number of the early Christians : we shall see how widely divergent were the systems of Jewish and Pauline Christianity, and how discrepant and tentative are the accounts given by St. Paul and by the author of the Fourth Gospel of the mystical nature of Christ, whom they tried to identify with different mysterious potencies supposed by the Jewish-Alexandrian philosophers to be coexistent with God. And if we pursue the history of the Church a little farther, we shall find many more things to startle us. We shall find, for instance, the most renowned apologist of early Catholic times, a materialist, holding the materiality not of the soul of man only, but of God also. " Nihil enim "—these are this Father's words—" si non corpus. Omne quod est, corpus est." Thus we see,' said the Doctor cheerfully, looking round him with a smile of benignant triumph, and blinking with his eyes, ' that difference of opinion about the dogmas of religion is nothing new. It existed in the Jewish Church ; the phenomenon was only prolonged by Christianity. Later Judaism and primitive Christianity were both made up of a variety of systems, all honestly and boldly thought out, differing widely from each other, and called by the honourable appellation of heresies : and of these, let me remind you, it is the glory of the Church of England to be composed likewise.'

The doctor here paused to open out a slip of paper that was gummed to the margin of his sermon-book ; and then proceeded in a softer and a more appealing tone.

' Nor is this all,' he went on ; ' not only are all these things so confused and doubtful ; but we now see that, in the face of recent criticism, we cannot even be quite sure about any of the details of the divine life of our Lord. But in all this '—the doctor's voice here became yet more aërial, and he fixed his eyes upon the painted ceiling of the theatre, as though he were gazing on some glorious vision—' in all this there is nothing to discompose us. We can be quite sure that He lived, and that He went about doing good, and that in Him we have, in the highest sense, everlasting life.

' Let us then no longer fight against the conclusions of science and of criticism, but rather see in them the hand of God driving us, even against our will, away from beliefs and teachings that are not really those of His Son. If we do not do this—if we persist in identifying the false Christianity with the true—the false, when it is at last plucked rudely away from us, as it must be, will carry away a part of the true with it. And as long as we are in this state of mind, we are never for a moment safe. We can never open a philological review, or hear of a scientific experiment, without trembling. Witness the discussions now engaging so much public attention on the subject of animal automatism, and the marvellous results which experiments on living subjects have of late days revealed to us; a frog with half a brain having destroyed more theology than all the doctors of the Church with their whole brains can ever build up again. Thus does God choose the " weak things of this world to confound the wise." Seeing then, that this is the state of the case, we should surely learn henceforth not to identify Christianity with anything that science can assail, or even question. Let us say rather that nothing is or can be essential to the religion of Christ which, when once stated, can be denied without absurdity. If we can only attain to this conception, we shall see truly that this our faith is indeed one " that no man taketh away from us." '

' If we be thus once " stablished in the faith," all human history, and the history of Christianity especially, will assume for us a new sacredness and a new significance. We shall recognise gladly its long struggles of growth, and its struggles for existence, and see how in all these were at work the great principles of evolution. We shall see how Christian perfection emerged gradually out of imperfection—nay, that it was only through imperfection that this perfection was possible. For although, as we now know, all the various theological systems that have sprung up about Christianity, and have been so long current, are not Christianity, and most of them, indeed, not even sense—yet it was through these that true Christianity made its way, and extended itself in a corrupt and ignorant world. For the world has been given from age to age just so much of the truth as it has been able to bear, and it is only, let us remember, from receiving it tempered in this wise proportion, that it has been able to receive it at all. But these times of the world's probation are now passing away. It is now at length ceasing to be under " tutors and governors; " it is learning to " put away childish things." It is coming to a sense that it is now fitted to receive Christ's truth first, and without any admixture or wrappage of falsehood. And so, as it looks back over all the various opinions once so fiercely agitated about religion, it recognises in all of them a common element of good, and it sees that all theologians and all sects have really agreed with one another, and been meaning the same thing, even when they least expected it. Nor is it, as modern study is shewing us, varieties of Christianity only that this deeper unity underlies, but all other religions also. It has been well observed by a great Roman Catholic writer now living, that whenever any great saintliness of life is to be observed amongst infidels and heretics, it is always found to be due to the presence of certain beliefs and rules which belong to the Catholics. And in like manner, we may say too, that whenever any great saintliness of life is to be observed amongst Catholics, it is due to the presence of certain beliefs and rules that belong to the infidels and the heretics—and indeed to all good men, no matter what their religion is.

'Such are the views that all the most enlightened men of our own day are coming to. But the process is gradual; and meanwhile let us not rebuke our weaker brethren, if for the present "they follow not after us;" let us rather bear with them, and make all allowance for them; for we must remember, as I have said before, that those evils to which they still cling, but from which we, under God's mercy, are trying to free ourselves, have done good service in their time; and that even such doctrines as those of eternal punishment, or of sacerdotal absolution, or the subtleties of sacramental systems, or the mystical paradoxes of the Athanasian Creed, have assisted in the evolution of the good—have been, in some sense, "schoolmasters to bring men to God." And even if we do occasionally come across some incident in the history of our religion—some doctrine or body of doctrines, which seems, humanly speaking, to subserve no good end at all—such as our own Thirty-nine Articles—let us not suffer such to try our faith, but let us trust in God, believing that in His secret councils He has found some fitting use even for these, because we know how many things there are, in every branch of enquiry, that we cannot explain, and yet we know that nothing happens but by those immutable and eternal laws which our Heavenly Father has Himself ordained, and of which He is Himself the highest synthesis.

'And now,' said the doctor, with a fresh briskness in his voice, 'I shall pass on to that wider point to which I have already alluded, which is indeed that which I wish chiefly to impress upon you, and to which all that I have hitherto said has been preparatory. We have come to see how genuine Christianity has been enabled to grow and extend itself only through an admixture of what we now recognise as evil. And seeing this, we shall be led on to a conclusion that is much wider. It has been said that it is the part of the devil to see in good the germs of evil. Is it not also the part of the devil not to recognise in evil the germs of good? May we not indeed say with St. Augustine, that absolute evil is impossible, because, if we look at it rightly, it is always rising up into good? And so, may we not recognise in all things the presence and the providence of God?

' Perhaps this view may at first sight seem difficult. Some of us may find that we have a certain amount of pride to swallow before we can cheerfully acquiesce in it. It is not an uncommon thing to find persons who secretly flatter their vanity by cherishing a gloomy view of the world and of mankind. But if we can only get free from these littlenesses, and attain to that view which I have indicated, it will enlarge and ameliorate our whole philosophy of life, and bring life and trust to us, in the place of doubt and despondency. Evil will then appear to us simply as undeveloped good—as something which we may acquiesce in without complaining—as something that has assisted in the development of whatever is good in the present, and which will itself one day become good in the future. Indeed it is not too much to say that all things, in a certain sense, existed first in the form of evil. It was not till after the Spirit of God had worked on the primeval matter that God pronounced the world to be " very good."

' And so, if we consider the subject thus, we shall learn to put a stop to all those fretful wailings over the badness of our own times of which we hear so much—wailings over the unbelief of our neighbours, the corruption of society, the misery of the poor, the luxury of the rich, or the decline of commercial morality. The present is an age of change, and is therefore at every turn presenting to us some new feature. But if these come to us in the apparent guise of evils, let us not uselessly bemoan them; but let us believe that they are, even if we cannot see that it is so, but the beginnings, the embryos of new good. Indeed, by the eye of faith, even in the present day, may be discerned the beautiful spectacle of good actually shining through evil. May we not, for instance, discern the well-being of the rich through the misery of the poor? and again, the honest industry of the poor through the idleness of the rich?

' If then these things be so, surely we may look on unmoved at the great changes and commotions that are going on around us, and the new forms that society, and thought, and politics are assuming, even although for the moment they may appear threatening. And if in this great storm our Master have fallen asleep, and no longer speak audibly to us, let us not be of little faith and fearful, and try to awaken Him with our foolish clamours; but let us trust all to Him, and follow His example. For really, if we do but trust in God, there is no ground for fear, but " all things work together for good to him that believeth." And, however the matter may strike us at first sight, the times we live in are really the times that are best fitted for us ; and we shall see, if we will but think soberly, that we could not, as a whole, alter anything in them for the better. I do not mean that we have not each of us his own work marked out for him to do ; but all this work is strictly in relation to things as they are. God has given to us the general conditions under which we are to serve Him, and these are the best and indeed the only conditions for us. Doubtless, if we each do the duty that lies before us, these conditions will be slowly and insensibly changed by us ; but we shall ourselves change also, as well as the conditions ; what I mean is, that supposing by a sudden act of will we could do what we pleased with the conditions of the age, we, being as we are, should not be really able to make the age better. We should not be really able to make it different. Any Utopia we might imagine would, if it were a thinkable one, be only our own age in a masquerading dress. For we cannot escape from our age, or add, except in a very small degree, anything that is really new to it. Nor need we wish to do so. Our age is for us the best age possible. We are its children, and it is our only true parent. But though we cannot alter our time at a stroke, so to speak, no, not even in imagination, we can all of us help to do so little by little, if we do cheerfully the duties that are set before us. And if we do this, which is what Christ bids us to do, then is Christ made manifest in us, and lives in the hearts of every one of us ; and in a far higher sense than any mere physical one, He is risen from the dead. And if He be not so risen in and for us, then are we indeed, as the Apostle says, " of all men most miserable."

· ' Let us therefore, with a large hope for the future, and a cheerful contentment with the present, be willing to leave the world in the hands of God, knowing that He has given us what conditions and what circumstances are best for us. Let us see all things in God, and let us become in Him, as Plato says, " spectators of all time, and of all existence." And thus, in spite of the difficulties presented to us by " all the evil that is done under the sun," we shall perceive that all things will, nay must, come right in God's own time ; and the apparent dualism of good and evil at last become a glorious unity of good. But let us remember also that " the Kingdom of God cometh not with observation ; " and I would conclude my sermon with certain memorable words spoken by Christ Himself, though unfortunately not to be found in the Gospels, but preserved to us by Clement of Alexandria. " The Lord," Clement tells us, " being asked when His kingdom should come, said, When two shall be one, and that which is without as that which is within, and the male with the female—neither male nor female."

'——And now——' (at the sound of this word the whole congregation rose automatically to their feet), ' I will ask you,' the Doctor went on after a pause, ' to conclude this morning's service by doing what I trust I have shown that all here may sincerely and honestly do. I mean, I will ask you to recite after me the Apostles' Creed.'

This appeal took the whole congregation quite aback. But there was no time for wonder. Dr. Jenkinson at once began ; nor was his voice the only sound in the theatre. Lady Ambrose, pleased, after all that she had heard the night previous, to make public profession of her faith, especially in a place where it could not be called in question, followed the Doctor audibly and promptly ; Miss Prattle followed Lady Ambrose ; Lady Violet Gresham, who was busy with one of her sleeve-links, followed Miss Prattle ; Lady Grace, from quite another part of the house, followed Dr. Jenkinson on her own account ; Mr. Stockton repeated the first clause in a loud voice, and then relapsed into marked silence ; Mr. Luke only opened his lips to sigh out audibly in the middle a disconsolate ' Heigh ho ! ' Mr. Storks blew his nose with singular vigour through the whole proceeding ; Mrs. Sinclair, just towards the end, tapped Leslie's arm gently with her fan, and said to him in a whisper, ' Do you really believe all this ? '

When all was over, when the Doctor had solemnly pronounced the last ' Amen,' he looked about him nervously for a moment, as if the question of how to retire becomingly suddenly dawned upon him. Luckily he perceived almost directly a servant standing in readiness by the curtain. The Doctor frowned slightly at the man ; made a slightly impatient gesture at him ; and Faust and the young witch again covered the preacher from the eyes of his congregation.

(To be continued.)

May and December.

THERE are flowers for me as for you, my darling,
    For both hath the wind a tale ;
For me the ice-wind, mourning and snarling,
    For you the sigh of the warm spring gale ;
White buds for both——the bridal wreath
Is yours, and mine is the decking of death.

Which is more blessed——the new incomer,
    Or she who leaves the ring ?
Spring must fear the toiling of summer,
    But winter dreams of a sweet new spring ;
I falter now, who tripped with the best ;
But the revel grew weary, and night brings rest !

May and December——we meet together ;
    You scarcely feel the yoke ;
I feel the loosening of my tether,
    Look for freedom and greeting my folk :
My hopes are blooming as yours, my child,——
There are bushes that blossom in winter wild.

The sweet white thorn in chill December,
    Somewhere down in the West,
Puts forth its buds——so men remember
    The spring-time, of all times the best,
And long for its coming——as I look out
For the coming spring, with never a doubt !
B. MONTGOMERIE RANKING.

MAY AND DECEMBER

MAY AND DECEMBER.

From Dreams to Waking.

BY E. LYNN LINTON.

CHAPTER I.

HER IDOLS.

' CHILD! your imagination will be your ruin. You live in a world that does not exist, and you see nothing as it is. I am sorry for you, for I know too well what you will have to suffer. But who can give another reason and common sense? We must all dree our own weird, and yours will be a heavy one!'

The speaker, Miss Morris, flicked out her flounces with a hopeless air, and, passing her hand over her eyes, sighed heavily. There was as much fretfulness as sorrow in this sigh; temper having the trick of pain, and a look of suffering making a very good mask for the feeling of displeasure. But Miss Morris, though observant, was not introspective, and had never come to that knowledge of herself which the sage said was the last and most difficult attainment of wisdom; hence she honestly believed that she was only sorry, and not in the least 'put out,' when she deprecated, as so often before, this inconvenient activity of fancy which made calls on her sympathy to which she could not respond.

The child, of whose bewildering imagination she spoke so plaintively, was her niece, Venetia Greville, a slender, fair-faced girl of seventeen, with a certain dreamy look in her large blue eyes, and that kind of settled sweetness in her smile which seemed as if she smiled more from what she thought and felt than from what she saw and knew; so far justifying her poor fretful, sickly, timorous aunt in her disclaimers, and, as she prophesied, threatening in the future that sorrow which comes to all dreamers before they wake and realise.

Those dreamy blue eyes, that settled sweetness of smile, were true tracings of the hidden writing. Venetia did live in a world of her own—which was by no means the world of ordinary human habitation—where she saw beauty that did not exist; virtue that her own mind only created; love-worthiness, greatness, nobleness, where were not even the shadows of divine things; where she made gods out of the clouds in the sky, and gave her worship to mist-wreaths that faded away as she looked.

Nevertheless, she was not as yet discouraged; and when one little cloud-god melted away and was lost, she created another which did as well. For among the needs of her young soul, that of enthusiasm about some person or some thing was the most imperative. This need had already led her into some troubles and a few follies, earnest of graver sorrows in the future when the *besoin d'enthousiasmer* should have given place to the more fatal *besoin d'aimer*; when the creation of an ideal for whom she should sacrifice herself, not only admire as from a distance—the worship of a god to whom she might bring the living incense of her love, not only watch as he floated through the sky—would be the terrible law of her life; when what was now the mere phantasy of her imagination would be then the main fact of her being.

As it was, her troubles had been comparatively slight and her follies unimportant; all the same, she had had the one and committed the other. Thus: last holidays, when she was sixteen, she had idealised the gardener's young daughter, a pretty, clever, facile kind of girl, who she persuaded herself was a genius in the rough, like one of the great of the earth born in obscure places, of whom she had been reading; a genius wanting only the aid of a friendly hand to strip away the rugged envelope and let the nobly fashioned soul go free. Full of this fancy, she had insisted on teaching the girl all that she herself knew, including music and drawing, French and physical geography. She made her holidays seasons of real hard work to herself and of infinite penance to Letty; till, tired out of her life by her lessons, and getting past the age when bread and jam rounded off the possibilities of human enjoyment, she went of her own accord as a nurse-girl at Farmer Rust's; and the last thing heard of the potential Hypatia, the hypothetical Vittoria Colonna, was that she had been seen flaunting through the streets of Belton on a market-day, hanging on the arm of a recruiting-sergeant, and, young as she was, evidently in that state when pewter rings like silver. Miss Morris, who had never much liked the girl, and who cordially detested all Venetia's crazes without having the courage or the energy to repress them, was cruelly delighted to tell her of these very coarse and clumsy feet of clay that had shown themselves beneath the petticoats of her genius. But poor Venetia cried herself sick, and to the last believed that Letty might have been made something of if only the right way had been taken and the right person had taken it.

Another time she persuaded her aunt to take into the house, and give fair trial to, a plausible, smooth-tongued, crafty young scamp, who came that way one bitter winter's evening, and told a pitiful story of a good place lost through the death of the mistress, and the impossibility of finding another without a character. He was put into buttons and made the page-boy of the establishment, much to cook's disgust—and cook knew the world as well as most. But he did pretty well, and was really handy and useful till he bundled all the silver into the best tablecloth and decamped in the night, never to be heard of again.

At school she had made an idol of Georgie Lawless, a big, lazy, imperious girl, who loved no one but herself, and treated poor adoring Venetia as living idols do treat their worshippers, nearly breaking her heart by her caprices and her cruelties, in preparation for the time when heartbreak would be a more serious matter than it was now. And she had done her best to idealise her aunt. But Miss Honoria Morris was scarcely cultivable ground, even for such a persistent enthusiast as Venetia. A peevish invalid with a sharp face and a grating voice, very querulous, very selfish, very prosaic, could scarcely be made into a saint or a heroine, try as hard as one would. Nor was her malady, which was liver, to be regarded as of those ethereal and refined sicknesses which are assumed to make folks liker to the angels than they are ever able to be when in good health and with pure blood. Neither could the girl exalt the pro-motherhood—for which her aunt received a handsome income, and got rid of her charge by sending her to school for nine months out of the twelve, and giving herself no kind of trouble about her for the three during which she was at home—into a subject for enthusiastic gratitude or poetic eulogy. There are things at which even the folly of youth becomes wise, and this was one of them. Wherefore, after a time, during which the girl had wrought hard to grow flowers on nether millstones, Aunt Honoria was laid aside like an old doll, and Venetia did what she could without her.

The present occasion of the girl's delight and the woman's rebuke was the prospect of a certain schoolfellow, one Graziella Despues, a Creole, who had been sent over from Cuba to the Misses Wynter at Noon Lodge, to perfect before bringing out. Venetia had heard from Kate Grant, a girl whose parents were in India, and who had no holidays, that the new arrival with the pretty name was the most beautiful, delightful little darling that had ever been seen. She wore earrings and rings, brooches, chains, charms and necklaces, like a grown-up woman, said little Kate, who already loved finery and possessed none; and she went out every morning and picked two flowers, one for her hair and one for her dress, and the Misses Wynter only smiled and said nothing ; and she talked the sweetest kind of broken English, and talked incessantly, all about Cuba and the lovely things that they had there—the flowers, and fruits, and trees, and birds ; and she had such eyes and such eyelashes—and was only about five feet high, with a waist that did not quite measure eighteen inches ; and, finally, that she, Kate, was so much in love with her !—and so would Venetia be when she saw her, for she was ever so much nicer than that great big Georgie Lawless. Which was mean of Kate, who was Venetia's shadow ; seeing that she too had worshipped at the Lawless shrine together with her model, and until the arrival of Graziella had held her supreme over all her rivals.

All this was enough to set the active imagination of Venetia in a flame, and to give her another idol in the clouds. A child of the sun, dark-haired, dark-eyed, who dressed herself in jewels and flowers like a daughter of the Incas, and had a name that was a poem in itself ; a creature so beautiful as Kate described ; so fascinating and good and delightful altogether as Venetia imagined ; how should she not love her ? how not make her on the spot her goddess to be worshipped, her queen to be obeyed ? In one half-hour she had created an ideal, as she had created others before ; and she counted the days between now and her return to school as a lover counts those which stand between him and his beloved.

'Oh, auntie, fancy ! a beautiful little thing from Cuba ; from that lovely country, that exquisite place !—why, they call it the Pearl of the Antilles !' she had said enthusiastically, after she had read Katie's letter. ' How delightful it will be ! She will be like a fairy among us all.'

For which outburst of baseless delight she had received the rebuke which begins this chapter, though the sole effect that it had on her was to send her back on herself, and to make her dreams silent instead of audible.

If Venetia's imagination had pictured the future in gold so far as her new schoolfellow was concerned, the reality of things brought her even more than she had anticipated. Graziella was the kind of girl to have warmed into activity a deader fancy than Venetia's. What, then, did she not do to one already disposed by temperament and that terrible ' need ' to find her a living poem, a human flower, a heroine out of a novel, a grace, a muse, a saint, and an angel all in one ?

Beautiful in a strange foreign way, but beautiful exceedingly ; with dark eyes surrounded by a fringe of lashes so long that they swept her rounded, olive-tinted cheeks ; a mouth like a rosebud ;

hair soft, thick, and black as night, falling to her feet when she let it loose; a figure as slight as the traditional sylph's, but of such exquisite proportions as made all others look coarse or meagre according to the line on which they differed; with a half-hidden fire beneath her graceful indolence; a passion, indicated rather than shown, penetrating her sweet caressing softness, which gave her that appearance of latent strength and unexplored possibilities, so attractive, so compelling, so mysterious to the imagination;—Graziella was soon the queen of the school, but reigning over none more arbitrarily than over Venetia. Her heart had gone down before the lovely little Creole as it had never yet gone down before anyone; and she transacted in little and in school-girl travesty the great drama of love which she was destined to enact in more serious fashion hereafter.

But things were not always smooth between the two friends; and, indeed, it was only the sweetness of Venetia's temper and the absolute sincerity of her devotion—the entire forgetfulness of herself and the delicate tact taught by truth and love together—that made matters bearable. For though Graziella had many virtues—the virtues which belong to a nature passionate and not ungenerous—she had a vice that went far to destroy all the good of these others, and that made her love more often a service of pain than of pleasure. She was jealous; fiercely, unreasonably, wildly jealous; jealous as only a Creole can be jealous—that is, as a savage for suspicion and a wild beast for cruelty. But she had fewer outbreaks with Venetia than she would have had with anyone else, because of this saintly devotion, this faithful absorption, and hourly dedication, which it was almost impossible for the most perverse ingenuity to distort or misunderstand. Sometimes, indeed, there were tremendous acts of trouble and tragedy to go through; but, on the whole, this school-girl romance brought as much happiness as it gave pleasure, for if the one was blessed in her worship the other was charmed to be worshipped.

So the days passed through summer and autumn, winter and spring, when Venetia, having reached the magic age of eighteen, was taken from Graziella and Noon Lodge to meet fortune and the future in the great world at home. The Creole, two years younger than the English girl, had to be kept for another twelve months under the Misses Wynter's fostering wing, when she too would be pronounced fit to fly on her own account, and to be eligible for balls and liable to lovers.

Of course it was a tremendous grief to Venetia to leave her young queen in the durance from which she, for her own part, had escaped. Though she disliked Noon Lodge, and did not love the

Misses Wynter, she would willingly have postponed her 'coming
out' for a year so that she might have kept with Graziella. But
fate is stronger than love, and the sacrifice had to be made. It
was agreed, however, that the Creole, who had only friends—no
acknowledged relations—in England, should spend half her holidays at Oak-tree House with Venetia and Miss Morris; and with
this the two friends had perforce to be content, and to make the
best of things as they stood. And as even Aunt Honoria—poor
peevish sickly body!—was, in a certain sense, fascinated by the
pretty little Cuban, the holidays were to be times of great delight.
Meanwhile, Venetia went out and enjoyed herself, and Graziella
wove her spells round others of her companions as well as round
her teachers, so that she succeeded in getting more pleasure and
less learning, more holidays, more indulgences, more caresses, and
fewer lessons, fines, or admonitions, than any other young lady in
the establishment. It was a way she had; a way which no one
yet had been found able to withstand, and which had, so far,
brought her what she wished and satisfied all her demands. It
remained to be seen whether, when fairly launched into the great
flood of life and the unknown, she would be able to steer her
precious bark as deftly as she had steered her toy boat, now in the
ponds and shallows; if she would be able to make men her slaves
as she had hitherto made her girl friends her servants, and compel
from them the love and adoration which she had won from these
others; if she would be still queen of her world, supreme, domi-
nant, and confessed; or—would she have to yield at times to
others?

CHAPTER II.

INITIATION.

THE return from school and formal 'coming out' of a pretty girl
of confessed amiability and a good fortune, is an event in a community which equals in importance the appointment of a new
curate, or the arrival of a crack regiment with an unmarried
colonel at its head. It is a kind of lottery, where the sanguine
see their success and the timid fear their failure; but where each
man who has the necessary conditions of celibacy and heartwhole-
ness is sure to think that fortune is impartial and chances equal,
and that the prize is as likely to be won by himself as by another.
This was the feeling which Venetia roused among the youth
of Belton Forest, where they all lived. She was the biggest prize
of their local matrimonial lottery on the female side of the lucky-
bag, and every unmarried man of the district—from little Tommy

Clarke, the doctor's son, to handsome Charley Mossman, of Belton Chace, through the gradations of Mr. Roughton, the curate, with a hundred and twenty pounds a year, and Captain Blakey, with his half-pay, grizzled beard and fifty years of experience—had his dreams about Venetia Greville, and his speculations as to whether it was worth his while to decide on making her his wife or no. Before she had been three months at Oak-tree House, she had received five offers of marriage. Five sane and stalwart English gentlemen had thrown themselves at her feet and besought her to bless them with her hand; each swearing that it was for love of her own sweet person only, and all with tongues discreetly silent on the Three per Cents., where her fortune was invested; though, to do them justice as men of business, all had turned their eyes that way, and each had studied the money article in the 'Times,' and decided on the investments that he would make when he had the control of things, and had raised the three per cent. to six.

Venetia, however, did not see her hero in any of the five; which was a blessing; though rather a surprise to her aunt, knowing as she did the girl's fatal facility for idealizing, and the extreme likelihood there was of her investing with every kind of heroic attribute some commonplace creature with a good manner and fluent speech, who should strike the key-note of her character cleverly and gain her heart by deluding her imagination. But nothing of this had happened yet; the girl's fate was still to come.

It came before long: how should it not? Writing school-girl love-letters to Graziella, and going out to such balls and picnics, such lawn-parties and water-parties as were given in the neighbourhood, was all very well; but even when alternated with spells of dry study on the off-days, and a sincere love of music and painting at all times, they were not interests of such dimensions as necessarily excluded others. On the contrary, the more the girl's nature was stirred, the more likelihood of deeper movement when the chance came. And so it happened when Ernest Pierre-point came down to pay a visit to Charley Mossman, his old Eton friend and college chum, and the bachelors of Belton Forest gave a ball to the neighbourhood, with Venetia Greville, the mistress of Oak-tree House, as the queen and acknowledged belle.

Anyone might be forgiven for idealising Ernest Pierrepoint. Even elderly women learnt the trick, and men themselves were not exempt. It was not only that he was handsome—Charley Mossman was that too, and Captain Blakey, though grizzled and fifty, had once been an Adonis, and was a ' fine figure of a man ' still; nor was it only that he was clever—Mr. Roughton, the curate, had been a double-first, and, like some one else more famous, had forgotten more than anyone else in the place had ever known. If Ernest Pierrepoint played on the flute divinely, so did little Tommy Clarke ; if he sketched like a master, so did James Butterworth ; and as for athletics, great as he was in all manly sports, he had his equals and his masters among the young men of Belton Forest ; so that it could not be on this account that he was accepted as king of his company wherever he appeared. No, it was for something far more subtle, far more indefinable ; for a certain grace of manner, a charm of voice, a chivalrous deference to women which yet did not put him at odds with men with whom he was *bon camarade* on all points ; for the most perfect sweetness of temper ; for a tact so delicate as to be almost a sixth sense ; for a pleasant power of talk which was bright without being gaudy fireworks, animated and not noisy, interesting and not scholastic ; and above all, for an appearance of curiously graceful guilelessness which set people at their ease at once, and was as far removed from the ordinary bluff British honesty which treads on your toes without apology, and slaps you in the face without regret, as was his breeding from that of a country hawbuck, or his person from that of a good-looking prize-fighter. In a word, he was a hero ready made to hand ; a young Apollo whom nymphs and goatherds might adore, and who, while accepting his position, gave no sign that he smelt the incense which, for his own part, he burnt as liberally as it was offered.

'You must present me, Charley, to your fair friend Miss Greville,' he had said, as they drove to the ball ; and Charley, who was really smitten, as the phrase goes, said ' of course,' joyfully thinking that now he should have a friend at court, who would sound his praises judiciously, and make Miss Greville understand his merits better than she seemed to have understood them as yet.

He had no fear of Ernest on his own account. He had always understood that there was an attachment between him and a pretty cousin, with paternal consent refused because of the relationship : but which was an effectual barrier to any other *affaire*, and so rendered him safe under the head of rivalry ; else perhaps he would not have said ' of course ' so joyfully, nor even have asked him down to Belton Chace at all. As it was, however, as soon as Venetia and her aunt came into the room, he went up to them with his friend, and presented in due form Mr. Ernest Pierrepoint to Miss Greville.

A waltz was just beginning, and Venetia's card was clear ; there was no reason, therefore, why she should not be whirled away on the arm of Charley Mossman's friend, though Charley had designed to dance this first waltz with her himself—had expressly saved himself for it—had been looking forward to it for some days as a thing that should somehow mysteriously advance him in the difficult path of her good favour, and make them happy—he scarcely knew why. But Ernest, in that unconscious innocent way of his, took her from under his very eyes; and Charley was left to console himself as he best could for his disappointment. Had it been any but Ernest, that disappointment would have been very bitter: but his fidus Achates, his friend and prospective champion—well, if not himself, this other was the next best that could be found. And with this Charley comforted himself, and waltzed with Emily Backhouse instead of with Venetia; which at least pleased one of the persons concerned. For Emily Backhouse had a tender heart, and Charley Mossman had once set his seal on it, a little carelessly, perhaps; but the impression remained, and poor Emily did not seek to rub it off.

Venetia had never enjoyed an evening as she enjoyed this. Ernest Pierrepoint seemed to consider himself specially told off for her service, and Charley Mossman shared his duty. This did not trouble her; though it made poor Emily uncomfortable enough; for the young heiress liked the good-hearted squire with his frank English face and pleasant voice, and had somewhat idealised him into her brother in a hazy kind of way—a distant and indistinct relationship which she did not care to make clearer, but which set her at her own ease and made him feel not the least in the world at his. He would have been better pleased if she had been less friendly; and the brotherly quality which she found in him was the last that he aspired to possess. But Mr. Pierrepoint—ah! that was another thing altogether. He was something that she had never seen before, and that she prized accordingly; for what virtue is so great as that of novelty?

The varied experiences of travel; proficiency in art and music; love of poetry and literature; a handsome face, a sympathetic voice, a charming manner, deferential, flattering, full of that subtle sense of manly protection and personal submission, of intellectual supremacy and the confession of moral inferiority, which is above all others the most delighted in by women from men—it was impossible that Venetia, romantic, enthusiastic, with the need of hero-worship woven in with the very fibres of her being, and just at the age when the sentiments are stronger than the perceptions, should not find her hero in Ernest. Here, it seemed to her, was the culmination of her ideal, the highest perfection to which the modern man could reach. A man who had shot lions in Africa and studied art in Rome; who had met the redskins on their war-path in Nebraska, and acted French proverbs in a Parisian salon; who spoke of a Polish princess with a sigh, and of an English countess with familiar affection; and who now treated her, a country girl just home from school, as if she had been a princess herself, raising his beautiful eyes to hers with that look of courteous adoration and tender respect for which he was famous among the women who knew him; was it to be wondered at if she let her fancy go free, and, led by its flickering light to unsafe places, made for Mr. Ernest Pierrepoint a temple where she placed him on her pedestal as the Best whom the chances of life had as yet sent her? Had she been asked, she would have added—or could ever send her!

They talked of all sorts of things; or rather, Ernest talked and Venetia listened. It never occurred to her that the exploits of which he told her so simply, so much as matters of course, looking for praise no more than if he had said that he had walked down Regent Street on a fine May morning, were based on but slender foundations of fact if embellished with a large amount of that which was not fact; that his hairbreadth escapes had been adventures wherein the danger had been infinitesimal and the way of escape a good broad cart-road, with stout hedges on either side; and that the only lions which he had ever seen were those in the Zoological Gardens. But then he had really missed the chance of making one of a sporting party for the interior of Africa, which two of his friends had joined; so if not the rose, he had been near it; and he took their true adventures as good models for his false ones. All this was unknown to her; and she would not have believed any nineteenth century Ithuriel who had told her. And as Ernest was not all bad—if vain and untruthful, a flirt and insincere, neither malicious nor evil-hearted—she had none of those mysterious instincts which are said to belong to the sex in its years of simplicity by way of protection against ignorance. Hence, she gave herself *tête baissée* to belief; and with belief to admiration.

'I hope that I may be allowed to call on you to-morrow?' Ernest said with his sweetest air, as they finished the last waltz and he was taking her a small promenade in the lobby before handing her to her aunt.

Had the ball been held in a private house, with a conservatory attached, he would have taken her there; but being in the large room of the principal hotel, there was nothing but a passage flanked with flowers for the more tender episodes of the evening.

'We shall be very happy to see you,' answered Venetia, her eyes on the ground. 'Do you stay long at the Chace?'

She held her breath to hear his answer. She scarcely realised how sorry she would be if he should give back a negative.

'That depends,' he said, looking at her almost as if he were asking her a question. 'There is nothing special to call me away at this moment; and there may be something to keep me here?'

Venetia smiled. 'I am glad of that,' she returned girlishly; and looked up with a pair of bright blue happy eyes, which just then seemed to him the loveliest that he had ever seen in woman. Even the Polish princess of whom he spoke with a sigh, even the countess so familiarly dear, had not such eyes as this sweet flower-faced country girl, this nymph in white silk and pale blush roses, who looked up into his face smiling, and said so frankly she was glad that he was not going away soon.

'And I am glad too,' he said in a rather lower voice than was necessary; but it gave a meaning and an emphasis, which was what he desired. 'I have found too much to enchant me to care to leave Belton Forest just yet.'

'It is a very pretty country,' said Venetia, embarrassed, she scarcely knew why.

'Very; but I was thinking of the people, not the place,' said Ernest, always in the same low tone of voice; as if the hydrangeas and dracænas lining the walls were so many unfriendly ears which he must baffle if he could.

Venetia felt that she must say something. It was difficult to know what; but difficulties have to be conquered, and thoughts must be dug for if they will not come up of themselves.

'Yes,' she said, looking vaguely round towards the ball-room door; 'we have a very nice society here.'

'I do not know much of the society; I only know that some people here are more than nice, are delightful, enthralling, enchanting,' he returned; and though Venetia was but a school-girl yet, and neither vain nor conscious, she could not be so stupid as not to see that he meant her to take this to herself, and to believe that it was her society which he eulogised so warmly.

'I think we had better go to my aunt,' she then said with a perceptible trouble in her face and eyes.

Though it was pleasant to admire this wonderful stranger as the hero of her dreams, the embodiment of manly excellence, she was not in any way desirous that he should admire her. That would have implied a higher degree than any that she had yet taken in the initiation through which we all have to pass; for to such a nature as hers imaginative and impersonal hero-worship comes long before the need of loving, while the need of loving comes long before that of being loved; which, indeed, with women of Venetia's stamp is never at any time so strong as this other.

'I will take you,' answered Ernest, who knew his alphabet too well to go too fast, and who understood the signs of a girl's timidity as well as he understood those of a woman's fervour.

On which the two walked demurely to where Miss Morris was waiting for her niece in the cloak-room; and Mr. Pierrepoint made no further advances, unless it might be called an advance to say, 'I shall do myself, then, the honour of calling on you to-morrow,' as he handed Venetia into her carriage, dexterously leaving Miss Morris to poor Charley.

There was little doubt but that he would keep his word. Easily attracted but eminently unstable, each new face seemed to him the loveliest of the series; and though none had yet been found strong enough to hold him, he had always a floating idea that here, in this latest beauty, he had at last found his fate. He thought so now with Venetia Greville, and blew his cigar smoke into rings, which somehow reminded him of the pretty little fringe on her forehead, though there was no kind of resemblance between the two; and saw the pure forms of her profile outlined in all sorts of incongruous things, and wherever he turned. Evidently he was what men call hard hit; but he kept his thoughts to himself, and Charley Mossman did not see which way they tended.

The next day, then, both young men went off to Oak-tree House to enquire if Miss Greville was very much fatigued after last night's ball, or if the known delicacy of Miss Morris had been increased by the cares of her chaperonage and the lateness of the hour to which those cares extended. They found the one alone in the garden, the other in her room and invisible; and each in his heart did *not* bless the peccant liver which revolted against a vigil prolonged to four o'clock in the morning, and by which he was denied the chance of the tête-à-tête that he had hoped for. For Charley, Orestes, had determined to manœuvre so that Ernest, his Pylades, should take the old lady off his hands and leave him with the young one; and Pylades had determined the same thing on his own account—with more likelihood of success. For between the two men, the balance of skill in the more delicate tactics of life certainly hung to Ernest's side.

Not much was to be done, however, by either at the present moment; for each doubled on the other, and spoilt the running which he could not make for himself. If Charley talked of next season's hunting and hoped that Miss Greville would sometimes come to the covert side, Ernest dexterously threw the conversation into art and suggested a day's sketching in some picturesque spot of which he claimed to be the discoverer. And Charley could not sketch, though Ernest could hunt.

When Charley spoke of getting up a water-party, Ernest seconded him enthusiastically, but turning to Venetia said,

' Ah, Miss Greville, you should have been at the last boating excursion that we made from Naples ; a large party of us in quite a procession of boats, with flags flying and that sweet Italian music ! The sea like lapis lazuli, the sky like one large opal, the splendid-looking fishermen, with their brown skins and picturesque dress, the girls with their magnificent faces, figures like so many goddesses, and eyes that were as bright as stars—that would have pleased you ! Colour, costume, climate, flowers, music, beauty— all the accessories perfect, and just such as would have enchanted a born artist, as you are ! '

The consequence of it was, that a water-party in grey and sombre England suddenly became to the girl's mind the very epitome of dulness, and that life seemed nowhere worth having save in beautiful Naples.

' See Naples and then die,' said Ernest dreamily.

' Better see it and live there ever after,' said Venetia, as dreamily.

' Ah ! give me old England ! There is no place like home,' cried Charley Mossman vigorously. ' England is the only country fit for a gentleman to live in ! '

' And the dungeon for artists ! ' sighed Ernest.

Venetia sighed too, she scarcely knew why ; but it seemed infinitely sad to her, first that Mr. Pierrepoint should feel England to be a dungeon at all, and next, that feeling it to be so he should be imprisoned in it. To her, too, it seemed at this moment as if the sun never shone here, that we had no flowers, no fruits, no sweet odours, no pleasant savours ; that we had never produced a poet nor an artist—nothing but blacksmiths and ploughboys, a few unimaginative young landed proprietors, and elderly ladies who suffered from congested livers. She looked at Ernest pityingly.

' Yes,' she said with a prettily pathetic air. ' England is, as you say, Mr. Pierrepoint, a dungeon for artists.'

' And the veritable assassin of poets ! ' he interrupted.

' Yes,' she assented.

' But the home of men ! ' said Charley Mossman, a little scandalised at the tone of the talk. ' Why, Ernest,' he continued, ' you are not a renegade to your own country, old fellow, are you ? Have the foreigners spoilt you so far as this ? '

Ernest smiled. There was a kind of compassionate superiority about his smile which Charley felt rather than saw.

'Improved me, you mean,' he answered; 'made me understand the worth of things rather than the unreal value of places—the grandeur of life, of humanity, of thought, rather than the narrow conception which we call patriotism. That is how I look at it, Charley.'

'And I don't,' said Charley curtly.

Briton of Britons, England was the ultimate to which national perfection could go, and he felt a slight on the mother-country as keenly as a personal insult, and indeed almost as a personal insult. But Ernest was his friend, and he could not be angry with him without graver cause than this.

'But Mr. Pierrepoint has travelled,' said Venetia gravely, raising her eyes to Charley's, and speaking with a certain intensity of remonstrance that had its effect.

This beautiful young man, who talked so sweetly on art and poetry, who had seen Naples, and made boating excursions with Polish princesses—he knew; and who was Charley Mossman, only a dull young English squire, that he should contradict?

'Travel is not everything, Miss Greville,' said Charley a little hotly. 'We have history too.'

'But Mr. Pierrepoint knows history as well as we do, and foreign countries better,' answered Venetia; and then remembering that she was in point of fact constituting herself the advocate of this comparative stranger, she stopped and blushed, and added: 'But really I am interfering in what I do not understand, and giving my opinion where I know nothing about the matter. Let us talk of something else—something that we shall agree on, and not have half-a-dozen ideas all clashing together!'

Which charming little womanly diversion each young man read according to his desire. Charley, that she did not want to oppose him, her old friend, in preference for a stranger; Ernest, that she did not wish to let her preference for him, a stranger, be too plainly seen by her old friend. Of a truth, Orestes and Pylades were playing odd cards to the lead!

After this the conversation languished. Retreat after the excitement of a skirmish seems often more dull than restful; and the young men were half afraid to show how dull they felt it by breaking into sword-crossing again. Soon after they took their leave; and Venetia found the day strangely heavy and oppressive when they had gone, and concluded that a storm was somewhere about—it was so lifeless, heavy, still; and then she wondered what a storm would be like at Naples, and pictured the boating expedition of which Mr. Pierrepoint had spoken, and wished that she had been there.

Chapter III.

UNEQUAL PLAYERS.

WITHOUT occupation or imperative duties, possessed of sufficient fortune to enjoy life in his own manner without thought or care for the future, if not rich enough to place himself among county magnates by the purchase of a large estate, Ernest Pierre-point had no other will to follow but his own, no other person to consult but himself. Hence, when he found that life was pleasant at Belton Forest, that Venetia Greville was more unsophisticated than the Polish princess, better tempered than the dear countess, and more beautiful than either, he decided on taking a house for the summer, and installing himself as one of the desirable bachelors of the neighbourhood—as an experience.

He had never lived in the country; being essentially a townbred man; and he thought that it would be good fun to give six months to the bucolics, as he called them—always excepting Venetia in his somewhat disdainful generalization, thanks to her fair face, sweet smiles, golden hair, and big blue eyes—and by the end of the time he would see what he had made of them and himself.

He knew one thing—that he would make love to Venetia after his own fashion. It would not be that vulgar, unmistakable kind of love, which, according to him, is fit only for common-place souls—thick-witted heads, destitute of poetry or delicacy of touch. No, it would be refined, subtle, suggestive love; love that should tantalize without satisfying; that should allow itself to be inferred rather than commit itself to confession; love that should pass over the girl's heart like the wind over an Æolian harp, awaking sweet sighs, responsive melodies in return; that should be like the sun on an opening bud, causing it to expand to its full perfection, to give out all its hidden perfume, all its secret beauty.

It was delightful to him to see her innocent face change like an April sky at his pleasure—become grave or gay, radiant or overcast, as he talked of life now with the melancholy of a man whose heart is in the grave, the sombre hopelessness of a phi losophy which has its roots in sorrow; now rolled out fine words and glittering ideas, vague, but all the time suggestive of beauty, of misty delight, no one knew why; of enthusiasm for no one knew what; but, by this very vagueness, appealing more power-fully than if they had been more distinct, to a mind so dreamy as Venetia's, so capable of erecting fairy palaces out of egg-shells.

Assuredly this was not the ultimate purpose for which Charley

Mossman had invited him to the Chace; but Charley, though inwardly annoyed at the sudden determination of Pylades, was an honest-hearted, generous kind of man, and held the doctrine of the best to win, like a true English gentleman as he was. If Ernest did really love Miss Greville, and that affair of his with his cousin was all off, he thought a little ruefully, and more than a little inclined to call himself ill names for his folly in asking him to the Chace at all—but, if he did really love her, and if she loved him—well! there was no help for it; he, Charley Mossman, was not going to be muff enough to break his heart for the loss of any woman in the world, nor cad enough to envy his friend the treasure which he had known how to win; by which it may be seen that the handsome young squire's condition was not desperate, and that Emily Backhouse had still a few 'lives' to the good.

Here, then, we have him, our handsome, agreeable, poetical *jeune premier*, installed at Acorn Bank, which the Hardmans, to whom it belonged, had been glad enough to let while they took their pleasure in Switzerland for the summer—notwithstanding Mrs. Hardman's fears for her furniture, and Mr. Hardman's reluctance to include the use of a shabby dogcart and a broken-down cob in the list of appliances and appurtenances for which he received about ten times their market value.

And it was extraordinary to Venetia how, since this arrangement had been made, the sun had seemed to her to shine every day, and the sky to be as blue as, surely, the sky of Italy itself! How glad, how happy she was! she used to think every morning when she woke, smiling, as at a friend, at the broad daylight streaming through her room. What a delicious day this has been—what a blessed thing it is to live! she used to think, with half a sigh, as she looked out on the stars for her last pleasure; and saw the lights of Acorn Bank shining in the distance; and remembered all that Mr. Pierrepoint had said to-day; and of the meeting that they were to have to-morrow at the old mill—for sketching, nothing more. If she had been required to give a reason for her happiness she would have been hard put to it, poor dreamy, enthusiastic Venetia! But youth does not reason, dreamers do not verify the truth of their visions, and enthusiasm contents itself with belief—passing over proof as altogether needless.

This old mill was one of the most picturesque features in the whole of the picturesque Belton country. The artist world had long known it, and more than one great man had tried his skill there in the contest between Art and Nature, the imitator and his original, wherein the former is so sure to be worsted, and the latter so inevitably the conqueror. But to Ernest Pierrepoint's view of things, it was quite the other way. He had always found Nature a very docile sitter, he used to say, laughing, and by no means an untranslatable original. All that you want is a poetic imagination and technical skill;, to be able to see correctly—so few people see, he would add, looking into the distance with his fine eyes fixed as if they indeed saw everything—and when you have learnt to see, then to transcribe courageously. This was all —surely nothing so very impossible !

And once, when he had said this, he turned· round to Venetia, and added in his sweet voice :

' *Your* eyes are made for seeing—seeing, I mean, in the artistic sense. Nature will keep no secrets from you; she gives them lavishly to all the souls who love ! '

' And I do love nature ! ' answered Venetia, with sudden embarrassment. She wished that she had said some other word instead of love.

Ernest smiled.

' How prettily you said that ! ' he exclaimed in his graceful, guileless way. ' It is such a charm when a woman speaks well,' he added, to poor Venetia's intense confusion, and a strange mixed kind of feeling, more pain than pleasure on the whole.

This was as they were walking through the wood to the mill, where they were to have an hour's sketching, and where Miss Morris was to have accompanied them. But Miss Morris had large ideas about trusting the young, and putting them on their honour, and all that kind of thing ; whereby she secured herself her afternoon nap, and saved herself from fatigue by throwing Venetia into peril of something worse than fatigue—into peril of a broken heart and a ruined life.

' You will make me vain if you flatter me,' she answered shyly.

' Shall I ? ' was his response. ' Would my words have so great an effect on you ? '

It was in Venetia's mind, as the right thing to say, ' Anyone's flattery would ; ' but her heart drove back even this very mild rebuke, and the utmost to which she could come in the way of repulse, was :

' You have seen so much more than I ; it is no wonder if your praise would have an effect on me.'

' Oh ! then I am only a living railway-ticket, an embodied lecture on the physical geography of the globe ? ' he said in a tone of disappointment and half-banter together.

She laughed confusedly, but her eyes were moist and tender.

Had she really hurt him? She would rather have hurt herself ten times over.

'I do not hold you quite like this,' she said a little humbly; and Ernest, for reasons, did not wish to press his victory too far.

'Thanks!' he cried pleasantly, and they went on for a while in silence; and when they began to talk again it was on indifferent subjects, till they came to the mill which they were to sketch in concert.

'This is just the day for us!' then said Ernest, as they settled themselves on the low stone wall facing the river and the ruined mill; there where they got the best view of the old wheel with grass and moss growing on its broken flanges, of the stately elm-tree shadowing both brook and building, of the thatched roof, starred with yellow stonecrop and rose root, with the swallows flying about their nests in the eaves, and the cattle standing knee-deep in the quiet pool. 'And just the circumstances,' looking at his companion tenderly.

'Yes, just,' answered Venetia, looking at the cows, but thinking of him.

After a pause, during which the two had arranged their boards, tried their colours, and sketched in their leading lines—careful, timid, and correct, as to Venetia's; bold, clever, and wrong as to Ernest's—the latter said, apropos of nothing:

'There is no true genius without strong sympathies. To understand, one must feel; and one cannot really feel without the power of living, as it were, in the mind, the soul of another; seeing through his eyes, loving as he loves, shrinking where he shrinks. Genius is in its nature universal; but only because it is sympathetic. It grows by love. The more the poet, the artist, loves, the higher is his genius. Nature recognises her own, and she gives tenfold for all that she receives. Is it not so?'

'Yes,' said Venetia, with a hushed kind of reverence in her voice.

Talk such as this was the spirit that led her into enchanted regions, nameless, formless, but none the less beautiful because they were not understood. All that she knew, all that she cared to know was, that when Ernest spoke to her like this, his melodious voice a trifle veiled, his eyes looking far before him, as if he, the spiritual seer of poetic things, discerned more than the grosser sort could see, his face as if radiant with the light of a nobler world than dullards, such as Charley Mossman, could reach—her soul seemed rapt away to heaven, where it floated in glory in the midst of beautiful forms and faint delicious music, making her almost sad, poor deluded dreamer ! with the intensity of her vague delight.

'How exquisite it is to be understood!' then said Ernest, turning his beaming eyes from the spirit-world where they had apparently been wandering on to the fair piece of humanity by his side. 'I have never yet met with one who seemed to understand me so well as you, Miss Greville. I have never seen anyone with such noble sympathies—such superb spiritual melodies !'

Venetia blushed, as her manner was, almost to tears.

'You are too indulgent to me,' she said timidly. 'I, who am only an unformed country girl, cannot deserve this praise from a man who has seen and known all that you have,' she continued, unmindful of his little rebuke so lately administered about the living railway-ticket and the embodied lecture. 'It is your own kindness to say so.'

'Pardon me, it is your own merit,' he answered. 'It is because of the very breadth and depth of my knowledge of life that I do say so. And if I, who have seen so much of the world, hang up my wreath against your door, you may be sure it is because I know that it is deserved.'

By which it may be seen that he too had forgotten it.

Venetia could not answer. To disclaim a compliment is sometimes more painful to modesty than to let it pass in silence. She did not want to have the appearance of arguing with Mr. Pierrepoint about her own perfections ; so she merely hung her head a little lower over her drawing, and wished that he would not talk of herself at all, and yet—though painful, it was a pleasant pain.

'That is the word,' continued Ernest; 'superb spiritual melodies. Others, of course, know more of life than, thank Heaven ! you do, Miss Greville—we do not want our snowdrops, our sweet maybuds, our violets, to be like flaunting poppies, like gaudy tulips, like bold, self-evident peonies ! And there are dreadful creatures who are scientific—logical reasoners, God help them, and us !—but nowhere have I met with so much exquisite sensibility, such a true artist-soul, such a lovely poet's heart !'

'You are very good,' murmured Venetia, oppressed with the desire to kneel at his feet and tell him, on her side, how great and noble and superior she thought him. But something that was not wholly spiritual held her back ; and all that she could do was to feel embarrassed, and to look divinely lovely but somewhat foolish.

More of this kind of thing went on during the two hours given to the sketching of the ruined mill, and Ernest found the time not ill-employed, It was a pretty pastime, that might lead to something more serious, who knows? He must be caught and caged some day, and Venetia Greville might as well be his captor and gaoler as another—if she suited on further acquaintance. Meanwhile it pleased him to make love in this vague and undefined manner. It committed him to nothing, and added to his store of knowledge, already considerable, as to the best way of dissecting a woman's heart without wounding his own. For one peculiarity of Ernest Pierrepoint's nature was that, however hard he might be hit, he was never really hurt—another, that his fancies invariably cooled on further knowledge, instead of growing warmer; and that the more he made a woman love him the less he loved her.

And all this while Venetia worshipped him as her hero, the embodiment of her highest manly ideas; and believed in his absolute sincerity as much as he believed in her absolute simplicity. It was an unequal match in the game of love; but such matches always are unequal where one plays with coolness and knowledge, and the other has only faith and fervour as the rules by which hearts are thrown away and the best trumps forced and lost. Faith and fervour, indeed, have been at all times impedimenta in the warfare of life. Seeing which some women fling them away altogether; and we can scarcely blame them !

There had never been so gay a summer at Belton Forest as was this. Every week something fresh and delightful was set afoot; chiefly by Ernest Pierrepoint and Charley Mossman; to which the neighbourhood gladly subscribed its attendance, and bought its pleasure at small cost. Of course Venetia was always one of the most desired and desirable guests, if aunt Honoria but rarely appeared—shuffling off the burden of her chaperonage on to any pair of matronly shoulders that would accept it, and even letting Venetia go under the escort of the young men alone rather than give herself the trouble of going with her.

The neighbourhood had naturally made up its mind as to the state of matters between Ernest and Venetia, and busied itself in conjectures as to when the marriage would take place. They were all sure that something was on foot, and that the two were engaged —or ought to be. There was no doubt as to the direction of their feelings—at least of hers, said the dowagers severely; and nothing but an engagement could justify the attentions which the one paid with such marked devotion, and the pleasure which the other showed in accepting them. Wherefore it was put down as a settled thing; and people began to ask each other whether they should congratulate Miss Greville before a formal announcement, or was it more proper to wait until the signal had been given by the authorities themselves? The women who had sons, generally

voted on the side of waiting; also a few who had daughters—with
a forlorn hope not yet beaten back, that things had not gone quite
so far as this, and that Jane and Mary, Ellen and Susan, had still
a chance—went with them. But the majority of the mothers with
marriageable daughters, for whom husbands were scarce to find,
were for shunting Miss Greville as soon as possible. Even if she
had secured a prize for her own hand, she would be one rival the
less for them if she was once fairly out of the way.

Meanwhile, Venetia on her own side never gave it a thought
whether she was engaged or not. She had come to the knowledge
by now that she loved this man, this hero of her dreams realised
in the flesh, with her whole heart, her whole strength; and she
was as sure of his love for her as of hers for him. Could he be her
hero and deceive her? Though he had never said anything
definite, distinct, yet his voice, his manner, had told her all. He
had suggested too much and too clearly not to mean her to understand him. She did not dishonour him so far as even to argue in
her own heart whether such and such things were or were not.
She knew; she was conscious; she trusted; she believed; she
loved; and she was sure that she was beloved.

So matters stood, when Graziella Despues wrote to her dear
friend and sister Venetia, telling her that scarlet fever had broken
out in the school, and that it was by Miss Priscilla's desire she
wrote to beg for an asylum at Oak-tree House, if her darling's
love could bear such a test—she, Graziella, having no place on
earth to go to, as her guardian was abroad, and she was thus practically homeless.

'It is a great shame of Miss Wynter to have scarlet fever in
her house!' cried Miss Honoria sharply. 'And very inconside-
rate to ask us to take Graziella. Good gracious! if she brings it
with her; why, we might both take it and die!'

'But the poor little thing might take it and die if she stays
there,' said Venetia; 'and that is more likely than that she
should bring it with her to us. I don't see how we can possibly
hesitate, auntie! It would be murder if anything happened to
her!'

The beautiful blue eyes filled up with tears. With her capacity for love, she could never be unfaithful to the old because of
the new; and not even Ernest himself could make her forget
Graziella.

'Did I say that we could?' returned her aunt snappishly.
'You always jump so absurdly to conclusions, Venetia! Of
course Graziella must come, more especially as she has been invited
already, and her visit, in the natural course of things, would have

taken place in a few weeks. I only say that it is very wrong of Miss Wynter to have allowed scarlet fever to break out, and that in my state of health it is a dreadful risk to run, dreadful !'

'Oh, I hope there will be no danger, auntie !' said Venetia lovingly. 'We will take all the care possible and perhaps no harm will come !'

'At all events, *you* will be satisfied to have your idol here; and if I have to suffer, I have ; that is all !' answered Miss Morris, with an angry sigh. 'So let us say no more about it. You are so fond of making a fuss, Venetia !'

With which she settled herself to her knitting dourly, while Venetia, feeling herself dismissed, went off to write to her friend, begging her to put herself in the train without a moment's delay, and come off to Oak-tree House—or rather to her home, under-lined three times—where she knew that she was more than wel-come, and where—story-telling Venetia !—they had no kind of fear. She had had scarlet fever ten years ago, and auntie was too old to take it. So the doctor said when it was raging at Belton the summer before last, and there was, of course, no danger now : —ending the letter with a great deal of love and verbal caressing, and putting in a postscript the salient point of all :—'We have a new resident here for the summer, a Mr. Pierrepoint—Ernest Pierrepoint—whom I am sure you will like, and who is sure to like you. We see a great deal of him.'

This was the first that Graziella had heard of her dear friend's last enthusiasm—Venetia having kept back her confidence on this matter with a reticence wholly unlike her usual self; in con-sequence of which, when she read this last announcement, Graziella, who, girl as she was, had more finesse and more suspicion than the average woman, and who was infinitely more developed than her years, thought at once there was something in it; and was prepared to find that something out.

'How sly !' she thought as she read the letter, a deep flush burning on her cheeks. 'So, this is what all her professions to me have ended in at last ! I was to be her dearest friend to the end of her life. I was her favourite, her second self, her beloved ; and here is this stranger, a person she has known only a few days, who has taken her away from me ! But I will show her what I think when I get there; and let her feel that I see and understand her treachery.' Then her thoughts took another turn. 'I wonder what this Mr. Ernest Pierrepoint is like ?' she said to herself, lean-ing back on the garden seat where she was sitting, half-closing her lustrous eyes as she watched the birds that came and went about her feet, and the shadows that fluttered on the flower-bed opposite. 'Perhaps he is handsome; perhaps he is in love with Venetia.' She sighed. 'I wonder if he is?—and I wonder if he will like me?'

It was one of those curious coincidences in life, of which there are so many, that at the moment when Graziella said these words to herself, Venetia was speaking to Ernest about her beloved friend —detailing her virtues, her beauties, her charms; and the Backhouse family were thrown into a state of the most intense excitement by the information that their half-brother, Colonel Camperdown—the son of Mrs. Backhouse by a former marriage—was coming home from India on sick leave, and would be at the Elms in about a week's time from this.

Here then was a new shifting of the kaleidoscope, a new shuffling of the cards; characters incorporated into the drama at present enacting which might change the whole face of things, and turn the current of events into a totally different channel.

(*To be continued.*)

Goldsmith's 'Deserted Village.'

THERE are scenes which once painted on the living canvas of the mind endure there for ever in colours unfading; there are names which to all the world, from youth to age, have a gentle magic in their sound, and become enshrined amongst the holiest remembrances of the heart. So it is with Auburn, once the 'loveliest village of the plain.' Who that has read Goldsmith's delightful poem has not wished himself away among those sequestered spots whose olden beauties it at once immortalises and sanctifies? What reader of it—straying by the more favoured haunts in his own vicinage when the first primroses of the year are in blow, or later, when all the apple-trees are shaken, and the orchardman's conical hut is deserted—has not been reminded of those bowers which the poet sighed after, in language the most touching and numbers the most harmonious?—

Where smiling spring its earliest visit paid,
And parting summer's ling'ring blooms delayed.

Many years have glided past since I first read the opening part of the *Deserted Village*. I built up illustrations to it from the retreats of my childhood with the wonted flexibility of youthful imagination, and the pictures thus created have held their places despite all else that has come and gone, until, at length, I have had an opportunity to compare them with what yet remains of the reality. This being so, it has occurred to me that the perusal of a few notes which I made on a recent visit to Auburn might be interesting to admirers of Goldsmith, more especially to that large class of rising students of literature whose time and opportunities for pilgrimages of this sort may be but limited, or all in the future.

The site of the 'Deserted Village' is on the road from Athlone to Ballymahon, about six miles from the former town; and as crops of new 'Auburns' are springing up round in all directions, it is necessary to mention the poet's name in order to be set on the proper track to 'Gooldsmith's Auburns,' as the Westmeath peasantry call it. The country north of Athlone is undulating, the view being shut out by ranges of low hills, many of them mere sand-hills; and along the Ballymahon road the ordinary parallel fences are missed in many places, so that the vagrant donkey has here now and then an opportunity to taste the stolen sweets of sundry pastures without let or hindrance. The slopes on either hand are starred over with the brightest of whitewashed cottages, and everywhere about the hawthorn and the sloe-tree form a multitude of pretty alleys, all redolent in the May-time with the breathings of those flowers that love to hide in the brambly dell in fellowship with the broad-leaved sorrel-tasted shamrock. The cottage-gardens, with here and there a lichen-diseased apple-tree, and currant and gooseberry bushes growing in many an out-of-the-way place, are sufficiently indicative of quiet happy scenes of other days whose mementos are departing one by one. Pursuing the road from Athlone northward for about three miles, in a recess at the left formed by the hills that skirt the banks of Lough Ree, we come upon Ballykeeran; and surely if I were to turn eremite, and to build me a cell at an agreeable distance from the din and glitter and ring of this working-day world, I would choose for a site some silent nook of that woody hollow. Truly it is a very silent place; the 'mournful peasant' seems to have led thence his humble band—how impelled it is needless to say; and much of the surrounding country blooms, not, however, 'a garden and a grave,' but a grazing farm and a panorama of modern villas. A mile farther on is Glasson, certainly one of the prettiest of Irish villages. It has a very modest-looking little church, and hardly a house is to be seen there whose walls are unadorned with creepers and trained rose-bushes. After all, happy is that village which sitteth within favour of aristocracy; the bird of beggardom doth not commonly build in the tree over against the grand gate. Such a place has usually a distinguished air: its environs have, according to Hall, a fostering influence on the muse. Beautiful scenery in a manner educates the poet. His special faculties are, indeed, often known to thrive wonderfully when the slough of adversity lies on his horizon on the one hand and the mountain of magnificence on the other. Even the wayfarer forgets the weariness of his feet while pausing to luxuriate amidst the riches of Nature tastefully disposed; and should he happen to recall the notorious couplet of Lord John Manners, while mentally repeating the last line of it, he is soothed into no little community of feeling with the noble writer by the home-felt present delight of shade or vista. Glasson owes much of its interest to its proximity to Waterstown, the demesne of Temple Harris. Waterstown House is very finely situated on an elevated position, commanding a most charming prospect in the happy combinations of wood and lake and hill which surround it.   It is reached by a long avenue, winding for great part of the way between palisades of beeches and lofty pines perfectly helical in growth. Fronting the house is an extensive parterre, exhibiting the most impressive elegance in the arrangement of its beds as well as in the variety of the flowers.   Among the paintings at Waterstown House is a portrait of Sir William Temple, so noted as a diplomatist and man of letters, and as the patron of Dean Swift.   Indeed, so far as we can discover, the Temple blood has long been duly appreciative of the fairness of the earth ; and Sir William tells us of his residence, Moor Park, in Surrey, that it was the sweetest place he had seen in his life at home or abroad.   About a mile north of Glasson the prospect is closed by the woods of Auburn House, the residence of a Mr. Adamson.   It is agreeably situated on a sheltered slope, but it has an air of certainly not very graceful neglect about it which, though promising the diversity of a fine group of ruins here in a few years, is sadly ominous, as indicating that ' southward the course of *the canker* hath its way.'   And now at last we are on the Pisgah whence we first obtain a view of that sacred region, the song of whose decay has floated over all the globe, and is breathed by thousands who have never set foot upon our shores. The road leads still north.   To the east, stretching parallel to it, is the ' neighbouring hill,' near the summit of which, conspicuous in the distance, is the ' decent church ' known as the rectory of Kilkenny West.   A decent chapel of more modern date tops another neighbouring hill in the parish of Bunowen, perhaps the only architectural improvement of recent years that the place can show.   At the west side of the road, a little way on, are the house and farm of Lissoy, where great part of Goldsmith's early days was spent.   The wide entrance avenue is bordered by youthful successors of the grand old elms that once overarched it with their boughs ; and at the farther end, with its front towards the road, is the ruined parsonage, of which, as it appears at present, a very correct illustration will be found in Chambers's ' Cyclopædia of English Literature.'   At the rear a few trees of the old orchard may yet be seen ; and, thanks to the farmer yclept ' James Grew,' who lives near it, the whole surroundings of the remains of the ' modest mansion ' are in keeping with the other associations of Auburn, and in accordance with the poet's line.   The house consisted of two stories, having each five windows, and according to Prior the basement is about sixty-eight feet by twenty-four.   From the situation of the fireplaces, I am disposed to say that the breadth of the kitchen or its substitute was no more than twelve feet.   The hearths are none of the hospitable Irish style ; there is nothing wide, generous, and inviting about them; and from thinking over their appearance, such as they must once have been, there need be little hesitation in declaring that a broken soldier would find the ingle of one of our peasant farmers a much more cheery haven on a winter's evening. About half a dozen aged trees to the right are all that now remain of the 'copse' of other days; and not even Darwin himself could trace any blossomed thing in the place to a garden flower, though he should suppose an evolution period of thousands of perennial cycles. As to the 'noisy mansion' by the blossomed-furze-fence, this has experienced the fate of all hedge-schools, and the commodious national school of Tobberclair at hand by all accounts well supplies its place. With our modern watchword, *mehr Licht*, perhaps the *donatio mortis causa* of Goethe, we are too often disposed to 'think our fathers fools as wise we grow,' and in all cases to associate with the term 'hedge-school' something inconceivably base and barbarous, forgetting its source and the tale its etymology tells of those sad penal times

> When, crouching 'neath the sheltering hedge, or stretched on mountain fern,
> The teacher and his pupils met—feloniously to learn.

Deeper thought must, however, awaken in the Irish breast grateful memory towards men who transmitted the vestal fire of the scholar, no matter how often in a smouldering state, from sire to son. True it is, that prototypes of the Firdramore seminary were but too numerous; yet must it, on the other hand, be admitted that, among the primary teachers of a bygone age, narrowness of surface was compensated for in most instances by a profundity not often to be met with in days like these. At all events, tradition testifies that the Lissoy pedagogue, Thomas Byrne by name, was none of your Ichabod Cranes or Van Bummels, but was indeed a light in his rustic circle; and whatever chagrin the impenetrable stupidity of 'poor Noll' when a schoolboy might have given the good man, the kind-natured poet in more favoured moments made up for it all.

At a little distance from the entrance to Lissoy, and at the same side of the road, is the very pool alluded to by Goldsmith, and the noisy geese were now as ever gabbling over it and on its margin as I passed. It is bordered by a few stunted hawthorn-bushes, having upon them a strange impress of eld. Over against it is a ruinous cottage, the residence of a 'wretched matron' whose tale of her own happier years assuredly merits a sympathetic listener:

> She only left, of all the harmless train,
> The sad historian of the pensive plain.

The fields near her cottage were, up to a recent period, covered with a deep embowering wood; but all this has been cut away, and now only the discoloured stumps remain, as if left to heighten the apparent desolateness of the scene.

Ascending an incline, which certainly deserves not the name of 'hill,' we come to the cross of the 'Three Jolly Pigeons,' where the ruins of the alehouse may be seen; also the sycamore on which the signboard of that little inn used to be so invitingly hung in years that are over. Here, too, at the opposite side of the road, grows a later representative of that famous hawthorn-bush, which, though no fragment of it now remains where those enviable old people would so often sit and chat, and where those artless loves were told by rustic lovers of long ago, yet bids fair to bloom in fancy's garden for ever. To the right, a little off the road leading north-west, are the hoary roofless walls of the once 'busy mill.' Most of the wheel has been taken away, doubtless by visitors, each scrap being in some sort as a faded palm-branch from one of 'the Delphian vales, the Palestines, the Meccas of the mind.' The old nether millstone alone is likely to endure for a while beneath the ceaseless agencies of change and decay. To enter the ruined mill one must step over the 'never-failing brook,' which, though indeed choked with sedges, still repeats its own solitary murmur, as if it would whisper to the wanderer,

> Men may come, and men may go,
> But I go on for ever.

It was evening, and the place was overcast with a marked loneliness; not even the corn-crake (for no nightingale visits Ireland—Spenser's nightingale is the sally-pecker) interrupted the stillness. I looked on Auburn for the last time; true, its bowers were not merely in ruin but obliterated, and the long grass waved on the mouldering wall and on the cheerless hearthstone and on the chimney-tops whitened by the rains of many a day. Just as I was about to turn on my homeward route, a sudden gush of sunlight streamed over all the prospect, far and away over moor and meadow and hill. There was for a moment round about such a brightness as the memory of old time sheds on an aged man's countenance; such a soft effulgence as needed but the lowing kine and the graceful milking-maiden's song responded to by the guileless swain, and the loud laugh (yes! ye stilted Meteyards and thou crabbed Carlyle) and the murmur of joyous voices near betokening a current of life flowing freely along, to rival in its influence on the mind and heart

> The light that never was on sea or land,
> The consecration and the poet's dream.

> J. O'BYRNE CROKE.

Juliet.

BY MRS. H. LOVETT CAMERON.

CHAPTER VII.

MR. BRUCE'S LETTER.

'You will let me sit here and write a letter, won't you, Colonel Fleming?' said Mrs. Blair, when Juliet, on her inopportune entrance, had effected a hasty retreat.

Of course Colonel Fleming was delighted to have Mrs. Blair's company. From his using it so much, the room had come to be looked upon as essentially his.

The lady sat down, dipped her pen in the ink, and began to write. Now and then she glanced at her companion, who, with a perfectly impassive face, sat apparently absorbed in the 'Saturday Review.'

It was not a very long letter, but the composition of it seemed to afford her a good deal of trouble, for she laid down her pen and pondered several times.

'You must be *very* urgent,' she wrote, 'for I fear Juliet is inclined to be headstrong, and to throw herself away in an entirely new and *most undeserving* quarter; it would be a dreadful mistake, —and with such a property. The responsibility rests almost entirely on yourself.' And then she signed her name and put up the letter in a faint-scented, grey-tinted envelope, which she sealed and addressed to 'Josiah Bruce, Esq., 199 Austin Friars, City,' with an underlined *Private* in large letters in the left-hand corner.

It was astonishing how affectionately devoted Mrs. Blair was to her step-daughter all that day. She hardly let her out of her sight; she was untiring in her efforts to amuse and entertain her; she offered to wind her wools, to play her accompaniments, to go out driving with her, and even to help her with her visits in the village.

Juliet was in such a strange exalted state of mind, that she was scarcely conscious of these unwonted attentions; but when the evening came, she found that she had not spoken a single word to her guardian since the morning.

When they went upstairs to bed, Mrs. Blair did a most unusual thing; she followed Juliet into her bedroom.

'Juliet, love, I have something to say to you; I fear, something you won't like,—something disagreeable.'

'One seldom does like disagreeable things, my dear Mrs. Blair. What is it that you are going to tell me?'

'Well, dear, it is about yourself. You don't generally like my advice even when it is best meant, I know; but still——'

'I am afraid I am not very amenable to advice,' said the girl, with a momentary softening towards the woman whose falseness she always instinctively fathomed with the clear-sightedness of a perfectly candid and sincere nature; 'you know I have had my own way so much; but I shall really be glad to listen to any advice you can give me.'

'Well, love, it is about Colonel Fleming and yourself.'

'What do you mean?' In an instant she was like a creature at bay, turning on her stepmother with flashing eyes.

'Don't get angry, Juliet; but do you think it is *quite* wise or prudent to sit so much alone in the library with Colonel Fleming in the morning? Of course you and I know what nonsense such a thing must be; but people are so stupid, and it gives rise to talk.'

'People! what people? and who talks?'

'Why, things are said in the house—in the servants' hall.'

'How *dare* they!' cried Juliet, frantically.

'Yes, of course, love, it is most impertinent; but you see servants notice things just like anyone else,' said Mrs. Blair deprecatingly.

'And how can you lower yourself to listen to tittle-tattle from the servants' hall, Mrs. Blair!'

'Hush, hush, my dear, don't scold at me; I never listen, never; as I always tell Ernestine, "don't bring things to *me*."'

'I hate that Ernestine!' broke in the girl passionately.

'Ernestine is a very valuable servant, and I don't intend to part with her,' said Mrs. Blair with a touch of temper, which, however, was instantly suppressed; 'but, my love, that is not the point; as I was saying, they *will* talk, and isn't it a pity to give occasion for such talk? Of course, you and I know how absurd it is, quite ridiculous, in fact; a man such years older than yourself, so grave and serious, and your guardian too; something almost improper in the idea, isn't there? and you half engaged to Cis Travers too!'

'Be good enough to leave Cis Travers's name out of the question, Mrs. Blair,' said Juliet, by this time fairly stamping with fury.

'I consider myself quite incapable of doing anything that is unseemly or unfitting to my position in this house, and I shall certainly not alter my conduct for any impertinent remarks which may be made upon it by your maid!'

'Well, dearest, don't be so angry about it; I am sure I only meant to give you a motherly hint, and you must not bear me a grudge for it, will you, darling?'

'Thank you; I dare say you thought it was your duty,' said Juliet, coldly; at which Mrs. Blair declared that she was a sweet, dear, warm-hearted, generous-souled darling, flung her arms round her, and kissed her almost with rapture, Juliet submitting to the operation with a very bad grace.

But afterwards the shot told, as Mrs. Blair, who understood her victim, probably knew that it would. For Juliet breakfasted in her own room the next morning, and then, it being a bright fine day, went straight out to the home farm and the village, and to call on the clergyman's wife, and did not come in till the luncheon bell was ringing. As she entered, she met Colonel Fleming in the hall.

'Why, where have you been hiding yourself all the morning?' he said, as he went forward to greet her.

'I have been out; I had to go into the village and to the farm.'

'You mustn't do that again. I can't spare you; I have wanted you all the morning,' he said, with a ring in his voice that sent a thrill of delight to her heart.

And then Mrs. Blair came sailing down upon them from above, and they all three went in to luncheon.

Juliet decided that she would not punish herself so foolishly another day; she would go into the library as usual the next morning.

But the next morning, fate, in the shape of a letter in a blue envelope that lay by Colonel Fleming's plate at breakfast time, intervened.

The letter ran thus:

Dear Sir,—I very much wish you would run up to town for a few days; to begin with, I should like you to meet Davidson about the sale of those small Dorsetshire farms, as we could settle it all so much better in a personal interview with him. I also much wish to have some talk with you about another matter that is most seriously on my conscience, namely, the Travers alliance. I have had a visit from young Mr. Travers himself, who has been good enough to honour me with his confidence, and I have also received a letter from his father on the same subject, and I think that you and I, my dear sir, shall be wanting in our duty to Miss Blair, and in our due regard for the maintenance of her very fine property, if we do not do our utmost to carry out her late father's wishes on this most important point.

I am, sir, yours faithfully, JOSIAH BRUCE.

Colonel Fleming read this letter over twice most carefully, and then laid it down by the side of his plate and went on with his breakfast in absolute silence.

'Can I have the dog-cart to take me to the station this morning to meet the 12.30 train, Juliet?' he asked, after some minutes.

'Certainly; but why?'

'I find I must go up to town to-day.'

'Then I will drive you to the station in my pony carriage; that will be much pleasanter, don't you think so?'

'No doubt, fair hostess; but I fear it is not possible, as I must take my portmanteau.'

'Your portmanteau! Why, I thought you meant for the day! For how long are you going?' said Juliet, laying down her knife and fork.

'I must be away a few days, perhaps a week,' he answered, not looking at her and speaking rather rapidly.

'A week!' she repeated, with a dull dismay in her voice.

'Yes, I have a good many things I ought to begin to see to. Time slips away so rapidly, and my leave will not last for ever; and now Mr. Bruce writes that he wants me to see about—about the Dorsetshire farms you have settled to sell. Yes, I think it will take me about a week. If you will kindly excuse me, I will go and see after putting up my things.' He spoke rather nervously, and rose to leave the room.

'Oh, let Higgs see to all that,' said Juliet, impatiently.

'Thanks; I will go and speak to him;' and he went.

Juliet sat still in a sort of stupor. A week! what an endless blank of days it seemed! what a sudden break in her fool's paradise! What could take him away from her like that for a whole week, with so much that was unspoken between them, and that last question that he had asked her still unanswered?

Almost before she had realized that he was going, she heard the sound of the wheels of the dog-cart driving up to the door, and she met the footman carrying down his hat-box and portmanteau, and he himself in stiff London clothes and a tall hat, following the man downstairs.

'Must you really be off?'

Poor child! A far less accurate observer of human character than was Hugh Fleming could hardly have failed to trace the despondency in her face and voice as she spoke.

'I must really, I am afraid; unless I want to lose my train,' he answered, smiling; 'but I shall come back, Juliet, certainly in a week, perhaps sooner; I shall come back.'

' You are sure?' she asked almost entreatingly; and he answered very gravely,

' Yes, in any case I shall come back.'

And then he jumped into the dog-cart, gathered up the reins, lifted his hat to her, and drove off; whilst she stood leaning against the open doorway, watching till he was out of sight. A tall graceful figure, clad in soft brown velvet, with large wistful dark eyes that seemed almost as if they might be full of tears as they looked after him.

Did he think, I wonder, as he looked back at her, of that other girl in her white dress, who had so stood under a honeysuckle archway on a midsummer's evening, twenty years ago?

Not much, I fancy.

How desolate and dull the house seemed to Juliet as she turned back into it again after he was gone! She wandered about aimlessly, not knowing what to do with herself. At last she went into the library, where everything reminded her of him.

His books, some of his papers, and his writing things lay scattered on the table where he was accustomed to sit; she fingered them lovingly one after the other, and then began to put them together, smoothing out the papers and putting them in order with a touch that was lingering and reverent, as if they had been relics.

Presently she caught sight of the portfolio of his drawings leaning up against the wall. She sat down on the floor in front of it, and began turning over the sketches eagerly until she found again the little crayon head she had first so ruthlessly torn and then so laboriously mended. Leaning her head on her hand and holding it out before her, Juliet Blair gazed long and intently at it.

Poor, pale, sweet face! now that she knew its story, how full of touching meaning were the blue eyes and the little timid mouth!

Poor little bride, dead on her wedding morning! was ever story so pitiful, so heart-rending as hers!

And yet her living rival, with her rich warm colouring and glorious eyes, with twice her beauty and ten times her talent, sat staring at the faint pale face with all the passion of unreasoning jealousy raging at her heart.

This was the girl who had possessed his first, his best affections, who was his ideal, his religion in woman, who had won from him that intense devotion of his early manhood which can never in any man be exactly reproduced again!

Was she unfortunate? was she poor? Nay, rather, most

fortunate, most blessed, most rich Annie Chalmers, to have known how to win his whole heart, to have possessed the first love of such a man as Hugh Fleming, even if with her life she had paid the forfeit of such intense, such unspeakable joy!

For, what was left to her—to Juliet Blair? Nothing but the wreck of a heart that had scarcely even now recovered that early shock; the fragments of a life that was broken up and spoilt; the tangled thread that might never possibly be entirely made straight again. And was she sure even of this? Alas! no.

I do not think that, from what you have seen of my Juliet, you will misunderstand her when I tell you that there was little pity, little compassion in her heart towards that poor dead girl, whose story nevertheless had affected her in the telling; but only a great envy and a great bitterness of soul.

Meanwhile Colonel Hugh Fleming was leaning back in a first class smoking carriage of the Great Western Railway with a cigar in his mouth, going through a course of the most unpleasant self-examinations.

Was he a blackguard? he asked himself angrily; had he no sense of honour left, that he must go and stay in a girl's house as her guardian, and then try to steal her heart as a lover?

She with all her money, and he with nothing save his Indian appointment! What had he been doing? what had he been thinking about? Over what precipice had his selfishness well-nigh hurried him when Mr. Bruce's timely reminder had recalled him suddenly to his senses? Good heavens! was this honour? was this conscientiousness? was this fulfilling the responsibility her father had delegated to him? What opprobrious names would there not be rightly cast at him by everybody belonging to her, were he to do this mean, base deed, and take advantage of his position with her to gain possession of her wealth!

Ah! but the child was learning to love him! could he not read it in those dark eyes that could hardly meet his, in her burning cheeks and trembling lips, and still more in all the little flashes of temper and jealousy that betrayed her secret to him a hundred times a day? Only learning as yet, he trusted; she would unlearn the lesson soon enough if he showed her how; her pride, her spirit would carry her through it. Alas! why was she not poor like himself? why was she clogged with all these riches? Oh God! but it was hard to have such happiness once more within his reach, and this time to have to push it away from him with his own hands!

When he got to town he put himself into a hansom and went straight down to Austin Friars.

Mr. Bruce was in, and delighted to see him.

He plunged at once into all the advantages of the 'alliance,' as he would call it. It would be the making of the property; just what was always wanted to render it the finest and most valuable in the county. The families had always been friendly, and her father had set his heart on it; he had at least a dozen letters from old Mr. Blair by him now on this subject; he would show them to Colonel Fleming if he liked.

Colonel Fleming would waive that; he was quite ready to take Mr. Bruce's word for it; but what, might he ask—what did Mr. Bruce imagine that *he* could do in the matter?

' Why, urge it upon her, my dear sir, urge it upon her.'

' I——what can I say? Surely you are the person——'

' Not a bit of it, Colonel; not a bit of it. She doesn't mind me more than an old woman. Now, she has the greatest respect and reverence for you, I know very well; and affection too, I think.'

' Yes, yes, very likely,' interrupted Hugh hurriedly; ' still I cannot see that anything I can say will make any difference to her.'

' You have great influence with her, I am sure you have; and besides you are the person to speak; it will come with authority from you. It is clearly your duty, Colonel Fleming, if you will excuse my saying so.'

' Of course, of course, Bruce; say no more about it; but Miss Blair is not docile.'

' Not at all, sir, not at all; and that reminds me. Do you know of any low attachment she is likely to have formed lately?' asks Mr. Bruce, quite unconscious that the 'undesirable person' alluded to in Mrs. Blair's letter, which by the way he carefully kept dark, was no other than Colonel Fleming himself.

' Low attachment!' repeated that gentleman in amazement; ' certainly not; I never heard of such a thing, and should think it quite impossible; what can you have heard?'

' Ah, well, I certainly did not think much of it myself, but rumours are always getting about, and will as long as she is unmarried; the girl should have a husband—nothing will really be right on the place till she is married.'

' Still,' objected the Colonel, ' I do not see that you can force her into marrying against her will.'

' Certainly not; but young women, my dear sir, as you and I know well, are very easy to influence. A few judicious words about duty and responsibility and so forth, and they come round as nicely as possible; they only want management.'

Colonel Fleming had his own views on the subject of whether young women were manageable or not, but he did not think it necessary to impart them to worthy little Mr. Bruce.

'I do not think,' he said as he rose to go, 'that you will find that Miss Blair is a lady who will do violence to her feelings from any such motives.'

'Violence—no, indeed, Colonel; I did not think of any violence in the matter. Young Mr. Travers has been with me, and from what he told me of their last interview, I should be inclined to think—well, perhaps it might be a breach of confidence —but still, as you are her guardian——'

'Tell me by all means, Mr. Bruce,' said Colonel Fleming eagerly; 'what had she said to him ?'

'Well, she had certainly given him a slight repulse, but Mr. Cecil Travers did not strike me as a hopeless lover at all; he seemed assured that with time and your assistance—in fact, my dear sir, as I said before, I believe the cause only wants a few judicious words from yourself to be won ;' and Mr. Bruce rubbed his hands together and smiled at his visitor in the most satisfied and delighted manner.

Colonel Fleming gravely assured him that he would endeavour to do his duty to Miss Blair in this as in every other respect, and then took his leave.

He wandered westwards in the lowest possible spirits; he dropped in at his tailor's and his banker's on the way, which did not take him very long, and then sauntered into the East India Club and ordered himself a solitary dinner. A few old friends nodded to him as he went in. One asked him when he was going back to India, and he answered, with a sort of half groan, as soon as possible. On which Major-General Chutney—whose wife had come home hoping to cut a splash, which she found herself unable to do in a remote semi-detached stucco villa in Notting Hill, and consequently led her lord along a path that was anything but bordered with roses—answered that he was quite right; he only wished *he* could get back there ; 'the old country is a mistake, Fleming, depend upon it, quite a mistake.'

And Hugh echoed his words gloomily, 'Yes, a mistake altogether ; how is your wife ?'

'Thanks, Mrs. Chutney is well, poor thing ; perhaps,' added the general insinuatingly, 'perhaps—ahem, as you are in town, you might look in upon her ; it would gratify her very much to see an old friend : here is my card.'

Hugh took the card and promised to call on the lady if he had time, wondering vaguely as he did so in what possible way it could gratify her, whilst his friend departed with many internal chuckles at the stroke of policy he had achieved.

'Very clever that of me about the calling,' he said to himself, rubbing his hands gleefully together, 'she'll like that, I know; shouldn't wonder if it kept her in a good temper for a week— shouldn't wonder a bit!'

For Hugh Fleming happened to have a first cousin who was a lord; a lord whose name was frequently to be seen in the 'Morning Post' in connection with other much greater names than his own. And although this was a fact to which my hero himself seldom gave a thought, and which it may be said that he had almost forgotten, seeing that his cousin had never done anything for him, nor ever given him anything beyond occasionally his lordly hand to be shaken, and once, many years ago, a day's covert shooting in his preserves; still the fact of his cousinship remained, and Major-General Chutney well knew that his better half was not at all oblivious of it. To be able to say in familiar converse with the ladies of her acquaintance, 'Colonel Fleming called on me to-day; such a dear fellow! an old friend of the General's and a first cousin of Lord So-and-so, you know, my dear, whose name I daresay you have often seen in the papers in attendance on His Royal Highness,' would certainly be very gratifying indeed to the soul of Mrs. Major-General Chutney!

Left alone at the club, Hugh Fleming ate his dinner in moody silence, and wondered what on earth he should do with himself in town during the week he had said he should be away.

Truth to say, he had named that time for his absence because he had thought it good both for himself and for her that he should be away as long as possible, and not at all because of the amount that he had to do.

In fact, he had hardly any thing to do. He was to go again the next day to see Mr. Bruce about the Dorsetshire farms; he had already visited his banker and his tailor; it was hardly possible that he should go more than once again to see these gentlemen. He went to call next day on his only London relatives, an uncle and aunt living in Cavendish Square, from whom he had not even any expectations, and who were almost more surprised than pleased at his visit; and he did actually, with a view to killing time, go and call on Mrs. Chutney, in which amusement he suc- ceeded in expending the whole of one afternoon, as that good lady, with true Indian hospitality, insisted on having up a refreshment tray, although it was but three o'clock in the day, and forced him into the consumption, much against his will, of a large slice of seed cake and a glass of very bad sherry. Finally he had his hair cut, and wandered up and down Bond Street and Pall Mall aimlessly and miserably for the whole of one day; and then he could stand it no longer. Two days short of the week he had promised to be away, he paid his hotel bill, packed up his portmanteau, drove to the station, and took his place in the midday express; which would bring him down to Sotherne in time for dinner, with an insane and perfectly unreasonable joy sadly unbefitting his mature years and the general seriousness of his aspect.

Chapter. VIII.

THE FIRST OF NOVEMBER.

It was on one of those days when Colonel Hugh Fleming was away up in London that 'a southerly wind and a cloudy sky' ushered in the first of November.

Of all the three hundred and sixty-five days of the year the first day of November was to Squire Travers the most solemn and the most important.

The first meet of the season was held, according to a time-honoured custom, on a small triangular-shaped common surrounded by three cross roads, and having in the centre a fine group of elm trees, known by the name of Waneberry Green.

Here, by eleven o'clock in the morning on the eventful day, were gathered together half the county-side. There were eight or ten carriages full of ladies on the road by the side of the turf—Lady Ellison driving her roan ponies with her daughter-in-law beside her; Mrs. Blair, in sables and a Paris bonnet, leaning back in the Sotherne barouche in solitary grandeur; fat, good-tempered old Mrs. Rollick, with her three plain but jolly daughters crammed up in the antiquated yellow family chariot, all four laughing and talking very loud indeed all at once, side by side with the Countess of Stiffly, very thin and angular, sitting bolt upright in her brand new carriage, and casting withering glances of contempt and disgust at 'those horrible Rollick girls;' and many other representatives of the county families. Besides these there were also most of the smaller fry of the neighbourhood.

The parsons had come out to see the fun, with their wives and daughters, in unpretending little pony carriages; and the farmers' wives, in wonderful and gorgeous colours, driving themselves in their high tax-carts.

And then there were a goodly company of riders. Ladies of course in any number, most of them having merely ridden over to see the meet and to flirt with the men, though some few had a more business-like air, and looked as if they meant going by and by.　Conspicuous amongst these latter is Juliet, on her three-hundred-guinea bay horse, side by side with Georgie Travers on her old chestnut.

Juliet with her face flushed rosy with the wind, and her beautiful figure shown off to full advantage by her perfectly fitting habit and by the splendid horse on which she is mounted, looks as lovely a picture as anyone need wish to see, and is the centre of an admiring group of red-coated horsemen; but Georgie is a little nervous and anxious, and keeps looking about for Wattie Ellison, who has not yet appeared.

The Squire of course is in great force, riding about from group to group, talking to the ladies in the carriages, waving his hand to this or that new-comer, consulting his watch every minute, and trotting rapidly up and down as full of business as a general on the eve of a battle.

'Isn't your Wattie coming?' asks Juliet aside of Georgie, for her woman's wit has long ago guessed her little friend's secret. 'Ah, there he is, coming up to us now; how well he looks in pink! How do you do, Mr. Ellison? here is Georgie getting quite pale and anxious because you are so late!' and Juliet nods pleasantly as the two lovers with smiles and blushes take up their position at once side by side.

And now the clatter of hoofs is heard on the left, and, headed by Ricketts the huntsman, and backed up by the two whips, in a deep, compact, and mottled mass, the pack of hounds comes trotting quickly on to the scene.

Then at once all is bustle and excitement; the Squire gives the word, on go the hounds to draw the woods to the right, crack go the whips, too-too-too goes the horn, and with much hurry and commotion the whole body of riders follow in the wake of the master.

Then there is the usual waiting about at the cover side, the gleam of red coats dotted about the field turns the grey background of brushwood and the sombre ploughed field into a holiday scene, all voices are hushed in the suppressed excitement of the moment, save only the Squire's, who swears roundly at everything and everybody within hearing, whilst the hounds draw silently but closely through the wood.

Then all at once a whimper is heard, soon deepening into a mellow chorus: 'Tally ho! Gone away! gone away!'

In a moment the hounds have burst from the wood, and after them dash the whole company helter-skelter, as fast as their horses can lay legs to the ground.

Such a confusion at the first few fences!

Some refuse, some jump on each other, some make for gates, whilst the timid riders turn back, and those who are left with the first flight settle themselves down to their work in earnest, and soon disappear over the shoulder of the hill.

In an incredibly short space of time Waneberry Green is deserted. The carriages have all driven off, some few to follow for a mile or two along the lane in hopes of coming across the hounds again, but most of them to turn in the direction of their respective homes. The lookers-on and followers on foot, who often see a good deal of the fun, have all disappeared; not a living soul is left; and the rooks, who have been disturbed from their haunts by the morning's noise and commotion, come cawing contentedly back to the elm trees in the middle of the little common.

They had a good run that morning, and foremost in the field was of course Georgie Travers, pressing close in her father's wake, and followed near by by Wattie Ellison. Georgie knew every inch of the country, every gap, every gate, every ditch.

She picked her own line with a cool head and scientific reckoning, she knew better than to waste her own strength or her horse's at the beginning of the day with unnecessary exertions, but when there did come an unavoidable thick-set bullfinch or a stiff bit of timber, Georgie put the chestnut's head well at it, rammed in her little spurred heel, set her teeth hard, and was over it in a manner that made every man round her turn for an instant to admire.

Juliet Blair did not ride to hounds after this fashion. I am not sure that she would not at heart have considered it rather *infra dig.* for the owner of Sotherne Court to go rushing over hedges and ditches during the whole day in the reckless way that little Georgie Travers did.

Juliet followed for a little way in a leisurely lady-like manner, followed by her groom, and keeping rather aloof from the ruck of the hunt, till they came to the first check, and then she turned her horse's head into a side lane, left the hounds behind, and went for a quiet ride on her own account.

Just when she was going home, and long after she thought she had left every trace of the hunt behind her, she suddenly came upon Georgie and young Ellison riding side by side down a narrow lane with their heads and hands suspiciously close together.

' Halloa, Georgie! I left you in the front; how do you come here?'

' I got thrown out!' said Georgie, blushing, ' and we have lost the hounds; have you seen anything of them?'

' Nothing whatever, and I don't suppose you want to see them, you very disgraceful young people!' said Juliet, laughing, as she cantered by.

Georgie and her lover rode on slowly.

'You will tell your father to-night, Georgie?' said the young man.

'Yes, I think I had better; but papa has been very worried lately by Cis.'

'What has poor Cis been doing now?'

'Why, Juliet has refused him again,' said Georgie, laughing.

'I am sure I am not surprised; how can your father expect her to have him?'

'Well, I don't know, but even now papa won't give up the idea; he is very savage with Cis, and it is a good thing the poor boy is away. Certainly Cis inherits papa's dogged determination if he inherits nothing else, for he won't give her up a bit. I rather like him for it. Oh Wattie, Wattie!' she cried suddenly, 'there are the hounds; come along.'

And Georgie was over the hedge in a minute and away, as a gleam of scarlet and white through a break in the woodland told them that they had again fallen in with the lost hunt.

Such a run they had in the afternoon! thirty-five minutes without a check; it quite eclipsed the little spurt of the morning.

It was very late that afternoon when Georgie and her father, stiff, tired, and muddy, dismounted at their own hall door, and limped into the house, whilst their steeds, looking tucked up and draggled, were led away to their well-earned gruel.

Little Flora came flying down stairs three steps at a time to meet them.

'Have you killed a fox, papa? where is his head?' she cried, clinging to her father's muddy coat tails.

Mrs. Travers, following slowly, lugubriously said it was a mercy they hadn't broken their necks this time, as if they were in the habit of doing so.

'Oh papa!' cried little Flora, 'do let me ride with you some day on Snowflake; I know I could go quite well without a leading rein.'

'So you shall, my little girl,' said the Squire, lifting her up and kissing her, 'I'll make another Georgie of you some day, when she goes and marries, and leaves her old daddy!' and the old man winked and nodded at his eldest daughter in a manner that made her quite hopeful about the confession that was hanging over her.

'Please go and take off your dirty things, Georgie, and make haste,' said her mother. 'Flora, you naughty child, you have covered your nice clean frock with mud; and I wish, Mr. Travers, you wouldn't put such ideas in the child's head; I am sure one daughter rushing about all day with a pack of men, and unsexing herself among stable boys is enough in a family. I hope to see Flora grow up a lady like her sister Mary.'

'Stuff and nonsense!' growled the Squire fiercely; 'there isn't one of 'em can hold a candle to Georgie; I won't hear her abused, ma'am. Unsexed, indeed! did ye ever hear such a word! d'ye want her to ride in a flannel petticoat? is it her wearing breeches that you mind?'

'Don't be so coarse, Squire,' said his wife, looking deeply offended, whilst her spouse retired into his dressing-room with a loud guffaw of certainly rather unrefined laughter.

It was in the evening, after dinner, when the Squire had retired to his study to smoke his nocturnal pipe that Georgie came and stood at the back of her father's chair.

'Papa, I have something to say to you,' she began, softly stroking the top of his bald head.

'What is it, my girl? I suppose you want another hunter this winter: well, I have been thinking myself the chestnut is looking a little bit shaky on his fore-legs, though there's no doubt he carried you well to-day, very well—couldn't have gone better; but still I know he won't last for ever. There's that brown mare, I meant her for you, and—there, I'll give her to you outright for your own; but I suppose you'll be wanting another. Well, if you're a good girl I'll see what I can do for you.'

'But, papa, it isn't about horses at all,' said Georgie timidly.

'Not about horses!' he exclaimed, looking up at her. 'Well, what is it, eh?'

'You—you said to-day, papa—perhaps some day I might—I might think about marriage.'

'Eh? what, what! marriage, is it? Ah, my girl, I shan't know how to part with you, but I won't be selfish; never fear, my dear, the old man won't be selfish. I won't say nay to any good man who will make my little girl happy and keep her as well mounted as she deserves to be. Who is the man? out with it, Georgie; who is the happy man?'

'Oh, papa, I am afraid it isn't at all a good match for me, not so good as you would like, but he is such a dear fellow, and I am so very fond of him.'

'Well—out with it; who is he?' said her father impatiently.

'Wattie Ellison!' faltered the girl, hanging down her head.

'*What!*' thundered the Squire, jumping up from his chair and turning round on her—whilst his best meerschaum pipe fell shattered at his feet. '*What!* how dare you mention that good-for-nothing young scoundrel to me? how dare you think of such a thing? confound his impudence! so that's what all your riding about together has come to, is it! I wouldn't have believed it of you, Georgie, I wouldn't have believed it!'

'Oh, papa, don't be so angry,' cried Georgie, tearfully clasping her hands together, 'indeed we couldn't help loving each other.'

'Loving! pack of nonsense. I am ashamed of you, Georgie. You don't suppose any father in his senses would allow his daughter to marry an idle young pauper like that. How dare he lift his eyes to you! how dare he make love to you! that's what I want to know. Of all the dishonourable, mean, base, contemptible young blackguards——'

'Papa, papa!' cried Georgie frantically.

'Oh ay, I mean what I say, and a good horsewhipping is what Mr. Wattie Ellison deserves, and that's what I would like to give him, and kick him out of the house afterwards, the impudent young scoundrel!'

And at this very moment the footman opened the door and in an impassive voice announced 'Mr. Walter Ellison.'

At this most unexpected and undesirable appearance on the scene of the young gentleman under discussion, poor Georgie went very nearly out of her mind with despair.

The Squire, speechless with fury, and almost foaming at the mouth, literally flew at the throat of his would-be son-in-law, and, seizing him by the collar of his coat, shook him as a terrier shakes a rat.

'What d'ye mean by it? How dare you, you scoundrel? You d—d young rascal!' he panted out breathlessly, whilst Georgie rushed at him to defend her attacked lover.

'I don't see that I need be so dreadfully sworn at, sir,' said Wattie as soon as he was able to speak. 'It is not my fault that your daughter is so charming that I could not help falling in love with her, and if you would allow us to be engaged we could wait, and I dare say I could get something to do, and you would help us a little perhaps.'

'I'll see you d—d before ever I give you or her a farthing, sir, of that you may be sure; and as to allowing her to be engaged to you, I'd as soon allow her to be engaged to Mike the earthstopper, quite as soon—much sooner, in fact.'

'Hush, hush, papa!' here broke in Georgie, with a very white face. 'You need not say any more—you will be sorry for having spoken like this by and by.'

'I shan't be a bit sorry. I mean every word I say. When this young gentleman goes out of the house this evening, I forbid him ever to come into it again. I forbid you ever to speak to him or write to him, or hold any communication with him whatever; if you do, I will disown you for my daughter, and never speak to you again; and I tell you, Georgie, that sooner than see you married, or even engaged, to such an idle, profitless good-for-nothing as this young man, I would rather by far see you in your coffin.'

There were a few moments' silence in the little room when the Squire finished speaking, and then Georgie, white to her very lips, but brave and resolute as the little woman always was where courage and resolution were wanted, went straight up to her lover.

'You hear what papa says, Wattie; don't stop here any longer, it is no use, he will never allow it, we must just make the best of it and submit. He is my father, and I wouldn't disobey him for worlds. You had better go right away, my poor boy, and try and forget me. Yes, don't shake your head, Wattie; if it's impossible, we shall perhaps learn with time and with absence to get over it. Oh Wattie, give me one kiss and say good-bye!' And she put both her arms round her lover's neck and kissed and clung to him sobbing, whilst her father stood by, looking on, but saying never a word, with a sort of choke in his throat of which he felt half ashamed.

'Good-bye, my love—God bless you, Wattie; as long as you are alive I will never marry any other man on earth. Go now,' and she pushed him with her own hands gently out of the room and closed the door upon him.

'My own brave good girl!' said the Squire when he was gone, attempting to draw his daughter into his arms, but Georgie shrunk away from him.

'Don't touch me, don't speak to me,' she said, and then sat down till she heard the front door close with a slam, and Wattie's footsteps die away on the gravel walk outside.

Then she got up and moved rather unsteadily towards the door. The Squire sprang forward and held it open for her, looking at her wistfully, almost entreatingly, as she passed out; but she fixed her eyes in front of her and did not look at him.

And somehow, when she was gone and he was left alone, although his daughter had given up her lover and promised to obey him, and although he had sworn his fill at the young fellow and had not even been answered again, the old man did not feel very triumphant; he did not seem to have had the best of it at all in the encounter that was just over, but rather very much the worst of it. He had a vague idea that he had taken an inglorious part altogether, and felt rather small and contemptible in his own eyes.

'Nonsense, nonsense,' he said to himself at last, 'of course I was quite right—quite right—any father in my place would have done the same—impudent young scoundrel! and how was I to know the girl would take it in that meek way ? girls don't generally. I didn't like the look in her face, though, when she went out. I hope it won't make any difference between her and me, though. Oh, she'll get over it fast enough ! I think I'll give her a new saddle ; she wants one badly—yes, I'll do that for her ; that will please her, I know.'

And no sooner had this brilliant idea come into his mind than he sat down and wrote to his saddler in London to send down as soon as possible a new lady's saddle of the very best that money could buy.

When he had directed and stamped this letter, and dropped it into the letter box outside in the hall, he felt happier in his mind, and went upstairs and joined the rest of his family in the drawing-room, but Georgie was not there.

No word was said between Georgie and her father of what had passed between them either the next day nor any of the days that followed. The girl went about her duties as usual, but very quietly and unobtrusively. She wrote her father's letters and read the papers to him and walked up to the stables and kennels with him as she was always accustomed to do, but silently, listlessly, without any of her natural energy and enthusiasm. You could see there was no longer any pleasure or spirit in her life for her. She was not in the least sulky, she was perfectly sweet and gentle and sub-missive to her father, and when the new saddle came down she showed as much affectionate gratitude to him as he could possibly have expected, and yet everything was different.

There was no longer that unity in thought and purpose, that perfect confidence that had always bound the two together in a tie that resembled a devoted friendship rather than the relation which father and daughter generally bear to each other.

The next hunting day Georgie, much to her father's relief, for he had been dreadfully afraid that she might refuse to go out, appeared at breakfast as usual in her habit. She rode the new brown mare, who, although she fidgetted a good deal at starting, and lashed out once or twice at the covert side in an unpleasant looking way, still, when she was once fairly going, certainly acquitted herself as if she knew her business.

Wattie Ellison was not there, and Georgie and her father both overheard Sir George Ellison say, in answer to some enquiries after him, that his nephew had taken a fit of industry and gone to town to court fortune in his old chambers in the Temple.

To Juliet Blair the girl said a few words concerning her trouble. Juliet saw at once that something had gone wrong with her little friend.

'What has happened, Georgie?' she asked in a whisper, as the two found themselves side by side during a check in a deep lane. 'You look so miserable.'

'I *am* miserable, Juliet,' answered the girl, and her lip quivered. 'It is all over between me and Wattie; he has gone away; papa won't hear of it; he was very angry.'

'What a shame! why should he be angry? I am sure Wattie is a man anybody might be proud of.'

'Thanks, Juliet dear, but papa was quite right,' answered Georgie, loyal as ever to her father; 'I knew he would not allow it. You see, Wattie has no money and no prospects whatever; one's sense tells one it was impossible.'

'How I wish I could help you!' cried Juliet, ever ready for a generous action. 'Now, don't you think I could make you a good fat allowance, just to start you in life, you know? You wouldn't be proud, I know, for after all half the use of money is that now and then one can make somebody one cares for happy—don't you think we could manage it?'

'I am afraid not, you dear good Juliet! not that I should be proud a bit; but you see papa would not hear of such a thing, nor Wattie either; that is the worst of these men,' added Georgie with a sigh.

'What, not even if I was your sister-in-law?' said Juliet, laughing.

'Ah yes, then, perhaps. Oh dear, Juliet, how I wish you could manage to marry Cis. Papa would be so pleased; poor papa! it is hard on him that both his children give him so much trouble and anxiety in their love affairs.' At this instant a halloa was heard, and Juliet, who was going home, waved her hand in farewell to her friend, who put the brown mare neatly over a stile and galloped off across a grass field to join the hounds.

CHAPTER IX.

COLONEL FLEMING ADVISES HIS WARD.

'I WONDER when he will come back,' said Juliet to herself as she rode slowly up to her own hall door. 'Not till the day after to-morrow, I suppose.'

It still wanted two days of the week he had said he would be away, and Juliet, as she dismounted and went in, felt that she had never known a week to be so interminably long as this one had been.

She went into the little morning room. The short winter afternoon was drawing in, and the room was but dimly lighted by the flicker of the firelight.

'Let us have some tea,' said Juliet, flinging down her hat and gloves on the table and ringing the bell, and then she stooped down in front of the fire and began warming her hands.

Somebody rose from the sofa in the half light and came and stood behind her on the hearth rug. She thought it was her step-mother.

'I am very cold,' she said.

'Are you?' said a voice that was certainly not Mrs. Blair's.

She jumped up with a glad cry of surprise.

'Hugh!' she exclaimed in her delight, unconsciously calling him by his christian name for the first time, and holding out both her hands to him; and he took the hands and held them tight in his own, and then, with an impulse which he was unable to resist, drew her suddenly towards him and kissed her once on the forehead.

Ah! How many days were to pass away ere ever his lips repeated that unexpected and all too deliciously sweet caress!

'You are glad to see me again, then?' he asked, as Juliet drew back from him a little confusedly.

'Yes, so glad,' she answered looking away from him with brightly crimsoned cheeks. 'I had no idea you were here. What brought you back sooner than you expected?'

'The three-thirty express. My business was over; there was no longer any reason for my staying away.'

And then Higgs and the footman came in with the tea-tray and the candles, followed almost immediately by the rustle of Mrs. Blair's silk dress along the passage.

'Why, Colonel Fleming!' exclaimed that lady, 'when did you come back? I never heard you arrive! Why, how quickly you have done all your London business; how much more lively I should have thought it must be for a man to be up in dear delightful London, with all the clubs, and Bond Street, and the shops, and the theatres, than down in the wilds of the country with only two women to amuse him; shouldn't you have thought so, Juliet?'

'You underrate your own fascinations, Mrs. Blair!' said Hugh with a gallant bow, whilst Juliet, still thrilling from head to foot with the memory of that kiss, busied herself silently at the tea-table.

About that same kiss Hugh Fleming took himself afterwards very seriously to task. It was not at all in the programme of grave coldness and guardian-like severity of demeanour which he had drawn out for himself, and was quite incompatible with that stern line of duty and high principle to which he had determined most strictly to adhere. It was wonderful how, at the first sight of that graceful girl, with her small dark head and soul-inflaming eyes, all these good resolutions had melted and vanished away, and left him so weak that he had not been able to resist even the small temptation of kissing her.

It was only by going over and over again all the old arguments of honour and duty and right feeling during the course of a somewhat restless and sleepless night, that Hugh Fleming could at all bring himself round again to the very proper determination which Mr. Bruce's arguments and his own conscience had succeeded in implanting deeply in his mind.

He must do this hard duty by her : he must plead his rival's cause ; he must if possible persuade her to look more favourably on Cis Travers's suit, and then he had better get himself back to India as quickly as he could ; for to stop by and see her married to another under his eyes was surely a pitch of self-torture and self-abnegation which could not possibly be required of him.

'Will you come out and take a turn in the garden with me, Juliet?' he asked of her as they rose from breakfast the next morning ; 'it is a nice bright day for a stroll, and I have something to say to you.'

Juliet gladly consented and went to fetch her hat.

They wandered out together towards the shrubberies, talking lightly first of one thing, then of another ; Hugh, like a coward, delaying the evil moment as long as possible. Did he guess, perhaps, how rudely his hand was to tear away all her brightest dreams?

At last there was a sudden pause in their talk, and Hugh began hesitatingly :

'I said I had something to say to you.'

'Yes?' she said enquiringly, breaking off a little branch of crimson-berried yew from the hedge along which they were walking.

'It is perhaps a difficult subject for me to broach to you, Juliet, and one which I can hardly dare hope you will listen to from me, but it has been forced upon my conviction of late that it is perhaps my duty to speak to you very plainly indeed upon this matter.'

'Why should you not speak plainly to me?' she answered, looking down at the red berries in her hand and fingering them nervously.

'It is the matter of your marriage,' he said gravely.

And then she answered, with, poor girl! heaven knows what a beating heart, and with all the hopes and fears of a glad love trembling in her low broken voice, 'Speak to me as plainly as you will; speak to me from your heart, Colonel Fleming, not as guardian to ward, but as man to woman ; that is how I shall like you best to speak.' In a moment it had flashed across her that because she was rich and he was poor, because he was her guardian and she his ward, therefore it was that he hesitated to speak what was in his heart towards her.

'Unfortunately, my dear Juliet,' he answered after a moment's silence, during which every demon that understands the art of temptation had fought a pitched battle within him and been defeated—'unfortunately, it is exactly as a guardian to a ward that I wish to speak to you. I think you have hardly given the subject of a marriage with Cecil Travers as much attention and consideration as the idea demands from you.'

The crimson berries dropped from her nerveless fingers upon the path and every vestige of colour faded from her face.

Colonel Fleming went on, speaking rather rapidly.

'I had no idea until lately how very much your poor father's heart was set upon it, and how completely the match was of his own planning and arranging for you.'

No answer, only Juliet walked on rather faster by his side.

'Cecil Travers is certainly a most steady and deserving young fellow, and is, as I need not remind you, very much attached to you personally. He is, I am sure, quite above any sordid considerations, and will value you for yourself and not for your money, as so many of the men you will meet in the world might do. Don't you agree with me?'

Still no answer ; Miss Blair walks rapidly on.

'From what Mr. Bruce tells me,' continued Colonel Fleming, ' and from what, indeed, I know myself of your affairs, it would be certainly a great advantage for the two properties to be united ; it appears that the whole of those outlying farms in the Lynedale valley, which now form part of Mr. Travers's property, did in point of fact actually belong to your great grandfather, who sold them very much beneath their value to the Travers family in order to pay the debts of a younger son. Now, such a proceeding was of course an iniquity, and if you can in any way repair and make up for the sins of your ancestors by restoring the property to its original fair dimensions it is no doubt incumbent on you to do so. *Noblesse oblige,* my dear Juliet ; in your position of responsibility you are not quite the free agent which young ladies are generally supposed to be in these matters, and you owe a certain distinct duty, not only to your predecessors, but also, if I may be allowed to say so, to those that are to come after you.'

Then Colonel Fleming comes perforce to an end of his arguments, having, in fact, nothing more to urge.

'You are well primed, Colonel Fleming!' cries Juliet sarcastically. 'Mr. Bruce has supplied you with the usual stereotyped sentences. I have heard all that you have been saying a great many times before;' and she laughed a short, dry, and not pleasant laugh.

'I don't know, if the things are true, that they are any the worse for having been said before,' says her guardian, almost humbly.

And then Juliet stops short in her walk and turns upon him with angry flashing eyes—

'And do you mean to say, Colonel Fleming, that you, of all people on earth, advise me to marry Cecil Travers?'

'Really, Juliet——' he begins hesitatingly, quailing somewhat before her righteous wrath.

'Answer me!' she cries, stamping her foot, 'do you wish me to marry Cecil Travers?—Yes or no, answer me!' and Hugh, not daring for his own sake to answer her 'No,' replies—'Yes.'

'May God forgive you for that lie!' answers Juliet, and deliberately turning her back upon him, she walks away into the house.

Things after that are very uncomfortable indeed at Sotherne Court for several days. Juliet is deeply, bitterly offended with her guardian, and will not speak to him more than she can possibly avoid.

That he should have spoken to her as he did, ignoring all that had passed between them of tender meaning and unspoken sympathy, was in itself a bitter source of grief to her, but that he should have deliberately insulted her by pleading the cause of his rival, is a thing which Juliet thinks, and perhaps thinks rightly, that no woman ought ever wholly to forgive to the man whom she loves.

By some mysterious means of her own, whether it is by letters from Mr. Bruce, or whether Ernestine's powers of observation have again been called into requisition, I am not prepared to say, but certain it is that Mrs. Blair is conscious not only of the coolness that exists between Juliet and her guardian, but also is perfectly aware of the cause for that coolness.

And this state of things affords her intense satisfaction.

Mrs. Blair, as has probably been seen long ago, divined that the interest which Colonel Fleming took in Juliet exceeded that amount of interest which a guardian may legitimately feel for a young lady who is in the position of his ward.

It seemed to Mrs. Blair that, given a man with no private fortune, and in a position of great intimacy in the house of a young lady largely gifted with all the good things of this world, what more natural than that the poor man should do his best to gain possession of those good things ?

Now, that Colonel Fleming should marry her step-daughter would not at all have suited Mrs. Blair's views for her own future arrangements.

Colonel Fleming was not a man over whom Mrs. Blair felt she could obtain the smallest influence ; she knew instinctively that he disliked and mistrusted her ; and as Juliet did the same, anything like an understanding between the two would probably be at once the signal for her own departure from the very comfortable quarters in which she was at present installed.   Although, with a weak youth like Cecil Travers, the widow felt that things would probably be very different, still I am not sure but that to put Cecil prominently in the foreground, in order to keep other and more formidable rivals at bay, was more her object than to urge on a marriage either with him or with anyone else.   She felt that, if she could get Colonel Fleming safely back to India without his having proposed to Juliet, she would have gained a great deal.

Unconsciously, honest little Mr. Bruce, whose faith in the claims of the ' Travers alliance ' was part of his creed with reference to Miss Blair, played into the widow's hands with a promptitude and unsuspiciousness for which she was constantly invoking blessings on his worthy head.   And she had yet another advocate— of which, however, she was quite unaware—in the scrupulous feelings of honour and delicacy which formed a part of Colonel Fleming's character.   Instead of being a fortune-hunter, as in her own mind Mrs. Blair had designated him, he was, on the contrary, ready to sacrifice not only his own happiness, but also Juliet's, if need be, sooner than in any way to court a woman whose wealth was to him only a disadvantage, and not in the very least a temptation.

After that conversation in the garden in which Colonel Fleming had given his advice so very ineffectually to his ward, his manner to her became entirely changed ; he was continually on his guard with her, constantly watching his own words and actions, so that he became reserved and even cold and distant to her.

Juliet fretted vainly over this change.   To her impulsive, affectionate nature such an alteration in one who had hitherto been uniformly kind and indulgent to her was inexpressibly painful. Her own resentment against him had been but short-lived, and had he but met her half way, she would have been only too glad to have forgotten all that he had said, and have let everything be as usual between them.

Things were in this state when a dinner party which had been for some time in contemplation took place at Sotherne Court.

Sir George and Lady Ellison, Mr. and Mrs. Travers and Georgie, and the Rollick family, were among the guests.

A country dinner party is not as a rule a lively entertainment; the conversation is purely of local topics, and to a stranger the ins and outs of county gossip are apt to be inexpressibly wearisome.

It is bad enough at dinner, but after dinner, in the drawing-room, when the ladies are left alone, it is ten times worse. Lady Ellison gets hold of a young married woman, to whom she proceeds to unfold her views on the nourishment of very young infants. Mrs. Blair descants on the superiority of French ladies-maids to Mrs. Travers, who thanks God piously that she never had a fine ladies-maid at all, either French or English ! Presently two of the Miss Rollicks good-naturedly go to the piano and warble a duet.

' Oh, were I on the zephyr's wing ! ' trill out these substantial maidens together, which makes Georgie Travers wickedly whisper that, if they were, they would very speedily tumble down ; Mrs. Rollick sits by, fanning her portly person placidly, and smiling sweetly at her offspring, whilst Juliet and Georgie whisper together in a corner about poor Wattie.

' My dear,' says Mrs. Rollick, who has a knack of making awkward remarks, nodding pleasantly across to Juliet,—' My dear,' how long is that very good-looking guardian of yours going to stay here ? '

Juliet is angry with herself for getting red as she answers, ' As long as I can keep him, I hope.'

' Ah ! ' says the good lady, nodding and winking, ' if I were you I would try and keep him altogether ; perhaps that is what you mean to do, eh ? '

Here Mrs. Blair remarks casually, ' I believe that Colonel Fleming's leave is nearly over, Mrs. Rollick; he will be returning to India almost immediately, I fancy.'

And for once, although she hates her for saying it, Juliet feels grateful to her step-mother.

She gets up and goes over to the Miss Rollicks, who have just ended their duet, and asks them to sing another, which they eagerly and joyfully proceed to do.

' I know a maiden fair to see ! ' said Miss Arabella Rollick, archly smiling round on the company generally.

'ARE YOU STILL ANGRY WITH ME?' SHE ASKS.

'Beware! take care!' echoes Miss Eleanor Rollick in a deep lugubrious contralto.

'She's fooling thee!' continues Miss Arabella, confidentially winking down the room.

And then there is a commotion at the door, and all the gentlemen come in very close together, turn round just inside the room, and go on with what they were talking about before they came in.

Lady Ellison and the young married woman hastily push their chairs apart and finish off their last confidences on the subject of the infants in a whisper.

The Squire has button-holed Sir George Ellison in the doorway, and is saying in a loud voice, ' Unless we can improve our breed of horses, sir, unless we can improve the breed, the country *must* go to the dogs!'

'Ah, we must improve the breed of dogs then, ha! ha!' says Sir George, with a feeble attempt at a mild joke, endeavouring to sidle away from his tormentor and to get into the middle of the room—a stratagem which the Squire immediately circumvents by backing in front of him, holding him tight by the arm, and talking at the top of his voice.

Mr. Rollick, who is very small and thin, and altogether gives one the idea of a man much sat upon by the females of his family, is telling the young married woman's husband, who is a curate, for the third time, that the crop of mangel wurzels is remarkably fine this year, ' re—markably fine.' The curate, whose interest in that vegetable is not absorbing, answers rather irrelevantly, ' Exactly so!' and looks round the room to see if his wife is sitting in a draught, which is his prevailing anxiety. Two young officers who have come over from the neighbouring garrison town stand for a moment together, and ejaculate to each other, ' Deuced good sherry!' and ' Deuced fine gal!' the latter remark being pointed at Juliet; after which the Rollick girls, having come successfully to the end of ' Beware,' bear down upon these gentlemen from the opposite side of the room, and carry them off in triumph into separate corners, there to torment them at leisure.

Lastly Hugh Fleming saunters into the room, looking very much bored, glances for one moment at Juliet, and then sinks down into a low chair by the side of Georgie Travers, to whom he has taken rather a fancy.

Squire Travers having backed himself into the middle of the room, still discoursing noisily by the way upon the breed of horses, catches his foot in the folds of Mrs. Rollick's amber-satin gown, among which he flounders about hopelessly, and nearly tumbles headlong on to that lady's portly lap.

Juliet goes laughingly to his rescue, and then, with a view to the release of the much-enduring Baronet, carries him off to a distant sofa for ' a talk.'

The Squire is pleased with the attention ; he is very fond of Juliet, and always looks upon her in the light of his future daughter-in-law. ' My little Georgie looks well, doesn't she ? ' he says, looking across to his daughter.

' Not at all, Mr. Travers,' answers Juliet remorselessly ; ' I never saw her look less well ; she looks as white and ill as possible ; I am afraid you have been giving her something to fret about lately ! '

' Eh, eh what ! what's the girl been grumbling about ? you don't really think she looks ill, do you, Miss Juliet ? ' This is said anxiously. Juliet answers that she really does think so, and the Squire scratches his thin grey hair, and mutters—' God bless my soul ! I can't let her go and marry a young pauper without a farthing, you know ! '

' No, but you might give her a little hope,' pleads Juliet.

' Well, and are you going to give me a little hope about my boy ? ' says he, dexterously turning the tables on her ; ' answer me that, Miss Juliet, and then I'll see what I can do for Georgie—not before, mind, not before ! ' And the argument is so unanswerable that Juliet is not able to continue the discussion.

And then, to everybody's relief, Lady Ellison's carriage is announced, and there is a general move ; everyone saying, as they wish good-night, what a pleasant evening they have spent, and no one honestly thinking so, except the Rollick girls, who have made great way with the two officers, and got them to promise to come over to lunch next Sunday.

The last of the carriages drives off, and as Mrs. Blair goes up to bed, Juliet lingers a moment in the hall, and presently Colonel Fleming comes out to her ; she lifts her eyes to his with a sort of dumb entreaty for mercy.

' Are you still angry with me ? ' she asks gently.

' Angry ! what can you be thinking of ? how could I be angry with you ? ' Something makes him more than half inclined to take her into his arms then and there, but he resists the temptation, and only says half playfully, half tenderly—' Go to bed, child, and don't take such silly ideas into your head ! '

And Juliet sprang upstairs with a blither step and with a lighter heart than she had had for some days.

(To be continued.)

DR. ROOKE'S ANTI-LANCET.

All who wish to preserve health, and thus prolong life, should read Dr. Rooke's "Anti-Lancet, or Handy Guide to Domestic Medicine," which can be had GRATIS from any Chemist, or POST FREE from Dr. Rooke, Scarborough.

Concerning this book, which contains 168 pages, the late eminent author, Sheridan Knowles, observed:—"It will be an incalculable ... to every person who can read and think."

CROSBY'S BALSAMIC COUGH ELIXIR

Is specially recommended by several eminent Physicians, and by Dr. ROOKE, Scarborough, Author of the "ANTI-LANCET."

It has been used with the most signal success for Asthma, Bronchitis, Consumption, Coughs, Influenza, Consumptive Night Sweats, Spitting of Blood, Shortness of Breath, and all Affections of the Throat and Chest.

Sold in bottles at 1s. 9d., 4s. 6d., and 11s. each, by all respectable Chemists, and Wholesale by JAMES M. CROSBY, Chemist, Scarborough.

☞ Invalids should read Crosby's Prize Treatise on "Diseases of the Lungs and Air-Vessels," a copy of which can be had GRATIS of all Chemists.

MAYFAIR SHERRY.
36 par doz
C. WARD & SON
CHAPEL St WEST MAYFAIR.
LONDON,
36 p. doz
MAYFAIR SHERRY

SWANBILL CORSETS.
(REGISTERED.)

FRENCH CORSET (14 bis B).—The Swanbill (Registered).—A full deep Corset, especially for ladies inclined to embonpoint. The Swanbill is most effective in reducing the figure and keeping the form flat, so as to enable ladies to wear the fashionable vêtements of the day; busk 13½ inches long. Price 14s. 6d. Finest quality, 21s.

FRENCH CORSET (20 bis B).—The Swanbill (Registered).—A shorter Corset than the former, with busk of similar shape, but intended for ladies who do not require so deep a Corset; busk 11 inches long. Price 14s. 6d.

Send Size of Waist with P.O. Order to prevent delay and inconvenience.

MRS. ADDLEY BOURNE,
LADIES' OUTFITTER, &c., 37 PICCADILLY,
OPPOSITE ST. JAMES' CHURCH.

(Bernard & Co.'s, Leith Distillery, Scotland.)
THE ENCORE WHISKY
(THE DOUBLE DISTILLED).
THE PUREST AND MOST WHOLESOME OF ALL WHISKIES.

Lancet—
'Very wholesome and pleasant Whisky.'

British Medical Journal—
'All injurious substances completely removed.'

Medical Times—
'Very wholesome and pleasant, and may be safely recommended.'

Medical Press—
'Very pure and wholesome.'

Sanitary Record—
'Deserves a wide-spread reputation.'

Public Health—
'Should be in general use.'

Food and Fuel Reformer—
'All who value their health should use it.'

Professor Tichborne—
'Perfectly free from all impurities.'

Dr. Bartlett—
'Purest Whisky I ever examined.'

Dr. Paul—
'Thoroughly wholesome.'

Dr. Stevenson Macadam—
'Very pure, and exceedingly fine quality.'

Please see that Bernard & Co.'s Labels are on all Bottles. Every Gallon guaranteed the same.

WHOLESALE DEPOT, THREE CROWN SQUARE, BOROUGH, S.E.

MAPLE & CO.

TOTTENHAM COURT

Illustrated Catalog

CARPETS—FURNITURE—BEDD

£5. 5s. SILK COSTUMES

Bodice Made. Silk Recommended for Wear.

Plates of Styles and Patterns of Silk Free on Application.

JAMES SPENCE & CO.,

76, 77, 78, & 79 ST. PAUL'S CHURCHYARD.

SIGNAL VICTORY AT YORKSHIRE

Awarded the only Medal. All Compet

TAYLOR

PATENT SEWING MAC

ARE THE

DRESSMAKING

bring simple to
work, quiet in
to get out of o
purchasers. If
Taylor's P
chines from
respectfully
for a prospe
97 CHEAPS

JOHN HEATH'S

POSTAL TELEGRAPH PEN.

OLD COUNTY HAND PEN

OBLIQUE NIB — TURNED UP NIB

WILL SUIT EVERY HAND

IN 6d. & 1/- BOXES AT ALL STATIONERS.

BY POST FOR 7 OR 13 STAMPS

BIRMINGHAM

Reckit

Pa

Possesses the follow-
ing advantages :—

1st.—Great Strength.
2nd.—Exceeding Beauty
of Tint.
3rd.—Great Economy in
use.
4th.—It cannot rot or
injure the linen.

Patronised by the Laundresses of the
and Duchess of
To be had of all respectable Grocers,

CADBURY

COC

ESS

The reason why so many are unable to take Cocoa is, that this variety commonly sold are mixed with Starch, under the plea of rendering them suitable ; while really making them thick, heavy, and indigestible. This may be easily detected, for if Cocoa thickens in the cup it proves the addition of starch. Cadbury's Cocoa Essence is genuine, it is therefore three times the strength of these Cocoas, and a refreshing Beverage like Tea or Coffee.

PURE. SOLUBLE. REFRESHING

Vol. XXX.

No. 118

PRICE ONE SHILLING.

BELGRAVIA

A LONDON MAGAZINE

AUGUST
1876

CHATTO & WINDUS, PICCADILLY, LONDON, W.

All rights reserved

Johnston's

'Quite free from Adulteration.'
—*Lancet.*

Corn Flour

'Is decidedly superior.'
—*Lancet.*

Is the Best.

THE GREAT PURIFIER AND RESTORER OF HEALTH.
BOWEN'S ANTISEPTIC TONIC-SALINE

Imparts to the system Nature's great purifier—OZONE, thereby cleansing the blood from all *effete* or poisonous matter, preventing fermentation in the stomach, and ensuring perfect digestion. It is the most efficacious remedy ever discovered for the cure of Indigestion, Bilious and Liver Complaints, Nervousness, Nervous and Bilious Headache, Skin Diseases, Eruptions, Scurvy, Scrofula, and Wasting Diseases; and it makes a pleasant and refreshing drink, which may be taken habitually with meals with the greatest advantage.

The TONIC-SALINE does NOT lower the system like some Natural Mineral Waters, Aerated Waters, Citrate of Magnesia, and Seidlitz Powders; but, on the contrary, it invigorates the Nerves and Muscular System, purifies and enriches the Blood, animates the Spirits and Mental Faculties, and ensures Good Health.

Emigrants and Travellers abroad should always keep a supply, as it is the only true preventative of, and cure for, Fevers, Dysentery, Cholera, Diarrhœa, and Sea Sickness.

CAUTION.—Although there are several preparations similar in appearance to mine, yet they are of an *entirely different composition.* This being the ONLY Saline medicine that does NOT lower the system, it will be found superior to any other for counteracting the depressing effects of hot weather.

Sold at 2s. per Bottle by all Chemists and Medicine Dealers, or sent to any address for 24 Stamps by the Sole Proprietor—
J. H. BOWEN, 91 WIGMORE ST., CAVENDISH SQUARE, LONDON, W.

TOURISTS AND TRAVELLERS.

Ladies visiting the seaside, rinking, driving, or otherwise exposed to the scorching rays of the sun or heated particles of dust, will find

ROWLANDS' KALYDOR

Most cooling and refreshing to the face, hands, and arms: it eradicates all Sunburn, Freckles, Tan, Stings of Insects, &c. 4s. 6d. & 8s. 6d. per bottle.

ROWLANDS' ODONTO

Whitens the Teeth and prevents and arrests their decay. 2s. 9d. per box.
ASK ANY CHEMIST, PERFUMER, OR HAIRDRESSER FOR ROWLANDS' ARTICLES.

KINAHAN'S LL WHISKY

KINAHAN & CO. find that, through the recommendation of the Medical Profession, the demand for their

CELEBRATED OLD LL WHISKY

for purely medicinal purposes is very great. They think therefore it will be satisfactory the Public to read the following EXTRACTS OF THE ANALYSIS of the LL W from the eminent Analyst, DR. ARTHUR HILL HASSALL:—"I have very carefully an fully analysed Samples of this well-known and popular Whisky. The sam and mellow to the taste, aromatic and ethereal to the smell.—The Whisky nounced to be pure, well-matured, and of very excellent quality. The Medi may feel full confidence in the purity and quality of this Whisky."

20 GREAT TITCHFIELD STREET, OXFORD STREET, LONDON.

'HE TOOK THE BODY AND DROPPED IT INTO THE WATER.'

BELGRAVIA.

AUGUST 1876.

GOOD STORIES OF MAN AND OTHER ANIMALS.

BY CHARLES READE.

3. Suspended Animation.

A JOURNAL called the 'Los Angelos Star' recorded the following incident at the time it occurred :

A gentleman in that city had a very large and beautiful tom cat, which he had reared from a kitten. It was now five years old, and the two animals were mutually attached. Every morning, when the servant brought in the water for his master's tub, Puss used to come in and sit at the side of the bed, and gaze with admiration at his employer, and sometimes mew him out; but retired into a corner during the tubbing, which he thought irrational, and came out again when the biped was clothed and in his right mind.

One day the cat was seen in the garden tumbling over and over in strong convulsions, which ended in its crawling feebly into the house. The master heard, and was very sorry, and searched for the invalid, but could not find him. However, when he went up to bed at night, there was the poor creature stretched upon the floor at the side of the bed, the very place where he used to sit and gaze at his master, and mew him out of bed.

The gentleman was affected to tears by the affectionate creature's death, and his coming there to die. He threw a handkerchief over poor tom, and passed a downright unhappy night. He determined, however, to bury his humble friend ; and no time was to be lost, the weather being hot. So, when his servant came in to fill his tub, he ordered a little grave to be dug directly, and a box to be found of a suitable size to receive the remains.

Then he got up ; and, instead of tubbing, as usual, he thought

he would wash poor tom's body for interment, for it was all stained
and dirty with the mould of the garden.

He took the body up, and dropped it into the water with a
souse.

That souse was soon followed by a furious splashing, that sent
the water flying in his face and all about the room, and away flew
the cat through the open window, as if possessed by a devil.   Nor
did the poor body forgive this hydropathic treatment, although
successful.   He took a perverse view, and had never returned to
the house 'up to the time of our going to press,' says the 'Los
Angelos Star.'

The cat is not the only animal subject to suspension of vital
power.   Many men and women have been buried alive in this
condition, especially on the Continent, where the law enforces
speedy interment.   Even in Britain—where they do not shovel one
into the earth quite so fast—live persons have been buried, and
others have had a narrow escape.   I could give a volume of
instances at home and abroad.   One of them an Archbishop, who
was actually being carried in funeral procession on an open bier,
when he came to, and objected—in what terms I know not ; but
the Scotch have an excellent formula in similar cases.   It runs
thus : 'Bide ye yet, mon ; I hae a deal mair mischief to do
firrrst !'

Two recent English cases I could certify to be true : one, a little
girl at Nuneaton, who lay several days without signs of life ;
another, a young lady, not known to the public, but to me.   She
was dead, in medicine ; but her mother refused to let her be buried,
because there was no sign of decomposition, and she did not get
so deadly cold as others had whom that mother had lost by death.

This girl remained unburied some days, till another of God's
creatures put in his word ; a fly thought her worth biting, and
blood trickled from the bite.   That turned the scale of opinion,
and the girl was recovered, and is alive to this day.   However, the
curious reader, who desires to work this vein, need go no farther
than the index of the 'Annual Register' and the 'Gentleman's
Magazine.' As for me, I must not be tempted outside my immediate
subject.   The parallel I shall confine a very large theme to is
exact.

At the opening of the century the public facilities for anatomy
were less than now.   So then robbing the churchyards was quite
a trade ; and an egotist or two did worse ; they killed people for
the small sum a dead body fetched.

Well, a male body was brought to a certain surgeon by a man he had often employed, and the pair lumped it down on the dissecting table, and then the vendor received his money and went.

The anatomist set to work to open the body; but, in handling it, he fancied the limbs were not so rigid as usual, and he took another look. Yes, the man was dead: no pulsation either. And yet somehow he was not quite cold about the region of the heart.

The surgeon doubted; he was a humane man, and so, instead of making a fine transverse cut, like that, at which the unfortunate author of 'Manon Lescaut' started out of his trance with a shriek, to die in right earnest, he gave the poor body a chance; applied hartshorn, vinegar, and friction, all without success. Still he had his doubts; though, to be frank, I am not clear why he still doubted.

Be that as it may, he called in his assistant and they took the body into the yard, turned a high tap on, and discharged a small but hard-hitting column of water on to the patient.

No effect was produced but this—which an unscientific eye might have passed over—the skin turned slightly pink in one or two places, under the fall of water.

The surgeon thought this a strong proof life was not extinct; but, not to overdo it, he wrapped the man in blankets for a time, and then drenched him again, letting the water strike him hard on the head and the heart in particular.

He followed this treatment up, till at last the man's eyes winked, and then he gasped, and presently he gulped, and by-and-by he groaned, and eventually uttered loud and fearful cries, as one battling with death.

In a word, he came to, and the surgeon put him into a warm bed, and, as Medicine has its fashions, and bleeding was the panacea of that day, he actually took blood from the poor body. This ought to have sent him back to the place from whence he came—the grave, to wit; but somehow it did not: and next day the reviver showed him with pride to several visitors; and prepared an article.

Resurrectus was well fed, and, being a pauper, was agreeable to lie in that bed for ever, and eat the bread of science. But, as years rolled on, his preserver got tired of that. However, he had to give him a suit of his own clothes to get rid of him. Did I say years? I must have meant days.

He never did get rid of him; the fellow used to call at intervals, and demand charity, urging that the surgeon had taken him out of a condition in which he felt neither hunger, thirst, nor misery; and so was now bound to supply his natural needs.

However, I will not dwell on this painful part of the picture, lest learned and foreseeing men should, from the date of reading this article, confine resuscitation to quadrupeds.

To conclude with the medical view.   To resuscitate animals who seem dead, but are secretly alive, drop them into water from— or else drop water on them from—A SUFFICIENT HEIGHT.

The New Republic;

OR, CULTURE, FAITH, AND PHILOSOPHY IN AN ENGLISH COUNTRY HOUSE.

BOOK II. (*continued*).—CHAPTER II.

THE blinds were half-down in the dining-room, to keep out the brilliant summer sun, and the luncheon table shone whitely in the soft gloom, looking very cool and refreshing with its green ferns and flowers and its day-lit glimmer of glass and silver. The guests dropped in by ones and twos. Dr. Jenkinson alone was absent. He had been up late last night, writing his sermon, or, to speak more truly, doctoring up an old one; he had, too, been at more than usual pains in the delivery of it; and what with these two labours, and the gas-light, and the draughts upon the stage, he was now suffering from a head-ache which inclined him to keep his room. This was soon generally known, and an unlooked-for prospect of freely discussing the sermon at luncheon dawned accordingly upon nearly every one.

Mr. Stockton and Miss Merton were amongst the first in the dining-room. Both had gone up to one of the open windows, and slightly raising the blind, were looking out at the lovely view before them—the sea, the marble terrace, and the green shrubs; and were listening to the clear singing of a bird. Mr. Stockton had been much struck with the strictly prosaic style of Dr. Jenkinson's discourse, and he had been secretly contrasting this with the more impassioned character of his own mind. The contrast was now specially brought home to him by his own deeply-moved feelings as he thus looked out upon Nature; and, as he exclaimed ' Beautiful!—beautiful!' several times in a half-whisper, he trusted that the expression which he put into the word conveyed some notion to Miss Merton of all that was going on within him. Presently Lady Ambrose entered, saying in a severe voice to some one who was behind her, ' No; I certainly don't think that Dr. Jenkinson has much poetry.' Mr. Stockton was only half-conscious that he heard these words; still, he did hear them; and in some occult way they wrought in his active mind, for he put his hands into the pockets of his coat-tails, he slightly raised his head, and exclaimed suddenly in his singularly melodious voice, still looking out of the window—

> Sweet bird, whose warble, wild and sweet,
> Rings Eden through the budded quicks,
> Oh, tell us where the senses mix !
> Oh, tell us where the passions meet !

He looked round for some response from Miss Merton ; but she was gone. He only—what somewhat disconcerted him—heard Mrs. Sinclair, who had just entered, saying to the man nearest her, ' I always thought what a very odd question that was to ask a bird—a bird, of all creatures.'

The man nearest her happening to be Mr. Storks, she met with no response.

Mr. Stockton moved towards the table.

' No,' he said, looking towards Lady Ambrose as he seated himself ; ' I'm afraid our friend's *forte* is certainly not poetry.'

' Surely,' said Donald Gordon with extreme solemnity of manner and only a slight twinkle in his eye, ' his *forte* is something far better. Poetry can only make us happy for a little while. Such doctrines as we have heard this morning ought to make us happy always.'

Lady Ambrose herself was in doubt what, altogether, to think of the matter. More than half her heart inclined her to look upon Dr. Jenkinson as a valuable ally ; but there was yet, all the while, a fatal something that whispered to her a vague distrust of him. She was therefore waiting anxiously to hear what would be said by others, before taking any side herself ; her mind all the while being busy with the profoundest questions. This suspense of judgment produced a certain gravity and depression in her, which was visible on her face, and which seemed to communicate itself to nearly every one at her end of the table. For Lady Ambrose was a communicative woman. Her spirits, good or bad, were generally caught by those near her. Mr. Herbert's spirits, however, seemed to need no one else to depress them. Low, slow, and melancholy, his accents at once caught the ear of Lady Ambrose.

' I have heard to-day,' he said to Mrs. Sinclair, who was sitting next him, ' an entirely new and in every way memorable doctrine, which I never heard before from the mouth of man, woman, or child ; nor can I tell by what steps any human being could have arrived at it. I have heard that the world—the world as it is— could not be better than it is ; that there is no real sorrow in it— no real evil—no real sin.'

' Poor Dr. Jenkinson ! ' said Mrs. Sinclair, also in a melancholy voice ; ' I suppose he has never loved.'

' I'm sure you ought not to say so,' said Leslie, ' considering the attentions he paid you last night.'

' Ah ! ' said Mrs. Sinclair, with a peculiar shadowy smile flickering over her face, ' that was only gallantry, Mr. Leslie. I'm sure that was not real love.'

Lady Ambrose was very indignant with Leslie for having given the conversation this turn. She was anxiously waiting to hear what Mr. Herbert would say more. But Mr. Herbert relapsed into silence. Mr. Stockton's voice, however, became at this moment audible ; and Lady Ambrose turned all her attention to him.

' The whole teachings of that school,' he was saying—his voice also was melancholy—' have always seemed to me nothing more than a few fragments of science imperfectly understood, obscured by a few fragments of Christianity imperfectly remembered.'

Lady Ambrose still remained in doubt.

' You forget,' said Leslie, ' that Dr. Jenkinson's Christianity is really a new firm trading under an old name, and trying to purchase the goodwill of the former establishment.'

Lady Ambrose's faith in the doctor began to strengthen. She felt sure at that moment that whatever Leslie spoke lightly of would be something of which she would approve. Again, however, Mr. Herbert's accents arrested her.

' It is simply,' he was saying to Mrs. Sinclair, evidently alluding to the same subject—' it is simply our modern atheism, trying to hide its own nakedness, for the benefit of the more prudish part of the public, in the cast grave-clothes of a Christ who, whether He be risen or no, is very certainly, as the angel said, not here.'

Lady Ambrose was again in doubt.

' All discussion of such subjects seems to me but a diseased activity,' said Mr. Rose, raising languidly a white, deprecating hand.

Lady Ambrose was bewildered.

' In his main point,' said Mr. Storks with severe dogmatism, ' putting aside his quasi-religious manner of expressing it—which, considering his position, may be pardoned—I conceive Dr. Jenkinson to have been entirely right.'

The mind of Lady Ambrose at once cleared. This fatal commendation of Mr. Storks confirmed her worst suspicions. The gloom on her face deepened, and she had a look almost of distress about her as she turned to Laurence.

' You look tired,' he said to her.

' No,' said Lady Ambrose, wearily : ' at least, perhaps I am a little. Do you know, I always think one feels rather dull if one doesn't get the letters one expects.'

' Perhaps you don't know,' said Laurence, ' that the letters you got this morning were only those of last night's post. Our Sunday letters we are obliged to send for, and they don't generally come till later on in the day.'

' Really!' exclaimed Lady Ambrose, with surprise. A smile slowly spread over her face; her frank eyes lit up again. ' The Duchess couldn't have forgotten it,' she said to herself half-consciously. Strangely enough, a new warmth, it seemed, had dawned upon her, and her ice-bound gloom began to thaw—to thaw only, however, not to evaporate. It did not go; it only became voluble.

' Do you know, Mr. Laurence,' she said, ' I have been thinking over and over again about many of the things that were said last night; and I really am afraid that the world is getting very bad. It is very sad to think so; but, with all this infidelity and wicked-ness of which we hear so much, I'm afraid it is true. For my own part, you know, there is nothing I dislike so much as to hear the Bible profanely spoken about; though, of course, I know one is tempted sometimes to make jokes out of it oneself. And then,' Lady Ambrose added—her ideas did not always follow one another in the strictest order—' hardly a week passes without some new scandal. I had a letter only this morning, telling me all the particulars about Colonel Eardly and poor Lady Arthur. And that man, you know—just fancy it!—it will not be very long before we shall be obliged to receive him again. However,' said Lady Ambrose, with a slightly more cheerful accent, ' that sort of thing, I believe, is confined to *us*. The middle classes are all right—at least, one always hears so.'

At this moment Lord Allen's voice was heard.

' But now,' Lady Ambrose went on to Laurence, very slightly moving her head in the direction of Lord Allen, and speaking in a low tone, ' how different *he* is!'

Lady Ambrose had the greatest admiration for Lord Allen, though her acquaintance with him had hitherto been of the slight-est; and Laurence, not knowing how to respond to all her late re-marks, was glad that her attention was thus called elsewhere.

' Don't you think,' Allen was saying, half addressing himself to Mr. Herbert, half to Mr. Luke, ' that, though things as they are in our days may be worse than they have ever been before, there are yet in the minds of our generation ideas of things as they might be, that are in advance of what has ever been before? I know quite well that society now is without any definite structure; and that it is the hardest thing in the world for one member of the body politic to perform its functions with regard to the others. I feel this every moment. I feel, too, how utterly without a religion we are ' (Lady Ambrose started)—' at least, a religion that one man can express to another, and that can enable men to act in concert. But, in spite of all this, it seems to me that a higher class of conceptions, both of religion and morals, is forming itself in the minds of thinking men—a purer, more unselfish morality, a more liberal social system.'

'Perfectly true, Lord Allen,' said Mr. Luke, 'perfectly true! It is indeed the very essence of the cultured classes to be beyond their time—to have, indeed, every requisite for making everything better, except the practical power. As you say, what man's life ought to be—what true morality is—what is true sense, and what is true nonsense—these are matters never at any time distinguished so truly as by some of us in the latter half of the nineteenth century. Only, unfortunately,' said Mr. Luke, sighing slowly, and looking round the table, 'the dense ignorance of the world at large hampers and hinders such men as these, so that all that their teaching and their insight can do, is only to suggest a Utopia in the future, instead of leading to any reality in the present.'

'All my happiness is in a kind of Utopia,' said Mrs. Sinclair, dreamily.

'Yes—yes,' said Mr. Luke, wearily; 'so in these days must be the happiness of all of us—except that of the world at large.'

Mr. Storks was here heard clearing his throat. With an ominous pugilistic smile he turned towards Mr. Luke.

'Are you quite sure,' he said, 'that the reason why your friends do nothing practical is not because they will build Utopias? I, as I have already said, entirely hold with Dr. Jenkinson that the world is as good as it can be—has, indeed, been always as good as it could have been—has, that is, been always persistently progressing by one constant course of evolution. I don't myself profess to be a student of history; but, as far as I at all understand its teachings, the one thing it most clearly shows to us is, that what strikes a superficial observer as simply the decadence of old orders of things, is really, under the surface, the birth of the new. Indeed,' said Mr. Storks, shrugging his shoulders, ' of course it must be so. We are all part of Nature ; and, little as we think it, we are all working together by invincible and inviolable laws. Nature will have her own way; and those who have studied her carefully know that her way is always the best. Even supposing we could transplant ourselves into some different, some more advanced, state of society —pooh!—do you think we should be any happier there? As

much happier, I suppose, as you or I should be if we were translated into the heaven our nurses used to tell us of, where nothing
was done but to sing Tate and Brady's psalms with the angels to
all eternity. The air of our own age is the only air fit for us.
In any other we should languish.'

'I languish in this,' said Mr. Luke, looking up to the
ceiling.

Scarcely were the words out of his mouth than Mr. Saunders
exclaimed, in his most excited and shrillest voice, ' I deny it—I
entirely deny it ! '

Mr. Luke was thunderstruck. Even Mr. Storks was taken
aback by the audacity of the contradiction ; and as for the rest of
the company, they could not conceive where on earth Mr. Saunders
had left his manners. Mr. Storks, however, was still more astonished, and still less pleased, when he discovered, as Mr. Saunders
proceeded, what was the real meaning of his speech.

'I entirely deny,' Mr. Saunders went on, ' that the ways of
Nature are the best ways. I maintain, on the contrary, that
Nature is the most odious of things—that the whole universe is
constructed on the most hateful principles ; in fact, that out of
the primordial atoms only one good thing has developed itself,
and that is the one thing that is usually opposed to Nature—the
reason of man.'

Mr. Storks turned sharply round, and stared at Mr. Saunders,
with an indescribable expression that at once reduced the young
man to silence ; and then said to him, in a voice of grim unconcern,
' May I trouble you for the mustard ? ' The unexpectedness of
this utterance completed the discomfiture of Mr. Saunders. Mr.
Storks took some mustard, and then again addressed himself to
Mr. Luke.

' You see,' he said, 'what I take to be civilisation is the gradual
self-adaptation of the human organism to its environment—an
adaptation which must take place, and any attempts to hinder
which are simply neither more nor less than disease. Progress is
a thing that will continue despite the opposition of individuals.
Its tendencies are beyond the control of individuals, and are to be
sought in the spirit of the age at large,—not—if you will forgive
me the word—in the crotchets of this or that thinker. And it
seems to me to be the hopeful and distinguishing feature of the
present day, that men are learning generally to recognise this
truth—that they are learning not to cry out against progress, but
to investigate its grand and inevitable laws, and submit themselves willingly to them. And the tendency of our own day is, I
am proud to say, a tendency towards firm, solid, verifiable knowledge,

and, as a result of this, towards the acquisition of a firm and solid happiness also.'

'To me,' said Mr. Herbert, 'it seems rather that the only hope for the present age lies in the possibility of some individual wiser than the rest getting the necessary power, and in the most arbitrary way possible putting a stop to this progress—utterly stamping out and obliterating every general tendency peculiar to our own time. Mr. Storks will perhaps think me very foolish. Perhaps I am. I freely own that I could more easily tell a good action if I saw it, than a good piece of protoplasm, and that I think the discovery of a holy moral law, by which an individual may live, of infinitely more importance than the discovery of all the laws of progress in the world. But let Mr. Storks despise me, and not be angry with me——'

'My dear sir,' interposed Mr. Storks, with a gruff courtesy, 'why should I do either the one or the other?'

'Because,' said Mr. Herbert, slightly waving his hand, and speaking with great emphasis, 'had I only the power, I would myself put a forcible stop to all this evolution. I would make a clean sweep of all the improvements that the present day so much vaunts. I would collect an army of strong, serviceable, honest workmen, and send them to blow up Manchester, and Birmingham, and Liverpool, and Leeds, and Wolverhampton——'

'And all the artisans in them?' asked Mr. Storks.

'Well,' said Mr. Herbert, smiling, 'I would, perhaps, give the artisans notice of this gunpowder plot of mine. And yet their existence has always presented a painful difficulty to me. For if there is no other life, I think they have a very bad time of it here; and if there is another life, I think that they will certainly be damned. But it is not only Manchester and Birmingham that I would blow up. I would blow up also every anatomical museum in the land, save such as were absolutely necessary for the use of professional doctors. I would destroy every railway, and nearly every steam-engine; and I would do a number of other things of a like sort, by way of preparing the ground for a better state of society. Indeed, so far am I from believing that an entirely different and better state of society is unthinkable, that I believe it to be not impracticable; and I am at the present moment collecting money, from such as will here and there confide in me, for the purpose of purchasing land, and of founding a community upon what seem to me to be true and healthful principles—a Utopia, in fact—a state in which I trust may be realised once again upon the earth those two things to which we are now such strangers—order and justice.'

'I once began a book about justice,' said Laurence, ' on the model of Plato's Republic.'

'What is Plato's Republic ? ' said Lady Ambrose. 'Tell me.'

'It is a book,' said Laurence, 'which describes the meeting of a party of friends, who fell discussing high topics just as we are doing, and, amongst others, What is justice ? '

'What ! ' exclaimed Lady Ambrose. 'Did not they know that ?'

' You forget,' said Laurence, 'that this was very long ago.'

'To be sure,' said Lady Ambrose ; 'and they were of course all heathens. Well—and what conclusions did they come to as to the nature of justice ? '

' At first,' said Laurence, 'though Socrates himself was amongst them, they were all completely at a loss how to define it. But at last they hit upon the notion of constructing an ideal perfect state, in which of course justice would be lurking somewhere. Now there are in life, Plato says, four great virtues—wisdom, courage, temperance, and justice ; and no sooner has the ideal state been constructed, than it appears that three of these virtues are specially illustrated and embodied, each in a particular class of citizens. Thus, wisdom is speedily embodied in the theoretical politicians and religious speculators of the day ; courage is embodied in the practical men who maintain and execute the regulations and orders of the philosophers ; and temperance is embodied in the commercial and industrial classes, who loyally submit themselves to their betters, and refrain from meddling in matters that are too high for them. And now, where is justice ? In what class is that embodied specially ?'

' In the judges and the magistrates and the policemen,' said Lady Ambrose.

'No,' said Laurence ; ' it is peculiar to no class. It resides in all. It is that virtue which enables the others to exist and to continue.'

' But surely,' said Lady Ambrose, ' all that is not what we mean by justice now?'

' Certainly not,' said Laurence ; ' and my book was designed to investigate what justice is, as it exists now. I, like Plato, constructed a state, making it, however, a real rather than an ideal picture. But when I had done this, I could find no earnest thinking class to represent wisdom ; no class of practical politicians that would carry out even the little wisdom they knew, and so represent courage ; and certainly no commercial or industrial class that would refrain for a single day from meddling in matters that were too high for them, and so represent temperance. So I analysed life in a somewhat different way. I divided it into happiness, misery, and justice. I then at once discovered that the rich represented all the happiness of which we are now capable, and the poor all the misery; and that justice was that which set this state of things going and enabled it to continue.'

'Ah, Laurence!' exclaimed Mr. Herbert, clapping his hands gently in sad soft applause, 'I like that. I wish you had worked out this idea more fully.'

'Suppose,' exclaimed Leslie, suddenly, 'that we try this afternoon to construct a Utopia ourselves. Let us try and embody our notions of life as it ought to be in a new Republic.'

'Well,' said Lady Ambrose, 'I am not a Conservative; I don't object. I'm sure at any rate that there is much we could all of us alter, if we only had our own way.'

'Much,' said Lady Grace, with severe briskness.

'Much,' said Miss Merton, with a soft, half serious smile.

'Much,' said Lord Allen, catching eagerly at the idea.

'Well, then,' said Laurence, 'let us all do our best to give those airy somethings, our aspirations, a local habitation and a name.'

The majority of the company took very kindly to the proposal. Lady Grace was especially pleased, as it seemed to provide at once a whole afternoon's occupation for the party; and it was arranged accordingly that after luncheon they should adjourn for castle-building to a shady spot in the garden.

CHAPTER III.

LAURENCE'S gardens, which had been laid out and planted with great care by his uncle, were in what had been designed to be a highly classical style. There was formal made ground in many places—broad flights of steps flanked by gods and goddesses, long straight terraces set with vases and Irish yews. Busts of orators, poets, and philosophers, with Latin inscriptions, glimmered in groves of laurel; and scaly Tritons, dappled with green lichens, spouted up twinkling water in the middle of gleaming basins. But Nature here had been too strong for art. The uneven character of the ground had conquered all efforts at any general formality. Walk led into walk without any order; the artificial ground gradually died away into natural undulations; everywhere the eye lost itself in a confusion of luxuriant foliage; the velvet of the green turf was entirely English; the smell of English flowers was in the air. The whole place seemed, indeed, a wilderness of Romance, into which the classical element had quite melted—as it does in Goethe's Helena—and the steps, terraces, statues, and Latin inscriptions, impressed the mind only as a soft sigh for the past, that could not even conjure back a shadow of its reality.

The gardens to-day were looking at their loveliest. There was an unusual freshness in the warm summer air. Beyond the green shrubs the sea shone bright and blue; and through the shrubs the sea-breeze moved and whispered.

Guided by Lady Grace, the guests gradually converged after luncheon towards the appointed spot, straggling thither by various ways, and in desultory groups. Laurence strolled slowly on behind with Miss Merton, choosing a path which none of the others had taken.

'How delicious this is!' said Miss Merton, lifting her hat to enjoy the breeze upon her forehead. 'Nobody could be in bad spirits in a place like this. There is something so fresh and living everywhere, and even when we lose sight of the sea we still hear it.'

'Yes,' said Laurence. 'I believe these gardens are like Keats's island. There is no recess in them

Not haunted by the murmurous sound of waves.'

'And how exquisitely everything is kept!' said Miss Merton, as they turned up a narrow winding walk, thickly set on either side with carefully-trimmed laurels.

Everything was, indeed, as Miss Merton said, kept with the most perfect care. Not a weed was on the grey gravel; not a single laurel twig called for pruning. Every vase they passed was full of the most delicious flowers; birds sang overhead in the branches of limes and of acacia-trees. Everything seemed to be free from care, and to be laughing, light of heart, in the bright weather.

'I am taking you this way,' said Laurence, 'because I want to show you what I think may interest you.'

As he spoke these words, a sudden bend in the walk brought them face to face with something that gave Miss Merton a sudden sensation of surprise. It was a small classical portico built in a style of the most severe simplicity, through which by an iron gate one passed into an open space beyond. What surprised Miss Merton on seeing this was the singular sense of desolation and dreariness that seemed all at once to come over her. The iron gates before her were a mass of rust; the portico, which had once been white, was weather-stained into a dismal grey; the stone, too, it was built of, was scaling off in almost every place, and the fragments lay unheeded as they had fallen upon the ground.

Here, amongst everything that spoke of the utmost care, was one object that spoke of entire forgetfulness and neglect. They approached in silence, and Miss Merton looked in through the bars of the rusty gate. The scene that met her eyes was one of greater desolation still. It was a circular plot of ground, fenced round by a low stone wall that was surmounted by spiked railings. It looked as though it might have been once a flower garden, but it was now a wilderness. Outside its boundary rose the rare and beautiful trees of the happy-tended shrubberies. Inside were nettles, brambles, and long weedy grass. Nothing else was visible in this desolate enclosure but three cypresses, apparently of various ages, the two smaller planted near together, the third, and by far the largest, standing apart by itself.

Miss Merton was quite at a loss what to make of this strange spot; and, as Laurence was feeling in his pocket for the key, she asked him if it had anything to do with breeding pheasants.

' Do you see what is written above the gate ? ' said Laurence.

Miss Merton looked, and detected a dim inscription, whose letters still retained a glimmer of fading gold.

' Can you read it ? ' said Laurence.

> ' Neque harum, quas colis, arborum
> Te, præter invisam cupressum,
> Ulla brevem dominum sequetur.

" Of all these trees which you love so, the hated cypress only shall follow its master, and be faithful to him in his narrow house." But come—let us go inside, if you are not afraid of the long grass.'

They passed through the gate, which gave a low wail upon its hinges, and Miss Merton followed Laurence, knee-deep in grass and nettles, to the smallest of the three cypress-trees. There Laurence paused. At the foot of the tree Miss Merton saw a flat slab of marble, with something written upon it; and for the first time she felt certain that she must be in a place of graves.

' This,' said Laurence, pointing to the little cypress, ' was planted only five years ago, ten days before the poor old man died who now sleeps under it. That is the inscription he himself chose, and he had that very stone slab brought to his bedside to look at during his last illness. This is my uncle's grave.

> Omnis moriar, nullaque pars mei
> Vitabit Libitinam.

" I shall wholly die, and there is no part of me that will escape the Venus of death." That, and that alone, he chose to have written over him.'

Laurence spoke with much feeling, and for a moment covered

his eyes with his hands. Miss Merton was so much surprised that she hardly knew what response to make.

'But does nobody take any care of this place?' at last she said.

'No,' said Laurence. 'By his own last orders, nobody. But come—you must look at this too.' And he motioned her towards the neighbouring cypress.

At the foot of this, almost hidden by the long grass, Miss Merton saw something that surprised her still more strangely. It was the statue of a woman half reclining in a languid attitude on a block of hewn marble. The figure was full and beautiful, and the features of the face were singularly fine; but there was something in the general effect that struck one at the first moment as not pleasing. What slight drapery there was, was disposed meretriciously over the rounded limbs; on the arms were heavy bracelets; one of the hands held a half-inverted wine-cup, and the other was laid negligently on a heap of coins. But what jarred most upon the feelings was the face, with its perfect features. For a cold sneer was fixed upon the full mouth and the fine nostrils; and the eyes, with a leer of petulant sensuality, seemed to be fixed for ever upon the flat neighbouring gravestone.

'This cypress,' said Laurence, 'is much older than the other. It was planted twenty years ago; and twenty years ago the original of that statue was laid beneath it. She was one of the many nameless ladies who from time to time shared his fortunes at the house here. She was, too, by far the loveliest. But she was at the same time the hardest, the coarsest, the most mercenary of all her race. He knew it too—knew it thoroughly. He read her through and through, with a keen, cynical humour. And yet all the same she intoxicated him—she distracted him. He squandered so much money upon her that she had made a large fortune out of him, when suddenly she caught a chill and died. She died here, and here she was buried; and all his feelings about her—many of his feelings, too, about himself—you may read in this statue. It was all done exactly as he directed. The attitude, the drapery, the wine-cup held in one hand, and the money in the other, are there by his express direction; and by his direction, too, that face, with its lovely features, leers and sneers at him for ever, as he rests in his neglected grave. See, too, there is the epitaph which he chose for her—

> Lusisti satis, edisti satis, atque bibisti;
> Tempus abire tibi est.

" You have wantoned enough with me—you have eaten enough of

my substance—you have drunk enough of my champagne : 'tis now high time for you to go."'

'What strange inscriptions!' said Miss Merton, absently, half bewildered by the whole scene.

'Let us come now to the third tree,' said Laurence, 'and you shall see what is overshadowed by it.'

They passed across the enclosure to the largest of the three cypresses, and at the foot of that Miss Merton discovered a third grave-stone, also with a poetical inscription. 'You can read that,' said Laurence, ' without help of mine.'

Miss Merton looked, and read the following lines, which were not new to her :

> A slumber did my spirit seal,
> I knew no mortal fears.
> She seemed a thing that could not feel
> The touch of earthly years.
>
> She knows no motion now, nor force,
> She neither feels nor sees,
> Rolled round in earth's diurnal course
> With rocks, and stones, and trees.

'Here,' said Laurence, ' is the oldest grave of all. Its date is that of the tree that stands beside it, and that was planted forty years ago. Under that stone lies the only woman—except myself, almost the only thing—that the old man ever really loved. This was in his young days. He was only thirty when she died ; and her death was the great turning-point of his life. She lived with him for two years, in a little cottage that stood on the very spot where he afterwards built the villa. She has no name, you see, on the grave-stone, and I had best not give her any. She was some one's wife, but not his. This is her story. I have her miniature somewhere, which one day I should like to show you. It is a lovely dark face, with liquid, spiritual eyes, and under it are written two lines of Byron, which might have been composed for her :

> She walks in beauty like the night
> Of cloudless climes and starry skies.

Well, there she lies now ; and the old man's youth lies buried with her. It was her death that made him a philosopher. He built this great place here, and laid out these gardens half to kill his grief for her, and half to keep alive her memory ; and here, as you see, he buried her. She gave up all that was best in her for the love of him. He gave up all that was best in him for the loss of her.'

'And is this place left quite uncared for?' said Miss Merton, looking around her.

'It is left,' said Laurence, 'as he ordered it should be. All

through him ran a vein of curious scoffing, of which he was himself
the object : and one of his special orders was that, when he was
dead and buried, no further care of any kind should be spent upon
this spot. The grass and weeds were to be left to grow wild in it,
the rails to rust, the portico to decay and crumble. " Do you
think," he said to me, " that I know so little of life as to flatter
myself that any single creature will regret me when I am gone, or
even waste a thought upon me ? I do not choose, as Christians do,
to rest for ever under a lie ; for their tombs are lying monuments
that they are remembered ; mine shall be a true one that I am
forgotten. Yes," he said, " it makes me laugh to think of myself
—me, who have built this house and planted these gardens which
others will enjoy—rotting in the midst of it all, under thorns and
brambles, in a little dismal wilderness. And then, perhaps,
Otho," he would say to me, " some of your friends who will walk
about these gardens in a year or two—Christians, no doubt, with
the Devil knows what of fine sentiments about faith and immor-
tality—will look in through the bars of the gate, and be shocked at
that honest wilderness, that unconcealed neglect, which is the only
real portion of those that have been." But during his last illness he
softened just a little, and admitted that I, he did believe, cared for
him, and might, when he was dead, every now and then think of
him. " And so," he said, " if you care to do it, come every now and
then, and scrape the moss from my inscription, and from the two
others. But that is all I will have you do—that, and nothing
more. This little will express all that it is possible that you
should feel for me." I promised him to do no more than that, and
that I do.'

Laurence was a man who was at times readily moved, and his
voice was now tremulous and low with feeling.

' Poor old man ! ' he went on, as they passed out of the gates,
and were again in the bright, trim garden ; ' he thought he was a
calm, hard philosopher—a Roman of the Empire—a master artist
in life, who knew each most delicate shade of beauty and of pleasure, and who could lay any phantom of sorrow with a sneer or an
epigram. To himself, I believe, he appeared as the union of three
characters, Petronius, Seneca, and Voltaire. He fancied that he
belonged to times before his own ; but he belonged in reality to
times after them. If he was Roman at all, as he always fancied
himself, he was Roman only in that sombre ennui that through all
his later years oppressed him—an ennui that always kept him
seeking for enjoyments, and that turned the enjoyments into ashes
as soon as he possessed them. He was what I suppose would be
called a man of pleasure ; but he was at heart what such men

always must be if possessed of any power of mind—a man of sorrows. Perhaps I am rather morbid in the way in which I think of him; but he always seems to me as a type of what the world is very soon coming to. He was without hope, without principle. He had an exquisite appreciation of every kind of pleasure, from the highest to the lowest; but his higher pleasures only made him despise the lower ones; and the lower ones he only sought for that he might drown the higher. Look! do you see that white stone pavilion there with the glass doors? He would sit there for days, looking out at the sea or at his flowers, or drawing, reading, or writing. The place is just as he left it, and inside are all his favourite books and papers. However, here we are close to the others. I am afraid we are rather late. Don't you hear them all talking?'

A turn of the path, as Laurence spoke, brought them upon the spot where nearly the whole party were already assembled, disposed in an easy group upon the grass. The place was an amphitheatre of velvet turf, set round with laurels and all kinds of shrubs; in the arena of which—if one may so speak—a little fountain splashed cool and restless in a porphyry basin. Overhead the blue summer sky was screened by the whispering shade of tall trees; and above the dark laurel leaves the fresh sea was seen in the distance, an azure haze full of sparklings. The whole scene, as Laurence and Miss Merton came upon it, was curiously picturesque. The various dresses made against the green turf a soft medley of colours. The ladies were in white and black and pale yellow, green and crimson and dove-colour. All the men, except Mr. Luke, were in shooting coats; and Mr. Saunders, who wore knickerbockers, had even pink stockings. And here, as the lights and shades flickered over them, and the gentle air breathed upon them, they seemed altogether like a party from which an imaginative onlooker might have expected a new Decameron.

There is one thing more to be noticed. A small gravel path ran round the top of the amphitheatre; and on this stood three figures, not mixing with the group below them. Two of these, who stood together, were Mr. Herbert and Mr. Rokeby. The third, who stood quite apart, with his hands in his pockets, and a grim smile on his face, was Mr. Storks. Miss Merton immediately joined the group, whilst Laurence addressed himself to the three gentlemen who seemed so little inclined to identify themselves with the general movement. As he was doing this, two more absentees made their appearance—Donald Gordon, with Dr. Jenkinson leaning on his arm.

The Doctor paused and surveyed the group. He smiled hesitatingly for a moment, and at length sat himself down by the side of

Mrs. Sinclair. She was certainly looking very bewitching in a grey Gainsborough hat, and was at that moment casting down her long eyelashes, whilst engaged with the sixth button of her glove.

'So here,' said Donald Gordon to the Doctor, 'they are to construct their ideal state out of the materials of the real.'

'Well,' said the Doctor, who was just preparing something pleasant to say to Mrs. Sinclair, 'I don't mean to say that there is not much anarchy, much sin, much frivolity to be wished away; but I don't think that we, constituted as we are, could devise a better age. Indeed, I don't think we could devise a different one. You see, we are necessarily limited by the circumstances that have created us.' Here the Doctor abruptly broke off, and with a tremulous solicitude begged Mrs. Sinclair to let him button her glove for her.

Meanwhile, all the ladies, with the exception of Mrs. Sinclair, had fallen, under Lady Grace's vigorous guidance, to discussing the higher education of women, or rather of woman—how her life might be made nobler, worthier, more significant.

'Now, Mr. Laurence,' exclaimed Lady Ambrose at last, dangling her hat in her hand, 'do come and put a stop to this. You see what a woman's parliament would be if we ever have one, which my husband thinks not at all impossible.'

'Don't you hear,' said Mrs. Sinclair to Leslie, 'you're wanted. Come now, begin and talk cleverly. We're all listening.'

'I think, Laurence,' said Dr. Jenkinson, who was a little piqued at finding how readily his fair neighbour turned away from him, 'I think, if you are going to construct a republic, you should have some Socrates to conduct your argument; otherwise you will never get on.'

'Well,' said Laurence, 'will you be our Socrates?'

'No,' said Dr. Jenkinson, who had noticed that Mr. Storks who was still standing by himself, and Mr. Herbert and Mr. Rokeby who were still standing together, were all three of them regarding the party with a certain expression of pity. 'No, I think not. Get started, and perhaps soon I will come back and see how you are getting on. I must go for a few minutes to speak to Mr. Storks. But remember—you must get a Socrates.'

At last, after some discussion, it was decided that the Socrates should be Robert Leslie.

'See,' said Mrs. Sinclair, 'I told you you would be wanted to talk cleverly.'

'Well,' said Leslie, 'if I am, you must listen and admire. Come, now, promise me this: that for this afternoon you will be my friend for better for worse; and that you will not be shocked at anything I may have occasion to say.'

'I will do my best,' said Mrs. Sinclair. 'And now, Mr. Leslie, don't you think you would be more comfortable if you sat a little farther off? or Lady Grace, of whom I am already afraid, will begin to think we're flirting.'

'And now, Mr. Leslie,' said Lady Ambrose, 'I hope you feel equal to pouring oil on these troubled waters; though I very much doubt if you know what extremely troubled waters a lot of women like ourselves are. Here is one of us who thinks that everything will go well if women can only learn to paint flowers on white dessert plates, and get fifteen shillings apiece for them.'

'And I,' said Lady Grace, smiling good-naturedly, 'was just saying that they ought all to be taught logic.'

'Perfectly true,' exclaimed Mr. Saunders, putting up his spectacles to see who had spoken.

'And Miss Merton,' said Lady Ambrose, 'thinks that we should all be taught to walk the hospitals, or be sick-nurses.'

'I should not so much mind that,' said Mrs. Sinclair, 'in war time, if one had any one fighting in whose life one really took an interest. I once thought, Mr. Leslie, that that might really be my mission, perhaps.'

'But,' said Lady Ambrose, 'how are we to build a castle in the air together, if we are all at cross purposes like this?'

There did, indeed, seem little probability of our friends setting to work at all, until Leslie slightly raised his voice, and said:

'In spite of all our differences, I think we shall be able to agree together, if you will listen for a moment to me. It is quite true that we all of us look upon life in different ways, and from different standpoints. We have all of us different and even clashing views in philosophy, politics, and religion. Our views of a perfect or a good state, one might expect, will differ very widely; and it would seem almost hopeless to try and make them agree. But I believe that our differences are often more outward than inward, and I believe the thing may be done. For there is one point on which I think we may all meet on amicable terms. We shall all admit, I suppose, that in a perfect state all the parts will be perfect, and each part will imply and involve all the others. Let us, then, first begin to see what it is that we really desire society to be—the lives we ourselves should like to live—our hopes—our aims—our pleasures—and see afterwards what is implied in these.'

'And is that all,' said Allen, 'that is needed to make the world perfect—that a very small section of it—which I suppose

you mean by society—is to be able to enjoy itself in the most refined way possible?　Are we to take no care first of any of the
really high aims in life?　Are we to let religion go without even
enquiring first if it be worth keeping?'

'We shall come to that afterwards,' said Leslie.　'If we want
a religion, depend upon it, it will be implicit in our notions of a
perfect state of society.'

'I confess I don't see that,' said Lady Ambrose.　'I think if
we don't take care of religion ourselves, it is only too apt to slip
away from us.'

'I think I see,' said Miss Merton.

'Well,' said Lady Ambrose, who was by this time in excellent
spirits, having just had a promise from Lord Allen to stay next
autumn with her in the country, 'I dare say it's all right.　And
so now, Mr. Leslie, we are to say, each of us, what we think is the
essence of good society, are we?　Well—I say the absence of dull
and vulgar people.'

'Art,' said Mr. Rose.

'Reason,' said Mr. Saunders.

'Unworldliness based on knowledge of the world,' said Miss
Merton.

'Wait a moment,' said Laurence; 'we are going too fast. This
is not what Mr. Leslie means.'

'No, no,' said Mr. Saunders.　'Let us get rid of what is evil
before we introduce what is good.　I should begin by getting rid
of every belief that is not based upon reason, and every sentiment
whose existence cannot be accounted for.'

'And I,' said Mr. Rose, 'of a certain failing which Aristotle
says has no name.'

Every one stared at Mr. Rose in alarmed amazement.

'I mean,' he went on slowly, 'the absence of æsthetic enthusiasm.'

'Here we go,' said Lady Ambrose, 'all over the place.　Come,
Mr. Leslie, you must pull us together again.'

'Seriously, then,' said Leslie, 'since I am to be the leader in
this business, don't we all of us here think that the present times
are out of joint?　We feel that this life is not what it might be.
We feel every day oppressed and hampered in a thousand ways.
Wherever we go we are met with scandals, vulgarities, corruptions.
We look in vain for possibilities of a higher and nobler, even of a
more refined, life.　We are always longing for something different.
We know what is good, and what is choice-worthy; but we cannot
choose it.'

'In other words,' said Mr. Luke, 'the age lacks, as a whole, practical culture. If the life of the world were guided by true culture, it would satisfy all our highest aspirations.'

'At any rate,' said Miss Merton, 'culture is a very good thing. I suppose we all of us admit that?'

'Of course,' said Lady Ambrose.

'And not only,' said Mr. Luke, 'are the inner aspects of life in this melancholy state, but its outer aspects are also, beyond parallel in any other age, hideous and chaotic. Now, as Mr. Leslie, very wisely as I think, advises us to work from the outward and the concrete, to the inward, might we not begin by considering for a few moments how the outward material aspects of our lives might be bettered for us? I am thinking particularly of our towns, and our town life.'

'Come,' said Leslie, 'let us have a political division of labour. May I be allowed to name Mr. Rose our commissioner of public works, and ask him to build us the city which is to be the centre of our regenerated England?'

Here at last was something definite; and the proposal was gladly welcomed.

'Well,' said Mr. Rose, 'since you refer this matter to me, I shall very gladly give you my views upon it; more especially as they are not mine only, but are shared now by an increasing body of men, who are slowly, and little by little, re-deciphering the spell by which the Beautiful may be again conjured back to us, and by which our eyes may be opened so that we discern its beauty.'

'Of course,' said Leslie, 'we presuppose in our society all external resources, so far as we need them—wealth, position, and so forth. Given all these, we are going to see what is the highest and noblest thing which in these days we can imagine life becoming—in other words, by what standards of possible good we condemn the present condition of things as bad. Mr. Rose will begin to show us.'

(To be continued.)

All in All.

Be calm, O wind, and gently blow,
  Nor rouse the waves to motion ;
Ye clouds, veil not the bay so low :
  My love sails o'er the ocean.

Out, boatman, out !   The wind will rise,
  The yawl will find it stormy.
Ay, thrice thy fee !   Her flag, it flies:
  My love looks waiting for me.

Blow on, ye winds ; and mope, you drone :
  Who cares for storm or weather !
My love, my own, no more alone,
  We walk the down together.

G. L. RAYMOND.

Juliet.

BY MRS. H. LOVETT CAMERON.

CHAPTER X.

THE MELODIOUS MINSTRELS.

WHEN Cecil Travers had met with that rebuff from the lady of his affections which has been recorded in a previous chapter, he had not been at all sorry to carry out her parting injunctions.

Broadley House became, so to speak, uninhabitable for Squire Travers's only son, and Squire Travers himself had taken care to make it so. During the two days that he had remained at home after having been refused by Juliet, Cis ardently wished himself anywhere but under the paternal roof.

His father sneered and scoffed at him all day long.

He wasn't surprised that no sensible girl would have him; he shouldn't wonder if he hadn't had the pluck to ask her right out; he supposed he went whining and whimpering to her like a school-girl instead of speaking up to her like a man; girls, especially spirited, clever girls, like Juliet, couldn't abide mollycoddles—and so on, till Cis very nearly lost his temper; and it was a pity that he didn't quite do so, for his father would have respected him ten times more if he had.

Finally, Cis having declared that he was not at all hopeless of eventual success, his father answered that it was like his vanity to say so; but that he was very glad to hear it, for he intended to see Juliet Blair his daughter-in-law before he died; and that, if Cis stuck to her like a man, and asked her often enough, she was quite certain to give in at last.

The upshot of it was, that old Mr. Travers gave his son a liberal cheque, and told him to go up to London, away from his molly-coddling mother, and see if he couldn't get some sense into his head, and see a little life.

Cis accordingly, feeling very much like the prodigal son, pocketed his cheque, and, nothing loth to escape from the storms of home life, went his way up to London.

There, as has been seen, he visited Mr. Bruce, took that gentleman considerably into his confidence, and felt much cheered and consoled by the very hopeful view which he took of his prospects, and also by the eager partisanship for his cause evinced by the worthy solicitor.

Mr. Bruce, like Mr. Travers senior, was of opinion that perseverance was the main thing required, and that, if the young lady was but asked often enough, she was certain to yield at the end.

Only of course time must be given.

'Take your time, my dear Mr. Cecil,' he said, assuringly; 'take your time; ladies never like being hurried. A little management is all that is required, and plenty of time.' And Cis, as he wished him good-bye, felt almost triumphant already.

Cis, left to his own resources in London, was not nearly so much a fish out of water as he was in his own home. He belonged to a young University Club, in its first stages, and here he was sure to meet plenty of his friends—men of his own college and of his own standing, who did not know nor care that he could not sit a horse, but who did know and were mindful of that first in 'mods.' of which his own father had spoken so disparagingly, and amongst whom he had in consequence some reputation for talent.

These young gentlemen—whose whiskers, like Cecil's, were small, and whose heads were for the most part filled with inordinate vanity, coated over with a thin layer of information—nevertheless counted themselves among the rising minds of their time.

When they met together they discoursed eagerly upon the principal religious and political subjects of the day, and honestly believed that their opinions were altogether new and original, and were destined to exercise a great and lasting influence on the history of their country.

Amongst these young men, Cis found himself quite an authority. Instead of being snubbed, sneered at, and sat upon from morning till night, his opinion was asked, and he was attentively listened to when he gave it; he made little speeches, and they were enthusiastically cheered; and altogether he was conscious of being considered by his clique to be a very clever and rising young man. So true is it that a prophet hath no honour in his own country!

All his friends were not, however, of the same stamp. One day, as he was wandering idly down Piccadilly, staring in at the shop-windows, a tall young fellow, in loose ill-made clothes, and with a ragged red beard, stopped suddenly before him, exclaiming—

'Surely you must be little Cis Travers!'

'So I am, at your service—and you? Why, it's David Anderson! We haven't met since we left school—fancy your remembering me!'

'I should have known you anywhere. What are you doing in town—nothing? You must come to my diggings. Won't you? What are you going to do to-night? Nothing particular—I thought so; well, then, you must positively come to our meeting. We hold our weekly meeting to-night.'

'Who are *we*?' asked Cis.

'Why, the "Melodious Minstrels,"—our musical society, you know. Of course you are fond of music?'

'Ye—s, I suppose so,' said Cis, doubtfully, recollecting that he was rather fond of listening to Juliet's singing.

'Yes, of course you are; every one with a soul loves music. Well, then, I can promise you a treat to-night: none of your trash, I promise you—real, good, first-class—the music of the future, you know,—Wagner, and Beethoven, and Schumann too. Here's the address,' giving him a card on which was inscribed—'Herr Franz Rudenbach, 114 Blandford Street.'

'But, my dear Anderson,' objected Cis, 'how on earth can I go to this place, and who is Herr Rudenbach?'

'Oh, he is our conductor and fiddler, you know, and with *such* a daughter! perfectly lovely! plays like an angel! You'd come for the daughter if you knew what she was like, I can tell you!' And Mr. David Anderson lifted up his hands and eyes, smacked his lips, and went through other gymnastic exercises indicative of his extreme admiration of the lady in question.

'You must come, you know, Cis; you'll be delighted. Nine o'clock sharp, mind; be sure you come. Good-bye;' and Mr. Anderson bolted swiftly round the corner of the street.

Cis felt very dubious about the evening's entertainment; but, when the time came, partly moved by curiosity concerning the fair Miss Rudenbach and partly through a wish to please his old schoolfellow, he found himself, a little after nine o'clock, at the indicated house in Blandford Street.

As he went up the narrow stairs of the dingy little house, a strange Babel of sounds met his ear: scrapings of violins, too-tooings of cornets, mixed with noises the like of which he had never heard before, made him imagine that a farmyard had been let loose in the room above him.

As he reached the top step a guttural German voice cried out—

'Now then, gentlemen. One, two, three, four—off!' And the performers started.

It was Beethoven's Toy Symphony. And anyone who remembers his impressions on hearing this performance for the first time will understand the absolute amazement with which Cis Travers, to whom it was a complete novelty, listened at the doorway.

He thought at first that he had stumbled on a company of lunatics. Ten young men were grouped around the piano, each armed with a different so-called 'instrument.' One had a child's drum, another a penny trumpet, another a whistle, one had a row of bells on a stick, another a sort of tambourine; but the most awful instrument of all was a small box, exactly like the stand of a child's toy dog, which when pressed emitted two sharp, short deafening squeaks, supposed to imitate the note of the cuckoo.

When all these varied instruments burst into play at once, with doubtful tune and most uncertain time, the effect was simply Pandemonium. Herr Rudenbach stood in the midst, with his bâton, and shouted 'Time, time!' at every bar, whilst his daughter Gretchen slaved away at the piano. Innocent, blue-eyed Gretchen, with her calm sweet face, and her smooth brown Madonna-like head! Cis Travers could not but acknowledge that David Anderson had shown his good taste in admiring her. She looked so out of place, so superior to her surroundings, like some garden flower grown up by chance in a field of weeds.

Wonders were never to cease that evening. Looking round the room towards the six or eight young men who composed the audience, Cis was astonished to recognise Wattie Ellison lounging back in an arm-chair and sketching Gretchen's profile in his pocket-book.

David Anderson, who was gravely playing the tambourine— indeed, the intense gravity of all the performers struck Cis at once as something very ludicrous, considering the ridiculous childishness of the instruments on which they were performing—David nodded at Cis over his music, and went on with his playing, and Cis sidled up to Wattie.

'Are they all mad, Wattie? and how on earth do you come here?' he whispered.

'I might ask the same,' answered Wattie in the same tone. 'Aren't they idiots? But it is very amusing, and little Gretchen's face is perfect. I am going to paint an historical picture; I don't know quite what the subject is to be, I haven't settled —the massacre of St. Bartholomew, or the burning of Joan of Arc, or something of that kind. I think I shall make something of it, and I want Gretchen's face for one of my figures. That is what I am here for; I am studying it. It's miserable

'TIME! TIME!'

work losing all the hunting season for this sort of thing, isn't it?
How are your people, Cis?'

Here the Toy Symphony came providentially to an end, and
David Anderson went up to speak to his old schoolfellow, and
introduced him to Herr Rudenbach, who bowed and smirked upon
him with exaggerated humility, whilst Gretchen came forward in
her grey stuff dress, made high up to the neck, and spoke a few
gentle words to him.

Then two young gentlemen played a duet on two violins,
which was really a very creditable performance, and was boister-
ously clapped and vociferously encored by the rest of the community; after which an unpretending little tray of refreshments
was brought in and handed round—lemonade and gin and water,
the latter beverage being generally preferred; slices of pound-
cake, and dry untempting-looking sandwiches from the ham-and-
beef shop round the corner, which were nevertheless partaken of
with avidity by the guests.

'Come home to my rooms, Cis,' said Wattie Ellison when,
having feasted upon the above-named refreshments, the little
society prepared to break up; and, linking his arm within that of
Georgie's brother, he carried him off with him to the Temple.

But that was by no means the last of Cis Travers's visits to the
house in Blandford Street, nor to the meetings of the 'Melodious
Minstrels.'

Partly through sheer idleness, partly through a certain pleasure
in playing the great man among a set of men who, being chiefly
city clerks or else embryo solicitors, looked up to him as to a
superior order of being, Cis grew rather fond of dropping in during
these weekly musical performances.

And little Gretchen got to look for his coming. With the
instinct of true refinement, she learnt at once to distinguish him
and his friend Wattie Ellison from the other young men, of David
Anderson's stamp, who came to her father's rooms. Cis was kind
to her, and took pains to talk to her and to be interested in her.
And he was to her as a god.

It was very pleasant to him to be so regarded. In the present
sore and wounded state of his heart and feelings, consequent upon
his rejection by Juliet Blair, it was inexpressibly soothing to him
to be worshipped and waited upon by any woman so young and so
pretty as Gretchen Rudenbach. This girl did not snub him, nor
laugh at him, nor pity him [with irritating compassion, nor call
him 'poor Cis' to his face, as if he were an inferior being. She
sat and gazed at him in speechless worship, or spoke to him, in
low timid tones, of her daily life, and cast adoring, respectful looks

at him when he talked to her or gave her advice, in a manner which no young fellow could possibly fail to find excessively flattering; he was grateful to her for her devotion, and began in return to pay her many little attentions. He brought her flowers and poetry books, and copied out music for her; once or twice he called at the house in the morning and found her at home; and having one day met her accidentally in the street, on her way to give a music lesson to two little girls, where she went three times a week, Master Cis carefully ascertained the exact route which she invariably followed on her way thither, and then found that, by some extraordinary coincidence, he was always turning up at unexpected corners of the street just at the moment when the little quietly-dressed music teacher appeared in sight.

Gretchen began to confide her little troubles and experiences to this kind-mannered young gentleman.

She told him that her father was not very kind to her, and that she was not at all happy in her home. Her mother, she said, had been a real lady—an English girl, who had run away with her father from the school at which he had been music teacher. As long as her mother lived, although she was a very unhappy woman, in very bad health, little Gretchen had been still not altogether uncared-for and unloved, but since her death the poor child had had but a troublous life of it with her father. From what she told him, Cis gathered that Herr Rudenbach, although he spoke kindly to his daughter before others, was rough and harsh to her when they were alone. He was avaricious and greedy of gain, looking upon his child and her talent for music solely as a means whereby he might make money out of her, of which he gave her hardly enough to clothe herself, whilst he himself spent every farthing that he could lay hands on upon his own selfish and not very respectable pleasures.

Gretchen also confided to Cis that David Anderson was anxious to marry her, and owned to him that, although she did not care for him in the least, she was half ready to do so in order to escape from the unhappiness which she endured at home.

But here Cis became quite eloquent in his remonstrances and admonitions. It was, he declared, the greatest sin a woman could be guilty of to marry a man she did not love. How could she possibly hope for a blessing on a union entered into from so unhallowed a motive? She must not dream of marrying David Anderson—it would be an absolute wickedness! She must promise him solemnly never to consent to become the wife of a man she did not love, and who was so utterly unsuited to her as honest David.

And Gretchen tearfully, timidly, and blushingly gave the required promise ; and heaven knows what wild impossible hopes dawned in the poor child's heart as she did so!

Cecil Travers was doing her a dreadful and incalculable injury. He was not in the smallest degree in love with her. Was he not as much in love with Juliet as it was possible for a man to be? He did not want little Gretchen for himself, but he did distinctly object to David Anderson having her. Men are very frequently found to resemble closely the typical dog in the manger.

And women are very slow to see this; they cannot understand a man being full of jealous objections to another man from any motive save one. Gretchen fancied (and who shall say she was to blame?) that because Cis was hotly, unreasonably indignant against David Anderson for wanting to marry her, therefore he must necessarily be desirous of doing so himself—whereas, as we know very well, nothing was farther from Cis Travers's thoughts than such a mésalliance.

David Anderson, although he had been educated at the same country-town school where Cis Travers had been sent for two years before going to Eton, was not exactly in the same rank of life as our young friend. He was the son of a worthy and respectable Glasgow merchant, who had given him a fairly good education and had got him a junior partnership in a young but rising firm in the city, dealing in hemp and flax. It was a splendid opening for young Anderson; for although his share of the profits was at present exceedingly small, in the course of a few years they would probably be much enlarged, and he would be in receipt of a very good income.

There was nothing in the world to prevent his marrying Gretchen Rudenbach, if he felt so disposed. His old parents were homely, simple-hearted people, who had no other wish than for their David's happiness ; and they would have welcomed such a sweet, gentle-mannered girl as she was with delight and affection. And David would have made her an excellent husband; but, alas for her! there came between herself and this rough but honest red-bearded suitor the vision of a tall, pale, gentleman-like youth, with blue eyes and yellow locks, who met her in her daily walks, who gave her paternal advice coupled with fraternal sympathy, and who, by occasionally pressing her hand sentimentally and looking at her tenderly, completely turned the head of the simple-natured little maiden.

One day, as the two were sauntering together down Wigmore Street, they came suddenly upon Wattie Ellison, who only nodded to them as he passed, but who looked back at them rather curiously after they had gone by.

'What can Cis Travers be walking about with little Gretchen for, I wonder?' he muttered to himself as he walked on; and Wattie came to the conclusion that Cis must be taken to task on this matter.

CHAPTER XI.

GRETCHEN GETS INTO TROUBLE.

WATTIE ELLISON'S rooms in the Temple do not, as it will be imagined, belong to himself. They are the property of a well-to-do bachelor friend, who seldom visits them, and who lends them to Wattie whenever he cares to come and occupy them. Wattie is one of those lucky men who always fall on their legs in these matters. He has friends by the score: friends with moors in Scotland, friends with fishing in Norway, friends with shooting in Norfolk, and friends to give him mounts in 'the shires;' and one and all of these friends are ready and anxious to welcome him and to give him of their best, whenever he may feel inclined to come to them.

And so, amongst others, he has of course a friend who has nice airy rooms, conveniently situated in the Temple, and who is only too delighted to place them at Wattie's disposal.

Wattie, who has been reading for the bar ever since he reached man's estate, comes to these pleasant chambers occasionally, by fits and starts as it were, whenever a sudden fit of industry is upon him, takes possession of his friend's household gods, gives pleasantly-spoken orders with a smile on his handsome face to his friend's old man and woman, who are left in charge, and who are ready to work their old fingers to the bone in the service of such a winsome-mannered, liberal-handed young gentleman; and, taking down his friend's musty law-books from their shelves, sets to work with a will, and burns the midnight oil in the study thereof.

And accordingly, when his utter rejection by Georgie Travers's father drove him in honour from the neighbourhood in which she lived, Wattie thought he would go up to London and toil at the law-books again. He had romantic ideas of remaining buried in hard study for several years, and then of bursting out suddenly into a Coleridge or a Cairns, when, having realised a large fortune and been raised to the top of his profession by his perseverance and genius, he would go down triumphantly to Broadley, and claim Georgie for his wife.

He set to work very hard indeed; for the first week he made himself almost ill by the ardour and energy which he threw into his labours. For the first week—after that, he began to find it rather monotonous. It occurred to him that, as he had a good deal of talent for painting, the fine arts might possibly open out a quicker road to fortune and to fame than the bar could do. At all events, the study would be pleasanter and more attractive in every way. Accordingly the law-books were replaced on their shelves, and the friend's rooms were quickly transformed into a studio. If, argued Wattie, he were suddenly to present to the world a striking and original picture, full of genius and talent, would not his fortune be as good as made? Why condemn himself to years of dry and uninteresting study when possibly a few months of much more congenial work might place him on 'the line' on the Royal Academy walls, and lead him at once to a comfortable income and to Georgie Travers? And, even supposing he should not succeed and his picture be a failure, why then he could always go back to the law-books, for after all a few months more or less would not make much difference in the long run.

It was just at this stage of his proceedings that he stumbled across Cis Travers in Blandford Street.

Wattie Ellison was exceedingly cordial to Cis; he had never taken very much notice of him when they were both down in the country together, but here up in London they met like old friends.

Georgie's brother was a person whom Wattie Ellison could not fail to find exceedingly interesting to him. When Cis sat in his friend's rooms writing to his sister, Wattie, without actually sending her any direct message, would suggest little allusions to himself and give bits of information or make little skilful enquiries, which Cis would duly report as he wrote.

'Wattie says he is going to do such and such things,' or 'Wattie has been asking me how your new mare goes, and what you have been doing this week,' and so on; and then, when Georgie's answers came, you may be sure that all these little remarks were noticed and commented upon, and that the letter was as freely read by Wattie as by her brother.

Cis was fond of Georgie, for she had always been good to him and protected him from his father, and he was glad to do a good turn for her. Moreover, he became very fond of Wattie Ellison, and the two young men frequently spent their evenings chatting together in those pleasant Temple chambers, whilst Wattie, with a bit of charcoal, sketched out numberless rough designs for his great picture on a white board upon an easel hard by, and then asked Cecil's advice upon them. Cecil invariably said of each that it was very nice; and then Wattie shook his head and said it did not please him yet, rubbed it all out, and began it over again.

The same evening of the day when Wattie had met Cis and Gretchen walking together in Wigmore Street, the two young men were as usual sitting together over the fire in the Temple rooms, when Wattie said, rather suddenly—

'Do you intend playing Faust to our little friend Gretchen, Cis?'

'Eh, what? What on earth do you mean?' said Cis, getting rather red.

'Don't you think it rather a pity to walk about with the child? And I saw you buying those flowers for her the other day at Covent Garden. She is an innocent little soul; one wouldn't wish her to get into any trouble.'

'There's no question of any Faust, as far as I am concerned, I assure you,' said Cecil, earnestly, leaning forward in his chair and staring into the fire. 'Why, you can't think so for one moment!'

'Well, I am glad of it; at the same time she may get fonder of you than is good for her, poor little girl, and it may put ideas into her head and give her hopes.'

'Hopes? My dear Wattie, you don't imagine that Gretchen can expect me to marry her?' cried Cis, laughing.

'There's no knowing what a woman won't expect when a young man begins describing to her his views of marriage, as I heard you doing the other evening,' said Wattie.

'Oh! as to that, you know, one can't allow her to throw herself away upon a boor like David Anderson, and I was giving her a little advice.'

'Why should she not marry David? he would make her an excellent husband,' replied his friend.

'My dear Wattie, what a sin it would be! Such a pretty, refined, gentle little thing to be wasted on a great rough fellow like that!'

'It would be a very good match for her. I don't see where she would get a better,' persisted Wattie.

'Good heavens! how can you suggest such an outrageous combination? Beauty and the Beast would be nothing to it!' and Cis began impatiently walking about the room.

At this moment there was a slight scuffle outside the door, and in another instant the stern-visaged old woman who 'did for' Mr. Ellison broke in upon the tête-à-tête of the two friends with the information, which she delivered with evident disapproval of such proceedings, that a young woman was wishing to see Mr. Travers.

She was almost immediately followed by a small figure, wrapped in a long black cloak, who, brushing past her into the room, fell at Cis Travers's feet in a passion of hysterical tears.

'Good heavens, Gretchen!' cried Cis. 'What on earth is the matter? what has happened? Here, Mrs. Stiles, go and fetch this young lady a glass of sherry.' And Wattie helped Cis to raise the sobbing girl and to place her on a chair.

'It is my father!' sobbed the girl. 'Oh, Mr. Travers, save me from him! He has beaten me so dreadfully, and he has turned me out of the house. Look here!' and she turned up her sleeve and showed the two horrified young men a sight that made them both shudder.

Her arm, once round and white and smooth, was covered with fearful bruises and bleeding wounds, and hung almost helplessly by her side.

'And my back is worse!'

'Good heavens, Gretchen, how dreadful!' exclaimed Wattie Ellison, in great dismay. 'What was the reason of it? what made him so brutal to you?'

'Alas! it was because I have lost my situation as music teacher. I am sure I did no wrong, did I, Mr. Travers, by walking with you? But Mrs. Wilkins, the lady whose little girls I was teaching, saw me with you to-day, and she saw me once before, she says; so she came this evening and told my father I was a bad girl, and that she would not have me to teach her children any more—and father was dreadfully angry, and beat me and then turned me out of doors, and oh, do help me! What shall I do?'

Cecil looked at his friend in blank dismay. This was what his mistaken kindness had brought upon her.

'Why on earth did you come here? had you no woman friend to go to?' asked Wattie, almost angrily, of the weeping girl.

'No, no one; and I knew Mr. Travers would take care of me, he is so kind to me. I haven't a friend in the world but you,' she added, looking up imploringly at Cecil.

'What shall we do, Cecil? Shall we take her back to old Rudenbach?' asked Wattie, in great perplexity.

'Oh no, no, no!' cried Gretchen, imploringly. 'I can never, never go back to him. If you knew how cruel he is, how often he beats me and kicks me, you would not want me to go back—I would rather beg my way in the streets. But, dear Mr. Travers, may I not stay here?'

She was evidently as innocent as a baby; no idea of any wrong or impropriety in coming alone at ten o'clock at night to throw herself upon the mercy and charity of two young men ever for an instant crossed her mind. Cecil was kind to her, and she loved him devotedly; so in her trouble she had come straight to where she knew he was likely to be found, and, having found him, she trusted herself implicitly to his protection.

No two young men were ever placed in a more awkward predicament. Here was this girl suddenly thrown upon their hands, without a friend in the world but themselves, and common humanity compelled them to take care of her. Cecil, moreover, felt himself responsible for the whole situation. It was his fault that the poor child had got into such a dreadful scrape; it was his foolish sentimental flirtation which had cost her her place and had made her brutal father turn her out of doors, and Cis felt in a perfect despair of misery and self-reproach as he reflected upon it.

Wattie Ellison forbore to reproach him. Fortunate it was that Mrs. Stiles was on the premises, and the two young men retired to consult with her over what was to be done.

Mrs. Stiles began by being exceedingly stiff and virtuous. She had never heard of such proceedings, she said, as a young woman coming alone to a gentleman's chambers in the middle of the night; she didn't know how she, Mrs. Stiles, a respectable woman, could mix herself up at all in such doings,—with sundry other cutting remarks of the same nature; but when the whole of Gretchen's story had been circumstantially related to her, and when she had seen the poor girl's maimed and bruised condition, feelings of humanity and charity awoke in her ancient bosom; and old Stiles, coming in at this juncture, proved a valuable ally, and suggested several useful and practical ideas.

Between the four it was settled that Mrs. Stiles should carry off Gretchen in a cab to the house of a cousin of her own—a certain Mrs. Blogg, who kept a small baker's shop in a street leading out of the Strand, and who, ‘ for a consideration,’ which Cecil Travers eagerly offered to make as liberal as could be desired, would, she thought, take in Gretchen for a few days until it could be further decided what to do for her.

This idea was immediately carried out. Poor little Gretchen, much bewildered and rather reluctant, was carried off by the stern but by no means unkind old woman. Cis wanted to go with them; but Wattie, who had more sense and more knowledge of the world, would not allow him to do so. Mrs. Blogg, a fat, shrewd-faced woman, with a sharp eye to the main chance, fingered the instalment of two sovereigns sent by Cis with greedy joy, and consented as a favour to take in the young woman.

And between them both the poor girl was put to bed.

But when Cis went the next morning to enquire after his protégée he found that Mrs. Blogg had in much alarm sent for the nearest doctor, as Gretchen had awakened in high fever and was quite light-headed.

For nearly a fortnight the poor child lay in raging fever and burning thirst between life and death, and then her youth asserted itself and the disease left her, to live, but oh! so weak and pale, such a poor little shadow of her former self, as made even the heart of the hired nurse whom Cecil had engaged to tend her ache with pity at the sight.

Meanwhile our two friends had not been idle in her service. They had, in the first place, repaired to Blandford Street, there to find that the wretched old German music teacher had departed and utterly vanished, leaving no direction behind him nor clue as to where he was to be found.

'And a good job, too!' said his indignant landlady, 'although he do owe me for five weeks' rent, and for three pound ten as he borrowed of me just the day before he went; but a more disrespectable drinking beast never came into an honest woman's house; and I am glad he's gone, even though I've lost the money. I am right down sorry for the poor young lady, that I am, and if I'd been at home he shouldn't have turned her into the streets; but then I was out, and never knew nothing about it till I got home an hour after and found that furrin beast lying dead drunk on the landing.'

No more information being obtainable in this quarter, the two friends began seriously to discuss what should be done with poor Gretchen.

Cis Travers's funds were getting low, and he hardly knew how he should be able to go on supporting the girl if she were to be ill much longer.

Driven at last to desperation, he wrote to his father, and, vaguely stating that he had got into a little difficulty in which his honour was concerned, besought him to ask him no questions but to send him a cheque for fifty pounds at once.

The Squire was delighted with this letter from his son. It so happened that there had been a Newmarket meeting the previous week; and the sport-loving old man settled it in his own mind at once that Cis had been lured into making some imprudent bets, for which this sudden and mysterious demand for money was to pay. Any iniquity connected with horses and horse-racing was pardonable in the old man's eyes. He was positively enchanted.

'The boy is coming round at last!' he said to himself, with a chuckle; 'I shall make something of him yet; that sending him to London by himself was a fine idea!'

And when Georgie came into his room he said to her, with quite a beaming face—

'Cis wants money ; he has been getting into trouble; he has been to Newmarket and lost his money, the young rascal!'

'To Newmarket!' repeated Georgie, in amazement. 'Are you sure, papa?' For Cis had corresponded pretty regularly with his sister of late, and certainly there had been nothing in his letters to lead her to suppose that horse-racing had in any way formed part of his pleasures.

'I tell you he has been to Newmarket,' repeated the Squire, doggedly, for he was determined to believe it ; and he turned the key of his cash-box and took out his cheque-book, filled up a cheque for seventy pounds, and sat down and wrote a mild exordium to his son on the evils of betting if you backed the wrong horse, which letter considerably surprised and puzzled that young gentleman when he received it.

Georgie had her own opinions on the subject of what the money was wanted for, but she did not think it necessary to impart them to her father. She pulled old Chanticleer's ear, and the ancient hound winked his one eye gravely at her as much as to say, 'We know better, don't we?'

'So we do, old boy!' said Georgie, in answer, half aloud; and left the Squire to his own delusions and to his letter.

But, although Cecil could make neither head nor tail of his father's letter, the meaning of his father's cheque was clear and very delightful, for with it he could do everything he wished for little Gretchen.

He and Wattie soon hit upon a plan for her. There was an old governess whom Wattie knew, who had once lived with the Ellisons, and who had now settled down in a little house in Pimlico, where she thankfully took in lodgers to eke out her small income.

This lady, Miss Pinkin by name, would, they soon found out, gladly receive Gretchen Rudenbach when she was well enough to leave Mrs. Blogg's not very comfortable mansion. Cecil was to pay for her lodgings and for the hire of a cottage piano for her use until she was well enough to begin her teaching again. Miss Pinkin's educational connection enabled her to ensure at least two or three young pupils for the girl at once, and in time she would, they hoped, get many more.

Gretchen, on being consulted, thankfully and meekly acquiesced in anything and everything that Cis had settled for her; and when she was well enough to be moved she took up her abode in Miss Pinkin's upper-floor rooms, and under that lady's care soon became strong enough to begin her work.

Cis took Wattie's advice, and went but very seldom to visit his little protégée. The poor child was very sad. She sat and watched for him day after day at her window, and when day after day passed, and he did not come, she wept miserable tears in her loneliness. Now and then, once perhaps in a fortnight, he did come and see her, and then Gretchen became a transformed being; her pale face was suffused with a blush of delight as he entered, her heavy eyes became bright with happiness, and her gratitude and love for her young benefactor beamed out in every look and word.

But Cis was very prudent, and was determined not to put himself again in the wrong concerning her; only it did annoy him considerably to hear that David Anderson had tracked her to her new abode, and was constantly visiting her and repeatedly urging her to become his wife.

He might have made himself quite at ease concerning this. Gretchen was in no danger of becoming Mrs. David Anderson.

'I do not think about him,' she would say to Miss Pinkin when that good lady urged her not to turn a deaf ear to so advantageous an offer.

'But you do think about Mr. Travers, I am afraid, Gretchen,' the ex-governess would say severely, 'although he is far above you in station, and is not likely to think about you.'

And to this accusation Gretchen could give no answer whatever.

Chapter XII.

REJECTED AND LEFT.

With her feet on the fender, the last new novel on her lap, and her eyes fixed on the fire, Juliet Blair is sitting one evening in the twilight in the little morning-room to which she is accustomed to resort for her five o'clock tea.

It so happens that an emissary from Madame Celeste in Bond Street, armed with cardboard boxes of every size and shape, has with much commotion arrived half-an-hour ago at the house, having come down from London by the afternoon express with an entirely new selection of Parisian bonnets, hats, and head-dresses, for inspection.

Mrs. Blair, who would barter her soul away for a French bonnet, has retired with Ernestine to her bedroom to unpack and look over all these treasures, and it is possible that Colonel Fleming is not altogether unaware of these arrangements nor of the superior attraction which retains the widow upstairs.

For he shortly afterwards steals into the morning-room and, drawing a chair in front of the fire, sits down by the side of his ward.

Juliet makes room for him with a smile, and then for several minutes neither of them speak.

'I have been doing a very unpleasant duty this afternoon,' says Colonel Fleming, at last.

'Yes?' from Juliet, enquiringly.

'I have sent off a letter that I have too long delayed writing. I have written to secure my return passage to India in the "Sultana," which is advertised to sail in a fortnight.'

'What!' Juliet starts to her feet. 'To India—are you mad! What have you done? The letters are not gone!' and she makes a step to the door.

He puts out his hand to stop her. 'I am afraid they are, Juliet; the bag was just going as I came in; but even if they were not, it could make no difference. I have quite made up my mind that it is high time I went back.'

'Surely this is a very sudden determination you have come to,' said Juliet, trying to speak calmly.

'Not at all; I have been thinking of it for some time,' he answered; 'only it was no use talking about it until I had made up my mind to go; and now the deed is done,' he added, with a half sigh.

'I do not see that the mischief is in any way irremediable,' she answers, speaking quickly. 'It is easy to write to-morrow, and retract your letter of to-day. Colonel Fleming, I entreat you to think better of it; we cannot let you leave us like this, indeed we cannot!'

'You are very good,' he begins, rather formally; 'but I have not acted without due thought, I assure you.'

And then all her self-control forsakes her, and she bursts into a wail of despair, clasping her hands entreatingly—'Oh! why, why should you go? are you not happy here?'

'Yes, I am happy—too happy, perhaps,' answers Hugh, gloomily; 'but one doesn't live for happiness, unfortunately. I have quite finished all that I came home to do for you, Juliet; and now I am only wasting my time and my life here.'

'But why need you ever go back? Why not throw up your Indian appointment, and stay at home?' she asks, despairingly.

Colonel Fleming smiles. 'I don't quite see my way to that, Juliet. I am not likely to get anything else so good at home, or indeed anything at all, good or bad; all my interest is in India, and this appointment of mine is a very good one. You forget that I am a poor man. I should not have enough of my own to live like a gentleman in England.'

Juliet was leaning up against the mantel-piece with her arms folded upon it, and her head bent down upon them. He could not see her face—the firelight flickered red and warm over her dusky head and her bowed figure ; something in the utter despair of her attitude touched him strangely.

As he finished speaking, she raised herself abruptly and began walking rapidly up and down the room behind him.

'You must not go, you shall not go!' she kept on saying aloud. He would not look round at her, perhaps because he could not trust himself to do so. He sat leaning forward on his chair and staring fixedly into the fire.

Then all at once she came and stood behind him ; her heart beat so that she could hardly stand ; her voice trembled so that she could scarcely speak ; her very hands, which she laid one on each of his shoulders, shook as they rested there.

There was no light in the room but the firelight, and they could not see each other's faces.

'Hugh! don't go. Why should you go ? Have I not enough for us both ? Stay and share everything that I have—dear Hugh!'

And to her trembling words there succeeded an utter silence in the little room.

Why had she not worded it otherwise ? why had she not said, 'I love you ; stay for my sake, because I cannot live without you.'

Then, indeed, he could hardly have withstood her ; then, indeed, for her sake as well as for his own, he must have taken her to his heart at once and for ever. But a something of maiden bashfulness and reserve, even in that moment of impulse, when in her despair she had let him see too much perchance of what was in her heart, had kept her back from the actual confession of her love.

She had spoken of her money! Ah, fatal, miserable mistake! She had brought up before him the one thing that in his own mind stood as an insuperable barrier between them, the one thing that for honour's sake bade him hold back and leave her.

Rapidly there flashed through his mind the utter impossibility of what she had asked him to do—'to stay and share all that was hers!' How could he do so? how could he, her guardian, place himself in the utterly false position of her lover ?

Still he did not speak. Ah, will no good angel prompt her to fall at his feet and to cry, 'I love you!'

The opportunity is gone. Hugh turns round, and takes her hands—gentle hands, that were still on his shoulders.

'My dear Juliet'—and his voice betrays some unwonted emotion —'you are, I think, the most generous-minded woman I have ever met—but——'

'Ah, say no more! say no more!' she cries, wrenching away her hands from his grasp and burying her face in them.

'Do you not recollect, my child,' he says, very gently and tenderly, 'do you not recollect that I am your guardian, and you my ward? In such a position, that I should accept any gift or loan of money from you is utterly impossible.'

He had wilfully misinterpreted her meaning! With bitterest shame she saw that he misunderstood her purposely—that he spoke of her money where she had meant herself! Was ever woman subjected to such soul-degrading humiliation?

She, Juliet Blair the heiress, the owner of Sotherne, young, beautiful, and talented, had made a free offer of herself to this man whom she had been weak enough to love. She had offered herself —and—had been rejected!

With flashing eyes and burning cheeks she turned upon him.

'Say no more, pray, Colonel Fleming. I am truly sorry that I should have offended you by offering to lend you money. As you say, I should have remembered that between you and me such a transaction was impossible. Pray forgive me, and rest assured that I shall be very careful not to offend you again by the repetition of such a proposition.'

Her voice was full of scorn, and as she ceased speaking she made him a sweeping bow and left the room; and, hurrying upstairs into her own bedroom, she flung herself down upon the sofa and burst into a fit of passionate tears.

Bitter tears of anger and self-reproach over her own abased pride and mortified self-esteem! What demon had prompted her to speak those miserable words? Why had she committed the fatal, irretrievable error of wooing instead of waiting to be wooed? And the worst of it was that it was all a mistake! She had thought herself loved, and she had been awakened rudely to find herself scorned and rejected! For that he had really misunderstood her she could not for one instant delude herself into believing. In his pity and his compassion he had answered her about her money, feigning to ignore her true meaning—which, alas, she had all too plainly betrayed!

To any woman the position would have been a sufficiently painful one; but to Juliet Blair, with her proud spirit and independence of mind, such thoughts were absolute torture.

There was no untruth in the statement which she made to her maid, when that functionary entered her mistress's room to put out her dress for dinner, that she had such a frightful headache that she felt quite unequal to going downstairs again, and that she would have a cup of tea in her room and then go to bed.

But when this message was brought downstairs to the two who were awaiting her appearance to go in to dinner, Colonel Fleming offered his arm in silence to the widow, and became very grave and silent indeed.

Not all Mrs. Blair's blandishments, backed up with an entirely new head-dress just come from town, could extract from her companion more than the most absent monosyllables.

When it came to the mistress of the house being forced to keep to her room because of his presence—for it was thus that he interpreted her absence—Colonel Fleming felt that something must be done. Sotherne Court was no longer a fitting abode for him.

After dinner was over, he studied Bradshaw attentively for some minutes, and then, going into the library, rang the bell for Higgs.

' Higgs, can I have the dog-cart to-morrow morning to meet the eight o'clock train ? '

' Yes, certainly, sir.'

' Very well, then : will you send James to my room to pack my things. I find that I am obliged to go up to town rather suddenly to-morrow.'

' Yes, sir—sorry you are obliged to go, sir ; we all hoped you would have stayed,' said the old man, lingering for a minute to poke the fire and sweep up the hearth. ' I'll send James at once, sir.'

And Higgs went his way to the back region, where, to the select community in the housekeeper's room, he gave it as his opinion that Miss Juliet had ' given the Colonel the sack ; and more's the pity, says I, for a nicer, pleasanter-spoken gentleman than Colonel Fleming never stopped in the 'ouse ! '

Colonel Fleming and James the footman were busy packing up for the best part of the night.

' He'll never come back no more,' said James to his superior, when at last he was dismissed ; ' he's packed up every stick and every straw ; he's not coming back no more, Mr. Higgs.'

It did not behove Higgs to lower his dignity by confiding to one of the under servants his views of the part which he supposed Miss Blair to have played in this sudden departure. He contented himself with gruffly desiring James to ' clean up that there mess, and to go to bed and be quite sure he called the Colonel in plenty of time the next morning ; ' an injunction which James, mindful of parting tips, was not at all likely to forget.

When Juliet awoke at eight o'clock the next morning, her maid stood by her bedside with a cup of tea, and on the tray lay a small sealed note.

'Colonel Fleming desired me to give you this note, miss, before he went.'

'Before he went! is he gone?'

With what a sudden, faint sinking of the heart she asked the question! but how foolish! Of course he had only gone up to town for the day.

The maid, perfectly unconscious of her mistress's agitation, said cheerfully that, yes, the Colonel was gone, and that she had heard Mr. Higgs say he had started in plenty of time, and was sure to have caught the train.

Juliet waited feverishly until the girl had left the room, and then tore open the note. It ran thus:

'Forgive me for leaving you so suddenly without a word of farewell or of thanks for all your hospitality and goodness towards me; but you will not, I know, think me ungrateful. After all that has passed between us, I do not think I could have stayed any longer under your roof, and I have thought it best to leave you thus without the spoken farewell that must have been full of pain to us both. God bless and reward you, dear Juliet, for all your generosity and affection towards me. I can never forget either; and, if ever you think of me in future years, do me at least the justice to believe that it is not inclination, but duty and honour alone, which have told me to leave you.

'I do not know where I shall stay in town, but I will write to you again before I leave England.'

Mrs. Blair and Ernestine were as yet deep in the mysteries of rouge and crimping-irons, when, preceded by a short, sharp knock, the door was flung open, and Juliet entered hurriedly, with an open letter in her hand.

'My dearest Juliet!' cried the widow, hastily flinging a dressing-cape over the small collection of pots, and phials, and camel's-hair brushes that stood on the table near her—'how you startled me! What on earth is the matter?'

'Did you know that Colonel Fleming was going away this morning?' asks Juliet, shortly.

'Going away? No, certainly not; has he gone?' answers Mrs. Blair, with an astonishment too real to be feigned.

'Yes, I have just had this note from him to say he is gone; and I don't know if you are aware of it, but he starts for India in a fortnight.'

'No, indeed; I had no idea of it. So he is gone! very rude of him, I must say, to go without wishing us good-bye.' Mrs. Blair has some difficulty in concealing the satisfaction she feels at this unexpected piece of news.

'Not rude at all; he is suddenly called away—it is perfectly natural. Of course he could not wake us all up at so early an hour,' answers Juliet.

'What does he say? Let me see the letter,' says her step-mother, stretching out her hand for the note; but Juliet does not dream of giving it to her.

'There is nothing in it that would interest you,' she says, folding it up slowly and replacing it in its envelope. 'Besides, he says he will write again from town.'

'Ah, he will write again?'

'Yes, so he says.'

'Then perhaps, Juliet, you will leave me to finish my dressing, as there is nothing very serious the matter, and it upsets my nerves to be obliged to talk so early in the morning. Go on with my hair, Ernestine.'

And Juliet goes.

Somehow that promise that he will write again prevents her from despairing.

That letter, she thinks, will in some way make up to her for all the suspense and uncertainty of the present. It is impossible that he can intend to leave her like that for years, perhaps indeed for ever. Vaguely, indistinctly, as women see such things, she begins to see the duty and the honour by which he has said he considers himself bound; but, woman-like, she does not think very seriously of them. Has he not at the same time more than implied that his inclination would lead him to stay with her? Do not such words mean that he loves her? And if so, then what need she fear?

What does a woman care for duty or for honour when set in the balance against love? Love in her mind outweighs every-thing; give her love, and she laughs at every other earthly consideration. To Juliet, with her impulsive, enthusiastic mind, and her passionate temperament, it seemed impossible that so cold-blooded a thing as honour could in any man's mind win the day against love.

He would come back to her, she said to herself; he would not be able to stay away; a few days of waiting, and then he would come back to her, as he had come back before, sooner even than she had dared to hope for him.

She read his letter over and over again, she pressed it gladly to her heart and her lips, for she could not, possibly she would not, see in it a farewell.

And Hugh Fleming up in London is pacing objectlessly up and down Piccadilly and Pall Mall, wondering what he shall say to her, and feeling more and more angry with himself for having left her, and more and more inclined to go back to her by the next train.

Curiously enough, he does not feel at all sure that Juliet does indeed love him. Even her last interview with him, when she had of her own accord offered him everything, had but partially opened his eyes. He knows her to be impulsive and impetuous, and generous to a fault. What more likely than that such a woman, fond of him as she undoubtedly was, should in a moment of exaltation be carried away into offering more than she intended or realised?

Should he be right or justified in taking advantage of that moment of weakness?

Had he known how completely and utterly the girl's heart was given over to him, he would certainly never have left her; but he did not know it—he knew, indeed, that if he chose he might win her, but he did not understand that she was already won.

He wandered about the streets, trying to settle in his own mind how he should write to her—or whether, indeed, he should write to her at all; and at last he decided that he would give himself one more chance of happiness.

He turned into the Club, and sat down and wrote to her.

He begged her to tell him truly if indeed what she had said to him had been the voice of her own heart—or merely an impulse of generosity; he told her that he loved her passionately, entirely, devotedly, with a love that he never thought to feel again after the death of his first love, and which she, Juliet, alone had had power to waken in him. But he told her at the same time that every feeling of honour, of duty, and of delicacy bade him leave her; that her money stood between them like a wall; and that, moreover, his own peculiar position as her guardian made it almost a breach of trust to the dead that he should aspire to be her lover. One consideration alone, he said, could surmount these objections —the consideration of her happiness. If, indeed, she loved him so entirely that without him she could not live nor be happy, then indeed, and then only, would he throw all these most weighty objections to the winds, and devote his whole existence to her: And in this case he entreated her to write to him at once and recall him to her side; but if it was not so, if it was merely a grateful affection, a generous friendship, or even but a brief-lived fancy, which had made her for one short hour imagine that she loved him—in that case he prayed her to put his letter into the fire, and to send him no answer whatever to it; he should know too well how to interpret her silence. He concluded his letter by naming to her the very latest date at which he could receive an answer from her in town before starting for Southampton, and by telling her that up to the very last minute he should still not despair, but hope to hear from her.

Even when he had directed and stamped this letter, Colonel Fleming did not immediately post it. He was still so doubtful about the wisdom and the propriety of writing to her at all that he walked about with the letter in his pocket the whole of the next day. It was only on the third day that, having, I think, previously tossed up a sovereign, drawn lots from a number of blank slips of paper for one marked slip, and made use of sundry other most childish and undignified tricks of chance, in every one of which the luck came to the same decision, he finally determined to send the letter, and, going out with it on purpose, dropped it himself into the pillar-post.

And then he waited—at first confidently and patiently—then, after a day or two, less confidently, but still patiently—then with restless impatience, and finally, as the days slipped away one after the other, and the posts came in in regular succession, and brought him many others, but never the one letter he looked for—finally his waiting became despair.

The last day of his stay in England dawned. He was obliged to go about his business to a few shops and to his banker's—but all day long he kept returning to his hotel to ask feverishly if there were no letters for him, to receive ever the same answer—none.

Then late in the afternoon he went to see a friend whom he could trust, and charged him solemnly to go the last thing at night, and again the first thing in the morning, to his hotel, after he had left, and, if he found there any letter for him with a certain postmark, to telegraph to him on board the 'Sultana,' at the Southampton Docks, to stop his starting.

The friend promised faithfully—and then he could do nothing more, and he was obliged to go down to Southampton. To the last he would not give up hope; he watched and watched all that night and all the next morning from the vessel's side, long after he had gone on board, for anything in the shape of a telegraph boy; and he would not have his things taken into his cabin, nor settle even that he was going, until the very last.

And then all at once the anchor was raised, and it was too late.

And as the good ship 'Sultana' steamed slowly over the grey waves of Southampton Water in the early morning, and stood out to sea in a light and favourable wind, Colonel Hugh Fleming beneath his breath cursed his native land, and Sotherne Court, and Juliet Blair, with deep and bitter curses.

' She does not know how to love—she could not stand the test. Her pride has ruined us both ! '

And he turned his back on the white shores of the old country, and set his face fixedly and determinedly towards that far Eastern land to which he was bound.

(*To be continued.*)

The Lunar Hoax.

BY RICHARD A. PROCTOR.

Then he gave them an account of the famous moon-hoax, which came out in 1835. It was full of the most barefaced absurdities, yet people swallowed it all ; and even Arago is said to have treated it seriously as a thing that could not well be true, for Mr. Herschel would have certainly notified him of these marvellous discoveries. The writer of it had not troubled himself to invent probabilities, but had borrowed his scenery from the 'Arabian Nights' and his lunar inhabitants from 'Peter Wilkins.'— OLIVER WENDELL HOLMES (in *The Poet at the Breakfast-Table*).

In one of the earliest numbers of 'Macmillan's Magazine,' the late Professor De Morgan, in an article on Scientific Hoaxing, gave a brief account of the so-called 'lunar hoax'—an instance of scientific trickery frequently mentioned, though probably few are familiar with the real facts. De Morgan himself possessed a copy of the second English edition, of the pamphlet, published in London in 1836. But the original pamphlet edition, published in America in September 1835, is not easily to be obtained. The proprietors of the New York 'Sun,' in which the fictitious narrative first appeared, published an edition of 60,000 copies, and every copy was sold in less than a month. Lately a single copy of that edition was sold for three dollars seventy-five cents.[1]

The pamphlet is interesting in many respects, and I propose to give here a brief account of it. But first it may be well to describe briefly the origin of the hoax.

It is said that after the French revolution of 1830 Nicollet, a French astronomer of some repute, especially for certain lunar observations of a very delicate and difficult kind, left France in debt and also in bad odour with the republican party. According to this story, Arago the astronomer was especially obnoxious to Nicollet, and it was as much with the view of revenging himself on his foe as from a wish to raise a little money that Nicollet wrote the moon-fable. It is said further that Arago was entrapped,

[1] On the occasion of my first visit to America, in 1873, I for the first time succeeded in obtaining a copy of this curious pamphlet. It had been mentioned to me (by Emerson, I think) as an amusing piece of trickery played off by a scientific man on his brethren ; and Dr. Wendell Holmes, who was present, remarked that he had a copy in his possession. This he was good enough to lend me. Soon after, a valued friend in New York presented me with a copy.

as Nicollet desired, and circulated all over Paris the wonders related in the pamphlet, until Nicollet wrote to his friend Bouvard explaining the trick. So runs the story, but the story cannot be altogether true. Nicollet may have prepared the narrative and partly written it, but there are passages in the pamphlet as published in America which no astronomer could have written. Possibly there is some truth in De Morgan's supposition that the original work was French. This may have been Nicollet's; and the American edition was probably enlarged by the translator, who, according to this account, was Richard Alton Locke,[1] to whom in America the whole credit, or discredit, of the hoax is commonly attributed. There can be no doubt that either the French version was much more carefully designed than the American, or there was no truth in the story that Arago was deceived by the narrative; for in its present form the story, though clever, could not for an instant have deceived any one acquainted with the most elementary laws of optics. The whole story turns on optical rather than on astronomical considerations; but every astronomer of the least skill is acquainted with the principles on which the construction of optical instruments depends. Though the success of the deception recently practised on M. Chasles by the forger of the Pascal papers has been regarded as showing how easily mathematicians may be entrapped, yet even M. Chasles would not have been deceived by bad mathematics; and Arago, a master of the science of optics, could not but have detected optical blunders which would be glaring to the average Cambridge undergraduate.

But to turn to the story itself.

The account opens with a passage unmistakably from an American hand, though purporting, be it remembered, to be quoted from the ' Supplement to the Edinburgh Journal of Science.' ' In this unusual addition to our journal, we have the happiness of making known to the British public, and thence to the whole civilised world, recent discoveries in astronomy which will build an imperishable monument to the age in which we live, and confer upon the present generation of the human race a proud distinction through all future time. It has been poetically said ' [where and by whom?] ' that the stars of heaven are the hereditary regalia of man, as the intellectual sovereign of the animal creation. He may now fold the zodiac around him with a loftier consciousness of his mental supremacy.' To the American mind enwrapment in the star-jewelled zodiac may appear as natural as their ordinary oratorical references to the star-spangled banner; but the idea is

---

[1] This Locke must not be confounded with Richard Locke, the circle-squarer and general paradoxist, who flourished a century earlier.

essentially transatlantic, and not even the most poetical European astronomer could have risen to such a height of imagery.

Passing over several pages of introductory matter, we come to the description of the method by which a telescope of sufficient magnifying power to show living creatures in the moon was constructed by Sir John Herschel. It had occurred, it would seem, to the elder Herschel to construct an improved series of parabolic and spherical reflectors 'uniting all the meritorious points in the Gregorian and Newtonian instruments, with the highly interesting achromatic discovery of Dolland' (*sic*). This is much as though one should say that a clever engineer had conceived the idea of constructing an improved series of railway engines, combining all the meritorious points in stationary and locomotive engines, with *Isaac* Watts' highly ingenious discovery of screw propulsion. For the Gregorian and Newtonian instruments simply differ in sending the rays received from the great mirror in different directions, and Dollond's discovery relates to the ordinary form of telescopes with large lens, not with large mirror. However, accumulating infirmities and eventually death prevented Sir William Herschel from applying his plan, which 'evinced the most profound research in optical science, and the most dexterous ingenuity in mechanical contrivance. But his son, Sir John Herschel, nursed and cradled in the observatory, and a practical astronomer from his boyhood, determined upon testing it at whatever cost. Within two years of his father's death he completed his new apparatus, and adapted it to the old telescope with nearly perfect success.' A short account of the observations made with this instrument, now magnifying six thousand times, follows, in which most of the astronomical statements are very correctly and justly worded, being, in fact, borrowed from a paper by Sir W. Herschel on observation of the moon with precisely that power.

But this great improvement upon all former telescopes still left the observer at a distance of forty miles from the moon; and at that distance no object less than about twenty yards in diameter could be distinguished, and even objects of that size ' would appear only as feeble, shapeless points.' Sir John ' had the satisfaction to know that if he could leap astride a cannon-ball, and travel upon its wings of fury for the respectable period of several millions of years, he would not obtain a more enlarged view of the more distant stars than he could now possess in a few minutes of time ; and that it would require an ultra-railroad speed of fifty miles an hour for nearly the livelong year, to secure him a more favourable inspection of the gentle luminary of the night ; ' but ' the exciting question whether this " observed " of all the sons of men, from the days of Eden to those of Edinburgh, be inhabited by beings, like ourselves, of consciousness and curiosity, was left to the benevolent index of natural analogy, or to the severe tradition that the moon is tenanted only by the hoary *solitaire*, whom the criminal code of the nursery had banished thither for collecting fuel on the Sabbath-day.'[1]   But the time had arrived when the great discovery was to be made, by which at length the moon could be brought near enough, by telescopic power, for living creatures on her surface to be seen [1] if any exist.

The account of the sudden discovery of the new method, during a conversation between Sir John Herschel and Sir David Brewster, is one of the most cleverly conceived (though also one of the absurdest) passages in the pamphlet.   ' About three years ago, in the course of a conversational discussion with Sir David Brewster upon the merits of some ingenious suggestions by the latter, in his article on Optics in the " Edinburgh Encyclopædia," p. 644, for improvements in Newtonian reflectors, Sir John Herschel adverted to the convenient simplicity of the old astronomical telescopes that were without tubes, and the object-glass of which, placed upon a high pole, threw the focal image to a distance of 150 and even 200 feet.   Dr. Brewster readily admitted that a tube was not necessary, provided the focal image were conveyed into a dark apartment and there properly received by reflectors. . . .   The conversation then became directed to that all-invincible enemy, the paucity of light in powerful magnifiers.   After a few moments' silent thought, Sir John diffidently enquired whether it would not be possible to effect *a transfusion of artificial light through the focal object of vision*!   Sir David, somewhat startled at the originality of the idea, paused awhile, and then hesitatingly referred to the refrangibility of rays, and the angle of incidence. Sir John, grown more confident, adduced the example of the

---

[1] The nurses' tale is, that the man was sent to the moon by Moses for gathering sticks on the Sabbath, and they refer to the cheerful story in Numbers xv. 32–36. According to German nurses the day was not the Sabbath, but Sunday. Their tale runs as follows : ' Ages ago there went one Sunday an old man into the woods to hew sticks. He cut a faggot and slung it on a stout staff, cast it over his shoulder, and began to trudge home with his burthen. On his way he met a handsome man in Sunday suit, walking towards the church. The man stopped, and asked the faggot-bearer : " Do you know that this is Sunday on earth, when all must rest from their labours ? " " Sunday on earth or Monday in heaven, it's all one to me ! " laughed the woodcutter. " Then bear your bundle for ever ! " answered the stranger. " And as you value not Sunday on earth, yours shall be a perpetual Moon-day in heaven ; you shall stand for eternity in the moon, a warning to all Sabbath-breakers." Thereupon the stranger vanished ; and the man was caught up with his staff and faggot into the moon, where he stands yet.' According to some narrators the stranger was Christ ; but, whether from German laxity in such matters or for some other reason, no text is quoted in evidence, as by the more orthodox British nurses. Luke vi. 1–5 might serve.

Newtonian reflector, in which the refrangibility was corrected by the second speculum, and the angle of incidence restored by the third.'

All this part of the narrative is simply splendid in absurdity. Hesitating references to refrangibility and the angle of incidence would have been sheerly idiotic under the supposed circumstances; and in the Newtonian reflector (which has only two specula or mirrors) there is no refrangibility to be corrected; apart from which, ' correcting refrangibility ' has no more meaning than ' restoring the angle of incidence.'

' " And," continued Sir John, " why cannot the illuminated microscope, say the hydro-oxygen, be applied to render distinct, and, if necessary, even to magnify, the focal object ? " Sir David sprung from his chair ' [and well he might, though not] ' in an ecstacy of conviction, and, leaping half-way to the ceiling, exclaimed, " Thou art the man ! " Each philosopher anticipated the other in presenting the prompt illustration that if the rays of the hydro-oxygen microscope, passed through a drop of water containing the larvæ of a gnat and other objects invisible to the naked eye, rendered them not only keenly but firmly magnified to dimensions of many feet ; so could the same artificial light, passed through the faintest focal object of a telescope, both distinctify (to coin a new word for an extraordinary occasion) and magnify its feeblest component members. The only apparent desideratum was a recipient for the focal image which should transfer it, without refranging it, to the surface on which it was to be viewed under the revivifying light of the microscopic reflectors.'

Singularly enough, the idea here mentioned does not appear to many so absurd as it is in reality. It is known that the image formed by the large lens of an ordinary telescope or the large mirror of a reflecting telescope is a real image ; not a merely virtual image like that which is seen in a looking-glass. It can be received on a sheet of paper or other white surface just as the image of surrounding objects can be thrown upon the white table of the camera obscura. It is this real image, in fact, which we look at in using a telescope of any sort, the portion of such a telescope nearest to the eye being in reality a microscope for viewing the image formed by the great lens or mirror, as the case may be. And it does not seem to some altogether absurd to speak of illuminating this image by transfused light, or of casting by means of an illuminating miscroscope a vastly enlarged picture of this image upon a screen. But of course the image being simply formed by the passage of rays (which originally came from the object whose image they form) through a certain small space, to send *other* rays (coming from some other luminous object) through the same small space, is not to improve, but, so far as any effect is produced at all, is to impair, the distinctness of the image.   In fact, if these illuminating rays reached the eye, they would seriously impair the distinctness of the image.   Their effect may be compared exactly with the effect of rays of light cast upon the image in a camera obscura ; and, to see what the effect of such rays would be, we need only consider why it is that the camera *is* made 'obscura,' or dark.   The effect of the transfusion of light through a telescopic image may be easily tried by any one who cares to make the experiment.   He has only to do away with the tube of his telescope (substituting two or three straight rods to hold the glass in its place), and then in the blaze of a strong sun to direct the telescope on some object lying nearly towards the sun. Or if he prefer artificial light for the experiment, then at night let him direct the telescope so prepared upon the moon, while a strong electric light is directed upon the place where the focal image is formed (close in front of the eye).   The experiment will not suggest very sanguine hopes of good result from the transfusion of artificial light.   Yet, to my own knowledge, not a few who were perfectly well aware that the lunar hoax was not based on facts, have gravely reasoned that the principle suggested might be sound, and, in fact, that they could see no reason why astronomers should not try it, even though it had been first suggested as a joke.

To return, however, to our narrative.   'The co-operative philosophers, having hit upon their method, determined to test it practically.   They decided that a medium of the purest plate-glass (which it is said they obtained, by consent, be it observed, from the shop-window of M. Desanges, the jeweller to his ex-majesty Charles X., in High Street) was the most eligible they could discover.   It answered perfectly with a telescope which magnified a hundred times, and a microscope of about thrice that power.'   Thus fortified by experiment, and 'fully sanctioned by the high optical authority of Sir David Brewster, Sir John laid his plan before the Royal Society, and particularly directed to it the attention of his Royal Highness the Duke of Sussex, the ever munificent patron of science and the arts.   It was immediately and enthusiastically approved by the committee chosen to investigate it, and the chairman, who was the Royal President' (this continual reference to royalty is manifestly intended to give a British tone to the narrative), 'subscribed his name for a contribution of 10,000*l.*, with a promise that he would zealously submit the proposed instrument as a fit object for the patronage of the privy purse. He did so without delay ; and his Majesty, on being informed that the estimated expense was 70,000*l.*, naively enquired if the costly instrument would conduce to any improvement in *navigation.* On being informed that it undoubtedly would, the sailor king promised a *carte blanche* for any amount which might be required.'

All this is very clever. The ' sailor king ' comes in as effectively to give *vraisemblance* to the narrative as ' Crabtree's little bronze Shakspeare that stood over the fire-place,' and the ' postman just come to the door with a double letter from Northamptonshire.'

Then comes a description of the construction of the object-glass, twenty-four feet in diameter, ' just six times the size of the elder Herschel's ; ' who, by the way, never made a telescope with an object-glass. The account of Sir John Herschel's journey from England, and even some details of the construction of the observatory, were based on facts ; indeed, so many persons in America as well as in England were acquainted with some of these circumstances, that it was essential to follow the facts as closely as possible. Of course, also, some explanation had to be given of the circumstance that nothing had before been heard respecting the gigantic instrument taken out by Sir John Herschel. ' Whether,' says the story, ' the British Government were sceptical concerning the promised splendour of the discoveries, or wished them to be scrupulously veiled until they had accumulated a full-orbed glory for the nation and reign in which they originated, is a question which we can only conjecturally solve. But certain it is that the astronomer's royal patrons enjoined a masonic taciturnity upon him and his friends until he should have officially communicated the results of his great experiment.'

It was not till the night of January 10, 1835, that the mighty telescope was at length employed upon our satellite. The part of the moon selected was on the eastern part of her disc. ' The whole immense power of the telescope was applied, and to its focal image about one half of the power of the microscope. On removing the screen of the latter, the field of view was covered throughout its entire area with a beautifully distinct and even vivid representation of *basaltic rock.* Its colour was a greenish brown; and the width of the columns, as defined by their interstices on the canvas, was invariably twenty-eight inches. No fracture whatever appeared in the mass first presented ; but in a few seconds a shelving pile appeared, of five or six columns' width, which showed their figure to be hexagonal, and their articulations similar to those of the basaltic formation at Staffa. This precipitous cliff was profusely covered with a dark red flower, precisely similar, says Dr. Grant, to the Papaver Rhœas, or Rose Poppy, of our sublunary cornfields; and this was the first organic production of nature in a foreign world ever revealed to the eyes of men.'

It would be wearisome to go through the whole series of observations thus fabled, and only a few of the more striking features need be indicated. The discoveries are carefully graduated in interest. Thus we have seen how, after recognising basaltic formations, the observers discovered flowers: they next see a lunar forest, whose 'trees were of one unvaried kind, and unlike any on earth except the largest kind of yews in the English churchyards.' (There is an American ring in this sentence, by the way, as there is in one, a few lines farther on, where the narrator, having stated that by mistake the observers had the Sea of Clouds instead of a more easterly spot in the field of view, proceeds to say : 'However, the moon was a free country, and we not as yet attached to any particular province.') Next a lunar ocean is described, 'the water nearly as blue as that of the deep sea, and breaking in large white billows upon the strand, while the action of very high tides was quite manifest upon the face of the cliffs for more than a hundred miles.' After a description of several valleys, hills, mountains and forests, we come to the discovery of animal life. An oval valley surrounded by hills, red as the purest vermilion, is selected as the scene. 'Small collections of trees, of every imaginable kind, were scattered about the whole of this luxuriant area; and here our magnifiers blessed our panting hopes with specimens of conscious existence. In the shade of the woods we beheld brown quadrupeds having all the external characteristics of the bison, but more diminutive than any species of the bos genus in our natural history.' Then herds of agile creatures like antelopes are described, 'abounding on the acclivitous glades of the woods.' In the contemplation of these sprightly animals the narrator becomes quite lively. 'This beautiful creature,' says he, 'afforded us the most exquisite amusement. The mimicry of its movements upon our white painted canvas was as faithful and luminous as that of animals within a few yards of the camera obscura. Frequently, when attempting to put our fingers upon its beard, it would suddenly bound away as if conscious of our earthly impertinence; but then others would appear, whom we could not prevent nibbling the herbage, say or do to them what we would.'

A strange amphibious creature, of a spherical form, rolling with great velocity along a pebbly beach, is the next object of interest, it is presently lost sight of in a strong current setting off from the angle of an island. After this there are three or four pages descriptive of various lunar scenes and animals, the latter showing a tendency, singular considering the circumstances, though very convenient for the narrator, to become higher and higher in type as the discoveries proceed, until an animal somewhat of the nature of the 'missing link' is discovered. It is found in the Endymion (a circular walled plain) in company with a small kind of reindeer, the elk, the moose, and the horned bear, and is described as the biped beaver. It 'resembles the beaver of the earth in every other respect than in its destitution of a tail, and its invariable habit of walking upon only two feet. It carries its young in its arms like a human being, and moves with an easy gliding motion. Its huts are constructed better and higher than those of many tribes of human savages, and, from the appearance of smoke in nearly all of them, there is no doubt of its being acquainted with the use of fire. Still, its head and body differ only in the points stated from that of the beaver; and it was never seen except on the borders of lakes and rivers, in which it has been observed to immerse for a period of several seconds.'

The next step towards the climax brings us to domestic animals, 'good large sheep, which would not have disgraced the farms of Leicestershire or the shambles of Leadenhall Market; we fairly laughed at the recognition of so familiar an acquaintance in so distant a land. Presently they appeared in great numbers, and, on reducing the lenses, we found them in flocks over a great part of the valley. I need not say how desirous we were of finding shepherds to these flocks, and even a man with blue apron and rolled-up sleeves would have been a welcome sight to us, if not to the sheep; but they fed in peace, lords of their own pastures, without either protector or destroyer in human shape.'

In the mean time, discussion had arisen as to the lunar locality where men, or creatures resembling them, would most likely be found. Herschel had a theory on the subject—viz., that just where the balancing or libratory swing of the moon brings into view the greatest extent beyond the eastern or western parts of the hemisphere turned earthwards in the moon's mean or average position, lunar inhabitants would probably be found, and nowhere else. This, by the way (speaking seriously), is a rather curious anticipation of a view long subsequently advanced by Hansen, and for a time adopted by Sir J. Herschel, that possibly the remote hemisphere of the moon may be a fit abode for living creatures, the oceans and atmosphere which are wanting on the nearer hemisphere having been drawn over to the remoter (on this hypothesis) because of a displacement of the moon's centre of gravity. I ventured in one of my first books on astronomy to indicate objections to this theory, the force of which Sir J. Herschel admitted in a letter addressed to me on the subject.

Taking, then, an opportunity when the moon had just swung to the extreme limit of her balancing, or, to use technical terms, when she had attained her maximum libration in longitude, the observers approached the level opening to Lake Langrenus, as the narrator calls this fine walled plane, which, by the way, is fully thirty degrees of lunar longitude within the average western limit of the moon's visible hemisphere. 'Here the valley narrows to a mile in width, and displays scenery on both sides picturesque and romantic beyond the powers of a prose description. Imagination, borne on the wings of poetry, could alone gather similes to portray the wild sublimity of this landscape, where dark behemoth crags stood over the brows of lofty precipices, as if a rampart in the sky ; and forests seemed suspended in mid-air. On the eastern side there was one soaring crag, crested with trees, which hung over in a curve like three-fourths of a Gothic arch, and, being of a rich crimson colour, its effect was most strange upon minds unaccustomed to the association of such grandeur with such beauty. But, whilst gazing upon them in a perspective of about half a mile, we were thrilled with astonishment to perceive four successive flocks of large winged creatures, wholly unlike any kind of birds, descend with a slow even motion from the cliffs on the western side, and alight upon the plain. They were first noticed by Dr. Herschel, who exclaimed : " Now, gentlemen, my theories against your proofs, which you have often found a pretty even bet, we have here something worth looking at. I was confident that if ever we found beings in human shape it would be in this longitude, and that they would be provided by their Creator with some extraordinary powers of locomotion." . . . We counted three parties of these creatures, of twelve, nine, and fifteen in each, walking erect towards a small wood near the base of the eastern precipices. Certainly they *were* like human beings, for their wings had now disappeared, and their attitude in walking was both erect and dignified. . . . They averaged four feet in height, were covered, except on the face, with short and glossy copper-coloured hair, lying snugly upon their backs, from the top of the shoulders to the calves of the legs. The face, which was of a yellowish flesh colour, was a slight improvement upon that of the large orang outang, being more open and intelligent in its expression, and having a much greater expansion of forehead. The mouth, however, was very prominent, though somewhat relieved by a thick beard upon the lower jaw, and by lips far more human than those of any species of the simia genus. In general symmetry of body and limbs they were infinitely superior to the orang outang ; so much so, that, but for their long wings, Lieutenant Drummond said they would look as well on a parade ground as some of the old Cockney militia. . . . These creatures were evidently engaged in conversation ; their gesticulation, more particularly the varied action of their hands and arms, appeared impassioned and emphatic. We hence inferred that they were rational beings, and, although not perhaps of so high an order as others which we discovered the next month on the shores of the Bay of Rainbows, that they were capable of producing works of art and contrivance. . . . They possessed wings of great expansion, similar in construction to those of the bat, being a semi-transparent membrane united in curvilinear divisions by means of straight radii, united at the back by the dorsal integuments. But what astonished us very much was the circumstance of this membrane being continued from the shoulders to the legs, united all the way down, though gradually decreasing in width ' (very much as Fuseli depicted the wings of his Satanic Majesty, though H.S.M would seem to have the advantage of the lunar Bat-men in not being influenced by gravity [1]). 'The wings seemed completely under the command of volition, for those of the creatures whom we saw bathing in the water spread them instantly to their full

---

[1] Milton's opinion may be quoted against me here ; and as received ideas respecting angels, good and bad, the fall of man, and many other such matters, are due quite as much to Milton as to any other authority, his opinion must not be lightly disregarded. But though, when Milton's Satan ' meets a vast vacuity ' where his wings are of no further service to him,

> ' All unawares
> Flutt'ring his pennons vain, plumb down he drops
> Ten thousand fathoms deep, and to this hour
> Down had been falling, had not by ill chance
> The strong rebuff of some tumultuous cloud,
> Instinct with fire and nitre, hurried him
> As many miles aloft,

yet this was written nearly a quarter of a century before Newton had established the law of gravity. Moreover, there is no evidence to show in what direction Satan fell ; ' above is below and below above,' says Richter, ' to one stripped of gravitating body ;' and, whether Satan was under the influence of gravity or not, he would be practically exempt from its action when in the midst of that ' dark, illimitable ocean ' of space,

> ' Without bound,
> Without dimension, where length, breadth, and height
> And time and place are lost.'

His lighting ' on Niphates' top,' and overleaping the gate of Paradise, may be used as arguments either way. On the whole, I must (according to my present lights) claim for Satan a freedom from all scientific restraints. This freedom is exemplified by his showing all the kingdoms of the world from an exceeding high mountain, thus affording the first practical demonstration of the flat-earth theory, the maintenance of which led to poor Mr. Hampden's incarceration.

width, waved them as ducks do theirs to shake off the water, and then as instantly closed them again in a compact form. Our further observation of the habits of these creatures, who were of both sexes, led to results so very remarkable, that I prefer they should be first laid before the public in Dr. Herschel's own work, where I have reason to know they are fully and faithfully stated, however incredulously they may be received. . . . We scientifically denominated them the Vespertilio-homo or Bat-man; and they are doubtless innocent and happy creatures, notwithstanding that some of their amusements would but ill comport with our terrestrial notions of decorum.' The omitted passages were suppressed in obedience to Dr. Grant's private injunction. 'These, however, and other prohibited passages,' were to be presently 'published by Dr. Herschel, with the certificates of the civil and military authorities of the colony, and of several Episcopal, Wesleyan, and other ministers, who in the month of March last were permitted, under stipulation of temporary secrecy, to visit the observatory, and become eye witnesses of the wonders which they were requested to attest. We are confident that his forthcoming volumes will be at once the most sublime in science, and the most intense in general interest, that even issued from the press.'

The actual climax of the narrative, however, is not yet reached. The inhabitants of Langrenus, though rational, do not belong to the highest orders of intelligent Lunarians. Herschel, ever ready with theories, had pointed out that probably the most cultivated races would be found residing on the slopes of some active volcano, and, in particular, that the proximity of the flaming mountain Bullialdus (about twenty degrees south and ten east of the vast crater Tycho, the centre whence extend those great radiations which give to the moon something of the appearance of a peeled orange) 'must be so great a local convenience to dwellers in this valley during the long periodical absence of solar light, as to render it a place of popular resort for the inhabitants of all the adjacent regions, more especially as its bulwark of hills afforded an infallible security against any volcanic eruption that could occur.' Our observers therefore applied their full power to explore it. 'Rich, indeed, was our reward. The very first object in this valley that appeared upon our canvas was a magnificent work of art. It was a temple—a fane of devotion or of science—which, when consecrated to the Creator, is devotion of the loftiest order, for it exhibits His attributes purely free from the masquerade attire and blasphemous caricature of controversial creeds, and has the seal and signature of His own hand to sanction its aspirations. It was an equi-angular temple, built of polished sapphire, or of some resplendent blue stone, which, like it, displayed a myriad points of golden light twinkling and scintillating in the sunbeams. . . . The roof was composed of yellow metal, and divided into three compartments, which were not triangular planes inclining to the centre, but subdivided, curbed, and separated so as to present a mass of violently agitated flames rising from a common source of conflagration, and terminating in wildly waving points. This design was too manifest and too skilfully executed to be mistaken for a single moment. Through a few openings in these metallic flames we perceived a large sphere of a darker kind of metal nearly of a clouded copper colour, which they enclosed and seemingly raged around, as if hieroglyphically consuming it. . . . What did the ingenious builders mean by the globe surrounded by flames? Did they by this record any past calamity of *their* world, or predict any future one of *ours* ?' (why, by the way, should the past theory be assigned to the moon and the future one to our earth ?). ' I by no means despair of ultimately solving not only these but a thousand other questions which present themselves respecting the objects in this planet; for not the millionth part of her surface has yet been explored, and we have been more desirous of collecting the greatest possible number of new facts, than of indulging in speculative theories, however seductive to the imagination.'

After this we have an account of the behaviour of the Vespertilio-homo at meals. ' They seemed eminently happy, and even polite ; for individuals would select large and bright specimens of fruit, and throw them archwise across to some friend who had extracted the nutriment from those scattered around him.' However, the lunar men are not on the whole particularly interesting beings according to this account. ' So far as we could judge, they spent their happy hours in collecting various fruits in the woods, in eating, flying, bathing, and loitering about the summits of precipices.' One may say of them what Huxley is reported to have said of the spirits as described by spiritualists, that no student of science would care to waste his time enquiring about such a stupid set of people.

Such are the more interesting and characteristic portions of a narrative, running in the original to forty or fifty pages like those of this magazine. In its day the story attracted a good deal of notice, and, even when every one had learned the trick, many were still interested in a *brochure* which was so cleverly conceived and had deceived so many. To this day the lunar hoax is talked of in America, where originally it had its chief—or, one may rather say, its only real—success as a hoax. It reached England too late to deceive any but those who were unacquainted with Herschel's real doings, and no editors of public journals, I believe, gave countenance to it at all. In America, on the contrary, many editors gave the narrative a distinguished place in their columns. Some indeed expressed doubts, and others followed the safe course of the 'Philadelphia Inquirer,' which informed its readers that 'after an attentive perusal of the whole story they could decide for themselves;' adding that, 'whether true or false, the narrative is written with consummate ability and possesses intense interest.' But others were more credulous. According to the 'Mercantile Advertiser' the story carried 'intrinsic evidence of being an authentic document.' The 'Albany Daily Advertiser' had read the article with unspeakable emotions of pleasure and astonishment.' The 'New York Times' announced that 'the writer (Dr. Andrew Grant) displays the most extensive and accurate knowledge of astronomy; and the description of Sir John's recently improved instruments, the principle on which the inestimable improvements were founded, the account of the wonderful discoveries in the moon, &c., all are probable and plausible, and have an air of intense verisimilitude.' The 'New Yorker' considered the discoveries 'of astounding interest, creating a newer era in astronomy and science generally.'[1]

In our time a trick of the kind could hardly be expected to succeed so well, even if as cleverly devised and as well executed. The facts of popular astronomy and of general popular science have been more widely disseminated. America, too, more than any other great nation, has advanced in the interval. It was about two years after this pamphlet had appeared, that J. Quincy Adams used the following significant language in advocating the erection of an astronomical observatory at Washington: 'It is

[1] The *Sun* itself claimed to have established the veracity of the account in a manner strongly recalling a well-known argument used by orthodox believers in the Bible account of the cosmogony. Either, say these, Moses discovered how the world was made, or the facts were revealed to him by some one who had made the discovery: but Moses could not have made the discovery, knowing nothing of the higher departments of science; therefore, the account came from the only Being who could rationally be supposed to know anything about the beginning of the world. 'Either,' said the *New York Sun*, speaking of a mathematical problem discussed in the article, 'that problem was predicated by us or by some other person, who has thereby made the greatest of all modern discoveries in mathematical astronomy. We did not make it, for we know nothing of mathematics whatever; therefore, it was made by the only person to whom it can rationally be ascribed, namely Herschel the astronomer, its only avowed and undeniable author.' In reality, notwithstanding this convincing argument, the problem was stolen by Locke from a paper by Olbers, shortly before published, and gave the method followed by Beer and Mädler throughout their selenographical researches in 1833–37.

with no feeling of pride as an American that the remark may be made, that on the comparatively small territorial surface of Europe there are existing more than 130 of these lighthouses of the skies; while throughout the whole American hemisphere there is but one.' At present, some of the finest observatories in the world belong to American cities, or are attached to American colleges; and much of the most interesting astronomical work of this country has been achieved by American observers.

Yet we still hear from time to time of the attempted publication of hoaxes of greater or less ingenuity. It is singular (and I think significant) how often these relate to the moon. There would seem to be some charm about our satellite for the minds of paradoxists and hoaxers generally. Nor are these tricks invariably detected at once by the general public, or even by persons of some culture. I remember being gravely asked (in January 1874) whether an account given in the ' New York World,' purporting to describe how the moon's frame was gradually cracking, threatening eventually to fall into several separate fragments, was in reality based on fact. In the far West, at Lincoln, Nebraska, a lawyer asked me, in February of the present year, why I had not described the great discoveries recently made by means of a powerful reflector erected near Paris. According to the ' Chicago Times,' this powerful instrument had shown buildings in the moon, and bands of workers could be seen with it who manifestly were undergoing some kind of penal servitude, for they were chained together. It was clear, from the presence of these and the absence of other inhabitants, that the side of the moon turned earthwards is a dreary and unpleasant place of abode, the real ' happy hunting grounds ' of the moon lying on her remote and unseen hemisphere.

As gauges of general knowledge, scientific hoaxes have their uses, just as paradoxical works have. No one, certainly no student of science, can thoroughly understand how little some persons know about science, until he has observed how much will be believed, if only published with the apparent authority of a few known names, and announced with a sufficient parade of technical verbiage; nor is it so easy as might be thought, even for those who are acquainted with the facts to disprove either a hoax or a paradox. Nothing, indeed, can much more thoroughly perplex and confound a student of science than to be asked to prove, for example, that the earth is not flat, or the moon not inhabited by creatures like ourselves; for the circumstance that such a question is asked implies ignorance so thorough of the very facts on which the proof must be based, as to render argument all but hopeless from the outset. I have had a somewhat wide experience of paradoxists, and have noted the experience of De Morgan and others who, like him, have tried to convince them of their folly. The conclusion at which I have arrived is, that to make a rope of sand were an easy task compared with the attempt to instil the simpler facts of science into paradoxical heads.

I would make some remarks, in conclusion, upon scientific or quasi-scientific papers not intended to deceive, but yet presenting imaginary scenes, events, and so forth, described more or less in accordance with scientific facts. Imaginary journeys to the sun, moon, planets, and stars ; travels over regions on the earth as yet unexplored ; voyages under the sea, through the bowels of the earth, and other such narratives, may, perhaps, be sometimes usefully written and read, so long as certain conditions are fulfilled by the narrator. In the first place, while adopting, to preserve the unities, the tone of one relating facts which actually occurred, he should not suffer even the simplest among his readers to lie under the least misapprehension as to the true nature of the narrative. Again, since of necessity established facts must in such a narrative appear in company with the results of more or less probable surmise, the reader should have some means of distinguishing where fact ends and surmise begins. For example, in a paper I once wrote, entitled ' A Journey to Saturn,' I was not sufficiently careful to note that while the appearances described in the approach towards the planet were in reality based on the observed appearances as higher and higher telescopic powers are applied to the planet, others supposed to have been seen by the visitors to Saturn, when actually within his system, were only such as might possibly or probably be seen, but for which we have no real evidence. In consequence of this omission, I received several enquiries about these matters. ' Is it true,' some wrote, ' that the small satellite Hyperion ' (scarce discernible in powerful telescopes, while Titan and Japetus on either side are large) ' is only one of a ring of small satellites travelling between the orbits of the larger moons ? '—as the small planets travel between the paths of Mars and Jupiter. Others asked on what grounds it was said that the voyagers found small moons circling about Titan, the giant moon of the Saturnian system, as the moons of Jupiter and Saturn circle around those giant members of the solar system. In each case, I was reduced to the abject necessity of explaining that there was no evidence for the alleged state of things, which, however, might nevertheless exist. Scientific fiction which has to be interpreted in that way is as bad as a joke that has to be explained. In my ' Journey to the Sun ' I was more successful (it was the earlier essay, however); insomuch that Professor Young, of Dartmouth College (Hanover, N.H.), one of the most skilful solar observers living, assured me that, with scarcely a single exception, the various phenomena described corresponded exactly with the ideas he had formed respecting the probable condition of our luminary.[1] But I must confess that my own experience was not, on the whole, favourable to that kind of popular science writing. It appeared to me that the more thoroughly the writer of such an essay has studied any particular scientific subject, the less able must he be to write a fictitious narrative respecting it. Just as those ignorant of any subject are often the readiest to theorise about it, because least hampered by exact knowledge, so I think that the careful avoidance of any exact study of the details of a scientific subject must greatly facilitate the writing of a fictitious narrative respecting it. But, unfortunately, a narrative written under such conditions, however interesting to the general reader, can scarcely forward the propagation of scientific knowledge, one of the qualities claimed for fables of the kind. As an instance in point, I may cite Jules Verne's ' Voyage to the Moon,' where (apart, of course, from the inherent and intentional absurdity of the scheme itself), the circumstances which are described are calculated to give entirely erroneous ideas about the laws of motion. Nothing could be more amusing, but at the same time nothing more scientifically absurd, than the story of the dead dog Satellite, which, flung out of the travelling projectile, becomes a veritable satellite, moving always beside the voyagers ; for with whatever velocity the dog had been expelled by them with that same velocity would he have retreated continually from their projectile abode, whose own attraction on the dog would have had no appreciable effect in checking his departure. Again, the scene when the projectile reaches the neutral point between the earth and moon, so that there is no longer any gravity to keep the travellers on the floor of their travelling car, is well conceived (though, in part, somewhat profane); but, in reality, the state of things described as occurring there would have prevailed throughout the journey. The travellers would no more be drawn earth-

[1] I had at the same time the good fortune to satisfy in equal degree, though quite unexpectedly, an English student of the sun, who at that time bore me no great goodwill. Something in the article chanced to suggest that it came from another, presumably a rival, hand; while an essay which appeared about the same time (the spring of 1872) was commonly but erroneously attributed to me. Accordingly, a leading article in *Nature* was devoted to the annihilation of the writer supposed to be myself, and to the lavish and quite undeserved laudation of the article I had written, which was selected as typifying all the good qualities which an article of the kind should possess. Those acquainted with the facts were much amused by the mistake.

wards (as compared with the projectile itself) than we travellers on the earth are drawn sunwards with reference to the earth. The earth's attracting force on the projectile and on the travellers would be equal all through the journey, not solely when the projectile reached the neutral point; and, being equal on both, would not draw them together.   It may be argued that the attractions were equal before the projectile set out on its journey, and therefore, if the reasoning just given were correct, the travellers ought not to have had any weight keeping them on the floor of the projectile before it started, 'which is absurd.'   But the pressure upon the floor of the projectile at rest is caused by the floor being kept from moving; let it be free to obey gravity, and there will no longer be any pressure: and throughout the journey to the moon, the projectile, like the travellers it contains, is obeying the action of gravity.   Unfortunately, those who are able to follow the correct reasoning in such matters are not those to whom Jules Verne's account would suggest wrong ideas about matters dynamical; the young learner who *is* misled by such narratives is neither able to reason out the matter for himself, nor to understand the true reasoning respecting it.   He is, therefore, apt to be set quite at sea by stories of the kind, and especially by the specious reasoning introduced to explain the events described. In fine, it would seem that such narratives must be valued for their intrinsic interest, just like other novels or romances, not for the quality sometimes claimed for them of combining instruction with amusement.

The Signal.

THE day is come for the ship to sail, and for John to go to sea,
And his aged mother is fretting with the bairnie on her knee;
The morning meal is scarcely touched; and the wife is still for
    sorrow,
For her good man will soon be gone, and she will be lone to-morrow:
Black clouds are lowering in the sky, but between them streams
    the sun,
With the light of hope in the dark time that for her is just
    begun.
Oh, may his heart keep as true as hers, and the ship in safety run!

And now they are waiting on the beach, and John, with uneasy
    breath,
Is fearing to say the sad Farewell—farewell, the shadow of death;
They have little to say, and little know of writing in the books,
But though they have lack of words, they can talk to each other
    with looks;
They can feel the heart in the hand, and read what is written in
    eyes;
They can tell of their joys and their sorrows in kisses and in sighs,
And so can they speak to each other without the words of the wise.

There is the good ship, the Mary Ann, at her moorings in the bay;
And a boat is grating on the sand, and ready to sail away
To the waiting ship with John and his mates. Ah, there's the
    signal gun!
And the husband turns to kiss his wife, and they to each other run:
It is over at last, and her good man is with the other tars;
She will, weeping, watch the good ship go till the dark clouds
    hide the spars;
And then for long lonely nights by the sea below the silent stars.

GUY ROSLYN.

From Dreams to Waking.

BY E. LYNN LINTON.

CHAPTER IV.

GRAZIELLA.

'SWEETER than ever!' was Venetia's first thought of her pretty little friend as she met her at the station, and Graziella appeared at the door of the carriage with her indolent grace and helpless air, part appealing, part commanding; as if she expected heaven and earth to come to her aid—or, at all events, men of all sorts to give her a helping hand. 'How glad she was that the dear little thing had come!' thought again the loving, good, unselfish heart, as the Creole was safely lifted from the carriage and deposited on the platform by the master himself. 'What a delightful summer they would have together—Graziella, Ernest, and herself! Could anything be more perfect?'

As they drove home, Venetia's lap encumbered with her friend's multitudinous wraps and belongings, while in Graziella's were some of the most beautiful flowers to be found in the Oak-tree garden, her thoughts carried her into a rose-coloured heaven where she saw themselves as a triad of faith, love, and friendship; Ernest loving Graziella partly for her own sweet sake and partly because she, Venetia, loved her so much; and Graziella loving Ernest for the same cause and in the same way. And she herself? She stood between the two as the link and partaker on both sides;—happy, oh how happy! for the love that she bestowed, for the love that she received, and for that of which she was the blessed and believing medium.

But while she dreamt this, Graziella, looking into her face smiling and silent as if her love were too big for words, her happiness needed no expression, thought for her own part: 'I wonder what we shall do this year? I hope it will be amusing; but the people here are rather mopy and Venetia herself is mopy too. And I wonder what this Mr. Pierrepoint of hers is like; and if he is very much in love with her; and if he will admire me. I should think he would. Venetia is not looking very well, I think. That hat is not becoming to her; mine is a beauty; and I know that I am just now in my best looks.'

Aloud she said:

'Darling, dearest Venny, how glad I am to be with you again, and how sweet it was of you to have me! What a happy time we shall have together, just like the old days when no one had come between us!'

'And no one has now,' Venetia answered, tenderly.

'Oh yes, there has!' sighed Graziella. 'No one can love two people exactly alike; and I am not the first with you now, as I used to be.'

'You are, Gracie; you are!' said Venetia.

'Am I?' said the Creole, with a sudden light in her eyes. 'Shall I put you to the test?'

'You might—I should not fail you!' answered her friend; and Graziella, sliding her hand under Venetia's arm, clung to her caressingly, and said:

'And I believe you, Venny—my own Venny, now and always!'

'Now and always,' echoed Venetia, who, having no portion of that strange sense of hidden things known as second sight, believed Graziella's spoken words in their entirety and knew nothing of those left unsaid in the cradle of the thought. Alas for the poor dreamers who build their world out of the mist and the rainbow, and do not see the precipices and the quicksands at their feet!

Belton Forest had seldom been so rich in social novelties as it was at this time. It could scarcely be said that either Ernest Pierrepoint or Venetia had palled on the people as yet; while Graziella, who had been here once before when she and Venetia were mere school-girls and not out, now came before the world as a beautiful young lady in the position of a prize, and with possibilities of fascination unfathomed and unknown.

Then there was Colonel Camperdown at the Elms; practically a stranger, though he had been born here and all the world that was old enough remembered him some five-and-twenty years ago as a troublesome young scamp in the tadpole stage, with a smile that took the heart clean out of the women and that made even the men forgive his delinquencies, which were many; with a curly crop of bright brown hair, and a pair of honest eyes that looked up frankly into your face while he confessed to some boyish enormity with that unflinching honesty which earns a thrashing oftener than does the half-hearted whine for pardon of a coward.

All the world too remembered his going through the regular gradations from tadpole to pickle, and all the rest of it, till he emerged into his final condition as a smart young officer who flashed into their dull world once or twice, like a nineteenth-century Apollo disguised as Mars; when his local light was suddenly eclipsed by that inexorable War Office which sent him off to India as one of the Cornelia's gifts of which the mother country is so prodigal. Now, when he came back at thirty-three, with bad health and an illustrious name, he came back as one practically unknown; one whom the neighbourhood was proud to honour, and whom those who were so inclined might put in unfriendly contrast with Mr. Ernest Pierrepoint. For whatever the merits of this other might be, he had not that passport to the consideration of a country community, of having been known to the people from his birth. And we all know how very much superior to every kind of foreign potentate are the local *aristoi*, even of the lowest degree.

Somehow, though there were other possibilities and other *dramatis personæ*—e.g. little Tommy Clark, the doctor's son who played Schumann and Chopin with real feeling and comprehension; Mr. Baughton, the curate and as some one once called him a very 'dungeon of learning;' Captain Blakey on half-pay, though with fifty years at his back, admirably preserved and a fine figure of a man still; the Backhouse girls at the Elms and the Fenton boys at the Limes—every one felt that the real interest in the social drama enacting and to be enacted for the summer, did and would lie in Venetia and Ernest Pierrepoint, Graziella and Colonel Camperdown. Perhaps Charley Mossman might be thrown in to make the running, as they say on the turf, with Emily Backhouse as the consolation prize of failure; but the true drama would be played out by these four. How would they act? Would they fit themselves together according to the arrangement assigned by common consent? or would any two of them perversely try for the same *rôle*, and thus destroy the balance of forces as at present constituted, and create confusion in the plan of order? This was what remained to be seen; and meanwhile the curtain drew up and the play began.

The feasts of our ancestors have left an indelible impress on us, their descendants; and the libations which it was obligatory on the old heathens to pour out to the gods are transferred, by survival, to the throats of our friends. Colonel Camperdown's return was therefore the signal for a succession of dinners and suppers, where each house would regulate its bill of fare after the same set pattern, and where the company would be as little varied as the dishes. And the one who headed the series was Charley Mossman. The married people were somewhat disconcerted by his precipitancy; and more than one lady said that it was a great piece of presumption on his part; and that, if he had understood the world and the proprieties as he ought, he would have waited until the rector, or some one of like authority, had sent out invitations before he had taken it on himself to give Colonel Camperdown a dinner. He was always putting himself forward, that young man; and really some one ought to take him down and give him a lesson. Nevertheless, those who hit him hardest behind his back accepted his invitation 'with pleasure,' and his dinner promised to be as great a success as the ball had been before it.

Among the guests were of course Ernest Pierrepoint and the two girls from Oak-tree House. This was the first time that Graziella and Ernest had met, or that Colonel Camperdown had seen this third member of the triad—poor Venetia's holy alliance, in which she believed with such touching good faith, such pathetic power of idealising and making beautiful that which was her own creation only, built upon the slenderest foundations.

As the host's most intimate friend, Ernest occupied the place of ' mistress ' in the middle of the table, opposite the well-looking, good-natured young squire. He had had assigned to him one of the dowagers; but to make amends, Graziella, fairy-like, exquisitely beautiful Graziella, had been placed on his other band. In spite of his generous sentiments about the best to win, and the like, Charley had indemnified himself for the social exigencies which had burdened him too with a dowager, and the most awful of them all, by giving himself Venetia on his left. Perhaps under this arrangement lay a half-unconscious hope that the race was not quite over, and that Graziella might—who knows?—effect a diversion. Ernest was notoriously fickle, and he, Charley, did not think that there was a real engagement between him and Venetia. It might be; but he did not think it. Apparently, to himself however, he placed Venetia on his left as the respect due to the heiress of the place, and so was able to eat his dinner with a clear conscience.

Meanwhile Colonel Camperdown, at the head of the table, surveyed the feast which had been made for him with an air of general benevolence. Inwardly he asked himself why he should be required to give himself an indigestion because he had come from India in shaky health and his townsfolk were glad to see him; but outwardly he was resigned and amiable enough, and soon found his interest in looking at Venetia and Graziella. They were beautiful enough to attract any man; and the Colonel was far too true a gentleman to be indifferent to the charms of women. It is only churls who are that. And as he had just come home and was as yet profoundly indifferent to local politics, save where he knew the people, he had heard nothing of the undercurrent of things; and would not have cared if he had been told. He had not fathomed his half-sister Emily's liking for Charley Mossman, nor Charley's now waning, now rekindling, devotion to Venetia. He knew nothing of the unspoken affair between her and Ernest Pierrepoint, which the world had settled to its satisfaction long ago; while he was ignorant who was this pretty little dark-haired creature with eyes like dusky stars, a waist that a man could span with his two hands, and that look in her face which seemed as if she was destined to make the sorrow of those who loved her—that look which belongs to the women who have passion, coquetry, jealousy, love of love, and the need of supremacy, but who all the time lack truth and depth—that look which burns the hearts of men like fire, but which never gives them peace.

He gave however a good deal of silent attention to the two girls; rather to the loss of his immediate neighbours, whom, being uninteresting, he somewhat neglected; and before the dinner was over he had made out two things for which he took to himself the credit of a discoverer: one, that this good-natured host of theirs admired Miss Greville immensely; the other that Miss Greville did more than admire Mr. Pierrepoint. For the pretty little dark-haired, bright-eyed stranger he had no difficulty in finding a theory to fit. She belonged to Ernest Pierrepoint. It was the necessity of circumstance—the apportionment of fate. The two had that sure but undefinable affinity which goes by the name of being made for each other. And Colonel Camperdown believed in affinities.

Miss Greville, with her sweet pure face, was not, so he thought, 'made' for this handsome but, to him, not fascinating young man. There was something about him that struck Harold Camperdown —a man of the world, but an upright gentleman as well—as not quite straight, not quite real. The lacquer was well laid on; but it was lacquer, it was not gold; and the Colonel found it out. It irritated him, he scarcely knew why—only that the best men are small, the strongest weak, in the matter of a pretty woman's regard—to see the loving glance, the happy, trustful smile which Venetia every now and then sent across the table to her two friends; while Graziella played off her sweetest airs on Ernest, and Ernest played off his most fascinating wiles on Graziella, till the two got more and more absorbed in each other and less and less mindful to reply to her pretty telegraphy. And who was this young fellow, thought the Colonel in secret displeasure, that he should have for his own share the two prettiest girls at the table, while every one else had to be content with a dowager or a dowdy? The Colonel had the strongest desire in the world to cut out this handsome, but to him artificial and unreal, young fellow in the good graces of one or other of his fair friends ; and he looked at both girls critically as he asked himself which? For the moment he could not answer. He would have to see them a little closer—know them a little better, before he could make up his mind ; but he did make up his mind that Ernest Pierrepoint should not have both at his feet, and that he would lower his objectionable crest by so much.

Meanwhile, had Ernest and Graziella given words to the main thread of their thoughts, with him it would have been :

' What a beautiful little creature ! what a perfect specimen of her kind ! How pale my Venetia looks to-night ! All the colour seems to be washed out of her. She is more lily-like, more statuesque than ever—very lovely all the same—yet what a delightful contrast this rich colour and hidden fire makes with her ! What a lucky fellow he will be whom this little enchantress will one day love ! '

With her the chant would have run simply thus :

' Venetia has deceived herself, poor thing ! This handsome man does not really love her ; and he will love me.'

In articulate speech their conversation was all about Cuba and flowers, starry nights and burning days ; of the children of the sun and the children of the mist ; of the coldness, the fogs, the absence of colour and of sunlight in England ; of the want of finesse and keen comprehension in the English people—specially in English women, and of these specially in the very fair women ; of the eloquence of eyes—dark eyes the most eloquent ; of the exquisite gift of beauty—dark beauty the most exquisite ; of the strange sympathies of souls ; and of the heavenly charm there was in finding something absolutely perfect to one whose nature was so refined, attuned to such superior melodies as not to be satisfied with anything short of perfection. It was the fountain springing in the desert, the tree in the wild waste that Byron speaks of, and that only such men as Ernest Pierrepoint could fully appreciate. And of such men as he there were few to be found—about as few as there were such exquisite examples of human perfection as she.

In short, he unfolded all the well-worn embroideries which he had formerly unfolded for the benefit of Venetia, simply changing the key of colour ; while Graziella took them up and played with them, turning aside his compliments with a grace, a dexterity which to most people would have seemed, in view of her youth and inexperience, utterly appalling as a forecast of the mature future that had to come,

To Ernest, however, it was enchanting; not the less so because so wholly different from Venetia. He was a good Catholic in the way of women; and would have blushed to have owned himself incapable of adding to the number of his canonisations. He had never understood why one should hold the way against another; why admiring a blonde should hinder him from making love to a brunette; why, having won the heart of Venetia, he should not try to win that of Graziella. The two things were distinct and different; as different as were the natures of the two girls themselves. Venetia had accepted everything in child-like faith, in simple sweetness of trust; Graziella fenced and parried and refused either to understand or to accept. The one had satisfied the man's vanity by the surrender of her deepest love, her idealising adoration, with very little trouble of trying on his part; the other piqued and disowned, and by its very difficulty made the final victory a thing to be desired and pursued. The one had been the facile conquest of a heart; the other was the keen encounter of wits—which at this moment was the more exciting of the two.

Venetia's love so frankly given, so ingenuously shown, had been delightful enough to Ernest while quite fresh, and while she was the prettiest girl in the place; and perhaps had no other distraction turned him aside he would have finally drifted into an engagement which would not have been entirely his voluntary choice. Now, when she had a rival, beautiful, dexterous, full of subtlety and fire, of languid grace and trenchant words, the softer fascinations of his Beautiful Lady, his Beatrice, his lily, as he used to call her, came to be somewhat pale and tame; and before the dinner was well over the young man had decided that it was absolutely necessary for his happiness, and to maintain the rightful balance of things, that he should make Graziella Despues in love with him:—when he would be better able to determine how true was his love for Venetia than he could possibly do now, without such an alternative.

Nevertheless he was not minded to lose Venetia's heart for this adjustment of the balance, this scientific determination of the dynamics of love. If gratitude for love had no more vitality with him than with the average man, vanity had. Wherefore, when he came into the drawing-room in the last detachment of gentlemen, and found Colonel Camperdown seated opposite to Venetia, talking pleasantly to her while she leaned back in her compartment of the ottoman and answered him with smiles and graceful girlish cordiality, a flood of jealousy rushed over him, and he felt all the man's natural desire to hold what he had already grasped, and to allow of no rivals near the throne where he had once been seated. Graziella, a little apart, was surrounded by half the young men in the room; but he let that pass. He was suddenly indifferent to her; hers being an affair of the future. The affair of the present was this conversation of Venetia with Colonel Camperdown, and the necessity that he was under of making spokes that should check the play of intrusive wheels.

He knew his power; and when he also drew a chair opposite to the girl, and entered into the conversation afloat between her and the Colonel, it was no surprise to him, however soothing to his pride, to see her sweet face brighten from brow to chin, and the trustful eyes raise themselves to his with that look of innocent worship which said so plainly where she placed him and how she held him. He smiled with a certain air of acknowledged proprietorship which set Colonel Camperdown's teeth on edge, as he bent forward to speak to her with a familiarity of tone and bearing not quite in such good taste as he prided himself on possessing. But Venetia said nothing of the impertinence. She only accepted the familiarity as affection; and so went home happy—as those are who live in fools' paradises, and whom false love and a mocking fortune cheat into smiles with empty dreams.

Graziella, who had seen and understood the whole of this little comedy, could scarcely be called as happy as her friend. Woof and warp of her character were alike shot through and through with jealousy, with the imperious need of domination. But being young she had still the tender germs of something that, with great care and cultivation, might eventually have passed muster for a conscience; and was thus desirous to be a little on the right side of the thorny hedge of honour. Hence, when they reached home, and the evening with its opening possibilities was at an end—while Ernest was making his smoke-rings into vapoury likenesses of Graziella's lovely little curls—Venetia's forgotten; while Colonel Camperdown was asking her people to tell him about that fellow—who he was and what he was doing here—in a tone of profound contempt and with feelings in harmony with his tone; while Charley Mossman was taking himself to task for folly on the one hand, in that he was running after a shadow which would never take substance and be caught, and for bad faith on the other, in that he was trying to cut out Pylades—Graziella, leaning back in her easy chair, Venetia kneeling by her side, suddenly raised herself into a sitting posture, broke off their girlish talk on this and that and him and her, and said abruptly:

'Venny, are you engaged to Mr. Pierrepoint?'

At the first instant Venetia thought to say 'Yes.' She felt

engaged to him ; and feeling stands for fact with the poor deluded creatures who are what is called in love.   But a moment's reflection made her blush and hesitate.   Apparently so simple, it was in point of fact a difficult question to answer ; almost impossible, indeed !   Was she engaged ?   Yes and No !   But she could not say this Yes and No to Graziella, looking at her so intently with eyes no longer languid, liquid, veiled, but opened to their fullest ; burning, fiery, intense, eyes that seemed as if they went down into her very soul.

'Are you, Venny ?' repeated the Creole, in a voice deeper than was usual with her.

'Not exactly,' stammered Venetia, turning away her head and suddenly becoming very white.

'Not exactly?   What an answer !   You must be one or the other.   Which do you mean, Ven ?' said Graziella, with disdain.

'Well, I mean that we understand each other,' she replied, looking now into Graziella's face.

'No! what you mean is, that you are in love with him and that he has not made you an offer,' returned Graziella.   'Has he made you an offer, Ven ?'

'Not in plain words,' was the answer spoken with a sudden spasm of pain and dread.

Graziella laughed.

'What a dear, stupid thing you are !' she said, prettily, crouching back in her easy chair in her old supple, graceful attitude. 'You are two years older than I, and ten years younger.   I am not a young lady out in the world as you are, I am only a schoolgirl ; but I know things a thousand times better.   If Mr. Pierrepoint has not made you an offer in plain words he has not made you an offer at all, and you are not engaged.'

'He certainly has not made me an offer,' said Venetia, still with that pain about her heart; 'but I can trust him, and we understand each other,' she repeated.

Graziella shrugged her shoulders.

'If it were my affair I would rather have it distinct than taken on trust,' she said, her eyes flashing with their fierce jealous light. Then she veiled them beneath their heavy lids and curling lashes, and added, caressingly : 'But you are quite safe, Venny ; no one could take him from such a darling as you are.'

'Do you think so?' said Venetia, with a sudden sense of relief. 'It is not that however, but that he is too good and true to deceive me ; and he has made me feel that he loves me.'

'All the same, he is free and so are you,' was Graziella's reply, made slowly,

'And I would not care to keep him by a promise if he was not kept by inclination,' said Venetia, tenderly.

'Ah! you are more unselfish than I am. I would not let any one go who had once made love to me as you say Mr. Pierrepoint has to you!' said Graziella, passionately. 'What has once been mine shall always be mine; no other person shall have it or take it from me. You, Venny, shall never have another friend; and the man who has once said he loved me shall never have another lover. I would kill him;—and you too, if you did!'

'You will never have cause to kill me, darling,' said Venetia, smiling. 'I could not have another friend like you, and no one could desert you for any one else.'

Graziella laughed softly.

'Well! one day I shall put your prophecy to the proof,' she said, in her most caressing manner. 'I daresay I shall not die before I have heard some one say he loves me.'

'A dozen!' said Venetia.

'One would be enough, if *the* one,' said Graziella, with an air of resignation.

And then they both laughed and kissed each other; and so parted for the night: Venetia happy as the happiest, quite recovered from that vague dread which had possessed her when brought face to face with the fact that Ernest never had really made her an offer, never had done more than suggest, insinuate, make her believe in his love;—Graziella, with a serene conscience saying to herself:

'They are not engaged, so there is no dishonour in trying!'

CHAPTER V.

SHADOWS.

WOULD that sketch of the old mill ever be finished? It had been such a pleasant labour of love to the two young people principally concerned, that really they had not the courage to put the finishing strokes to their work, even though they might have found some other such patient sitter for their pastime. The old mill had come to be to Venetia like a sweet and sacred depository of her thoughts, her happiness, her love. She had no wish to leave it for any other; to make, as it were, a second temple that would want something of the holiness, the entirety of this. Wherefore it was that when Graziella·came the sketches were still incomplete, and she was thus admitted into the adytum as the third member of poor Venetia's trinity of faith, love, and friendship.

But before they went on the expedition which was to form,
as it were, a stage or landing-place in their relations together,
Ernest was a great deal at Oak-tree House, where, if he made
love to Venetia, he certainly did not forget Graziella whose power
of fascination over him grew daily stronger and was daily more
clearly shown.   This was perhaps Venetia's happiest time.   It
was the fulfilment of her dream, the perfect satisfaction of her two
great affections ; and as the intimacy between these two dear ones
of her life increased, so did her delight.   So far as things had
gone yet she had not the smallest pretext for uneasiness ; and she
was not of the kind to make pretexts that were not supplied by
events.   If they liked each other, each loved her, and the harmony
of all three was absolutely perfect.

One day, however, Ernest proposed that the old mill should be
again 'attacked,' to see what they could make of its lights and
shadows, its bounding lines and tender curves; and of course
Graziella was now to be one of the sketchers, together with her
friend and the 'uncommitted' lover of that friend.

'You sketch, of course ?' said Ernest, turning to Graziella,
after he had made the proposition to Venetia and Venetia had
accepted it with her tender smile and radiant face.

The pretty little Creole whose trees were like cabbages and
her clouds like rocks, whose cows were like rhinoceroses, and her
men forked radishes, lifted up her lovely eyes and said : 'Oh yes,
I sketch, of course!' with as much coolness and courage as if she
had been a member of one of the water-colour societies, and looked
to be some day pricked for A.R.A.

On which Ernest professed himself enchanted, but not surprised.   He had divined as much, he said with his flattering
smile ; which meant that to his mind Miss Despues must necessarily have all the arts as well as all the graces of womanhood—
that she must have poetry, intellect, the creative faculty and
technical skill, as well as star-like eyes, a waist that you could span,
adorable hands and feet, hair like a dusky veil, and beauty and
perfection all round.   After which pleasant little swinging of the
censer—Venetia standing by looking at Graziella lovingly, and so
glad that Ernest Pierrepoint saw her charms so clearly !—the two
girls put on their hats, brought out their books, and the three set
off.

Of course it was only right.   Venetia understood that quite
well and had not a reproach to make.   Graziella was the stranger
and the friend, and Ernest ought to pay more attention to her
than to herself.   She was too secure to need assuring ; but Graziella—that was different ! No, it was quite right ; and not a shade

of jealousy or distrust stirred the calm lake of her gentle mind when Ernest busied himself with the Creole, chose for her the best place after endless difficulties and as much serious deliberation as if the happiness of a life had depended on the nice conjunction of shade and convenience—arranged her shawl, her book, her lights and her lines, and devoted himself to her with the same fervour, the same absorption, as he had formerly shown to Venetia.

She, 'poor darling' as Graziella repeatedly called her, while laughing at the little sacrifices that she was required to make, so far from being exalted and attended to to-day was put under strict requisition for her friend's benefit. Her best sketching pencil, her shawl because it was the softest, the stone which Ernest had brought from some little distance as a footstool—all were begged for Miss Despues by Ernest; and Venetia had no wish to refuse. It agreed too well with her unselfish temper, with her love for the little queen of the hour, with her liking to do as Mr. Pierrepoint wished, and with her desire to make Graziella happy; so that this transfer of care only echoed her own thoughts and wishes, and she was glad to see the man whom she loved so kindly occupied with her dearest friend.

Nevertheless, down in the remotest corner of her heart she wished that Ernest would speak to her a little more than he did —just a little more—not to deprive Graziella but to be included. If her place was between these two, as she had said to herself, she felt somewhat more crushed than she had anticipated. She was less the link than the obstacle; or rather less the link than the wedge, which was being a little set aside. And again, though no more vain than she was jealous or self-seeking, it hurt the artistic sense in her, the consciousness of truth, to be told that Graziella's botch had the true artistic feeling, while her really good and careful study was too cold, too timid, the shading here wrong, the lines there out of drawing. They had been tender, delicate, suggestive, sweet; but each day has its adjectives, and those which were told off to Venetia to-day were not the choicest.

All this was nothing more than a vague feeling, an unformed thought; like the beginning of pain to a person asleep and before awaking has brought with it consciousness. She was not suffering actively, she merely felt that something was out of tune and that she was not quite so happy as usual.

While they were sitting there, Ernest talking apparently for the benefit of both but in reality addressing himself to Graziella, they heard a footfall come softly through the bushes and the bracken by the water's edge, and Harold Camperdown drew in sight, a rod in his hand, and a fishing basket at his back, whipping the stream for trout. Seeing the triad sitting there, he left the water and came up to the wall, leaning his arms on the parapet while he spoke to them all, but looked especially at Venetia. Her face, too much the mirror of her feelings for her peace, perhaps for her dignity, though gentle as always—that was of necessity —was a little saddened and overcast; while Graziella's dark eyes burned and beamed beneath their lashes like one on the secret track of a coming triumph; and Ernest had that air which a man puts on when he is doing his best to fascinate a woman—that air which women love as the expression of his desire to please, and which men among themselves denounce with disdain as 'coxcombry.' But then men are jealous, and resent each other's successes.

Some contradictious demon put it into Harold Camperdown's head to adopt a flirting manner that was not quite his way to women; to pay compliments of a rather glaring kind to Graziella, half in fun as to a child, half in earnest as to a woman; to praise her sketching—which cost him something—but, though a fine fellow enough, he was no purist and slipped into the smaller sins without much consideration; to look into her eyes with an admiration somewhat too boldly expressed in his own; while every now and then he gave a more serious attention, a more chivalrous and respectful heed to Venetia, and made her feel rather than openly conveyed his admiration. All this irritated Ernest horribly; and all the more so as Colonel Camperdown had a kind of high-handed indifference about him which expressed the most supreme disregard of Mr. Pierrepoint's likings and dislikings —a manner which men understand so well among each other, and which even women see plainly enough.

Though Ernest was so sure of Venetia that he had no fear of her wandering into strange pastures, he nevertheless disliked intensely all that looked like interference with his rights—however vague that interference, however shadowy and unexpressed those rights; while as for Graziella, his newest fancy and therefore the most coveted for the time, he was even more indignant that any man should presume to trespass here on ground which he wished to fence in for himself—while he took time to consider which of the two he would cultivate. In the days to come he might be glad of some one to take one or other of these two fair ones off his hands, but for the present he wished to keep them both safe, and in the balance. Hence he was indignant exceedingly; and to Venetia put on the airs of a martyr a little out of temper, while to Graziella he redoubled all his powers of fascination, and made her feel herself a prize for which two men were contending—the choice left in her own hands.

Colonel Camperdown was not the kind of man to care for the displeasure of any other man in the matter of women, or indeed of aught else ; so he flirted with Graziella and talked to Venetia as much as he wished—and a great deal more than poor Venetia liked ; and after he had spent half-an-hour pleasantly enough in this pastime he took his leave, and Venetia's punishment began.

This was the first time that Ernest had been angry with her since their acquaintance—that perilous acquaintance which had ripened into such disastrous depth of love with her !—the first time that a ripple had come on the smooth surface of their intimacy ; the first time that she had felt 'in disgrace,' or been other than his Queen and his Beautiful Lady. It was something so strange to her to watch the change that had suddenly come over Mr. Pierrepoint ; to see him turn away from her, devoting himself to Graziella with feverish absorption while ignoring her herself as if she did not exist ; to feel that all her pretty little tender efforts for reconciliation went for nothing, and that, though not rough nor brutal—which was not his way—her hero was decidedly cross and unappeasable,—that at first she could hardly take it in. What did it all mean ? If she entered into the conversation which he was keeping up with Graziella, he withdrew from it, or answered only exactly so much as and no more than the nicest politeness demanded. If she asked him, as she did once : 'Is this right, Mr. Pierrepoint ? ' handing him her drawing-book, he looked at the work coldly, and gave it back to her with an indifferent : 'Oh yes ! it will do ! ' as if it really did not signify how she rendered that old mill with its broken wheel and mossy roof, as if what she did were unworthy more serious consideration. But meanwhile he almost oppressed Graziella with his cares, eager as she was for adulation ; and made the contrast in his manner to the two so evident, that those weak and sickly germs of what might have become a conscience were just a little painfully stirred. Graziella was well content to be the first, as, she said to herself, she deserved to be by virtue of her beauty, but Venetia need not have been made such a very bad second so suddenly ! The lower place would have to come, but the descent might have been a little more gradual. Nevertheless she was not going to quarrel with Mr. Pierrepoint because he chose to pay her a little more attention than he chose to pay Venetia, who was a great goose for showing how much she loved him. ' It never answers ! ' said Graziella to herself, made wise by temperament if not by experience ; so she received all his cares and his compliments with the

most enchanting manner of right, and as if she were wholly unconscious of any cause whereby her friend should feel hurt.

This pitiful little comedy went on till the afternoon was at
an end—the longest afternoon that Venetia had ever spent ;—
would that preliminary sketch of Graziella's never be done ?—when
the necessities of social existence contained in the dinner hour
made themselves felt, and the terribly divided triad had to return
home. Even then Ernest did not relent ; and when he shook
hands with the girls and wished them good-bye, he said to
Graziella, keeping her hand while looking into her face with an expression of the most intense interest and entreaty in his own :
' And to-morrow, Miss Despues ? May I have the happiness of
giving you another lesson to-morrow ? Not that you need much
instruction, but I am a little more used to the brush than you.'
To Venetia he only said : ' Good evening, Miss Greville,' coldly,
scarcely holding her hand at all.

The consequence of which was that Venetia, being no strong-
minded woman who could whistle her love down the wind without
much more trouble than she would have in throwing away an old
dress when she was tired of it, but being simply a very affectionate,
very tender, and entirely feminine girl desperately in love, went
upstairs to her own room and cried till her pretty blue eyes were
swollen to about half their ordinary size, her dear little nose red and
unsightly, and her fair, sweet, flower-like cheeks patched with red
and white and green and purple all in the wrong places. Which
means that, being unhappy, she made herself more unhappy still,
and added personal disfigurement to mental distress.

To all of which Graziella was discreetly blind. But she had
never made herself so charming to her friend as she did this
evening; never been so thoroughly the little heroine of romance,
that poor Venetia's idealising fancy had made her. It did a little
towards soothing the unhappy child in this her first initiation into
the anguish of love; but it did not do much. The heart is not
like a pint bottle, imperial measure, which can hold only so much,
and so much, and which thus cannot be filled with gall by one
when another has poured into it honey up to the neck—which
can love only one at a time, and feel only one set of feelings at a time.
Graziella was not Ernest, and her sweetness could not undo his
displeasure. It simply soothed for the moment in view of
Graziella herself; but the sting left by Ernest remained and
smarted as bad as ever.

The only allusion which Graziella permitted herself to make
to the facts of the day, she made when they were parting for the
night. After she had wished her friend good-night, and when she

had got to the door of the room, the handle in her hand, she turned round, and said with a certain under-current of disdain, finely marked beneath the surface tenderness :

' I would not cry if I were you, Venny dear ; you will only spoil your face and do no earthly good to yourself or any one else. If you have offended any one, crying all by yourself will not make you good friends again ; and if you have been unlucky enough to fall in love with a flirt, making yourself ugly will not make him constant. Good-night, darling, and don't be a goose.'

Which little exordium, touching the spring of poor Venny's trouble, made her cry plentifully for the next two hours, when, weak and sick, she fell asleep and went through a series of uncomfortable dreams.

The next day immediately after luncheon Ernest appeared at Oak-tree House, radiant and re-established. He had slept off his ill-temper, and he did not wish to punish his poor Beatrice, his Beautiful Lady, too heavily for what after all was not her fault. So he entered the drawing-room where the two girls sat ; Graziella, graceful and indolent, curled up on a chair half asleep, slowly fanning herself between times, and at intervals taking up the flowers with which her lap was full like a second Maimouna ; Venetia working hard at some horribly crabbed passages in Jean Paul, the better to distract her errant thoughts—handsome, serene, æsthetic, flattering, delightful as ever. The first glance into his face was sufficient to show Venetia that the cloud had passed ; and when he came up to her and took her hand in his, and held it softly, gently, tenderly as his manner was, and lowered his handsome eyes on her with their old look of admiration, and spoke to her with his old accent of tenderness—that accent which was in itself a confession, a caress—the grave of her sorrow was closed, and her soul went back to the heaven of joy in which it had been living for all these later weeks. She lifted her eyes to him—those sweet loving eyes—and a smile that made her look for the moment like an angel broke over her face, as she faintly returned the pressure of his hand ; and so ratified the treaty of peace that he offered.

All of which Graziella saw between her half-closed lids, and took her measures accordingly ; not by pouting, not by coolness, not by making herself unpleasant in any way, but by the most exquisite sweetness, the most playful good temper, the most fascinating brightness—that was her manner of revenge, the method which she took to break one chain and forge another ; and her common sense told her that it was a more desirable method than the one of coolness and overt jealousy—at least at this stage of affairs.

She was right.   That vagrant fancy of Ernest's, wandering
now here, now there, and never settled anywhere for long, was
more caught by Graziella's piquant indifference than it had been
ever troubled by Venetia's frank bestowal ; all the same, he loved
the latter well to-day, and the three set out to the old mill once
more, apparently as well assorted as Venetia's hope and fancy had
made them.   Venetia was happy in the renewal of confidence and
affection between her and Ernest ; Graziella was happy in the
consciousness of a contest where she would come off victorious ;
and Ernest was happy—what man would not have been ?—with
one pretty girl whom he liked and who loved him, and another
whom he admired and wanted to make love him.   It was the soft
and tender twilight and the brilliant flush of dawn in the same
horizon ; and surely that was enough to fall to one man's share !

They were sitting on the wall, all in high spirits, Ernest paying much devotion to each, when as yesterday Harold Camperdown came up the river, fishing for trout.   As yesterday, the
human attraction on the wall overcame that of the fish in the
waters, and the Colonel left the river to greet the sketchers and
join in a conversation where, good and gallant as he was, no one
wanted him.   He talked as he had talked before, with lightness
and laughter to Graziella, with interest and respect to Venetia.
But this time the Creole, having decided on her action, scarcely
answered, and Ernest took no part in the conversation at all ; so
that the whole burden of the hour rested on Venetia ; by which
her uncommitted lover made a fair excuse to himself for withdrawing Graziella out of danger, and for leaving the other to herself and the Colonel.

Saying a little abruptly, 'The shadows are all wrong for
you to-day, Miss Despues, and if you do not mind coming with
me, I will show you a lovely nook which, I think, will make even a
better picture than this : we will not be long, Miss Greville,'—he
offered his hand to Graziella, to assist her in the difficult task of
putting her delicate little feet to the ground, and the two went off
together ; Venetia feeling herself this time abandoned, which was
almost worse than being somewhat unpolitely snubbed.

She felt herself grow pale as they turned and left.   Was her
heaven to be closed to her again, and so soon ?   Why had this
man come between them a second time ?   What had she done that
he should trouble her peace so cruelly ?   Ah ! how she wished
that he would go, and that she could then show Ernest that she
had no attraction for any man but himself. and that none but him
had any for her !   But the Colonel seemed to have no intention of
going.   On the contrary, he placed himself in a still more con-

venient attitude, and his face had a marked expression of pleasure, as if certain uncongenial elements had been withdrawn. Even Venetia, preoccupied as she was, could not fail to see the change which stole over him, and which she wished that she had not seen. It embarrassed her, and made her feel treacherous against her wish to Ernest.

'Has Mr. Pierrepoint been here long?' began the Colonel, carelessly. But he watched the sweet troubled face bending over the sketch-book while he spoke, though apparently he was absorbed in pulling off the bells of a foxglove that grew against the wall, and snapping them between his fingers.

'About two months,' answered Venetia.

'Did you know him before he came?' was the second question, still made carelessly.

'No,' said Venetia. 'He was—he is Mr. Mossman's friend.'

'A school friend?'

'Yes.'

'I never saw him before I came here, but I have heard of him,' continued Colonel Camperdown, picking a fresh bell. 'A man in my regiment knew him. I remember all about him, now.'

'Yes?' said Venetia; and she said no more. She did not care to ask this man what he knew of Ernest Pierrepoint, what he had heard of him. If true it could be nothing but good; if bad, then it was a falsehood. All the same, she felt it would be disloyal to ask the question; so she said nothing, but went on with her painting which she was rapidly ruining past redemption.

'Yes,' continued the Colonel, in a quiet matter-of-fact kind of voice; 'a man in my regiment knew him only too well. He broke the heart of his favourite sister—killed her as much as if he had put a knife to her throat. Ask him to tell you the story of Amy Craven, and hear what he will say. It was a bad business, Miss Greville.'

'You have heard only one side, Colonel Camperdown,' answered Venetia, with energy. 'You can have heard only one side. Are you just to condemn any one on partial hearsay?'

'There cannot be two sides to such a story,' he said, looking at her steadily.

'Mr. Pierrepoint might say there were,' she replied, with a sudden flash of scorn and anger.

'Do you think so, Miss Greville? Can there be two sides to the story of a man making a girl love him till he had got entire possession of her very soul, then suddenly flinging her off for a fresh fancy whom he abandoned in the same way? Can there be two sides to the history of a man who goes through the world ruining the happiness of women with no more compunction than an entomologist has in catching butterflies ? Mr. Pierrepoint's history is well known ; and no man who had the smallest regard for his sisters, his daughters, or his wife, would allow him free access to his house. Fortunately for my sister Emily, she has not touched that miserable thing he calls his heart ! If she had, I tell you, Miss Greville, I would have shot him before I would have let him tamper with her as he did with poor Amy Craven ! Men know what word to give to such a man ; it is scarcely one to be said before ladies.'

'Then it is not one to be hinted at before me, who am Mr. Pierrepoint's friend,' said Venetia, looking at the Colonel as steadily as he looked at her.

'You are loyal,' he answered, tenderly but very sorrowfully. 'I admire you, Miss Greville ; but I am sorry for you—bitterly sorry !'

'You have no cause to be,' she answered, proudly.

'Poor girl !' he said, softly. 'Remember, I have warned you.'

'I thank you, but I repudiate your warning,' was her reply, her head still held high and her eyes fixed on his.

She said this just as Graziella and Ernest turned the corner and Ernest finished a long speech about the daughter of the sunny south in these words : 'If I had to paint my ideal of a woman, she should be small, dark, soft yet full of passion and fire ; she should have foreign blood in her, and be eminently un-English ; she should have eyes like yours, Miss Despues, and hair like the dusky night—as yours is ; hands and feet as small as yours ; a voice soft and low like yours ; and she should come from some beautiful island in the southern seas, bringing with her the sweet association of flowers, sunshine, and beauty !'

'What a charming person she would be !' said Graziella, simply, as they came in sight of Venetia looking at Harold Camperdown fixedly in the face ; their arrival making her crimson with a strange guilty blush as if she had been caught in some fault.

'What a bold man Colonel Camperdown seems to be !' then said Graziella, under her breath, as they drew near ; and Ernest answered viciously :

'He is a cad !'

Soon after this the Colonel wished them all good-day, and went on up the river with his fishing ; when the shadows suddenly found themselves right and the sketching continued with vigour. But Ernest, struck by that fixed look of Venetia's into Harold Camperdown's face which he caught as he came up, and staggered for a moment into the doubt : Was she absolutely safe after all ? did not repeat his experiment of yesterday. On the contrary, he had never been more charming than he was now. It seemed as if he wished to wipe away to the last and faintest line the remembrance of the displeasure which had caused her so much pain ; as if his love wished to atone for his jealousy. So Venetia read it, and in her reading made herself blessed as of old.

Thus the hours passed without a flaw ; and even Graziella, jealous and exacting as she was, did not grudge her friend the attentions which she was beginning to regard as her own dues. She judged Ernest by herself, and took it to mean the careful covering of a tender plant, the intentional hypocrisy of a man who does not wish the truth to be seen just yet. It was the right thing to do at this part of the play, she thought approvingly ; but soon there must be a change in the method if things were to go smoothly between them. A triumph, to be a triumph for Graziella, must be one transacted in full view of the public !

(To be continued.)

Mrs. Godolphin.

SPEAKING of the white pond-lily, Nathaniel Hawthorne remarks:
'It is a marvel whence this perfect flower derives its loveliness
and perfume, springing, as it does, from the black mud over which
the river sleeps, and where lurk the slimy eel and the speckled frog
and the mud-turtle, whom continual washing cannot cleanse. It
is the very same black mud out of which the yellow lily sucks its
obscene life and noisome odour. Thus we see, too, in the world
that some persons assimilate only what is ugly and evil from the
same moral circumstances which supply good and beautiful results—
the fragrance of celestial flowers—to the daily life of others.'
Very similar appear to have been the reflections of the virtuous
Evelyn on contemplating the pure and saintly character developed
by his charming and accomplished friend, Margaret Blagge, afterwards Mrs. Sidney Godolphin, in the ineffably foul and corrupt
atmosphere of the Court of Charles II. Indeed, he candidly
avows that it was some time before he could bring himself to
believe that any maid of honour accustomed from her childhood to
such scenes of ribaldry and licentiousness, could possibly have preserved an abiding sense of religion and virtue. Though his picture
of the Court as it existed and wallowed in vice, only a week previous
to the death of the merry but graceless monarch, is well known, it
may not be amiss to reproduce it as a moral counterpart of the
reeking and polluted pond whence the fragrant water-lily derived
its beauty and perfume.

'I can never forget,' he wrote, 'the inexpressible luxury and
profaneness, gaming and all dissoluteness, and as it were total forgetfulness of God (it being Sunday evening) which this day
se'nnight I was witness of; the King sitting and toying with his
concubines, Portsmouth, Cleveland, Mazarin, &c., a French boy singing love songs in that glorious gallery, whilst about twenty of the
great courtiers and other dissolute persons were at basset round a
large table, a bank of at least 2,000l. in gold before them, upon
which two gentlemen who were with me made reflections with
astonishment. Six days afterwards all was in the dust.'

And yet in the midst of such hideous and degrading circumstances an orphan girl succeeded in keeping herself unspotted from the world, and in so comporting herself in every relation of life that on her death, in the twenty-sixth year of her age, the afflicted Evelyn wrote in his diary :—

' Never was a more virtuous and inviolable friendship; never a more religious, discreet, and admirable creature, beloved of all, admired of all, for all possible perfections of her sex. She is gone to receive the reward of her signal charity, and all other her Christian graces, too blessed a creature to converse with mortals, fitted as she was by a most holy life to be received into the mansions above. She was for wit, beauty, good-nature, fidelity, discretion, and all accomplishments, the most incomparable person. . . . Her husband, struck with unspeakable affliction, fell down as dead. The King himself and all the Court expressed their sorrow. To the poor and miserable her loss was irreparable, for there was no degree but had some obligation to her memory.'

Margaret Blagge, born on August 2, 1652, was the youngest daughter of Colonel Blagge, Groom of the Bedchamber to Charles I., and among the first to take up arms in defence of his sovereign. In the year after the setting-up of the Royal Standard at Nottingham he is mentioned as being in command of a regiment, and it is matter of history how gallantly he defended Wallingford Castle, marching out with all the honours of war, after capitulating to Sir Thomas Fairfax by the King's authority. Colonel Blagge was also present at the fatal fight at Worcester, and was one of the small band who accompanied the fugitive prince. On the inevitable dispersion of his companions at Boscobel, Charles II. entrusted his diamond George, the same which his father had worn and consigned to Bishop Juxon, to his faithful ' Tom Blague,' as he used to call him, and before his discovery and arrest near Stafford, the Colonel contrived to conceal the precious charge beneath a heap of chips and dust. The historic ' bauble' was brought by Isaac Walton to Colonel Blagge when a prisoner in the Tower, and was carried off by him when he effected his escape, and finally restored to its rightful owner. The brave soldier died within six months after the Restoration, leaving a widow and four daughters with comparatively limited means, his landed property in Suffolk having been sacrificed to the Royal cause. It is pleasant to be able to add, that both Charles II. and his brother the Duke of York took a kindly interest in the welfare of the bereaved children; and Margaret, then only eight years of age, was, in particular, warmly befriended by the noble families of Berkeley and Villiers. It is related of her that, while yet quite a child, she was taken to Paris by the Duchess of Richmond and confided to the

Countess of Guildford, Groom of the Stole to the Queen Mother. Refusing, however, to go to Mass, she was harshly treated by the Countess, until an opportunity occurred of sending her back to her mother, with whom she resided until the plague broke out, when she was taken into Suffolk. From her earliest infancy, Margaret Blagge displayed strong devotional tendencies, which she confirmed by a course of study very unusual at her tender age. So precocious, indeed, were her attainments in godly learning, that Dr. Gunning, Bishop of Ely, felt justified in administering to her the Holy Sacrament before she had attained her twelfth year. It was about this time that the Duchess of York expressed a desire to receive the young child as a maid of honour, and from such a quarter a request was well-nigh tantamount to a command.

As her biographer observes, ' this was indeed a surprising change of air, and a perilous climate for one so very young;' but so guarded and discreet was she in all her ways, that, instead of catching any taint herself, she exercised a wholesome influence over her companions, many of whom were her seniors, and by her evident sincerity and prudence won the love and respect of all who formed her acquaintance. To her unhappy mistress she was affectionately attached, and tended her closely during the trying period of her last illness, when she was neglected by her own husband, and abandoned to the tortures of religious doubts and apprehensions.

On the death of the Duchess, Mistress Blagge—to use the phraseology of that period—was appointed, though not yet sixteen, maid of honour to the Queen ; a distinction coveted by the noblest maidens in the land, though little to the taste of the pious and, for her age, ascetic damsel. So fearful was she of erring even in trifles, that she drew up a set of rules for her daily conduct, in private as well as in public, prescribing certain prayers and reflections for the occupation of her mind while dressing and undressing, and a suitable deportment in church, at meal-times, and when in attendance on her Majesty in the drawing-room. It might be a very prudent restriction, though not highly complimentary to the King, never to permit herself to speak to him, except in brief reply to a direct question; nor could any denunciation of the morals and manners of the Court have been more pointedly severe than this young creature's resolution to take no part in filthy conversation, but rather to express her disapproval by the increased gravity of her demeanour. She also resolved not to meddle with what did not concern her, to refrain from idle curiosity and vain questionings, to keep a watch over her tongue, and to speak simply, truthfully, and without affectation.

' On festival eves,' she wrote, ' I resolve to dine at home, and to repeat all the Psalms I know by heart, reserving my reading or part of my prayers till night ; and sup with bread and beer only.' On Wednesdays and Fridays she took no nourishment until after evening prayers, and, as will presently be seen, carried much too far the mortification of the body. She was, besides, too much given to self-examination, and aimed at a theoretic perfection unattainable by human nature. Her distaste for frivolous amusements, her simplicity of dress in her leisure hours, and her avoidance of the society of courtly gallants, were no doubt primarily a matter of temperament, but became habitual as the result of wise reflection. At the same time she was no austere fanatic, nor averse from lively converse on secular topics. In truth, she was not less admired for her wit, her lively but good-natured raillery and her rare talent of mimicry, than for her beauty and virtue. It is perhaps scarcely surprising that Evelyn should have hesitated for a time to credit the genuineness of such exceptional excellence, combined with so much grace and liveliness, and have felt even some degree of repulsion from what appeared to savour of consummate hypocrisy. No long time, however, elapsed before he was constrained to recognise the habitual purity of her thoughts, words, and actions, and could only wonder to meet with a being so young, so charming, so universally admired, surrounded by such overwhelming temptations, and yet so wholly free from spot or blemish. Circumstances brought him into such close contact with this peerless maid of honour, to whom his wife was, besides, affectionately attached, that he could not fail to perceive that there was not the slightest disguise, concealment, or affectation about either her outer or inner life. Great accordingly was his delight when, one day, she opened herself out more unreservedly than usual, and lamented that she had no friend to whose sympathy she could confide all her joys and sorrows, her thoughts, hopes, and perplexities. She admitted that there was one who was ' nearer and dearer still,' but it was with gratitude she accepted Evelyn's offer to be to her as ' a guide, philosopher, and friend.' There is something whimsically romantic in the incident itself as related in his Memoir of Mrs. Godolphin, and he almost seems to have been for the moment half ashamed of the sentimental *rôle* he had undertaken to fill. He relates how he sketched something intended to represent an altar, above which she wrote, ' Be this the Symbol of Inviolable Friendship,' signed ' Marg. Blagge,' with the date ' October 16, 1672,' and underneath ' For my Brother E——.' Upon which he said to her, partly in jest, partly in earnest, ' The title that has consecrated this altar is the Marriage of Souls and the Golden Thread that ties the hearts of all the world;' and then went on to dilate on the new duties and responsibilities she had

laid upon herself. On the morrow she wrote to him a touching
letter, in which she begged him to look upon her as his child as
well as a friend, and she herself always evinced towards him the
love and reverence due to a parent. 'Her friendship to me,' he
pathetically exclaims, ' was passing the love of women.'

As already casually remarked, Margaret Blagge was no longer
heartfree, but at a very early age had plighted her troth to Sidney
Godolphin, subsequently raised to the peerage and appointed First
Commissioner of the Treasury. He is described by Lord Macaulay
as extremely cautious and reserved, and of a grave deportment,
though his tastes were in reality of a low and frivolous order, his
favourite amusements being horse-racing, card-playing, and cock-
fighting. On the other hand, he was indefatigably laborious, clear-
headed, and thoroughly conversant with finance. His character
was happily hit off by Charles II. when he said, ' Sidney Godolphin
is never in the way and never out of the way.' Though from his
boyhood brought up in the impure atmosphere of the Court, he
had sense enough to appreciate the loveliness of such a being as
Margaret Blagge, and the watchful Evelyn admits that during the
long probation of nine years these two were ' the most entire and
faithful lovers in the world.' Being much employed about the
King's person, Mr. Godolphin was unable to marry his betrothed
so soon as both desired, and at times she seriously contemplated
breaking off the engagement and devoting herself to a life of
religious celibacy. These fits of despondency or devotional exaltation were strenuously and successfully combated by Evelyn ; but
nothing could induce her to remain at Court after completing her
seventh year of attendance, though it was with some difficulty
she obtained their Majesties' consent to her retirement, and it
was with sincere regret that her companions and, indeed, the whole
Royal Household bade her farewell. The faithful Evelyn waited
upon her as her escort from Whitehall to Berkeley House. ' All
her household stuff,' he says, ' besides a Bible and a bundle of
Prayer Books, was packed up in a very little compass, for she
lived so far from superfluity that she carried all that was valuable
in her person ; and though she had a courtly wardrobe, she affected
it not, because everything became her that she put on, and she
became everything that was put upon her.' Her spirits rose at
the prospect of having more time for study and reflection, though
under that aspect there proved to be little change for the better in
her new life. Although nominally mistress of her own actions, she
was expected by the Duchess to assist in entertaining her company,
and to make herself generally agreeable. So irksome, however,
became the constant dissipation in which she was compelled to

participate, that she more than once talked of paying a visit to her sister, Lady Yarborough, in Yorkshire, preparatory to retiring into a life of seclusion at Hereford under the spiritual guidance of the Dean, whom she regarded as her 'ghostly father.' To all such projects her Grace turned a deaf ear, positively refusing to part with her, and she was even constrained to take the principal part in a brilliant masque that was enacted before their Majesties on December 15 and 22, 1674. As maid of honour, Mistress Blagge had, with great reluctance, more than once had occasion to display her rare histrionic talents, which were greatly assisted by a clear, correct enunciation and a peculiarly musical voice. The masque in question was entitled 'Calisto, or the Chaste Nymph,' and was composed by John Crowne. The other performers were the Princesses Mary and Anne, daughters of the Duke of York, and each in her turn Queen of England, Lady Henrietta Wentworth, Countess of Sussex, Lady Mary Mordaunt, and Mistress Jennings, afterwards Sarah Duchess of Marlborough. Among the dancers were the Duke of Monmouth, Lord Dumblaine, and Lord Daincourt, while even the chorus and the female dancers consisted of ladies of high rank and breeding. To Margaret Blagge was entrusted the leading part of the Goddess Diana, in which she acquitted herself to the admiration of the entire Court. Her dress alone cost upwards of 300*l.*, and the jewels with which she was covered were valued at 20,000*l.* Owing to the pressure of the crowd she had the misfortune to lose a valuable diamond belonging to the Countess of Suffolk, and which could nowhere be found though the stage was carefully swept. The Duke of York, however, perceiving her trouble, very handsomely enabled her to replace the loss by a gem of equal value. Whenever the exigencies of her part did not require her presence on the stage, she retired into a corner and read a book of devotions, and 'whilst the whole theatre were extolling her, she was then in her own eyes not only the humblest, but the most diffident of herself and least affecting praise.' As soon as the performance was over, and without waiting for supper, she hurried off to Berkeley House and to her oratory, 'whither,' says Evelyn, 'I waited on her, and left her on her knees, thanking God that she was delivered from this vanity, and with her Saviour again. "Never," says she, "will I come within this temptation more whilst I breathe."'

On May 16, 1675, Margaret Blagge was privately married to Sidney Godolphin in the Temple Church, the Duchess of Berkeley honouring the ceremony with her presence, but the affair being kept a profound secret for reasons that do not very clearly appear. On this solitary occasion our heroine is represented in very unfavourable colours. Notwithstanding her vows of eternal friend-ship and implicit confidence, she not only kept this momentous event from Evelyn's knowledge, but was guilty of the duplicity of leading him to believe that she still sighed for a life of celibacy and religious retirement. It was as Mistress Blagge that she accompanied the Duke and Duchess of Berkeley to Paris, on his Grace proceeding thither as ambassador; and as she refused to go to the French Court or mix in the gaieties of the capital, it is not much to be wondered at that the Duchess grew somewhat impatient of her puritanism. She herself longed to return to England, it may be in the hope of being publicly recognised by her husband as his wedded wife: ' I am weary of my life,' she wrote to Evelyn. ' I have here no time for my soul. Cards we play at four hours every day: whoever comes to visit, I must be by to interpret: wherever a certain lady goes (if my Lady Hamilton be not at hand), I must trudge: so that poor I can scarce say my prayers, and seldom or never read.' Earnestly she desires to be restored to her own people and her own God; and, after enumerating the various occupations of her time, concludes with the touching adjuration: ' O pity, pity me, dear friend!' In the following spring she availed herself of an opportunity of returning to England, and in the first instance placed herself under the roof of her relative Dr. Warnett, in Covent Garden. It was now she disclosed her marriage to Evelyn, and besought his pardon with such manifest contrition that the worthy man had no choice but to condone her equivocation and deceit.

Shortly afterwards she was joined by her husband, and the youthful couple removed to Berkeley House, where they received the congratulations of their friends and relatives. Here they remained until March 31, 1677, when they took possession of the ' pretty habitation ' in Scotland Yard, which Evelyn had prepared for them. How Mrs. Godolphin fared in her married life may be partly divined from the following extract from a letter written by her to Evelyn from her new abode:

' Lord, when I this day considered my happiness in having so perfect health of body, cheerfulness of mind, no disturbance from without, nor grief within, my time my own, my house quiet, sweet, and pretty, all manner of conveniences for serving God in public and private; how happy in my friends, husband, relations, servants, credit, and none to wait or attend on but my dear and beloved God, from who ₁I receive all this; what a melting joy ran through me at the thoughts of all these mercies, and how did I think myself obliged to go to the foot of my Redeemer and acknowledge my own unworthiness of His favour!'

In another letter she protested that she had 'little to wish for but a child, and to contribute something to my friends' happiness, which I most impatiently desire.' For two years, however, her yearnings remained ungratified, so that, despairing of issue of her own, she adopted an orphan girl, 'whom she tended, instructed, and cherished with the tenderness of a natural mother.' Her chief anxiety centred in her 'dear man,' who was subject to frequent attacks of fever; but under no circumstances did she forget the poor and afflicted, and only a short time before her coveted confinement she sent Evelyn 70*l.* from her private purse to distribute among the most needy. Her staunch friend Lady Mordaunt happening to call upon her one day about that time, found her with eyes swollen with weeping. In reply to her sympathetic enquiries Mrs. Godolphin told her that she had been writing a letter to her husband, asking him to grant her one request should she die in childbirth. She had put everything in order, she added, and was prepared 'against all surprises.' But, though strongly impressed with the belief that her constitution was too weak to carry her through the illness that awaited her, she preserved her cheerful equanimity to the very last, and divided her time between her religious exercises and social obligations. She was unusually solemn, indeed, on one occasion about a month before her confinement, during a visit paid to her by her attached friends Evelyn and Lady Mordaunt; but then she had just ceased from sorting and arranging her various papers and letters, and was longing 'after that glorious state where,' said she, 'I shall be perfectly at repose and sin no more.'

On September 3 a man-child was born into the world, and, as noted in Evelyn's diary, 'was baptized in the Chamber by the name of Francis, the susceptors being Sir William Godolphin (head of the family), Mr. John Hervey, Treasurer to the Queen, and Mrs. Boscawen, sister to Sir William and the father.' The latter speedily arrived from Windsor, and all things promised for the best. Four days later, however, the young mother was seized with a fever just then very prevalent, and on the following forenoon, being Sunday, a note from her husband was handed to Evelyn during divine service, couched in this plaintive strain :

'My poor wife is fallen very ill of a fever, with lightness in her head. You know who says the prayers of the faithful shall save the sick; I humbly beg your charitable prayers for this poor creature and your distracted servant. Londor Saturday, nine o'clock.'

Evelyn and his wife at once took boat for Whitehall, and arrived in time to soothe the last hours of the dying saint. Though still able to recognise her old friends, her mind wandered a good deal, and she was often disturbed by strange fancies; but not a single improper word or allusion ever escaped from her lips, as so frequently happens in such cases, and her spotless soul passed unscathed through the ordeal of delirium.   There might possibly have been a chance of saving her life, had the physicians promptly attended to her husband's impatient summons; but one stood upon etiquette, another took no notice of the message, and when at last a doctor did make his appearance it was too late to do any good. As her biographer quaintly remarks, 'she was now in a manner spent, and no't could phisitians doe when neither the cupping nor the pigeons, those last of remedies, wrought any effect.'   Erysipelas breaking out on her back, neck, and arms, her strength entirely forsook her, and cordials seemed to have lost their virtue. In the course of the following day, September 9, 1678, her gentle spirit took its flight peacefully and tranquilly, and her only regret was for those she left behind to bewail her departure.

When the afflicted widower had recovered from the swoon into which he fell on becoming sensible of his irreparable loss, his sister Mrs. Boscawen placed in his hands the letter written by his wife under the presentiment of her early death.   In this she assures him, that ' of all earthly things you were and are the most dear to me ; and I am convinced that nobody ever had a better or half so good a husband.'   She touchingly begs his forgiveness for her many imperfections, for her errors in the management of his household, for her ' vanity of humour ' in being too often splenetic and melancholy.   She prays God to bless and comfort him, and then asks him to sanction a few legacies to her servants, and especially one to her waiting-woman of 100*l.*, ' the use of which being six pounds a year, she may live at her father's house upon, if she will, for I fear she will scarce get anybody to bear with her want of good service as I have done.'   She desires that her child may be confided to Mrs. Boscawen or Mrs. Penn, who would be ' careful of its better part.'   She further requests that he will lay out 100*l.* in the purchase of rings for his five sisters, 'to remember me by.' ' Think of me,' she continues, ' with kindness, but never with too much grief.'   She is anxious that her funeral should be simple and inexpensive, though she confesses to a wish to lie with the Godolphins ' among your friends;' and, as the journey by land to Cornwall would take both time and money, she suggests that her body should be sent round by sea : she is willing, however, to be buried anywhere that may be most convenient to himself.   ' If you should think fit to marry again, I humbly beg that the little fortune I brought may be first settled upon my child, and that as long as any of your sisters live, you will let it (if they permit) live with them; for it may be, though you will love it, my successor will not be so fond of it as they, I am sure, will be.' It is almost needless to state that the utmost respect was paid to her dying wishes. Her devoted friend Evelyn, who was appointed her trustee, undertook the entire management of the last sad ceremonies, the bereaved husband being for a while totally incapacitated for taking any part in the active duties of life.

'Having closed the eyes,' writes the sorrowing diarist, 'and dropped a tear upon the cheek of my dear departed friend, lovely even in death, I caused her corpse to be embalmed and wrapped in lead, with a plate of brass soldered thereon, with an inscription, and other circumstances due to her worth, with as much diligence and care as my grieved heart would permit me; I then retired home for two days which were spent in solitude and sad reflections.'

'*September* 17.—She was accordingly carried to Godolphin in Cornwall, in a hearse with six horses, attended by two coaches of as many, with about thirty of her relations and servants. There accompanied the hearse her husband's brother Sir William, two more of his brothers, and three sisters; her husband was so overcome with grief that he was wholly unfit to travel so long a journey until he was more composed. I went as far as Hounslow with a sad heart, but was obliged to return upon some indispensable affairs. The corpse was ordered to be taken out of the hearse every night, and decently placed in the house, with tapers about it, and her servants attending, to Cornwall; and then was honourably interred in the parish church of Godolphin. This funeral cost not much less than 1,000*l*.'

A pensive melancholy seems to have been the only shade to the radiant qualities that constituted the charming character of the deceased lady. Some time before her last illness she presented Evelyn with her likeness, in which she was depicted sitting on a tombstone adorned with a sepulchral urn, and she appears to have taken almost a morbid pleasure in meditations of a sad and depressing order. This might perhaps be partly attributable to her excessive abstemiousness. She had been compelled, indeed, to abate something of her self-imposed mortifications during the season of Lent; but even on festival days she fared sparingly, choosing the driest and leanest morsels of meat, unflavoured by any kind of sauce or condiment. When remonstrated with, and told that her health was being injured by her austerities, she would merrily reply that she was 'as strong as a lion,' or that 'she could be fat in three days' if she wished it. Being once reproved by

Evelyn for fasting on a Church festival, she said : ' As to fasting on a festival, I had not done it but that I had for it the opinion of a learned and reverend bishop, who told me it was not a fasting day of our own making ; we might, when a fast and a feast of the Church meet, feast at church and fast at home ; which I did, and it was a good day with me. I could be content never to dine so long as I live, so as I might spend every day like that.' The Scriptures she knew almost by heart, and was well versed in Dr. Hammond's Annotations and other practical books of a pious character. She herself composed a large quantity of prayers, meditations, hymns, and discourses on various religious subjects. Among her original writings was the following ' Morning Hymn,' which, if somewhat too ecstatic, is at least joyful and not unmusical :

> Up and be doing! Sleep no more.
> Hark! who is knocking at the door?
> Arise, my fair one, come away ;
> For thee I wait: arise and pray.
> Shake off thy sleep: behold! 'tis I :
> Canst thou love that, when I am by?
> Vain thoughts, presume not to come near;
> You'll find no entertainments here :
> My love has sworn—her vows are past—
> That I shall be her first and last.
> Rise then, my dearest, come and see
> What pleasures are reserved for thee.
> I come, dear Lord. Behold, I rise :
> Beyond all pleasures Thee I prize.

On the Lord's Day she manifested a peculiar joyfulness ; but few things caused her greater annoyance than the ' impertinent visits ' and idle amusements which were then customary on Sunday evenings. The recreation she herself chiefly affected on that day was a quiet walk in the garden or the fields, diversified by visits to the poor. Notwithstanding her youth, she went without fear and without attendance to prisons and hospitals, and into noisome and squalid streets, strong in her conscious rectitude. She also employed a widow of a pious character but in very humble circumstances to find out cases of real distress worthy of relief. Evelyn, too, was oftentimes her almoner, and was able to testify from his personal knowledge that at different times she had released thirty debtors from gaol, and paid the fees of many 'prentice lads. During the season of Lent she occupied herself in cutting out and making up garments for the poor, while some one read to her upon religious subjects. She was an admirable housekeeper, strictly methodical, and frugal in order to be generous. She ' never went on score,' but settled all her accounts every Saturday evening.

Endowed with quickness of apprehension, a retentive memory, a sound judgment, and great natural eloquence, she could not fail to be sought after by all who needed advice or consolation. And, strange as it may seem, she was much consulted by the ladies of the Court in matters pertaining to dress and finery, especially for masques and balls, her taste being recognised as most accurate and refined. Cards she utterly detested, though often forced to play, and generally she was very fortunate; but her winnings were always given to the destitute.

In her diary appears the following entry, dated June 2, in reference to a loss she had sustained at cards : 'I will never play this half-year but at three-penny omber, and then with one at halves. I will not. I do not vow, but I will not do it. What! lose money at cards, yet not give to the poor! 'Tis robbing God, misspending time, and misemploying my talents ; three great sins. Three pounds would have kept three people from starving a month. Well, I will not play.' To curb a natural tendency to wit and raillery, she pinned up papers in all sorts of places inscribed with some grave maxim or admonition; but with all her watchfulness over herself she still remained ' the most harmless and diverting creature in nature.' Children were particularly fond of her, and she would sit for hours reading and talking to the sick, the peevish, and the discontented. ' She would sing and play and act and recite and discourse, prettily and innocently, a thousand harmless and ingenious purposes to recreate old and melancholy persons, and divert the younger.' In short, it was truly said of Mrs. Godolphin that ' never was there a more unspotted virgin, a more loyal wife, a more sincere friend, a more consummate Christian; add to this, a florid youth, an exquisite and natural beauty, and gracefulness the most becoming.'

JAMES HUTTON.

Joshua Haggard's Daughter.

BY THE AUTHOR OF 'LADY AUDLEY'S SECRET.'

CHAPTER XXIII.

'A STORM WAS COMING, BUT THE WINDS WERE STILL.'

No life could have been more self-contained than Naomi's in this fair summer time. She claimed sympatny from no one, but bore the anguish of her widowed heart in a resolute silence. From Cynthia she shrank, with a feeling that was more nearly akin to aversion than she would have liked to confess to herself. Womanly instinct had fathomed the mystery of Oswald's defection. She had looked back, and remembered, and weighed looks and tones of his, which had but faintly impressed her at the time, but which now, considered by the light of his subsequent conduct, had fullest significance. His heart had gone astray, and it was to Cynthia, her father's wife, that truant heart had wandered—not with deliberate sinfulness; she could not believe him deliberately wicked. The tempter had set this snare for him, and he had weakly yielded. Cynthia's childish beauty, Cynthia's innocently simple ways, had allured him from the straight path of righteous dealing. He had struggled, poor sinner, fought and striven with the Evil One, and, finding the powers of darkness too strong for him, had turned and fled. It was wisest, it was best so.

Naomi loved him with so fondly indulgent an affection—a passion so unselfish—that she could find it in her heart to forgive him for having fallen away from her. She could pardon and pity him, though he had taken the light and glory out of her life, and left her world empty as an exhausted crater. But she could not so easily forgive Cynthia. Her father's wife should have been above suspicion, unassailable by temptation. And if Cynthia had not shown some tokens of weakness, Oswald would surely have been stronger. Cynthia, the wandering waif, cherished and garnered by the most generous of men, should have loved her husband with a love strong enough to shield her from the possibility of temptation; and yet in this false wife's pallid face, in the heavy eyes, and sad set lips, Naomi read the secret of a guilty sorrow. She, Cynthia, grieved for the absent one—she shared Naomi's sacred grief, she intruded upon that privileged domain of fond regret. The knowledge of this silent distress made Naomi angry and unforgiving.

One evening in the beginning of August, soon after Joshua's reading of 'Werther,' Naomi walked alone in Pentreath Wood. Such lonely evening rambles were her melancholy comfort, and this wood her favourite resort. Her wild garden had been neglected of late. It was too narrow for her grief. Jim, or Aunt Judith, or Cynthia, might intrude upon her at any moment. But here, in this wide shadowy wood, she was really alone—no one to spy out her tears or offer humiliating pity—no companions but the stars high up yonder, shining through over-arching beech and oak—the unknown life in brambles and underwood, dry fern, and last year's leaves, which were stirred now and then mysteriously by those unfamiliar creatures that make merry at nightfall, or by the distant hoot of some ancient owl, sounding ghostlike in the dimness, or the red-brown cattle lying in the grassy hollows and sheltered corners, restful but unsleeping.

Here Naomi could nurse her grief as she pleased. She could bring forth her sorrow from its hiding-place, and cherish and caress it, as if it had been a fondly-loved child. Here she recalled Oswald's looks and tones, when she had believed him true, and lived over again the happy days in which he had been all her own, the time before Cynthia came and brought sorrow and shameful thoughts into Joshua Haggard's peaceful home. Every turn and wind of the dear old wood, every veteran oak, ferny bank, and knoll and hollow, was associated with that lost lover, and aided fancy to conjure up his image. Here he had read 'Ivanhoe,' here 'Marmion.' Here, in a lazy mood, he had lain stretched at full length, and told her the story of Caleb Williams, and how he had once seen Kean play the part of Sir Edward Mortimer, in the *Iron Chest,* at the little theatre in Exeter. Here, leaning against the silvery bark of this giant beech, he had recited Byron's 'Isles of Greece'—thrilled with a fervour which was almost inspiration. Oh, happy, irredeemable hours—the dead departed delights of life !

Here, on this August evening, Naomi walked and meditated. It was a dim and hazy twilight, with a pale new moon shining faintly behind the tree-tops in a sky of translucent grey. The young trees, and the underwood beneath them, had a ghostly look in this half light. It might have been a scene made up of shadows.

Bitter, beyond all measure of common bitterness, to remember the days—but a little while ago—when Naomi and her lover had roamed in this very wood, when there was but the red-brown glow of coming foliage on the leafless beech boughs, and the chestnut fans were still unfolded, and the anemones whitened the hollows, and the blue dog-violets smiled up at the blue April sky. Cynthia had been with them always—the fair young sick-nurse in her neat grey gown and little Quaker cap. She had been with them. sharing all their talk; and Naomi had nothing suspected, nothing doubted. It was only now that she understood the drama in which her own part had been so sad a one—only now that she could fathom the meaning of that low subdued voice—those pauses of silence, and lapses into dreamy thoughtfulness, which had marked Oswald's manner during this time.

' It was then he began to care for her,' she told herself. ' God help and pardon them both! I do not believe that either entered deliberately upon this path of sin. But if Cynthia saw that he was so weak—so wicked—she ought to have left the Grange at once; she ought never to have seen him again. It was her duty.'

Easy enough to say this, but a moment's reflection showed Naomi that it would have been no easy thing to do. To avoid temptation thus would have been to create a scandal. And Oswald had made no confession of his weakness. Those subtle differences in his tones and looks may have been meaningless for Cynthia.

' No,' thought Naomi, with a burst of very human passion, ' she must have understood them; his words and looks must have been clear to her—for she loves him.'

Pondering thus—as she had pondered on many an evening since her lover's desertion, travelling over and over again the same sad pathway of thought—Naomi came to the skirt of the wood, and from the wood into the park, where the trees stood far apart, and the smooth sward rose and fell in gentle undulations. She could see the house from this point. How lonely it looked, how deserted; a gloomy dwelling that might have been so bright!

' I was to have been a fine lady, with a drawing-room and a conservatory,' Naomi said to herself, full of bitterness; 'and coaches were to come rolling over that gravel drive, where the weeds grow so thickly. And there were to be lights in all those windows; and music sounding in the night—a life like fairy-land. Poor Oswald! How he used to talk of our future! And he was true then—he meant all he said. Oh, my dearest, my dearest,' she murmured, with clasped hands; 'I wanted no lights or music; I wanted no grand visitors—no bliss other than this common world can give, while I had you! My life would have been all happiness, had Providence made you the poorest of God's poor, and our home a hovel, and our days full of toil, if we had only spent them together—if you had only been true to me.'

She stopped, with tears rolling down her cheeks—tears that gushed forth unawares at the sweet sad thought of what life might have been. She stood looking straight before her with those tear-dimmed eyes,—looking at the dull old house.

Not a gleam of light! Yes; the heavy hall door opens slowly, she sees the dim lamp within. A figure comes out of the dusky porch, and walks at a leisurely pace along the broad gravel terrace at the side of the house.

Naomi gave a faint awe-stricken cry, as if she had seen a ghost —a cry so faint that it could not reach the ears of yonder solitary muser, pacing the gravel path with bent head. She turned, and hurried back to the wood, and was quickly lost in the darkness of that green mystery of oak and beech ; and then, secure from observation, walked slowly home, meditating upon what she had seen.

He had come back—he who had said his path of life was to lie in other lands—he, the self-banished exile, the new Childe Harold. Why had he come? and was it for long? How was it that the village had not been aware of his coming, and made his return common talk—an inevitable consequence of such knowledge? Had he any purpose in returning secretly—in hiding himself from his little world? Naomi was perplexed and troubled by these un-answerable questions.

It was late when she entered the little parlour at home. Prayers were over, and the family were seated in the usual formal array round the temperately furnished board. The huge junk of single Gloucester, about the size and shape of one of those granite slabs which bestrew the path of the adventurous tourist who tempts the perils of the Loggan Rock, stood up in the centre of the table like a family idol, round which the family had assembled for evening worship. The brown beer-jug—simulating a portly figure in a three-cornered hat—occupied its accustomed corner. Everything was precisely as Naomi remembered it in her earliest child-hood. The quiet monotony of life had never been disturbed by new crockery, or a change of form and colour in the vulgar de-tails of existence. The Druids could hardly have lived more simply than this Methodist household.

And now that the mainspring of life was broken, this sordid sameness seemed odious ; nay, almost unbearable. Naomi looked at the familiar home picture with a shudder. Affection gave it no beauty in her eyes to-night. A fair enough picture of domestic peace from the outside, if there had been any one in the street to contemplate that candle-lit circle through the window; some vagabond, perchance, homeless, and deeming that there must be bliss in a home. Yet, save honest Jim, who sat munching his bread-and-cheese with a countenance of equable discontent, there was no member of that family circle whose bosom was not racked by anguish or passion.

'Half-past nine, Naomi!' exclaimed Joshua, looking up reproachfully, as his daughter came into the room. 'The first time I've read prayers without you since I can remember—except when you've been ill. What has kept you so long?'

'I've been frightened,' answered Naomi, looking not at her father, but at Cynthia. 'I was in Pentreath Park, and I thought I saw a ghost.'

'A ghost, Naomi? I thought you were too good a Christian to believe in such folly.'

'Saul saw a ghost,' interjected Jim, with his mouth full of lettuce, 'and you wouldn't say that was folly.'

'Saul lived in days when God taught His children by miracles.'

'And if Providence chose to send a ghost to Combhollow, who's to hinder it?' cried Jim, with unconscious irreverence. 'I'm sure ghosts are wanted—people are wicked enough. I dare say the Cock Lane ghost would have done a deal of good if a pack of busybodies hadn't made her out an impostor. And there are the ghosts that worried the Wesley family. You can't fly in *their* faces.'

'Sit down to your supper, Naomi,' said Joshua, rebuking Jim's flippancy by a grave disregard which was more crushing than remonstrance; 'you ought not to be wandering about so late of nights. It is not respectable.'

Naomi sighed and made no answer. Those weary ghosts in Dante's nether world wandering in their circles of despair might have felt very much as she did, had any accuser charged them with levity or unseemly conduct. She looked at her father with eyes full of a wondering reproachfulness, as if she would have said, 'Can you, who know my burden, upbraid me?'

'What about the ghost?' asked Aunt Judith, sweeping her crumbs into a neat little heap with the back of her knife. 'Don't tell me it was Mr. Trimmer. Sally had the impudence to hint at his walking, only last Sunday night; but I think I stopped her tongue.'

Mr. Trimmer was a retired miller who had died of dropsy 'up street,' and who was supposed to be not quite comfortable in his mind about the division of the property which he had left behind him, about which there had been some squabbling among his nephews and nieces. This disagreement of the miller's heirs had given rise to the report of ghostly visitations—of an erratic and unconsecutive character—on the part of the miller.

' I won't swear to his having walked,' cried Jim, eagerly ; ' but there have been groans heard down at the red mill. *That* I can vouch for, because Joe Davis's father heard it coming home from his work last Saturday night.'

' Why, Trimmer hadn't worked the mill for ten good years,' exclaimed Aunt Judith. ' What could he want down there ? '

' To look after the money he'd buried,' replied Jim, with conviction. ' You may depend that what he's left behind him above ground isn't half what he's left beneath.'

' Was it Trimmer ? ' asked Judith, letting her natural love of the marvellous get the better of common sense.

' No,' answered Naomi ; ' it was nothing but fancy, I dare say. The mists were rising—white clouds of vapour that looked like the shadows of the dead.'

' Let there be no more said upon the subject,' said Joshua, sternly. ' It is sinful to dwell upon such folly. Eat your supper, Naomi, and let there be none of these evening wanderings.'

It is not easy to eat when one is bidden. The home-made bread, sweet as it was, seemed bitter to Naomi's parched mouth. She drank a long draught of water and held her peace, and there was silence till the end of the meal. Naomi lifted her downcast eyelids once or twice, and looked at Cynthia with thoughtful scrutiny. There was nothing in the young wife's countenance to betray any knowledge of Oswald's return to the Grange. There was only that settled sadness which had become a part of the sweet face lately.

' She will know very soon, I dare say,' thought Naomi, bitterly. ' It is not to see me that he has come back.'

Her heart burned with indignation, as if Cynthia had, by some unholy witchcraft, some subtle silent exercise of womanly artifice, lured the false lover back to her net. She could not give her credit for innocence, or even for helpless unconscious yielding to a guilty love. No, it was her fault that Oswald had gone astray. Had she been strong in purity of heart, Oswald would never have been so weak.

When the time came for bidding good night, and Cynthia approached with her pretty pleading look and rose-bud mouth ready to kiss, Naomi turned away from her stepmother with a stony face and left the room in silence. Cynthia looked after her wonderingly, but said not a word. She knew but too well what it meant. Oswald's treachery had made a lasting breach between them. Her only hope was that Joshua had not seen that cruel repulse. But he had seen it, and formed his own conclusions thereupon.

CHAPTER XXIV.

FULL OF SCORPIONS.

' WILL he come, will he come to see me ? '

This was the question which Naomi asked herself when she arose next morning, to see another peerless summer day smiling at her, but to feel none of the joy of harvest, only a heart as dull and desolate as if she had awakened to find herself amidst some dwindled hope-forsaken band hemmed round by cruel Arctic seas. What was summer to her, or harvest, or all the common joys of life —joys that gladden hearts which are *not* broken ?

All through the feverish wakeful night the same doubt had agitated Naomi's mind. Might not her lover have repented and returned to her ? So blessed a thing was just possible. He had loved her dearly once ; surely that old love could not die. He had often told her that love was deathless. Fancy had gone astray, perhaps, and love had been true all the time. Absence had taught him that she was still dear. Oh, how tenderly she would have welcomed the returning prodigal, could she but be sure of his repentance, sure that her love could even yet make him happy ! Thus argued hope ; but despair took the other side. He had come back in secret, for some evil purpose. He had come back to see Cynthia.

This day would show if he meant well or ill. If well, he would not fear to show himself at Mr. Haggard's house. He would come, and make peace with his betrothed. Oh ! long hours of waiting, between morning prayer and noontide—hours in which the simple household tasks were performed while the girl's heart was given to alternate hope and despair ! Would he come ? Would he prove true and good, despite of all that had gone before ?

Noon came, and dinner, and afternoon, and he did not appear. Hope died in Naomi's breast. She went about the house listlessly, yet was too restless to sit long at her work. It happened to be a busy afternoon in the drapery department, and Aunt Judith was too well employed behind the counter to observe her niece's idle moving to and fro, or else there would have been the small bitterness of that maiden lady's lectures superadded to the great bitterness of Naomi's despair.

Cynthia and Jim were in the garden. Those two were very friendly just now. The poor little stepmother clung to the honest outspoken lad in this time of cloud and brooding storm. Naomi's coldness cut her to the heart. She felt that there was a great gulf between her and her husband. Of Judith's dislike and distrust she was inwardly assured.

But Jim seemed fond of her, and he was of her husband's flesh and blood. The poor little timid soul went out to him in its loneliness.

'Do you really like me, James?' she asked to-day, as they were tying up the carnations in the long garden border, Cynthia's small face shaded by a big dimity sun-bonnet.

'Liking isn't the word, Cynthia,' answered the boy. 'I'm uncommonly fond of you; and if you'd only summon up a little spirit and make Aunt Judith give up the housekeeping, I should have a still better opinion of you. Why should she stint us to one or two puddens a week, and those as hard as brickbats; and a fruit pasty once in a blue moon, when the garden's running over with gooseberries and may-dukes? It isn't her place to order the puddens. It's yours. It was all very well to be trodden under her foot when we were orphans, but you're our mother now, and you ought to stand by us. Why don't we have bacon and fried potatoes for breakfast, like Christians? She'd let a whole side go rusty before she'd give us the benefit of it. And my father sits at the table and starves himself, and quotes William Law to show that starvation is a Christian duty. I've no patience! I'm sure I wonder I've grown up the fine young man I am, upon such short commons.'

Jim came into the house half-an-hour later, and found Naomi in the parlour. She was standing by the window, idle, her work in her hands, staring absently at the bend in the road yonder, by which Oswald used to come, on Herne the Hunter. Poor old faithful Herne! the tears came into her eyes when she thought of him. He had been turned out to grass, and she had seen him looking over gaps in the hedge, a haggard, unkempt beast. She had called him, and coaxed him, and held out her hand to invite his approach, and he had come with a shy, sidelong gait close up to her, and then shot off like a sky-rocket before she could caress his honest grey nose.

Jim burst into the parlour like a whirlwind.

'I thought you was fond of those hart's-tongues I got for you?' he exclaimed, breathless with indignation.

'So I am, Jim; very fond of them.'

'Then you'd better get a bit of black stuff out of the shop and make yourself a mourning gown!'

'Are they dead?'

'They're as near it as anything in the fern line can be—as yellow as the inside of a poached egg, and half eaten by snails. How long is it since you've been in the wilderness?'

'I don't know: a few days—a week, perhaps.'

'You're a nice young woman for an industrious brother to toil for! The place is as dry as an ash-pit. What's the use of my getting you fine specimens, if this is the way you treat 'em? There's the parsley fern crinkled up like a bit of whitey-brown paper. Cynthia and I have been giving the things a good dowsing; but they've been shamefully neglected. I should have thought you could have found time to look after them. *You're* not in the business,' concluded Jim, with a superior air.

'Don't be cross, Jim,' faltered Naomi, gently. 'It was wrong of me to neglect the ferns that you've taken such trouble to set for me; but I have not done any gardening lately; I have not been feeling well enough——'

And here Naomi burst into tears—Naomi, with whom tears were so rare.

Jim had his arms round her in a moment, and was hugging her like an affectionate bruin.

'There, there, there!' he cried; 'don't fret. I oughtn't to have been so cross. You've had your troubles lately—father going and breaking off your marriage without rhyme or reason. Nobody ever heard of such tyranny. I'll be sworn William Law, the father of Methodism, is at the bottom of it. Suffering is good for us. It's blessed to deny ourselves. And my poor little sister mustn't marry the man she loves! Cheer up, Naomi; it will all come right in the end, I dare say, though things are going crooked now. Don't worry about the wilderness. Cynthia and I are making things tidy—weeding and watering, and training the creepers over the rock-work. You can come down and look at us, if you like. It will cheer you up a bit!'

'I'll come presently, Jim, dear,' answered Naomi, drying her tears.

'Be sure you do,' said Jim; and then he hurried back to his work.

Naomi sat in the parlour for a quarter of an hour or so. She shed no more tears, but sat with dry eyes looking straight before her.

Why had he come back? Not for her—oh, not for her!

The day was nearly done. She could hear the rattling of teacups in the pantry. Sally was getting her tray ready. That meant half-past four o'clock. Naomi rose, with a long heavy sigh, and went out into the garden. It was to please her brother she went. There was no pleasure or interest for her in earth or sky.

She walked slowly down the long straight garden path, where the clove carnations and double stocks were in their glory, and through the little orchard to the wilderness. Jim was hard at work—the perspiration running down his forehead, his coat off and his shirt-sleeves rolled up to the elbow—dividing great tufts of primroses and overgrown hart's-tongue. Cynthia was on her knees weeding, a pretty picture of youth and fairness in the yellow sunlight.

Naomi stood and looked at her. What was the charm in her which had lured that false lover? Could the eye of another woman see the bait that had won weak and fickle man, the enchantment which had wrought alike upon the strong man in his meridian of knowledge and wisdom and the youth in his folly?

Yes ; the charm revealed itself even to the cold eye of a resentful rival. It was not so much absolute beauty which allured in this nameless waif as a soft and gracious innocence, a flower-like loveliness, that stole upon mind and heart unawares.

She charmed the senses, as roses and lilies do in the early morning, while the dew is still on them. She appealed to the eye, and held it, like some picture which, in a long gallery, stands out from all other images, and transfixes the spectator. She stole upon the soul like music.

Nor was it this outward charm of perfect fairness and grace only which attracted. The soft loveableness of her disposition accorded with the tender grace of her beauty. She had the clinging affectionateness of a soft and yielding nature ; a humility of spirit which made her ready to reverence the strong ; a tenderness of heart which inclined her to pity the weak. In one word, she was loveable—a woman created to be adored.

Naomi stood and looked at her, full of bitter thoughts. For the first time in her life she envied the gifts of another. She felt all the good things that Providence had given her of no account when weighed against the bewitchment of fair looks and winning ways.

'How wicked I am growing!' she thought, shocked at her own bitterness.

'There!' exclaimed Jim, pulling down his shirt-sleeves ; 'I think I've done a tidy afternoon's work. You'll have oceans of primroses next year, Sis.'

'If they don't all die,' said Naomi, not hopefully. 'Do you think it's quite the right time for moving them?'

'Primroses!' cried Jim. 'As if you could hurt a primrose! I know what I'm about, sister. They wouldn't take any harm by my moving if they were the delicatest flowers in a hot-house.'

He pulled on his coat, put away trowel and rake, and came out of the wild garden into the orchard. Cynthia rose too, with an absent-minded sigh, and followed him.

'Now, look here, little stepmother,' he said, in his patronising way, 'you'd better go in and make yourself tidy for tea, while I show Naomi what I've done to her primroses.'

Cynthia obeyed without a word, and left them. Jim tucked his sister's arm under his own, and began to perambulate the orchard.

'What's the matter, Jim?'

'Cheer up, old woman; I've got some good news for you. I won't see you trampled upon, not if I can help it. I won't have your early affections blighted, and young Pentreath sent to the right-about, if I can prevent it. Don't be afraid, Sis. I'll stand by you.'

'Jim, what do you mean?' cried Naomi, piteously.

'I've got a letter for you.'

Naomi's heart leapt with sudden overwhelming joy. He had written. Thank God, thank God! She was not utterly forgotten.

'A letter, Jim?' clasping his arm rapturously. 'How did it come?'

'How should it come? He brought it himself, of course.'

'And gave it to you? You saw him? Dear, dear Jim, tell me all about it. How is he looking? Ill or well?'

'White and fagged; as if he'd been going to the—well, you know—all the time he's been in London. I only just caught a glimpse of him above the wall.'

'And he gave you the letter——'

'No, that's the fun of it. He didn't see me. It was just as I came back to the wilderness after I left you in the parlour. Cynthia was sitting reading on the bench yonder. Just as I came to the gate, I saw a pale face look over the wall; and then a white hand went up and threw something over. It fell among the ferns, not a yard from stepmother. But she never saw it; that was the lark. Her nose was in her book—poetry or some such trash. I gave a whistle, and off went my gentleman like a shot—scared away.'

'And what became of the letter?'

'Why, I picked it up unbeknown to Cynthia, when her back

was turned. It's wrapped round a stone. There's no address on it—too artful for that—but I knew the party it was meant for.'

'Are you sure it's for me?' asked Naomi, trembling a little. That exceeding great joy fainted in her heart. A letter unaddressed —and thrown at Cynthia's feet!

'Of course it's for you. Stepmother sat with her back to the wall, and her head and shoulders smothered in that great sun-bonnet of hers. He might easy take her for you.'

'Give me the letter, dear,' said Naomi, with suppressed eagerness.

He handed her a little parcel—a goodish-sized pebble packed neatly in a sheet of letter paper, and carefully sealed with the well-known coat-of-arms which had hung a year ago from the Squire's fob.

'Ain't you going to read it?' demanded Jim, as his sister stood looking at the packet.

'Not just yet, dear. I had rather read it when I'm quite alone.'

'Oh my!' ejaculated Jim. 'For fear some of the love should run over, like clouted cream that hasn't set properly. What it is to be in love! Well, Sis, I'll leave you to the enjoyment of your love-letter, while I go and clean myself.'

He ran off, leaving Naomi alone in the orchard. Fear held her hand for a moment, though hope whispered that this little packet was full of comfort and sweetness. It had fallen at Cynthia's feet, said fear. Was it not possible that it had been meant for Cynthia?

She broke the seal and carefully unfolded the sheet of Bath post—the fair wide paper which our forefathers used when letters were worth having.

It was a letter of three pages, written by a hand which betrayed its owner's emotion. Naomi's eyes shone with an angry light as they hurried over the lines. There was a name written here and there—a hateful name that told her the letter was not for her. 'My Cynthia.' 'My Cynthia—mine by that mutual love which is our mutual sorrow.'

'Villain and traitor!' cried Naomi, with a burst of passion which transformed her.

Had he stood before her in that moment, and she armed, she could have stabbed him. This Naomi, who could have laid down her life to accomplish some good and great thing, was—for this one instant—capable of murder.

Such cruel perfidy, such heartless treachery, such shameless iniquity, outraged her sense of justice. It seemed to her as if Heaven had created a monster.

She had not yet read the letter, but Cynthia's name stood out from the tremulous lines as if it had been written in fire. Slowly, with her hand pressed against her burning forehead, in the effort to keep brain and understanding clear, she addressed herself to the hateful task.

She would know the lowest deep of man's infamy : a lover who could forsake his sworn love; a man, calling himself gentleman, who could try to seduce a good man's wife.

The letter was incoherent, passionate—despair's foolish appeal against fate :

I must see you once again—yes, dearest, at whatever hazard to you or me— at whatever cost. I have made up my mind to live and die far away from the dear place that holds you. The wide, bleak, barren sea shall roll between me and my beloved. I am going to America : that is far enough, surely ! Death could part us no wider than the Atlantic. I shall look at that great sea and think how the green waves roll up the golden sands of home and kiss your feet; how the white spray blows into your hair and caresses you like a cloud; and I am no Jove to be in that cloud, love. I shall be severed from you for ever. But before I sail for the other side of the sea I must see you once more ; yes, Cynthia —my Cynthia—mine by that mutual love which is our mutual sorrow—I must see you once more, clasp your hand and say farewell ; bless you, and be blessed by you. Trust me—trust me—my beloved—with but one meeting. There shall no evil word be spoken ; you shall not even hear me complain against fate. I will only take your hand in mine and say good-bye. Vain blessing, you will say ; but, dearest love, the memory of that moment will comfort me in weary days and nights to come. I would but know that you pity, and forgive, and pray for me ; and that—if Fate had willed it so—you might have loved me. It will be like a parting between two friends when one is doomed to die. I shall think the executioner is waiting at the door and the death-bell ready to toll. Oh, dear love, by thy tender and pitying heart, I adjure thee, grant me this last prayer ! Thy Werther, despairing unto death, pleads to thee !

I have come back to Devonshire for this only—to see thee once more. I have taken my passage for New York. All is settled ; nothing can alter my decision. I am not weak enough, or guilty enough, to remain within reach of thee. I thought that in London I might forget, but your image followed me everywhere I went ; in crowds or in solitude you were always near ; nothing but a lifelong exile can cure my wound, or expiate my guilt.

Let me see you, beloved one. I shall contrive to convey this letter to you by some means in the course of to-day. Meet me to-morrow afternoon ; and to-morrow night, by the coach which starts from the First and Last at eight o'clock, I will leave Combhollow for ever. Your afternoons are always free ; I shall wait for you, from two to four o'clock, on the common beyond Matcherly Wood, near the old shaft. It is rather far for you to come, but I think it is the safest place for our meeting. No one ever comes there but a stray cow-boy in quest of his cattle.

Come, dearest ; it is the only boon you can bestow upon one whose heart you have broken unawares.

Yours till death,
OSWALD.

This was the letter. Naomi read it slowly to the end, then folded it neatly and put it in her pocket.

A shrill shriek from the house door roused her from abstraction.
'Naomi, are you coming?' at the top of Aunt Judith's high-pitched voice.

'We never do have our teas like Christians, nowadays!' complained Miss Haggard, as Naomi came into the parlour breathless. 'Have you seen another ghost, girl?' she asked, staring at her niece. 'You look as white as a yard of calico. Here's your father not home to his tea again; that makes the third time this week.'

'He is attending to his duty, no doubt, aunt.'

'Who says he isn't? But I wish he could contrive to combine duty with punctuality at meals. I hate a disorderly table.'

Joshua came in just as they had finished their meal. His large cup of tea had been put on one side for him, covered with a saucer. He sat down in his arm-chair and drank his tea in silence. He was looking exhausted and weary.

'I am afraid you have had a hard afternoon's work, Joshua,' Cynthia said, sitting down beside him timidly.

'I have been in the house of death, my dear; that is always trying to weak humanity. And I have walked a long way in the sun.'

Naomi sat by the window darning Jim's stockings. Aunt Judith washed her tea-things, and then retired to the drapery department. Joshua leant back in his chair, with closed eyes. Cynthia took up a book; it was Milton's 'Paradise Lost,' one of the few imaginative works of which Mr. Haggard did not disapprove.

They sat thus for some time, in a silence only broken by the lowing of distant cattle and the gentle lapping of summer waves upon the pebbly beach. Then Jim looked in at the door and called Cynthia. She rose quickly and went out to him, and Naomi was alone with her father.

This was the opportunity she had been waiting for. After reading Oswald's letter she had come to a desperate resolve. These lofty natures have a touch of hardness in their composition sometimes; a sense of immunity from sin and weakness makes them stony-hearted judges of erring humanity. Oswald's wrongdoing had awakened that latent element of hardness in Naomi's nature. She thought she was only doing her duty in taking desperate measures. Or was it jealousy which put on a mask and called itself justice? She took the letter out of her pocket, and looked at her father. He was not asleep, only resting with closed eyes.

'Father,' said Naomi, in a low voice, 'here is a letter which has come to me by accident, and which I think you ought to see. It is from Oswald to your wife.'

She put the letter into his hand and left him; she dared not await the issue of her act.

CHAPTER XXV.

' FAREWELL, CONTENT.'

JOSHUA read the letter slowly, every word going to his heart like the thrust of a knife. He had been told that a man had addressed a confession of guilty love to his wife, and the knowledge that this thing had been had preyed upon him like a corroding poison. But, even in all he had suffered since Judith's revelation, he had never realised the greatness of the wrong as he did now with the betrayer's letter in his hand, the audacious confession deliberately set down in black and white.

'He dared to write this!' he muttered. 'He dared—to my wife! Oh, God! how low she must have fallen in his esteem before he wrote this letter.'

Here was the cruellest sting. Could Oswald have penned this passionate appeal had he not been sure of a hearing? Did not this letter imply that he knew himself beloved? Ay, there were the abhorrent words burning the paper: 'Our mutual love, which is our mutual sorrow!' This villain made very sure that he was loved. Must he not have been so assured before he dared to ask an honest woman to grant him a secret meeting?

Joshua Haggard sat with the letter in his hand, and a look in those dark eyes of his—a lurid fire under black, lowering brows—which would have struck terror to the hearts of his admiring flock could they have seen their shepherd in his lonely agony. What was he to do—how find revenge great enough for this gigantic wrong? Revenge was not the thought in his mind; retribution, justice, rather, was what he demanded. He felt himself like Orestes, privileged, nay appointed, to slay. The furies might come afterwards, but in this present hour it seemed to him that he might claim this man's blood.

That gentlemanlike institution, the duel, was in full force in Joshua's day. Had he been a man of the world, nothing would have been clearer or more easy than his course. But for the shepherd of souls, the preacher of peace, to take up the sword! Would it not be the renunciation of those principles for which he had lived? How often from his pulpit had he anathematised the slayer of his brother, hurled his thunders against that corrupt society in which murder could be deemed honourable!

He sat with the letter in his hand, and all was dark before him. Could he ever trust his wife again?—believe in her purity, cherish

with a fond and almost fatherly pride that sweet and girlish innocence, that utter ignorance of evil, the freshness and beauty of
life's morning, which had first won his love ?   Never more ; never
more !   His Eve had gathered the fatal fruit ; the serpent had
lifted his venomous crest from among the flowers ; the glory of
life's paradise had faded.   Never more could he love, or worship,
or trust.   Henceforth he must hold her loathly.   If this letter
had reached her, how would she have received it ?   Would she
have listened to the tempter's pleading ?   Would she have stolen
in secret to meet him, to hear his poisonous vows, to pity his weak
unmanly lamentings ?

'I should like to know that,' he said to himself; 'I should
like to know how she would have answered this letter.'

And then it occurred to him that he might easily put her
to the test.   The seal had been broken, but the paper round it
was untorn.   It would be easy to re-seal the letter, making the
second seal just a little larger than the first.   And Cynthia would
not examine the outside of the letter too closely.

He lighted a candle and re-sealed the violated letter; then
paused for a moment or so, wondering how he should get it
conveyed to his wife. 'She shall find it somewhere,' he thought.
'Her guilty conscience will tell her it is from her lover.   He may
have written to her before, perhaps.   God only knows the greatness of her sin—God who made us, and knows the blackness of
our unregenerate hearts.   And I thought that there could be
one exempt—one free from humanity's universal taint.   Fool, fool,
fool !'

He went slowly upstairs to the bedchamber, the airy, orderly
room, with its substantial old-fashioned furniture, and look of
homely comfort—the room that had once been his father's.   There
hung the old grocer's turnip-shaped silver watch on the mahogany
stand upon the mantelpiece, ticking with as lusty a beat as when
its sturdy proprietor carried it in his ample drab-cloth fob.   There
were the samplers which testified to the industry and skill of Joshua's
mother and Joshua's wife—the pyramidal apple-trees innocent
of leaves—the angular figures of Adam and Eve in the garden, with
a curly serpent standing on tip-tail between them.   The evening
sun shone into the room, and glorified the gaudy sunflowers on the
chintz bed furniture, and glittered on the brazen handles of Joshua's
escritoire.   A bowl of freshly-gathered roses and carnations on the
table perfumed all the room.   Joshua knew whose busy hand had
plucked the flowers, and the sight of them smote him with an
aching pain.   Oh, wounded heart, for which every new thought was
a new torture !

The escritoire stood open, and there was 'The Sorrows of Werther,' lying where he had placed it after his long night of waking. There had been no need for Cynthia to hide the book any more. It had told its story.

Joshua's sombre glance lighted on the volume. 'Accursed book that taught them to sin!' he exclaimed; 'they might never have fathomed the wickedness of their own hearts but for thee.'

This was hard upon the innocent and noble Charlotte, the misguided but generous Werther.

A thought full of bitterness and anger came into Joshua's mind as he looked at 'Werther.' He would put Oswald's letter between the leaves of that detested book. She would find it there, he felt assured; the book was her own love story, it talked to her of her lover. He could fancy her hanging over the pages—sucking poisonous sweetness from every line. Werther and Oswald were, in Joshua's mind, one.

He put the letter in the book, and was going slowly downstairs, when he stopped, with his hand upon the banisters, and pondered for a minute or so.

The thought came over him that he could not pray with his household, or teach, or exhort them to-night. It was as if an evil spirit were at his shoulder forbidding him that holy and familiar exercise. He felt that it would have been a kind of profanation to lay his hand upon the Bible, that anchor of his life, which had never before seemed insufficient mooring for his wind-driven bark.

'Not to-night,' he muttered to himself—'not to-night.'

He called over the stairs to his daughter, who had just come in from the garden.

'Tell your aunt to read a chapter and a psalm, Naomi,' he said; 'I am too ill to come downstairs again to-night.'

Naomi hurried to him, full of apprehension.

'Dearest father, what is the matter? Can I do anything? can I get you anything?'

Conscience smote her. Why had she afflicted him by the sight of that wicked letter? It would have been better to have taken it to Cynthia and spoken words of Christian reproof and warning. Why had she made him, her dearest upon earth, to suffer?

'No, my dear, you can do nothing. It is the mind that is ill at ease, not the body. My soul is too dark to hold communion with her God. The blow has been heavy.'

'Dear father, it was so wicked of me to show you the letter—an evil, revengeful act. And, after all, the sin may not be so deep as it seems to us. They are but children—weak, foolish, easily led astray. Let us pity and forgive them.'

' I may come—some day when I am old and doting—to pity
her. I can never forgive him.' He put his daughter aside, went
into his bedroom, and shut the door. Naomi dared not follow him.
She went slowly downstairs, greatly troubled.

It is one thing to launch the thunderbolt, and another to survey
the ruin the bolt has made.

Joshua Haggard turned his face to the wall and gave himself
up to darkest thoughts. He rose soon after daybreak, and his first
look was directed to ' Werther.' The letter was gone. Yes ; there
was nothing now between the pages but a few faded rose-leaves,
and withered fern tendrils, which marked a favourite passage here
and there.

He looked from the book to his wife, lying with her face turned
from the light, and one round white arm, dimpled like a young
child's, thrown above her head. Was she sleeping placidly with
that guilty secret in her breast, or only pretending to sleep ? He
could not tell.

' She is all dissimulation,' he thought, ' fairest seeming, sweetest
show—bitter as ashes within ! '

Chapter XXVI.

' WE TWO STOOD THERE WITH NEVER A THIRD.'

IN the sultry August afternoon—earth glorious in the full
power of the sunshine— Oswald Pentreath went up to Matcherly Common. It was a long walk and a hot one, but in this
land of beauty there were many welcome spots of shade—cool lanes
shadowed by tangled greenery, natural arcades of oak and hawthorn, wild apple and elderberry, from which he could look out
on the glittering sea, almost intolerable in its sunlit splendour.
There was the wood to cross ; a deep and cool retreat, where inter-
woven boughs made summer days seem a perpetual even-song. Only
here and there stole a shaft of vivid light through the beechen
branches ; while here and there the ruddy fur of a squirrel flashed
like a flying gleam of colour through the gloom.

Oswald walked slowly, his hands clasped behind his back, giving
himself up to the soft influence of the scene and hour, and thinking of Cynthia.

Would she grant his prayer? Would she meet him ? Love
and hope said yes—and the thought of the meeting was rapture,
though despair lay beyond it. He was to die to-night—or at least
all of him that made life worth having—but he was to be happy
first ; happy for the briefest flash of time in which he could hold

her in his arms and press one kiss upon her innocent brow, and bless her and leave her.

The thought that his letter might reach the wrong hands had not occurred to him. He had seen Cynthia sitting in the wilderness, and had thrown his letter almost at her feet; Jim's approach had made him retreat rather suddenly, but it had never struck him that Cynthia might not see the letter and that Jim might.

The common was on high ground rising above the wood—a broad tract of undulating land clothed with furze, and with a pool of water here and there, just like that stretch of heath, far away, where Joshua Haggard had found his second wife. The mines, whose deserted shafts disfigured this billowy expanse of golden bloom, had not been worked since Watt first applied steam to mining. They had yielded well enough in their day, had made some men rich and ruined others; and there stood the ruined engine-houses with their tall chimneys, wide apart across the common, like sentinel towers on the coast of a golden sea.

Cynthia was there. Oswald found her sitting on a yellow bank at the base of the abandoned shaft, sitting with a book open in her lap trying to read. She started up, as he came towards her, with a frightened look, as if his coming had been a surprise to her, and stood before him very pale and with clasped hands.

'Dearest, best, how shall I thank you?' he cried, taking her hands and kissing them in a rapture of gratitude.

'Do not thank me at all, Oswald—indeed I am afraid I have done very wrong in coming; you ought not to have asked me, you ought never to have come back to Combhollow, unless it was in your heart to be true to Naomi. Oh, Oswald, why can you not love her as she deserves to be loved, as you did once love her? She is so good, so noble, like my dear husband in all high thoughts. Why cannot your heart come back to her? Why should we all be miserable because you are inconstant?'

The poor little soul had come here to say this. She had come with a clear and honest purpose in her mind—come to bring the wanderer back to the path of duty.

'Can a man help his fate?' said Oswald, gloomily. 'It is my fate to love you. I shall love you till I die. But don't be frightened, Cynthia; I will be the cause of misery to none of you. I am going to America, my mind is quite made up on that point.'

'And you will break Naomi's heart. If you could see the change in her since you left us you could not help being sorry.'

'I am sorry. My soul is sick with its burden of sorrow. But my heart cannot go back to Naomi. It never was hers. I never knew what love meant till I loved you. I made the fatal error of

'SHE WAS THERE.'

mistaking affection for love. I am sorry for her; sorry that I have wronged so noble a creature; sorry for the loss of that peaceful life which I once thought to share with her. But I cannot go back. You might as well ask me to be a child again. The star of my manhood shone upon me when I saw you.'

'I wish I were wiser,' said Cynthia, sadly; 'I wish I could speak as I feel I ought to speak; I might convince you then, perhaps.'

'Not if you had the eloquence of Brougham and the wisdom of Bacon. Naomi and I are parted for ever, dearest, and at her own desire. It is best that it should be so. Providence has been good to me in loosening a bond that would have made two lives miserable.'

And then he said no more about Naomi, but began to talk of himself, and love, and fate, and parting, and despair. Foolish words that have been said so often, empty breath for the most part, bearing no result upon this earth save idle sorrow and wasted tears, yet which mean so much for the speaker and the one who listens. Cynthia had come there to hear no such passionate complaints and protestations. She had come, intent upon delivering her pious lecture—talking to him of grace and redemption, and the sacred stream which washes away all sin—and winning him back to duty and Naomi. Yet she lingered and heard him. It was the last time; they were parting for ever. Who should blame them for this one half-hour, which would stand hereafter like a chasm in the life of each, parting youth and passion from sober age and duty? It could matter to no one that they had met thus and thus parted.

'You will try to lead a good life?' pleaded Cynthia, when Oswald had told his pitiful story—told how he had honestl striven to forget her, and had failed; 'you will cling to the cross? Oh, let me think when you are far away, across that wide cruel sea, that your soul is safe, that you are one of the elect—that I shall meet you where the seas are jasper, and the glory of the Lamb lights the shining streets. You will try to be good, Oswald? Promise me that!'

'I would wear raiment of camel's-hair and a hempen girdle for thy sake, dearest.'

'You will go to chapel—church is so cold and dull. It has no awakening power, it does not call the lost home. You will seek out some stirring preacher, like Joshua, and let him lead you to the sheltering rock, and you will drink the living water and be saved.'

Oswald looked down at the fair young face, lifted to his with such utter earnestness; not one thought of earth in the pleading soul—only thorough and implicit belief in something higher and better than earth, a prize to be struggled for and won.   In the Greek race called the lampadrome, in which the runners carried lighted lamps in their hands, they were the winners who reached the goal with their lamps still burning.   So in the Christian race, the light once quenched, there is but little hope for the runner.   It might be safely said of Cynthia, as she looked up at her lover with truthful innocent eyes, charging him to be thoughtful for eternity, that her lamp still burned with purest light.

Oswald looked down at her through a mist of tears.

'Yes,' he said, 'for your sake I will try to go to heaven.   I have been careless of these things.   I meant to let Naomi make me a Christian, but she was to have had all the trouble.   But for your sake, to meet you hereafter in a fairer world, to see this dear face again shining amidst the angel faces, I will struggle, I will strive to make my life worthier and better!'

'God bless and comfort you, and establish you in well-doing,' said Cynthia; 'and now good-bye.   I must not stay a moment longer.   I have been too long already.'

She looked at her watch.   Four o'clock, and she had three miles to walk before five.   There would be much astonishment and questioning if she was not punctual in her appearance at the tea-table.

'You will let me walk through the wood with you?'

'No; what would be the use?   I have said all I had to say. It would only make us more unhappy.'

'It would give us one more hour together,' said Oswald—'an hour in paradise.'

'The Christian's paradise is to be reached by thornier paths than those through Matcherly Wood,' answered Cynthia, with a reproving air.   'Good-bye, Oswald.'

Her earnestness dominated him, weak and childish as she looked, with the fair hair clustering in tiny baby curls under the shady cottage bonnet.   Very soft and gentle, but very firm at the same time she seemed, in her simple straightforwardness of purpose; and Oswald obeyed her.

'Since it must be so, then, good-bye,' he said, gloomily.   'I promised that I would be content with a brief farewell, such as condemned criminals have.   You have given me a little sermon into the bargain.   I ought to be more than satisfied.   Farewell, my best beloved; the seas will roll between us soon, and there will be nothing left for me but the picture and memory of to-day— nothing but the dreams that haunt my pillow—the sweet unreal presence of her I love.'

He took her to his breast; she having no more force to resist those circling arms than a lily to recoil from the hand that gathers it; took her gently and solemnly to his heart, and pressed his lips on the white forehead. It was a long and fervent kiss; but if there was passion in it, that passion was no low or sensual feeling, only the passion of a great love and a deep despair.

'Bless you, my darling!' he cried. 'God bless you, and guard you, and make all days and paths pleasant and peaceful for you, when I am far away.'

And so they parted—for ever. Unhappily, there was one who saw the lingering meeting, the fond embrace, the fervent kiss, but could not hear the words that went with them.

CHAPTER XXVII.

'IT IS A BASILISK UNTO MINE EYE.'

TRANQUIL and monotonous days hung like a cloud upon the little household of Combhollow. The daily round of labour—of eating and drinking in a spare and Spartan fashion—of praying and preaching, went on with pitiless regularity; but of household joys there were none, of family love but little. A gloomy change had come over Joshua Haggard. He was still the enthusiastic apostle of Primitive Methodism—a man ready to go out and preach the gospel in wild and barbarous places, to be the bearer of glad tidings to those who despised and rejected such messengers, to be hooted by a brutal rabble, if need were, and driven from village to village at peril of his life, and to escape from his persecutors by the skin of his teeth, as John Wesley did, more than once, in his long and difficult career. He was ready to endure all things. Day by day his discourses grew more fervid, but alas! more darkly fraught with a message which was not glad tidings—the message of an offended and an avenging God. Christ, the Saviour, was almost excluded from the preacher's exhortations. When he talked of man's Redeemer it was as of one who turned His face from a sinful world, in which there were very few to be saved. If he had lived in that awful time before the Deluge, when all the earth was peopled with reprobates, he could hardly have been more despairing of humanity's ultimate destiny.

His flock were in no wise offended by this gloomy view of their spiritual condition, although it implied so mean an opinion of their personal merits and conduct. The more vehemently threatening Joshua Haggard's sermons became, the more eagerly the sinners crowded to hear him. It was as if they liked to hear themselves upbraided and denounced. Perhaps everybody saw the barbed shaft fly straight to the gold of a neighbour's heart, and did not feel it rankling in his own. When Joshua talked of the frivolity and extravagance of an unregenerate race, Mrs. Pinter thought of Mrs. Mivers's last new bonnet, which was clearly a superfluous and culpable outlay; such bonnet not being due to Mrs. Mivers, from an economic point of view, until Advent Sunday, whereas the lady had flaunted it before the disapproving eyes of the flock early in October. If Joshua denounced sensuality and the vile indulgence of earthly desires, Mrs. Pentelow's thoughts flew at once to the Polwhele family, who were known to have hot suppers—squab pies, and other savoury meats—every night in the week. You could see the grease oozing out of their complexions on warm Sunday afternoons, as if digestion as well as respiration were a function of the skin.

From the day when he gave up humanity for lost, and plainly told them so, Joshua's popularity increased in a marked degree. The darker his doctrine grew, the better his congregation liked to hear him. It was not milk for babes which they wanted, but strong meat for men of iron thews and sinews, and women with vigorous constitutions and masculine strength of mind. They liked to hear that the Devil was among them, at their shoulders, prompting them to evil, fighting for the mastery of their souls.

'I can see him, I can feel his presence,' cried Joshua, in a passion of despairing ecstasy. 'He is among us; his sulphurous breath burns me with a foretaste of eternal fire; his whisper hisses in my ear as the serpent's hiss stole into the ear of Eve. He will not loose his hold. He is fighting for the possession of my soul; he is striving to drag me down into the pit. What shall I do to be saved? How shall I win the fight against so omnipotent an adversary—omnipotent to destroy—omnipotent to enthral and enchain souls? He wants to people hell, my brethren. He is not content with his victory over willing sinners; the profligates and harlots are too pitiful a prey for him! He wants to have the virtuous man in his net. He would have liked to get John Wesley, or George Whitefield, or William Law. He tried for them as he is trying for us. He is a fallen angel himself, and it pleases him to entrap men of high estate—to take the Christian in his toils—to make the white scarlet, and the wool like unto blood.'

Naomi heard and shuddered. Was this her father who had preached infinite faith in God's mercy, in Christ's redeeming grace? He talked now as if mankind were abandoned as a prey to the Evil One, with no guardian and champion to protect and save; no all-merciful Judge to adjust the balance; as if humanity, forgotten by God, were left to struggle single-handed against the devices of the Great Enemy. Of our ever-interceding Redeemer, of guardian angels, and ministering spirits, and saints who had fought and conquered, Joshua now rarely spoke. He described a world given over to the Prince of Darkness.

Nor was this the only change which Naomi beheld with remorseful grief, believing herself in somewise to blame for this gloomy transformation. In his home as well as in his pulpit the minister was a new man. It was not in his nature to become a domestic tyrant. He interfered with no one's liberty or comfort; but he sat in his domestic circle like a statue; he banished all cheerfulness by his silent presence, he breathed an atmosphere of gloom.

Even Judith regretted this alteration in her brother's temper, though she had been apt in happier days to think him far too easy and indulgent a father. She, like Naomi, had her moments of remorse, thinking the change her work. Better perhaps if she had held her tongue about that foolish young man, and let time and Providence cure him of his folly. Naomi's marriage would have been a feather in the family cap; and although Miss Haggard had been disposed to begrudge her niece this exaltation, it was a trial to receive the condolences of friends whose affected sympathy thinly disguised their inward satisfaction. Yes, taking all things into consideration, Judith was sorry she had not held her peace. She had acted for the best, of course. When had she ever done otherwise? But the worst had come of it instead of the best.

Cynthia bore her cross and made no murmur, and had neither kindness nor pity from any one except James Haggard, who thought it a hard thing that his pretty young stepmother should lead so dreary a life. She had not even the business and the delightful consciousness of increasing profits to console her; nor the power to restore exhausted nature with a surreptitious handful of figs or pudding-raisins when the dinner had been more than usually Spartan. James was sorry for the 'poor little woman,' as he called her, and was kind to her always, for which grace she rewarded him with heartfelt affection.

But her husband—the teacher, master, and friend, whom she had loved so dearly, reverenced so deeply, and to whom, even when weak enough to pity and return Oswald's romantic passion, she had always rendered homage and affection—had withdrawn his favour from her; he loved her no longer; he was doubtless sorry that he had linked himself to so weak and useless a creature.

'What am' I in his life?' she asked herself, in deepest despondency. 'I cannot even keep his house for him; others do that. I sit by his fireside a useless intruder. He will not let me share in his higher life; if I ask him about the books he reads, or talk to him about our religion, I can see a cold and disdainful sneer upon his lip. Sometimes I think that he is getting to hate me.'

This thought was poison. Cynthia searched her life to see in what article of it she had offended her husband, and could discover no cause for his anger. That she had erred in letting Oswald love her, in letting her heart go out to him, she knew, and had repented of her sin with many tears; and, having bidden the sinner an eternal farewell, deemed that error a thing of the past, repented of, and in somewise atoned. She did not believe that jealousy was the cause of her husband's estrangement. Jealousy was allied to love, and her great fear was that Joshua hated her. She did not know that there is a kind of jealousy, and that which has its root in the deepest love, which puts on the garb of hate, and has not seldom culminated in murder—such jealousy as made Othello strike Desdemona before the Venetian emissaries, the passion of strong natures.

She endured her husband's unkindness with a sweet submission which might have softened a sterner temper than Joshua's, and would assuredly have melted him but for the corroding influence of a sleepless jealousy—jealousy of the past—jealousy of a ghost—for the departed Oswald was nothing more than a shade.

Joshua had said no word to his daughter about Oswald's letter. All through that day on which Cynthia went to Matcherly Common, Naomi had been full of anxiety and fear. How would her father act? Would his anger against Oswald take any violent shape? That was assuredly a contingency to be dreaded, an evil she had not foreseen when she gave Joshua the letter. But passion is fatally blind. The harm being done, she could see the possible danger plainly enough.

All through the long summer day she was restless and watchful, fearing she knew not what, or, rather, not daring to tell herself what she feared. The morning went by very quietly: Cynthia sitting in the parlour, sewing; Naomi busy about her usual household labours. She went in and out of the parlour a good many times, and always found Cynthia in the same attitude, working assiduously at that fine stitching which would have tried older eyes.

Had Joshua spoken to his wife about the letter?

Yes. Naomi thought he had. There was one bright spot of

colour on Cynthia's pale cheek that told of agitation studiously suppressed. Once when Naomi spoke to her she answered ab-sently. She must know something about the letter, Naomi thought.

After dinner, Cynthia went up to her bed-room, and came down again five minutes afterwards with her bonnet on. It was a busy afternoon in the shop. Aunt Judith and Jim had returned to their duties, and Joshua had gone out. There was only Naomi in the parlour, when Cynthia came down ready for her walk.

'I am going for a long walk, Naomi,' she said. 'I shall be home by tea-time.'

There was no fear of Naomi offering to accompany her step-mother. They had not walked together since Oswald Pentreath's departure. Day by day the gulf had been widening.

This walk of Cynthia's set Naomi wondering. Could she be gone to meet Oswald? That seemed of all things most unlikely. Joshua had the letter; it was Joshua who would keep the appoint-ment. And then, oh God! who would tell what might be the issue of the meeting!

Naomi went about the house and the garden like a wandering spirit for the next hour, and then it seemed to her that this suspense was beyond endurance; she must follow her father to the old shaft—she made very sure that he had gone there—she must be on the spot or near it, whatever harm was to come. Oh, why had she given him that shameful letter? Blind and wicked rage which prompted so wild an act!

'Did I want to make my father's life miserable, or to bring evil upon Oswald?' she cried. 'Yes, I was wicked enough for anything yesterday; I was mad with anger and jealousy.' She put on her bonnet, and went out, unseen even by Sally, who was washing in the cool brick-floored back kitchen. The sun was blazing upon the neat little town. The white houses were of a dazzling brightness, the sweet-williams and red roses shone like spots of fire, the ruddy glow of the forge looked pale against the sun-glory. Naomi took no heed of the heat; she walked rapidly to the end of the lane that led to Matcherly and then ran along the shaded narrow way till she came to the edge of the wood. Here she paused for a little, breathless and exhausted. They would be coming homewards by this time, she thought. Cynthia and Oswald, and he who had gone perhaps to watch their meeting—or to disturb it. She might come face to face with her false lover. Her heart beat wildly at the thought.

There was one central path through the wood, a clearly defined cattle track, which, she felt assured, would be taken by any one going in the direction of the old shaft. It was easy to skirt this broad grassy track by a narrow footway that wound through the underwood, and among the smooth silvery beech boles and the rugged greenish grey oak trunks. The path ran like a thread through the bracken. By this narrow way Naomi went swiftly, till she came to the rising ground that sloped upwards to Matcherly Common. Here she chose her post of espial behind a sturdy old oak, bearded with grey lichen, and half strangled with ivy—a Methuselah of trees, from which time had lopped limb after limb, but which still held numerous arms aloft, like a woodland Briareus, and seemed to threaten or denounce surrounding Nature. So one might fancy some prophetic Druid transformed into a tree, dumbly prophesying evil to come upon the earth.

Sheltered by this broad trunk, which stood waist high in hawthorn and bracken, Naomi waited to see her father and Oswald pass by and to be assured that all was well with them. They would hardly fail to return by the cattle track; it was the only direct path to Combhollow, and on either side the underwood was too thick and wild for the perambulation of anything but the furred and feathered inhabitants of the forest.

She waited for what seemed a long and weary time; then, a little after four o'clock, she saw Cynthia go by, walking slowly. She was very pale, and the white wan cheeks bore the trace of tears: but she had a resigned look, as of one whose soul is not lost to peace.

'She has been to meet him,' thought Naomi. 'And yet she does not look like a shameless sinner.' Then Naomi began to pray that Joshua might not have seen that clandestine unholy meeting—that he might have been spared the temptation to any evil act.

The time she had to wait for her father's coming hung heavily, so great had become that burden of nameless dread. Yet it was but half an hour after Cynthia had gone by that her husband came slowly along the forest glade, and passed within a yard of the tree behind which his daughter was watching.

She rose as he approached, and stood leaning against the bulky old trunk, gazing at her father's face as she had never looked before at anything under God's heaven. Never had any other spectacle so thrilled, so frozen her being, as this one view of a familiar countenance. To have looked in the face of the dead would have been less awful.

White to the lips, and with big drops of sweat upon brow and cheek, the mouth rigid, the dark eyes almost hidden under the lowering brows—Joshua, the Christian preacher, the man sure of election and grace, passed under the flickering lights and shadows ; like some horrible vision of sin and vengeance, passed, and was gone. Naomi leaned against the tree, her hands clasped, her eyes gazing at the empty air, the shaft of afternoon sunlight upon which a million atoms, each a life, danced and sparkled; yet still seeing that blanched and awful face—the face of a man who had come straight from some hideous death-scene ; the face of a man burdened with the secret of a crime.

'Oh, God !' cried Naomi, with an overmastering despair, 'why didst thou create us, predestined sinners, judged, doomed before we were born ! The best of us, the most earnest, the truest, the noblest, given over a prey to the Evil One ! My father, even my father, lowest, blackest of sinners ! '

She stood in the same attitude, supported by the mossy trunk; stood as in a trance, and saw the sunlight dip lower behind the black branches and change from gold to rose, from rose to crimson, from deepest red to tenderest purple. She watched these changes in a kind of semi-consciousness and a strange feeling of uncertainty as to her own identity ; this Naomi Haggard leaning against a tree seeming to her—the actual entity—to be a forlorn and stricken creature sorely to be pitied. She pitied herself and was sorry for herself with a half-scornful compassion. And so she waited, in a dreamy watchfulness, till nature gave way and she sank, worn out, into a heap at the foot of the tree.

Here, faint and exhausted but not unconscious, she still watched, till thick night came down upon the wood, and she heard the owls hooting and saw the rabbits running within a few feet of her resting-place. Only when the darkness closed round her did she rise and go home, too familiar with the wood to lose her way even in the deep shadow of a woodland night-scene. She went homeward slowly, caring little who might question or wonder at her absence.

And in all the time of her watch she had not seen Oswald Pentreath go by.

(To be continued.)

An Invocation.

I.

Stay with me, Poesy ! playmate of childhood !
　Friend of my manhood ! delight of my youth !
Roamer with me over valley and wild wood,
　Searching for loveliness, groping for Truth !
Stay with me, dwell with me, spirit of Poesy ;
　Dark were the world if thy bloom should depart ;
Glory would cease in the sunlight and starlight,
　Freshness and courage would fade from my heart.

II.

Stay with me, comfort me, now more than ever,
　When years stealing over me lead me to doubt
If men, ay ! and women, are all we believed them
　When we two first wandered the green earth about !
Stay with me, strengthen me, soother, adorner,
　Lest knowledge, not wisdom, should cumber my brain
And tempt me to sit in the chair of the scorner,
　And say, with sad Solomon, all things are vain !

III.

Stay with me, lend me thy magical mirror,
　Show me the darkness extinguished in light ;
Show me to-day's little triumph of Error,
　Foiled by to-morrow's great triumph of Right !
Stay with me—nourish me—robe all creation
　In colours celestial of amber and blue ;
Magnify littleness—glorify commonness—
　Pull down the false, and establish the true !

IV.

Stay with me, Poesy ! Let me not stagnate !
　Despairing with fools, or believing with knaves,
That men must be either the one or the other,
　Victors or victims—oppressors or slaves !
Stay with me, cling to me, while there is life in me !
　Lead me, assist me, direct and control !
Be in the shade what thou wert in the sunshine,
　Source of true happiness—light of my soul !

CHARLES MACKAY.

June, 1876.

Dr. ROOKE'S ANTI-LANCET.

All who wish to preserve health, and to prolong life, should read Dr. Rooke's "Anti-Lancet, or Handy Guide to Domestic Medicine," which can be had GRATIS from any Chemist, or POST FREE from Dr. Rooke, Scarborough.

Concerning this book, which contains 168 pages, the late eminent author, Sheridan Knowles, observed:—"It will be an incalculable boon to every person who can read and think."

CROSBY'S BALSAMIC COUGH ELIXIR

Is specially recommended by several eminent Physicians, and by Dr. ROOKE, Scarborough, Author of the "ANTI-LANCET."

It has been used with the most signal success for Asthma, Bronchitis, Consumption, Coughs, Influenza, Consumptive Night Sweats, Spitting of Blood, Shortness of Breath, and all Affections of the Throat and Chest.

Sold in bottles at 1s. 9d., 4s. 6d., and 11s. each, by all respectable Chemists, and Wholesale by JAMES M. CROSBY, Chemist, Scarborough.

☞ Invalids should read Crosby's Prize Treatise on "Diseases of the Lungs and Air-Vessels," a copy of which can be had Gratis of all Chemists.

MAYFAIR SHERRY.

36 per doz.

C. WARD & SON
CHAPEL St WEST MAYFAIR.
LONDON.

36 per doz.

MAYFAIR SHERRY.

SWANBILL CORSETS.

(REGISTERED.)

SWANBILL CORSET (Registered). 14 bis, N.B.—A full deep Corset, especially for ladies inclined to *embonpoint*. The Swanbill is most effective in reducing the figure, and keeping the form flat, so as to enable ladies to wear the fashionable *vêtements* of the day; busk 13½ inches long. Price 14s. 6d. Finest quality, 21s. Scarlet, 15s. 6d.

SWANBILL CORSET (Registered). 51 bis, —Hand-made. Perfect in shape, and producing—even in indifferent figures—that graceful *contour* which is the distinguishing feature of the present style of dress; busk 13 inches long. Price 31s. 6d. Send Size of Waist with P.O. Order to prevent delay and inconvenience.

Mrs. ADDLEY BOURNE, Ladies' Outfitter, &c.,

37 PICCADILLY (opposite St. James's Church); & 76 RUE ST. LAZARE, PARIS.

(Bernard & Co.'s, Leith Distillery, Scotland.)

THE ENCORE WHISKY

(THE DOUBLE DISTILLED).

THE PUREST AND MOST WHOLESOME OF ALL WHISKIES.

Lancet—
'Very *wholesome* and pleasant Whisky.'
British Medical Journal—
'All injurious substances completely removed.'
Medical Times—
'Very *wholesome* and pleasant, and may be safely recommended.'
Medical Press—
'Very pure and wholesome.'
Sanitary Record—
'Deserves a wide-spread reputation.'

Public Health—
'Should be in general use.'
Food and Fuel Reformer—
'All who value their health should use it.'
Professor Tichborne—
'Perfectly free from all impurities.'
Dr. Bartlett—
'Purest Whisky I ever examined.'
Dr. Paul—
'Thoroughly wholesome.'
Dr. Stevenson Macadam—
'Very pure, and exceedingly fine quality.'

Please see that Bernard & Co.'s Labels are on all Bottles. Every Gallon guaranteed the same.

WHOLESALE DEPOT, THREE CROWN SQUARE, BOROUGH. S.E.

MAPL & CO.
TOTTENHAM COURT

Illustrated Catalogue

CARPETS—FURNITURE—BEDDIN

£5. 5s. SILK COSTUMES

Bodice Made.   **Silk Recommended for Wear.**

Plates of Styles and Patterns of Silk Free on Application.

JAMES SPENCE & CO.,
76, 77, 78, & 79
ST. PAUL'S CHURCHYARD.

JOHN HEAT

YE OLD COURT HAND PEN

OBLIQUE NIB   TURNED U

WILL SUIT EVERY

IN 6ᵈ & 1/ BOXES AT ALL ST

BY POST FOR 7 OR 13

BIRMINGHA

SIGNAL VICTORY AT YORKSHIRE EXHIBITION.
Awarded the only Medal. All Comers beaten.

TAYLOR'S
PATENT SEWING MACHINES
ARE THE BEST FOR
DRESSMAKING AND FAMILY USE,

being simple to learn, easy to work, quiet in action, not liable to get out of order. Intending purchasers, if unable to obtain Taylor's Patent Sewing Machines from local Dealers, are respectfully requested to send for a prospectus to
97 CHEAPSIDE, LONDON, E.C.

Reckit

Pai
Bl

Possesses the following advantages ;—

1st.—Great Strength.
2nd.—Exceeding Beauty of Tint.
3rd.—Great Economy in use.
4th.—It cannot rot or injure the linen.

Patronised by the Laundresses of the and Duchess of Edinburg
To be had of all respectable Grocers, Oil

CADBURY'
COC
ESS

The reason why so many are unable to take Cocoa is, that the varieties commonly sold are mixed with Starch, under the plea of rendering them soluble; while really making them *thick, heavy,* and *indigestible.* This may be easily detected, *for if Cocoa thickens in the cup it proves the addition of starch.* CADBURY'S Cocoa Essence is genuine, it is therefore three times the strength of these Cocoas, and a refreshing Beverage like Tea or Coffee.

PURE, SOLUBLE, REFRESHING

Spottiswoode & Co. Printers, New-street Square, London.

Vol. XXX.

No. 119

BELGRAVIA

A
LONDON MAGAZINE

SEPTEMBER
1876

CHATTO & WINDUS, PICCADILLY, LONDON. W.

All rights reserved

J. & P. COATS'
SEWING
COTTON.

BEST SOFT 6-CORD SEWING COTTON.
SUITABLE FOR ALL SEWING MACHINES.

EXTRA GLACÉ COTTON.
This Cotton being greatly improved in quality and finish, will be found unsurpassed for Machine or Hand Sewing.

On Reels, 100, 200, or 300 Yards.

CROCHET OR TATTING COTTON,
Unsurpassed in Quality.

To be had of all Wholesale & Retail Drapers throughout the United Kingdom.

Johnston's
Corn Flour
Is the Best.

'Quite free from Adulteration.'
—*Lancet.*

'Is decidedly superior.'
—*Lancet.*

ROWLANDS' ODONTO

Whitens the teeth and prevents and arrests their decay. 2s. 9d. per box.

ROWLANDS' MACASSAR OIL

Prevents the hair falling off or turning grey, and eradicates scurf and dandriff.
Price 3s. 6d., 7s., 10s. 6d. (family bottles equal to four small), and 21s.

Ask any Chemist, Perfumer, or Hairdresser for Rowlands' Articles, and avoid cheap imitations.

KINAHAN'S LL WHISKY.

KINAHAN & CO. find that, through the recommendation of the Medical Profession, the demand for their

CELEBRATED OLD LL WHISKY

for purely medicinal purposes is very great. They think therefore it will be satisfactory to the Public to read the following EXTRACTS OF THE ANALYSIS of the LL Whisky from the eminent Analyst, Da. ARTHUR HILL HASSALL:—"I have very carefully and fully analysed Samples of this well-known and popular Whisky. The samples were soft and mellow to the taste, aromatic and ethereal to the smell.—The Whisky must be pronounced to be pure, well-matured, and of very excellent quality. The Medical Profession may feel full confidence in the purity and quality of this Whisky."

20 GREAT TITCHFIELD STREET, OXFORD STREET, LONDON.

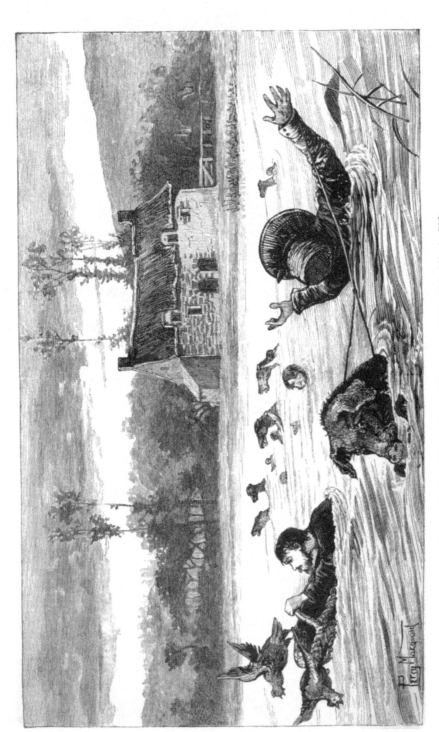

MAN'S LIFE SAVED BY FOWLS, AND WOMAN'S BY A PIG.

BELGRAVIA.

SEPTEMBER 1876.

GOOD STORIES OF MAN AND OTHER ANIMALS.

BY CHARLES READE.

4. Lambert's Leap.

NEAR Newcastle is Sandy-ford bridge, thirty-six feet above the river, which, like many Northern streams, is seldom quite full, but flows in a channel, with the rocky bed bare on each side : an ugly bridge to look up to ; or to look over, driving by.

In Scotland and the North of England, when our wise ancestors got hold of so dizzy and dangerous a place, they made the most of it ; with incredible perversity they led the approach to such a bridge either down a steep, or nearly at right angles. They carried Sandy-ford lane up to the bridge on the rectangular plan, and thereby secured two events, which were but the natural result of their skill in road-making, yet, taken in conjunction, have other claims to notice.

At a date I hope some day to ascertain precisely, but at present I can only say that it was very early in the present century, a young gentleman, called Lambert, was run away with by his horse ; the animal came tearing down Sandy-ford lane, and, thanks to ancestral wisdom aforesaid, charged the bridge with such momentum and impetus that he knocked a slice of the battlement, and half a ton of masonry, into the air, and went down after it into the river, with his rider.

The horse was killed ; Mr. Lambert, though shaken, was not seriously injured by this awful leap. The masonry was repaired ; and, to mark the event, these words, 'LAMBERT'S LEAP,' were engraved on the new coping-stone. The road was allowed to retain its happy angle.

December 5, 1822, about 11, forenoon, Mr. John Nicholson, of Newcastle, a student in surgery, was riding in Sandy-ford lane.

His horse ran away with him, and, being unable to take the sharp turn for such cases made and provided, ran against the battlement of the bridge. It resisted this time, and brought the horse to his knees; but the animal, being now thoroughly terrified, rose and actually leaped, or scrambled, over the battlement, and fell into the rocky bed below, carrying away a single coping-stone, viz., the stone engraved ' LAMBERT'S LEAP.' That stone was broken to pieces by the fall; the poor young man was so cruelly injured that he never spoke again; he died at seven o'clock that evening—but the horse was so little the worse, and so tamed by the fall, that he was at once ridden into Newcastle for assistance.

The reversed fates of the two animals, and the two incidents happening within an inch of each other, have earned them a place in this collection.

Richardson's ' Local Historian's Table Book' relates the second leap, and refers to the first, which is also authenticated.

5. Man's Life Saved by Fowls, and Woman's by a Pig.

MEN'S lives have been sometimes taken, sometimes saved, by other animals, in ways that sound incredible until the details are given.

Here is a list that offers a glimpse into the subject, nothing more :

1. Several ships and crews destroyed by fish.
2. Two ships and crews saved by fish.
3. One crew saved by a dog.
4. Many men killed by dogs, and many saved.
5. Many men killed by horses, and many saved.
6. Men killed, and saved, by rats.
7. Man killed by a dead pig.
8. Woman saved from death by a live pig.
9. Man saved by fowls.
10. Ditto by a crocodile.
11. Ditto by a lady-bird.
12. One man executed by the act of a horse.
13. Crows leading to the execution of murderers.
14. A man's life saved by an ape.
15. Ditto by a bear.
16. Ditto by a fox.

Some of these sound like riddles, and are at least as well worth puzzling over as acrostics and conundra.

I will leave the majority to rankle in my reader, and rouse his curiosity. But I feel he is entitled to some immediate proof that the whole list is not a romance; so I will relate 8 and 9, by way of specimen.

And here let me premise that, as a general rule, I exclude from this collection all those wonderful stories about animals, which are found only in books specially devoted to that subject. Those writers are all theorists : men with an amiable bias in favour of the inferior animals. This tempts them to twist and exaggerate facts, and even to repeat stale falsehoods, which have gone the round for years, but never rested on the evidence of an eye-witness.

On the other hand, when some plain man, who has no theory, writes down a story at the time, and on the spot, and sends it off to a newspaper or other chronicle of current events, where it lies open to immediate contradiction, then we are on the *terra firma* of history.

Example.—Here is a letter written on the spot, and at the time, to a newspaper, and transferred from that newspaper to the 'Annual Register':—

Extract of a Letter from Nottingham.

January 9, 1761.

On Tuesday se'nnight Mr. Hall's servant of Beckingham, returning from market, and finding the boat at Gainsborough putting off from shore full of people, was so rash and imprudent (to say no worse of it) as to leap his horse into the boat, and with the violence of the fall drove the poor people and their horses to the farther side, which instantly carried the boat into the middle of the stream and overset it.

Imagine you see the unfortunate sufferers all plunging in a deep and rapid river, calling out for help and struggling for life. It was all horror and confusion ; and during this situation the first account was despatched, which assured us that out of eighty souls only five or six were saved. By a second account we were told that there were only thirty on board, but that out of these above twenty had been drowned. This was for some time believed to be the truest account ; but I have the pleasure to hear by a third account, that many of those, who were supposed to be lost, have been taken up alive ; some of them at a great distance from the ferry ; and that no more than six are missing, though numbers were brought to life with difficulty. It was happy for them that so many horses were on board, as all who had time to lay hold of a stirrup, or a horse's tail, were brought safe to shore.

A poor man, who had a basket of fowls upon his arm, was providentially buoyed up till assistance could be had, and he, after many fruitless attempts, was at last taken up alive, though senseless, at a distance of four hundred yards from the ferry.

A poor woman who had bought a pig, and had tied one end of a string round its foot and the other round her own wrist, was dragged safe to land in this providential manner.

Observe—I am better than my word; for I have thrown you in the circumstance that the horses saved the rest: certainly in this particular business the lord of the creation does not show that vast superiority to the brutes which he assumes in some of his sculptures and nearly all his writings; Butler's ' Analogy' included. The animal that makes the mischief by his folly is a man: the animals that prove incompetent to save their own lives are the men. All the other animals in the boat, down to the very pig, turn to and pull the lords and ladies of the creation out of the mess one of these peerless creatures had plunged them all into.

·

Swedenborg's Visions of other Worlds.

BY RICHARD A. PROCTOR.

IF it were permitted to men to select a sign whereby they should know that a message came from the Supreme Being, probably the man of science would select for the sign the communication of some scientific fact beyond the knowledge of the day, but admitting of being readily put to the test. The evidence thus obtained in favour of a revelation would correspond in some sense to that depending on prophecies; but it would be more satisfactory to men having that particular mental bent which is called the scientific. Whether this turn of mind is inherent or the result of training, it certainly leads men of science to be more exacting in considering the value of evidence than any men, except, perhaps, lawyers. In the case of the student of science, St. Paul's statement that 'prophecies' 'shall fail' has been fulfilled, whereas it may be doubted whether evidence from 'knowledge' would in like manner 'vanish away.' On the contrary, it would grow stronger and stronger, as knowledge from observation, from experiment, and from calculation continually increased. It can scarcely be said that this has happened with such quasi-scientific statements as have actually been associated with revelation. If we regard St. Paul's reference to knowledge as relating to such statements as these, then nothing could be more complete than the fulfilment of his own prediction, 'Whether there be prophecies, they shall fail; whether there be tongues, they shall cease; whether there be knowledge, it shall vanish away.' The evidence from prophecies fails for the exact inquirer, who perceives the doubts which exist (among the most earnest believers) as to the exact meaning of the prophetic words, and even in some cases as to whether prophecies have been long since fulfilled or relate to events still to come. The evidence from 'tongues' has ceased, and those are dust who are said to have spoken in strange tongues. The knowledge which was once thought supernatural has utterly vanished away. But if, in the ages of faith, some of the results of modern scientific research had been revealed, as the laws of the solar system, the great principle of the conservation of energy, or the wave theory of light, or if some of the questions which still remain for men of science to solve had been answered in those times, the evidence for the student of science would have been irresistible. Of course he will be told that even then he would have hardened his heart; that the inquiry after truth tending naturally to depravity of mind, he would reject even evidence based on his beloved laws of probability; that his 'wicked and adulterous generation seeketh "in vain" after a sign,' and that if he will not accept Moses and the prophets, neither would he believe though one rose from the dead. Still the desire of the student of science to base his faith on convincing evidence (in a matter as important to him as to those who abuse him) does seem to have something reasonable in it after all. The mental qualities which cause him to be less easily satisfied than others, came to him in the same way as his bodily qualities; and even if the result to which his mental training leads him is as unfortunate as some suppose, that training is not strictly speaking so heinously sinful that nothing short of the eternal reprobation meted out to him by earthly judges can satisfy divine justice. So that it may be thought not a wholly unpardonable sin to speak of a sign which, had it been accorded, would have satisfied even the most exacting student of science. Apart, too, from all question of faith, the mere scientific interest of divinely inspired communications respecting natural laws and processes would justify a student of science in regarding them as most desirable messages from a being of superior wisdom and benevolence. If prophecies and tongues, why not knowledge, as evidence of a divine mission?

Such thoughts are suggested by the claim of some religious teachers to the possession of knowledge other than that which they could have gained by natural means. The claim has usually been quite honest. The teacher of religion tests the reality of his mission in simple à priori confidence that he has such a mission, and that therefore some one or other of the tests he applies will afford the required evidence. To one, says St. Paul, is given the word of wisdom; to another, the word of knowledge; to another, faith; to another, the gift of healing; to another, the working of miracles; to another, prophecy; to another, the discerning of spirits; to another, divers kinds of tongues: and so forth. If a man like Mahomet, who believes in his mission to teach, finds that he cannot satisfactorily work miracles—that mountains will not be removed at his bidding—then some other evidence satisfies him of the reality of his mission. Swedenborg, than whom, perhaps, no more honest man ever lived, said and believed that to him had been granted the discerning of spirits. 'It is to be observed,' he said, 'that a man may be instructed by spirits and angels if his interiors be so open as to enable · him to speak and be in company with them, for man in his essence is a spirit, and is with spirits as to his interiors; so that he whose interiors are opened by the Lord may converse with them, as man with man. *This privilege I have enjoyed daily now for twelve years.*'

It indicates the fulness of Swedenborg's belief in this privilege that he did not hesitate to describe what the spirits taught him respecting matters which belong rather to science than to faith; though it must be admitted that probably he supposed there was small reason for believing that his statements could ever be tested by the results of scientific research. The objects to which his spiritual communications related were conveniently remote. I do not say this as desiring for one moment to suggest that he purposely selected those objects, and not others which might be more readily examined. He certainly believed in the reality of the communications he described. But possibly there is some law in things visionary, corresponding to the law of mental operation with regard to scientific theories; and as the mind theorises freely about a subject little understood, but cautiously where many facts have been ascertained, so probably exact knowledge of a subject prevents the operation of those illusions which are regarded as supernatural communications. It is in a dim light only that the active imagination pictures objects which do not really exist; in the clear light of day they can no longer be imagined. So it is with mental processes.

Probably there is no subject more suitable in this sense for the visionary than that of life in other worlds. It has always had an attraction for imaginative minds, simply because it is enwrapped in so profound a mystery; and there has been little to restrain the fancy, because so little is certainly known of the physical condition of other worlds. Recently, indeed, a somewhat sudden and severe check has been placed on the liveliness of imagination which had enabled men formerly to picture to themselves the inhabitants of other orbs in space. Spectroscopic analysis and exact telescopic scrutiny will not permit some speculations to be entertained which formerly met with favour. Yet even now there has been but a slight change of scene and time. If men can no longer imagine inhabitants of one planet because it is too hot, or of another because it is too cold, of one body because it is too deeply immersed in vaporous masses, or of another because it has neither atmosphere nor water, we have only to speculate about the unseen worlds which circle round those other suns, the stars; or, instead of changing the region of space where we imagine worlds, we can look backward to the time when planets now cold and dead were warm with life, or forward to the distant future when planets now glowing with fiery heat shall have cooled down to a habitable condition.

Swedenborg's imaginative mind seems to have fully felt the charm of this interesting subject. It was, indeed, because of the charm which he found in it, that he was readily persuaded into the belief that knowledge had been supernaturally communicated to him respecting it. 'Because I had a desire,' he says, 'to know if there are other earths, and to learn their nature and the character of their inhabitants, it was granted me by the Lord to converse and have intercourse with spirits and angels who had come from other earths, with some for a day, with some for a week, and with some for months. From them I have received information respecting the earths from and near which they are, the modes of life, customs and worship of their inhabitants, besides various other particulars of interest, all which, having come to my knowledge in this way, I can describe as things which I have seen and heard.'

It is interesting (psychologically) to notice how the reasoning which had convinced Swedenborg of the existence of other inhabited worlds is attributed by him to the spirits. 'It is well known in the other life,' he says, 'that there are many earths with men upon them; for there (that is, in the spiritual life) every one who, from a love of truth and consequent use, desires it is allowed to converse with the spirits of other earths, so as to be assured that there is a plurality of worlds, and be informed that the human race is not confined to one earth only, but extends to numberless earths. . . . I have occasionally conversed on this subject with the spirits of our earth, and the result of our conversation was that a man of enlarged understanding may conclude from various considerations that there are many earths with human inhabitants upon them. For, it is an inference of reason that masses so great as the planets are, some of which exceed this earth in magnitude, are not empty bodies, created only to be carried in their motion round the sun, and to shine with their scanty light for the benefit of one earth only; but that they must have a nobler use. He who believes, as every one ought to believe, that the Deity created the universe for no other end than the existence of the human race, and of heaven from it (for the human race is the seminary of heaven), must also believe that wherever there is an earth there are human inhabitants. That the planets which are visible to us, being within the boundary of our solar system, are earths, may appear from various considerations. They are bodies of earthy matter, because they reflect the sun's light, and when seen through the telescope appear, not as stars shining with a flaming lustre, but as earths, variegated with obscure spots. Like our earth, they are carried round the sun by a progressive motion, through the path of the Zodiac, whence they have years and seasons of the year, which are spring, summer, autumn, and winter; and they rotate upon their axes, which makes days, and times of the day, as morning, midday, evening, and night. Some of them also have satellites, which perform their revolutions about their globes, as the moon does about ours. The planet Saturn, as being farthest from the sun, has besides an immense luminous ring, which supplies that earth with much, though reflected, light. How is it possible for any one acquainted with these facts, and who thinks from reason, to assert that such bodies are uninhabited?'

Remembering that this reasoning was urged by the spirits, and that during twelve years Swedenborg's interiors had been opened in such sort that he could converse with spirits from other worlds, it is surprising that he should have heard nothing about Uranus or Neptune, to say nothing of the zone of asteroids, or again, of planets as yet unknown which may exist outside the path of Neptune. He definitely commits himself, it will be observed, to the statement that Saturn is the planet farthest from the sun. And elsewhere, in stating where in these spiritual communications the 'idea' of each planet was conceived to be situated, he leaves no room whatever for Uranus and Neptune, and makes no mention of other bodies in the solar system than those known in his day. This cannot have been because the spirits from then unknown planets did not feel themselves called upon to communicate with the spirit of one who knew nothing of their home, for he received visitors from worlds in the starry heavens far beyond human ken. It would almost seem, though to the faithful Swedenborgian the thought will doubtless appear very wicked, that the system of Swedenborg gave no place to Uranus and Neptune, simply because he knew nothing about those planets. Otherwise, what a noble opportunity there would have been for establishing the truth of Swedenborgian doctrines by revealing to the world the existence of planets hitherto unknown. Before the reader pronounces this a task beneath the dignity of the spirits and angels who taught Swedenborg, it will be well for him to examine the news which they actually imparted.

I may as well premise, however, that it does not seem to me worth while to enter here at any length into Swedenborg's descriptions of the inhabitants of other worlds, because all that he has to say on this subject is entirely imaginative. There is a real interest for us in his ideas respecting the condition of the planet because those ideas were based (though unconsciously) upon the science of his day, in which he was no mean proficient. And even where his mysticism went beyond what his scientific attainments suggested, a psychological interest attaches to the workings of his imagination. It is as curious a problem to trace his ideas to their origin as it sometimes is to account for the various phases of a fantastic dream, such a dream, for instance, as that which Armadale, the doctor, and Midwinter, in ' Armadale,' endeavour to connect with preceding events. But Swedenborg's visions of the behaviour and appearance of the inhabitants of other earths have little interest, because it is hopeless to attempt to account for even their leading features. For instance, what can we make of such a passage as the following, relating to the spirits who came from Mercury?—— ' Some of them are desirous to appear, not like the spirits of other earths as men, but as crystalline globes. Their desire to appear so, although they do not, arises from the circumstance that the knowledges of things immaterial are in the other life represented by crystals.'

Yet some even of these more fanciful visions significantly indicate the nature of Swedenborg's philosophy. One can recognise his disciples and his opponents among the inhabitants of various favoured and unhappy worlds, and one perceives how the wiser and more dignified of his spiritual visitors are made to advocate his own views, and to deride those of his adversaries. Some of the teachings thus circuitously advanced are excellent.

For instance, Swedenborg's description of the inhabitants of Mercury and their love of abstract knowledge contains an instructive lesson. ' The spirits of Mercury imagine,' he says, ' that they know so much, that it is almost impossible to know more. But it has been told them by the spirits of our earth, that they do not know many things, but few, and that the things which they know not are comparatively infinite, and in relation to those they do know are as the waters of the largest ocean to those of the smallest fountain ; and further, that the first advance to wisdom is to know, acknowledge, and perceive that what we do know, compared with what we do not know, is so little as hardly to amount to anything.' [1] So far we may suppose that

[1] It is noteworthy how Swedenborg here anticipates a saying of Laplace, the greatest mathematician the world has known, save Newton alone. Newton's remark that he seemed but as a child who had gathered a few shells on the shores of ocean, is well known. Laplace's words, ' *Ce que nous connaissons est peu de chose* ; *ce que nous ignorons est immense*,' were not, as is commonly stated, his last. De Morgan gives the following account of Laplace's last moments, on the authority of Laplace's friend and pupil, the

Swedenborg presents his own ideas, seeing that he is describing what has been told the Mercurial spirits by the spirits of our earth, of whom (during these spiritual conversations) he was one. But he proceeds to describe how angels were allowed to converse with the Mercurial spirits in order to convince them of their error. 'I saw another angel,' says he, after describing one such conversation, 'conversing with them; he appeared at some altitude to the right; he was from our earth, and he enumerated very many things of which they were ignorant. . . . As they had been proud on account of their knowledges, on hearing this they began to humble themselves. Their humiliation was represented by the sinking of the company which they formed, for that company then appeared as a volume or roll, . . . as if hollowed in the middle and raised at the sides. . . . They were told what that signified, that is, what they thought in their humiliation, and that those who appeared elevated at the sides were not as yet in any humiliation. Then I saw that the volume was separated, and that those who were not in humiliation were remanded back towards their earth, the rest remaining.'

Little being known to Swedenborg, as indeed little is known to the astronomers of our own time, about Mercury, we find little in the visions relating to that planet which possesses any scientific interest. He asked the inhabitants who were brought to him in visions about the sun of the system, and they replied that it looks larger from Mercury than as seen from other worlds. This of course was no news to Swedenborg. They explained further, that the inhabitants enjoy a moderate temperature, without extremes of heat or cold. 'It was given to me,' proceeds Swedenborg, 'to tell them that it was so provided by the Lord, that they might not be exposed to excessive heat from their greater proximity to the sun, since heat does not arise from the sun's nearness, but from the height and density of the atmosphere, as appears from the cold on high mountains even in hot climates; also that heat is varied according to the direct or oblique incidence of the sun's rays, as is plain from the seasons of winter and

well known mathematician Poisson:—'After the publication (in 1825) of the fifth volume of the Mécanique Céleste, Laplace became gradually weaker, and with it musing and abstracted. He thought much on the great problems of existence, and often muttered to himself, "*Qu'est ce que c'est que tout cela!*" After many alternations he appeared at last so permanently prostrated that his family applied to his favourite pupil, M. Poisson, to try to get a word from him. Poisson paid a visit, and after a few words of salutation, said, "J'ai une bonne nouvelle à vous annoncer: on a reçu au Bureau des Longitudes une lettre d'Allemagne annonçant que M. Bessel a vérifié par l'observation vos découvertes théoriques sur les satellites de Jupiter." Laplace opened his eyes and answered with deep gravity, "*L'homme ne poursuit que des chimères.*" He never spoke again. His death took place March 5, 1827.'

summer in every region.' It is curious to find thus advanced, in a sort of lecture addressed to visionary Mercurials, a theory which crops up repeatedly in the present day, because the difficulty which suggests it is dealt with so unsatisfactorily for the most part in our text-books of science. Continually we hear of some new paradoxist who propounds as a novel doctrine the teaching that the atmosphere, and not the sun, is the cause of heat. The mistake was excusable in Swedenborg's time. In fact it so chanced that, apart from the obvious fact on which the mistake is usually based—the continued presence, namely, of snow on the summits of high mountains even in the torrid zone—it had been shown shortly before by Newton, that the light fleecy clouds seen sometimes even in the hottest weather above the wool-pack or cumulus clouds are composed of minute crystals of ice. Seeing that these tiny crystals can exist under the direct rays of the sun in hot summer weather, many find it difficult to understand how those rays can of themselves have any heating power. Yet in reality the reasoning addressed by Swedenborg to his Mercurial friends was entirely erroneous. If he could have adventured as far forth into time as he did into space, and could have attended in the spirit the lectures of one John Tyndall, a spirit of our earth, he would have had this matter rightly explained to him. In reality, the sun's heat is as effective directly at the summit of the highest mountain as at the sea-level. A thermometer exposed to the sun in the former position indicates indeed a slightly higher temperature than one similarly exposed to the sun (when at the same altitude) at the sea-level. But the air does not get warmed to the same degree, simply because, owing to its rarity and relative dryness, it fails to retain any portion of the heat which passes through it.

It is interesting to notice how Swedenborg's scientific conceptions of the result of the (relatively) airless condition of our moon suggested peculiar fancies respecting the lunar inhabitants. Interesting, I mean, psychologically. For it is curious to see scientific and fanciful conceptions thus unconsciously intermingled. Of the conscious intermingling of such conceptions instances are common enough. The effects of the moon's airless condition have been often made the subject of fanciful speculations. The reader will remember how Scheherazade, in 'The Poet at the Breakfast Table,' runs on about the moon. 'Her delight was unbounded, and her curiosity insatiable. If there were any living creatures there, what odd things they must be. They couldn't have any lungs nor any hearts. What a pity! Did they ever die? How could they expire if they didn't breathe? Burn up? No air to burn in. Tumble into some of those horrid pits, perhaps, and break all to bits. She wondered how the young people there liked it, or whether there were any young people there. Perhaps nobody was young and nobody was old, but they were like mummies all of them—what an idea!—two mummies making love to each other! So she went on in a rattling, giddy kind of way, for she was excited by the strange scene in which she found herself, and quite astonished the young astronomer with her vivacity.' But Swedenborg's firm belief that the fancies engendered in his mind were scientific realities, is very different from the conscious play of fancy in the passage just quoted. It must be remembered that Swedenborg regarded his visions with as much confidence as though they were revelations made by means of scientific instruments; nay, with even more confidence, for he knew scientific observations may be misunderstood, whereas he was fully persuaded that his visions were miraculously provided for his enlightenment, and that therefore he would not be allowed to misunderstand aught that was thus revealed to him.

'It is well known to spirits and angels,' he says, 'that there are inhabitants in the moon, and in the moons or satellites which revolve about Jupiter and Saturn. Even those who have not seen and conversed with spirits who are from them, entertain no doubt of their being inhabited, for they, too, are earths, and where there is an earth there is man; man being the end for which every earth exists, and without an end nothing was made by the Great Creator. Everyone who thinks from reason in any degree enlightened, must see that the human race is the final cause of creation.'

The moon, being inhabited then by human beings, but being very insufficiently supplied with air, it necessarily follows that these human beings must be provided in some way with the means of existing in that rare and tenuous atmosphere. Tremendous powers of inspiration and expiration would be required to make that air support the life of the human body. Although Swedenborg could have had no knowledge of the exact way in which breathing supports life (for Priestley was his junior by nearly half a century), yet he must clearly have perceived that the quantity of air inspired has much to do with the vitalising power of the indraught. No ordinary human lungs could draw in an adequate supply of air from such an atmosphere as the moon's; but by some great increase of breathing power it might be possible to live there: at least, in Swedenborg's time there was no reason for supposing otherwise. Reason, then, having convinced him that the lunar inhabitants must possess extraordinary breathing apparatus, and presumably most powerful voices, imagination presented them to him accordingly. 'Some spirits appeared overhead,' he says, 'and thence were heard voices like thunder; for their voices sounded precisely like thunder from the clouds after lightning. I supposed it was a great multitude of spirits who had the art of giving voices with such a sound. The more simple spirits who were with me derided them, which greatly surprised me. But the cause of their derision was soon discovered, which was, that the spirits who thundered were not many, but few, and were as little as children, and that on former occasions they (the thunderers) had terrified them by such sounds, and yet were unable to do them the least harm. That I might know their character some of them descended from on high, where they thundered; and, what surprised me, one carried another on his back, and the two thus approached me. Their faces appeared not unhandsome, but longer than those of other spirits. In stature they were like children of seven years old, but the frame was more robust, so that they were like men. It was told me by the angels that they were from the moon. He who was carried by the other came to me, applying himself to my left side under the elbow, and thence spoke. He said, that when they utter their voices they thunder in this way, 'and it seems likely enough that if there are any living speaking beings in the moon, their voice, could they visit the earth, would be found to differ very markedly from the ordinary human voice. In the spiritual world their thunderous voices have their use. For by their thundering the spirits from the moon terrify spirits who are inclined to injure them, so that the lunar spirits go in safety where they will. To convince me the sound they make was of this kind, he (the spirit who was carried by the other) retired, but not out of sight, and thundered in like manner. They showed, moreover, that the voice was thundered by being uttered from the abdomen like an eructation. It was perceived that this arose from the circumstance that the inhabitants of the moon do not, like the inhabitants of other earths, speak from the lungs, but from the abdomen, and thus from air collected there, the reason of which is that the atmosphere with which the moon is surrounded is not like that of other earths.'

In his intercourse with spirits from Jupiter, Swedenborg heard of animals larger than those that live on the earth. It has been a favourite idea of many believers in other worlds than ours, that though in each world the same races of animals exist, they would be differently proportioned; and there has been much speculation as to the probable size of men and other animals in worlds much larger or much smaller than the earth. When as yet ideas about other worlds were crude, the idea prevailed that giants exist in the larger orbs, and pygmies in the smaller. Whether this idea had its origin in conceptions as to the eternal fitness of things or not, does not clearly appear. It seems certainly at first view natural enough to suppose that the larger beings would want more room and so inhabit the larger dwelling-places. It was a pleasing thought that, if we could visit Jupiter or Saturn, we should find the human inhabitants there

> In bigness to surpass earth's giant sons ;

but that if we could visit our moon or Mercury, or whatever smaller worlds there are, we should find men

> Now less than smallest dwarfs, in narrow room
> Throng numberless, like that pygmæan race
> Beyond the Indian mount ; or fairy elves,
> Whose midnight revels, by a forest side
> Or fountain, some belated peasant sees,
> Or dreams he sees.

Later the theory was started that the size of beings in various worlds depends on the amount of light received from the central sun. Thus Wolfius asserted that the inhabitants of Jupiter are nearly fourteen feet high, which he proved by comparing the quantity of sunlight which reaches the Jovians with that which we Terrenes receive. Recently, however, it has been noted that the larger the planet, the smaller in all probability must be the inhabitants, if any. For if there are two planets of the same density but unequal size, gravity must be greater at the surface of the larger planet, and where gravity is great large animals are cumbered by their weight. It is easy to see this by comparing the muscular strength of two men similarly proportioned, but unequal in height. Suppose one man five feet in height, the other six ; then the cross section of any given muscle will be less for the former than for the latter in the proportion of twenty-five (five times five) to thirty-six (six times six). Roughly, the muscular strength of the bigger man will be half as great again as that of the smaller. But the weights of the men will be proportioned as 125 (five times five times five) to 216 (six times six times six), so that the weight of the bigger man exceeds that of the smaller nearly as seven exceeds four, or by three-fourths. The taller man exceeds the smaller, then, much more in weight than he does in strength ; he is accordingly less active in proportion to his size. Within certain limits, of course, size increases a man's effective as well as his real strength. For instance, our tall man in the preceding illustration cannot lift his own weight so readily as the small man can lift his ; but he can lift a weight of three hundred pounds as easily as the small man can lift a weight of two hundred pounds. When we get beyond certain limits of height, however, we get absolute weakness as the result of the increase of weight. Swift's Brobdingnags, for instance, would have been unable to stand upright ; for they were six times as tall as men, and therefore each Brobdingnag would have weighed 216 times as much as a man, but would have possessed only thirty-six times the muscular power. Their weight would have been greater, then, in a sixfold greater degree than their strength, and, so far as their mere weight was concerned, their condition would have resembled that of an ordinary man under a load five times exceeding his own weight. As no man could walk or stand upright under such a load, so the Brobdingnags would have been powerless to move, despite, or rather because of, their enormous stature. Applying the general considerations here enunciated to the question of the probable size of creatures like ourselves in other planets, we see that men in Jupiter should be much smaller, men in Mercury much larger, than men on the earth. So also with other animals. But Swedenborg's spirit visitors from these planets taught differently. ' The horses of our earth,' he says, ' when seen by the spirits of Jupiter, appeared to me smaller than usual, though rather robust ; which arose from the idea those spirits had respecting them. They informed me that among them there are animals similar, though much larger ; but that they are wild, and in the woods, and that when they come in sight they cause terror though they are harmless ; they added, that their terror of them is natural or innate.' [1]   On the other hand, the inhabitants of Mercury, who might be thirteen feet high yet as active as our men, appeared slenderer than Terrene men. ' I was desirous to know,' says, Swedenborg ' what kind of face and person the people in Mercury have, compared with those of the people on our earth. There therefore stood before me a female exactly resembling the women on that earth. Her face was beautiful, but it was smaller than that of a woman of our earth ; she was more slender, but of equal height ; she wore a linen head-dress, not artfully yet gracefully disposed. A man also was presented. He, too, was more slender than the men of our earth ; he wore a garment of deep blue, closely fitted to his body without folds or flowing skirts. Such, I learn, were the personal form and costume of the humans

---

[1] The reason assigned by Swedenborg is fanciful enough. ' In the spiritual sense,' he says, ' a horse signifies the intellectual principle formed from scientifics, and as they are afraid of cultivating the intellectual faculties by worldly sciences, from this comes an influx of fear. They care nothing for scientifics which are of human erudition.'

of that earth. Afterwards there was shown me a species of the oxen and cows, which did not indeed differ much from those on our earth, except that they were smaller, and made some approach to the stag and hind species.' We have seen, too, that the lunar spirits were no larger than children seven years old.

One passage of Swedenborg's description of Jupiter is curious. 'Although on that earth,' he says, 'spirits speak with men' (i.e. with Jovian men), 'man in his turn does not speak with spirits, except to say, when instructed, *that he will do so no more,*' which we should regard as a bull if it were not news from the Jovian spirit world. 'Nor is man allowed to tell anyone that a spirit has spoken to him; if he does so, he is punished. Those spirits of Jupiter when they were with me, at first supposed they were with a man of their own earth; but when in my turn I spoke with them, and thought of publishing what passed between us and so relating it to others, then, because they were not allowed to chastise me, they discovered they were with a stranger.'

It has been a favourite idea with those who delight in the argument from design, that the moons of the remoter planets have been provided for the express purpose of making up for the small amount of sunlight which reaches those planets. Jupiter receives only about one twenty-seventh part of the light which we receive from the sun; but then, has he not four moons to make his nights glorious? Saturn is yet farther away from the sun, and receives only the ninetieth part of the light we get from the sun; but then he has eight moons and his rings, and the nocturnal glory of his skies must go far to compensate the Saturnians for the small quantity of sunlight they receive. The Saturnian spirits who visited Swedenborg were manifestly indoctrinated with these ideas. For they informed him that the nocturnal light of Saturn is so great that some Saturnians worship it, calling it the Lord. These wicked spirits are separated from the rest, and are not tolerated by them. 'The nocturnal light,' say the spirits, 'comes from the immense ring which at a distance encircles that earth, and from the moons which are called the satellites of Saturn.' And again, being questioned further 'concerning the great ring which appears from our earth to rise above the horizon of that planet, and to vary its situations, they said that it does not appear to them as a ring, but only as a snow-white substance in heaven in various directions.' Unfortunately for our faith in the veracity of these spirits, it is certain that the moons of Saturn cannot give nearly so much light as ours, while the rings are much more effective as darkeners than as illuminators. One can readily calculate the apparent size of each of the moons as seen from Saturn, and thence show that the eight discs of the moons together are larger than our moon's disc in about the proportion of forty-five to eight. So that if they were all shining as brightly as our full moon and all full at the same time, their combined light would exceed hers in that degree. But they are not illuminated as our moon is. They are illuminated by the same remote sun which illuminates Saturn, while our moon is illuminated by a sun giving her as much light as we ourselves receive. Our moon then is illuminated ninety times more brightly than the moons of Saturn, and as her disc is less than all theirs together, not as one to ninety, but as sixteen to ninety, it follows that all the Saturnian moons, if full at the same time, would reflect to Saturn one-sixteenth part of the light which we receive from the full moon.[1] As regards the rings of Saturn, nothing can be more certain than that they tend much more to deprive Saturn of light than to make up by reflexion for the small amount of light which Saturn receives directly from the sun. The part of the ring which lies between the planet and the sun casts a black shadow upon Saturn, this shadow sometimes covering an extent of surface many times exceeding the entire surface of our earth. The shadow thus thrown upon the planet creeps slowly, first one way, then another, northwards and southwards over the illuminated hemisphere of the planet (as pictured in the 13th plate of my treatise on Saturn), requiring for its passage from the arctic

---

[1] Similar reasoning applies to the moons of Jupiter, and it so chances that the result in their case comes out exactly the same as in the case of Saturn; all the Jovian moons, if full together, would reflect only the sixteenth part of the light which we receive from the full moon. It is strange that scientific men of considerable mathematical power have used the argument from design apparently supplied by the satellites, without being at the pains to test its validity by the simple mathematical calculations necessary to determine the quantity of light which these bodies can reflect to the planets round which they travel. Brewster and Whewell, though they took opposite sides in the controversy about other inhabited worlds, agreed in this. Brewster, of course, holding the theory that all the planets are inhabited, very naturally accepted the argument from design in this case; and Whewell, in opposing that theory, did not dwell at all upon the subject of the satellites. But in his 'Bridgewater Treatise on Astronomy and General Physics,' he says, 'Taking only the ascertained cases of Venus, the Earth, Jupiter, and Saturn, we conceive that a person of common understanding will be strongly impressed with the persuasion that the satellites are placed in the system with a view to compensate for the diminished light of the sun at greater distances. Mars is an exception; some persons might conjecture from this case that the arrangement itself, like other useful arrangements, has been brought about by some wider law which we have not yet detected. But whether or not we entertain such a guess (it can be nothing more), we see in other parts of creation so many examples of apparent exceptions to rules, which are afterwards found to be capable of explanation, or to be provided for by particular contrivances, that no one familiar with such contemplations will, by one anomaly, be driven from the persuasion that the end which the arrangements of the satellites seem suited to answer is really one of the ends of their creation.'

to the antarctic regions and back again to the arctic regions of the planet, a period nearly equal to that of a generation of terrestrial men. Nearly thirty of our years the process lasts, during half of which time the northern hemisphere suffers, and during the other half the southern. The shadow band, which be it remembered stretches right athwart the planet from the extreme eastern to the extreme western side of the illuminated hemisphere, is so broad during the greater part of the time that in some regions (those corresponding to our temperate zones) the shadow takes two years in passing, during which time the sun cannot be seen at all, unless for a few moments through some chinks in the rings, which are known to be not solid bodies, but made up of closely crowded small moons. And the slow passage of this fearful shadow, which advances at the average rate of some twenty miles a day, but yet hangs for years over the regions athwart which it sweeps, occurs in the very season when the sun's small direct supply of heat would require to be most freely compensated by nocturnal light,—in the winter season, namely, of the planet. Moreover, not only during the time of the shadow's passage, but during the entire winter half of the Saturnian year, the ring reflects no light during the night time, the sun being on the other or summer's side of the ring's plane.[1] The only nocturnal effect which would be ob-

---

[1] The reader who cares enough about such subjects to take the necessary trouble, can easily make a little model of Saturn and his ring system, which will very prettily illustrate the effect of the rings both in reflecting light to the planet's darkened hemisphere and in cutting off light from the planet's illuminated hemisphere. Take a ball, say an ordinary hand ball, and pierce it through the centre with a fine knitting-needle. Cut out a flat ring of card, proportioned to the ball as the ring system of Saturn to his ball. (If the ball is two inches in diameter, strike out on a sheet of cardboard two concentric circles, one of them with a radius of a little more than an inch and a half, the other with a radius of about two inches and three-eighths, and cut out the ring between these two circles.) Thrust the knitting-needle through this ring in such a way that the ball shall lie in the middle of the ring, as the globe of Saturn hangs (without knitting-needle connections) in the middle of his ring system. Thrust another knitting-needle centrally through the ball square to the plane of the ring, and use this second needle, which we may call the polar one, as a handle. Now take the ball and ring into sunlight, or the light of a lamp or candle, holding them so that the shadow of the ring is as thin as possible. This represents the position of the shadow at the time of Saturnian spring or autumn. Cause the shadow slowly to shift until it surrounds the part of the ball through which the polar needle passes on one side. This will represent the position of the shadow at the time of mid-winter for the hemisphere corresponding to that side of the ball. Notice that while the shadow is traversing this half of the ball, the side of the ring which lies towards that half is in shadow, so that a fly or other small insect on that half of the ball would see the darkened side of the ring. A Saturnian correspondingly placed would get no reflected sunlight from the ring system. Move the ball and ring so that the shadow slowly returns to its first position. You will then have illustrated the changes taking place during one half of a Saturnian year. Continue the motion so that the shadow passes to the other half of the ball and finally surrounds the other point through

servable would be the obliteration of the stars covered by the ring system. It is strange that, this being so, the spirits from Saturn should have made no mention of the circumstance; and even more strange that these spirits and others should have asserted that the moons and rings of Saturn compensate for the small amount of light directly received from the sun. Most certainly a Swedenborg of our own time would find the spirits from Saturn more veracious and more communicative about these matters, though even what *he* would hear from the spirits would doubtless appear to sceptics of the twenty-first century to be no more than he could infer from the known facts of the science of his day.

But Swedenborg was not content merely to receive visits from the inhabitants of other planets in the solar system. He was visited also by the spirits of earths in the starry heaven; nay, he was enabled to visit those earths himself. For man, even while living in the world, 'is a spirit as to his interiors, the body which he carries about in the world only serving him for performing functions in this natural or terrestrial sphere, which is the lowest.' And to certain men it is granted not only to converse as a spirit with angels and spirits, but to traverse in a spiritual way the vast distances which separate world from world and system from system, all the while remaining in the body. Swedenborg was one of these. ' The interiors of my spirit,' he says, ' are opened by the Lord, so that while I am in the body I can at the same time be with angels in heaven, and not only converse with them, but behold the wonderful things which are there and describe them, that henceforth it may no more be said, " Who ever came from heaven to assure us it exists and tell us what is there ? " He who is unacquainted with the arcana of heaven cannot believe that man can see earths so remote, and give any account of them from sensible experience. But let him know that spaces and distances, and consequently progressions, existing in the natural world, in their origin and first causes are changes of the state of the interiors; that with angels and spirits progressions appear according to changes of state; and that by changes of state they may be apparently translated from one place to another, and from one

which the polar needle passes. The polar point which the shadow before surrounded will now be seen to be in the light, and this half of the ball will illustrate the hemisphere of Saturn where it is midsummer. It will also be seen that the side of the ring towards this half of the ball is now in the light, so that a small insect on this half of the ball would see the bright side of the ring. A Saturnian correspondingly placed would get reflected sunlight from the ring system *both by day and by night*. Moving the ball and ring so that the shadow returns to its first position, an entire Saturnian year will have been illustrated. These changes can be still better shown with a Saturnian orrery (see plate viii. of my Saturn) which can be very easily constructed.

earth to another, even to earths at the boundaries of the universe; so likewise may man as to his spirit, his body still remaining in its place. This has been the case with me.'

Before describing his visits to earths in the starry heavens, Swedenborg is careful to indicate the probability that such earths exist. ' It is well known to the learned world,' he says, ' that every star is a sun in its place, remaining fixed like the sun of our earth.' The proper motions of the stars had, alas! not been discovered in Swedenborg's day, nor does he seem to have been aware what a wild chase he was really entering upon in his spiritual progressions. Conceive the pursuit of Sirius or Vega as either sun rushed through space with a velocity of thirty or forty miles in every second of time! To resume, however, the account which Swedenborg gives of the ideas of the learned world of his day. ' It is the distance which makes a star appear in a small form; consequently' (the logical necessity is not manifest, however) ' each star, like the sun of our system, has around it planets which are earths; and the reason these are not visible to us is because of their immense distance and their having no light but from their own star, which light cannot be reflected so far as to reach us.' ' To what other end,' proceeds this most convincing reasoning, ' can be so immense a heaven with such a multitude of stars? For man is the end for which the universe was created. It has been ascertained by calculation that supposing there were in the universe a million earths, and on every earth three hundred millions of men and two hundred generations within six thousand years, and that to every man or spirit was allotted a space of three cubic ells, the collective number of men or spirits could not occupy a space equal to a thousandth part of this earth, thus not more than that occupied by one of the satellites of Jupiter or Saturn: a space on the universe almost undiscernible, for a satellite is hardly visible to the naked eye. What would this be for the Creator of the universe, to whom the whole universe filled with earths could not be enough' (for what?), ' seeing that he is infinite.' However, it is not on this reasoning alone that Swedenborg relies. He tells us, honestly beyond all doubt, that he knows the truth of what he relates. ' The information I am about to give,' he says, ' respecting the earths in the starry heaven is from experimental testimony; from which it will likewise appear how I was translated thither as to my spirit, the body remaining in its place.'

His progress in his first star-hunt was to the right, and continued for about two hours. He found the boundary of our solar system marked first by a white but thick cloud, next by a fiery smoke ascending from a great chasm. Here some guards appeared, who stopped some of the company, because these had not, like Swedenborg and the rest, received permission to pass. They not only stopped those unfortunates but tortured them, conduct for which terrestrial analogues might possibly be discovered.

Having reached another system, he asked the spirits of one of the earths there how large their sun was and how it appeared. They said it was less than the sun of our earth, and has a flaming appearance. Our sun, in fact, is larger than other suns in space, for from that earth starry heavens are seen, and a star larger than the rest appears, which, say those spirits, ' was declared from heaven ' to be the sun of Swedenborg's earthly home.

What Swedenborg saw upon that earth has no special interest. The men there, though haughty, are loved by their respective wives because they, the men, are good. But their goodness does not appear very manifest from anything in the narrative. The only man seen by Swedenborg took from his wife ' the garment which she wore, and threw it over his own shoulders; loosening the lower part, which flowed down to his feet like a robe (much as a man of our earth might be expected to loosen the tie-back of the period, if he borrowed it in like manner) he thus walked about clad.'

He next visited an earth circling round a star, which he learned was one of the smaller sort, not far from the equator. Its greater distance was plain from the circumstance that Swedenborg was two days in reaching it. In this earth he very nearly fell into a quarrel with the spirits. For hearing that they possess remarkable keenness of vision, he 'compared them with eagles which fly aloft, and enjoy a clear and extensive view of objects beneath.' At this they were indignant, 'supposing,' poor spirits, ' that he compared them to eagles as to their rapacity, and consequently thought them wicked.' He hastened to explain, however, that he ' did not liken them to eagles as to their rapacity, but as to sharp-sightedness.'

Swedenborg's account of a third earth in the star-depths contains a very pretty idea for temples and churches. The temples in that earth ' are constructed,' he says, ' of trees, not cut down, but growing in the place where they were first planted. On that earth, it seems, there are trees of an extraordinary size and height ; these they set in rows when young, and arrange in such an order that they may serve when they grow up to form porticoes and colonnades. In the meanwhile, by cutting and pruning, they fit and prepare the tender shoots to entwine one with another and join together so as to form the groundwork and floor of the temple to be constructed, and to rise at the sides as walls, and above to bend into arches to form the roof. In this manner they construct the temple with admirable art, elevating it high above the ground. They prepare also an ascent into it, by continuous branches of the trees, extended from the trunk and firmly connected together. Moreover, they adorn the temple without and within in various ways, by disposing the foliage into particular forms; thus they build entire groves. But it was not permitted me to see the nature of these temples, only I was informed that the light of their sun is let in by apertures amongst the branches, and is everywhere transmitted through crystals; whereby the light falling on the walls is refracted in colours like those of the rainbow, particularly blue and orange, of which they are fondest. Such is their architecture, which they prefer to the most magnificent palaces of our earth.'

Other earths in the starry heavens were visited by Swedenborg, but the above will serve sufficiently to illustrate the nature of his observations. One statement, by the way, was made to him which must have seemed unlikely ever to be contravened, but which has been shown in our time to be altogether erroneous. In the fourth star-world he visited, he was told that that earth which travels round its sun in 200 days of fifteen hours each, is one of the least in the universe, being scarcely 500 German miles, say 2,000 English miles, in circumference. This would make its diameter about 640 English miles. But there is not one of the whole family of planetoids which has a diameter so great as this, and many of these earths must be less than fifty miles in diameter. Now Swedenborg remarks that he had his information from the angels, 'who made a comparison in all these particulars with things of a like nature on our earth, according to what they saw in me or in my memory. Their conclusions were formed by angelic ideas, whereby are instantly known the measure of space and time in a just proportion with respect to space and time elsewhere. Angelic ideas, which are spiritual, in such calculations infinitely excel human ideas, which are natural.' He must, therefore, have met, unfortunately, with untruthful angels.

The real source of Swedenborg's inspirations will be tolerably obvious—to all, at least, who are not Swedenborgians. But our account of his visions would not be complete in a psychological sense without a brief reference to the personal allusions which the spirits and angels made during their visits or his wanderings. His distinguished rival, Christian Wolf, was encountered as a spirit by spirits from Mercury, who 'perceived that what he said did not rise above the sensual things of the natural man, because in speaking he thought of honour, and was desirous, as in the world (for in the other world every one is like his former self), to connect various things into series, and from these again continually to deduce others, and so form several chains of such, which they did not see or acknowledge to be true, and which, therefore, they declared to be chains which neither cohered in themselves nor with the conclusions, calling them the obscurity of authority;' so they ceased to question him further, and presently left him. Similarly, a spirit who in this world had been a 'prelate and a preacher,' and 'very pathetic, so that he could deeply move his hearers,' got no hearing among the spirits of a certain earth in the starry heavens; for they said they could tell ' from the tone of the voice whether a discourse came from the heart or not;' and as his discourse came not from the heart, 'he was unable to teach them, whereupon he was silent.' Convenient thus to have spirits and angels to confirm our impressions of other men, living or dead.

Apart from the psychological interest attaching to Swedenborg's strange vision, one cannot but be strongly impressed by the idea pervading them, that to beings suitably constituted all that takes place in other worlds might be known. Modern science recognises a truth here; for in that mysterious ether which occupies all space, messages are at all times travelling by which the history of every orb is constantly recorded. No world, however remote or insignificant; no period, however distant—but has its history thus continually proclaimed in ever widening waves. Nay, by these waves also (to beings who could read their teachings aright) the future is constantly indicated. For, as the waves which permeate the ether could only be situated as they actually are at any moment through past processes, each one of which is consequently indicated by those ethereal waves, so also there can be but one series of events in the future as the sequel of the relations actually indicated by the ethereal undulations. These, therefore, speak as definitely and distinctly of the future as of the past. Could we but rid us of the gross habiliments of flesh, and by some new senses be enabled to feel each order of ethereal undulations, even of those only which reach our earth, all knowledge of the past and future would be within our power. The consciousness of this underlies the fancies of Swedenborg, just as it underlies the thought of him who sang—

> There's not an orb which thou beholdst
> But in his motion like an angel sings,
> Still quiring to the young-eyed cherubim.
> But while this muddy vesture of decay
> Doth grossly close us in, we cannot hear it.

The G. B. C.

A TALE OF A TELEGRAM.

BY JAMES PAYN.

I DO not as a rule engage in commercial speculation; but my dear friend Jones insisted with such eloquence upon the success that must indubitably follow upon the establishment of the Great Butter Company—an association formed for the manufacture of that commodity out of a material which shall be nameless, but which was by no means so precarious and open to adulteration as cream, and the supply of which was practically inexhaustible—that I suffered the name of Martingale to appear, for a consideration, on the list of directors.

It is a name well known in society, and was up to that time untainted by connection with trade; unless, indeed, the swopping and sale of chargers—for which I will back myself against any cavalry officer in Her Majesty's service—may be considered by the pedantic as coming under that head. As for the City, I knew nothing more about it than that it was a locality lying east of Cox's, the army agent's, which was the limit of my personal experience in that direction. I have always breathed quite another atmosphere— that of Pall Mall; I wish I could say a purer one; but the fact is, that the atmosphere of the smoking-rooms both at 'the Rag' and the 'Junior' are, towards the small hours of the morning, when my own day is by no means finished, something appalling. I had three hundred a year for directing the Butter Company; and it was far easier work, I am bound to say, than were the old duties in my regiment, for which I was paid a precisely similar sum. Once a month the chairman called for me in his brougham, and deposited me at the offices in Cornhill, where, after an excellent luncheon (of which our butter formed no ingredient), I attached my autograph to certain documents; a proceeding which, I believe, is technically termed 'passing the accounts.' There were some persons of my acquaintance and profession—persons I have reason to believe who had themselves applied for directorships, and faile d

— who did not scruple to call the Great Butter Company a slippery concern, and who affected to give me friendly counsel to get out of it ; but I was too well accustomed to the system of military exchanges not to perceive their drift : their object was of course to be gazetted in my stead. I listened to their jokes about ' Martingale the man of business ' every time I returned from an expedition to Cornhill with even more than my usual good-nature, for I had twenty-five golden reasons in my pocket—the directors were paid monthly—for sticking to the Butter. And I believe the Butter would have stuck to me, had it not been for my own fault— if I can call that a fault which was the most extraordinary piece of ill-fortune that ever befell a fellow, and solely through another fellow's being too clever by half.

Well, I say the G. B. C.—as we who belong to it were accustomed to call it, as the chairman said, ' out of affection and euphony,' but so far as I was concerned, for mere shortness—was a little ' talked about '; it had its detractors, and even its enemies. People shook their heads at it (especially when they tasted the butter), and prophesied we should not last ; and it was necessary to advertise considerably to get new customers. Our business lay rather with new ones than old ones, perhaps ; but it was gradually getting spread over the country—though thinly spread, like butter upon bread at school.

So long as we were harmonious amongst ourselves, said the chairman, or, at all events, washed our dirty linen at home—did not attack one another in the papers, as so many boards of directors are wont to—we should be all right ; but if once there should be mistrust of one another, he would not answer for the consequences. ' Let only the Great Butter Company be true to itself,' said he, during the peroration of the most powerful speech I ever remember to have heard from any man *sitting,* ' and I do not hesitate to affirm that the days of dairymen are numbered.' For though I am still under an obligation of secrecy as to the material of which our butter was composed, I may say it had nothing in common with dairies—except a little water. Enough, however, of commercial details.

When playing at pool in the early autumn one night at the Club, I had the misfortune to lose—neither my money nor my life, for I am amazingly careful of both, but—my self-possession, and somehow or other got inveigled into a promise to go down to old Slowcombe's to shoot, upon the first of October. It was a foolish thing to do, for Slowcombe is a bore, and I happened to owe him a little money ; and when a man is both a bore and a creditor, it is intolerable to be under the same roof with him, more especially

if it be his own.   There were some excuses for me, for in the first
place there were so few men in town that we were obliged to ask
Slowcombe to make up the pool, and secondly, when one owes a
fellow money one is bound to be civil to him.   We got talking of
pheasants, and the old fellow asked me if I liked pheasant-
shooting, and when I said yes, ' Then come,' said he, ' and have a
shy at mine.'   I no more suspected Slowcombe of having any
pheasant-shooting to give away than of keeping a roulette-table at
Hampton Court races ; he was a stodgy, pursy, plethoric old fellow,
who had been in the yeomanry for a day or two (just to get a
qualification for the Club), and had then rested on his laurels.   Still,
when a man farms his own land, there is always a temptation to
get *something* out of it, and it seemed he had grown pheasants.
I ought to have been more prudent, and I will another time, or
my name is not Martingale.

I am, however, a man of my word, and I never thought of
breaking my promise to Slowcombe, until I heard him ask another
man, and then another, to come down and enjoy themselves
among his covers, and *both of them refused point-blank.*   They
did not owe him money, as I did ; but it struck me that they
were more decided in their negatives than the occasion demanded.

' Why don't you go down to poor old Slowcombe's ? ' said I
to one of them, a man I should have liked as a companion in such
an expedition : ' he means well and is quite harmless.'

' Harmless !   By Jove ! that is just what he isn't,' was the unexpected reply.   ' Why, last year was the first, according to his
own confession, that he ever took gun in hand, and he shot Brooks
of ours in the leg at fifteen yards in one of his own turnip-fields.
You don't mean to say you never heard Brooks tell the story about
his leg, and how Slowcombe made game of it ? '

I did not like to say that I myself had promised to go down to
Slowcombe's, but I made up my mind from that moment that I
wouldn't go.   I am not a family man, but I respect myself, I hope,
as much as if I was ; and I wasn't going to be blown to pieces by an
old rhinoceros like that, in a field of swedes.   My difficulty was
to find an excuse ; for the other men's refusals—and his own
knowledge perhaps of why they wouldn't come—had made Slowcombe ' touchy ' ; and when I had hinted that I couldn't be quite
sure of being with him on the First, he had made an allusion to
the little matter of business between us, which I felt to be equivalent
to ' play or pay '—Come to Ploughshire (for he lived among the
clodhoppers), or settle my account.

At last I hit upon a plan.   He knew that I was connected
with the Great Butter Company, and had often sounded me as to

its prospects; but I could never persuade him to invest in it. 'If it's such a real good thing, you had better stick to it yourself, Martingale, and let nobody else in.' I didn't like the remark about letting people in; but I was not in a position to quarrel with Slowcombe. He parted from me on the last day but one of September, telling me he wanted twenty-four hours to get his guns ready, and impressing upon me the best train by which to start for Ploughshire on the morrow. The next morning (the 30th), I wrote him this letter from the Club:

My dear Slowcombe,—I am exceedingly sorry to disappoint you—and still more so to disappoint myself—but I regret to say that my proposed visit to you has been knocked on the head. The enclosed telegram will explain itself. Nothing but the most urgent business would have prevented my keeping my engagement; and I feel confident, from the ideas you have often expressed to me respecting the necessity of attending strictly to the G. B. C., I need no further apology for my absence. You will, doubtless, have many another gun with you, and if the phrase of 'the more the merrier' can be applied to pheasant-shooting, that of 'the fewer the better cheer' is certainly still more to the purpose. A fuller bag will, I hope, compensate for the absence of yours most faithfully,

MARMADUKE MARTINGALE.

Then leaving the envelope open, I proceeded to concoct the telegram:

From the Secretary of the Great Butter Company (Limited), Cornhill, to Marmaduke Martingale, Esq., Military, Naval, and Militia Club, Pall Mall.—Defalcations have been discovered in the Company's accounts. I am therefore compelled to summon an extraordinary meeting of the Board of Directors for Wednesday next, when your presence will be indispensable.

I gave this composition to the Club commissionaire, an active, intelligent fellow whom I had often employed, and sent him off to the nearest telegraph office. I calculated that it would return to me—in telegraphic form—in about a quarter of an hour at furthest. But as it happened, it did not. I had an engagement for that afternoon at Hurlingham, and was obliged to leave the Club before the arrival of the expected document. However, as I knew it must come, and could place the utmost confidence in the porter, I left my letter with him, instructing him to place the telegram inside it as soon as it came to hand, and then to post it.

The next morning, I found upon inquiry that this had been done, and thought no more about the matter. The day after, a note, as I had expected, arrived from Slowcombe; the contents of which, however, I did not expect:

Sir,—I am astonished that you should have the assurance to send me that telegram from your place of business. If you imagine because your secretary has 'bolted,' and the 'blessed concern' (as your friend terms what I had understood from you to be a sound commercial association) has ' burst up,' that I shall not be disposed to press for my hundred pounds, you are very much mistaken. I have placed the matter in the hands of my solicitor, and remain—Yours obediently,

THOMAS SLOWCOMBE.

Had I taken leave of my own senses, or had Slowcombe taken leave of his ? ' Bolted,' ' burst up,' ' blessed concern '? No such words, I am sure, had ever been contained in my telegram. What on earth did it all mean ? I did a thing which I had never done before, except upon the first Monday in every month—I hurried to our place of business in the City as fast as a hansom could take me; and found the shutters up. The office of the G. B. C. was closed—just as though the Company had been defunct. Upstairs, however, I found the chairman looking at a heap of bills and gnawing his moustache.

' This is a pretty piece of work, Captain Martingale,' said he; ' and we have to thank you for it.'

' To thank *me?*' cried I. ' What do you mean ? Is *everybody* gone mad ? I have done nothing—*nothing.*'

' Perhaps you didn't send a telegram to our secretary about "defalcations ?" Here it is.' And he tossed me over the message I had sent from the secretary to myself—*transposed.* That respectable and intelligent commissionaire had, it seemed, taken it for granted that I had made a mistake in sending a telegram to myself, and substituted the word ' from ' for ' to,' and ' to ' for ' from.' He thought, doubtless, he was doing a very clever thing, and one for which I should be much indebted to him.

The secretary really had, it seems, ' defalcated ' in a small way, and getting my telegram (instead of my getting *his*), he thought all was discovered, so laid his hands on everything he could, and decamped. It was the chairman himself who had wired the news to me in that familiar style, which had so incensed Slowcombe : ' Our secretary has bolted, and the blessed concern has burst up.'

The Great Butter Company, in fact, was nowhere, thanks to my little device for avoiding pheasant-shooting. The secretary would probably never have fled, but only have gone on defalcating slowly, but for my alarming message : as it was, everything was precipitated, including the compulsory payment of my debt to Slowcombe. It was altogether a miserable fiasco ; and when I hear fellows talking about the splendid results of civilisation, and ' Look at the electric telegraph, for example!' and 'the corps of commissionaires!' I say to myself—— But never mind what I say. I have told enough to make it understood why I should not agree with them.

Quips and Cranks at our Club Window.

BY AN OLD ENTHUSIAST AND A YOUNG CYNIC.

No. I.—POOR LIZZIE.

You swear I loved you dearly once—
   Perhaps! my pretty Lizzie;
But then was then—and now is now:
   I'm busy—very busy!

You'd like to have a thousand pounds!
   Good girl, your brain is dizzy!
But mine is calm, and knows the world:
   I'm busy—very busy!

You'll try your rights! you'll go to law!
   Your lawyer's clever! *Is* he?
Well! give the man my best respects,
   I'm busy—very busy!

No. II.—PROGRESS.

We travel faster than we did
   A hundred years ago,
And send by wire and not by road
   Our messages of woe:
Or else the price of stocks and shares
   And wool and calico.
We conquer Time, make light of Space,
   And every passing day
Snatch some new force from Nature's hand,
   And teach it to obey.
But are we happier than our sires,
   Or brave and good as they?
Speak up, old History! tell the truth!
   Give us the yea—or *nay*!

QUIPS AND CRANKS.

¡No. III.—AN ADIEU.

GOOD-NIGHT, sweet Sorrow,
  Until to-morrow,
And then we shall dwell together again;
  I've known thee long,
  Like a mournful song,
  Till thou'st grown a part
  Of my innermost heart,
And a nestling bird on my pillow of pain.
  Sweet little Sorrow,
Come back to-morrow;
I've learned to love thee—remain, remain!

No. IV.—A DIALOGUE.

IN DEEP WATER:

FAIR-WEATHER friends, that sought me once,
  I fail to reach the shore;
Thick darkness shrouds the face of heaven,
  And angry tempests roar.
Idle is all your good advice:
  I want a rope— a hand—
A heart—a will—a little skill
  To draw me to the land.

THE FAIR-WEATHER FRIENDS:

Rope, did you say? we have no rope;
  We drove you not to sea;
You drifted out into the storm:
  Drift out of it, say we!

No. V.—DUBIOUS.

  How can an earnest man be born
  In an age of jest and scorn,
  That mocks at greatness if it comes,
  Or noses it with twiddling thumbs?

  How can a mighty bard appear
  Amid incessant jibe and jeer,
  When seriousness is out of season,
  And Laughter lords it over Reason?

  Who can revive a rotting time?
  Who can make jewels out of slime?
  Or who upon a mountain stand
  If nothing *is*, but shifting sand?

QUIPS AND CRANKS.

No. VI.—THE POOR OLD MILLIONAIRE.

I've fifty thousand pounds a year,
    Palace and park and tower,
Horses and hounds, and yachts and friends,
    And all the pomp of power.
Peer of the noblest in the land,
    Men call me great and high,
And never think I am so poor
    That I'd be glad to die.
I cannot eat, I cannot drink,
    For sharp arthritic pain,
And dread neuralgia kills my sleep
    And maddens all my brain.
Oh, give me health, ye dreadful Fates,
    To earn my bread and beer !
For sleep and appetite and peace,
    And fifty pounds a year,
I'd sink my thousands in the sea,
    Never to re-appear !

No. VII.—THE WORTH OF WISDOM.

Should the day come when men of sense
Shall be, like Dodos, born no more,
And genius vanish from the earth—
Lost as the Mastodons of yore :
How long would last the human race
To hold its high accustomed place?
A hundred years ?   I greatly doubt
If fifty would not snuff it out !
Or leave such scope for fools to revel,
That if no Flood made all things level,
The wars, the crimes, the lusts of men,
Would bring the jungle back again !

No. VIII.—EUTHANASIA.

Poor and mean are our thoughts of Death,
    The world's a wheel in a rut ;
And men still think as their fathers thought,
    With scarcely an ' if ' or a ' but.'
To me, kind Death seems a lady fair,
    A teeming mother, well wed,
Whose children inherit another world—
    The new-born, beautiful dead.
Born with a glory unperceived
    By us on the gloomy shore,
Children that sport in their Father's light,
    And know their Mother no more !

No. IX.—MONEY OR NO MONEY.

I WOULD have money for this verse of mine,
  To buy my loaf, my cordial, or my vest,
To hold my head aloft i' the morning shine,
  And pay my way as fully as the rest.
But if the money comes not?   Well! 'tis pity
  To me, but not to others.   Still, I'll rhyme,
And envy not the magnates of the city,
  Whose only music is the guineas' chime;
They have their present comforts : so have I.
  Has not the lark, to the bright heaven upsoaring,
As much enjoyment in the clear blue sky,
  As money-grubbers o'er their ledgers poring ?
All things that live bear more or less of burden ;
Song is its own reward, work its own guerdon.

No. X.—NUT-CRACKING.

WHEN I could crack a nut
  With the molars in my jaws,
With teeth all white and steadfast
  And innocent of flaws,
I laughed at angry Fortune,
  Made light of coming sorrow,
Was happy all to-day,
  And careless of to-morrow.
I trusted men and women,
  And women most, maybe !—
Oh, pleasant was that spring time
  To my teeth and me !
But now, when teeth are shaky,
  And going one by one,
I find, like Israel's monarch,
  Small good beneath the sun.
I cannot crack a nut,
  I cannot find a truth,
Or man, or lovely woman,
  Like those I found in youth.
Put back, O cruel Fortune,
  Thy sword into its sheath,
Let me believe in something,
  And contradict my teeth !

Joshua Haggard's Daughter.

BY THE AUTHOR OF 'LADY AUDLEY'S SECRET.'

CHAPTER XXVIII.

'AND YET I FEEL I FEAR.

UNDER that quiet surface which life wore in Joshua Haggard's household there were troubled waters.

Naomi had never forgotten the awful look in her father's face that afternoon in the wood. It haunted her in all places and at all seasons. The impression it had made upon her mind would not pass away. What it meant she knew not—dared not shape the thought in her mind—but she was very sure that it meant evil of some kind, evil to her father's soul, wrong to Oswald.

If she could have known for certain that Oswald had carried out the intention set forth in his fatal letter to Cynthia, she would have been, comparatively speaking, at ease and happy. But of this she knew nothing. Whether he had really gone to America, how and when he had left Combhollow, of these things she was ignorant. Cynthia might know, perhaps, but not even to set these anxious fears at rest could Naomi stoop so low as to seek for any information about her lover from the woman for whose sake she had been abandoned. No, if Cynthia knew anything for certain, the knowledge must remain locked in her breast. Save in the merest outward and ceremonial form, a bare civility in every-day intercourse, there could be no contact between Naomi and her stepmother. The gulf that sundered these two was impassable.

Oswald's letter had stated that he meant to leave Combhollow by the night coach. He had not gone by that coach, for James Haggard, who was fond of an evening stroll when the shutters were up, and who took a lively interest in other people's business, had watched the departure of the coach on that particular evening, and entertained his family at the silent supper-table with a detailed account of that exciting event in the every-day life of his town.

'There was only one inside, and that was old Mrs. Skevinew,

who is going to Exeter to see her married daughter,' said Jim ;
' she had three bandboxes, two umbrellas, a pair of pattens, and a
pair of the new-fashioned clogs—she bought 'em of Aunt Judith
the day before yesterday—a hamper of peas, a green goose, a basket
of eggs, a tin of clouted cream, a red cotton handkerchief full of
bullaces, two pasties done up in brown paper, and a pig's cheek.
Won't her friends be glad to see her ? '

' Who were the outsides ? ' asked Judith.

Jim ran over the names, checking them off on his fingers.

' Was there no one else in the coach ? ' asked Naomi, looking
at her father, who sat in his usual place with bent brows, neither
eating nor drinking.

' No one.'

He had not gone by that coach then, thought Naomi.   But
presently it occurred to her that Mr. Pentreath's return to Combhollow having been a secret and underhand proceeding, he would
hardly care to leave the place under the broad glare of his town's-
people's eye.   The departure of the coach from the First and Last
Inn was a public event.   To leave by that vehicle, at that point
of departure, and not be seen, came hardly within the limits of
possibility, unless a man had got himself hidden away in the boot
before the spectators assembled ; no, if Oswald had made up his
mind to travel by that coach, he had doubtless walked on to some
quiet spot, to be taken up as the mail passed.

This reflection quieted Naomi's fears in some measure, yet did
not set her heart at ease.   Her father's face haunted her like some
unholy image sent by Satan to suggest evil.   What had passed
between Joshua and that weak sinner—what violence of upbraiding
had the minister used against his wife's lover ?   That there had
been an angry meeting of some kind Naomi did not doubt.   Only a
wild indulgence of evil passion, only an utter abandonment of himself to man's omnipresent tempter, could have conjured up such a
look in Joshua Haggard's face.   The dark mind of the spirit of
evil was there reflected.   The lurid gleam in those darkly brooding eyes was the red glare caught from the open doors of hell.

There had been hard words spoken, words of hatred and fury,
perchance even some open act of violence, a blow struck by that
strong hand of Joshua's, who might have spurned the sinner as if
he had been the tempter himself, in his base form of serpent.
But it was over, and Joshua had doubtless begun to repent of his
violence, and Oswald was on his way to a distant world to begin
a new and wiser life.

' God keep him and guard him and lead him aright,' thought
Naomi, ' and make him a good and great man.   I could bear the

pang of parting with him, could I feel secure about his happy future here and in the better world.'

Oh, empty life from which he had vanished for ever—oh, dreary days which hung upon this young spirit like a burden, and weighed her down to the dust. Yes, verily, to the dust; so that, in her utter weariness, she felt as if it would be a good and pleasant end of all things to lie down in some lonely corner of the land— lie face downward among the fern and wild flowers, and wait for death. Surely the dark angel would take pity upon her joyless fate, and come and fold her in his sheltering wings, and comfort and cure her.

'There is no other comfort, no other cure,' she said, forgetting all the old pious lessons in her despair, forgetting even to do good to others in the sharpness of her pain.

She sought for consolation from no one—not even from honest Jim—who was distressed at seeing such blank hopeless faces in his home, and was eager, after his rough and ready fashion, to administer comfort.

'Come, Naomi, cheer up and be bright, like a sensible girl,' he would say. 'There's as good fish in the sea as ever came out of it, and though you've missed landing a fine salmon through father's foolishness, you'll have your net full by-and-by, I'll warrant. A good-looking, straight-built lass like you will never want a sweetheart.'

'Jim, if you talk to me like that I shall hate you!' cried Naomi. 'I shall go single to my grave, and you know it, or if you can think otherwise of me, you're not worthy to be my brother.'

'Hoity-toity!' cried Jim, 'what fine notions run in our family! Here's father refusing the lord of the manor for his son-in-law, and you talking of dying an old maid because your first affections have been blighted. Why, if my first love takes a wrong direction, I shall turn my heart into the right road, as easily as I guide grey Dobbin down a lane where he doesn't want to go. Just a shake of the reins or a touch of the whip, and off we start.'

Crushed by this weariness of life, Naomi strove notwithstanding to do her duty. Even Aunt Judith found no room for complaint with Naomi or Cynthia, unless haggard eyes and pale faces, and low voices with no joyous ring in them, were sufficient ground for upbraiding. The household work was faithfully performed. The starching and ironing, the dusting and beeswaxing, the sewing and darning were duly done. Cynthia had finished her dozen of shirts, without a gusset set awry, a seam puckered, or one deviation from a right line in the pearl-like stitching of collars and wristbands; and now she had taken to knitting Joshua's grey

woollen stockings, which was a pleasantly dreamy occupation calling for very little exercise of the intellectual faculties till one
came to the heel. She used to sit in the garden or the wilderness
in the calm September afternoons, with a grave quiet face bent
over her flashing needles—a face that told of an abiding sorrow.
The Miss Weblings would scarcely have recognised their cheerful
sunny-faced little maid in the serious young matron, with a complexion almost as white as her cap. Joshua rarely saw that
patient figure sitting in his place on the grass plat, for he had
been growing more and more indefatigable in his visitations
among the scattered members of his flock, walking great distances
to lonely homesteads or labourers' cottages, or, when not thus occupied, spending his afternoons in solitary wanderings by the
wild seashore, holding commune with his troubled soul.

Save at family prayer, and at meals, he was now seldom seen
in his own house, while he had almost wholly deserted the shop.
Aunt Judith bewailed this falling away from the good old habits
which had made Haggard's the leading commercial institution in
Combhollow. The salvation of one's soul was a vital transaction,
doubtless ; but a man secure of his calling and election in eternity could well afford to attend to his temporal business, instead
of wandering about in desolate places like John the Baptist, without having anyone to baptise.

' He might as well live on the top of a pillar like St. Simon
What's-his-name, and have his meals sent up to him by a ladder,'
said Judith contemptuously, ' if his mind is never in his business. We're always running out of things now, for want of proper
attention to the stock.'

To Naomi it was a small thing that her father should be indifferent to loss and gain, and turn his back upon the business by
which his father and grandfather had maintained their importance and respectability in the little town. The change she saw
in him was more alarming than this neglect of daily duties—a
change which she associated involuntarily with that bitter day on
which she had seen his gloomy murderer's face pass by her in the
woodland dimness.

In the autumn evenings, when she could escape from the joyless house, Naomi felt herself drawn, as by a magnet, to Pentreath
wood. It was not that she found peace there, or consolation.
She loved the shadowy scene as a place in which she could feed
her grief, and haunted it as an inconsolable mourner haunts the
burial-ground where lies her dead. How desolate the place seemed
in the season of earth's decay, all the winding ways deeply strewn
with the red-brown leaves, soft and soddened in the hollows where

the autumn rains lay longest; frogs croaking in the marshy places, and a dead snake lying here and there among the brambles.

It was not often that Naomi went within sight of the deserted house, where the old servants lived on in a lazy seclusion, waiting their master's bidding; almost as slumberous a household as that which slept for a hundred years in the old fairy story, only that here there was no lovely princess shining like a jewel in the innermost chamber of the castle. Here were only empty rooms, and dust and loneliness.

One evening early in October, Naomi roamed a little farther than she had intended, and found that, to reach home in decent time, she must take the nearest way, which was across the park, and out into the road by the park-gate. This would take her very near the house.

It was a fine bright evening. The sun had set redly behind the trees before she had entered the wood, and now the moon had risen and was shining over the great sea yonder—a lovely evening, mild and peaceful. She was loth to go back to the lighted room at home, and her father's evening lecture, now always of so gloomy a character as to minister to her despair, rather than to lift up her soul from its depth of sorrow.

The hall-door stood open, and a light burned dimly within. Old Nicholas, the butler, was sitting in the porch. He recognised Naomi as she skirted the outer garden, and got up quickly and came after her.

'I beg your pardon, Miss Haggard, but seeing you go by just now, I made bold to follow you. Have you heard any news of the young Squire? I've wanted to ask sometimes when I've been up at the shop, to get my bit of tea and sugar, but your father wasn't about, and I don't like to ask your Aunt—she's apt to be snappy.'

'No, Nicholas, we have had no news. You would be more likely to hear of your master than we.'

'Deary, now! I knew there was something wrong when he came down here so sudden, and told me I was to say nothing about it, and he was going off to Ameriky, and I was to keep the place in order agen Mr. Arnold came home, and then he was to be the master here. A power of changes to happen in such a short time, ain't it, Miss? I feel as if the world was topsy-turvy, somehow. The poor old master gone! He was dreadful near, to be sure, but I'd got used to him, and I misses his fidgety pinching ways, looking after every candle-end, and such a nose of his own if he suspected we was frying a bit of bacon for supper. Well, he's gone where scraping and saving won't help him, poor gentleman. There's no candle-ends in the heavenly Jerusalem.'

AND YOU HAVEN'T HEARD NOTHING, MISS?

Nicholas sighed despondently, as if he doubted whether an immortal home, in which cheese-paring could not be practised, would satisfy his departed master.

'And you haven't heard nothing, Miss?'

'Nothing,' answered Naomi. 'But there is hardly time for anyone to have had a letter yet—is there, Nicholas?'

'I can't say, Miss. Perhaps not. It were the beginning of August when he went away, warn't it? and here we are in October. I suppose there wouldn't be time; and yet I begin to feel oneasy in my mind about him. There was something queer about his going away, you see!'

'How do you mean?' asked Naomi, looking at him intently.

'Well, you see, he says to me, "Nicholas, you get they two big trunks down to the coach this evening, and that there bag." The trunks was what he'd packed his clothes and books in, and such like, that morning, purpose to take them with him to Ameriky. "I shall walk on ahead, and let the coach pick me up this side of Henbury turnpike," he says. "But you get they trunks safe in the boot," says he. So the gardener and I puts 'em in a barrer and wheels 'em down, and gets 'em safe packed into the boot afore seven o'clock.'

'Well, what then?' asked Naomi, with suppressed eagerness.

'What then, Miss Haggard? Why, they trunks and that there bag is in the young Squire's room now—come back, like a bad penny!'

'Come back?'

'Yes. The coach never picked him up this side of Henbury turnpike. The coachman never set eyes upon him all along the road. When he got to Exeter, there was no one to take to they trunks, no directions left about 'em, so he just brought 'em back; and if the young Squire be gone to Ameriky, he be gone without his luggage. Lord, Miss, how you do trimble! I hope there's nothing wrong, but it comes over me sometimes that things ain't altogether right!'

'He may have changed his mind at the last,' said Naomi falteringly. 'He may not have gone to America!'

'Perhaps not, Miss; but wherever he's gone, he's gone without his luggage—even the carpet-bag, with his razors and night-clothes.'

'He may have had other luggage in London.'

'He had a black portmanteau at the inn where he'd been stopping in London, but it wasn't a big one. It wouldn't have been luggage enough for Ameriky, or anywhere else in foreign parts. And then the books and things that he was so fond of, and his writing-desk, [and most of his clothes—all in they big boxes. It's odd he didn't send for 'em.'

' He may not want them.'

' But it's queer for him not to want 'em all this time. And if that there coach didn't pick him up—and we know it didn't—how did he get away? Nobody saw him leave, nobody heard of him. Lord a mercy, Miss, how white you be! I didn't ought to say such-like things, but it weighs so heavy on my mind. It's a comfort to talk about it. The London lawyer he sends me down my wages monthly, and board wages for me and the others in-doors. We might live on the fat of the land if we chose, only our constitutions have got used to pinching and we likes it. We couldn't have a better place, only they two trunks weighs upon my mind, and I shan't feel easy till I've had a letter from my master.'

What comfort could Naomi give him—she whose thoughts were full of fear? She went home and found the family circle waiting for her. It was past the customary prayer-time by ten minutes or so.

' Rambling again, Naomi!' said her father severely, and then opened his Bible and began to read a chapter of Jeremiah, which he afterwards expounded, dwelling darkly on all that was darkest in the text. The prayer that followed was rather a cry of self-abasement and desolation than a supplicatory address, curiously different from that simple and single-minded appeal which the Divine Teacher dictated to His disciples. Joshua asked for no common wants of common life ; he pleaded not to be forgiven as freely as he forgave—but he grovelled in the dust before an angry God, and heaped ashes upon his head, and abased himself with humility which touched the confines of fanaticism.

' What kept you out so long, Sis?' asked James, when they were seated at supper.

' Nicholas, the butler at the Grange, stopped me to ask about his master. He is very anxious about him.'

' Why?' asked her father sharply.

' Because he has been away so long, and has not written.'

Cynthia lifted her languid eyes, large with sudden terror.

' How could anyone get a letter? He has not been gone three months. And even if there were time enough, why should he write to Nicholas?' said Joshua.

' Nicholas is anxious about him, anyhow,' answered Naomi.

She said nothing about the luggage left behind, which was the chief cause of the old servant's uneasiness.

' Well, all I can say is that a young man with such a property as that was a fool to go to America,' remarked Jim conclusively.

It was a generally accepted fact by this time that the young Squire had gone to America, and there were various versions of his motive for this exile. The male gossips inclined to the idea that he and Naomi had quarrelled, and that this lovers' quarrel had been the cause of his departure; the female portion of the community pinned their faith upon the young man's fickleness. He had repented of his engagement to the grocer's daughter, and had gone away to avoid its fulfilment.

'It was all very fine while his father was living, and likely to live to a hundred, and he hadn't a five pound note,' said Mrs. Spradgers. 'He knew that Mr. Haggard was a warm man, and he might do worse than marry Naomi; but it was quite another thing when the old gentleman went off and the property turned out better than young Mr. Pentreath had ever expected. It's only natural he should look higher. Circumstances alter cases.'

The year wore to its close, and yet there came no tidings of the young Squire. There was, perhaps, no reason why he should trouble himself to write to anyone at Combhollow, argued Naomi, trying to shake off that burden of unquiet thoughts which oppressed her. He could hardly be expected to write to his old servants; he had provided for their comfort through his London solicitor. His rents were collected by a local agent and paid to the same man of business. There was no one at Combhollow who had any right to expect letters from him. He had broken away from all his old moorings, and begun a new life in a new country. He was happy, perhaps, amused and interested by the novelty of his surroundings—occupied—adventurous, a light-hearted traveller, while her thoughts of him were so full of gloom.

'Why cannot I banish him from my mind altogether?' she asked herself. 'It is a sin to dwell thus persistently upon an earthly loss. "If thy right hand offend thee, cut it off." He came between me and heaven—for I loved him too well. Even now that he is far away, the thought of him binds me down to earth. Why cannot I forget him?'

There was another question in her mind which hardly shaped itself in direct words: 'Why cannot I forget my father's face that day in the wood?'

The new year began, and there was no change in the quiet household, save a change in Cynthia which had been so gently wrought that it was invisible to the eyes that saw her daily. The minister's young wife had faded and drooped since that troubled summer-time of the year just gone. The slender figure had lost its graceful curves, the white arm was no longer round and full, the oval of the cheek had fallen, and the blue-veined lids drooped languidly over the gentle eyes, in which there was a look that seemed to plead for pity or forgiveness.

Joshua's popularity was at its height this winter. Those stirring sermons—those eloquent theological fulminations—acted on his hearers as a stimulant and a tonic. People flocked to hear him from distant villages. He was proud of his popularity, lifted up and exalted by the idea that he was bringing sinners home to God, fighting hand to hand with the devil and all his angels. He lived apart from his own household, a stranger among them, though sitting by the same fireside. It was as if they were people of old time giving shelter to a prophet. They scarcely dared speak to him, but approached him with an awful respect. It was an understood thing that he had no more to do with the business which had in years past occupied half his time and some portion of his care. James now took the helm in the commercial vessel, and felt that he was of the stuff that makes great captains. Joshua seemed hardly aware of the change that had come over his life. He was a dreamer and lived in a world of dreams.

So the year began, and it was early spring again, and Naomi felt that her youth was gone, and that the years could bring her nothing but age and death. They would come and go and make no difference in her life. They held no promise, they knew no hope.

Chapter XXIX.

THE WANDERER'S RETURN.

It was March—just a year since the old Squire had been stricken with his fatal illness. The daffodils were blooming in sunny places. There was a faint tinge of green upon the hedgerows.

Naomi was sitting alone in the twilit parlour in the calm grey evening. She had done all her daily duties, and could afford to rest from her toil. She looked at the familiar scene—the glimpse of sea, the curve of the road winding up the hill towards Pentreath Grange—with sad, hopeless eyes. No bright harbinger of joy would ever come to her by yonder road, down which she had seen the Squire's funeral train slowly descending with wind-tossed plumes and scarves less than a year ago.

' I had such a strange sense of loss that day,' she thought, remembering the dismal procession, and her own feelings as she watched its approach. ' I seemed to know that the end of my happiness had come ; that change, or sorrow, or death was near.'

Twilight deepened, and the scene took a shadowy look. Who was this walking down the hill at a leisurely pace, with a careless easy gait which seemed familiar? Nay, it was familiar, for it set

Naomi's heart beating vehemently; it made her cold and faint. This was no peasant returning from his work. She knew how the Combhollow population carried themselves. This tall slim figure, so straight and yet so easy of motion—was no son of the soil, no hard-handed agricultural labourer, no fisherman smelling of tar and sea-weed, with wet raiment all glistening and scaly.

She stood up, and opened the window—stood with the chill March breeze blowing upon her pale terror-stricken face. This time she felt verily as if she were seeing a ghost.

'He has come back,' she thought. 'He is not dead. Oh, foolish fear! Oh, wretched doubt of the best and truest upon earth! He is safe; and has come back again. I shall see him once again—living and happy. My God, I thank thee!'

The figure came nearer. Yes, it was Oswald Pentreath. She saw the well-remembered face in the dim light. How well he looked; how strong; how brave! Travel and strange countries had improved him. His chest had expanded—he walked with a firmer step—held his head higher. And he was coming to her father's house—boldly; with no stealthy approach. He came as a man who had done no evil, and had no cause for fear.

'He is cured of his folly; he is my true and noble lover once again. Oh God, Thou art full of mercy; Thy love aboundeth.'

The familiar figure was close at hand. There was nothing but the narrow front garden between him and Naomi; yet now there was a strangeness—her heart grew lead. The young man looked up at the house enquiringly, like a stranger who reconnoitres an unfamiliar place. He glanced up and down the street —quite empty of humanity at this moment, the solitary young woman with a basket, who had constituted its traffic a minute ago, having just gone indoors—then looked again at the house, and became conscious of Naomi's pale face at the window.

'I beg your pardon,' he began courteously. 'Is this Mr. Haggard's?'

Life-long sorrows are not so keen as a sudden stab like this— an arrow that pierces the heart and kills its hope for ever. It was not Oswald's voice. There was a likeness in the tone; that family resemblance so often to be found in the tones of kindred; but these tones were more decided—rougher. They lacked the poetic languor—the gentle sweetness—of Oswald's utterance. This speaker was one who had commanded men on the high seas; not the musing idler who had wasted half his life lying listlessly in summer woods, or wandering with his rod beside autumn's swollen streams.

It was not Oswald. For the space of half a minute, the surging blood in Naomi's brain almost blinded her. For an instant or so reason faltered, and she was on the verge of unconsciousness. Then the strong young soul resumed her power, and she comprehended that this was no shade from Avernus, but her lost lover's sailor brother, the Squire's runaway son.

'Yes,' she answered, with a steady voice, 'this is Mr. Haggard's house. Do you want to see my father?'

'Ah, then you are Naomi,' cried the stranger eagerly. 'I think I would rather talk to you than to your father. You can tell me more. I have only just come home, and I am very unhappy about my brother. May I come in, please?'

How friendly, how dear his voice sounded in its resemblance to the voice of Oswald. The familiar tones comforted Naomi, somehow, after that bitter disappointment just now. Her heart was lifted up from its despair. Arnold had come home—Arnold would find out all about his beloved brother.

At that thought a sudden dread came upon her, like a vision of doom.

If there were any guilty mystery in Oswald's fate, would not his brother bring the deed to light? Her shapeless fears rose up like gorgons and confronted her.

She opened the door for Arnold, and stood dumbly as he came in and held out his hand to her.

'How deadly cold your hand is!' he exclaimed. 'I'm afraid I startled you coming so suddenly. People say I am very like my brother. And I daresay you are anxious about Oswald.'

He had gone into the parlour with her, and seated himself with a familiar friendliness close to the chair into which Naomi had sunk, scarcely able to stand.

'Yes; I have been very anxious,' she said faintly.

'I can see that. Please God, there is no real cause for fear, though old Nicholas has frightened me a little by his raven-like talk. The last letter I had from my brother was written in London, on the fourteenth of July. He urged me to come home, and told me he had some thoughts of going to America; and that, if he went, I was to take care of the estate in his absence; and to consider myself master, and so on, in his generous reckless way—as ready to give up all his privileges as Esau was to swop his birthright against a dish of lobscouse. This letter has been following me from port to port, and I only got it nine or ten weeks ago at Shanghai, where my ship was waiting for a cargo. I went straight to Oswald's London agent when I left the docks; but he could tell me nothing, except that my brother had made all arrangements for a long absence from England. He was to have sailed for New

York on the fourteenth of August. But a thing that puzzled this lawyer fellow a little was that Oswald should have drawn no money since he left home. "He may have taken plenty with him," said I —for you see Oswald was brought up to make a little money go a long way, or to do without it altogether mostly. "So he may," said the lawyer; "but I find that young men generally do draw a good deal of money when they've got any sources to draw upon— and even, sometimes, when they have not. It's a way they have." This made me rather uneasy, and I came down here as fast as those blundering coaches, which hardly do five knots an hour, could bring me. And the old house looked so lonely and dismal without Oswald, that the mere sight of it made me miserable; and then old Nicholas's raven croakings made me worse—so I came straight off to you for comfort.'

'I can tell you nothing,' answered Naomi, with a sigh.

'Nicholas told me you had received no letter. That's strange, certainly. He would have written to you before anyone, I should think.'

'No, I had no right to expect any letter from him. I expected none.'

'What—not as his betrothed wife?'

'Our engagement was broken off some time before he went. Did you not know?'

'Not a word. His last mention of you was full of affection— not in his latest letter, by the way, but in the one which told me of my father's death. I was to come home, and be very fond of you, and we were all to be happy together.'

'Yes, I know,' said Naomi, with a pang of bitterest remembrance. How often had Oswald talked to her of union and love and happiness —sweet domestic joys which Arnold was to share!

'But why was your engagement broken off?' asked the sailor bluntly. 'Did you quarrel?'

'Quarrel? No.'

'He must have behaved very ill, then.'

'No, no. It was my father's wish. I obeyed my father in setting Oswald free. And he accepted his liberty—he was grateful for his release. Love does not always last a lifetime: there is a difference, you see. I think that he once loved me, but——'

Here the tears rained down upon her trembling hands. Arnold drew nearer to her, and gently pressed one of those cold hands with a brotherly kindness.

'My poor girl—my sister that was to have been! He behaved badly, I'm afraid. There was something wild and queer in his last letter, and then that sudden resolve to go to America! I ought to have seen that things had gone wrong with him.　Poor Oswald!　And I expected to see him so happy with you.'

'Providence willed it otherwise.　I was too happy with him, I think: too much absorbed in the joys of this world.'

'Why should we not be happy in this world?　God would never have made so fair a world for a scene of suffering.　You can't. imagine—you stay-at-home people—how beautiful this earth is.　The birds and animals and reptiles and insects are happy.　All free creation enjoys itself, from its birth till its death.　Why should man be wretched, or the source of misery in others?　Why should Providence be offended because you and my brother loved each other and were happy?'

Naomi could not answer.　It was an article of her religion that Heaven disapproved of too much earthly bliss.

'But you must have known where he was going—he told you his plans surely?' asked Arnold.

'No, I knew nothing of his intentions—directly,' answered Naomi, a faint blush dyeing her pallid cheek.

'Did you not see him when he came back to the Grange in the beginning of August?　He came to bid you good-bye, I suppose!'

'No, I did not see him.'

'Then why did he come back to Combhollow at all?　I can hear of nothing that he did in the way of business, except to pack those trunks, which he left behind him after all his trouble.　What was the motive of his return?'

'Indeed, I cannot tell you,' faltered Naomi, sorely distressed.

Arnold looked troubled.　He got up and walked up and down the narrow parlour, as he had walked his quarterdeck in many an hour.of doubt and difficulty.

'I can't understand it,' he said.　'It is the strangest business altogether.　Why did he come back and pack his trunks, and have them taken to the coach, and why did he not appear to claim them?　If he did not leave by the coach, how did he get away?'

'There are vessels that sail between Rockmouth and Bristol, are there not?' suggested Naomi.　'He may have gone that way.'

'A slow roundabout way for him to choose, after making up his mind to go by the coach.　I begin to feel as anxious as Nicholas.　Oh, my dearest Oswald, where are you, and why this mystery?　God grant that he is safe and happy somewhere!　God grant there has been no foul play!'

At these words Naomi's face took a deathlike hue.　But the room was too dark for Arnold to see the change.

'If harm of any kind has happened to him, Heaven help the

wrongdoers, for they shall have no mercy from me! I'll hunt them down. But no, I won't think it. I won't believe that he has come to an untimely end. The brother who carried me in his arms, and was so gentle and loving, and whom I loved, God knows, with all my heart, though I left him! How I have looked forward to our reunion, and counted upon it, and built upon it in all these years. And I come back to find him far away, and his fate a mystery.' He threw himself into a chair and sobbed aloud, honest manly tears coming from a true and brave heart.

It was Naomi's turn to comfort now. She bent over him, and laid her hand lightly on his shoulder.

'Pray do not say that evil has befallen him,' she said. 'He may have changed his mind as to his way of travelling at the last; who can tell what trifling thing may have influenced him?'

'What did he do with himself all that day?' asked Arnold. 'Nicholas tells me that he left the Grange before one o'clock, and the coach was not to pick him up till after eight in the evening. Where was he? With whom did he spend his time? He seems to have no friends in Combhollow but you and your family, and he was not with you?'

'No.'

'Cannot you help me to find out where he was?'

'No, I cannot.'

'That's a pity. If I could only find out the people who saw the last of him here, they might enlighten me as to his intentions. I must see what I can do elsewhere. I came to you naturally for help; but then I did not know your engagement was broken off.'

Sally brought in the lighted candles, and started and stared at sight of the sea-captain.

'Don't be frightened, Sally,' said Naomi; 'this is Captain Pentreath, the Squire's brother.'

'Lor' sakes!' faltered the hand-maiden, 'I took he for the young Squire's ghost.'

'Is your father at home?' asked Arnold presently; 'I should like to see him.'

'No, it is his class-night; he will not be home for nearly an hour. And I know he could tell you nothing more than I have told you,' added Naomi.

'Perhaps not, but he might advise me; I have heard that he is a superior man. I should like to see him: I'll call to-morrow. Good-night, Naomi—I may call you Naomi, I hope, for my brother's sake? He told me to think of you as a sister.'

'I should like you to think me so still, if you can,' Naomi answered gently. And then he pressed her hand, and was gone.

There was some kind of comfort in the sailor's friendliness, in this brave, strong, manly figure, suddenly introduced into the dull scene of a sorrow-shadowed life. He was so like Oswald, and yet so unlike. And he loved his brother so dearly. Oswald's fate would be no longer a mystery. All those unspoken fears, which had preyed upon her like a consuming disease, would be proved vain and foolish. He was safe, he was happy in some strange land. There needed only a little energy and cleverness to find out all about him, and Arnold would supply both.

Then there flashed upon her the memory of that awful moment in the wood, when she saw her father go by with a look upon his face that seemed to her like the brand of Cain, full of awful meaning.

Chapter XXX.

' WHERE IS THY BROTHER ? '

' Father,' said Naomi at supper-time, ' Captain Pentreath has come home, and wants to see you to-morrow.'

' Captain Pentreath ! ' echoed Joshua, staring at her blankly ; ' who's he ? '

' Oswald's brother.'

' Oh, Arnold, the younger son ; the boy who ran away to sea ? He's come home, has he, to take possession of the estate ? That's a good thing.'

' Not to take possession, father ; to take care of the old place, perhaps. He has no right to take possession in his brother's lifetime.'

' Not unless he had stayed away seven years without being heard of,' interjected Jim, the English mind having a firm grip upon this idea of seven years.

' Why should anyone suppose him dead ? ' asked Naomi with a look that was half indignant, half apprehensive ; ' he has only been away a little more than six months. His brother has come home to look for him ; he is determined to find him.'

' What's the use of looking for him at Combhollow, when everybody knows he's gone to America ? ' cried Jim.

' I mean that Captain Pentreath is going to find out all about his brother, when and how he left England.'

' Poor worm ! ' exclaimed Joshua with lofty scorn. ' His brother's fate is in the hands of God. As if he could make or mend it ! '

' But he has a right to know, father, and it is natural he should be anxious.'

' That shows he belongs to the unregenerate,' said Jim, glad to

have a fling at the creed which had been forced upon him before
he was able to form his own estimate of its merits, like vaccina-
tion. 'If he were sure of his own election, he needn't care a toss
what became of his brother ——.'

'In time, perhaps not,' said Joshua, with an awful look; 'but
how dreadful to know him lost in eternity. Better to remain
for ever ignorant of the fate of those we love than to be sure of
their condemnation.'

'Judge not, that ye be not judged,' said Naomi, for the first
time in her life daring to lift up her voice against her father.
'Who can be sure of another's condemnation? It is blasphemy to
say such a thing.'

'What new Daniel is this?' exclaimed Joshua, scornfully. 'Is
my daughter going to be my teacher? I tell you, Naomi, there
are some sins which cannot be repented of. There is a guiltiness
which seals the sinner's doom, and sends him, self-convicted, to
receive his Maker's sentence.'

'I have no fear that Oswald would be such a sinner,' answered Naomi, meeting her father's dark look with defiant eyes.
'Weak, erring, led astray by one more erring than himself—yes,
he might be these, but not a deliberate offender, not obstinately
guilty!'

What was this new feeling which made her talk to her father
as if she was arguing with an adversary? She felt a thrill of
horror at her own audacity. But she was not mistress of herself
when her father spoke harsh words of Oswald Pentreath. Reason
grew clouded and the voice of passion cried aloud in defence of
her lost lover. He was weak, and she would not let the strong
man spurn him. He was absent, and she would not hear him
condemned.

Cynthia sat silent, and heard them talk of the man who had
loved her too well, whose only sin and sorrow was to have let his
heart go out to her as a young bird flies from its nest into the
glad new world. He had loved her, and that love had darkened
his life. She could see him looking down at her, as on that last
day, passion-pale, bidding his eternal farewell. What a dream it
had been—so fair, so sweet, so unreal! She had suffered herself to
be beloved, and to love again, and in this dreaming, half-unconscious state had tasted an ineffable happiness. She did not regret
this lost dream-world; she would not have recalled its vanished
sweetness; she was honestly repentant of her sin against the
husband she honoured; but the past was ineffaceable—a part of
her being.

> I cannot but remember such things were
> That were most precious to me.

Though full of anxious thoughts, Arnold Pentreath brought brightness and pleasant days to the old Grange and all who came within his influence. His candid intelligent face, the frank heartiness of his manners, with just a dash of the seaman's bluntness, and that firm straightforwardness which comes from the habit of commanding others and restraining oneself—all these things gave him immediate mastery over the simple folks at Combhollow. The old servants worshipped him. He had been the most daring and mischievous of the two brothers, in boyhood, and naturally the most popular. He had defied his old father, and had won golden opinions from the household by his juvenile mutinies. He came back a man, broad-shouldered and strongly built, bronzed and battered a little by all kinds of climates and hard weather, but all the handsomer, in the eyes of a sea-loving population, for his sunburnt cheek and the stubborn crispness of his hair. He was fonder of his fellow-men than Oswald had been, and, instead of dreaming over Childe Harold in Pentreath Wood, was out and about all day, tramping along the lanes, making acquaintance with every hind who worked upon his land, tossing cottage children in his strong arms, with a kindly word for every one he met.

He had not been three days at the Grange before the fact of his return was known far and wide, and brought all manner of applicants to the old house to ask favours which no agent would grant. He heard all complaints with an equable good nature, and lent his attention to the smallest detail. The slates blown off the homestead in ' they high winds—now do'ee see what you can do for us, Squire.' The granary thatch which had ' cotched fire ' in such a mysterious way after last midsummer's thunder-storm, that old Farmer Westall was firmly convinced it was the work of Nancy Dowben, the witch.

' For she be a witch, Squire,' said the farmer, ' that's well beknownst. And I do say as it ain't right a spiteful old woman like she should be allowed to meddle with forked lightning.'

' Well, farmer, if it was witchcraft fired the barn, you can't expect me to pay for new thatching it ? ' argued Arnold.

' But look'ee now, Squire. It was the ould gentleman, your feyther, brought it on us. All they witches bore an evil eye towards him. He were so hard upon 'em, and that screwy, never a drop of milk or a faggot to give 'em.'

' Wasn't it you, now, that refused old Nancy the faggots, Farmer Westall ? ' suggested Arnold.

' Well, now, you're a bit of a conjurer yourself, Squire. There was one day as the ould ooman come for some wood to bile her kittle, and I wasn't in the best of tempers, for our ould sow had etten up seven pegs, and I thowt it was some o' Nancy's work, so I calls out, "Now jist look yere, Nancy; you had a faggot, yesterday, and another the day afore that, and I didn't make that stack o' wood o' purpose for you, old lady." So she gives a sniff and a grunt, and off she goes, and it wasn't a week from that when the lightning caught the thatch o' my biggest barn. And I'm a man with a long fambly, Squire, and I've had the roof covered up anyhow with some old boards and a bit of tarpaulin ever since, because Bill Stowell, the thatcher, asks a mort o' money before he'll make a good job of it!'

'We'll see what can be done, farmer. Perhaps I might go halves in the expense, if the barn was roofed in to my satisfaction. I'm only a steward, you see—a kind of deputy for my brother.'

Farmer Westall sighed and looked glum. Old Nicholas, the butler, had infected most of his acquaintance with his own dismal ideas about the absent lord of the manor. It was a general opinion that the vessel in which Oswald had sailed for America had gone to the bottom.

'There are some folks that 'll never get no luck out o' the sea,' said the voice of public opinion as represented by the fishermen of Combhollow. 'Remember that storm, and the way the "Dolphin" went to pieces. The two sailors was saved easy enough, but the Squire would have been drownded or knocked to pieces on they rocks but for Joshua Haggard. And what were the use of saving him? He never did no good to the Haggards; and here he is gone down to the bottom, as sure as fate. It was what were meant from the fust, and there's never no good in flying in the face of Providence. You may save a ship's cargo—that's man's business—and an honest way of providin' for a fambly: but they as is aboard the ship is in the care o' Providence, and it's clean blasphemy to risk your life in fishing of 'em out of the water!'

Captain Pentreath had exhausted his resources, and had found no clue to his brother's proceedings after that August noontide in which he had left the Grange, with the avowed intention of going to Exeter—on his way to London—by the evening coach. Arnold had gone back to London, and had seen the solicitor again, and had made his enquiries in every likely and unlikely direction, but he had learned nothing. The London lawyer did not know the name of the vessel in which Arnold had booked his passage to New York. His client had told him nothing, except that he had made up his mind to go to America, and that he wanted his affairs administered in his absence. The household at the Grange was to suffer no alteration, and when Arnold came he was to be master.

'Until your return!' the lawyer had said to him.

' My return is an event of the remote future,' Oswald had replied ; ' I may never return.'

Arnold went to Liverpool, and the result of his researches there convinced him that Oswald had not left that port in any vessel bound for America, unless he had sailed under an assumed name. From Liverpool he went to Cork—from Cork he went by water to Bristol—from Bristol westward to Plymouth ; and the most searching enquiries at these places resulted as his enquiries had resulted at Liverpool. There was no trace of Oswald Pentreath's passage to America to be found in any shipping office. He went back to the Grange sorely depressed, for his brother's fate was beginning to assume a hue of mystery which gave room for the darkest fears.

His conversation with Joshua Haggard had told him nothing more than he had already learned from Naomi. The minister had received him with a chilling reserve which held him at arm's length. The frank outspoken sailor wondered that his brother could have written to him so warmly in praise of such a man.

He called on Joshua the day after his return from his round of enquiry.

' This is a bad business, Mr. Haggard,' he began, plunging at once into the subject nearest his heart ; ' I have found out enough to feel very sure that my brother has not gone to America.'

Joshua's grave countenance betrayed no surprise. ' Why, the fellow is not a man but a machine,' Arnold thought indignantly.

' You don't seem to understand what a serious question this is,' said Arnold. ' If my brother did not go to America last August, what has become of him ? '

' That is a question that I cannot be expected to answer, Captain Pentreath. We are all in God's hands. In life or in death He deals with us as seemeth best to Him. He may have appointed your brother for an evil end. You had best be content to leave all to Him.'

' Do you mean that if my brother has come to an evil end, I am to let his murderer go scot-free ? ' cried Arnold, indignantly. ' Do you think that I shall fold my hands and wait for Providence to avenge my brother ? Why, if I did, God would have the right to ask of me as he did of Cain, " Where is thy brother ? " You do not know how dearly we two loved each other, Mr. Haggard.'

' " Vengeance is mine, I will repay," ' quoted Joshua solemnly ; ' be sure that if your brother has been murdered, an idea I do not for a moment entertain, his assassin has suffered or will suffer as heavy a punishment as any vengeance of yours could inflict.'

' May God make conscience an undying worm to feed upon his soul ! ' said Arnold. ' But it shall be my business to bring his body to the gallows.'

Joshua heard him in silence. He sat with folded hands, and a countenance as mysterious in its solemn thoughtfulness as the head of Memnon.

'Come, Mr. Haggard, you must be able to give me some help in this matter, if you choose,' urged Arnold passionately; 'my brother was your daughter's lover—her affianced husband, till you, for some motive of your own, forbade their marriage. There is a story underlying that act of yours—a story that might cast some light upon my poor brother's fate. You must have had strong reasons for such a step. A man of your principles would hardly be governed by caprice. Tell me honestly, as one who has a right to ask, what that reason was.'

' I can give you no details upon that point,' answered Joshua, after some moments of profound thought, 'but I will tell you broadly that I had reason to disapprove of your brother's conduct in relation to another woman. I had reason to know that his heart had gone away from my daughter. He would have kept his promise, and married her, and would have believed that he was acting as a man of honour; but he would have lied at God's altar, and his marriage would have offended Heaven.'

' You believe that my brother's heart had gone astray?'

' I know it.'

' Then, for heaven's sake, tell me all you know. This love affair may throw light upon his after conduct—may give us the clue to his present whereabouts. There would be a false delicacy—an absolute cruelty—in hiding anything from me—from me, his brother, who am distracted by the most hideous apprehensions.'

' I can tell you nothing more,' answered Joshua, with a stern resoluteness which chilled Arnold to the heart. ' I am withholding no knowledge which could help you in the smallest degree. Your brother sinned—and is gone. You must be content to know no more than that.'

' I will not be content,' cried the sailor, vehemently. ' You are juggling with me—you, a preacher of God's Word, who ought to be truthful as the day. But I forgot—the prophets were dark of speech, and God taught His chosen people by dreams and allegories, and you seek to imitate those mysterious ways. Have you no human pity—as a man and a Christian—for a brother's grief for a lost brother? You could tell me something that would make this mystery clear; and you lock your lips, and abandon me to the agony of uncertainty. My brother respected, admired—nay, loved you, Mr. Haggard.'

This wrung a sigh from a breast which Arnold had deemed marble.

'I tell you I am withholding nothing that could give you comfort,' said Joshua, looking downward with fixed and gloomy brow. 'I deplore your brother's fate, and the mystery which surrounds it. Yet for your sake—for the sake of my daughter who loved him—I say, May the veil never be lifted!'

'Why?'

'Because I fear he came to a bad end.'

'You must have some reason for that fear. You know something,' exclaimed Arnold, breathlessly.

'I am guided by my knowledge of his character—of his condition of mind last summer.'

'You think he destroyed himself?'

'I do.'

Arnold bowed his face upon his clasped hands; his strong frame was shaken by the agony of that momemt. To have stayed away from his brother all the days of his youth—to come home full of hope and pleasure—and to be told this! The cup was bitter.

When Arnold looked up, Joshua Haggard was gone.

He stayed in the empty room, looking out into the windy March street—where one old woman was tightening a three-cornered shawl across her skinny shoulders—with eyes that saw not, and thinking over Joshua's words.

What did they mean? How much, or how little? Was this idea of Oswald's suicide a mere speculation on the minister's part, or had he sound evidence on which to found his conclusions?

'It is too bad of him to leave me in the dark,' mused Arnold. 'I have a right to know everything that can be said or thought about my brother. He is a hard-hearted scoundrel. These over-pious men are adamant. And yet he saved my brother's life at the risk of his own. Oswald told me the story, and the fishermen here are never tired of talking about it. Don't let me forget that. The man is better than his speech. And he tells me he is keeping nothing back. But to think that my brother took his own life—that he was wretched enough to find the coward's last release from difficulty! I will not believe it.'

He rose to depart; but before he got to the door, Naomi came in, and they stood face to face, both startled, both agitated by this sudden meeting, natural as it was.

'Oh, Naomi, I want you,' cried the sailor, taking both her hands, and looking into the pale face with beseeching earnestness. 'I want you to advise, to comfort, to enlighten me. I have been talking to your father, and he has almost broken my heart. Tell me, for pity's sake, the truth, dear, as sister to brother. Say that you do not believe Oswald killed himself.'

'Killed himself?' she echoed, growing very white. 'No. Who says so—who thinks so?'

'Your father.'

'My father says that—my father believes that?'

'Yes, dear. He told me so five minutes ago. Only say that you don't believe it.'

'I do not!' she answered with flashing eyes. 'I know that he was unhappy, but I cannot believe—I will not believe—that he could be so weak—so guilty. No, there was no such thought in his mind. He had made his plans for beginning a new life; he had taken his passage for America.'

'You know that from himself?' cried Arnold eagerly.

Naomi bowed her head in assent.

'God bless you, sister!' said the sailor. 'You have comforted me more than I can say. You knew him—you loved him.'

'With all my heart and soul—too much for duty, or peace, or righteousness.'

'And you think he really did go to America?'

Naomi's troubled face took a still deeper shadow.

'I know he meant to go; he may not have gone after all.'

'Yet it was strange that he should not have left by the coach, after telling Nicholas that he meant to go that way. Very strange that he should leave those trunks behind him after packing them.'

'He may have changed his mind at the last. He was troubled in mind, and might be careless about things which people in an ordinary state of mind would consider important.'

'True, my dear. How clearly you see everything. Yes, that was so. And he sailed from some small port, perhaps—or from the other side of the Channel, Havre or Brest. The fact that I cannot trace him is worth nothing. We will wait and hope, Naomi; hope for your husband and my brother's return.'

'For our brother's return,' answered Naomi, with a tender gravity. 'He can never again be more to me than a brother: and to the end of my life I shall love him with a sister's love.'

'Poor fellow!' said Arnold dreamily; 'he threw away a jewel above all price when he lost you.'

(*To be continued.*)

Lady-Troubadours and Courts of Love.

BY F. HUEFFER.

THE north of France was the birth country and chief seat of epic poetry in the middle ages. The *chanson de geste*, the *roman*, the *fabliau*, bear witness to consummate grace of narrative diction. Even the lyrical effusions of the *trouvères* frequently take the form of the monologue or dialogue. The poet loves to hide his own personality under the mask of a fictitious character. This is different with the troubadour, the poet of Southern France. He is the lyrical singer *par excellence*, speaking in his own undisguised person, and of his own subjective passion. His *canzo* is the song of love, and even in his *sirventes*—that is, a song of political or personal satire—he often breaks off abruptly, ' for now,' he says, naïvely, ' I must sing the praise of my lady.' In a poetry so thoroughly imbued with one prevailing passion, and in the civilisation of which this poetry is the utterance, woman naturally occupied a most important place. But to define this place is a matter of some difficulty. The poems of the troubadours themselves give us but scanty information in this respect. We there hear a great deal of the incomparable charms of Provençal ladies ; their lovingkindness is extolled, or their cruelty complained of. But in a few cases only are we enabled to realise from generalities of this kind an individual human being with individual passions or caprices. It would, indeed, be impossible even to decipher the numerous *senhals* or nicknames under which the poets were obliged to hide the real names of their lady-loves from the watchfulness of evil tongues and cruel husbands, but for the aid of the Provençal biographies of the old troubadours, which in most cases offer a welcome clue to the identity of these pseudonymous flames.

It is by this means that we hear of the beautiful ladies of Provence—such as the three sisters, Maenz of Montignac, Elise of Montfort, and Maria of Ventadorn—praised in impassioned song by Bertran de Born, Gaucelm Faidit, and other troubadours ; and of that lovely lady with an unlovely name Loba, (she-wolf) of Penau-

tier, who turned the fantastic brain of Peire Vidal, and sent him
into the wilderness clad in a wolf's skin—a practical pun on the
name of his mistress. From such hints as may be found in these
biographies and other contemporary sources, I have tried to form
a tangible idea of a Provençal lady of the twelfth or thirteenth
century; of her position in society ; and, most of all, of her decisive
influence on the poetry of the troubadours. Does the reader care
to know ?

What was the type of the lady of Provence of whom so much
has been said in verse and prose? Was she a demure, well-con-
ducted person, clad in sober colours, mending stockings and cutting
bread-and-butter for the children; a model housewife, in fact, such
as might be found in a best-possible world of Mrs. Lynn Linton's
devising? Or was she, on the other hand, a progressive-minded
female, despising the frivolities of society, and thirsting for medical
degrees and the franchise, or whatever may have been the mediæval
equivalents of these much-desired prerogatives ? I fear that even
Margarida de Rossilho, 'the lady most praised of her time for all
that is praiseworthy and noble and courteous,' would have fallen
far short of these divergent ideals of our latter days. Her main
purpose of existence was—shocking though it may sound—altogether not practical, but ornamental. It was her choice and her
duty to wield in a society only just emerging from barbarism the
softening influence to which we owe the phenomenon of a highly
finished literature and of an astonishing degree of social refinement at the very outset of the mediæval epoch. Whether this
result was altogether unworthy of woman's mission in the history
of civilisation graver judges must decide.

There is extant, dating from about the middle of the thirteenth
century, a curious poem in rhymed couplets entitled, 'L'essenhamen
de la donzela que fe N' Amanieus des Escas com apela dieu d'amors;'
Anglice : ' Instruction to a young lady, composed by Sir Amanieu
des Escas, called God of Love.' In this treatise we are supplied with a minute account of the accomplishments expected
from a well-educated young lady, and of the bad habits most prejudicial to her character. The poet is supposed to be addressing
a noble damsel living at the court of some great baron, as a sort
of ' lady-help' to his wife ; this being a not unusual, and undoubtedly a most efficient, method of polite education in Provence.
The young lady has accosted Amanieu on a lonely walk, asking for
his advice in matters fashionable. This the poet at first refuses to
tender ; alleging that ' you (the damsel) have ten times as much
sense as I, and that is the truth.' But, after his modest scruples
are once overcome, he launches forth into a flood of good counsel.

He systematically begins with enforcing the good old doctrine of 'early to rise;' touches delicately on the mysteries of the morning toilet, such as lacing, washing of arms, hands, and head, which, he sententiously adds, ought to go before the first-mentioned process; and, after briefly referring to the especial care required for teeth and nails, he leaves the dressing-room for the church, where a quiet, undemonstrative attitude is recommended; the illicit use of eyes and tongue being mentioned amongst the temptations peculiarly to be avoided.   Directions of similar minuteness assist the young lady at the dinner-table; the cases in which it would be good taste, and those in which it would be the reverse, to invite persons to a share of the dishes within her reach are specified; and the rules as to carving, washing one's hands before and after dinner, and similar matters, leave nothing to be desired.   'Always temper your wine with water, so that it may not do you harm,' is another maxim of undeniable wisdom.

After dinner follows the time of polite conversation in the *sala* (drawing-room), the arbour, or on the battlements of the castle; and now the teachings of Amanieu become more and more animated, and are enlivened occasionally by practical illustrations of great piquancy. 'And if at this season,' he says, 'a gentleman takes you aside, and wishes to talk of courtship to you, do not show a strange or sullen behaviour, but defend yourself with pleasant and pretty repartees.   And if his talk annoys you, and makes you uneasy, I advise you to ask him questions, for instance: "Which ladies do you think are more handsome, those of Gascony or England? and more courteous, and faithful, and good?"   And if he says those of Gascony, answer without hesitation: "Sir, by your leave, English ladies are more courteous than those of any other country." But if he prefers those of England, tell him Gascon ladies are much better behaved; and thus carry on the discussion, and call your companions to you to decide the questions.'   I defy any modern professor of deportment to indicate a more graceful and appropriate way of giving a harmless turn to a conversation, or cutting short an awkward *tête-à-tête*.

And the same sense of tact and social ease pervades the remainder of the poem, which consists chiefly of valuable hints how to accept and how to refuse an offer of marriage without giving more encouragement or more offence than necessary.   Upon the whole, it must be admitted that 'Amanieu des Escas, called God of Love,' although undoubtedly a pedant, is the least objectionable and tedious pedant that ever preached 'the graces' from the days of Thomasin of Zerclaere to those of Lord Chesterfield.   But the important point for us is the enormous weight attached to these rules of etiquette in the education of the Provençal lady. Again and again the advantages of *cortesia, avinensa,* and whatever the numerous other terms for a graceful, courteous behaviour may be, are emphasised : ' even the enemy of all your friends ought to find you civil-spoken,' the poet exclaims in a fit of polite enthusiasm. However exaggerated and one-sided this point of view may appear to the reader, he ought to remember that in primitive societies the code of ethics can be enforced alone by the power of custom ; the derivation, indeed, of our word ' morality ' from the Latin *mores* is by no means a mere etymological coincidence.

Prepared by an education such as I have tried to sketch in the above, the lady generally contracted a marriage at an early age ; the choice of a husband being in most cases determined by her parents, or her feudal overlord. In the higher classes of society— and these alone concern us here—her own inclination was taken into little account. Her position at the head of a great baron's family was by no means an easy one. She had to soften the coarse habits and words of the warlike nobles ; and, on the other hand, to curb the amorous boldness of the gay troubadours who thronged the courts of the great barons. The difficulties and temptations of such a situation were great, and further increased by the perfect liberty which, in ancient as in modern France, married ladies seem to have enjoyed. Indirect, but none the less conclusive, evidence establishes this point beyond doubt. We hear, for instance, of ladies travelling about the country without attendance ; like the pretty wives of Sir Guari and Sir Bernart, whom Count William of Poitiers deceived by acting a deaf-and-dumb pilgrim. Even the dueña, as a regular institution at least, seems to have been unknown in Provence. There certainly were jealous husbands who tried to protect their wives from gallant intrusion by watchfulness and strict confinement. The husband of the lovely Flamenca, in the charming romance of that name, is an example of such fruitless care. But his fate could not invite imitation ; and the universal horror expressed by all gallant knights and ladies at this fictitious instance and at some real instances of similar cruelty sufficiently proves the high degree of personal freedom enjoyed by the ladies of Southern France.

That this freedom was frequently abused is, unfortunately, no matter of doubt. France is not, and never has been, a prosperous climate for the growth of wedded happiness. The heroines of all the love-stories connected with the history of the troubadours are, indeed, with not a single exception that I am aware of, married ladies. This fact is certainly of deep significance, but its importance ought not to be overrated. We must remember that the troubadours and their biographers were by nature and profession inclined to magnify the force and extension of the *grande passion*. Frequently they may, and in some cases we positively know that they did, mistake gracious condescension for responsive passion; and to accept all their statements *au pied de la lettre* would be about as advisable as to judge the institution of marriage in modern France solely by the works of Flaubert and Ernest Feydeau. In many cases, however, the perfect innocence of the relations between the troubadour and the lady he celebrates is fully acknowledged by all parties. It was the privilege of high-born and high-minded women to protect and favour poetry, and to receive in return the troubadour's homage. It is in this beautiful character, of an admirer and patroness of the literature of her country, that I wish first to consider the lady of Provence. In the choice of an individual instance of the relation alluded to, I have been guided by a feeling of historic, not to say poetic, justice.

History and fiction have vied with each other in painting the picture of Eleanor, wife of Henry II. of England, in the darkest colours. The former convicts her of faithlessness to two husbands, and of conspiracy with her own sons against their father ; the latter charges her with the murder of Rosamond Clifford. Any redeeming feature in such a character ought to be welcome to the believer in human nature. Her connection with Bernart de Ventadour, one of the sweetest and purest of troubadours, is such a feature. The poet came to her court in sorrow. The lady he loved had been torn from him, and it was by her own desire that he left her and the country where she dwelt. He now turned to Eleanor for comfort and sympathy, and his hope was not disappointed. The old Provençal biography of Bernart is provokingly laconic with regard to the subject. 'He went to the Duchess of Normandy,' it says, ' who was young and of great worth, and knew how to appreciate worth and honour, and he said much in her praise. And she admired the canzos and verses of Bernart. And she received him very well, and bade him welcome. And he stayed at her court a long time, and became enamoured of her and she of him, and he composed many beautiful songs of her. And while he was with her King Henry of England made her his wife, and took her away from Normandy with him. And from that time Bernart remained sad and woful.'

This statement is incorrect in more than one respect, and may be cited as an instance of the desire on the part of the ancient biographers to give a dramatic, and at the same time an erotic, turn to the stories of their heroes. The allegation of the poet's prolonged courtship of the Duchess of Normandy being interrupted by the lady's marriage with Henry is self-contradictory, for the simple reason that she became Duchess of Normandy and took up her residence in that country in consequence of this identical marriage, which took place in the same year of her separation from Louis VII. of France. Moreover, all the songs known to us as having been addressed by the poet to Eleanor, are written after Henry's accession to the English throne. One of these songs, in which Bernart calls himself 'a Norman or Englishman for the king's sake,' was most likely composed in England, where Bernart had followed the court of his supposed rival.

These same songs tend also to throw grave doubts on another statement of the old manuscript—that with regard to the mutual passion between lady and troubadour. It is true that his devotion frequently adopts the language of love; but there is no evidence to show that this love was returned by anything but friendship and kindness. He never boasts of favours granted, as troubadours were but too prone to do, and the joyful expectation expressed in one of his poems is evidently and confessedly a hope against hope. One somewhat obscure remark of the poet seems to indicate that King Henry did not regard the matter in an altogether innocent light. The line reads thus in the original Provençal : ' Per vos me sui del rei partitz ; ' which means, ' For your sake I have parted from the king,' and seems to indicate some sort of disagreement between the poet and the lady's husband. But, supposing even that Henry's jealousy were proved by this vague hint, we are not for that reason obliged to adopt his suspicions. Internal evidence points strongly towards a different relation—a relation much more common between the ladies and poets of Provence than is generally believed, and which is marked by fervent admiration on the one side, and by helpful and gentle, but inapproachable, kindness on the other.

Frequently, however, the case was different. Not all ladies were inexorable ; not all troubadours contented with a purely ideal worship. Ardent wooings led to passionate attachments, and lovers' bliss was frequently followed by lovers' quarrels. Such quarrels—or, it might be, differences of opinion on abstract points of love and gallantry—were not unusually discussed in a poetic form ; the 'tenzo,' or 'song of contention,' being especially reserved for this purpose. It was mostly on occasions of this kind that ladies took up the lute and mingled their voices with the chorus of Provençal singers. The names of fourteen gifted women have in this manner become transmitted to us—a very modest figure, seeing that the entire number of the troubadours is close upon four hundred. But even of these fourteen lady-troubadours few, if any, seem to have been professional or even amateur poets. The works of most of them are exceedingly few in number, consisting, in several cases, of a single song or part of a *tenzo*. This reticence on the part of the ladies cannot be praised too highly; it explains to us at the same time their position in the literary movement of their time. Literature in the twelfth and thirteenth centuries was a lucrative and honourable calling, followed by many members of the poorer nobility and of the lower classes. Professional singers of this kind, technically called *joglars* to distinguish them from their richer amateur brethren, naturally depended on their productions for a livelihood. Hence the number and hence also the occasional coldness and formality of their songs.

But this was different with women. With them poetry was not an employment, but an inward necessity. They poured forth their mirth or their grief, and after that relapsed into silence. Even Clara of Anduse, the brilliant and beautiful lady who conquered the obstinate indifference of Uc de St. Cyr, the celebrated troubadour, and who is described as ambitious of literary fame, does not seem to have sinned by over-production. Only one of her songs remains to us, and there is no reason to believe that time has been more than usually destructive to her works.

The only lady-troubadour of whose poems we possess a sufficient number to allow of a fair judgment of her capability is the Countess Beatrice de Die. She may also serve to illustrate the essentially subjective conception of the art of poetry which marks the phase in literature alluded to. The unvarying subject of her poems is the story of her love; without this passion she would have remained mute. Her first song is the embodiment of new-awakened happiness; her last a dirge over hopes dead and forlorn.

The Countess de Die, says the old manuscript, 'was the wife of Guillem de Poitou, a good and beautiful lady; she became enamoured of Rambaut of Orange, and wrote many fine poems of him.' This Rambaut was the third ruler of that name of the county of Aurenga or Orange, in the south of France, from which the Dutch line of the house of Nassau derived its name. The English Jacobites, by the way, were considerably out in their etymological reckoning when they derisively squeezed the orange.

Rambaut is well known as the author of numerous poems, some of them rather coarse in character. One of his songs is metrically curious by the poet relapsing at the end of every stanza into a few lines of prose, in which admirers of Walt Whitman will perhaps discover rhythm. In another poem he gives an elaborate prescription for gaining the hearts and bending the minds of women, quite in the spirit of the coarsest scenes of the *Taming of the Shrew.* The apparent disagreement of the poet with his own rules expressed in one stanza does not much alter the case in his favour, neither can we consider his calling one of his lady-loves by the nickname 'my Devil' a sign of refinement on his part. The exaggerated and boldly uttered opinion of his own poetic power is an additional unpleasant feature of Rambaut's character. His songs to Beatrice de Die, of which several remain, are marked by extravagant gallantry rather than by true feeling. It may, for instance, be doubted whether the lady had much reason to be pleased with compliments of this kind: 'The joy you give me is such that a thousand doleful people would be made merry by my joy. And on my joy all my relations could live with joy without eating.'

The reader will notice the frequent repetition of the word 'joy,' which occurs once in every line of the stanza. This is an instance of the artificial trifles on which many troubadours, Rambaut of Orange foremost amongst the number, prided themselves. A similar metrical contrivance is found in another song by our poet, most likely also addressed to the Countess de Die. It is called the '*rim dictional*,' and consists of the combination, in the rhyming syllables, of two words which can be derived from each other by either adding or deducting one or more syllables. Thus, for instance, the feminine and masculine forms of the adjective and participle *at-ada*, *ut-uda* stand in the relation of 'dictional rhymes.' It is sadly significant to see that this silly contrivance has been adopted by Beatrice de Die in the song which expresses the fulness of her loving bliss. Perhaps it would be too bold to conjecture without additional evidence that, in this as in so many cases, the teacher had developed into the lover ; but this sign of intellectual dependence is at any rate highly characteristic.

Unfortunately, the serene sky of her happiness was soon to become overclouded. We can distinctly recognise the mutual position of the lovers. Count Rambaut, if he had at any time felt a serious passion for Beatrice, soon got over that weakness. In vain he tries to hide his apathy from the keen glance of the loving woman. She is appeased for the moment by his grandiloquent vows of eternal devotion ; but soon her suspicion awakes again with renewed strength. Such are the feelings which have inspired the admirable *tenzo* respectively ascribed to Rambaut and Beatrice, but most likely composed by both of them in alternate stanzas of reproach and excuse. The poet, taxed with indifference and fickleness, explains that the rareness of his visits is caused by his fear of the evil tongues and spies ' who have taken my sense and breath away.' But the lady is little impressed with this tender care for her reputation. 'No thanks do I owe you,' she says, 'for your refusing to see me when I send for you, because of the harm I might suffer through it. And if you take greater care of my welfare than I do myself, you must forsooth be over loyal; more so than the Knights of the Hospital.' Only by the most extravagant promises of amendment is the poet enabled to gain from the lady the qualified concession : 'Friend, I will trust you so far, so that I find you true and loyal to me at all times.'

A second song of the countess marks a further stage of this unfortunate amour. The poet has now dropped the mask ; the lady is deserted—deserted for another love. The sight of her misery is pathetic, although, perhaps, less dignified than would be the silent pride of a noble-hearted woman. But pride is strange to the heart of poor Beatrice. Her desire is not to upbraid, but, if possible, to regain, her truant lover ; and nothing she considers beneath her dignity that may attain this sole desire of her heart. Abject flattery of her lover and even the praise of her own beauty are resorted to by her with a naïve openness which, somehow, makes us forget her utter want of dignity. There is the true ring of simple pathos about her poem, which I have tried to retain as far as possible in the subjoined literal rendering of three of the stanzas :

It is in vain, this silence I must break ;
The fault of him I love moves me to speak.
Dearer than all the world he is to me ;
But he regards not love nor courtesy,
Nor wisdom, nor my worth, nor all my beauty—
He has deceived me. Such my fate should be,
If I had failed to him in loving duty.

Oh, strange and past belief that in disdain,
Your heart, O friend, should look upon my pain ;
That now another love should conquer you,
For all that I may say, that I may do.
Have you forgotten the sweet first communion
Of our two hearts? now sorely would I rue
If by my guilt were caused this last disunion.

The noble worth, the valour you possess,
Your fame and beauty add to my distress.
For far and near the noble ladies all,
If love can move them, listen to your call.
But you, my friend, whose soul is keenest-sighted,
Must know who loves you, and is true withal.
And ah ! remember now the troth we plighted.

The reader need hardly be told that this touching appeal proved in vain. We have another song of Beatrice, in which she deplores the final loss of her friend. It is remarkable that even now no word of anger escapes her lips. She blames herself for a reticence of feeling which, if she had possessed it, might have averted her fate. This is the first stanza of the plaintive ditty:

> Ah, sadly, sadly do I miss
> A knight of valour once mine own!
> To all at all times be it known,
> My heart was his—was only his.
> Foolishly my secret keeping,
> I hid my love when he was near;
> But in my heart I held him dear,
> Day and night, awake and sleeping.

And here we must take leave of the beautiful Beatrice de Die. She is not without interest from a psychological point of view, and represents the literary capabilities of her class by the intensely subjective character of her work, which is the immediate outgrowth of her feeling.

There is yet one other important character in which I should wish to introduce the lady of Provence to the gentle reader. It has already been pointed out that to her influence the refinement of manners and the high conception of the duties of gallantry in the early middle ages are mainly due. But nowhere did her gentle sway exercise a more irresistible power than in that truest domain of womanhood—love. This love was little restrained in Provence by the legitimate bounds of marriage, but it was not altogether lawless for that reason. There were certain rules of conduct instinctively felt rather than definitely formulated, but which, nevertheless, no lady or gallant cavalier could transgress with impunity. Discretion, for instance, was a demand most strictly enforced by these self-imposed laws of the loving community. No lady of self-respect would have accepted the services of a knight who had failed in this respect to a former mistress. Neither was it thought compatible with good principles for a lady to deprive another lady of her lover. Inquiries into the antecedents of intended cicisbeos were of frequent occurrence, and only where a troubadour could prove his ' being off with the old love' could he hope for a favourable reception of his vows. We indeed know of one case where a lady, although herself desirous of the services of a poet, effects his reconciliation with a rival beauty. But this loyal feeling did not extend to that bugbear and scapegoat of gallant society in Provence—the husband. No amount of verbal falsehood or hypocrisy was thought unjustifiable in the endeavour to dupe his well-founded suspicion. His resentment of injuries received was, on the other hand, punished by the general interdict of polite society. Such, at least, is the no doubt somewhat highly coloured picture drawn by Provençal poets and romancers.

To the great influence of noble ladies on public opinion and to the *esprit de corps* evinced by their recorded words and doings we have to trace back the general and time-honoured idea of the ladies' tribunal, or ' court of love.' To us in England Chaucer's poem of that title has sanctioned the name ; and a prettier picture can hardly be imagined than that drawn by many old and modern writers of an assembly of beautiful women sitting in judgment on guilty lovers, and gravely deciding knotty points of the amorous code. The slight tinge of pedantry in such a picture adds to its mediæval quaintness. The only drawback is that, like so many other pretty and quaint pictures, it has no counterpart in the reality of things ; not as far, at least, as the south of France and the times of the troubadours are concerned. Friederich Diez, the lately deceased great philologist, to whom the history of Romance litera-ture and languages owes so much, has once and for ever destroyed the fable of the ' courts of love ' in connection with the troubadours. This was done in 1825 ; but ever since the exploded notion has gone on producing fresh and powerful shoots in the fertile soil of periodical, and generally unscientific, literature. It is, indeed, one of the few dainties of Provençal composition which have been frequently and *ad nauseam* dished up to the general reader of this country.

The state of the case is briefly this :—

In 1817 the well-known French scholar, M. Raynouard, pub-lished his large collection of Provençal poems, entitled *Choix des Poésies originales des Troubadours.* In the second volume of this work he has inserted a long and elaborate inquiry of his own into the subject of the ' courts of love.' He determines the period of their duration to have been the time from the middle of the twelfth to the end of the fourteenth century or thereabouts, and gives a somewhat minute description of the legal and polite customs observed at these extraordinary tribunals. According to him, the members of the court were noble ladies guided by a written code of love, their decisions again constituting precedent. An appeal to a different tribunal was admissible. The parties had, as a rule, to plead their cause in person ; at other times, however, written documents— affidavits, as we should say—were accepted, the latter frequently taking the form of the *tenzos* already alluded to in the above. To these tenzos, therefore, we ought to look for some confirmation of these statements; and, according to Raynouard, such confirmation is forthcoming in more than sufficient abundance. It is the custom in these songs of contention for the two disputants to refer their case to the arbitration of third parties. ' This tenzo will last for ever,' says one troubadour, after having exhausted his arguments. ' Let us take our cause to the Dauphin ; he will decide and conclude it in peace.' But here is the rub. The umpires mentioned on this and many other occasions are always one or two individuals, generally friends of the contending parties, or else well-meaning and courteous persons, men or women, who decide according to the rules of common sense, or quote the opinions of celebrated troubadours by way of law and guidance. Not once is a ' court of love' mentioned in these tenzos, nor, indeed in any other poem, by a genuine troubadour. The expression as well as the thing was unknown to them. Both belong to a much later time.

The period of spontaneous production in the literature of most nations is followed by that of classification. Byzantine scholarship and Athenian tragedy belong to different phases of intellectual life. When the poetry of the troubadours began to decay, grammarians and metrical scholars sprang up, and artificial poetry flourished at the *Jeux Floraux*. In the same sense it may be said that ' courts of love' could not exist where love itself was alive. The laws of gallantry were inscribed in the hearts of ladies and troubadours while the brilliant, buoyant life of Southern France was in its acme. When this civilisation was crushed, when these beautiful times lived but in the remembrance of a few, it might become necessary to preserve in dead formulas and codes the remnants of a better past. But even in the fourteenth and fifteenth centuries the south of France seems not to have been a favourable soil for the ' courts of love,' as certain amateur societies of gallant and literary ladies and gentlemen then began to be called. The chief witness on the subject, Andreas Capellanus, who quotes several sentences delivered by these *curiæ dominarum*, seems to refer chiefly to the north of France. Another Frenchman, Martial d'Auvergne, an advocate in Paris, has introduced the technical language of the law into these amorous discussions ; much to the edification of his contemporaries (he lived in the fifteenth century), to judge from the number of editions published of his work.

The sober truth arrived at by these and many other considerations too long to mention, may be summed up thus : 'Courts of love,' as established tribunals with written codes, are altogether fictitious. Amateur societies of that name occur in the late middle ages, but chiefly in the north of France. To the troubadours the name and essence of ' courts of love' were entirely unknown.

A Ballad of Dreamland.

BY ALGERNON CHARLES SWINBURNE.

I HID my heart in a nest of roses,
  Out of the sun's way, hidden apart ;
In a softer bed than the soft white snow's is,
  Under the roses I hid my heart.
  Why would it sleep not ? why should it start,
When never a leaf of the rose-tree stirred ?
  What made sleep flutter his wings and part ?
Only the song of a secret bird.

Lie still, I said, for the wind's wing closes,
  And mild leaves muffle the keen sun's dart ;
Lie still, for the wind on the warm sea dozes,
  And the wind is unquieter yet than thou art.
  Doth a thought in thee still as a thorn's wound smart ?
Does the fang still fret thee of hope deferred ?
  What bids the lids of thy sleep dispart ?
Only the song of a secret bird.

The green land's name that a charm encloses,
  It never was writ in the traveller's chart,
And sweet as the fruit on its tree that grows is,
  It never was sold in the merchant's mart.
  The swallows of dreams through its dim fields dart,
And sleep's are the tunes in its tree-tops heard ;
  No hound's note wakens the wild wood hart,
Only the song of a secret bird.

ENVOI.

In the world of dreams I have chosen my part,
  To sleep for a season and hear no word
Of true love's truth or of light love's art,
  Only the song of a secret bird.

From Dreams to Waking.

BY E. LYNN LINTON.

CHAPTER VI.

UNCERTAIN WHICH.

AFTER this little brush of jealousy on the part of Ernest there was, as it were, a lull in the affairs of the Holy Alliance; when it might have seemed as if Venetia's fond idea had really some groundwork of reasonableness in it, and was going to work well for all concerned. The three were for ever together; and for some days, owing to the marvellous ability of Ernest, who could make love to two girls, bosom friends and inseparable companions, yet not allow either to be jealous of the other, and to the loyal trustfulness of Venetia which rendered it impossible for her to suspect what was not clearly displayed before her eyes, the harmony of their relation was as remarkable as it was charming.

The subtle tact of the one, and the innocent acceptance of the other, sufficed during these first days for even Graziella's jealous exclusiveness and passionate desire of public supremacy. Ernest made her understand in a thousand secret ways that she was his light and his life, his queen and his poem, his idol and his beloved : only he could not say so just yet in the market-place, because of certain obstructive reasons why; but it would come—it would come ; and Venetia seemed to acquiesce in this transfer of attention and poetic idolatry from herself to her friend, and even to carry her own love as increase of tribute to the little queen of the day whom they both desired to honour. For, as Graziella argued, she could not be such an absolute idiot as not to see that Ernest paid her— the Cuban—as much devotion as he had ever given to herself; and if she was not jealous, then she must be acquiescent; and if not vexed, nor sad, nor sorry, then pleased or, at best, indifferent. So things went merrily forward ; and all three were satisfied if two of those three were deceived.

The summer was at its height ; with burning days but evenings fresh, cool, and delightful, when the young men and maidens of the Forest turned out from boudoir and smoking-den, garden and drawing-room, for rowing parties on the river, for riding parties through the woods and lanes, for impromptu dances got up at small expense, less trouble, and much pleasure at one or other of the houses in the neighbourhood. It was the merriest time that the place had ever known, and years after would be remembered as the ideal summer—the summer *par excellence* of all the summers that had ever been or ever would be—the summer when Mr. Pierrepoint was at Acorn Bank and that beautiful little Miss Despues was staying with Miss Greville at Oak-tree House, when Colonel Camperdown had come home from India, and when everybody was marrying everybody—at least in public belief. At all events, when Mr. Pierrepoint was marrying Venetia Greville almost as certainly—according to the world which ruled the fate of individuals and nations alike at the Forest—as if he had been already called in church, and was only waiting now for the cake to be baked and the ring to be bought.

But by degrees the neighbourhood began to take umbrage at the postponement of its prophecy; to think things badly managed and itself most shamefully tricked; and to find in Graziella a possible cause of hindrance to what, now that there seemed to be a barrier slowly rising in the air, it declared was the most perfect marriage that could be made, and one that every member of the place had wished, foreseen, and done his or her best to help forward. Soon it began to wonder which of the two girls this omnivorous young man meant to take at last; for the astutest observer would have been puzzled to say which he did really prefer. It wondered, too, how Venetia liked his divided attentions and evident admiration of Miss Despues. But after all that was no affair of theirs, said the neighbours with more anger than philosophy in this repudiation; and if Miss Greville chose to put up with only half a lover and had no dislike to share him with her friend, that was her look out, not theirs. It was to be supposed that she knew what she was about, and had her compensations.

Still, they did not approve of it, and thought that it would be more becoming in the young man if he did away with all this uncertainty, and married and settled once and for all. This kind of irresolution, and now one and now another, till no one could make out which, was not their idea of a love affair at all; and they made no scruple of saying so—when well out of hearing of the principals. Onlookers are so impatient at the slow progress of events! They want all the histories in which they take an interest to be transacted by telegrams; and delay, so far from whetting their curiosity, only sharpens their annoyance.

But Mr. Ernest Pierrepoint evidently did not mean to hurry

himself in his choice. He enjoyed his position thoroughly, and did not care to curtail it. But slowly and almost imperceptibly things began to change, a little—just a very little. Graziella's jealous need for triumph and confession began to be a trifle unappeasable by secret assurances of the uncommitted kind, and Ernest had sometimes hard work to keep her in good humour yet not blow the whole thing prematurely into the air; Venetia began to feel as if a kind of veil made of cobwebs, but all the same a veil, was being slowly woven between her and Ernest; and Colonel Camperdown began to come to Oak-tree House so often, and to join the three inseparables so unfailingly whenever they appeared in public, that the world in its turn began to make guesses as to 'which?' in his favour, just as it had already made the same guess in Ernest's. But the Colonel's outward manner being as impartial to each, before folk, as was Mr. Pierrepoint's, conjecture had a fine time of it, and assurances were as positive as the ignorance on which they were founded was absolute.

Nothing annoyed Ernest more than this intrusion into their circle of a man whom he felt to be in every way his superior, and the only one who had the power to make him uncomfortable. He wanted to be absolute master of his own domain; to hold those two young hearts in his power—waiting on his word—until, if ever, it should please him to make up his mind which he would bless with his final choice; and the frequent presence of a man like the Colonel, handsome in the best manner of masculine beauty, high-spirited, straightforward, honourable, disturbed him more than he used to acknowledge. Charley Mossman he could afford to despise;—as he phrased it in his own mind, 'give him long odds and beat him;'—but Harold was another kind of rival altogether, and of him he was sincerely afraid.

He was the more vexed and perplexed because he could not say anything. Even to Venetia he did not dare now to show jealousy or annoyance; for this would have implied more than he wished her to understand, as things were—his ties with her loosening daily, those with Graziella becoming daily tighter. All the same, he was disgusted and annoyed; which helped not a little in the spinning of that cobweb veil slowly weaving between him and Venetia.

Coming one day to Oak-tree House with a copy of Longfellow in his pocket, he found Harold Camperdown already before him, seated on the sofa beside Graziella, while Venetia was on a low chair fronting them, reading poetry to the two girls from a book in manuscript. Now, reciting in all its forms was one of Ernest's special acquirements. He acted, declaimed, read poetry to perfection; and this art, and singing, were not his least effective vehicles of love-making. Consequently he looked on the Colonel as a poacher, and resented his presence in his preserves, with his unlawful nets and snares in manuscript rhyme, as men who hold preserves naturally do resent the presence of poachers. For the first time since that famous day at the mill, his jealous temper got the better of his discretion, and he showed the anger that he felt. He was offended, cool, abrupt, and generally disagreeable. He spoke with ill-concealed bitterness to Graziella; to Venetia he scarcely spoke at all; and to Colonel Camperdown his manner suggested pistols and seconds, were pistols and seconds things of modern English usage. Graziella, who did not care for Harold Camperdown at all, save as a spur in the side of Ernest, had no desire whatsoever to be implicated in his misdeeds, to the loss of her shifty adorer's delightful homage; and Venetia, loving, tender-hearted Venetia, was by turns distressed that the one should have been annoyed and the other perhaps affronted. But Colonel Camperdown, himself the cause of all this hidden turmoil and secret vexation, was provokingly cool and indifferent. The suggested association of pistols and seconds fell harmless on him; the abrupt and decidedly insolent manner of the offended hero troubled him no more than the angry chirp of a hedge-sparrow or the barking of a toy terrier. His own manner indeed was to the full as annoying as Ernest's, and his airs of manly superiority, put on, it must be said, for the express purpose of offence, made the young fellow fume and rage; and all the more as there was, in effect, a kind of duel which they were fighting out in the presence of the girls—with the Colonel in the better place, and himself at a disadvantage.

'You like poetry, I think, Mr. Pierrepoint?' at last said Harold, the 'Mr.' slightly accentuated.

'As a man of some education, I suppose I do,' answered Ernest with a short laugh.

'This is a volume of unpublished poems, written by a friend of mine,' said the Colonel, flirting the leaves of the book between his fingers.

'Written by a friend of yours?' put in Venetia as a diversion. He had not spoken of their authorship before.

'Yes,' he answered; 'by a man in my regiment—Frank Craven,' raising his eyes suddenly to Ernest's face, and speaking in a rather loud and very distinct voice. 'The brother of that poor sister of his, Amy, who died less than two years ago. I think you knew her, Mr. Pierrepoint?'

'Slightly,' said Ernest with a visible effort.

Colonel Camperdown laughed; a laugh as short, and hard, and unpleasant as Ernest's had been.

'Adverbs are useful parts of speech,' he said satirically; 'but sometimes more useful than exact.'

He looked at Venetia while he spoke, and met her eyes raised with grave rebuke to his. She thought him cruel and unjust, and longed to say aloud what she thought—to throw the shield of her loving faith round the man whose peace he was so rudely assailing—to tell him to his face that he was mistaken, had been deceived, and that Ernest Pierrepoint, full of noble thoughts and elevated sentiments, loving art and poetry and nature and humanity, had never committed a baseness—was as incapable indeed of committing one as was Harold Camperdown himself. And for all his enmity to the man whom she loved, Venetia gave him credit for honesty and rectitude.

Ernest's eyes, roving and unquiet, caught the look that passed between Colonel Camperdown and Venetia—the man who tormented and the woman who adored him. Not having the key, he read the riddle wrong. It seemed to him more a mutual understanding than assertion determined to justify itself on the one side, and disbelief answering back with deprecation on the other. And the result of this false reading on him, was to make him resolve to be more lover-like to Venetia than he had been of late, determined as he was to hold her against all comers until he himself should decide on giving her her liberty—that liberty which she would then feel to be desolation and desertion.

'Who was Amy Craven?' asked Graziella innocently, and of no one in particular, but in a sufficiently loud voice to arrest Ernest's attention, for all that he had turned to Venetia and had begun by a discourse with her on the beauty of trust and the shameful sin of doubt in those who loved and were beloved—trust to the death—trust in spite of all appearances.

'Ask Mr. Pierrepoint,' said Colonel Camperdown in a loud voice; adding, with a sudden flash, 'remembering only that her brother is an intimate friend of mine, and that it may be my duty to report what is said.'

'I have no wish to say anything,' said Ernest, holding his head high. 'There are times—and reasons—when a man feels himself bound to be silent on all relating to a woman.'

'I agree with you,' the Colonel answered. 'As, for instance, when the man has behaved like a scoundrel.'

'Exactly,' said Ernest, with admirable indifference; 'when he has, as you say, behaved like a scoundrel. Or' (playing with his

watch-guard) ' when the family has angled for a *bon parti,* and he
has seen through their schemes, and drawn off in time.'

' And the girl comes off the worst in either case,' said Graziella
with sweet compassion. ' Like this poor Amy Craven?' turning
to Colonel Camperdown.

' Yes ; like this poor Amy Craven : killed by a modern Adonis,'
he answered bitterly, fixing Ernest with his eyes.

' " Adonis " might say sacrificed through the shameless haste
of her friends,' retorted Ernest ; ' friends who wished to press
and hurry, and were not content to wait until things had cleared
themselves, and liking had ripened into love—friends who showed
their mercenary designs too clearly, and so spoilt their own market
by their greed.'

' You are prepared to defend that view of the case to Captain
Craven when he comes home this autumn ?' Harold asked with
an unmistakable sneer.

' To a dozen Captain Cravens,' returned Ernest. ' You may
write and tell him so.'

Then lowering his voice, he went on with his conversation with
Venetia ; and Graziella, in revenge, flirted with the Colonel to the
bounds of indiscretion for the rest of their joint stay.

What had not been done with Venetia had been done surely
enough with Graziella—that is, she understood how things had
been, and the truth of Mr. Pierrepoint's relations with poor Amy.
The Creole read the whole story as clearly as if it had been transacted in her sight. Reading it, she determined that this kind of
thing should never happen to her; and that the present indecision
must be brought to an end. It should be one or other of the two
now in the balance; and that soon and without subterfuge. She would
not be made now first and now second ; to-day queen, to-morrow
subordinate, at the will and whim of any man. Mr. Pierrepoint
must make up his mind which it was to be ; and now, at once.
This story of the girl, ' killed by Adonis,' as Colonel Camperdown had said so emphatically, proved to her more than ever the
kind of man Ernest was ; and though she was in no sense revolted
by the knowledge, yet she was as it were put on her mettle by
the fact that no one had hitherto been able to secure him. That he
had jilted others, and was playing fast and loose with Venetia as
well as with herself, made her merely resolute to prove herself
stronger than all the rest ; and that where he had done as he liked
with others, he should be mastered and enchained by her. Wherefore she took her resolution and decided on her measures ; and
gave Mr. Ernest Pierrepoint clearly to understand, during the
latter part of his visit, that she was intensely disgusted with him

—horribly indignant—and that he would win no more smiles or
sweet looks from her until—what?

This kind of dumb warfare lasted for some days, and with other
things made Ernest's life just now one of more pain than pleasure.
The Creole's coldness distracted him as much as her former delicate
allurements had charmed; and when Colonel Camperdown came
about her and Venetia, seeming to travesty his own indecision and
double attraction, he was nearly beside himself with jealousy—
now on account of the one whom he loved, now on account of the
one who loved him. Yet for all this, he could not make up his
mind to take the final and irrevocable plunge. Graziella secured,
Venetia was lost; and to a vain man, as he was, this was a fact
by no means to be desired. Still, something must be done. For
these last three days Graziella had scarcely spoken to him, but had
seemed to devote herself to Harold Camperdown with maddening
amiability; and Charley Mossman, whose hopes had suddenly re-
vived with respect to Venetia, was like a faithful dog with something to guard, never far from her side.

Of a surety something must be done, thought Ernest, part
rueful, part savage; but what? One must be chosen; but which?
Venetia had money, position, and staying-power, but Graziella was
most to his taste. Venetia had a love that would last for his life;
Graziella a passion that, if it lasted only for a month, would make
that month better than fifty years of any other joy.

So he sat and smoked and pondered; and while he pondered,
big, good-natured Charley Mossman came in with something of
tremendous importance on that good mind of his, and which he
wanted to get off it as soon as possible.

There was to be a small dance at Oak-tree House to-morrow
evening; one of those country-house impromptu evenings which
are the pleasantest things in the world, and more delighted in by
young people than more formal gatherings. Poor old Charley,
who had no more real knowledge of how to win a woman's love
than he had of the signs which tell when it is won and when it is
hopeless, had determined to have it out, first with Ernest and then
with Venetia. Double-dealing in such matters was by no means
in his line, and he wanted to get a clear view of how things stood,
and what was his true horizon.

'Look here, old fellow!' he said a little abruptly, when he
had filled his favourite pipe and settled himself to serious business,
both of talk and smoke. 'Look here! I have not interfered with
you while I thought you loved her and she you; but lately I've
lost the track somehow, and I think that you have too. Neither I
nor any one else can make out which of the two you are after, if,

indeed, you are after either; and it's hard lines on those of us who love one or other, and feel ourselves cut out—shut out, I ought rather to say—by a kind of dog-in-the-manger affair which won't take for itself, and won't let others take for themselves. So now I give you fair warning!'

Ernest laughed lightly.

'Well, Charley, old man, I never did think you an orator,' he said with perfect pleasantness; 'but I did think you could do something better than this bit of tangle, which it would take Œdipus himself to unravel. In plain English, and little of it, what do you mean?'

'Miss Greville—' said Charley, with a pleasantness not quite so perfect as his friend's.

'Yes?—and after?'

'I love her, and I will ask her to be my wife.'

'Good! But why say this to me? I am not Miss Greville's father, nor guardian.'

Charley looked at him, with his clear honest blue eyes, a little sadly.

'That's hardly straight, Ernest,' he said. 'You know as well as I do that you have been philandering round her ever since you came; and you know too as well as I do, that when I thought you were in earnest and that she was too, I held off. But now, when you seem to be as much taken up with the other—Miss Despues, I mean—a fellow feels free to cut in if he can.'

'All right!' said Ernest cheerfully, blowing his cigar-smoke into concentric rings. 'Win her if you can! The best to win always.'

'And it is all the same to you?' asked Charley.

'Who makes love to Miss Greville?—all the same,' said Ernest with a short laugh; 'you or any other—win her if you can!'

'Does that mean that no one can, Ernest? Are you so safe as that?' asked Charley.

'It means just what interpretation you choose to put on it,' was the reply. 'It means, either that I am safe and so defy you all; or, that I have no pretensions in that quarter, and so leave the ground free to you all. It means anything or nothing, just as you please; the sequel alone shall enlighten you!' laughing again with a certain metallic hardness in the ring of his voice that did not sound much like pleasure and light-heartedness.

'I should have thought you would have treated me fairer than this,' said Charley, turning away his head.

He did not like to think ill of Pylades, but this kind of thing was not quite his idea of manly fairness. He was conscious in his own heart of having been very fair indeed towards Ernest, absurdly so, perhaps; and it hurt him to be met with this want of candour in return. Also it seemed somehow an ill-turn done to Venetia, and that was worse than want of fairness to himself.

Nothing more however could be got out of Ernest; and, after talking with great volubility on a dozen and one subjects that had not the slightest interest for either of them, the young squire took his leave, and Ernest went on with his cigar and his meditations, perfectly satisfied that Charley Mossman had not the ghost of a chance with Venetia Greville so long as he chose to keep her to himself. He wished that he could have been as sure about Graziella and the Colonel; but the Creole's nature was different altogether from her friend's, and pique might lead her to do what neither jealousy nor heartbreak could win from the other.

Whatsoever the end might be he knew as well as some others that it was drawing near that end; and that things would not go on much longer as they were now. To-morrow! Would to-morrow be the fatal Ides of March? Something was in the air that seemed to foretell a crisis, just as something in the air foretells a storm; and more than one looked to the Oak-tree House dance as to the Rubicon which must be passed now or never. Charley Mossman had made up his mind that he would ask Venetia once for all if she thought that in the far distant future, and after infinite pains and love on his part, she would learn to look upon him with affection—the poor fellow's demands were fearfully modest !—Graziella had made up hers that Mr. Pierrepoint should make up his; and Venetia, whose spirits had risen to the highest point of happiness during these last few days, when the cobweb veil seemed to have got suddenly cleared away and Ernest, repelled by Graziella, had been her own once more, thought that surely now her doubts and perplexities would be at an end, and that Ernest would tell her in unmistakable terms what he had already told her in vaguer if more delicious ways, that he loved her—loved her once and for ever—and had chosen her before the world as his wife.

CHAPTER VII.

THE DIE CAST.

THE two girls had never looked more beautiful, each in her own way, than they did to-night at the Oak-tree House 'little dance.' Perhaps Venetia carried off the palm in the opinion of most, hers being that kind of beauty which speaks as much to the heart as to the eye, while Graziella was of the sort which touches the senses and warms the imagination more than it stirs the finer emotions

It was so much loveliness of the flesh, exquisite enough if you will; but that thing which goes by the name of Soul was somehow left out of the catalogue.

Still, people are not too severe on that thing which goes by the name of Soul—or rather on the want of it—when the subject is a lovely little girl with such a face and figure as Graziella's; and after all, extreme youth supplies something that makes a very good imitation of spirituality, and that disposes men to be charitable. Nevertheless, in spite of the Creole's surpassing loveliness, it was evidently Venetia's hour of triumph; for everyone seemed fascinated to-night by the young heiress and mistress of the house—she who, until Graziella's coming, had been without a rival near her throne.

Charley Mossman, with his clumsy resolution to try a fall with fortune before he had made sure of his footing—to reap his harvest before he had even sown the grain—hung about her like the faithful dog which was his type; all the old aspirants who had presented their petitions and been dismissed seemed to think that renewed signatures might bring reversed readings, and that they had still the traditional hope which clings to life; and Colonel Camperdown, as well as the rest, formed part of her body-guard, and looked as if he too had ideas like the rest. All of which piqued Ernest Pierrepoint still more into the semblance of his first devotion, and made him feel that none of them should take from him the prize that he had won; and that he would show them all how easily he could distance the best among them, when he chose to exert his power.

'What have you done to yourself to-night?' he said in an undertone to Venetia, as he carried her off on his arm. 'I have never seen you look so lovely—so divinely fair as you do. What is it?'

Venetia raised her eyes with a happy smile that soon passed into a still happier bashfulness.

'I have done nothing to myself,' she said prettily; but her voice and face added to her words: 'It is only my love for you, and yours for me, that has glorified me.'

'I wish it had been something that you knew how and why,' said Ernest, still speaking below his breath; 'then I might make sure of having you always as you are to-night.'

'I feel well—and happy; that is all,' faltered Venetia shyly.

He pressed her to him lightly.

'You are happy because you are an angel,' he said.

'No,' said Venetia; 'because my friends are good to me.'

'Am I one of them?' he whispered.

'Yes,' she said, also in a whisper.

' And always shall be ? '

' If you wish it—always,' she said.

' Would anyone relinquish you who had once held you?' returned Ernest. ' Ask yourself, is there a friend you have who would care to let you go, when once you had laid your dear hand in his, and given him the privilege of—caring for you ? '

' I hope some would not,' she faltered.

' None,' was his reply, again lightly pressing her to his breast ; and then the waltz began, and Venetia in her fairest moment of happiness and love felt how good a thing it was to live.

Now she felt sure that she was beloved, and that she would soon be engaged in the face of the world. Ernest was too noble to trifle with a woman's honest affection which he had taken pains to win. And he knew that her affection was honest, and given only because distinctly, if covertly, sought. Yes, it was all right now, poor Venetia thought, as, the dance ended, she looked round the room with her big blue happy eyes, and saw Ernest bending down to Graziella, speaking to her as if with entreaty, while Colonel Camperdown stood at a little distance pulling his moustache, and looking as if waiting his turn to offer adulation.

Meanwhile Charley Mossman came tumultuously to where Venetia was standing, and carried her off on his arm, as Ernest had done less than half an hour ago ; and before the dance was over had asked her to be his wife with no more idea of tact or management than if he had been asking her to give him a rose or to sell him a pony.

When Venetia heard him plead, she shrank back with the same feeling of desecration that she would have had if she had been married. It was something so infinitely shocking to her that Ernest's friend should ask for the love of Ernest's—engaged wife. Had Colonel Camperdown, for instance, or anyone else not so intimately bound up with Mr. Pierrepoint, come to her knees and begged for her grace, she would have been more pitiful, less revolted ; but in the injustice of her own purity—her own certainty, she was hard on Charley, and answered him with so much passion of negation that he saw something more than mere refusal stirred her.

' Tell me only one thing, Miss Greville,' he said pitifully, looking at her with his honest face full of pain : ' are you engaged to Ernest ? '

' Yes—or almost,' said Venetia severely ; and then relenting, she added : ' I thought you knew.'

' No, I did not,' he answered.

' No ? Then I am sorry I spoke so harshly,' she said, tenderly apologetic.

Hardness was so foreign to her, it pained her so much to be forced by sterner virtue into its use, that it was a relief to her heart to apologise. What she had done by conscience she shrank from by nature; and she was so glad that now nature and conscience might be once more in accord!

'I am glad if you are happy,' said the poor fellow ruefully. 'I am not one of those, Miss Greville, that envy another man because he has been more fortunate than myself. Ernest is a fine old fellow, and will make you happy; but I wish he had been franker with me.'

'Thank you,' said Venetia with a glowing face, ignoring the last part of his remark. 'And you will forget this little mistake, and be, as you have always been—our best friend—our brother?'

'Yes,' said Charley, gallantly suppressing himself.

He pressed her hand in a frank, sisterly way.

'Thank you,' she said again prettily. 'And I too will forget this evening, and we will both go on as if it had never been.'

'You are an angel,' said the young man, gulping down something in his throat that was half choking him; and then they went on with the dance as if nothing had happened, and the fortunes of a life had not been cast and decided on the die of the moment.

Seated in a corner Graziella watched the circumstances of the evening, and made her comments, and took her measures accordingly. She saw, with eyes that burned like fire, the homage of which her friend was the centre; and she said to herself that she would have her revenge somehow, and prove where the larger power of attraction lay. She saw Charley Mossman's fair English face beam and brighten with excitement as he edged his broad shoulder through the little throng, and wrote his name on Venetia's card for the first dance disengaged; she saw Harold Camperdown, cool, calm, but with an odd look of waiting in his face, write his three times over; and then Ernest, a little flushed, and with that air which seemed to join the entreaty of a slave with the command of a master, broke through them all, and taking Venetia's hand, led her away as his by right. And seeing all this she took her decision, and determined on what she would and would not do. What she would do was to make Colonel Camperdown in love with her if she chose; what she would not do was to accord the faintest grace to Ernest Pierrepoint, until he had decided which. If Venetia was blind to the fact that he was playing fast and loose with them, she was not; nor was she inclined to let the game go on. One or the other—whichever he chose; but it should be one or the other, else no more smiles, no more grace from her.

Graziella was not the girl, young as she was, to go back on her intentions. Once made, she held to them pretty firmly; and when Ernest came to her, after he had made things as he considered straight with Venetia, and begged her for the honour of a dance, he was met by a refusal—and a refusal that meant everything.

'I am engaged,' said Graziella, dropping her eyes; not with that tender bashfulness which cannot raise them to the beloved face—that fond and failing look which is so delightful to the man who loves—but coldly, scornfully, as if he were beneath her regard and she too much pre-occupied or too much disgusted to care to hold any terms with him.

'Which, then, may I have?' asked Ernest in his sweetest tones.

'None; I am engaged for all,' said Graziella, opening and shutting her fan while looking at Colonel Camperdown, standing a little apart, pulling his moustache, watching and waiting.

'For all?' incredulously.

'Yes, for all,' said the Creole, raising her heavy lids and looking at him for one single instant with a flash of superb scorn and pride.

'I am unfortunate,' said Mr. Pierrepoint with as much coldness as her own.

She smiled, but did not speak. It was a disagreeable smile, and meant to convey the assurance that if Ernest felt himself unfortunate, she did not hold herself to be pitied. If it was a misfortune to him that she could not dance with him, it was none to her. His substitutes were quite as much to her liking, and perhaps more so.

All of which Ernest understood as clearly as if her thoughts had been put into words instead of looks. He was too well versed in that kind of language not to be able to read it accurately; and Graziella knew as well as he what he thought and what he divined. There was no chance of propitiation at this moment; and, besides, a waltz was beginning—the waltz which poor Charley took as the springboard for his wild leap in the dark—when Colonel Camperdown came up to Graziella, and bore her off before the eyes of Ernest Pierrepoint, as it seemed to him, with insolent triumph and security.

All through the evening this dumb quarrel between Graziella and Ernest raged with unabated bitterness. She would not speak to him nor dance with him; while she kept Harold Camperdown chained to her side, till the dowagers looked from one to the other, and wagged their heads in wrath at the sight of such early and pronounced depravity. After the little comedy had continued for nearly the whole evening—Ernest paying the most marked attention to Venetia, Colonel Camperdown to Graziella—Ernest suddenly gave way. What Charley Mossman's expressed intentions had aroused on the one side, so did the Colonel's apparent designs on the other; and after a moment's hesitation, the final step was taken. Ernest went into the conservatory; and there, tearing a leaf out of his pocket-book, wrote a few lines in pencil rapidly.

He looked flurried and disturbed enough while he wrote; but when he came back to the room he had the air of a man who has once more taken possession of events.

A quadrille was forming. It was one of the dances for which he had engaged Venetia. He went up to her, lover-like, smiling; and she received him with a face as eloquent of happiness as of love. She was blessed, supremely blessed, to-night. All the clouds were swept away, and she had only sunshine and joy, as of old. He offered his arm, and they took their places, and found themselves *vis-à-vis* with Graziella and Harold.

A sudden light came into Ernest's face, and he looked strangely resolute, yet not ungentle. At the first meeting of their hands in the chain, Graziella let only the tips of her fingers pass lightly over his sleeve; but the next time he took her hand wholly in his —and when he left it, he had slipped into it a folded bit of paper. Then he went back to Venetia, and pressed her hand tenderly, and looked into her happy eyes lovingly. He was very glad that he had done this thing to Graziella; so glad, that it made him love Venetia all the more.

Then the evening came to an end, and the guests dispersed, after having made up a water party for to-morrow, in the moonlight.

When she had got rid of Venetia, who seemed, to her impatience, as if she would never go to-night, Graziella drew the crumpled bit of paper from her bosom where she had hidden it, and read, written in an agitated hand, these words:

' My darling, why do you frown on me? Light of my life, do you not know that I cannot live without your smiles? Take pity on the poor wretch who is at your feet—your slave and your over; and do not trample on the heart that is in your power.'

Graziella smiled.

' Yes, very pretty,' she said to herself. ' But all this is only what he has said to Venetia, and perhaps to a dozen others, twenty times over. If he wants me to love him, he must say so in plain words, and engage himself to me. I will not be caught by any man in the world who holds himself free and me only captive— like that silly Venetia; nor allow a man who does not commit himself to say anything to keep off others who might make one an offer—like Colonel Camperdown, for instance. I will make Mr. Ernest choose between us—Venetia and me—and then I will think of what to say to him. Dear, handsome, good-for-nothing fellow, it will be " Yes " I know—for a little while ! '

She said this just as Venetia laid her head on her pillow, a happy smile making her fair face like an angel's in its pure pleasure and loving content ; saying, in her turn :

' Ah, he does love me, I am sure of it ! There is some reason why he has not said so yet, but he will now. I am certain that he loves me, and that he will ask me to be his wife before long. He has made me feel too surely that I am loved not to let others know it too. He is too good and honourable to deceive, and that story of Amy Craven is not true. Colonel Camperdown is cruel. Ernest never deceived any woman ! '

The next evening was ideal ; warm, fresh and fragrant. The sun was within an hour of setting, when they all met at the river-side ; and when set, then the ruddy harvest moon would light up the old earth, almost like another sun. They were to row down the river as far as St. Herbert's Isle, a little island with the Hermi-tage, a ruined stone building whereof tradition made a holy retreat for some old-time saint, and modern manners an eating-place for parties of pleasure—a white-washed palimpsest for multitu-dinous writers of doggrel verse and undesignated initials, a resort for lovers—and a reason why for such an expedition as this.

The present party was composed of the usual members—the triad ; Charley Mossman, who had determined not to be down-hearted because he had been unsuccessful, and to keep his own counsel about that little talk during the waltz last evening ; Colonel Camperdown and his half sister Emily, with a married sister of his own and her husband—a Mr. and Mrs. Judge—to avert the wrath and secure the countenance of Mrs. Grundy. They had a long, narrow, four-oared river boat, and each gentleman took an oar, which prevented ' spooning,' and did not allow of even much eye-flirtation, seeing that the looks meant for one might be misinterpreted by another and would certainly be seen by all. No ; there was no special flirting during the row. The girls sang glees and part songs ; and the men, resting on their oars, put in bass or tenor as nature had endowed them. Graziella was half lying on a kind of divan made of the softest cushions and three parts of the shawls, looking divinely lovely, Ernest thought, as every now and then she stole a conscious languid look at his handsome face through the fringe of her dark lashes—a look that seemed to promise as well as to prepare him for the better things to come. Emily Backhouse trailed her fingers through the water and caught the water-lilies as they floated by ; Mrs. Judge, a cheery, bright-eyed little woman with a couple of babies and not an ounce of sentiment, made conversation for a dozen; and Venetia at the stern—fair, sweet, placid, and blessed—steered with rare technical skill.

So they went merrily down the stream, to all appearance the happiest and most careless-hearted boatload to be found in all England. At last they came to St. Herbert's Isle, and shot the boat alongside the broken little pier that served as a landing-place. The men made it fast to the posts, and the girls stepped ashore, just as the moon rose above the horizon, and began to carve the world beneath in silver and ebony.

At first they were all in a loosely amalgamated body together. Those who wished to choose their companions were afraid to be precipitate, and waited for the pairing to appear a matter of accident rather than of design; and those who had no such desire kept with the rest and unintentionally prevented disintegration. But presently, partly because the path grew narrow, and partly because the natural impatience of man made uncertainty and a longer delay unpleasant, the loosely amalgamated body separated into pairs; and Ernest found himself by the side of Graziella, while Harold Camperdown took military possession of Venetia.

Unselfish and unsuspicious though she was, Venetia could not help feeling one acute pang of disappointment as her lover, or rather the man whom she loved, passed away into the shallow of the woods, side by side with her friend. 'The influences of soul and sense' had thrilled her to-night as they long ago had thrilled guileless Géneviève; and her imagination had pictured all sorts of beautiful eventualities for herself. But Ernest, engaged in an animated conversation which apparently engrossed him, wandered into a by-path with Graziella; and the last words that Venetia heard were, 'art—poetry—music—rapture.'

Then she felt the blood leave her face, and a sickness such as she had never known before gather round her heart. Life, the solid earth, her friends, her love, all seemed to fail her; but she shook herself clear of her weakness, and turned to speak to her companion. She met his eyes fixed on her with a look full of acute tenderness and compassion, so that involuntarily her own filled up with tears. It seemed to her as if he had spoken, and said, 'Poor child!' Nothing however was said; and Venetia, loyally anxious that Ernest should not be condemned, put pressure on herself, and talked with a forced calmness, a false brightness that imposed only on herself. For him it was always in his heart, 'Poor child—poor child—she feels that she is deceived and knows that she has to suffer!'

Venetia and Harold Camperdown had taken a way that led round the island as a belt, not one of the radii converging on the

Hermitage. It was the same path as that taken by Ernest and Graziella, they having turned to the right—these others to the left. And thus it was that after some time they came to a cleared space, where, seated on a fallen tree, they saw in the bright moonlight Ernest Pierrepoint and Graziella Despues—he with his arm round her waist, she with her head resting on his shoulder—while they heard him say :

'My darling! my life! I love you! Sweetest Graziella, I have never loved before now!'

'And I love you,' said Graziella's flute-like voice exquisitely subdued.

Then their faces met; and Graziella received her first kiss of love from the man on whose loyalty her dearest friend had embarked the happiness of her youth.

'My darling, will you be my wife?' said Ernest with passion.

'Yes—Husband,' answered Graziella.

Venetia turned to Colonel Camperdown with a wild, scared look. She held out her hands as if asking for help; then with a little cry fell forward, and was caught by Harold just in time to save her.

'Mr. Pierrepoint!' he said in a loud, harsh voice; 'go to the Hermitage for my sister, Mrs. Judge. Miss Greville has fainted.'

(*To be continued.*)

This Day Last Year.

This day last year—was not the same thrush singing?
  We stayed our talk, and hushed our breath to hear ;
The bird's note quivered through our silent rapture,
  And broke upon our hearts—this day last year !

Silent we watched the self-same shadows deepen
  'Neath the young leaves that caught the straying light
Each bud, each blossom brought its tithe of gladness,
  Even the happy tears that blurred my sight !

Mutely we breathed the language of hands clasping ;
  No need for murmured vows or low replies ;
Each sun-flecked leaf, each sudden shadow passing,
  Cast some vague memory to our dreaming eyes.

To-day, I crave no thought of vanished sweetness,
  I do not ask for my lost love again ;
Only that some one throb of wakened yearning
  May thrill the numbness of my heart to pain.

I strain my ear. The song has lost its secret.
  My heart stirs not ; my weary eyes are dry.
I pray for tears, where once I dreamt but gladness :
  Has life—has death itself—a sadder cry !

L. B.

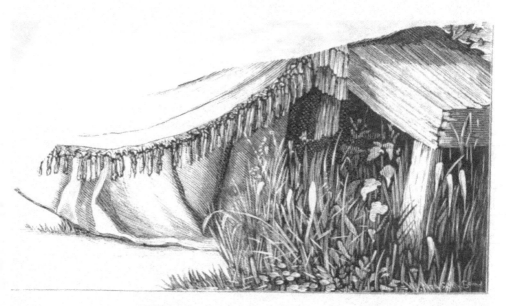

THIS DAY LAST YEAR

Only ..
  May thrill ..

I strain my ear. The song ha.
  My heart stirs not ; my weary eye.
I pray for tears, where once I dreamt bu.
  Has life—has death itself—a sadder cry !

THIS DAY LAST YEAR

The New Republic;

OR, CULTURE, FAITH, AND PHILOSOPHY IN AN ENGLISH COUNTRY HOUSE.

BOOK III.—CHAPTER I.

MR. ROSE, who had been lying down hitherto almost at full length on the grass, now raised himself with a dreamy slowness into a more upright posture, and plucked half-absently, as he did so, a flower of his own name that grew just behind him. For a moment he surveyed the whole party with a look of soft compassion; for a moment he dropped his eyelids, gazed on his flower tenderly, and buried his large white nostrils in the crimson petals. Then he looked slowly up again, and at length began to speak.

'London often drives me to despair,' he said somewhat abruptly, yet in a tone of plaintive melody, 'when I walk about it, and see how hideous its whole external aspect is, and what a dissonant population it is infested by. Consider for a moment what a beautiful thing city life might be, what a beautiful thing in other times it has been. Consider how the human eye delights in form and colour, and the ear in tempered and harmonious sounds; and then think for a moment of a London street! Think of the shapeless houses, the forest of ghastly chimney-pots, of the hell of distracting noises made by the carts, the cabs, the carriages —think of the bustling, commonplace, careworn crowds that jostle you—think of the frightful flaring placards that insult the eye!' Mr. Rose gave a soft groan. 'Who,' he went on, sighing and taking breath, 'can so much as look at an omnibus without a poignant pang? What would a Greek, what would an Athenian, have thought of a four-wheeled cab? On the Appian Way even——'

'I often ride in an omnibus,' said Lord Allen to Miss Merton.

'It is true,' said Mr. Rose, only overhearing the tone in which these words were said, 'that one may ever and again catch some touch of sunlight that will for a moment make the meanest object beautiful with its furtive alchemy. But that is Nature's work, not man's; and we must never confound the accidental beauty that Nature will bestow on man's work even at its worst, with the

rational and designed beauty of man's work at its best. And it is
this rational human beauty that I say our modern city life is so
completely wanting in. Indeed, it almost seems as if the air of
London sometimes took away from one the power of imagining
even that such beauty is attainable. The whole outer aspect of
the place seems to speak of a generation utterly gone wrong—altogether ignorant or careless of what is really precious in life.
Indeed, as I wander along our streets, pushing my way among the
throngs of faces—faces puckered with misdirected thought, or
expressionless with none—barbarous faces set towards Parliament, or Church, or scientific lecture-rooms, or government
offices, or counting-houses—I say, as I push my way amongst all
the sights and sounds of our streets, only one thing ever catches
my eye, that breaks in upon my mood, and warns me I need not
despair.'

'And what is that?' asked Allen, with some curiosity.

'The shops,' Mr. Rose answered, 'of certain of our upholsterers
and dealers in works of art. Their windows, as I look into them, act
like a sudden charm on me—like a splash of cold water dashed on
my forehead when I am fainting. For I seem there to have got a
glimpse suddenly of the heart of things ; and as my eyes rest on
the perfect pattern (many of which are really quite delicious;
indeed, when I go to ugly houses, I often take a scrap of some
artistic crétonne with me in my pocket as a kind of æsthetic smelling salts), I say, when I look in at their windows, and my eyes rest
on the perfect pattern of some new fabric for a chair, or for a win-
dow-curtain, or on some new design for a wall-paper, or on some old
china vase, I become at once myself again, and can turn once more
with a better heart to the hateful streets, and to the loud noises of
our own time ; for I then remember how many there are amongst
us who have deliberately turned their backs on all these things,
and have thrown their whole souls and sympathies into the happier
art-ages of the past. They have gone back,' said Mr. Rose, raising
his voice a little, 'to Athens and to Italy, to the Italy of Leo and
to the Athens of Pericles. To such men the clamour, the interests,
the struggles of our own times, become as meaningless as they
really are. To them the boyhood of Bathyllus is of more moment
than the manhood of Napoleon. Borgia is a more familiar name
than Bismarck. I know, indeed—and I cannot overpraise them—
several distinguished artists who, resolving to make their whole
lives consistently perfect, will, on principle, never admit a newspaper into their houses that is of later date than the times of
Addison ; and I have good trust that the number of such men is
on the increase—men I mean,' said Mr. Rose, raising his eyes to

the sky, 'who with a steady and set purpose follow art for the sake of art, beauty for the sake of beauty, love for the sake of love, life for the sake of life.'

'What, Mr. Rose!' exclaimed Lady Ambrose, 'do you mean to say that the number of people is on the increase who won't read the newspapers?'

'Why, the men must be absolute idiots!' said Lady Grace, shaking her gray curls, and putting on her spectacles to look at Mr. Rose.

Mr. Rose had by this time laid himself flat on his back, and was gazing upwards at the flickering foliage overhead.

'Yes,' he murmured, as though he were talking in his sleep; 'the spirit that rejects newspapers is, I believe, on the increase.'

There was a pause. In a moment he again roused himself, and proceeded in a way that made his audience think he had gone to sleep in good earnest.

'My hopes of the present generation,' he said, 'are also continually buoyed up by seeing what enormous sums are now given for really good objects.'

'That,' said Lady Grace, with some tartness, 'is true enough, thank God!'

'But I can't see,' said Lady Ambrose, whose name often figured in the *Times*, in the subscription-lists of advertised charities—'I can't see, Mr. Rose,' she said, speaking loud as if to awake him, 'any reason in that why we should not read the newspapers.'

'The other day, for instance,' Mr. Rose went on meditatively, not having listened to a word of either of these remarks, not, indeed, having realised that they were addressed to him—'the other day, for instance,' he said, 'I heard of eight Chelsea shepherdesses, picked up by a dealer, I really forget where—in some common cottage, if I recollect aright, covered with dirt, giving no pleasure to anyone—and these were all sold in a single day, and not one of them fetched less than two hundred and twenty pounds.'

'*I* can't help thinking they must have come from Cremorne,' said Mrs. Sinclair softly.

'But why,' said Mr. Rose, 'speak of particular instances? I just mentioned this because it happens to have been in my mind a good deal to-day. But we must all of us have friends whose houses are full of priceless treasures such as these—the whole atmosphere of whose rooms really seems impregnated with art.'

'To be sure,' exclaimed Lady Ambrose, feeling that she had at last got upon solid ground. 'By the way, Mr. Rose,' she said, with her most gracious of smiles, 'I suppose you have hardly seen

Lady Julia Hayman's new house in Belgrave Square? I'm sure that would delight you. I should like to take you there some day, and show it to you.'

'I have seen it,' said Mr. Rose, with languid condescension. ' It was very pretty, I thought—some of it really quite nice.'

'May I ask,' interrupted Mr. Saunders severely, 'what connection all this has with an ideal of an advanced state?'

'Listen,' said Mr. Rose, waving his hand gently. ' I have been just noting certain signs about us that an æsthetic philosophy of life, a pure *cultus* of the Beautiful, is again struggling to revive itself in the world—is even now trying to put its buds out in the middle of this present " winter of our discontent." Now, what you ask me to do is to shape some vision for us of what this higher æstheticism might do under happier circumstances, in the way of bettering the outer aspects of life ; and I think it very wise to begin with this ; for if we at once get free of the present scenery of existence, our imagination will be much less hampered. In my judgment, then, the first thing to be done—we confine ourselves, I suppose, to our own country—would be to remove London to some kindlier site, where it might be born anew, and become a fitter nursing-place for the society we desire to people it with.'

' Ah me ! ' sighed Mr. Luke, ' *cœlum non animum mutant.*'

'Pardon me,' said Mr. Rose, ' few paradoxes—and most paradoxes are false—are, I think, so false as that. There are really few single things that so distinctly give a tone to a man's existence as the colour of the skies he lives under. Thus much, at least, of sea-like our minds have. Come, then, with me to the south-west of England, and to the sea-coast, where the waves are blue, and where "the air is calm and fine;" and there, as the imagination is a quick workman, I can show you our metropolis already transplanted and rebuilt. Yes,' said Mr. Rose, closing his eyes and speaking in an Æolian whisper, ' I can fancy that I see it this moment, as it were from a distance, with its palaces, its museums, its churches, its convents, its gardens, its picture-galleries—a cluster of domed and pillared marble, sparkling on a gray headland. It is Rome, it is Athens, it is Florence, united and reanimated in these latter and distant days. Yes, there, under the stainless azure, the aloe-tree of beauty is again blossoming—again—I see it. For our architecture——'

' Yes,' said Mr. Luke, ' our architecture—let us hear about that.'

' Our architecture,' said Mr. Rose, ' will be of no style in particular. We shall have no style.'

' Good gracious ! ' exclaimed Mr. Leslie.

'No,' continued Mr. Rose, unmoved; 'we shall have no style in particular. Our style will be a *renaissance* of all styles. The architects of our state will not invent. They will do what is far higher. They will select—they will appropriate. They will go into the gardens of past ages, like bees,

Grata carpentes thyma per laborem,

and will collect there whatever of sweet or precious our own age can assimilate. It will matter nothing to them whether it be pagan or Catholic, classical or mediæval. They will be quite without prejudice or bigotry. To the eye of true taste, an Aquinas in his cell before a crucifix, or a Narcissus gazing at himself in a still fountain, are—in their own ways, you know—equally beautiful.'

'Well, really,' said Miss Merton, 'I can *not* fancy St. Thomas being a very taking object to people who don't believe in him either as a saint or a philosopher. I always think that, except from a Christian point of view, a saint can be hardly better described than by Newman's lines, as—

A bundle of bones, whose breath
Infects the world before his death.'

'I remember the lines well,' said Mr. Rose, 'and the writer you mention puts them in the mouth of a yelping devil. But devils, as far as I know, are not generally—except, perhaps, Milton's—conspicuous for taste : indeed, if we may trust Goethe, the very touch of a flower is torture to them.'

'Dante's biggest devil,' cried Mr. Saunders, to everyone's amazement, 'chewed Judas Iscariot like a quid of tobacco, to all eternity. He, at any rate, knew what he liked.'

Mr. Rose started, and visited Mr. Saunders with a rapid frown. He then proceeded, turning again to Miss Merton as if nothing had happened.

'Let me rather,' he said, 'read a nice sonnet to you, which I had sent to me this morning, and which was in my mind just now. These lines'—Mr. Rose here produced a paper from his pocket—'were written by a boy of eighteen—a youth of extraordinary promise, I think, whose education I may myself claim, I believe, to have had some share in directing.

Three visions in the watches of one night
Made sweet my sleep—almost too sweet to tell.
One was Narcissus by a wood-side well,
And on the moss his limbs and feet were white ;
And one, Queen Venus, blown for my delight
Across the blue sea in a rosy shell ;
And one, a lean Aquinas in his cell,

Kneeling, his pen in hand, with aching sight
Strained towards a carven Christ ; and of these three
I knew not which was fairest. First I turned
Towards that soft boy, who laughed and fled from me :
Towards Venus then ; and she smiled once, and she
Fled also. Then with teeming heart I yearned,
O Angel of the Schools, towards Christ with thee !

Yes,' murmured Mr. Rose to himself, folding up the paper;
' they are dear lines. Now, there,' he said, ' we have a true and
tender expression of the really Catholic spirit of modern æstheticism, which holds nothing common or unclean. It is in this spirit,
I say, that the architects of our state will set to work. And
thus for our houses, for our picture-galleries, for our churches—I
trust we shall have many churches—they will select and combine——'

' Do you seriously mean,' broke in Allen, a little impatiently,
' that it is a thing to wish for and to look forward to, that we
should abandon all attempts at original architecture, and content
ourselves with simply sponging on the past ? '

' I do,' replied Mr. Rose suavely ; ' and for this reason, if for
no other, that the world can now successfully do nothing else.
Any new—any spontaneous style of architecture is out of the question for us, just as we find it to be in our painting and our poetry.
The age we live in is of a kind that forbids us even to imagine such
a thing. We may, of course, talk about it, just as we may talk of
Heaven. But our talk will be like Hamlet's book, words—words
only. It will convey no pictures to our minds ; and we must stick
now to words that will convey pictures.'

' You say we have no good architecture now !' exclaimed
Lady Ambrose ; ' but, Mr. Rose, have you forgotten our modern
churches ? Don't you think them beautiful ? Perhaps you never
go to All Saints ' ?

' I every now and then,' said Mr. Rose, ' when I am in the
weary mood for it, attend the services of our English Ritualists,
and I admire their churches very much indeed. In some places
the whole thing is really managed with surprising skill. The dim
religious twilight, fragrant with the smoke of incense ; the tangled
roofs that the music seems to cling to ; the tapers, the high altar,
and the strange intonation of the priests, all produce a curious
old-world effect, and seem to unite one with things that have been
long dead. Indeed, it all seems to me far more a part of the past
than the services of the Catholics.'

Lady Ambrose did not express her approbation of the last part
of this sentiment, out of regard for Miss Merton ; but she gave a
smile and a nod of pleased intelligence to Mr. Rose.

'Yes,' Mr. Rose went on, 'there is a regretful insincerity about it all, that is very nice, and that at once appeals to me, "*Gleich einer alten halbverklungen Sage.*" The priests are only half in earnest; the congregations, even——'

'Then I am quite sure,' interrupted Lady Ambrose with vigour, 'that you can never have heard Mr. Cope preach.'

'I don't know,' said Mr. Rose languidly. 'I never enquired, nor have I ever heard anyone so much as mention, the names of any of them.'

'Do you seriously, and in sober earnest, mean,' Allen again broke in, 'that you think it a good thing that all our art and architecture should be borrowed and insincere, and that our very religion should be nothing but a dilettante memory?'

'The opinion,' said Mr. Rose, 'is not mine only, but that of all those of our own day who are really devoting themselves to art for its own sake. I will try to explain the reason of this. In the world's life, just as in the life of a man, there are certain periods of eager and all-absorbing action, and these are followed by periods of memory and reflection. We then look back upon our past, and become for the first time conscious of what we are, and of what we have done. We then see the dignity of toil, and the grand results of it, the beauty and the strength of faith, and the fervent power of patriotism; which, whilst we laboured, and believed, and loved, we were quite blind to. Upon such a reflective period has the world now entered. It has acted and believed already; its task now is to learn to value action and belief—to feel and to be thrilled at the beauty of them. And the chief means by which it can learn this is art—the art of a *renaissance.* For by the power of such art, all that was beautiful, strong, heroic, or tender in the past— all the actions, passions, faiths, aspirations of the world, that lie so many fathom deep in the years—float upwards to the tranquil surface of the present, and make our lives like what seems to me one of the loveliest things in nature, the iridescent film on the face of a stagnant water. Yes; the past is not dead unless we choose that it shall be so. Christianity itself is not dead. There is "nothing of it that doth fade," but turns "into something rich and strange," for us, to give a new tone to our lives with. And, believe me,' Mr. Rose went on, gathering earnestness, 'that the happiness possible in such conscious periods is the only true happiness. Indeed, the active periods of the world were not really happy at all. We only fancy them to have been so by a pathetic fallacy. Is the hero happy during his heroism? No, but after it, when he sees what his heroism was, and reads the glory of it in the eyes of youth or maiden.'

'Do you mean,' said Miss Merton, with a half humorous, half incredulous smile, 'that we never value religion till we have come to think it nonsense?'

'Not nonsense—no,' exclaimed Mr. Rose, in gentle horror; 'I only mean that it never lights our lives so beautifully as when it is leaving them like the evening sun. It is in such periods of the world's life that art springs into being, in its greatest splendour. Your Raphael, Miss Merton, who painted you your "dear Madonnas," was a luminous cloud in the sunset sky of the Renaissance, —a cloud that took its fire from a faith that was sunk or sinking.'

'I'm afraid that the faith is not quite sunk yet,' said Miss Merton, with a slight sudden flush in her cheeks, and with just the faintest touch of suppressed anger.

Mr. Saunders, Mr. Stockton, and Mr. Luke all raised their eyebrows.

'No,' said Mr. Rose, 'such cyclic sunsets are happily apt to linger.'

'Mr. Rose, you do talk most beautifully,' cried Lady Ambrose, 'but I am positively so stupid that I don't quite follow you.'

Mr. Rose changed his posture. He sat up and gave a little hem.

'I will try to make my meaning clearer,' he said, in a brisker tone. 'I often figure to myself an unconscious period and a conscious one, as two women—one an untamed creature with embrowned limbs native to the air and the sea; the other, marble-white and swan-soft, couched delicately on cushions before a mirror, and watching her own supple reflection gleaming in the depths of it. On the one is the sunshine and the sea-spray. The wind of Heaven and her unbound hair are playmates. The light of the sky is in her eyes; on her lips is a free laughter. We look at her, and we know that she is happy. *We* know it, mark me; but *she* knows it not. Turn, however, to the other, and all is changed. Outwardly, there is no gladness there. Her dark, gleaming eyes open depth within depth upon us, like the circles of a new Inferno. There is a clear, shadowy pallor on her cheek. Only her lips are scarlet. There is a sadness—a languor, even in the grave tendrils of her heavy hair, and in each changing curve of her bosom as she breathes or sighs.'

'What a very odd man Mr. Rose is!' said Lady Ambrose in a loud whisper. 'He always seems to talk of everybody as if they had no clothes on.'

'Yes,' Mr. Rose was meanwhile proceeding, his voice again growing visionary, 'there is no eagerness, no action there; and yet all eagerness, all action is known to her as the writing on an open scroll ; only as she reads, even in the reading of it, action turns into emotion, and eagerness into a sighing · memory. Yet this is she who is the lady of all gladness, who makes us glad in the only way now left us. And not only in the only way, but in the best way—the way of ways. Her secret is self-consciousness. She knows that she is fair ; she knows, too, that she is sad ; but she sees that sadness is lovely, and so sadness turns to joy. Do you see my meaning more clearly now, Lady Ambrose ? '

An amused good humour gathered twinkling in Lady Ambrose's grey eyes. She pursed up her mouth, and answered, ' No. No, Mr. Rose,' she said, shaking her head ; ' I'm afraid I must give it up ; ' and she gently brought one hand down on the other, as if to emphasise this statement.

Mr. Rose turned abruptly away from her, and addressed himself to the general company.

' Such a woman,' he went on, ' may be taken as a symbol not of our architecture only, but of all the æsthetic surroundings with which we shelter and express our life. Such a woman do I see whenever I enter a ritualistic church——'

' I know,' said Mrs. Sinclair, ' that very peculiar people do go to such places ; but, Mr. Rose,' she said with a look of appealing enquiry, ' I thought they were generally rather over-dressed than otherwise ? '

' The imagination,' said Mr. Rose, opening his eyes in grave wonder at Mrs. Sinclair, ' may give her what garb it chooses. Our whole city then—our new London that is to be,' he continued, clearing his throat, and looking round him, ' is in keeping with this spirit. It will be the architectural and decorative embodiment of the most educated longings of our own times after order and loveliness and delight, whether of the senses or the imagination. It will be, as it were, a resurrection of the past, in response to the longing and the passionate regret of the present. It will be such a resurrection as took place in Italy during its greatest epoch. As you wander through the streets of our city, through its groves, its gardens—as you contemplate its stately theatres, its galleries, its marble palaces, or as your eye is caught by its triumphal arches, such as that which Antonio San Gallo constructed in honour of Charles V., the whole will strike you as the expression of the finest and most varied culture of our age—as the embodiment of its most sensitive taste, and its deepest æsthetic measure of things. And there you will see men living, not madly struggling after the means to live. You will be distracted no longer by the noise or sight of trade or traffic ; nor in every spare space will your eyes be caught by abominable advertisements of excursion trains to Brighton, or of Horniman's, cheap tea. They will rest, instead, here on an exquisite fountain, here on a statue, here on a bust of Zeus or Hermes or Aphrodite, glimmering in a laurelled nook; or again on the carved marble gate-posts of our palace gardens, or on their wrought iron or wrought bronze gates. The wind of the spirit that breathes there will blow to us from all the places of the past, and be charged with infinite odours. There will be scarce an ornament of our buildings that will not deliciously quicken or cool the blood, or deliciously stimulate or assuage thought. Every frieze that runs round our walls, every clustered capital of a marble column, will be a garland or nosegay of associations. Indeed, our whole city, as compared with the London that is now, will be itself a nosegay as compared with a faggot; and as related to the life that I would see lived in it, it will be like a shell murmuring with all the world's memories, and held to the ear of the two twins, Life and Love.'

Mr. Rose here dropped his voice, as though he had said his say. Mr. Luke, however, would not leave him in repose.

'But we must,' said Mr. Luke, in a tone of chilly dissent, 'have trade and business going on somewhere.'

'And, Mr. Rose, you're not going to deprive us of all our shops, I hope?' said Lady Ambrose.

'Because, you know,' said Mrs. Sinclair, with a soft maliciousness, 'we can't go without dresses altogether, Mr. Rose. And if I were there,' she continued, plaintively, 'I should want a bookseller to publish the scraps of verse—poetry, as I am pleased to call it—that I am always writing.'

'Pooh!' said Mr. Rose, a little annoyed, 'we shall have all that somewhere, of course; but it will be out of the way, in a sort of Piræus, where the necessary καπήλοι——'

'A sort of what?' said Lady Ambrose.

'We must remember,' said Laurence, coming to Mr. Rose's rescue, 'that we are only considering now the most perfect way in which our highest class may live. Let us think that out first, and the other things will come afterwards.'

'But still,' said Lady Ambrose, 'Mr. Rose's city does not seem to me in harmony with modern life.'

'It is not in unison with modern life, certainly,' said Mr. Rose, 'if you mean that. But it is in harmony, which is a very different thing.'

'I don't say,' said Lady Ambrose, 'that it is not very beautiful of Mr. Rose to have thought of all this. But it is all somehow like a dream. And why must there be a lot of heathen gods and goddesses about the place, whom no one believes in, unless, perhaps,

it is Mr. Saunders? And why are our houses to be like the houses
of old Greeks or old Italians ? I like some things to be old—china,
for instance, and tapestry, and family portraits. But there really
is a limit. We can have too much of a good thing.'

Lady Ambrose's words flowed off her lips with a glib dogmatism. Mr. Rose answered with unusual earnestness.

' Such a city,' he said, ' is, indeed a dream, but it is a dream
which we might make a reality, would circumstances only permit
of it. We have many amongst us who know what is beautiful,
and who passionately desire it ; and would others only be led by
these, our streets and our houses might be such as Giulio Romano
or Giorgio Vasari, or Giulio Campi would have rejoiced to look at;
we might have metal-work worthy of the hand of Ghiberti and
the praise of Michel Angelo; we might rival Domenico Beccafumi
with our pavements——'

' No,' said Lady Ambrose ; ' this is all too deep for me.'

' Let me fill in Mr. Rose's outline,' said Laurence, ' and make
it a little more realistic.'

' Pray do,' said Mr. Rose, with a grave inclination of his head.

CHAPTER II.

' I DON'T think, Lady Ambrose,' said Laurence, ' that you'll find
Mr. Rose's city half so dream-like as you fancy. You will have
all the luxuries and amusements of modern life there—operas,
theatres, picture-exhibitions, balls, parties, parks and gardens to
walk and ride and drive in ; only everything will be more beautiful,
more harmonious than it is now. The present age, you know, has
taste of a highly-cultured and very sensitive kind, and the whole
aspect of Mr. Rose's city will be such as to satisfy and stimulate
this taste to the utmost. Our entire appreciation of the world's
past history, and of its present capabilities of beauty—our appreciation of its religions, its art, its heroisms—all this will be expressed
in our city's architecture—will be written visibly in marble for us,
in the open air, and under the blue sky. This really seems to me
to be as fit a place as any for the society which we wish to represent to ourselves. For consider, Lady Ambrose, before we go into
particulars about it, what the general characteristics of this society
will be. It will have to unite all the artistic and intellectual powers
that are now to be found amongst us—all the religious earnestness,
the sense of duty, the scientific and political enlightenment, the ever-
extending knowledge, the interest in our fellow-men, the zeal for
our own and for their progress—it will have to unite the best of
all this that we can at present dream of. But this is only half of

what we want.   It must be inspired further with all those gracious and liberal sentiments which are the peculiar heritage of an aristocracy at its best, and which spring from an inborn and hardly conscious sense of *noblesse oblige*; it must have, too—this will indeed follow from what I have said before—the utmost polish, ease and grace of manner, and the completest *savoir vivre.*   Our leading class will thus be an exemplar of human life at its highest possible beauty ; and our ideal city will be, as it were, a human flower-garden, not what London is now, a great wilderness where weeds and flowers grow together, and where the former half choke the latter.'

'Good,' murmured Mr. Rose, ' human flower-garden is good.'

'Well, Mr. Laurence, go on,' said Lady Ambrose.   ' I think I'm getting a little brighter.'

'I can fancy,' said Laurence, stretching himself out on the grass, and resting his cheek on his hand, ' that I am at this very moment walking along one of the streets of our city, under the shady trees that line it, and watching the people as they pass by. How distinguished they all look, and how much expression there is in their faces !   I am not naturally a bold man, but I can't help staring at the women, they are so lovely—they hold themselves so piquantly, and they are so exquisitely dressed.   Ah, what a vision has just passed by me !   what a hat!   what a figure !   what rich brown hair !   I can't help it.   I turn round, stand stock still, and gaze after her.   See, she has just turned into that house with the gate-posts of clouded yellow marble, a nymph and a satyr carved on each of them.   I hear her feet on the short gravel sweep.   Hark ! " The gates of heaven are closed, and she is gone."   As she passed me, I stared at her.   Was she angry that I did so ?   No, no—that could not be.   Her glance, on the contrary, seemed to seek and meet mine of its own accord.   I cannot resist it.   I must and will go after her.   How is it I do not feel shy ?   I cannot tell. Certain it is I cross the street.   I pass in between those yellow gate-posts ; I walk up the gravel sweep ; I stand in the echoing portico.   I ring the bell.   A curious foreign servant opens the door for me, with a dark complexion, and a livery that makes him look like a perfect picture.   His manners are faultless.   He does not ask me my name, but shows me in directly.   I find I am in a circular hall, with a domed ceiling, surrounded with frescoes and statues, and with a pavement like one I once saw at Pompeii.   On a marble table is a bust of Goethe, with a vase of flowers before it, placed like a votive offering.   Close beside it, thrown down carelessly, lies a book bound in delicious cream-coloured vellum.   But I can't stay to read the title.   I must follow the servant.   I pass into a wide corridor, and through the windows of it shines the sea. Plants in majolica vases are on either hand. On another table as I pass I see a heap of engravings lying, and oh! close beside them—how a delightful tremor runs all through my body—I see *her* bewitching hat lying, and her delicate gloves! An inlaid door is thrown open. I am in the drawing-room. The light is subdued and soft. I am in a cool bath of most delicately flower-scented air. I have at once a sensation that I am in an educated atmosphere, though as yet I am hardly conscious why. She is not in the room. The servant has gone to fetch her. I look about me. I am wooed on all sides by a concourse of soothing colours, from walls, furniture, flowers; and by a sense of the presence of books, works of art, and musical instruments. All are at first vague and indistinct; but as I gradually take stock of them, each has a separate and delightful message for me. Enchanted, charmed place! China, books, flowers—and in one corner a gilded harp, standing by a great azalea, a mass of scarlet blossoms! I examine the books first. What green morocco prize is this, lying under the shadow of a crimson rose, that hangs its head over a Venetian glass? It is "Candide." And this, on the little purple velvet table, near that pale lovely heath? It is Dante's "Inferno"—yes, and it is resting on Balzac's "Histoire de Treize." There are tempting books everywhere, placed about naturally, as though read, and kept for reading. Here is a case with cameos of the twelve Cæsars in it: and there is the second volume of Gibbon's "Rome." Here are Tennyson, Browning, and so forth—here I see Victor Hugo, Heine, a volume of Comte—and here—here by a low chair, an open volume of "Wilhelm Meister," with a rose thrown across the page, by way of a marker. And what is this? Close by a Strauss's "Life of Jesus" stands the photograph of a lovely child, with long glossy hair. But its eyes are quite closed—it is dead. Yes—and let into the velvet frame is a little case containing a lock of its fair hair, and under the picture is written in a woman's hand,

> Animula, vagula, blandula,
> Quæ nunc abibis in loca?

That clock on the chimney-piece is a Louis Quatorze—what an enchanted chime, as it strikes the hour of noon! How sweetly the quick silver notes fall in the scented silence, like the petals of a shaken rose tree! Welcome, my Montaigne! Is that you that I see in the book-stand—one volume of you? the other lying close by on the top of a "Contemporary Review"? And oh, my friend, my sweet companion "Tristram Shandy," do these delightful people not blush to have thee on their drawing-room tables? But—the door opens ; my heart grows tremulous, at the rustle of a woman's dress—that speaking rustle ! Ah ! see—she enters ! Yes, it is she—the eyes, the hair, and the pose of the flower-like head. How bewitchingly she enters ! How frankly she holds out her white hand to me ! " You are new to London," she says ; " I am charmed to see you ; and you will stay to luncheon, won't you ? " Am I making a good impression ? I hardly know how I answer her—and yet, I am not shy. " What an exquisite room ! " I say ; " I can't tell you how I am delighted with it." " Yes," she answers, " it is all my own arrangement. I like it myself, because, you know, I think it is a little like me." " I can fancy that," I answer, looking first round the room, and then at her. " Here," she says, moving towards the window, and touching a glass shade, " is one of the things that I am fondest of. We brought it last year from Corinth." I look and see that it is an exquisite Grecian vase, with a sacrificial procession on it ; and on the stand it rests upon I read these two lines :

> Thou yet unravished bride of quietness,
> Thou foster-child of silence and slow time.

" That vase," she says, making the prettiest little grimace with her mouth, and with a soft pathetic humour glimmering in her long-lashed eyes, "seems to take one back into the past like Hans Andersen's Goloshes of Happiness." My admiration of her grows momently. Her face is so full of expression ; her voice is so rich in varying cadences. She is a woman, I feel at once, who is the product of a double culture, life and books. Her books have been a comment on her life ; her life has been a comment on her books. She likes admiration, too—I feel sure of that. She sees I admire her, and she likes it.'

' Stay, my dear Laurence,' broke in Leslie. ' This lady is an old acquaintance of mine, and I, unperceived of you, have come in after you. You think me very much *de trop*, I can see that : and she herself receives me with a little embarrassment. But just then the husband enters—an oldish man, handsome, but with a slight limp—and he insists on your coming with him to see his library : and so—off you go, and I am left master of the occasion. " And so you are here again, are you ? " she says to me in a slow, languid voice, as soon as we are alone. Her manner, my dear Laurence, has quite changed since you left the room. Her eyes rest full upon mine for a moment, and then their long lashes droop a little, and cover them. " And what brings you here ? " she says. "Memories," I answer; "and what memories I surely need not tell you." " Memories ! " she repeats, in a low tone, looking out of the window. " Do you ever remember ? " " Try me," I say, "and see. It is ninety days to-day since first I saw you : it is eighty-nine days since first I kissed you : it is eighty-eight days since last I said good-bye to you." " You have a memory indeed ! " she answers, half sadly, half carelessly. " Why don't you exercise it on something more worthy of it ? But no," she adds, with more interest in her voice, " that is not to the point. How many other memories of the same sort have you, and of a yet later date ? How many other women have you been saying the same things to, that you once said to me ? I suppose you will say, No one." " No," I answer, " I'm afraid I can't say that. But this I can say," and I look wistfully at her, " that I have never since then said an improper thing to any woman but I wished you were by, and that I was saying it to you instead." " What ! " she exclaims, " Do you fancy I take such constancy as that to be a compliment ? Move a little farther off, if you please ! " I start at the sudden change of manner, and begin to fear I may have said something to offend her. " Do you stare ? " she goes on ; " do you look astonished ? Can you mistake my meaning ? Have you forgotten who I am ? My husband's limp in the passage should remind you that I am a married woman. It has reminded me." '

'I shall be shocked in another minute,' said Mrs. Sinclair, ' if you go on like this.'

'Poor woman,' said Miss Merton, ' why have you made her so unhappy ? '

'Well,' said Laurence, ' I have found our host charming ; but we have certainly not come back again before we were wanted.'

'See,' whispered Mrs. Sinclair to Leslie, 'Miss Merton is quite *en rapport* with Lord Allen. Just watch them whispering. Do you believe in animal—what do you call it ?—animal magnetism ? '

'Listen, Mr. Laurence,' said Allen in a moment, with a half-shy smile ; ' your host wants you and Mr. Leslie to go into the garden ; and whilst you are looking at the view, I have been asked to introduce Miss Merton to our hostess. It is done. I see they will get on together—in fact, I know it ; for fifteen minutes are over by this time, and Miss Merton has told me so. The first thing they talked about was flowers, and in our friend's tone was a subdued pathetic ring that Miss Merton at once detected—a sort of appealing music that is only given by sorrow. After a few minutes, she offered to show Miss Merton her boudoir. On the table where she read and wrote was a glass with a single rose in it, and a book left open. Miss Merton glanced at this, and saw that it was the ' Imitatio Christi.' Our friend blushed slightly as she saw Miss Merton looking at it, and said in a half apologetic tone, "I was trying to read a chapter of that this morning. I often look at it. But somehow I could not read much to-day. The air was so delicious that I was obliged to go out of doors and feel it, and breathe in all I could of it; and the fresh sea, with all its sparklings, looked as if it were waiting for something happy to happen." As she said this, Miss Merton turned her eyes upon her, saying nothing; only—she could not tell why—she felt her own eyes begin to moisten; and it seemed to her all of a sudden as if she understood our friend. Miss Merton made a slight movement towards her, and she towards Miss Merton. Miss Merton held out her hand to her, and she took it with a grateful pressure. Then in a moment Miss Merton's arm was round her waist. For a moment she looked at Miss Merton timidly and enquiringly, and then——'

'Stop!' suddenly exclaimed Mr. Saunders.

A quick blush shot over Allen's face. He stopped instantly; and for a few moments there was a general silence, disturbed only by Mr. Sinclair's saying in a whisper to Leslie,

'I think Lord Allen's sayings remind one a little of sisters' kisses, "insipid things, like sandwiches of veal." Do you recollect that verse of Hood's?'

Everyone was waiting in wonder to learn the reason of Mr. Saunders's unceremonious interruption. Mr. Saunders was, however, apparently too excited to proceed directly; and Lady Ambrose, a little unfairly, hastened to take advantage of a silence that had not been secured for her.

'Look here, Mr. Laurence,' she exclaimed; 'there is one thing I have been wanting to say all along. No doubt you will think me very stupid; but still I can't help fancying there is something in it. It seems to me that all this is—all this Utopia, I mean—that it is just a little—(it's very delightful, you know; I'm not denying that, remember) but it's—— '

'Well, Lady Ambrose?'

'Well, just a little bit *blue*. It is all too bookish, if you understand what I mean. Don't you know when anyone comes to see you in London, and will talk of nothing but books, one always fancies it is because he isn't—it's very uncharitable to say so, but still it's true—because he isn't very much in society, and doesn't know many people to talk about?'

'I always think it such a blessing,' said Lord Allen, 'to find anyone who will talk about books, and will not be perpetually boring one with vulgar gossip and scandal.'

'Oh, so do I,' said Lady Ambrose eagerly, 'but that was not what I meant exactly. I mean that I like men to ride, and shoot, and do what is manly, and take part in what is going on in the world;

and you know, when one meets them, I like them to be able to talk about what people *do* ; not only about what they think, or write, or discover—unless it is something *very* interesting. Philosophers and men of science are all very well of course, and no one can admire or respect them more than I do—not that I know any of them, by the way, unless you call poor old Lord Dash one; and I'm sure Mr. Laurence will agree with me that he's not very brilliant company, although he is an old dear, with his funny frilled shirts and his enamelled snuff-box. But still —' Lady Ambrose here suddenly recollected the presence of Mr. Stockton—' I only mean that I dislike stupid clever people. Mr. Stockton and I, I believe, are very good friends ; and who can be cleverer than he ? '

Mr. Stockton, who till that moment had not heard a word Lady Ambrose had been saying, having been busily engaged in showing Lady Violet Gresham a wood-louse through a pocket microscope, at this last sentence looked up in a little flutter of interrogatory surprise, and made Lady Ambrose a slight bow.

' But now about this bookishness,' went on Lady Ambrose, having somewhat confused herself, and laughing at her confusion, ' you know what I mean, Mr. Laurence, I'm sure you do. No one can delight in a book more than I ; but still—it is possible to be too literary, isn't it, as well as too anything else ? '

' Perfectly true, Lady Ambrose,' said Mr. Luke—Lady Ambrose was delighted—' people continually *are* too literary—to my cost I know it ; and that is because the world at large—what is called the reading world even more than the non-reading world— are helplessly at sea as to what books are, and what they really do for us. In other words, if you will forgive my harping as I do upon a single expression, they lack culture. And now,' said Mr. Luke, ' will you let me give you all a little bit of advice ? Here you have Mr. Rose's city (in which *carte blanche* is given you for all kinds of beauty and delightfulness) waiting to be peopled by society, I mean human life in its most perfect form, as we—the more thoughtful and gifted among us—are all more or less vaguely dreaming it might be. Now, if you really want to see what these dreams are—if you want to make their details really clear and instructive, begin first with examining, as carefully as may be, the highest culture of this present age of ours; for culture in its widest and truest sense is the bud, as it were, in which the flowers of our future lie enfolded for us. Let us see what are the ideas, the emotions, the conduct, that the most cultivated amongst us most admire and approve of, and we shall thus see what sort of new Republic it is that we are reaching out towards.'

Mr. Luke's proposal was received with general satisfaction.

' Admirably said ! ' murmured Mr. Rose; ' the bud in which the flowers of our future lie enfolded for us ! '

' Come,' said Lady Ambrose, ' this is just what I like. Let us all talk about culture.'

' Very well,' cried Mr. Saunders, who had been several times trying in vain to find a hearing, ' what I wished to say just now when I called out " Stop ! " I will draw your attention to by and bye—when you are tired,' he added, lying down as if he were going to sleep, ' of discussing culture, whatever that may be.'

' Yes,' said Lady Ambrose, ' whatever that may be. Had not we better, Mr. Luke, be quite clear first what we mean by culture, before we begin to talk about it ? You know, I think, it's always so much better to be accurate if one can, in one's use of language.'

' Well,' said Mr. Luke, with an august wave of his hand, ' let Mr. Laurence tell us all what culture is. No one can do so better than he. I, Lady Ambrose, have perhaps grown something too much of a specialist to be able to put these things in a sufficiently popular way.'

Laurence, with some diffidence, assented, and there was a general rustling on all sides of the party settling themselves more luxuriously on the soft grass.

' And now, Mr. Laurence,' said Lady Ambrose, ' begin at the beginning, please, and don't do as Lord Kennington did at the Eton and Harrow match the other day—go talking to me about " overs," and " long-stops," and what not, before I even knew the difference between " out " and " in." '

(To be continued.)

Juliet.

BY MRS. H. LOVETT CAMERON.

CHAPTER XIII.

THE SOTHERNE LETTER-BAG.

' ERNESTINE,' said Mrs. Blair to that talented damsel, during the course of the same day that Colonel Fleming had so suddenly left Sotherne Court,—' Ernestine, you are looking very pale.'

' Thank you, madame, my health is quite good.'

' That makes no difference,' persisted her mistress. ' You are looking very pale, and I am not at all easy about you.'

Here Mademoiselle Ernestine's gifted nature asserted itself, and she perceived that it was her duty to be pale and ailing.

' Oui, madame, perhaps I am a little souffrante; I have had some aches in my head.'

' Exactly so, Ernestine; and it is plain that you do not get enough fresh air; you want exercise, my good girl—a walk every day.'

' Madame is very kind—but I have not much time for a promenade.'

' Not during the day, perhaps; and that brings me to what I wish to say: I should like you to take a good brisk walk in the morning before you call me.'

' Madame!' exclaimed poor Ernestine, with rather a blank face at the prospect of an earlier rise from her much-loved bed.

' Don't interrupt me; it is dull I know for you to walk out so early without any companion or any object, but you might go along the high road; it is always dry that way; and then when you meet the postman you can come back, and if you like to take the bag from him, and bring it to me, to take my letters out, it will give you some little interest to go out for—and, Ernestine, you are a good girl, and I am very pleased with you. Look here! I have put out that black silk mantle of mine for you; it will make you a nice jacket, and there is a bit of real lace on it, which I will give you too.'

'How very amiable you are towards me, madame!' exclaimed the delighted maiden, as she took up the silk mantle.

'I am quite sure that an early walk will do you all the good in the world; there is nothing like the morning air.'

'Thank you, madame; and shall I begin to-morrow?'

'Certainly, I should like to see some roses in your cheeks as soon as possible. Here, put some scent on this handkerchief, and give me my gold eyeglass—that is all I want just at present; you may go now.'

Ernestine fully comprehended what was required of her. She carried off the silk mantle, which was almost new, and a very handsome present to give to a maid, and prepared herself honestly to fulfil her part of the bargain.

She understood that Mrs. Blair wished to have the first sight of the letter-bag; and she probably guessed that it was her object to find out whether Miss Blair received any letters from the departed Colonel Fleming.

Further than that, to do her justice, Ernestine's suspicions did not go.

It was the custom at Sotherne for the letters to be left at the lodge-gate about eight o'clock in the morning, by the walking postman, whence they were daily fetched by James the footman. Higgs the butler was supposed to keep the key; and when the letter-bag arrived, it was his duty to open it, and distribute the servants' letters to them, and then to lay the rest on the dining-room sideboard, save only Mrs. Blair's, which Ernestine always carried off to her mistress's room.

But Higgs, like many other good servants who have been long in their masters' confidence, was rather spoilt and lazy; he was fond of shirking as many of his lesser duties as he found he could, without detriment to his own dignity or his mistress's interests, hand over to the rather meek-spirited footman. Amongst other little duties, that of opening the post-bag, and distributing its contents, had of late years been completely entrusted to James.

The bag arrived just when Mr. Higgs was most comfortably enjoying his breakfast and his morning talk with Mrs. Pearse in the housekeeper's room. Higgs was fat, and Higgs was also getting old and lazy: it was therefore considerably easier, simpler, and less troublesome to himself in every way to give up the key to James; and, as he fetched the bag from the lodge, to let him also open it and distribute the letters.

Now, if there was one duty which James hated and detested above all other duties, it was that of fetching the post-bag from the lodge. Every morning, wet or dry, fine or foul, he had to trudge out after 'them dratted letters,' as he elegantly expressed it ; and as his own correspondence was of an exceedingly limited and most unexciting nature, being chiefly composed of bills for tobacco and beer from the village public-house, and petitions for money from a drunken old mother whom filial duty commanded him to support, he was not very much interested in its contents.

These sentiments, being freely spoken and concisely expressed pretty frequently before his fellow-servants, were well known to Mrs. Blair's French maid.

She also knew—for trust a woman, above all a Frenchwoman, to discover such matters—that James was consumed with an absorbing passion for herself. Acting upon the knowledge of these two facts, Ernestine set to work to make an unconscious instrument of her admirer.

'Monsieur Jams,' she said to him, with her sweetest smile, 'do you not dislike very much to fetch the bag with the lettres?'

' Ay, that I do, mam'zell,' answered her swain, earnestly; ' it just takes me off when everyone else is beginning their breakfasts, having to fetch them blessed letters ; and if there's one thing I can't abear, it's not being able to sit down comfortable to my meals.'

'Well, look at this, Jams—I will fetch it for you for a few days.'

' You, mam'zell ! '

' But yes. I have given a dress to Mrs. White, the woman at the lodge, to make for me, and I wish to go and see how she does do it every morning ; and if you will give me the key, I will go fetch the bag at the same time.'

'The key!' repeated James, rather dubiously; 'well, I don't know about that—I don't know as I ought to give you the key.'

' Oh yes, give me the key, for I expect a letter from a friend in Paris—what you call a lovere ; but he is dying,' she added quickly, seeing that James looked as firm as adamant at the mention of a rival.

' Ah, he's dying ! Are you sure of that ? ' he said, with a gleam on his face at the melancholy news.

' But yes, he dies, and perhaps he leaves me some money.'

' Ah, ah ! ' with a delighted grin.

' Yes ; and if he do, I can perhaps marry myself to one—whom I love much better ; ' and here Mademoiselle Ernestine glanced at her admirer with a most telling *œillade,* and then looked coyly down at the corner of her apron. ' So you see, Monsieur Jams, I am in impatience to see the lettres ; so please give me the key.'

'You mustn't let out to Higgs, then,' said the enraptured footman, clasping his beloved's hands, 'and you must give me a kiss.'

'If you give me the key,' said Ernestine, who had been prepared to use bribery and corruption.

The kiss was submitted to, and Ernestine walked off triumphantly with the key in her pocket.

'Qu'ils sont donc bêtes, ces hommes! Mon Dieu! qu'ils sont niais!' she muttered to herself as she went upstairs; and it must be confessed that, as far as James was concerned, she had some cause for her sweeping condemnation of the male sex.

The following morning Ernestine entered Mrs. Blair's bedroom soon after eight o'clock, triumphantly bearing the letter-bag and the key. That she had previously opened it and carefully looked over the contents herself, and then locked it up again, was of course a proceeding to which, under the circumstances, she considered that she had a perfect right, but which she did not think it necessary to impart to her mistress.

Mrs. Blair eagerly turned the key and tumbled out all the letters over the bed-clothes.

But there was nothing whatever to reward her curiosity: her own letters were only bills, and there were three for Juliet—one from Mr. Bruce, one from Georgie Travers (an answer probably to an invitation to lunch, which she knew Juliet to have sent to her), and the third was either a bill or a circular; there was certainly nothing from Colonel Fleming. She replaced all the letters, and Ernestine gravely took the bag from her hand, and carried it downstairs to James, who proceeded to distribute the contents as usual, and who was brought to acknowledge that it certainly made no difference who fetched it, and that he had much enjoyed eating his breakfast undisturbed. A second and a third morning Ernestine, undaunted by the wind and the rain, sallied forth wrapped in her waterproof cloak down to the lodge, and still there had been nothing to reward her energy nor to satisfy her mistress's curiosity. But on the fourth day, when the girl brought in the bag, she knew perfectly well, by a previous inspection, that there was a letter from Colonel Fleming to Miss Blair inside it. Mrs. Blair saw it, and pounced upon it the instant she opened the bag; it was impossible to mistake the large bold handwriting with which she was perfectly familiar, even had the crest and monogram on the seal been wanting to make assurance doubly sure.

She hastily slipped the letter under her pillow, waiting till Ernestine's back was turned towards her whilst she was pulling up the blinds and arranging the window curtains, to do so; then, taking out her own letters, she gave the bag back into her hand, and sent her away.

The instant she was alone, Mrs. Blair sprang out of bed, and, wrapping her dressing-gown around her, carried her prize to the light of the window.

Without a moment's hesitation she broke the seal, unfolded the letter, and began hastily reading through all poor Hugh's passionate love-words. She had but just finished it when she heard Ernestine coming along the passage with her hot water. She had only time to tear the letter once across, and throw it hastily on to the fire, when the door opened. The envelope and one torn half fell on to the blazing coals, and were rapidly consumed: but the other half, unseen by Mrs. Blair, fluttered aside, and slipped down behind the coalscuttle, where it remained between that household article and the wainscot, completely hidden.

'I did not ring,' said Mrs. Blair sharply to Ernestine, for she was angry at her untimely entrance.

'N'est-ce pas, madame? Ah, I beg pardon, I heard a bell: it must have been Mademoiselle Blair's bell; and I thought it was yours. Will you wait, madame, or shall I bring you your bath, as the hot water is here?'

Ernestine was not unmindful of the blazing papers on the fire, upon which she kept one eye whilst she spoke. Her entrance, it is needless to say, was not in the very least accidental; but had been, on the contrary, very carefully planned by her from the moment when she had ascertained that the letter for which her mistress was on the look-out had arrived.

She set about her duties of dressing and waiting upon Mrs. Blair with alacrity, and it was whilst bustling actively about the room that she caught sight of a small corner of white paper sticking out behind the coalscuttle.

When Mrs. Blair had completed her dressing and left the room, Ernestine flew to the coalscuttle, and triumphantly drew forth the torn half-sheet of Colonel Fleming's letter.

'Ah, mais c'est trop fort!' she muttered, with a slight compunction for Juliet. 'I would never have imagined she would have opened it and then burnt it. Ah, but it is shameful to that pauvre demoiselle!'

But, in spite of her compunctions, Ernestine did her best to decipher the mutilated letter, although, owing to her imperfect education, and to its fragmentary condition, she was not able to make out as much of it as she would have liked.

'I will keep him! he will be useful to me some day,' she said to herself, as she carefully folded it up and put it in her pocket.

Then she carried it upstairs to her own room, and wrapping it in a piece of silver paper, locked it up in a little cedar-wood money-box, side by side with her last quarter's wages, a packet of love-letters, chiefly in French, a withered bunch of violets given her by Adolphe, her first love, who had gone for a soldier and died in Algeria, and a pair of gold and pearl earrings, her greatest treasures, which, being very handsome, and having been presented to her by a French count, she was afraid to wear openly in the sterner moral atmosphere of an English family.

Meanwhile Juliet was waiting and watching day after day for that very letter, of which one-half lay upstairs in that box in the French lady's-maid's attic bedroom, and the other half was in ashes in Mrs. Blair's fire-place. She was too proud to show her anxiety ; she would not send for the letters to her bedroom, but every day she got up a little sooner, and hurried downstairs to see what the morning's post had brought her, every day to meet with a fresh disappointment.

At first she was so full of hope, that when his letter did not come she hardly made herself unhappy : she felt so sure he would write to her, so certain that he would keep his word. But when day after day passed and brought her no word, no sign from him, her heart began to be very heavy. She read and re-read the little note he had written to her before he left, and tried to comfort herself afresh with the assurance of that letter which he had promised to write to her. It was impossible, she said to herself, that he could break his word ! But she began to get restless and impatient ; she could settle to nothing : all her ordinary occupations and duties became hateful to her ; she could take no pleasure in any of them. She began to torment herself with all sorts of horrible conjectures. Could he be ill ? she wondered ; or, good heavens ! had there been any railway accidents the last few days in which he might have been disabled, or possibly worse ? and a hundred ghastly fancies and imaginations haunted her from morning till night.

Every day she longed ardently for the next to come, and when the next day dawned, it brought her still nothing—nothing.

Everyone knows the miserable suspense of that watching and waiting for news that will not come, that hope deferred which maketh the heart sick. Juliet tried to call pride to her aid ; but, although she said to herself, over and over again, that if he did not care, neither would she—that it was unworthy of her to waste tears and sighs on a man who could care for her so little as to leave her so heartlessly, that he could not be worth her love who treated her so cruelly—although she said these things to herself a hundred times a day, she found all such arguments singularly unavailing.

Pride is very little help to a woman who really loves.

And the days slipped away silently, swiftly—uneventful days of misery—whilst she waited in vain for that letter that was never to come, and for the answer to which Hugh Fleming up in London was eating his heart out with longings that were all in vain.

At last there came a day when Juliet and her stepmother sat together in the drawing-room—the girl with her work in her hands and her thoughts far away, and the elder woman reading the ' Times '—and the latter broke the long silence by saying suddenly,

' Did you not say the " Sultana " was the name of the ship Colonel Fleming was to go to India in, Juliet ? '

' Yes ; I think that was the name he mentioned,' she answered, rather faintly ; ' what about her ? '

' Oh, nothing,' replied her stepmother, unconcernedly ; ' only, I see that she has sailed, so I suppose he is gone. By the way, did he ever write to you again ? '

No answer. The room seemed to swim around her ; a mist was before her eyes ; she rose unsteadily, and began mechanically folding up her work. Like one in a nightmare she got herself out of the room, and staggered across the hall towards the staircase, and then one of the housemaids, passing along the corridor above, heard a heavy sound as of someone falling, and uttered a shriek of dismay at seeing her young mistress fall forward in a dead swoon in the hall below.

Her cries of alarm speedily brought assistance, and Juliet was carried up to her own room and laid upon her bed, whilst a groom was immediately sent off by the frightened Higgs to summon Dr. Ramsden to the mistress of Sotherne.

But Juliet was ill with a disease which it was beyond good Dr. Ramsden's skill to prescribe for.

When she recovered her senses after that short fainting fit, she came back to a state of misery and wretchedness compared to which the death-like unconsciousness of her deep swoon had been a merciful condition.

For nearly a fortnight the girl was almost beside herself with grief. She had not known till now how much, in spite of everything, hope had buoyed her up—how impossible, in the bottom of her heart, she had thought it for Hugh to leave her. But now that he was indeed gone utterly beyond recall, an absolute despair took possession of her. She knew him too well to believe he would come back ; he was dead to her, she felt—as much dead as if she

had seen him in his coffin.   In all the world that was before h r,
there would be no Hugh Fleming; others might fill her life or
occupy her thoughts, but never again he who must ever, come what
may, be first and dearest in her heart.

Ah, that long blank of years that stretches out hopelessly
greyly, before some of us—how shall we ever live through them!
How long life seems to those who miss out of it the one face that
can make it all too short!

Juliet Blair had none of those qualities that go to make an
heroic nature : she had little reserve or self-control ; hers was not the
character that could 'suffer and be still ;' she felt things too intensely, too acutely, for that calm suppression of all outward emotion which is the gift of colder natures.   She spent hours locked
up in her own room in paroxysms of tears, or sitting dry-eyed
staring into the fire with a white, scared, miserable face.   She
would see no visitors, and could hardly be persuaded to touch any
food ; and, to all enquiries as to what ailed her, she answered
wearily, ' I am ill ; let me alone—I am ill !'

The sight of her stepmother, who had so calmly and lightly
told her of Hugh Fleming's departure, became absolutely hateful
to her.   Sometimes she wandered about the house, or sat silently
for hours alone in the library, in his chair ; with her face buried
in her hands.   One day sitting thus, and leaning her elbows on
the writing-table, half unconsciously she pulled open one of the
drawers in front of her.   Some things of Colonel Fleming's were
still left inside : a few unimportant papers, a packet of envelopes
stamped with his crest, a little ivory penholder she had often seen
him use, and, right in the front, an old pair of dogsk   gloves,
moulded and shaped to the form of his hands as if he had just
pulled them off.   Juliet's fingers wandered over each and all with a
loving touch ! and then she remembered how once before she had
found his things lying about, in this very room, when he was away,
and how she had smoothed them and put them straight for him
with reverent hands ; only, *then* he had come back to her—but now,
now !—with a wail of despair she burst into a passion of bitter
tears.

By-and-by she took out of the drawer all the dear relics of
her lover—the gloves, the penholder, the envelopes and papers—
and carried them upstairs to her own room, and there, shower-
ing passionate kisses on each insensate object that had been his,
she locked them up in her dressing-case, by the side of that
short farewell note which was all of his that she could call her
own.

And they were a comfort to her.   Hitherto she had pos-

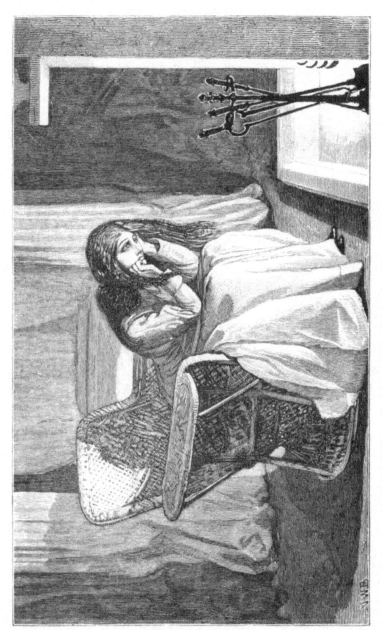

STARING INTO THE FIRE WITH A WHITE, SCARED, MISERABLE FACE.

sessed nothing that had belonged to Hugh Fleming, nor had she one single thing that he had given to her; and Juliet prized these things that she had found as her greatest treasures; for most women are insanely foolish over such relics of those they love.

As the days passed away Juliet Blair gradually recovered her self-possession; as the sorrow sank deeper and deeper into her heart, so it left her outwardly calmer. She wept no more; it would seem, indeed, as if the fountain of her tears had run itself dry.

By degrees she resumed her ordinary occupations; she rode and drove out, and paid visits as she had been accustomed to do; and Mrs. Blair, who had watched her misery with a good many pangs of conscience, and some uneasiness as to the result, breathed freely again, and congratulated herself upon having done quite the wisest and best thing for her step-daughter's welfare.

'She has quite got over it—very soon she will have forgotten his existence!' she said to herself.

But there was a change in Juliet which no one around her noticed, because none of those by whom she was surrounded loved her well enough to detect it.

She was altered. The old brightness, the old impatience were almost gone; her cheek was a shade paler, her sweet lips had a sadder droop: her step had lost something of its lightness, her eyes something of their fire; and to the end of her life these things never wholly came back to Juliet Blair.

But Mrs. Blair saw nothing of all this. In her suffering, as in her joy, the girl was alone—utterly alone.

Ernestine had discontinued her morning walks. Two days after the arrival and subsequent destruction of Colonel Fleming's letter, Mrs. Blair remarked to her maid that she looked so much better that there was no longer the necessity for that daily exercise which she had prescribed for her.

So Ernestine gave back the key of the letter-bag to James.

'Here, Monsieur Jams, is your key,' she said, shaking her head mournfully; '*he is dead!*' in allusion to the French lover.

'Dead, is he?' cried James eagerly; 'and the money—have you heard?'

'Alas!' said Ernestine, 'it is no use, my friend; the perfidious one has left it all to his cousin Annette.'

Chapter XIV.

WHAT THE BROWN MARE DID.

Soon after the departure of Colonel Fleming on his return voyage to India, a hard frost set in which stopped the hunting for a fortnight.

During this fortnight Squire Travers was intensely miserable; he spent his days in alternately tapping the barometer, and going out to look at the weathercock.

'I think it's half a point to the west of north, Georgie,' he would say excitedly, coming in from these excursions of inspection; 'just you come out and see.' And Georgie would obediently throw a shawl over her head, and run out into the keen, frosty air to stare up at the top of the house.

'Well'—doubtfully—'hardly, papa; and I am afraid the smoke is *very* due north, and that is the safest guide.'

'Not at all; the chimneys all want sweeping; that sends the smoke all ways at once. I stick to the weathercock—but you're right; there isn't much sign of its changing yet.'

And then the Squire would stroll disconsolately round to the stable, and go into every stall, and mutter grievous things below his breath as he gazed sorrowfully at each sleek-coated animal— dire words relative to the process of 'eating their heads off,'— that strange and mysterious feat which horses are supposed to accomplish in frosty weather.

'D'ye see any signs of its giving?' he would ask a dozen times of Davis, the stud groom, who followed him about from stall to stall, taking off the clothing from each idle hunter's back.

Davis, who was of a sanguine disposition, would remove the everlasting straw from his mouth, and answer cheerfully :

'Oh, bless you, yes, Squire; it can't last much longer. We shall have rain before night, most likely.' And though these enlivening prophecies had not as yet been fulfilled, the Squire pinned his faith to Davis, and derived much consolation from his hopeful assurances.

Georgie regretted the frost as well as her father, but not so keenly as she would once have done. A good deal of the pleasure had gone out of the girl's life since Mr. Travers had so sternly banished Wattie Ellison from her side. She never thought of rebelling against his decision; in the long run she felt sure he was right. But sometimes she found it hard to bear. Her letters from Cis were a great comfort to her; from them she learnt that her lover was well, and that he thought of her, and that he was, as Cis said, 'working hard;' and she, too, had her dreams of the fortune which his genius, in which she had unbounded faith, might some day achieve for her sake. Buoyed up by these hopes, she tried to bear her life cheerfully and patiently, and to be the same bright sympathising companion to her father as she used to be; but it had become an effort to her, and the Squire was dimly conscious of it. It made him irritable, and often sharp to her; her patient little face, with its somewhat sad smile, was a perpetual reproach to him. He knew at the bottom of his heart that he had not behaved quite fairly or rightly to his favourite child; he did not want to be reminded of it. He wanted everything to be as it was before that unwelcome episode about Wattie had taken place; and yet, somehow, everything was different, and the Squire did not like it.

He had numberless little ways of trying to make up to her for his one great injustice. He took to making her endless presents: first, there was the saddle; then a new hunting crop; then a set of gold horse-shoe studs; then a number of books he had heard her say she liked—almost every day something came down from town for Georgie: and she was very grateful to him. She smiled, and kissed him, and tried to look as pleased as he expected her to be; but all the while she saw through it all perfectly.

'Poor papa!' she would say to herself, with a sigh, as she carried away his latest present; 'poor papa! he wants to make it up to me.'

Georgie's hunting was, as ever, her greatest resource. It took her out of herself; and the active exercise was good for her, and prevented her from moping; so that when it was stopped perforce by the frost, she was nearly as anxious for a thaw as her father.

'It's a good thing the brown mare has laid up just now; she couldn't have chosen a better time,' said the Squire, cheerily, in family conclave one evening, trying to derive comfort from the smallest causes under the untoward state of the weather.

The brown mare, after she had been ridden for the first time, had caught a bad cold, which had prevented Georgie from using her since, for which she was not altogether sorry. Georgie was suspicious of the brown mare—there was not, when she was on her back, that complete understanding between the horse and his rider which it is thought should exist between the two to constitute a perfect mount.

If Georgie wanted to go one way, the brown mare had a

habit of wanting to go the other, and an unseemly struggle would ensue. True she was good-looking and fast, and withal an undeniable fencer ; but, in spite of all these good qualities, Georgie did not like her—she could not forget that Wattie Ellison had warned her against her.

When, therefore, the Squire congratulated himself upon the mare's being laid up during the frost in preference to any other time, Georgie answered that she was sorry she didn't go dead lame altogether.

' I can't imagine why you dislike her so,' said her father testily. ' She's a very nice mare. What's wrong with her, I'd like to know ? '

' Well, papa, I was told she had a bad character,' answered Georgie, looking down.

' Who told you ? ' and then his daughter turned very red, and was silent ; and the Squire knew perfectly well who it was that had told her. The discovery did not tend to improve the old man's temper.

' I will thank you not to go listening to tales against your father's horses from every ignorant young upstart who thinks he can give an opinion on what he knows nothing about,' he said angrily, and bounced out of the room, with a slam of the door behind him that made his wife jump and utter a little squeal like a shot rabbit, at which Flora laughed aloud behind her book of fairy tales.

' Your father is so rough,' said Mrs. Travers to her assembled daughters.

Mary sympathisingly agreed with her mother, as she made a point of doing on every occasion, having no independent will or opinion of her own, and Georgie looked miserably into the fire, and said nothing.

All the world was out of joint with poor Georgie just now ; there was no comfort for her anywhere. Everything was going wrong, with her parents, with Cis, and with herself—they were all at odds together, and there wasn't even the hunting to fall back upon, she reflected dismally !

A few days later Mrs. Travers and Mary went away together for a visit to an uncle in Devonshire, and the Squire was left with Georgie and the two little girls.

The weather was still frosty, and the old man still grumbled ; but things were rather better between the father and daughter ; the smaller-sized party, and the absence of the mother, who was always a firebrand in the family and never a peacemaker, made the home circle brighter and happier. During the last three

days of that long frost Georgie was almost the gay light-hearted
Georgie of old days; afterwards, when what was to come
was all over, it comforted the Squire to think that it had been
so.

It was during these three days that Georgie told her father
that she thought Juliet Blair was beginning to regret having sent
Cis away.

'No! do you really think so?' he said, quite eagerly; for this
was a scheme very near to his heart.

'I do indeed, papa; for I never saw anyone so altered
as Juliet is—she looks so ill and out of spirits; and the other
day, when I was lunching with her, she hardly spoke and ate
nothing. She is evidently very far from happy.'

It was strange that Georgie never once connected the sudden
departure of Colonel Fleming with Juliet's altered looks and spirits.
But the Travers family had so long considered Cis as her lover that
it did not readily occur to any of them that he might possibly have
a rival.

'Well, that would be good news, indeed,' said the Squire.
'Shall I write to him to come home?'

'Well, no—not yet. If she is coming round to him, it will be
because she misses him; and his absence is doing him more good
than his being here could do;—she asked after him, and seemed
pleased to hear about him.'

'I'm sure I'm glad to hear it. She's a nice girl; it would
be a great comfort to me if Cis married her. She would improve
him wonderfully; perhaps, too, she might make him keep on the
hounds when I am gone—she could do it, if anyone could,' added
the old man, with a half sigh.

'We won't think of that yet, papa dear,' said Georgie, coming
round behind him, and kissing the top of his bald head fondly as
she used to do in old days. 'I hope you will keep them yourself
for many a long year.'

The Squire pressed his daughter's hand for a minute, and
then dropped it hurriedly, as if ashamed of his unwonted
tenderness.

Like most male Britons past middle life, he was not prone to
give way to emotion; the only exhibition of feeling he indulged in
was that of anger. As for love and sympathy and religion and so
forth, the Squire would have said that they formed a part, no doubt,
of every Christian's nature; but he considered it unmanly, un-
English, and almost indecorous to speak of such things, or to give
any outward signs of their existence.

So when his darling child, with a little effusion of repentant affection, made her little loving speech and kissed him, he just pressed her hand for an instant, and then hastened to change the subject to safer grounds.

'Ahem! yes, my dear,' he coughed nervously; 'that puppy is growing very leggy; that wasn't half such a good litter as the last that Jenny had—nothing like.'

Georgie dragged up the puppy on to her lap by the scruff of his neck, with all his big weak-looking paws hanging feebly out in front of him, and a general depressed appearance, as if he expected shortly to be beaten, whilst his chances of beauty and usefulness were discussed.

And old Chanticleer, half jealous, half confiding, rested his grey nose and one heavy paw on his young mistress's knee, and blinked up lovingly at her with his one solemn brown eye.

Altogether it was an evening like old times that the two spent together in the dingy, cosy, little smoking den.

The next morning the wind had gone round to the south-west, and the frost was giving in every direction.

'Hurrah!' shouted the Squire, as he bounced into the breakfast-room, with the energy of a schoolboy. 'Hurrah! we shall hunt to-morrow if this goes on!

'Hurrah!' echoed Flora, who always made a noise at the smallest pretext for doing so, jumping round the room, and clapping her hands, till her father started off and chased her round the table.

And what a commotion there was all day!—the grooms and the whips rushing into the house for orders; the Squire giving contradictory directions every hour according to the aspect of the sky; messages going up to the kennels, messages to the stables, and post-cards to be written to every member of the hunt in the county.

Georgie had her hands pretty full.

About five o'clock in the afternoon a steady rain came on, which satisfactorily settled the question of the departure of the frost.

'I have told Davis to bring the mare round for you in the morning,' said the Squire to his daughter, coming in dripping wet from his last stable excursion, and taking off his shining macintosh in the hall—'she is all right again now, and it would do her good to be out.'

'She will be very fresh,' said Georgie dubiously. 'I would rather ride the chestnut.'

'What does being fresh matter? I have settled for you to ride her—don't let me hear any more nonsense about it. Have you written all those post-cards ?   Well, then, I want a stitch put into that thick white scarf; it works up at the back.   Go and fetch it, there's a good girl, and I will show you what it wants.'

And Georgie obeyed in silence.

The morning broke calm and mild and grey.   Georgie sprang from her bed, and peeped out from behind her window-blind at a green wet world, patches of water lying in the grassy hollows, and drops of moisture clinging on to every leafless branch in the garden.   No frost, at all events.

When she was nearly dressed, she drew aside the curtains, threw up the sash, and leant out of the window.

There was a sort of grey distinctness over the face of the earth.

The hills on the further side of the valley looked near and green ; every tree upon them stood out 'clearly against the sky ; the leafless woods were purple blue; not a breath was stirring—not a sound was heard ; only the chirrup of a robin, hopping about on the garden path beneath the window, and the distant tinkle of a sheep bell from the penned-up flock in the field below.

There was something depressing, almost solemn, in the leaden sky and chill green earth.

A heap of fresh-turned mould lay in the flower-bed beneath. The gardeners had been uprooting an evergreen killed by the frost; the brown earth lay wet and heavy by the side of the gaping trench, and the robin, lured there probably by hopes of fresh worms turned up with the soil, hopped lustily down into the dark-looking hole.

Georgie watched the bird idly, and then, with a little shudder, the thought flashed across her—

' How horrible it must be to be buried ! how wet and cold the earth looks ! '

And she turned hastily from the window.

'A letter for you, miss,' said the little housemaid who waited upon her, standing behind her as she turned round.

Georgie flushed crimson, for the letter was in Wattie Ellison's handwriting.

She tore open the envelope nervously, and read—

My dearest Georgie,—You know very well that no ordinary cause would make me risk your father's displeasure, by writing to you against his orders ; but what I have to say concerns him as well as yourself, and if you see fit you will no doubt show him this letter.   It is about your brown mare.   I have just seen a man who knew all about her down in Warwickshire.   He says she is a runaway, and not safe for any lady to ride.   She killed the man who last had her, by bolting with him into a wood, where his head was smashed against the branch of a tree, and that is why your father got her so cheap. Do tell him this, and I am sure he will agree with me that you must not ride her. I *entreat* you not to do so; if anything happened, he would never forgive himself. I must not write more to you—much as I long to.

Yours always devotedly,
Wattie Ellison.

Dressed in her habit, and holding this letter in her hand, Georgie came into the room where her father was already at breakfast.

'Papa, I have had a letter from Wattie.'

'What!' thundered the Squire, and the piece of bacon half-way to his mouth dropped off his fork back upon his plate. 'Georgie, how dare you?' and his face turned as red as his hunting coat.

'Well, papa, here is the letter; he wishes you to read it, and so do I—you will see that it is not a love-letter!' she added, with a little smile.

Her father took the letter from her hand and walked to the window with it, turning his back upon her as he read it.

And then he came back, crushed it up between both his hands, and flung it angrily upon the fire.

'It's all a d—d lie!' he said furiously.

'Papa!' cried the girl, in dismay, 'what can you mean? You don't suppose that Wattie——'

'Hold your tongue with your Wattie!' he answered savagely; 'don't you suppose I know what my daughter ought or ought not to ride, without being dictated to by an infernal young scoundrel who only wants to set her against her father?'

'O papa! that's not true—he never would do that; and if the mare isn't safe——'

'The mare *is* safe, I tell you!' shouted the old man; 'and if you don't ride her, you shall not ride at all—there!'

'But, papa——' began the girl.

'Hold your tongue; if you are too great a coward to ride, say so, and stop at home.'

Georgie turned very white, and set her lips hard.

'I am no coward, as you know,' she said, below her breath, and then sat down and poured herself out a cup of tea with a trembling hand, and began nibbling a bit of dry toast.

No more was said.

The horses came round to the door.

Standing on the doorstep, ready to mount, Georgie turned round and made one last appeal to her father.

'Let me have the chestnut just for to-day, papa,' she said entreatingly.

The Squire buttoned his gloves in silence, with a frown on his brow, before he answered her. The whole thing, he said to himself, was a plant—just a dodge for that good-for-nothing young pauper to set his own daughter against him—if he did not make a stand now at once, there would be no end to this sort of thing.

'Let me have the chestnut,' pleaded Georgie once more. He looked at her for one minute angrily, and then said shortly, 'No!'

Georgie put her hand on the pommel and her foot in Davis's outstretched hand, and vaulted lightly on to the brown mare's back.

'You see she goes quietly enough,' said her father, when they had gone for some little way along the road, and the mare had shown no signs of misbehaviour.

'We are not off yet!' answered Georgie, with a smile. And then she made an effort to talk about the weather and the state of the ground, as if nothing untoward had passed between them.

She shook off her vague apprehensions, which, after all, did not amount to nervousness, and with the fresh air and the pleasant exercise her spirits came back and her vexation wore off.

She was too good a horsewoman to be in reality in the least afraid. If it had not been her lover who had warned her, she would probably have laughed at the warning she had received. After all, thought Georgie, rousing herself from her depression with an effort, with such good nerve and such a firm seat as she had, and so accustomed as she was to ride every sort of animal, there could not be much risk for her, whatever bad qualities her horse might have.

By the time they had reached the 'King's Head,' a wayside public-house where the meet was to be held, she was too busy greeting friends, congratulating everybody on the thaw, discussing the chance of foxes, and the possibilities of a run, to think very much of Wattie's letter and its warning.

Juliet Blair was not out—a fact which Georgie was sorry for, as she had not seen her for some days; but there were plenty of men to crowd round and talk to her, for her well-known splendid riding secured her many admirers in the hunting-field.

There were no carriages full of ladies and no dawdling at the meet on this occasion—strict business was attended to.

The covert was drawn, a fox soon found, and then—off and away!

The brown mare behaved well during the early part of the day. True, she was somewhat fresh and excitable; she kicked at starting, refused once or twice, and bucked in a manner which would have unseated a less perfect rider; but, on the whole, she was not at all unmanageable in Georgie's strong little hands.

The afternoon was drawing in when, just as the Squire was thinking of bringing the day's sport to a close, a fresh fox was started, and the hounds set off at a good pace straight in the direction of Sotherne Court.

The Squire and Sir George Ellison were riding side by side well in front; only seven of the field were left, following close on the hounds, when straight in front of them, crossing their line at right angles, with her head well down and her tail up, shot the brown mare at a terrific pace, Georgie, with teeth set, sitting like a rock, but having evidently lost all control over her.

'All right!' she shouted back, as she passed, turning her head for one instant in the direction of her father.

'That mare has bolted with your daughter, Travers,' said Sir George.

'She's all right—she knows what to do,' said the Squire, looking after her a little anxiously, but keeping on his own way after the hounds.

And a momentary wish passed through his mind that Wattie Ellison were there to go and see after her.

A groom with a second horse was following a little way behind. The Squire turned round, and waved his arm to the man to follow after his daughter.

When they got over the fence into the next field, the Squire craned his neck forwards, and saw his daughter's slight figure, two fields off, being carried away in the opposite direction.

'She'll go along Dallerton Bottom,' said he to his companion.

'Dallerton Bottom!' repeated Sir George, and reined up his horse with a sudden jerk that sent him on to his haunches.

The Squire stopped too, with a bewildered face. 'What?' he said, in a puzzled way; and then suddenly he struck his hand to his forehead and cried out wildly,

'Good God! the gravel-pits!'

Not a word more passed between them. With one accord they turned their horses' heads, and pressed madly, eagerly forwards in the direction in which the brown mare had now utterly disappeared in the gathering twilight.

Fainter and fainter waxed the sounds of the hunt—faster and faster flew the grey hedges, and the shadowy woods, and the flat, even-coloured fields as they sped by them; but urge on their steeds and strain their eyes as they would, still there was no sign, no sound of her they sought!

And when at last, frantic with an unspoken fear, they flung

themselves from their horses and rushed in an agony of terror to gaze down over the yawning edge of the long row of disused gravel-pits that stretched half across the sheep-dotted meadow—what was it that they saw?

Down at the bottom a dark writhing object, but dimly seen through the gloom of evening—the brown mare in her dying struggles.

And close beside, a small figure crushed and crumpled up face downwards upon the dark damp earth—and quite motionless.

CHAPTER XV.

THE SHADOW OF DEATH.

JULIET BLAIR was sitting alone in the gloom of the twilight with her face pressed against the window, her eyes fixed on the damp shadowy garden without, and her thoughts very far away.

She was thinking of Hugh Fleming. Alas! when was she not thinking of him now? She was thinking that every minute she lived, and every breath she drew, were carrying him farther and farther away from her, more hopelessly out of her life; and, as she thought, slow miserable tears welled slowly up into her dark eyes, and dropped down unheeded upon her lap, heavily one after the other, like thunder drops in summer.

And then she thought of that other girl whom he had left alone behind, when he had gone out to India once before—only she had been left in her grave.

'Would God I too had been left there!' she cried bitterly to herself.

How much happier that dead girl had been than she was! To her had come no doubts, no spurned, crushed feelings, no agonies of hopeless separation; up to the last she had known no shadow over her love, no uncertainties in her glad young hopes. Her death must have been so sudden, so instantaneous, that probably she had been spared every pang of terror, every pain of parting; and yet, for hundreds who would pity poor dead Annie Chalmers, not one probably would pity the rich, handsome Juliet Blair, whose life was before her, whose world was her own, and whose heart was dead!

The garden into which she stared with blinded hopeless eyes, that saw not the objects on which they rested, grew greyer and dimmer. One by one the more distant trees and shrubs on the lawn sank away in the blackness of the coming night, and the bare bushes in the rose garden, lit up faintly by the fire-light from the room, gleamed weirdly out, like the gaunt tree shadows in Gustave Doré's pictures, against the dark background beyond.

And as Juliet rose from the window, with a little shiver at the dreary prospect, there came the sound of horses' hoofs clattering at full gallop up the drive to the front door, and, with a loud clanging peal, the hall bell was violently rung.

With a thrill of unaccountable apprehension, she threw open the door into the hall and listened, and at the same time Mrs. Blair, appearing on the staircase, called out nervously to her,

'What is it?'

The men servants had already gone to the door, and in another instant old Higgs came hurriedly back across the hall to find his mistress. She made a step forward to meet him.

'Who is it, Higgs?'

'It's Sir George Ellison's groom, miss; and oh, miss, he says there has been an accident!'

'An accident!' cried Miss Blair falteringly, whilst her step-mother ran hastily downstairs to hear. 'Who is hurt, Higgs? is it Sir George?'

'Oh no, miss—it is poor Miss Travers; and it was close by, in the field just below the village, that it happened, and so they are bringing her here, poor young lady!'

Juliet uttered one cry of dismay, and then her presence of mind came back to her. Without a moment's hesitation she went out to the door, and ordered the groom to ride off with the utmost speed to the town to summon Dr. Ramsden; then she sent for Mrs. Pearse the housekeeper; and a room on the ground-floor, which was occasionally used as a bachelor's bedroom, was hastily got ready, Juliet running about and helping the maids, and superintending every arrangement herself, with blanched cheeks and a beating heart.

She did not dare to think in what condition her poor little friend would be brought to her house. She had just gathered from the groom that Georgie was not killed; but she knew well that she must be very much hurt, as much by the man's frightened face as by his saying that they were carrying her up to the house on a hurdle.

Meanwhile Mrs. Blair sat uselessly trembling and wringing her hands on the lowest step of the stairs, with Ernestine standing over her, plying her with sal volatile and smelling-salts.

It made Juliet angry to see them there. She stopped for one moment as she sped past them with her arms full of pillows, and said impatiently,

'If your mistress is ill, Ernestine, take her upstairs at once

into her own room, and wait upon her there. You are very much
in the way where you are; I cannot have any faintings and
hysterics going on;' and she passed on.

'Ah, you have no heart, Juliet,' whimpered Mrs. Blair, affectedly; 'nothing seems to upset you. My nerves are so shaken
by this dreadful—dreadful——'

'Come into your room, madame,' interrupted Ernestine, thinking it wise to take Miss Blair's hint; 'it would be terrible for you
to be here when the poor demoiselle arrives.'

'Oh no—no! I couldn't see her!' cried her mistress, clinging
hysterically to her; 'take me away!'

And Ernestine did take her away safely up to her own bedroom,
where in time a strong cup of tea and a couple of nice hot buttered
muffins effectually restored her equanimity.

And presently they brought her into the house. From the
mist and darkness of the winter evening, into the light and warmth
and sweet scents of exotic plants in the hall, came the hurdle, with
its living, suffering freight, slowly, carefully carried between two
men. Close behind, with a white, scared face and chattering
teeth, half dragged along, half supported by Sir George Ellison's
strong arm, tottering and stumbling at every step, and staring
in front of him with fixed crazy-looking eyes, came Squire
Travers. Three or four gentlemen, with frightened awe-struck
faces, followed them, to see if they could be of any use.

And thus it was that Georgie Travers was borne over that doorway through which she had so often passed before—sometimes
tripping in lightly in her habit, jumping up the stone steps two at
a time; sometimes more soberly following in the wake of her
parents, in all the sheen of her silken evening garments; sometimes with soft laughter, if she came in with others; or sometimes whistling a merry little tune below her breath, if she came
in alone.

Often and often had she come up those steps and entered that
hall before, but never as she comes in now.

Georgie lies stretched flat out on the hurdle, half covered by
her father's scarlet hunting-coat. She is not unconscious; her
eyes, big and blue, are very wide open, and on her deathly white
face there are nevertheless two crimson fever patches, one on either
cheek—for they had poured half a flask of brandy down her throat
when they first found her.

As she catches sight of Juliet coming to meet her, she
begins to speak, weakly, wanderingly, with fever-stricken rapidity.

'Oh, is that you, Juliet? I can't think what they are bringing
me here for. I am not hurt badly, you know—only bruised

and stiff. Do tell papa I am not hurt. I know I could walk if they would let me try. I can't be hurt, you know, because I don't feel any pain to speak of—only so stiff. I'm just bruised and shaken a bit. If I could have got the mare's head round in time!—but I am not hurt, Juliet; do tell papa I am not hurt.'

And then they got her into the bedroom that was prepared for her; but when they lifted her off the hurdle on to the bed, she fainted dead away.

After a very little while Dr. Ramsden came dashing up to the door in his dogcart, and putting everyone out of the room save Mrs. Pearse, who was a useful sensible woman, and had been accustomed to illness, he proceeded to examine his patient.

Sir George Ellison, and the one or two friends who lingered hoping to hear a favourable account, waited in the dining-room, where Higgs, mindful even in the midst of the general confusion of the traditional hospitality of Sotherne Court, brought forth the best sherry and a round of cold beef, and pressed the downcast guests to allay the pangs of hunger and thirst.

Juliet took the Squire into her own little morning-room. There, with her own hands, firm but gentle, she fetched him a glass of wine, and cut him a tiny sandwich; and though at first he shook his head, somehow she persuaded him to take them.

'You must keep up your strength, dear Mr. Travers, for her sake,' she whispered; and the Squire obeyed her, and took the much-needed refreshment from her hands like a child.

'She will die—I know she will die!' he said, looking up piteously at her with his horror-stricken eyes.

'Oh no, don't say that! wait to see what Dr. Ramsden thinks,' she said soothingly. 'She said herself she was not in pain.'

'If you had seen her at first,' he said, with a shudder; 'and the height it was!—thirty feet at the least; and the mare—curse her!—was killed. And it is all my fault too—I made her ride the brute!' And then he laid his head down on the table in front of him, and groaned aloud. And so they waited.

Would the doctor never come out of the sick-room? At most it was only twenty minutes, and yet never did twenty minutes pass so slowly!

The old man sat quite still in front of the table, with his head bowed down on his arms; and Juliet stood by him, now and then stroking the poor grey head softly with her gentle hand, or stooping down to whisper something—some soothing, loving word, some fragment of a prayer, or some pitiful, helpful text from the Bible—anything that came into her head. Heaven knows if it did him any good, or even if he heard it—probably not; yet, in a dim, vague way, it gave him patience, and helped him over the agonising suspense of those awful twenty minutes.

And then Dr. Ramsden came in.

He was a grey-haired man, with keen, clever dark eyes and a kindly expression. He had known Georgie Travers from her childhood. What he had to say of her was certainly very grievous to him, more especially when the hard words must be said to an old friend like the Squire.

'I have made her a little more comfortable. I trust she will sleep,' he began nervously.

'Tell me the truth, Ramsden,' said the Squire; 'I had rather know the worst at once.'

'I am afraid, my dear friend, that the truth is the worst—the very worst!' he answered, in a very low voice.

'You mean, she must die?'

And the doctor nodded.

The old man staggered back with a groan, and leant against the wall with his face in his hands; but Juliet burst forth impetuously,

'It is impossible—quite impossible, at her age, and with her strong constitution. I will not believe it! We must send to London. I will telegraph at once. Tell me whom to send for, Dr. Ramsden—any one you like; but more advice we must have, and the very best that can be got.'

'My dear young lady,' said the Doctor laying his hand on her arm to detain her, for she had already gone to the door, 'you may send for every doctor in London, but they could not save her. It is a perfectly hopeless case—her spine is dislocated!'

And then Juliet, too, fell back in despair.

'You had better go to her, Mr. Travers,' said Dr. Ramsden, turning to the old man; 'she was asking for you; and had you not better send for Mrs. Travers?'

'Yes—yes, of course. Juliet, you will see to that, won't you?' said the Squire, rousing himself; and then he added in a frightened whisper, 'she is away from home, a long way off. Will there be time, do you think?'

'Yes; she may last about twenty-four hours. We must be very thankful that she is in no pain; and I don't think she will suffer much. She is perfectly conscious, only a little light-headed at intervals, from feverishness.'

All night long Juliet and the Squire sat by Georgie's sick-bed, one on each side.

She lay very quiet, wandering a little sometimes, but for the most part dozing uneasily, in short fitful snatches.

But neither of her watchers closed an eye all night.

During the silence of that long vigil, in the gloom of the darkened room, lighted only by the shaded lamp and the faint red flicker of the firelight, there passed through the Squire's mind many sad and bitter reflections.

He saw plainly now how hardly and selfishly he had treated his favourite child, and how gentle and dutiful she had been in her submission to him. With deep self-reproaches, he recalled his obstinacy and bad temper; he remembered how, by calling her a coward, he had goaded her on to ride the brute that had killed her; and ever the words, 'It is my doing—all my doing!' formed the miserable refrain of his thoughts.

When the morning broke, Georgie opened her eyes and spoke.

'Papa!'

'Yes, my darling?'

'I think I am going to die! tell me if I am?'

'Oh, my darling child,' began the Squire in a broken voice; and she interrupted him quickly.

'Never mind, papa. I know it. Poor papa!' and she stroked the grey head that lay bowed down on the bed beside her. 'Poor papa! I am so sorry for you; but you know it was a thing nobody could tell. I never should have believed that I couldn't hold the mare. Don't fret about it; it couldn't be helped. What has become of her?'

'The mare?'

'Yes!'

'She is dead,' answered the Squire, and a strong shudder at the recollection of that awful leap shook the little helpless frame. Presently she spoke again.

'You would not mind my seeing Wattie now—would you, papa?'

'My darling, no. Shall I send for him?'

'Yes; send for him, and for Cis too, at once,' she answered.

Juliet slipped from the room to send off the telegram, and Georgie seemed satisfied and dozed again.

There was a hushed suspense over the whole house. The servants went about on tip-toe; the doors were softly shut; the numberless neighbours who, as soon as day dawned, sent or came themselves to enquire, went round by the back way; not a bell was rung; not a voice was heard above a whisper; for over Sotherne Court hung a deep and awful shadow—the shadow of the angel of death.

(*To be continued.*)

Dr. ROOKE'S ANTI-LANCET.

All who wish to preserve health, and thus prolong life. should read Dr. Rooke's "Anti-Lancet, or Handy Guide to Domestic Medicine," which can be had GRATIS from any Chemist, or POST FREE from Dr. Rooke, Scarborough.

Concerning this book, which contains 168 pages, the late eminent author, Sheridan Knowles, observed:—" *It will be an incalculable boon to every person who can read and think.*"

CROSBY'S BALSAMIC COUGH ELIXIR

Is specially recommended by several eminent Physicians, and by Dr. ROOKE, Scarborough, Author of the "ANTI-LANCET."

It has been used with the most signal success for Asthma, Bronchitis, Consumption, Coughs, Influenza, Consumptive Night Sweats, Spitting of Blood, Shortness of Breath, and all Affections of the Throat and Chest.

Sold in bottles at 1s. 9d., 4s. 6d., and 11s. each, by all respectable Chemists, and Wholesale by JAMES M. CROSBY, Chemist, Scarborough.

☞ Invalids should read Crosby's Prize Treatise on "Diseases of the Lungs and Air-Vessels," a copy of which can be had GRATIS of all Chemists.

MAYFAIR SHERRY
36 per doz. C. WARD & SON, CHAPEL ST WEST MAYFAIR. LONDON. 36 per doz.
MAYFAIR SHERRY

SWANBILL CORSETS.
(REGISTERED.)

SWANBILL CORSET (Registered). 14 bis, B.—A full deep Corset, especially for ladies inclined to *embonpoint*. The Swanbill is most effective in reducing the figure, and keeping the form flat, so as to enable ladies to wear the fashionable *vêtements* of the day; busk 13¾ inches long. Price 14s. 6d. Finest quality, 21s. Scarlet, 15s. 6d.

SWANBILL CORSET (Registered). 51 bis, —Hand-made. Perfect in shape, and producing— even in indifferent figures—that graceful *contour* which is the distinguishing feature of the present style of dress; busk 13 inches long. Price 31s. 6d. Send Size of Waist with P.O. Order to prevent delay and inconvenience.

Mrs. ADDLEY BOURNE, Ladies' Outfitter, &c.,
37 PICCADILLY (opposite St. James's Church); & 76 RUE ST. LAZARE, PARIS.

(Bernard & Co.'s, Leith Distillery, Scotland.)
THE ENCORE WHISKY
(THE DOUBLE DISTILLED).
THE PUREST AND MOST WHOLESOME OF ALL WHISKIES.

Lancet— 'Very *wholesome* and pleasant Whisky.'

British Medical Journal— 'All injurious substances completely removed.'

Medical Times— 'Very *wholesome* and pleasant, and may be safely recommended.'

Medical Press— 'Very pure and wholesome.'

Sanitary Record— 'Deserves a wide-spread reputation.'

Public Health— 'Should be in general use.'

Food and Fuel Reformer— 'All who value their health should use it.'

Professor Tichborne— 'Perfectly free from all impurities.'

Dr. Bartlett— 'Purest Whisky I ever examined.'

Dr. Paul— 'Thoroughly wholesome.'

Dr. Stevenson Macadam— 'Very pure, and exceedingly fine quality.'

Please see that Bernard & Co.'s Labels are on all Bottles. Every Gallon guaranteed the same.

WHOLESALE DEPOT, THREE CROWN SQUARE, BOROUGH. S.E.

MAPLE
& Co.
TOTTENHAM COURT ROAD.
Illustrated Catalogue free.

CARPETS—FURNITURE—BEDDING.

£5. 5s. SILK COSTUMES

Bodice Made. Silk Recommended for Wear.

Plates of Styles and Patterns of Silk Free on Application.

JAMES SPENCE & CO.,
76, 77, 78, & 79
ST. PAUL'S CHURCHYARD.

John Heath's PENS

Over 200 patterns. In 6d., 1s., and 1 Gross Boxes at all Stationers. Selected sample Box, by Post, for 7 or 13 stamps.

BIRMINGHAM.

POSTAL TELEGRAPH PEN

TURNED UP NIB WILL SUIT ALL HANDS.

SIGNAL VICTORY AT YORKSHIRE EXHIBITION.
Awarded the only Medal. All Comers beaten.

TAYLOR'S
PATENT SEWING MACHINES
ARE THE BEST FOR
DRESSMAKING AND FAMILY USE,

being simple to learn, easy to work, quiet in action, not liable to get out of order. Intending purchasers, if unable to obtain Taylor's Patent Sewing Machines from local Dealers, are respectfully requested to send for a prospectus to 97 CHEAPSIDE, LONDON, E.C.

TRADE MARK.

Reckitt's Paris Blue

Possesses the following advantages;—

1st.—Great Strength.
2nd.—Exceeding Beauty of Tint.
3rd.—Great Economy in use.
4th.—It cannot rot or injure the linen.

IN SQUARES.

Patronised by the Laundresses of the Princess of Wales and Duchess of Edinburgh.
To be had of all respectable Grocers, Oilmen and Druggists.

CADBURY'S COCOA ESSENCE

The reason why so many are unable to take Cocoa is, that the varieties commonly sold are mixed with Starch, under the plea of rendering them soluble; while really making them *thick, heavy,* and *indigestible.* This may be easily detected, *for if Cocoa thickens in the cup it proves the addition of starch.* CADBURY'S Cocoa Essence is genuine, it is therefore three times the strength of these Cocoas, and a refreshing Beverage like Tea or Coffee.

PURE, SOLUBLE, REFRESHING

Spottiswoode & Co., Printers, New-street Square, London.

Vol. XXX.

No. 120

BELGRAVIA

A
LONDON MAGAZINE

OCTOBER
1876

CHATTO & WINDUS. PICCADILLY. LONDON.W.

THE GREAT PURIFIER AND RESTORER OF HEALTH.

BOWEN'S ANTISEPTIC TONIC-SALINE

Imparts to the system Nature's great purifier—OZONE, thereby cleansing the blood from all *effete* or poisonous matter, preventing fermentation in the stomach, and ensuring perfect digestion. It is the most efficacious remedy ever discovered for the cure of Indigestion, Bilious and Liver Complaints, Nervousness, Nervous and Bilious Headache, Skin Diseases, Eruptions, Scurvy, Scrofula, and Wasting Diseases; and it makes a pleasant and refreshing drink, which may be taken habitually with meals with the greatest advantage.

The TONIC-SALINE does NOT lower the system like some Natural Mineral Waters, Aerated Waters, Citrate of Magnesia, and Seidlitz Powders; but, on the contrary, it invigorates the Nerves and Muscular System, purifies and enriches the Blood, animates the Spirits and Mental Faculties, and ensures Good Health.

Emigrants and Travellers abroad should always keep a supply, as it is the only true preventative of, and cure for, Fevers, Dysentery, Cholera, Diarrhœa, and Sea Sickness.

CAUTION.—Although there are several preparations similar in appearance to mine, yet they are of an *entirely different composition*. This being the ONLY Saline medicine that does NOT lower the system, it will be found superior to any other for counteracting the depressing effects of hot weather.

Sold at 2s. per Bottle by all Chemists and Medicine Dealers, or sent to any address for 24 Stamps by the Sole Proprietor
J. H. BOWEN, 91 WIGMORE ST., CAVENDISH SQUARE, LONDON, W.

Johnston's

'Quite free from Adulteration.'
—*Lancet.*

Corn Flour

'Is decidedly superior.'
—*Lancet.*

Is the Best.

ROWLANDS'
MACASSAR OIL

Prevents the hair falling off. 3s. 6d., 7s., 10s. 6d. family bottles (equal to four small), and 21s.

ROWLANDS' EUKONIA,

A new and fragrant Toilet Powder for ladies, 3s. per box.

ROWLANDS
ODONTO

Whitens the teeth and prevents their decay, 2s. 9d. per box.

ROWLANDS' KALYDOR

Beautifies the complexion and eradicates cutaneous eruptions, 4s. 6d. per bottle.

Ask any Chemist, Perfumer, or Hairdresser for Rowlands' Articles, and avoid imitations.

KINAHAN'S LL WHISKY

KINAHAN & CO. find that, through the recommendation of the Faculty, the demand for their

CELEBRATED OLD LL WHISKY

for purely medicinal purposes is very great. They think therefore it will interest the Public to read the following EXTRACTS OF THE ANALYSIS of their Whisky from the eminent Analyst, Dr. ARTHUR HILL HASSALL:—"I have very carefully analysed Samples of this well-known and popular Whisky. It is soft and mellow to the taste, aromatic and ethereal to the smell.—The Whisky is pronounced to be pure, well-matured, and of very excellent quality. The Public may feel full confidence in the purity and quality of this Whisky."

20 GREAT TITCHFIELD STREET, OXFORD STREET.

'A WORD FIRST, IF YOU PLEASE, SIR.'

BELGRAVIA.

OCTOBER 1876.

GOOD STORIES OF MAN AND OTHER ANIMALS.

BY CHARLES READE.

6. Reality.

MISS SOPHIA JACKSON, in the State of Illinois, was a beautiful girl, and had a devoted lover, Ephraim Slade, a merchant's clerk. Their attachment was sullenly permitted by Miss Jackson's parents, but not encouraged : they thought she might look higher.

Sophia said, 'Why, la! he was handsome and good, and loved her, and was not that enough?'

They said, 'No; to marry Beauty, a man ought to be rich.'

'Well,' said Sophy, 'he is on the way to it; he is in a merchant's office.'

'It is a long road, for he is only a clerk.'

The above is a fair specimen of the dialogue, and conveys as faint an idea of it as specimens generally do.

All this did not prevent Ephraim and Sophia from spending many happy hours together.

But presently another figure came on the scene—Mr. Jonathan Clarke. He took a fancy to Miss Jackson, and told her parents so, and that she was the wife for him, if she was disengaged. They said, 'Well, now, there was a young clerk after her, but the man was too poor to marry her.'

Now, Mr. Jonathan Clarke was a wealthy speculator; so, on that information, he felt superior, and courted her briskly. She complained to Ephraim. 'The idea of their encouraging that fat fool to think of me!' said she. She called him old, though he was but thirty; and turned his person and sentiments into ridicule, though, in the opinion of sensible people, he was a comely man, full of good sense and sagacity.

Mr. Clarke paid her compliments. Miss Jackson laughed, and reported them to Slade in a way to make him laugh too.

Mr. Clarke asked her to marry him. She said no ; she was too young to think of that. She told Ephraim she had flatly refused him.

Mr. Clarke made her presents. She refused the first, and blushed, but was prevailed on to accept. She accepted the second and the third without first refusing them.

She did not trouble Ephraim Slade with any portion of this detail. She was afraid it might give him pain.

Clarke wooed her so warmly that Ephraim got jealous and unhappy. He remonstrated. Sophia cried, and said it was all her parents' fault—forcing the man upon her.

Clarke was there every day. Ephraim scolded. Sophia was cross. They parted in anger. Sophia went home and snubbed Clarke. Clarke laughed and said, ' Take your time.' He stuck there four hours. She came round, and was very civil.

Matters progressed. Ephraim always unhappy. Clarke always jolly. Parents in the same mind.

Clarke urged her to name the day.

' Never ! '

Urged her again.

' Next year.'

Urged her again before her parents. They put in their word. ' Sophy, don't trifle any longer. You are overdoing it.'

' There, there, do what you like with me,' said the girl ; ' I am miserable ! ' and ran out, crying.

Clarke and parents laughed, and stayed behind, and settled the day.

When Sophy found they had settled the day, she sent for Ephraim, and told him with many tears. ' Oh ! ' said she, ' you little know what I have suffered this six months.'

' My poor girl ! ' said Ephraim. ' Let us elope, and end it.'

' What ! My parents would curse me ! '

' Oh, they would forgive us in time ! '

' Never. You don't know them. No, my poor Ephraim, we are unfortunate. We can never be happy together. We must bow. I should die if this went on much longer.'

' You are a fickle, faithless jade ! ' cried Ephraim in agony.

' God forgive you, dear ! ' said she, and wept silently.

Then he tried to comfort her. Then she put her arm round his neck, and assured him she yielded to constraint, but her heart could never forget him ; she was more unhappy than he, and always should be.

They parted, with many tears on both sides, and she married Clarke. At her earnest request Slade kept away from the ceremony; by that means she was not compelled to wear the air of a victim, but could fling the cloak of illusory happiness and gaiety over her aching heart; and she did it, too. She was as gay a bride as had been seen for some years in those parts.

Ephraim Slade was very unhappy. However, after a bit, he comprehended the character of Sophia Clarke, *née* Jackson, and even imitated her. She had gone in for money, and so did he: only, on the square—a detail she had omitted. Years went on; he became a partner in the house, instead of a clerk. The girls set their caps at him. But he did not marry. Mrs. Clarke observed this, and secretly approved. Say she had married, that was no reason why *he* should. *Justice des femmes!*

Now you will observe that by all the laws of fiction Mrs. Clarke ought to have learned to her cost that money does not bring happiness, and ought to have been miserable, especially whenever she encountered the pale face of him whose love she valued too late.

Well, she broke all those laws, and went in for Life as it is. She was happier than most wives. Her husband was kind, but not doting; a gentle master, but no slave; and she liked it. She had two beautiful children, and they helped fill her life. Her husband's gold smoothed her path, and his manly affection strewed it with flowers. She was not passionately devoted to him, but still, by the very laws of nature, the wife was fonder of Jonathan than the maid had ever been of Ephraim; not but what the latter remaining unmarried tickled her vanity, and so completed her content.

She passed six years in clover, and the clover in full bloom all the time. Nevertheless, gilt happiness is apt to get a rub sooner or later; Clarke had losses one upon another, and at last told her he was done for; he must go back to California and make another fortune. 'Lucky the old folks made me settle a good lump on you,' said he. 'You are all right, and the children.'

Away went stout-hearted Clarke, and left his wife behind. He knew the country, and went at all in the ring, and began to remake money fast.

His letters were not very frequent, nor models of conjugal love, but they had good qualities; one was their contents—a draft on New York.

Some mischievous person reported that he was often seen about with the same lady; but Mrs. Clarke did not believe that, the remittances being regular.

But presently both letters and remittances ceased. Then she believed the worst, and sent a bitter remonstrance.

She received no reply.

Then she wrote a bitterer one, and, for the first time since their union, cast Ephraim Slade in his teeth. 'There he is,' said she, ' unmarried to this day, for my sake.'

No reply even to this.

She went to her parents, and told them how she was used.

They said they had foreseen it—that being a lie some people think it necessary to deliver themselves of before going seriously into any question—and then, after a few pros and cons, they bade her observe that her old lover, Ephraim Slade, was a rich man, a man unmarried evidently for her sake ; and if she was wise, she would look that way, and get rid of a mock husband, who was probably either dead or false, and, in any case, had deserted her.

'But what am I to *do*?' said Mrs. Clarke, affecting not to know what they were driving at.

'Why, sue for a divorce.'

'Divorce Jonathan ! Think of it ! He is the father of my children, and he was a good husband to me all the time he was with me. It is all that nasty California.' And she began to cry.

The old people told her she must take people as they were, not as they had been ; and it was no fault of hers, nor California's, if her husband was a changed man.

In short, they pressed her hard to sue for a divorce, and let Slade know she was going to do it.

But the woman was still handsome and under thirty, and was not without a certain pride and delicacy that grace her sex even when they lack the more solid virtues. 'No,' said she, ' I will never go begging to any man. I'll not let Ephraim Slade think I divorced my husband just to get him. I'll part with Jonathan, since he has parted with me, and after that I will take my chance. Ephraim Slade ? he is not the only man in the world with eyes in his head.'

So she sued for a divorce, and got it quite easy. Divorce is beautifully easy in the West.

When she was free, she had no longer any scruple about Ephraim. He lived at a town seven miles from her. She had a friend in that town. She paid her a visit. She let the other lady into her plans, and secured her co-operation. Mrs. X—— set it abroad that Mrs. Clarke was a widow ; and, from one to another, Ephraim Slade was given to understand that a visit from him would be agreeable.

'Will it ?' said Ephraim. 'Then I'll go.'

He called on her, and was received with a sweet, pensive tenderness. 'Sit down, Ephraim—Mr. Slade,' said she, softly and tremulously, and left the room. She had scarcely cleared it, when he heard her tell the female servant, with a sharp, imperious tone, to admit no other visitors. It did not seem the same voice. She came back to him melodious. 'The sight of you after so many years upset me,' said she. Then, after a pause and a sigh, 'You look well.'

'Oh, yes! I am all right. We are neither of us quite so young as we were, you know.'

'No, indeed' (with another sigh). 'Well, dear friend, I suppose you have heard. I am punished, you see, for my want of courage and fidelity. I have always been punished. But you could not know that. Perhaps, after all, you have been the happier of the two. I am sure I hope you have.'

'Well, I'll tell you, Mrs. Clarke,' said he, in open manly tones. She stopped him. 'Please don't call me Mrs. Clarke, when I have parted with the name for ever.' (*Sotto voce.*) 'Call me Sophia.'

'Well, then, Sophia, I'll tell you the truth. When you jilted me——'

'Oh!'

'And married Cl——who shall I say? Well, then, married *another*, because he had got more money than I had——'

'No, no. Ephraim, it was all my parents. But I will try and bear your reproaches. Go on.'

'Well, then, of course I was awfully cut up. I was wild. I got a six-shooter to kill you and the other.'

'I wish you had,' said she. She didn't wish anything of the kind.

'I am very glad I didn't, then. I dropped the six-shooter, and took to the moping and crying line.'

'Poor Ephraim!'

'Oh, yes! I went through all the changes, and ended as other men do.'

'And how is that?'

'Why, by getting over it.'

'What! you have got over it?'

'Lord, yes! long ago.'

'Oh, in—deed!' said she bitterly. Then with sly incredulity, 'How is it you have never married?'

'Well, I'll tell you. When I found that money was everything with you girls, I calculated to go in for money too. So I speculated, like—the other, and made money. But when I had once begun to taste money-making, somehow I left off troubling about women. And, besides, I know a great many people, and I look coolly on, and what I see in every house has set me against marriage. Most of my married friends envy me, and say so. I don't envy any one of them, and don't pretend to. Marriage! it is a bad institution. You have got clear of it, I hear. All the better for you. I mean to take a shorter road : I won't ever get into it.'

This churl then, who had drowned hot passion in the waves of time, and, instead of nursing a passion for her all his days, had been hugging celibacy as man's choicest treasure, asked her coolly if there was anything he could do for her. Could he be of service in finding out investments, etc., or could he place either of the boys in the road to wealth? Instead of hating these poor children like a man, he seemed all the more inclined to serve them that their absent parent had secured him the sweets of celibacy.

She was bursting with ire, but had the self-restraint to thank him, though very coldly, and to postpone all discussion of that kind to a future time. Then he shook hands with her and left her.

She was wounded to the core. It would have been very hard to wound her heart as deeply as this interview wounded her pride.

She sat down and shed tears of mortification.

She was aroused from that condition by a letter in a well-known hand. She opened it, all in a flutter :

'My dear Sophy,—You are a nice wife, you are! Here I have been slaving my life out for you, and shipwrecked, and nearly dead with a fever, and coming home rich again, and I asked you just to come from Chicago to New York to meet me, that have come all the way from China and San Francisco, and it is too much trouble. Did you ever hear of Lunham's dog that was so lazy he leaned against the wall to bark? It is very disheartening to a poor fellow that has played a man's part for you and the children. Now be a good girl, and meet me at Chicago to-morrow evening at 6 P.M. For if you don't, by thunder! I'll take the children and absquatulate with them to Paris, or somewhere. I find the drafts on New York I sent from China have never been presented. Reckon by that you never got them. Has that raised your dander? Well, it is not my fault ; so put on your bonnet, and come and meet

'Your affectionate husband,

'Jonathan Clarke.

' I sent my first letter to your father's house. I send this to your friend, Mrs. X——.'

Mrs. Clarke read this in such a tumult of emotions that her

mind could not settle a moment on one thing. But when she had read it, the blood in her beating veins began to run cold.

What on earth should she do? fall to the ground between two stools? No; that was a man's trick, and she was a woman, every inch.

She had not any time to lose, so she came to a rapid conclusion. Her acts will explain better than comments. She dressed, packed up one box, drove to the branch station, and got to Chicago. She bought an exquisite bonnet, took private apartments at a hotel, and employed an intelligent person to wait for her husband at the station, and call out his name, and give him a card, on which was written—

'*Mrs. Jonathan Clarke,*
At the X—— Hotel.'

This done, she gave her mind entirely to the decoration of her person.

The ancients, when they had done anything wrong, and wanted to be forgiven, used to approach their judges with dishevelled hair and shabby clothes—*sordidis vestibus.*

This poor, shallow woman, unenlightened by the wisdom of the ancients, thought the nicer a woman looked, the likelier a man would be to forgive her, no matter what. So she put on her best silk dress, and her new French hat bought on purpose, and made her hair very neat, and gave her face a wash and a rub that added colour. She did not rouge, because she calculated she should have to cry before the end of the play, and crying hard over rouge makes channels.

When she was as nice as could be, she sat down to wait for her *divorcé*; she might be compared to a fair spider which has spread her web to catch a wasp, but is sorely afraid that, when he does come, he will dash it all to ribbons.

The time came and passed. An expected character is always as slow to come as a watched pot to boil.

At last there was a murmur on the stairs; then a loud, hearty voice; then a blow at the door—you could not call it a tap—and in burst Jonathan Clarke, brown as a berry, beard a foot long, genial and loud, open heart, Californian manners.

At sight of her he gave a hearty 'Ah!' and came at her with a rush to clasp her to his manly bosom, and knocked over a little cane chair gilt.

The lady, quaking internally, and trembling from head to foot, received him like the awful Siddons, with one hand nobly extended, forbidding his profane advance. 'A word first, if you please, sir.'

Then Clarke stood transfixed, with one foot advanced, and his arms in the air, like Ixion, when Juno turned cloud.

'You have ordered me to come here, sir, and you have no longer any right to order me : but I am come, you see, to tell you my mind. What! do you really think a wife is to be deserted and abandoned, most likely for some other woman, and then be whistled back into her place like a dog! No man shall use *me* so!'

'Why, what is the row? has a mad dog bitten you, ye cantankerous critter?'

'Not a letter for ten months, that is the matter!' cried Mrs. Clarke, loud and aggressive.

'That is not my fault. I wrote three from China, and sent you two drafts on New York.'

'It is easy to say so : I don't believe it.' (Louder and aggressiver.)

Clarke (*bawling in his turn*). 'I don't care whether you believe it or not. Nobody but you calls Jony Clarke a liar.'

Mrs. Clarke (*competing in violence*). 'I believe one thing, that you were seen all about San Francisco with a lady. 'Twas to her you directed my letters and drafts : that is how I lost them. It is always the husband that is in fault, and not the post.' (Very amicably all of a sudden :) 'How long were you in California after you came back from China?'

'Two months.'

'How often did you write in that time?' (Sharply.)

'Well, you see, I was always expecting to start for home.'

'You never wrote once.' (Very loud.)

'That was the reason.'

'That and the lady.' (Screaming aloud.)

'Stuff! Give me a kiss, and no more nonsense.'

(Solemnly :) 'That I shall never do again. Husbands must be taught not to trifle with their wives' affections in this cruel way.' (Tenderly :) 'Oh, Jonathan, how could you abandon me? What could you expect? I am not old, I am not ugly.'

'D——n it all, if you have been playing any games!'—and he felt at the back of his neck for a bowie-knife.—Californian instincts!

'Sir!' said the lady in an awful tone, that subjugated the monster directly.

'Well, then,' said he sullenly, 'don't talk nonsense. Please remember we are man and wife.'

Mrs. Clarke (*very gravely*). 'Jonathan, we are not!'

'Damnation! what do you mean?'

'If you are going into a passion, I won't tell you anything; I hate to be frightened. What language the man has picked up—in California!'

'Well, that's neither here nor there. You go on.'

'Well, Jonathan, you know I have always been under the influence of my parents. It was at their wish I married you.'

'That is not what you told me at the time.'

'Oh, yes, I did! only you have forgotten. Well, when no word came from you for so many months, my parents were indignant, and they worked upon me so and pestered me so—that—Jonathan, we are divorced.'

The actress thought this was a good point to cry at, and cried accordingly.

Jonathan started at the announcement, swore a heartful, and then walked the room in rage and bitterness. 'So, then,' said he, 'you leave the woman you love, and the children whose smiles are your heaven; you lead the life of a dog for them, and when you come back, by God, the wife of your bosom has divorced you, just because a letter or two miscarried! That outweighs all you have done and suffered for her. Oh! you are crying, are you? What! you have given up facing it out, and laying the blame on me, have you?'

'Yes, dear; I find you were not to blame: it was—my parents.'

'Your parents! Why, you are not a child, are you? You are the parent of my children, you little idiot: have you forgotten that?'

'No. Oh! oh! oh! I have acted hastily, and very, very wrong.'

'Come, that is a good deal for a pretty woman to own. There, dry your eyes, and let us order dinner.'

'What, dine with *you*?'

'Why, d—n it, it is not the first time by a few thousand.'

'La, Jonathan, I *should* like ; but I *mustn't*.'

'Why not?'

'I should be compromised.'

'What, with me?'

'Yes; with any gentleman. Do try and realise the situation, dear. *I am a single woman.*'

Good Mr. Clarke—from California—delivered a string of curses so rapidly that they all ran into what Sir Walter calls a 'clishma-claver,' even as when the ringers clash and jangle the church bells.

Mrs. Clarke gave him time; but as soon as he was in a state to listen quietly, compelled him to realise *her* situation. 'You see,' said she, 'I am obliged to be very particular now. Delicacy demands it. You remember poor Ephraim Slade?'

'Your old sweetheart. Confound him! has he been after you again?'

'Why, Jonathan, ask yourself. He has remained unmarried ever since; and when he heard I was free, of course he entertained hopes; but I kept him at a distance; and so (tenderly and regretfully) I must you. *I am a single woman.*'

'Look me in the face, Sophy. You won't dine with me?'

'I'd give the world; but I *mustn't*, dear.'

'Not if I twist your neck round—darling—if you don't?'

'No, dear. You shall kill me, if you please. But I am a respectable woman, and I will not brave the world. But I know I have acted rashly, foolishly, ungratefully, and deserve to be killed. KILL ME, DEAR—you'll forgive me then.' With that, she knelt down at his feet, crossed her hands over his knees, and looked up sweetly in his face with brimming eyes, waiting, yea, even requesting, to be killed.

He looked at her with glistening eyes. 'You cunning hussy!' said he; 'you know I would not hurt a hair of your head! What is to be done? I tell you what it is, Sophy; I have lived three years without a wife, and that is enough. I won't live any longer so—no, not a day. It shall be you, or somebody else. Ah! what is that?—a bell. I'll ring, and order one. I've got lots of money. They are always to be had for that, you know.'

'Oh, Jonathan! don't talk so. It is scandalous. How can you get a wife all in a minute—by ringing?'

'If I can't, then the town crier can. I'll hire him.'

'For shame!'

'How is it to be, then? You that are so smart in dividing couples, you don't seem to be very clever in bringing 'em together again.'

'It was my parents, Jonathan, not me. Well, dear, I always think when people are in a difficulty, the best thing is to go to some very *good* person for advice. Now, the best people are the clergymen. There is one in this street, No. 18. Perhaps he could advise us.'

Jonathan listened gravely for a little while, before he saw what she was at; but, the moment he caught the idea so slily conveyed, he slapped his thigh and shouted out, 'You are a sensible girl. Come on.' And he almost dragged her to the clergyman. Not but what he found time to order a good dinner in the hall as they went.

The clergyman was out, but soon found : he remarried them, and they dined together man and wife.

They never mentioned grievances that night; and Jonathan said, afterwards, his second bridal was worth a dozen of his first ; for the first time she was a child, and had to be courted up hill ; but the second time she was a woman, and knew what to say to a fellow.

Next day Mr. and Mrs. Clarke went over to ——. They drove about in an open carriage for some hours, and did a heap of shopping. They passed by Ephraim Slade's place of business much oftener than there was any need, and slower. It was Mrs. Clarke who drove. Jonathan sat and took it easy.

She drives to this day.

And Jonathan takes it easy.

Echoes.

THE blithesome shepherd sings
 His artless songs,
And Echo's wandering voice
 The notes prolongs.
A maiden's eye strikes mine,
 My cheeks flush red,
And, like a flower oppressed,
 She droops her head.

I love the mystic voice
 That back again
Returns in purer tones
 The shepherd's strain.
I love the maid whose soul,
 Reflecting mine,
Would speak its kindling thoughts
 In looks divine.

Beau Feilding at the Old Bailey.

A CHAPTER OF MANNERS.

BY GEORGE AUGUSTUS SALA.

BETWEEN Truth and Falsehood, Thales of Miletus is said to have said—for all his words are lost, and even Mr. G. H. Lewes, to whom no science is a mystery, and who has written the lives of all the philosophers from Thales to Comte, can only quote the Milesian at second hand—there is the same difference as that which exists between the Eyes and the Ears. *Cœteris paribus*, it may be observed that between the history of a given epoch, and the authorised report of a trial at law relating to that epoch, there is as much difference as there is between Hearing and Seeing. It is for this reason that (being no judge of literary style, and feeling anxious only to arrive at a knowledge of veritable things) I continue to prefer Howell's 'State Trials' and the 'Old Bailey Sessions Papers' to Hume, Smollett, Lyttelton, Rapin, Tindal, Macaulay, Lingard, Froude, and Mrs. Markham. Let those who will read 'Little Arthur's History of England:' I would rather pin my faith to the Police Reports. I respect the scholars who can take delight in the weird legends of the 'Nibelungen-Lied' and the exquisite fancies of the 'Faerie Queene;' but give me the 'Gazette des Tribunaux.' An exemplary student in the compartment next to mine in the British Museum reading-room has just made out a ticket for a rare edition of the 'Romaunt of the Rose;' but I have made bold to trouble the courteous assistant for the 'Causes Célèbres,' in forty volumes small octavo.

The men and women who rise up before you—no pale, misty phantoms, but solid, breathing, vascular beings, so they seem, coming out of their shrouds of worm-eaten, type-indented paper—prevaricate and dissemble, equivocate and lie, in the witness-box, in the dock, or at the advocate's table, just as witnesses and prisoners and counsel fence and fib at this instant day; but, next to the revelation of the truth, there is nothing so edifying as the manifestation of palpable falsehood; and a convicted liar is, from many points of view, an interesting and instructive spectacle. You 'get at' humanity, as the saying is, in the 'Sessions Papers.'

No flowery, no malevolent, and no milk-and-water historian thrusts himself forward with his rose-tinted, his yellow-jaundice-smirched, or his eclipse-smoked glasses to impede your view of *Homo* yonder — of yourself, O my Uncle—testifying to that which is clearly as false as Michelet's story of Joan of Arc, but very often breaking down to exhibit all the meanness and wickedness, all the lust and avarice, the cowardice and cruelty that are within the testifier. Or, if there be an upright man and pure either on the bench or behind the spikes of the clock, he is lustrous very brightly and clearly indeed in the report of a trial at the Old Bailey. In that unadorned reproduction of the Talk of human animals, you have, almost, a mirror without a flaw. Such is not the case with Parliamentary reports : the gentlemen in the gallery strive to do their work honestly, but, whether they be conscious of it or not, it is contemporary history which they write, and the particulars of history are never trustworthy. The reporters are fain to condense, and occasionally to slur, our speeches, to bring the great Panjandrums of politics to the front, while the poor little *Dii minores* from Scotch burghs and elsewhere are left to shiver in the background far away from the cheery radiance of the footlights. Parliamentary reporters, too, are fain to dress up ungrammatical verbiage in grammatical garb ; coughing, stammering, and ' trying back ' are suppressed; the honourable gentleman who asserts that the population of Huntingdonshire is four hundred millions, that Cape Breton is an arm of the sea, or that Charlemagne flourished 800 B.C., is silently corrected. In a word, the reporters do their best to avoid writing down Sir John Falstaff, M.P. for Berks, an ass ; but when that estimable county member says a witty thing, they polish and point the *bon mot* that it may read the wittier. This is history-writing, but it is not truth-telling. Truth is naked, and in my opinion she is to be found oftenest in her most edifying undress in the ' Newgate Calendar.'

I have been led to the conclusions hereinabove expressed through some diligent researches which I have been making lately into the habits and manners of the curious excrescences of bygone society who were known as Beaux, Sparks, Fops, Macaronis, Bucks, Bloods, and what not : painted butterflies which, with corking pins transfixing their poor little shrivelled carcasses, are yet discoverable, all faded and dusty, in out-of-the-way glass cases of which only bookworms have the keys. History, naturally (in her purblind, conceited way), ignores the Beaux altogether, although they played often a very prominent part in the transactions of their time ; and even Macaulay, the strong-beaked, strong-taloned eagle who, when he could not light upon a lamb to carry to his eyrie, did not disdain, time and again, to swoop down on such very small deer as conies or field mice, has not much more to say about the most notable Beau of the seventeenth century (and the early part of the eighteenth) than that he was a worthless fop, married to a duchess who was a great-grandmother. The Beau in question was the notorious Robert Feilding, commonly called the ' Major-General ; ' and it appears to me that he was something, and a great deal, more than a fop.   The best evidence in the world—that of the Central Criminal Court—shows him to have been an amazing ruffian, hypocrite, and villain; and it is in those aspects that, with a pile of musty folios and dog's-eared pamphlets around me, I am looking admiringly at Beau Feilding holding up his rascally hand at the Old Bailey, as the Clerk of the Arraigns asks him how he will be tried.   Come along and be tried by the light of the ' Sessions Papers,' thou bigamous Beau.

There is no authentic portrait of the Beau extant that I am aware of ; although he seems to have been handsome enough, and at times to have had money (or the money of other people) enough to have sat to Lely or Kneller (the Beau's life was a long one), or at least to Michael Wright, or Edward Ashfield, or Gerard Zoust.   An elaborate pen-and-ink presentment of Feilding has, indeed, come down to us in the ' Orlando the Fair ' of the ' Tatler '—a bitter satire on the Beau's career and character, and the authorship of which (in Bohn's edition of 1842) is ascribed to Steele.   The lampoon, for it is little more, appeared in the fiftieth number of the ' Tatler,' published August 4, 1709 ; and the writer remarks that ' ten lustra and more ' were wholly passed ' since Orlando first appeared in the metropolis of this island.'   It was in 1706 that he met with that little mischance which led to his appearance at Justice Hall ; and, assuming that he was at least twenty when he first came upon town, he must have been on the verge of seventy when he married the great-grandmother Duchess of Cleveland, between whom and himself there was consequently no very great disparity in age.   Steele is enthusiastic as to the Beau's personal endowments.   We are told that his descent was noble, his wit humorous ; ' but to none of these recommendatory advantages was his title so undoubted as that of his beauty.   His complexion was fair, but his countenance manly ; his stature of the tallest, his shape the most exact ; and though in all his limbs he had a proportion as delicate as we see in the works of the most skilful statuaries, his body had a strength and firmness little inferior to the marble of which such images are formed.'   This is, indeed, very high eulogium, and, to my mind, it establishes a point to which I shall revert by-and-by.   The ' Tatler ' goes on to say that the Beau had been in the army.   A note in ' Bohn ' states that ' he embarked in the fortunes of King James II., who gave him the nomination of colonel, and for whom he raised a regiment in his native county of Warwick.'

This assertion is of the loosest, and is probably inaccurate. The only period at which the Beau could have 'embarked in the fortunes' of King James II. was during the brief time elapsing between the landing in England of William of Orange and the flight of James. Feilding was a Roman Catholic; still, he could scarcely have been an avowed Jacobite, since we find him openly living in a fine house in Pall Mall early in the reign of Anne; and in reality he seems to have enjoyed a kind of brevet rank, not as colonel, but as major-general, due to his services both in the British army and abroad. Steele says, 'his exploits in foreign nations and courts have not been regularly enough communicated to us to report them with that veracity which we profess in our narration.'[1] Possibly his military life abroad had been that of many other soldiers of fortune as good-looking and as scampish as he, in the splendidly Bohemian epoch during which he 'flourished.' From a scrap of internal evidence which came out at the Old Bailey, it seems likely that the Beau had in his youth served at Tangiers or thereabout. After describing his return to England to find that 'other Beaux born in his absence had made it their business to decry his furniture, his dress, and his manner,' Isaac Bickerstaff proceeds to recount that 'the Beauteous Villaria became the object of his affection.' The 'Beauteous Villaria' was Barbara Villiers, daughter and heiress of William, Viscount Grandison, of the Kingdom of Ireland. Glaringly notorious in history as Countess of Castlemaine and Duchess of Cleveland, as the mistress of Charles II. and the paramour of Jacob Hall, the rope-dancer—of *mille e tre*, to boot, indeed—she is described by Bishop Burnet as 'a woman of great beauty, but enormously vicious and ravenous; foolish, but imperious.' She seems, in short, to have possessed all Nell Gwynne's comeliness and impudence, without the wit and the kindliness of heart of that 'excellent wretch.' I find that among the Castlemaine's titles (patented to her in 1670) was that of Baroness of Nonsuch; yet there seems to have been plenty of Baronesses and non-Baronesses such as she in the exemplary reign to which we owe the Act of Parliament for the Better Observance of the Sabbath. She enriched the British peerage with a Duke of Northumberland, a Duke of Southampton, and a Duke of Grafton; and in the last-named instance a lineal descendant of Charles and Barbara survives to make us thank Heaven that we have a House of Lords. The profligate hag must have been about sixty-five years of age when Handsome Feilding courted, married, swindled, and beat her. The

[1] The mock gravity of the 'Tatler' is here manifestly imitated from the passage in Don Quixote in which Cervantes solemnly weighs the evidence regarding the real name of his hero: 'Pero esto importa poco á nuestra cuenta : basta que en la narracion del no se salga un punto de la verdad.'

first part of Steele's biography of the Beau concludes with a bit of ribaldry from which I have been fain to excise one or two passages which might grate fastidiously on prudish modern ears. He is supposed to be addressing a crowd of 'Britons under the age of sixteen,' who 'saw his grandeur and followed his chariot with shouts and acclamations.' They are supposed to be his illegitimate children. The Beau bids them go to school, and not lose their time by following his wheels. 'Hark ye, sirrah with the white hair,' he continues, 'I am sure you are mine. There is half-a-crown. Tell your mother this, with the half-crown I gave her long ago, makes five shillings. . . . Why, you young dogs, did you never see such a man before ?' ' Never such a man as you, noble general,' replied a truant from Westminster. ' Sirrah, I believe thee . there is a crown for thee. Drive on, coachman ! '   In the fifty-first number of the ' Tatler,' Steele continues and finishes the history of Orlando the Fair. The satirist banters the Beau on his assumption of martial manners, and describes him as calling for his tea by beat of drum, ordering his valet to shave him by sound of trumpet, and changing the call to boot and saddle when water was brought for his teeth.   But presently the poor Beau is pictured on his beam ends. ' An unlucky accident brought to his remembrance that one evening he was married before he courted the nuptials of Villaria.   Several fatal memorandums were produced to revive the memory of this accident, and the unhappy lover was for ever banished her presence to whom he owed the support of his first renown and gallantry. . . . Orlando, therefore, now raves in a garret, and calls to his neighbour skies to pity his dolours, and to find redress for an unhappy lover.'   And so ends this malicious banter, of which, by the way, is made up the bulk of the productions of those British essayists of the eighteenth century, to the study of whose scandal-magging ephemera we of the nineteenth are bidden to devote our nights and days if we would master the art of writing pure and elegant English.

So much for the Orlando the Fair of the ' Tatler '—an amusing enough lampoon, but one that, like a ' Portrait in Oil ' in the ' World,' must be taken with a great many grains—I had well-nigh said bushels—of salt.   Now for the Orlando of reality—the Beau of the Old Bailey.

You have to imagine yourself as a spectator in court at the Sessions House on December 4, 1706, when Robert Feilding, Esq., is indicted for bigamy in marrying Barbara, Duchess of Cleveland, his former wife being at the same time living. The prisoner being bidden to hold up his hand, to him the Clerk of the Arraigns, ' How sayst thou, Robert Feilding, art thou guilty of this indictment, or not guilty?' whereto quoth Robert, 'Not guilty;' and in answer to a further question from the Clerk as to how he will be tried, he makes the customary reply, 'By God and my country.' The jury are then sworn; but the prisoner foregoes his right of challenge, and they take their places in the box unquestioned. In the interests of name-lore, I am always curious concerning the nominal elements of old jury-panels; but among the appellations of the twelve honest men who sat in judgment on the Beau, I can only find two—Joseph Devenish and Thomas Yeamond—whose names strike unfamiliarly on the modern ear. The prisoner is qualified in the indictment as being late of the parish of St. James's (his residence was in Pall Mall), and he was charged with having on the ninth day of November in the year 1705, and in the parish aforesaid, taken to wife one Mary Wadsworth, spinster; and on the twenty-fifth of the same month of November with having, in the parish of St. Martin's-in-the-Fields (presumably at St. Martin's Church), feloniously and bigamously intermarried with the most noble Barbara, Duchess of Cleveland; his former wife, Mary Wadsworth, being then alive; 'against the Peace of our Sovereign Lady the Queen, her crown and dignity, and the form of the statute in that case made and provided.' Mr. Raymond and Sir James Mountague were counsel for the Crown, and the last-named learned gentleman drew the attention of the Court to the fact that the crime alleged against the prisoner being a felony, he was consequently deprived by law of the benefit of the assistance of counsel, but not of benefit of clergy in case of conviction; the practical result of which appears to me to have been, that the prisoner was to be denied the means of showing (through the acumen of his counsel) that he might be innocent; but that he was to be provided with a means of escaping punishment if he were found guilty. Sir Robert Mountague's elaborate history of the case in his opening speech I omit, as I hold it to be better (from the manners-painting point of view) to let the witnesses speak for themselves; so let us make haste to put Mrs. Villars into the box. Mrs. V. tells the Court that last year one Mrs. Streight comes to her lodgings about Bartholomew-tide, and leaves word that she would speak to her 'most particular,' adding that it will be 500l. out of her way if she does not come quickly. Whereupon Mrs. V. seeks out Mrs. Streight, with whom she has an interview in the presence of Major-General Feilding, and who tells her that there is a mighty rich and comely young widow named Mrs. Deleau newly come to town, with whom the Major-General would gladly enter into the bonds of wedlock. Does Mrs. Villars know Mrs. Deleau? Mrs. V. responds that she has no particular acquaintance with the widow, but that

'she used to cut her hair.'   'I am in love with her,' cries Orlando
the Fair ; 'and you must help me in my courtship.'   At a subsequent interview, the Major-General informs Mrs. V. that he has
learnt that Mrs. Deleau is worth 60,000*l.*, but that he does not
know where she lives.   Communicative Mrs. V. informs him that
the widow resides in Copthall Court, nigh to the Exchange, and
that she has a country house at Waddon, in Surrey.   Whereat says
the Beau that he is going to Tunbridge Wells, and that on his
way thither he will call at Waddon to see the gardens, and, if he
can, to have a view of the widow herself.   This, within a few days,
he accomplishes, or thinks so, at least ; and tells Mrs. Villars that,
in passing through the gardens, he has espied the widow at a casement ; and that, in order that she might have a perfect view of him
(conceited Orlando), he had taken divers turns, pulled out his watch
and set it by a sundial ; that he had come a roundabout route
through the country, and had almost murdered his horses to obtain
a sight of his beloved.   Impressionable Orlando !   As artful as he
was amorous, the stricken Beau instructed Mrs. Villars to tell the
widow that her Grace the Duchess of Cleveland had heard a great
deal of the beauty of the gardens and Waddon, and would fain have
a view of them.   To which gracious intimation the widow made
answer that she could refuse nothing to a lady of the Duchess's
quality ; but she begged that the visit to Waddon might be postponed for a week, as she, Mrs. Deleau, was going to see a horse-race
upon Banstead Downs.   This answer being conveyed to the Beau,
failed, it would seem, to please him.   He remarked that the Duchess
was sick, and had relinquished her intention of coming to Waddon ;
but that he himself would go to Banstead Races and endeavour to
see the widow.   He went accordingly ; but the 'widow hunt' was
not a successful one.   He bowed to the lady on the race-course, but
she did not return his salutation in an encouraging manner.   Then
he followed her to Epsom, and sent her a letter by a servant out of
livery ; but the coy (or prudent) Mrs. Deleau sent word that the
missive required no answer.   'I perceived,' continued Mrs. Villars,
'that he had no knowledge of Mrs. Deleau ; and so I acquainted
another young woman (Mrs. Wadsworth) with his inclination.   She
said that she did not expect to be so happy, but wished it might be
so.   (Here Villars was palpably lying.   Her aim was manifestly to
extort money from Feilding for marrying him with the widow Deleau.
Probably aware that the widow would have nothing to do with a
man of infamous character and notorious insolvency, Villars possibly thought that she could make some present profit out of him
by palming Mary Wadsworth (a pretty, disreputable adventuress)
upon him as the wealthy relict of Copthall Court.)   She told the

Bench vaguely that she did all she could to bring 'it' about, and that between Bartholomew-tide and Lord Mayor's day divers presents passed between 'them,' and that gifts were sent by Feilding through her to 'the lady.' The first *cadeau* was 'a gold apron struck with green.' 'He thought it was Mrs. Deleau all the while,' pursues the artful minx, 'but it was Mrs. Wadsworth.' Afterwards the Beau sent the sham widow 'a suit of white satin knots, and gloves, and other things;' and, at length, he desired that Mrs. V. would bring the widow to his lodgings. Mrs. V. brought Mrs. Wadsworth in a 'mourning-coach.' The sable vehicle was, I suppose, intended to be symbolical of Mrs. Deleau's recent bereavement. When Beau Feilding found himself in the presence of the sham widow of Waddon, 'he fell down upon his knees and kissed her, and expressed abundance of fine sentiments. He asked her why she stayed so long, and whether she loved singing. He said he would send for Margaretta to come up. When she came, Mr. Feilding bade her sing the two songs which he loved—the one was "Charming Creature," and the other "Ianthe the Lovely."'

A word concerning the singing woman. Margaretta, or La Margarita, is mentioned by Swift in a letter to Stella. 'We had a music meeting in our town last night. I went to the rehearsal of it; and there was Margarita and her sister, and another drab (oh, Mr. Dean!), and a parcel of fiddlers.' Mrs. Manley, in the 'New Atlantis,' relates some scandalous anecdotes touching the Margarita and Lord Nottingham, from whom the *cantatrice* to whom Swift applied so ungallant an appellation extracted, it is said, no less than 8,000*l*. I wonder how much Beau Feilding paid her for singing 'Charming Creature' and 'Ianthe the Fair.' Was it a guinea; or, haply, a kiss and a pack of fine promises? Handsome Feilding does not seem, at this time at least, to have been very flush of ready money. He was liberal enough, however, according to Mrs. Villars's showing, in the way of treating his favourites; for, the caterwauling of the hired singing-woman being finished, he sent out for 'two pints of wine and some plum-cake.' Then Margaretta seems discreetly to have vanished, and the Beau became hotly importunate that the pseudo-widow Deleau should marry him there and then. She declined (diplomatically enough), but promised to renew her visit on the following Wednesday; and she afterwards, by letter, changed the appointment to Friday, the 9th of November, Lord Mayor's day. The ladies being once more arrived at his apartments, the Beau came running in, and clasped the false Deleau in his arms, exclaiming that now nothing further was needed than the presence of a priest to make them both happy. The sham widow made some show of being shamefaced at this proposal, but the Beau, accustomed both in love and war to anticipate the Napoleonic maxim ' Frappez vite et frappez fort,' would take no denial, and went away, like Lord Grizzle in ' Tom Thumb,' not ' post haste for a license,' but to fetch a reverend gentleman, taking the precaution to lock the door of the chamber in which the ladies were. He had a French valet, one Boucher; and to this retainer he gave strict orders not to admit anyone until his return. In a short time he came back, bringing an ecclesiastic with him ' in a long red gown, lined with blue, a long beard, and a fur cap.' ' This,' quoth the Benedict Beau, ' is the holy father;' whereupon he bade Boucher lay the cloth, and they all went to supper, Monsieur Boucher being instructed to fetch a ' dish of pickles' from a neighbouring tavern. During the meal the sham widow evinced some doubts as to the reverend gentleman in the red gown and the long beard—a prodigious Guy he must have looked—being in proper orders; upon which his long-bearded reverence pulled a picture out of his pocket, about the bigness of a crown-piece, and showed it to her, saying that none but priests had such pictures; but the scrupulous Wadsworth (who, all sham widow as she was, evidently desired that this should be no sham wedding) desired another token; so, the rest of the servants being sent downstairs, the convenient Boucher was sent for ' water, salt, and rosemary, to make holy water.' These ingredients being brought, the Beau locked the door and put the key in his pocket. The priest in the red gown began to read something in Latin; but that most punctilious Wadsworth continuing to evince dissatisfaction as to the sufficiency of his orders, the Padre ' took from under his gown a piece of silk like a scarf that was marked with a cross in the middle, and said none but priests used such a thing.' The incredulous Wadsworth was convinced. She objected, however, to the Latin, and desired to be married in English, ' as well as he could.' The accommodating Padre asked Mr. Feilding ' whether he would have the gentlewoman to be his wedded wife.' Said the Beau, ' With all my heart.' Then he asked Wadsworth if she would have the gentleman to be her husband. Replies the cunning quean, ' Yes;' but ' faintly,' so Mrs. Villars said. ' But,' pursued the Beau, ' you don't say it as earnestly as I do. You must say " with all my heart and soul."' Which she did, and they were married. Boucher then brought up more wine, and, the whole party having refreshed themselves, the priest was discharged. The Beau saluted his wife as the ' Countess of Feilding,' at which she wept plenteously. Marriages are made in heaven, they say; and no married man, I apprehend, is prepared to deny *that* fact; yet I cannot help fancying that there was somebody present at this wedding, as ' best man,' whose extraction was of anything but a celestial one, and who (not to enter into too minute particularities) had horns, and hoofs, and a tail. After this precious ceremony, the 'Countess of Feilding' made frequent visits between her own residence (possibly in the hundreds of Drury) and Pall Mall. Her tastes do not seem to have been very luxurious, for on one occasion, finding that both the Beau and Monsieur Boucher were from home, she sent out for some supper for herself, which repast consisted of ' a pint of wine, some toasted cheese, and a bottle of oat ale.' A thirsty soul, this Countess. Mrs. Villars being asked by the presiding judge at what period Feilding discovered that he had been befooled, replied that it was in May, 1706. In the mean time, the real Mrs. Deleau's father had died, and it became town-talk that her fortune was much increased, that she was a 'great catch,' and that she was not yet re-married. The fury of the Beau was fearful. He took Mrs. Streight into a closet at the Duchess of Cleveland's (whom he had in the interim bigamously married) and sent for the perfidious Villars. I am sorry to say that this gentleman of fashion, family, and figure was mean and mercenary enough to demand that the presents he had made to the sham widow Deleau—the gold apron struck with green, the suit of white satin knots, and so forth—should be restored to him. I am sorrier to add that when the two women laughed in his face and called him a fool for his pains, this high-bred gentleman proceeded to beat them, asking, ' was that ' (meaning the Charming Creature Wadsworth) ' a fit wife for him ? ' ' And then,' added Mrs. Villars, ' he took a thing made of steel at one end, and a hammer at the other end, and told me that if I would not unsay what I had said of his marriage with Wadsworth he would slit my nose off. And that he would get two blacks ; the one should hold me upon his back, and the other should break my bones.' Decidedly, Beau Feilding must have seen service among the Moors at Tangiers. He had been one of Kirk's ' lambs,' perchance.

When Villars had finished her statement, the Beau in the dock asked her by what name Mary Wadsworth had passed during the performance of the marriage rites. ' By no name at all,' answered the ' discreet duenna.' To further questions from the prisoner, Mrs. Villars further admitted that he had never appeared in public with ' the Countess of Feilding.' Questioned by Judge Powel as to how the Duchess of Cleveland had become acquainted with the bigamous behaviour of her husband, Mrs. Villars replied that it came about in this wise. Not satisfied, apparently, with having beaten Mrs. Streight and Mrs. Villars, to say nothing of terrifying the latter with threats of the nose-slitting implement and the two blacks, the baffled brute who had been so completely tricked by a trio of female sharpers sent for the 'Countess of Feilding,' *alias* Wadsworth, to the lodge of the Duchess of Cleveland's house in Whitehall, and then and there beat her too (Wadsworth), badly. I have not much doubt either but that he had beaten the Duchess into the bargain, for Bishop Burnet records that he (Feilding) 'used her Grace with unhandsome severity.' Wadsworth manifestly did not like to be beaten; so she and the equally-bruised Mrs. Villars went away to the Duke of Grafton, one of the Duchess's bar-sinister sons, and told his Grace the whole scandalous story. The Cleveland family were, presumably, anxious enough to get rid of the Beau, and so made haste to prosecute him. When the prosecution had done with Villars, the clerk of a proctor in Doctors' Commons was called to prove that Feilding had gone to the ante-chamber of that temple of Hymen and Plutus to procure a copy of the will of the late Mr. Deleau, and after this evidence had been given there occurred in the proceeding that which modern reporters would style a 'sensational incident.' The real Mrs. Deleau was put into the box. That most desirable widow swore that she had no acquaintance whatever with Mr. Feilding; that she only knew Mrs. Villars as a servant of her hairdresser; that Mr. Feilding had once walked through her gardens; and that it was not she whom the Beau had seen at the casement, but another lady. The 'other lady' was sworn; but the reporter at the Old Bailey has had the discretion to omit her name from his account of the trial. The anonymous one corroborated the real widow Deleau's evidence, and vanished straightway into the Infinities. Who was she? Bah! who was your great-great-grandmother, my lord? You are as incompetent, haply, to enlighten us on that score as little Jack Chance, the parish foundling, can be.

Monsieur Boucher, the valet, made oath that on the 9th of November, 1705, 'he and his master' (*Ego et Rex meus*) had gone in Mr. Feilding's chariot to a linendraper's, at the sign of the Three Legs, in Cheapside, to see the Lord Mayor's show. Afterwards the Beau called on Sir Basil Firbrass, bidding his servant meet him later in the evening in Bond Street. Boucher deposed to the two ladies coming to Pall Mall at night in a mourning-coach; and here, according to Monsieur Boucher, it would appear that the house in Pall Mall was not Beau Feilding's own—he only lodged there at a Mrs. Heath's. For the rest, Monsieur confirmed the evidence of Mrs. Villars. He added that since he had left the Beau's service, he had become cook to General Webb's regiment. Ah! how the rats desert the sinking ship. At the period mentioned, the Duke of Marlborough's victorious army was swearing terribly in Flanders, and Webb's regiment was far away from England; but Monsieur Boucher had been sent for, express, by the Duke of Grafton to testify against Feilding. Evidently no expense had been spared by the grandees in Whitehall in order to get rid of the Beau. A Mrs. Martin, sister to Mrs. Heath, the lodging-house keeper in Pall Mall, remembered the mourning-coach, the coming of the long-bearded man in the red gown and the fur cap, and the ordering of the dish of pickles for supper. Mrs. Heath herself, being examined, ' put on airs ; ' and her evidence is delicious to read. She knew Major-General Feilding. She had heard that the Major-General received ladies of quality, but she never saw them, ' her family living retired from lodgers.' Mrs. Heath had heard of the man in red coming to the house, but the idea of a marriage had never entered her head. ' I did not believe it a marriage,' said she to the Court, ' but a conversion, because his man came down to my parlour, and asked for salt, and water, and rosemary, which occasioned these words, " Lord ! " says I, " I fancy they are making a convert of the woman upstairs." ' Adieu ! most excellent Heath.

Enter the Margaretta. Deposed that on a certain night in November she was sent for to do her vocal office. Sang several Italian songs and some English ditties ; among others, ' Ianthe the Lovely.' It was a favourite song with the Major-General. He said that he had the original of it, and that he had translated it from the Greek (fifth form, turn up your Anacreons ; I mean, your Tom Moores). Saw a gentlewoman in mourning with a velvet scarf. She was sitting by the fire. Did *not* see Mrs. Villars ; thought that if anyone else had been there, she must have seen them, for, quoth the Charming Creature, ' I was mistress of all the doors.' Exit the Margaretta. I fancy that she had a sneaking kind of liking for the Beau, and gave her evidence as softly as she could.

Was there ever such an Oyer of Women, and all to fix a felony upon one man ? It was as though the hand of Nemesis were in it. The wretched Beau had wronged women enough in his time, and *il était puni là par où il avait péché.* The pleasant vices had turned to cats of nine tails. ' Call Mrs. Price,' said the counsel for the Crown. Mrs. P. (who also lived at the Pall Mall lodging-house) seems to have been a lady of some discernment as regards sacerdotal vestments, for she qualified the queer accoutrement of the father as an ' Armenian habit.' Then a goldsmith and his man were called to prove the ordering of a gold wedding-ring by Feilding, and the engraving of it, according to his instructions, with a posy. To him succeeded Constantine Pozzi, a servant of the Austrian Ambassador (Emperor's Envoy he was then styled), Count Clam-Gallas ; and this sub-diplomatist made oath that the Beau had come to the Embassy in quest of a priest ; and, the Father in Red (who seemed to be peculiarly the man for his money) not being at home he had been fain to make shift with one Father Florence; only, his Red Reverence opportunely coming in, the Beau took him away blithely to the Pall Mall lodgings. A graphic account was given by one Mr. Paul, the keeper of Whitehall Gate, of sundry endearments which passed in his presence between the 'Countess of Feilding' and her husband. 'Mr. Feilding came to the Gate in a Chariot, and he lit out of it. There was a Hackney Coach brought two women. One of these Women got out of the Coach, and came up to Mr. Feilding. Mr. Feilding called her ——' well, what was the 'bitter word' applied in her wrath by the bereaved mother of poor young Lawrence to Lady Clara Vere de Vere? Mr. Tennyson may know, but I do not. It was not a polite word—of that you may be sure; and Beau Feilding was not polite to his spouse. 'The Lady called him Rogue (oh, fie!) and said she was his Lawful Wife; and Mr. Feilding, having a Stick, did Punch her with it. It happened upon her Mouth, and made her Teeth bleed.' The poor maltreated wench seems after this to have hurried to the King's Arms tavern at Charing Cross, where she sent in a drawer to Captain Eaton of the Guards, whom she knew. To him she related the story of her wrongs; and the gallant captain made haste to tell the Lord Duke of Northumberland, who lost no time in relating the affair to his Grace of Grafton; and a very pleasant afternoon must these scions of the sainted King Charles have spent with their immaculate mamma, the most noble Barbara, Duchess of Cleveland. Dear, dear me! what a highly-flavoured scandal it must have been: the villanous inquest at Balham was nothing to it.

Be it remarked that Mary Wadsworth-Feilding was present in Court throughout the trial, and that her identity was repeatedly established by different witnesses. She was not called, however, nor did the Father in Red make his appearance. The only material witness to the fact of the marriage having taken place was Mrs. Villars; and the question to determine was whether that gentlewoman was or was not worthy of belief. The Major-General in the dock being called upon for his defence, stoutly maintained that Mrs. Villars had told nothing but lies; that she had been flatly contradicted by the Margaretta as to her presence when 'Ianthe the Lovely' was sung; and that she was altogether a woman of infamous character, who had been in the custody of the Master of Bridewell and had there received the Correction of the House, and was thus unfitted to appear as a witness in a court of justice. Finally, he pleaded that Mary Wadsworth had already another husband, one Lilly Bradby, whom she had married in the Fleet; and the custodian of the Fleet Registers—a woman named Basset, who said that she likewise kept a public-house, and that she had 'several ministers' in her employ—produced a book containing an entry of the marriage in October, 1703, of Lilly Bradby of St. James's to Mary Wadsworth of St. Margaret's, Westminster. Mrs. Drinkwater, Mrs. English, Mrs. Gardiner (the accumulation of feminine testimony recalls the great case of Bardell *v.* Pickwick), came forward to declare that Mrs. Villars was a very naughty person; and the keeper of the Tothill Fields Bridewell proved that five years back he had had Mrs. Villars under lock and key, but that she had been excused the Correction of the House (*i.e.* a whipping) on the score of her being then in an interesting condition. There were some innuendoes of evidence, too, that the Duchess of Grafton had offered somebody 200*l.* to swear against Feilding; that the prosecution had covertly endeavoured to get possession of the Fleet register of the marriage between Bradby and Wadsworth, intending to destroy it; and, finally, that, after proceedings against Feilding had commenced, the Father in Red had been seen at dinner with the Duchess of Cleveland. Judge Powel summed up the case with great impartiality, telling the jury that, if they found Wadsworth's marriage with Bradby sufficiently proved, they must acquit the Beau, even if they likewise found that he had been married to the sham widow in Pall Mall.

The jury having been absent for some time, brought in their verdict 'that Mr. Feilding was guilty of the felony he stood indicted of.' Poor Beau!

Well, not so poor (in the sense of misfortune) as you might imagine. I suppose that by this time there can be little doubt in your mind, my dear reader, that the high-bred, handsome elderly gentleman at the bar was a heartless, knavish, ruffianly old scoundrel; that he had laid a cunning trap to catch a wealthy widow; and that when he found that he had been caught in another trap by knaves more artful than he, his brutish nature burst forth in menaces and blows among the poor fallen creatures who had foiled him. *He* a ' Beau '! He ' Orlando the Fair '! Why, he was as mean a skunk as —— : but I must not expose *Belgravia* to the risk of an action for libel.

The scamp had come into the dock provided with the Queen's warrant to suspend execution of the sentence in case he were found guilty; so the Court, by a ' *cur advisare vult*,' suspended judgment until the next sessions, and the convicted bigamist was liberated on bail. He was of ' gentle blood,' and had mixed in the best society; and that society evidently did not desire to bear too hardly on their embarrassed favourite. The Cleveland clique evidently did not want to ruin him. They only desired to get rid of him. On January 15, 1707, he came up again for judgment, and, waiving an exception which he had taken to the verdict, very coolly craved the 'benefit of his clergy.' Whether he was called upon to read a 'neck-verse' or not I do not find stated. Judgment was given that he should be burnt in the hand and discharged; but the hangman had no occasion to use his branding iron—the Beau was prepared for all eventualities. He produced her Majesty's warrant to stay execution; gave formal bail to come up again when called upon, and so left the Court scot-free. In the following May his marriage with the Duchess of Cleveland was solemnly annulled by the Ecclesiastical Court. It was scarcely worth while to put the proctors, and notaries, and the Right Worshipful Sir John Cooke, Doctor of Civil Laws, who read in fine law Latin the decree of nullity of marriage, to so much pains. Two years afterwards, the most noble Barbara, Duchess of Cleveland, died, and her handsome husband did not long survive her. I do not know whether he made a good end of it; but, in any case, the world was well quit of a scoundrel.

As I shut up the worm-eaten old parchment-bound tome which contains—with many other records of human crime and misery—the story of Beau Feilding, I feel as though I had been scanning, till my eyes were dim, a portfolio full of Hogarth's prints. Shutting those eyes, the darkened chamber sealed by the lids seems full of beaux and mohawks, seminary priests and captains of horse, gamblers, demireps, Fleet chaplains, tavern drawers, lords in blue ribbons, duchesses, and drabs. There is Kate Hackabout beating hemp on the Bridewell block, and wincing under the gaoler's rattan; there foul old Charteris prowling about the inn-yard in quest of prey for his lust; there Ophelia, in Dilke's play of 'The Pretenders,' 'taking a hackney-coach, scouring from playhouse to playhouse till she meets with some young fellow that has power enough to attack her, stock enough to treat her, and folly enough to be laughed at for his pains;' there Mirabel lounging with his friend in the Mall; there Beau Shamtown reading his old love-letters; there Sir Bellamour Blunt coming out of the chocolate-house with Vainthroat; there Lord Foppington dining at Lacket's, and 'stapping his vitals' because a dish no bigger than a saucer comes to fifty shillings; and there the 'Town Beau' in 'Chrysal' pawning his laced waistcoat for three guineas, repairing to a coffee-house at the Court end of the town, and then going home to supper on a Welsh rabbit and three pennyworth of punch. They are all present; ay, and the drunken Irish chairmen fighting over a fare in St. James's Street; and Tim Flick, the cutpurse, yelling at the cart's tail as the hangman lashes him; and poor Jack Road the highwayman (who could plead no benefit of clergy) swinging from Tyburn Tree. Surely, if 'laws are made for every degree,' he should have had a gentleman there to keep him company: Beau Feilding, to wit.

Juliet.

BY MRS. H. LOVETT CAMERON.

CHAPTER XVI.

HER LAST WORDS.

CIS TRAVERS was breakfasting at his friend's rooms in the Temple.

It was a bright clear morning; the sun streamed in through the big dusty windows, and lit up the dingy old rooms cheerily.

There were eggs, and kidneys, and muffins, all laid out on quaint old-fashioned blue china, in which Wattie took great pride, being somewhat of a connoisseur; a finely chased silver tea-pot, and curious-shaped sugar-bowl and milk-jug—like the china, relics of past extravagances; whilst on the fire the bright copper kettle steamed and fizzed away merrily.

It was altogether as daintily set out a little breakfast table as you could wish to see. And the two young men were in the best of spirits.

'Fetch me the kettle, Cis, and help yourself to kidneys,' says Wattie, standing up while he pours out the tea, after a fashion that male beings have, when they preside at the breakfast table. ' Did you see Gretchen last night ? '

'Yes, I looked in on my way home,' answers Cis, with his mouth full of muffin.

'Ah ! very imprudent of you,' says Wattie censoriously. ' Well, how is she getting on ? '

' Oh, first rate ; two new pupils since last week, and she looks as rosy and happy as possible. Do think ! the dear little girl offered me three pounds, to pay for the doctor's bill, she said. Of course I wouldn't take it.'

' I wish she wasn't quite so fond of you, and I wish she would marry David Anderson,' said wiser Wattie.

' Well, I don't, then—marry that boor, indeed ! '

' You had better take care that Miss Blair doesn't hear of

your evening visits to Gretchen; there would be an end of your chances *there*,' answered his friend.

'Well, of all the rubbish I ever heard you talk!' began Cis impatiently; and then there came a sharp knock, and Mrs. Stiles's head, in extreme dishabille, decorated with manifold whity-brown curl-papers, surmounted with a far from spotless cap, which, from its peculiar shape and crumpled appearance, suggested irresistibly the idea that she must have slept in it, was poked furtively in at the door.

'A tallygrum for you, please, sir,' said this lady, holding out the dusky pink missive in the corner of her apron.

'You may call it rubbish, Cis,' Wattie was saying, in answer to his friend's last remark, and laughing carelessly as he took the telegram from Mrs. Stiles's hand; and then he opened it leisurely, for nobody nowadays feels nervous at the sight of a telegram.

A minute of silence whilst he read, and then a cry of horror burst from his lips—

'Oh, my God!'

'What is the matter?' cried Cis, springing to his feet in amazement, as his friend turned as white as a sheet, and the pink paper fluttered to the floor.

Cis picked it up and read—

'From Miss Blair, Sotherne Court, to Walter Ellison, Esq., Harcourt Buildings, Temple.

'Georgie has had a bad accident. Come down at once to Sotherne, and bring Cis. Lose no time.'

They bore it well, as men do such sudden blows; Wattie, as might have been expected, being the least upset of the two.

'We shall catch the 11.25 if we look sharp,' he said as soon as he could speak, rapidly turning over the pages of Bradshaw.

'Go back to your rooms, and get your bag, Cis, and meet me at the station. You must look sharp, though—we have only thirty-five minutes.'

And Cis, who was shaking and trembling all over, obeyed him in silence.

Down at Sotherne Court, Georgie on her sick bed was moaning over and over again—

'Have they come yet? when will they be here? how much longer will they be?' in a weak, fretful voice.

On the bed by her side lay old Chanticleer. Early in the morning she had asked for him, and a messenger had been sent to Broadley to bring him over.

'Don't think me foolish,' she had said, 'but I should like him to lie on the bed where I can stroke him, poor old boy!' and her lightest wish was, of course, a law to those who watched by her.

The old hound lay with his head resting on his great white paws, gazing up at her fixedly and piteously, with every now and then a low whine of sympathy.

And who shall say that in that faithful canine heart there was not at least a partial knowledge of the dread change that was about to befall his young mistress?

Little Flora, who had been brought over with the dog, crouched at the bottom of the bed, trying to stifle her sobs.

'Don't cry, Flora,' said her sister once. 'Look here! I leave poor old Chanticleer to you; you will be very fond of him, won't you, for my sake? and don't forget to give the poor old boy his bread and milk in the morning—he will miss it so, if he doesn't get it; and now he has so few teeth, he likes it better than anything else. You will promise me not to forget it, Flora?'

'Yes, Georgie,' sobbed the little girl; and then Juliet drew her away into an adjoining room, and took her on her lap, and let her sob and cry upon her shoulder till she was fairly worn out.

By three o'clock the two young men had arrived. A faint flush came into Georgie's face when she was told that they had come.

'Papa,' she said, turning to her father, 'I want to see Wattie by himself—quite alone, with no one else in the room. May I? do you mind?'

And so they all left the room, and Wattie went in alone.

What passed between them during those solemn parting moments no one ever knew; no sound came from within the room to the ears of those who stood waiting outside the door; but, after about a quarter of an hour, Wattie came out, and rushed past them blinded with tears—out at the open hall door, away down the slopes of the garden, there to work away the first anguish of his sorrow by himself.

And presently the Squire went out after him. He found him lying prone at the foot of a tree, stretched along the damp grass.

'Wattie—my dear boy, my poor boy, do get up!'

The young man looked up with dim eyes, and a dazed white face; but when he saw that it was the Squire, he got up.

'Can you ever forgive me?' said the old man in a broken voice. 'It was I who made her ride the mare, though you had written to warn her against her. She didn't want to ride her, but I made her; it was my cursed obstinacy—and now I have killed her—I have killed my child!'

'Don't say that, sir!' said Wattie, passing his arm within the old man's; 'it is God's doing; no one was to blame; she was so good—too good to live!'

'Oh, my boy, how I wish I had let you be engaged to her—perhaps this might never have happened,' cried the Squire.

'We cannot tell,' answered Wattie gravely; 'at all events, such self-reproaches can avail nothing now. Come, sir, you look so ill and tired, take one turn down the garden with me—the fresh air will do you good—and tell me as we go how it all happened, for you forget that I know nothing beyond what the telegram has told me, and then we will go back to her.'

So the old man leant upon his arm, and told him all the pitiful story over again—everything from the beginning, all about Georgie's patience and goodness, and all about his own stubbornness and harshness to her. He poured out his whole heart to him, and the recital did him good.

When the two entered the house again they stopped short with one accord, and grasped each other's hands ere they went back into the sick room. Everything was forgiven between them; and from that hour to his dying day Squire Travers loved Wattie Ellison as his own son.

And after that they none of them left her room any more until the end. Towards four o'clock Georgie became very much weaker, and it soon grew evident to those around her that Mrs. Travers and Mary, who had a long cross journey, and could not possibly reach Sotherne before six o'clock, would not arrive in time to see her alive.

Dr. Ramsden came again for the second time that day, and suggested what he could to make her more comfortable: she did not suffer pain, only uneasiness; and then he was obliged to leave, promising to call again later.

It was Juliet who with gentle hands smoothed the pillows of the dying girl, and moistened her parched lips and bathed her hot head with cooling scents. Juliet had, like many impetuous restless women, an inborn genius for nursing the sick. Her step was soft but swift, her hand gentle but firm, and her eye quick and ready to see what was wanted. Georgie often glanced up at her gratefully, as, unweariedly patient, she bent over her to minister to the hundred little requirements of a sick bed.

After a long silence, broken only by the whispers of those around her, Georgie suddenly spoke in a strong clear voice:

'Juliet!'

'Yes, darling?'

'I want you to promise me to marry Cis; it would be such a

comfort to poor papa. I think it would almost make up to him for losing me. Give me your hand, Cis, and yours, Juliet; there, now say you will try and love him. I think I shall rest easier in my grave if you will say you will—it will be such a gleam of happiness by-and-by for poor papa!'

What could Juliet do?

Georgie had taken their hands—hers and her brother's, and had joined them together between her own little white ones. The one thought, poor child, in her weakened, bewildered brain, half dulled already by illness and approaching death, was that something should be done to comfort her father after she was gone.

How could Juliet over that death-bed speak of her own love-troubles—troubles that, in the awful excitement of the last twenty-four hours, seemed to have faded away into absolute insignificance? How could she vex that dying girl with doubts and perplexities?

What should she do?

Cis was gazing at her across the bed with big blue eyes, haggard with weeping and misery, and yet full of love and yearning to herself; and Georgie was saying over again, with the gentle impatience of those who are very ill—

'Come, Juliet, you will promise to marry him—won't you?'

And Juliet, driven to speak, and unable to speak as she ought to have done, whispered—

'Yes, Georgie dear, I will promise.'

The dying girl raised the two hands she held to her lips, whilst a faint gleam of pleasure stole over her pale face.

Then she called her father to her.

He half raised her up, and she rested her head upon his shoulder.

'Juliet will marry Cis, papa,' she said, 'and that will be a great comfort to you; now I shall die happier.'

After that she never spoke again.

In a little while she passed into that strange borderland of unconsciousness in which so many spend their last hours on earth.

Most awful, most solemn time of mystery, when the soul, whilst struggling to be free, hovers between earth and heaven, and the spirit, darkened and obscured, lingers still in the body it has already partially left!

Quite motionless were the watchers around her: her father supporting her head against his shoulder; her lover, with his hand fast locked in hers, kneeling by her side; little Flora, trembling and shivering with fright, close held in her brother's arms; and Juliet standing with bowed head at the foot of the bed.

And old Chanticleer was by her side, watching her silently with the rest.

And so, surrounded by those who had loved her in life, softly and painlessly Georgie Travers's gentle spirit passed away.

CHAPTER XVII.

A WINDY WALK.

CHRISTMAS had come and gone—Christmas, the saddest day in all the year for those who have suffered and lost—sad therefore to three-fourths of the population of the Christian world; for how many in every land are those who sorrow!

January was nearly over, the crocuses and snowdrops were cropping up thickly in bright compact rows in the Sotherne flower-borders, and down below in the valley the green grass had already grown up over Georgie Travers's grave.

Juliet Blair was wandering alone about the garden walks, with a sad, wearied face. Ever since that death-bed scene she had been perplexed by the one absorbing memory of that promise which had been wrung so unwillingly from her by her dead friend.

Was not a promise to a dying person the most solemn and binding of any promise that can be given? Would not the breach of such a promise be a dire and mortal sin, provoking the wrath of Heaven to fall in curses on the faithless promiser?

Was she in very truth bound to marry Cecil Travers?

She asked herself these questions over and over again a hundred times a day.

Nothing had been said to her by either Cis or his father upon the subject; but she knew well that they had not forgotten it, and she felt instinctively that they were but waiting for her to speak of it.

Juliet was very lonely in these days. Not one word had she received from that far-distant lover who had left her, as she thought, so cruelly and so heartlessly. Through Mr. Bruce she had, indeed, heard that he had arrived safely in India, and that he was well; but there had come no word to her from him. Through all these weary weeks she had pined and sickened to hear from him, and nothing came to her day after day, but the same dead, cold silence.

The conviction was forced upon her that he had treated her shamefully—that he had trifled with her—amusing himself by winning her heart, only to fling it back to her with scorn and mockery; and that now he had utterly forgotten her!

She had neither home-life nor home-love to fill up the great emptiness of her heart—and Juliet was one who could not live without love.

Her stepmother she absolutely disliked, and she had not a relation in the world with whom she was even on intimate terms; whilst poor Georgie, the one friend whom she had been fond of, and who had brought affection and sympathy into her life, had been taken from her by a sudden and awful death.

Juliet wondered vaguely why she had not been killed instead of her friend. Georgie's death had brought sorrow to so many, utter desolation to her old father, and scarcely less to her young lover. Whereas, if she, Juliet, had died in her place, who would have sorrowed for her—who would even have missed her?

How dreary and empty her life was! She looked at what might be her lot, if she chose—with a husband who would assuredly love her, and whose family were prepared to welcome her with open arms; such a marriage would be better, she thought, than this utter loneliness—and since the one man she cared for loved her not, why not marry Cis as well as any other?

At this point of her reflections, Mrs. Blair came across the garden to join her.

'How much longer are you going to smother yourself up in that horrid crape?' were her first words, pointing to her step-daughter's sable garments.

'Till Easter probably,' answered Juliet coldly.

Mrs. Blair lifted her hands and eyes. 'My dearest Juliet! really I think you over-strain your expression of feeling—it is not as if the poor thing had been any relation, you know.'

'I have told you before,' said Juliet impatiently, 'that I shall wear mourning for dear Georgie as if she had been my sister.'

'Your *sister*! ahem! my dear—that will be great encouragement for somebody we know, won't it?' said the widow slyly.

Juliet, with reddened cheeks, was silent for a moment, and then, with one of those sudden impulses to which she so often gave way, she said—

'You may as well know, Mrs. Blair, that I shall very probably marry Cecil Travers; so pray don't torment me any further about him.'

'My darling girl!' cried her stepmother, 'how charmed, how delighted I am! Pray let me congratulate you! And are you really engaged?'

'No, I am not engaged,' said Juliet, withdrawing herself from the encircling arms which her stepmother had rapturously flung around her. 'I am not engaged, so please don't mention it to anyone, but I believe I shall be shortly, and I don't wish to speak about it again.'

Here Higgs appeared on the lawn with a note for his mistress.

It was from Wattie, who was staying at Broadley, and ran thus:—

My dear Miss Blair,—It would be very kind of you if you would come over and see the Squire soon. He frets after you sadly; and sometimes I hardly know what to do with him. He is so utterly broken down, that it is quite distressing to see him. Cecil has a delicacy in asking you to come over; so I ventured to write to you on my own responsibility.

Yours very sincerely,

WALTER ELLISON.

'I shall drive over to Broadley this afternoon,' said Juliet, as she shut up this note and put it in her pocket; and after luncheon she started.

Things were indeed altered at Broadley House since poor Georgie's death.

To begin with, the Squire had given up the hounds; they had been taken by a sporting colonel, a new comer who had lately rented a place a few miles off. Everyone had entreated Mr. Travers to resign them only for the season, and not to give them up altogether. Even his wife could see how utterly lost and at sea he would be without this hitherto all-absorbing occupation of his life. But the old man was obstinate. No, no, he said, he should never be fit to be a master again. By-and-by, another year perhaps, he would potter out after the hounds on his old bay horse Sunbeam, just when the meets came handy; but as to keeping the hounds again! no, that he should never do! Besides, he added pitifully, how could he, with no one to write his letters or help him with the work?

So he sat all day long in his study, doing nothing, stooping forward with bent head and clasped hands in his chair, and looking as if ten years had gone over his head in as many weeks.

Flora often sat on the floor by his side, leaning against him, with her story-book and Chanticleer's head on her lap; but, though he liked to have her there, and sometimes put his hand down to stroke her fair curls, she was too young to talk or be much of a companion to him.

Cis was staying at home, but, though kind and gentle in his manner to his son, the Squire had no comfort in his society.

Wattie Ellison seemed the only one who could in any way rouse or interest him. When Wattie came down for a couple of nights, as he did almost every week, the Squire would take his arm and allow himself to be tempted out of doors round the garden, and sometimes even into the stables, and to Wattie he would talk as he could to no one else.

For hours together these two, to whom the dead girl was a living link of unfailing interest, would talk of her to each other, recalling her words and her doings, and all her sweet unselfishness.

No one save Wattie, the Squire felt, had ever appreciated his dead darling; her mother had snapped and scolded at her all her life; was it likely that she could sorrow for her properly now that she was gone? Cis had been too much of a milksop, and Mary too cold and selfish, to understand her; Flora alone of all her sisters had been devoted to her; but the Squire felt that Georgie had been more his child than any of his other children, and he was very jealous of her memory. He would never even mention her name to any of the others save only to Wattie, who had loved her and understood her, and who sorrowed for her intensely even as he did himself.

When Juliet went over to Broadley that afternoon, Mrs. Travers met her in the doorway.

'It is very good of you to come over to such a dull house,' said she, with that sort of sham self-depreciation which is so irritating because so unanswerable; 'I am sure there is little enough in this house of sorrow to amuse you.'

'Dear Mrs. Travers, as if I wanted amusement!' said Juliet, a little indignantly.

'Well, my dear, everything is changed here for us all, and poor Mary feels the dreadful depression very trying to her spirits. You have come to see the Squire? Ah, dear me! it is sad to see him, and my dear Cis is quite unable to rouse him at all. I hope, Juliet, you will say something to give him and us all a little hope and pleasure?' she added wistfully, for she too was anxious that her son should make this brilliant match with the rich Miss Blair.

When Juliet went into the study, and when she saw how the old man's face lighted up at her entrance, she felt quite a pang of self-reproach to think how seldom she had come over of late.

'Why, Juliet! this is kind of you; come, sit down here, my dear, by the fire, and warm yourself. Is it cold out?'

'Rather; I think it is inclined to be frosty.'

'You don't say so!' he exclaimed with a momentary eagerness, adding, however, immediately, with a sigh, 'not that it matters to me much now!'

Juliet took the chair that he drew forward for her and began talking to him of everything she could think of to interest and amuse him, just as one talks to a child, observing pitifully the while how tottering and aged he had become, and how drawn and white his once hale and robust face had grown.

Then Wattie came in for a little while and joined in the talk, and after he had gone Juliet asked suddenly, with something like a blush—

'And where is Cis?'

'Do you want him?' said the Squire eagerly; 'dear Juliet, do you want to see him?'

And Juliet answered, 'Yes, I do indeed.'

The Squire turned round to Flora, who was crouched up on the floor by the window with her arm round Chanticleer's neck, and told her to go and find her brother.

The child obeyed and left the room, the old hound following close at her heels as he used to at Georgie's.

'He is almost as fond of her,' said the Squire brokenly, looking after her, and alluding for the first time to his dead daughter.

'Yes, and she is growing so like dear Georgie; have you not noticed it? I think Flora will be a comfort to you some day, dear Mr. Travers.'

The old man shook his head.

'She is a good child—a good child; but she will never be like the other,' he answered, and then Cis came in.

'I have sent my carriage home, Cis,' said Juliet, as she shook hands with him; 'will you walk with me?'

'Juliet! do you mean it really?' cried Cis, flushing with pleasure.

'Yes, I do really,' she answered, smiling, and she shook hands with the Squire, and they both went out together.

For some minutes they went on side by side in silence. The fresh breeze blew briskly in their faces, as they walked quickly along, so that Cis found it difficult to keep his hat on, and was rather thankful that his companion did not speak to him. When, however, they turned out of the open park into the more sheltered lane, and Juliet still kept silence, Cis found that it was incumbent upon him to speak.

'Do you ever think of what poor Georgie said to us before she died, Juliet?' he asked timidly.

'I am always thinking about it, Cis,' answered Juliet, in her clear, steady voice.

'And what do you think of doing?' he asked nervously.

'What should you wish me to do?' said Juliet, smiling at him kindly.

'Do you mean to say—oh, Juliet, do you mean to say that you will marry me?' cried Cis, excitedly catching hold of both her hands, and forcing her to stand still, whilst his hat, left unsecured, took the opportunity of blowing off. Juliet laughed; it was so like the old awkward Cis of boyish days.

'Yes, Cis,—that is, if you will listen first to what I have to say; let us walk on, it is too cold to stand still. Cis, before I promise you anything, I want you to know the truth; the truth is that, though I am certainly fond of you, I do not love you as a woman ought to love her husband, and I am afraid I never shall. The reason is,' she added, lowering her voice,—'the reason of it is, that everything in my heart that I have had to give has been already given away.'

'Juliet! to whom?' faltered Cis.

'Ah, never mind that,' she answered, smiling; 'I am not bound to tell you that; never mind who it was, he is never likely to cross my path or yours again; and—I don't know why I need be ashamed to say it to you—but the truth is that my affection was misplaced, for it was never returned. Well, Cis, I am leading a profitless and aimless life. I have no domestic ties and no one to love me.'

'Oh, Juliet!'

'Hush, don't interrupt me, it is quite true; I have great need of some one who will be good to me. And when I know how anxious you are to marry me, and what a great deal of comfort I should give to your poor father by doing so, and above all how I have already promised our darling Georgie on her death-bed that I would be your wife, I cannot help thinking that by giving in to the earnest wishes of you all I shall at all events be doing some good to somebody, instead of wasting my life in selfish and profitless repinings. Cis, if you will be content to have me after this fashion, I will be your wife.'

And then Cis called her by every fondest, proudest name, and swore to her a dozen times that he cared not how she came to him so long as she would come, that he would spend his life in trying to prove his gratitude to her, that he had love enough for both, and that he would never expect nor exact of her more than she chose to freely give him.

'I don't quite know how we shall get on together,' she said, rather dubiously, when Cis had come to an end of his rhapsodies; 'I am afraid we are not very well suited to each other; but, at all events, we can try it.'

It was not a very ecstatic speech for a young lady to make to the man she was just engaged to, certainly; but Cis was not hurt, he was too intensely delighted at being engaged to her at all to think much of the manner in which she had bound herself to him.

He was at this moment occupied in debating within himself

whether it was or was not possible for him to venture to kiss her in the open high road along which they were progressing; but Juliet, who possibly suspected his intention, cut short these ambitious hopes.

'Now, Cis, go back to your father and tell him the good news; I can walk home very well from here.'

'May I not walk to the door with you?' said her lover, in dismay at so abrupt a dismissal.

'No, not to-day,' she answered, smiling and holding out her hand to him, and he could not do otherwise than leave her.

And Juliet walked on alone, a tall, dark figure in the gathering twilight.

'If he had not left me, I should never have done it,' she said to herself bitterly, ten minutes after she had parted with her affianced husband.

And, before a week was over, Miss Blair was regretting her engagement to Cecil Travers intensely and hopelessly, and she would have gladly given up ten years of her life to have been able to undo the work of that afternoon's walk.

But in a week it was too late. In a week every man, woman, and child in her native county knew of it; she had received the congratulations of half the neighbourhood; and——worst, most unbreakable chain of all——she had knelt by the Squire's arm-chair, and had been blessed and thanked, in broken trembling words, for her goodness in bringing back a gleam of pleasure and sunshine into his desolate and darkened life.

That was what bound her to Cis more securely than all her promises to him. And, to tell the truth, that was the one grain of pleasure and satisfaction she derived from her engagement.

Everything else about it revolted and horrified her; she seemed to see plainly now that the little gush of emotion and self-sacrifice which had been upon her that day had worn off; she knew how utterly unhappy such a marriage must be for her, how uncongenial poor Cis was to her in every way, and, worst of all, how vain it was to hope that her heart would ever belong in the faintest degree to anyone but to Hugh Fleming.

But the thought of old Squire Travers's delight, and of the pleasure which Cecil's family generally displayed at the news of his engagement, did in some measure reconcile her to it. She tried to persuade herself, and, indeed, she did honestly believe, that she was doing a good and unselfish action, and that a blessing would therefore rest upon her for it.

And she had one hope left.

'JULIET WALKED ON ALONE.'

As soon as she was engaged she wrote to tell Mr. Bruce, and requested him to write and inform Colonel Fleming of the fact, in order to ask for his formal consent to her marriage.

She had a wild, unreasonable hope that he would come home and save her from her fate—that he would never allow her to be taken utterly away from him, never suffer her to go without a struggle to retain her.

She little knew Hugh Fleming !

Two months passed away, and his answer came—in a note to Mr. Bruce, which that gentleman forwarded to her.

My dear Mr. Bruce,—I am very glad to hear such good news about Miss Blair. Pray give her my very hearty congratulations, and my sincere good wishes for her happiness ; as to my consent, that, you know, is merely a matter of form, as we have talked over this subject before, and you know that I quite approved of Mr. Travers as a suitable husband for my ward. Please send me all necessary papers to sign, with your instructions. You are very kind to wish me to be present at the wedding, but that is, I fear, impossible. I should like to hear when the day is fixed.

With kind remembrances to all,
Yours faithfully,
Hugh Fleming.

That was all.

That evening, when Cis came over to dinner, Juliet told him that she would keep him in suspense no longer, for that she would marry him in the month of May.

Chapter XVIII.

a wedding in may.

There was one person to whom the news of Cecil Travers's engagement came as a great shock, and that was Gretchen Rudenbach.

It was in a letter from Wattie that Gretchen first heard of it, for Cecil himself was too full of his new happiness to give a thought to the poor little music-teacher in Pimlico.

When Gretchen had finished reading Wattie Ellison's letter, she laid her head down upon the table-cloth, all among her poor little breakfast array, her cup of weak tea, and her untempting-looking bread-and-butter, and cried bitterly.

In the middle of these tears, in came Miss Pinkin.

Miss Pinkin wore a black front, and a tulle cap decorated with small lilac bows and tied under her chin with white gauze ribbons, and she was enveloped in a silk shawl of an old-fashioned pattern and colour, very tightly drawn around her spare figure ; she had a thin, angular face, and was altogether an austere-looking woman.

'Mercy me!' exclaimed this ancient virgin, lifting up both hands in amazement at the discovery of Gretchen in her woe. 'What on earth are you crying your eyes out for?' Gretchen wiped her eyes, but made no answer.

'I know very well what you are crying for,' continued Miss Pinkin, glancing severely at the open letter on the table. 'You are crying about a piece of news that ought to give you a great deal of pleasure, if you had a well-regulated mind. I, too, have had a letter from Miss Augusta Ellison, my old pupil, and she tells me that Mr. Cecil Travers is engaged to be married to Miss Blair of Sotherne. You ought to be very much pleased, you foolish girl, instead of crying like a water-spout, and laying your head down in your bread-and-butter plate, which isn't cleanly.'

Gretchen, at this well-merited reproach, lifted her head and pushed away the bread-and-butter to a safe distance.

'Because a young gentleman, *far* above you in station, has been kind to you when you were ill and homeless, you have been so silly as to allow your thoughts to dwell upon him in an indecorous manner.'

'You should not say that, Miss Pinkin.'

'But I must say so, Gretchen. When you were put under my charge, I determined to do my duty by you as if you were a young relative of my own. I must tell you that it is indecorous for a female to think of the other sex at all. I have never done so myself,' added Miss Pinkin, virtuously drawing herself up with conscious pride. 'Throughout my life I have made it a rule to myself to avoid rather than to seek the other sex; and look at me!' Gretchen did look at her, and mentally reflected that possibly the other sex had also found it more prudent to avoid than to seek that hard-featured visage. 'Look at me,' she continued; 'honoured, respected, and esteemed by all gentlemen; you would wish to be so too at my age, would you not, Gretchen?'

'I should wish to be loved too,' said the girl in a low voice.

'Hush, hush, my dear! I am shocked at you!' cried Miss Pinkin, throwing up her hands. 'A girl should never mention such a word in connection with gentlemen. Come, dry your eyes, and be thankful that it was only I who found you with such improper tears in them. What would people think to find you weeping over Mr. Cecil Travers's engagement? why, it would be shocking!'

'I am not ashamed of loving him,' said Gretchen, with scarlet cheeks; 'he is the only person in the world who has ever shown me any kindness; but for him I should have starved and died. If I did not love him, I should be a monster of ingratitude; but you make a mistake, Miss Pinkin, in thinking that I have lifted my eyes above my station. I have never dared to do so. I was crying because if he marries I shall hardly ever see him; but I am very glad to hear good news about him, and I hope he will be very happy.' The last words were spoken, for all her bravery, with a little choke in them, as Gretchen prepared herself to put on her bonnet and to go out on her daily rounds. And Miss Pinkin, although she thought her words most strange and forward, and turned up her eyes in wonder at what on earth the young women of the present day were coming to, yet felt a pang of pity as she watched the girl pass out, patiently and humbly, carrying her roll of music under her arm, with her sad white face bent downwards, and her eyes still swollen with tears.

Late that night, when her work was all over, and long after Miss Pinkin overhead was snoring the sonorous snores of the just, Gretchen Rudenbach sat up, by the light of her one candle, writing to the man whom she was not ashamed to own that she loved —a laborious letter, much pondered over, and all written in fine, delicate German-looking characters—the only foreign things about her were her name and her handwriting—a letter in which she invoked every good gift in heaven and earth upon her benefactor, and prayed that the good God would bless him and make him happy, as he deserved to be; and then she told him that she would never forget him, however many years she might live, but always remember him morning and evening in her prayers. She told him that she knew the woman he loved must be good and beautiful, and it made her, Gretchen, glad to think how happy and proud of his love his chosen bride must be; and lastly she told him that if ever he was sad, or sorry, or in trouble, if he would come to her, he would always find in her a devoted and faithful friend, who would at any time give her life to serve him and to comfort him.

Poor little high-flown letter; yet with truth and earnestness breathing out from every line! it was written with so many prayers and tears, and with such simple devotion of a love that only asked to spend itself, and expected nothing in return!

And Cecil Travers read it with a smile, thought first he would show it to Juliet, and then, with a better feeling, decided not to show it to anyone, but tore it to pieces and threw it into the fire, and then—forgot to answer it!

Meanwhile the preparations for Juliet's wedding went on apace. As it would be only six months after poor Georgie's death, it was, of course, to be a very quiet affair, but still it was impossible, on an estate like Sotherne, to prevent a certain amount of feasting and rejoicing among the tenantry and labourers. A dinner all classes in tents on the lawn, and a tenants' ball and fireworks in the evening, were unavoidable on such an occasion; and although Juliet herself would not be there, she had nevertheless all the settling and arranging to do beforehand.

And her trousseau was also, of course, in progress. Here she found an invaluable ally in her stepmother, who was quite in her element, and who was allowed to order silks, satins, and laces to her heart's content.

Time went on; Juliet was too busy to be unhappy; and she was too thorough a woman not to take an interest in the hundred and one details of her wedding preparations. She wrote her orders to tradesmen, her letters to friends, her list of guests—everything, in short, that was necessary to be done—with a sort of dazed, bewildered feeling of unreality running through it all. It was as if she were doing it for some one else, and not for herself. A sort of stagnation was in her heart; she was not happy, neither was she unhappy; she was simply very busy, too busy to think; and, even had she had the time, there was throughout a dumb stupor in her mind, as if all her feeling, thinking powers were extinct.

This lasted till four days before her wedding, and then an event happened which taught her painfully that her capacity for suffering was as keen as ever.

A box arrived for her. It was no uncommon event, for presents from acquaintances came to her every day now. But when Higgs brought in this particular box, Juliet knew, almost before she looked at the travel-stained direction, that it came from India.

'Take it up to my room and unfasten it, Higgs,' she said calmly to the man, whilst all the time her heart beat painfully.

In a few minutes she went upstairs, and locked her door. The box, with its lid off, was in the middle of the room. She knelt down in front of it; at the very top lay a note addressed to her in a large well-known handwriting. The envelope, simply directed to 'Miss Blair,' and without stamp or post-mark, seemed to bring him very near to her; it was as if his hand had only just laid it there. With a miserable hopelessness she opened it and read :—

My dear Juliet,—I send you a few trifles that I have chosen for you with great care, remembering the things you used to admire. Perhaps when this reaches you, you will be Juliet Blair no longer. May every blessing, and every joy that heaven and earth can give, be yours! In all probability I shall never meet you again, and I dare say I shall not trouble you with many letters; but I shall often think of you, dear child, oftener perhaps than you would imagine it possible. You have been a little harsh to me, Juliet. I will not blame or reproach you—you were probably full of your new happiness—it was not intentional, I know—you forgot—but oh, child, you might have written me *one* line—the coldest would have been less cold than your silence.

Yours always,

HUGH FLEMING.

The letter dropped from her fingers.

What did he mean? how could she have written to him, who had never written to her? in what had she been harsh to him?

Harsh! and to *him*, her love, her heart's darling! how could such a thing have been possible?

With set white lips, and lines of painful bewilderment on her forehead, she knelt, staring blankly in front of her.

Dimly, vaguely, there dawned upon her the possibility of the existence of some horrible misunderstanding between them; he had not forgotten her, he still thought of her with affection, and yet he accused her of forgetting, and he reproached her!—for what?

Was it possible that, in spite of his silence, his coldness, his desertion of her, he loved her even now?

But of what avail? was it not too late? With a low cry of despair she buried her face in her hands. Of what use were all her vague hopes and speculations now—now that it was too late?

Presently she roused herself to look at the contents of the box; one after the other she drew out richly-chased gold and silver ornaments, gorgeous-coloured cashmeres heavy with embroidery, and rare specimens of old Oriental china. All were lovely and in excellent taste—things, as he had said, that he knew she would like; yet Juliet turned away from the glittering array with positive disgust; the spicy odour of the sandal-wood shavings in which they had been packed, and which is so peculiarly Indian, made her turn sick and faint.

Why had he sent them? why had he written? Believing herself forgotten and scorned, she had been able to reconcile herself almost cheerfully to the life that was before her. But how was she to bear it, if by some dreadful, incomprehensible mistake, she was to discover that he loved her after all?

And again she puzzled and pondered, until her head ached with her thoughts, wondering what it was he meant, why he reproached her with silence and with harshness; to what did he allude? and she could in no way understand or answer these questions to herself.

There is an old superstition, of which probably on this occasion both bride and bridegroom were unaware, that a marriage in the 'Virgin's month,' the month of May, is unlucky.

And, certainly, the weather, to begin with, appeared anxious to carry out the old saying.

The 20th of May, Juliet Blair's wedding-day, was ushered in with a fine cheerless drizzle which by nine o'clock had settled down into a steady downpour.

Nevertheless, at as early an hour as five in the morning, a small person, cloaked and bonneted, and bearing a waterproof, an umbrella, and a little handbag containing a parcel of roughly-cut sandwiches and some ginger-bread nuts, came creeping cautiously down the staircase of a certain house in Pimlico.

At an angle of the stairs a door suddenly flew open, and an awful apparition—Miss Pinkin in her night-gown, with a frilled nightcap, and minus the black front—stood in a threatening attitude on the landing,

'Merciful heavens! what on earth are you doing? where in the name of common-sense are you going at five o'clock in the morning, disturbing honest folk in their beds? have you lost your wits, Gretchen Rudenbach?'

'I am going out,' answered that damsel humbly, yet with a sort of doggedness which quiet-mannered people often evince.

'Going out! at five o'clock! are you going to climb the lamp-posts to put out the gas-lights, pray?' which sneering display of ignorance concerning the habits of the London lamplighter caused Miss Rudenbach to smile.

'No, I am going to spend the day in the country, Miss Pinkin; don't keep me standing here—I shall lose my train.'

'*Where* are you going, may I ask?' and every frill on ·Miss Pinkin's night-cap seemed to stand erect with outraged virtue.

'To see a friend,' answered the girl defiantly.

'Humph!' snorted Miss Pinkin; 'you'll come to harm, Gretchen, as sure as my name is Sarah Anne Pinkin. I wash my hands of you. A friend, indeed! as if I didn't know where you are going! Go your own way. You'll come to harm, mark my words!' and shaking a warning finger at her refractory lodger, Miss Pinkin flounced back into the privacy of her bedroom.

Gretchen crept out alone into the deserted streets—to find a cheerless leaden sky, that harmonised well with the girl's own sad thoughts, and wet, muddy pavements, through which her ill-made boots splashed laboriously as she plodded along them. At so early an hour neither cabs nor omnibuses were stirring, and Gretchen had come out prepared to walk to the station. Her way lay across Hyde Park. The path was wet and sloppy; the wind drove the fine grey drizzle straight into her face, and blew her·shabby little black bonnet half off her head; and she had a difficulty in keeping up he umbrella. As she struggled painfully along, a solitary figure, coming from the opposite direction, passed her half-way in the middle of the Park.

Passed, and then looked back at her, and with a start recognised her.

'You! Gretchen!'

'Yes, it is I,' said Gretchen, shrinking a little aside as David Anderson's honest but rough face peered down under her umbrella.

'But where on earth are you going at this hour?'

'I am going to the station to catch an early train; please don't stop me, I have no time to lose,' she answered irritably, and hurrying on; but David Anderson kept pace beside her.

'I cannot let you walk alone; I will go with you,' he said, gently taking her bag out of her hand, and steadying the fluttering umbrella over her head with his stronger hand.

'Where are you going?'

'I am going into the country to spend the day; if I were to ask you so many questions, you would not like it. Pray, where are *you* going, and where do you come from?'

David Anderson, who, truth to tell, was coming home in the early morning from a very late and very riotous party at the lodgings of a friend, a late member of the now dispersed 'Melodious Minstrels' society, found the questions somewhat difficult to answer, and walked along by her side in snubbed silence.

How Gretchen hated this enforced companionship! There *was* a time when she had been almost fond of David Anderson; but of late she had learnt to regard him with aversion and disgust. She looked at him through Cecil Travers's eyes; she remembered that Cis had called him underbred, a snob and a boor, and that he had made her promise that she would never be so foolish as to throw herself away upon a man so thoroughly inferior to herself. On arriving at the Great Western Terminus, Gretchen insisted upon taking her ticket herself, while she had sent David away to secure a place for her in a second-class carriage. She did not want him to know where she was bound.

Poor David lingered ruefully by the carriage door till the train went off, hoping in vain for some kind word of thanks that would repay him for his wet walk; but Gretchen only gave him a careless nod as she was carried off, and the great rough fellow turned away with a deep sigh and something very like tears in his eyes.

It was the old story of cross-purposes everywhere. Elinor is in love with Charles, who does not even know it, but is sighing out his soul for Lady Blanche, who is as far above his reach as the moon, and who, moreover, nourishes a secret affection for young Dandy in the Guards, whilst that young gentleman, cruelly careless of the girl he might have for the asking, is passionately and hopelessly smitten with pretty Mrs. Lowndes, who has four children and a prosy husband, and who snubs young Dandy heartlessly, being herself bent upon the fascination of some one else; and so on—the wrong man is for ever pairing off with the wrong woman, till one is tempted to look upon the whole well-worn subject of love and its delights as the creation of a few high-flown and ignorant poetical gentlemen, and to ask, if it be indeed true that 'marriages are made in heaven,' why it is that, being confessedly for the most part such utter failures, the unconscious victims of these unsuccessful arrangements above are not allowed a re-adjustment of matters on earth? What a game of Puss-in-the-corner we should have, to be sure!

'Can you tell me the way to Sotherne Church, please?' asks Gretchen of the porter, as she is landed shivering in the rain on the little wayside station platform, and the train that has brought her disappears slowly in the distance.

'Straight on, miss,'—when does anyone give one any other direction to find one's way than that inevitable 'straight on?'— 'straight on as fur as you can see, and you'll come to the church; it will be wet walking for you, miss,' added the man, softened, perhaps, by the pretty, gentle face and the big, sad blue eyes.

The road, of course, was anything but 'straight;' it wound about like a serpent between its wet green hedges, and there were innumerable cross-roads intersecting it in every direction, so that Gretchen had to ask several times, and had some difficulty in finding her way.

Eventually, however, after about two miles' walk along the sloppiest and wettest of country lanes, she arrived at the village and the church.

Even at this early hour—it was but nine o'clock—it was evident that some unusual event was about to happen. The place was all astir, several triumphant arches of greenery had been erected across the road, and the village carpenters were still at work tying up the last branch of lilac, and tin-tacking securely the last breadth of bunting. Flags were flying from the public-houses and principal houses in the village, whilst the inhabitants in their Sunday clothes stood about in groups talking eagerly and excitedly of the coming festivities. The church doors were wide open, and Gretchen entered unmolested and took up her position in a sheltered nook close to the door, behind a stone pillar.

Some women were laying red cloth down the aisle, and presently, with a little commotion, the Vicar's bustling little wife came in with a big basket of flowers on her arm, with which she proceeded to decorate the altar.

Gretchen watched her with greedy eyes. What would she not have given to help her! she had a half-thought of going forward to offer her assistance; but shyness and prudence kept her back.

As Mrs. Dawson passed down the church again, she glanced sharply at the girl sitting alone, half-concealed behind the pillar. She knew every woman and girl in the parish of Sotherne, and in most of the parishes round, and Gretchen's face was strange to her; besides, she evidently belonged to a better class than any of the farmers' daughters about. Gretchen blushed deeply as she felt herself the object of such close scrutiny; and as she noticed the blush on the pretty, delicate features, and the downcast blue eyes, and the bent, smooth brown head, with its poor but perfectly lady-like covering, something of the real state of the case flashed through the mind of the clergyman's wife.

'Come down from town by the first train to see Cis Travers married!' was her mental reflection. 'Well, men *are* wretches, but I did think Cis Travers was too soft for that kind of thing—he is not half good enough for Juliet in any way, and now it appears he has not even been devoted to her! It all comes of his father's letting him be knocking about London so long by himself; it's a shocking bad thing for boys'—with a rapid thought of her own stalwart sons. 'I shall be careful not to let Tom and Charlie be turned out in London with nothing to do. Poor girl!' added the Vicar's wife to herself pityingly, as she trudged rapidly down the churchyard path to the vicarage gate; 'she looked modest and gentle enough; I dare say he has made her very unhappy—the wretch! Well, I don't think I shall say anything about it to the Vicar; he would be wanting to come out and reclaim her before breakfast, and that would make us all late; and besides, he would be sure to call her 'brazen woman' or 'daughter of sin,' or some horribly coarse name to her face, and that would do more harm than good: good men are so hard on women! and they never have any discrimination to distinguish between the vicious and the unfortunate—no, I will say nothing about it; besides, I really know nothing, it is only my own suspicions.' So saying, good little Mrs. Dawson, who, like many—alas, not most!—Christian women, had all a woman's tenderness towards a sorrowing fellow-woman, from whatever source her sorrows might come, shook off her wet cloak and stamped her muddy little toes in the vicarage porch, and went in to pour out her husband's tea, with never a word to that excellent but somewhat severe divine about the little strange girl who sat shivering in the church hard by, and who seemed to Mrs. Dawson's eyes to be the living impersonation of Cis Travers's London wickednesses—wickednesses of which you and I, my reader, know him to be guiltless.

I am not going to describe Juliet Blair's wedding. Weddings are but dismal things at best, and if anyone has a partiality for reading detailed accounts of them, of the demeanour and aspect of the ' blushing bride,' of the elaborate costumes of herself and her bridesmaids, and her friends' presents on the interesting occasion, they have but to study the last ' Court Journal,' where such scenes are weekly set forth in far better language and with far more knowledge of the subject than I should be at all likely to display.

Juliet Blair's wedding was exactly like anyone else's. There was the same fluttering in of well-dressed wedding guests, bustling backwards and forwards in and out of the pews to exchange whispered greetings with each other. The same gathering of prettily-dressed and moderately good-looking bridesmaids at the bottom of the church. The same awkward interval of suspense whilst the bride was anxiously awaited, during which Cis stood first on one leg, then on the other, and gnawed nervously at the ends of his straw-coloured kid gloves in the same helpless-looking way that every bridegroom invariably does, suggesting irresistibly the idea that, but for the best man—in this case, a very young Oxford friend—he must inevitably turn and flee. The best man, with a big button-hole flower, looks jaunty and self-important, as if the success of the whole ceremony depended mainly upon his exertions, although a passing thought of the speech which he will have to make by-and-by sends an occasional cold shudder down his back. Then the bride comes in on Sir George Ellison's arm, for, as she has no near relative, he, as an old friend of her father's, is to give her away. And there is the same scuffle of everybody getting into their places that always happens, and the ceremony proceeds with the same sniffles and snuffles from that female portion of the spectators who are invariably affected to tears without any known cause on such occasions.

There was nothing at all peculiar or striking in Juliet Blair's wedding; but to Gretchen Rudenbach, craning forward and straining her eyes and ears to catch every sight and every sound, it was a wedding different from every other wedding.

Presently the organ burst joyfully into the Wedding March, and the bride and bridegroom came down the aisle together, the school children flung flowers down before them as they came, and Gretchen pressed forward with the rest. Down at the bride-

BLACK RUPERT'S LEAP.

groom's feet there fell a little bunch of lilies of the valley that only last night had been fastened together in Covent Garden Market, and the next moment they were crushed—poor, innocent white blossoms !— beneath his heel.

And looking at his wife's face, cold, impassive, and almost despairing, Cis Travers, with a start, caught sight of a face beyond it, eager, yearning, wet with tears, and quivering with emotion, and in that moment the young bridegroom felt vaguely which it was of these two women that loved him best.

In another second Gretchen had shrunk back into her sheltering corner, and Cis was tucking his wife's white satin train into the carriage ; whilst she, with her heart on the other side of the world, was saying to herself—

'It is too late now—too late !   Oh, Hugh !   Oh, my darling, why did you ever leave me?'

(To be continued.)

Black Rupert's Leap.

Black Rupert, speed !   Your glossy neck,
That never yet has felt the lash,
Is ruffled with the hot foam's fleck.
Across the rolling prairie dash,
Although a double load you bear.

The sun-burnt grass was dead and dry,
A jealous enemy was near,
And from his bitter hate we fly.
Black Rupert, speed, by all that's dear !
To 'scape the fate we three may share.

Too late !—too late !   Your quivering flank
Heaves, and your blood-stained eyeballs glare;
And nearer yet come, hot and rank
The stifling smoke, and cruel flare
Of flames that race before the wind.

On ! Rupert, on !   For life or death !
The hand that loves you plies the whip;
And scorching torments suck the breath
That trembles on my darling's lip.
On ! Rupert, from the hell behind.

A falter !   Ah, the cruel lash !
A crash of stones—a gleaming light—
And in our front a fiery flash.
Thank God !   the torrent meets our sight
Amid the foliage which it fed.

A bound—a rushing through the air—
And Rupert's sinews, tried as steel,
Have borne us o'er the stream, and there
Safe by brave Rupert's form we kneel;
—But he is motionless and dead !

W. E. W.

The New Republic;

OR, CULTURE, FAITH, AND PHILOSOPHY IN AN ENGLISH COUNTRY HOUSE.

BOOK III.—CHAPTER III.

CULTURE could hardly have been discussed in a lovelier or more appropriate scene, nor could a more delicate or melodious voice have dwelt upon it than that of Otho Laurence. Every influence of the summer afternoon conspired to make all take kindly to the topic—the living airy whisper of the leaves overhead, the wandering scents of the flowers that the breeze just made perceptible, the musical splash of the fountain in its quiet restlessness, the luxury of the mossy turf as soft as sleep or rose-leaves, and a far faint murmur of church-bells that now and then invaded the ear gently, like a vague appealing dream. Mr. Saunders even was caressed by his flattered senses into peacefulness; the high and dry light of the intellect ceased to scintillate in his eyes; the spirit of progress condescended to take a temporary doze.

'Of course,' Laurence began, smiling with a little preparatory shyness, 'we can all understand the difference between a coarse common rustic palate, like that of the burly farmer, for instance, who just enjoys food in a brute way when he is hungry, and drink so long as it is spirituous at all times; and the palate of the true epicure, that is sensitive to taste as the nicest ear is to music, and can discriminate perfectly all the subtle semitones and chords of flavour. Well, transfer this image from the mouth to the mind, and there's the whole thing in a nutshell. There is culture and no culture. A person is really cultivated when he can taste not only the broad flavours of life—gulping its joys and sorrows down, either with a vulgar grimace of disgust, or an equally vulgar hearty voracity; but when with a delicate self-possession he appreciates all the subtler taste of things, when he discriminates between joy and joy, between sorrow and sorrow, between love and love, between career and career; discerning in all incidents and emotions their beauty, their pathos, their absurdity, or their tragedy, as the case may be.'

' You mean, then,' said Miss Merton, ' that a man of the highest culture is a sort of emotional *bon-vivant*? '

' That surely is hardly a fair way—' began Laurence.

' Excuse me, my dear Laurence,' broke in Mr. Luke, in his most magnificent of manners, ' it is perfectly fair—it is admirably fair. Emotional *bon-vivant*!' he exclaimed. ' I thank Miss Merton for teaching me that word!—for it may remind us all,' Mr. Luke continued, drawing out his words slowly, as if he liked the taste of them, ' how near our view of the matter is to that of a certain Galilean peasant—of whom Miss Merton has perhaps heard—who described the highest culture by just the same metaphor, as a hunger and a thirst after righteousness. Our notion of it differs only from his, from the *Zeitgeist* having made it somewhat wider.'

Miss Merton, in her inmost soul, did anything but return Mr. Luke's compliment, and consider his comment on her words as either admirably or perfectly fair. However, she held her peace. The thoughts of Lady Ambrose had been flowing in a slightly different direction.

' I want to ask one thing, too,' she said. ' I want to know why it is that whenever one hears it said, " Oh, So-and-so is a very *cultivated* person," one always expects to find him—well, almost half professional as it were, or at least able to talk of nothing but music, or painting, or books? I mean, a man who's *merely* a cultivated person, doesn't seem ever to be quite a man of the world, or to be much good in society, except when one wants him to talk on his own subjects—I hate people myself who *have* subjects—and then, ten to one, he doesn't know when to leave off. Now, Mr. Laurence, I see you want to interrupt me; but do let me say my say. A right amount of culture is of course delightful, and personally I don't much care for people who haven't got it. But too much of it—I'm sure, Mr. Laurence, you must agree with me at heart—is a mistake. And it seemed to me just now that you were expecting people to have rather too much.'

' Ah,' said Laurence smiling, ' I see the reason now why you accused me of making our state too bookish, when I dwelt on the books to be found in our Utopian drawing-room. You look on culture as some special kind of accomplishment or taste, like music; and you think that in some special way it is bound up with books; and books you look upon as something special also, beginning and ending with themselves; and unless I am much mistaken, you think that the more books a man has read, the more cultivated you may safely call him.'

' Not all books,' said Lady Ambrose, in an injured tone. ' Mr

Laurence, you shouldn't go about to misrepresent me so. It's very ill-natured of you. Of course I don't mean books of history, and things like that.'

'But what I want to impress on you,' said Laurence, ' is this: that culture, whatever its relation to books may be, is in no way a bookish thing—a thing for the library or the lecture-room, or a thing less in place at Hurlingham than at the South Kensington Museum. Nor is it in any sense a hobby, or a special taste, to be gratified at the expense of anything else. But it is a thing for men and women of the world, and of society; and it would be really only in the best society that we could look to find it in perfection.'

Lady Ambrose smiled, and looked more interested, and began to give Laurence her most intelligent attention.

'Still,' Laurence went on, ' culture and books have a good deal to do with one another; and since they are so bound up together in your mind, let us try to see at once what the relation really is. Let us begin, then, with that kind of culture which is most bound up with books—which, in fact, cannot be got without them—the culture, I mean, that comes from a knowledge of the past—from a knowledge of history, in short, or parts of history.'

Lady Ambrose here took Laurence fairly aback by the way in which she repeated the word ' History!'

'Well, judging from the results I have seen,' she said, with an unusual amount of decision in her voice, ' I can *not* say, Mr. Laurence, that I agree with you. And I think that on this subject I have a right to speak.'

'What can the woman be meaning?' said Mr. Luke to himself.

'It is not a fortnight ago,' Lady Ambrose went on, ' that I sat at dinner by a man—I won't tell you his name—who had not only read heaven knows how much history, but had written, I believe, even more than he had read. And what do you think this good man did during all the early part of dinner? Why, he did nothing but fume, and fret, and bluster, so that everyone was made uncomfortable because somebody said that King Harold was not quite so excellent a character as the late Prince Consort; and I heard him muttering, "What monstrous injustice! What monstrous ignorance!" to himself for nearly half an hour. I don't think I ever saw such a—I was going to say,' said Lady Ambrose, laughing softly, ' such a beast—but I won't; I'll say a bear instead. At last, however—I don't know how it came about—he said to me, in a very solemn voice, "What a terrible defeat that was which we had at Bouvines!" I said timidly—not thinking we were at war with anyone—that I had seen nothing about it in the papers. He gave rather a rude grunt, and made me feel dreadfully ignorant, and then he said to me very brusquely, " I had an excursus on it myself in the 'Archæological Gazette ' only last week." And, do you know, it turned out that the Battle of Bouvines was fought in the thirteenth century, and had, as far as I could make out, something to do with Magna Charta. Now, Mr. Laurence, if that's the sort of culture one gets from studying history, I'm glad I've forgotten even the names of the twelve Cæsars, and the dates of the kings of England. Besides, it makes one think what a serious thing it is to lose a battle, if people are to be made so cross about it six hundred years afterwards.'

' I quite agree with you,' said Laurence, 'that if that's the sort of culture one gets from history, we had better never open a history book again. But history, Lady Ambrose, has very little to do with the Battle of Bouvines, and nothing with the character of Harold. History, in its true sense, is a travelling in the past ; the best of histories are but the carriages or the steamboats you travel by ; your histories of dates and battles are at best but the Bradshaws and the railway-maps. Our past must be an extension of the present, or it is no real past. Now I expect, Lady Ambrose, that, in its true sense, you know a good deal more history than you are aware of. I saw you reading Saint-Simon yesterday evening, and you alluded to Grammont's Memoirs at dinner.'

' Oh, of course,' exclaimed Lady Ambrose, ' books like that ! But, then, they really give you such a notion of the times, and quite take you back to them.'

' Nothing is history that does not,' said Laurence.

Mr. Saunders, who was lying down with his hat over his eyes, and who seemed asleep, here made a little unquiet moan, and shuffled himself for a moment impatiently.

' Really,' said Lady Ambrose, brightening,' " il y a plus de vingt ans que je dis de la prose, sans que j'en susse rien." And so it seems that I have known history without suspecting it, just as M. Jourdain talked prose.'

' Well,' said Laurence, ' don't you see something of what history does for us, as men and women of the world, in the way of culture —history, this travelling in the past, as I have called it ? Think for a moment what our own age would seem to us if all the past, beyond the memories of our grandfathers, was a blank to us ; and then think how infinitely our minds are enlarged, how a freer air, as it were, seems to blow through them, even from that vague knowledge of the past afloat in the world, which we pick up here and there as we go along. Even that has an effect upon us. It makes us no longer merely *temporal* people, who are just as narrow-minded and dull as those merely *local* people—the natives of a neighbourhood—who wear gorgeous ribands at flower-shows in the country.'

Lady Ambrose smiled and nodded.

' Go on, Mr. Laurence—I can understand all this,' she said. ' But I want to hear a little more.'

' Well,' said Laurence, ' your own knowledge of the history of France and England during the last two hundred years—you know well enough how that has made you, in a certain sense, more a woman of the world. But your knowledge of history does not really end there. You know something of the feudal times. You know what a castle was like, what a knight was like, and what a monk was like; and you know something, too, of Rome, and Greece, and Palestine, and Egypt; and each of these names is really a little aerial chariot which carries your imagination back as you pronounce it into some remote age, when life was different from what it is now. So is the mind widened by even a little vague history. Or, just repeat to yourself such words as *France* and *Italy*, and think for a moment of the effect of them. They are not mere names—mere geographical expressions; but they are spells which evoke, whether you will or no, hosts of subtle associations, rising up like spirits out of the past centuries, and hovering in the air round you with their unbidden influence, and mixing with all your notions of Europe as it is now. Or, would you feel the matter more strongly yet, think, when you are travelling, what but for history would Venice be, or Athens, or Jerusalem? If it were not for history, would you find the same indescribable fascination in Rome?'

' I never was at Rome,' said Lady Ambrose. ' We're going there next winter with the Kenningtons.'

Laurence proceeded no further. Mr. Rose, however, whose imagination had been fired by all this talk about history, suddenly broke forth.

' History!' he exclaimed, ' why, but for history, what should we be now but a flock of listless barbarians, ὀνειράτων ἀλίγκιοι μορφαῖσι φυρόντες εἰκῇ πάντα? Is it not history that takes us back to Greece, and lets us find in Greece, after so many centuries, the chief teaching we, in our present case, need—how fair a thing life may be, how rich in harmonious freedom, and beauty of form, and love, and passionate friendship? Is it not history, too, that gives us that other teacher of ours—that strange child of Aphrodite and Tannhäuser—the Italian Renaissance? Is it not, indeed, by history alone that we in our day can learn anything of the more subtle and gorgeous dyes that life is capable of taking, and will, we may trust, yet again take? What, but for history, should we know,' cried Mr. Rose, ' of the χάρις of Greece, of the lust of Rome, of the strange secrets of the Borgias? Consider, too,' he said, sinking into a dreamier tone, ' of the bowers of quiet, full of sweet dreams, that history will always keep for us—how it surrounds the house of the present with the boundless gardens of the past—gardens rich in woods, and waters, and flowers, and outlooks on illimitable seas. Think of the immortal dramas which history sets before us; of the keener and profounder passions which it shows in action, of the exquisite groups and figures it reveals to us, of nobler mould than ours—Harmodius and Aristogeiton, Achilles and Patroclus, David and Jonathan, our English Edward and the fair Piers Gaveston, ἅμα τ᾽ ὠκύμορος καὶ ὀϊζυρὸς περὶ πάντων.'

' Wait a moment,' said Lady Ambrose, with a meditative smile.

Mr. Rose, not having fancied Lady Ambrose at all a person to understand or sympathise with him, stopped instantly, and looked at her with a mixture of surprise and pleasure.

' Wait a moment,' she said; ' I once knew the date of Piers Gaveston. I learnt it in a " Memoria Technica," when we had sentences to remember the dates by. *The Mad Sad Gaveston*, 1307. There, Mr. Laurence, I remember it now, you see. Isn't that right, Mr. Rose? I really do begin to think that I'm quite an historian.'

' At any rate,' said Laurence, ' you see now something of the sort of culture which history gives us; and you see, too—this is the chief point I want to impress upon you—that in history, and many other things as well, books are only the telescopes through which we see distant facts; and we no more become *bookish* by such a use of books than you became *optical* when you looked through your telescope in Gloucestershire, and saw Captain Audley, at the bottom of the park, proposing to your under-keeper's daughter.'

' I really do believe,' said Lady Ambrose, ' that that man is a little off his head. However,' she went on laughing, ' I give up about the bookishness, Mr. Laurence, and I dare say one really is the better for knowing something about history; but still, I can't help thinking that the chief thing to know about is, after all, the life about one, and that knowledge, just like charity, should begin at home.'

' There, Lady Ambrose,' said Laurence, ' we quite agree. That was the very thing I wanted to impress upon you. It is just this—to appreciate the life about us, and, I should add, to enrich it also, that is the whole and sole aim of culture. We only study the past to adorn our present, and make our view of it clearer.

And now let us put the past out of our minds altogether, and merely consider culture and the present. I tried to explain just now that we meant by a man of culture one on whom none of the finer flavours of life are lost—who can appreciate, sympathise with, criticise all the scenes, situations, sayings, or actions around him— a sad or happy love-affair, a charm of manner and conversation, a beautiful sunset, or a social absurdity. I declare,' said Laurence, ' I could tell better whether a man was really cultivated, from the way in which he talked gossip, or told a story, than from the way in which he discussed a poem or a picture.'

' Certainly,' said Leslie, ' I don't call a woman cultivated who bothers me at dinner first with discussing this book and then that— whose one perpetual question is, " Have you read So-and-so?" But I call a woman cultivated who responds and who knows what I mean as we pass naturally from subject to subject—who by a flash or a softness in her eyes, by a slight gesture of the hand, by a sigh, by a flush in the cheek, makes me feel as I talk of some lovely scene that she too could love it—as I speak of love or sorrow, makes me feel that she herself has known them ; as I speak of ambition, or *ennui*, or hope, or remorse, or loss of character, makes me feel that all these are not mere names to her, but things.'

' Do you call *me* cultivated, Mr. Leslie ? ' whispered Mrs. Sinclair, with a smile of plaintive humour, in a soft parenthesis.

' I mean,' said Leslie, finishing, ' I like to hear each key I touch make, not a dead thud, as on a piece of wood, but strike a musical string.'

'Good,' murmured Mr. Rose; 'that is good! Yes,' he continued, ' the aim of culture, if Mr. Leslie will lend me his nice metaphor, is indeed to make the soul a musical instrument, which may yield music either to itself or to others, at any appulse from without ; and the more elaborate a man's culture is, the richer and more composite can this music be. The minds of some men are like a simple pastoral reed. Only single melodies, and these unaccompanied, can be played upon them—glad or sad ; whilst the minds of others, who look at things from countless points of view, and realise, as Shakespeare did, their composite nature—their minds become, as Shakespeare's was, like a great orchestra. Or sometimes,' said Mr. Rose dreamily, as if his talk was lapsing into a soliloquy, ' when he is a mere passive observer of things, letting impressions from without move him as they will, I would compare the man of culture to an Æolian harp, which the winds at will play through— a beautiful face, a rainbow, a ruined temple, a death-bed, or a line of poetry, wandering in like a breath of wind amongst the chords of his soul, touching note after note into soft music, and at last gently dying away into silence.'

'Well, now,' said Laurence, speaking briskly, and in a matter-of-fact tone, for he was afraid that Mr. Rose's dreamy manner might confuse Lady Ambrose, 'since we see that the aim of culture is to make us better company as men and women of the world, let us consider a little further how culture is attained. We have just spoken of histories and other books, which merely bring us face to face with distant facts. We want to know now how, given the knowledge or experience of facts—the facts of the present especially—we are to convert this knowledge into culture. Mere experience will not do it. A woman may have had all kinds of experience—sorrow, and love, travel, remorse, distraction—and yet she may not be cultivated. She may have gone through everything only half consciously. She may never have recognised what her life has been. What is needed to teach her—to turn this raw material into culture? Here, Lady Ambrose, we come to our friends the books again—not, however, to such books as histories, but to books of art, to poetry, and books akin to poetry. The former do but enlarge our own common experience. The latter are an experience in themselves, and an experience that interprets all former experiences. The mind, if I may borrow an illustration from photography, is a sensitised plate, always ready to receive the images made by experience on it. Poetry is the developing solution, which first makes these images visible. Or, to put it in another way, if some books are the telescopes with which we look at distant facts, poetry—I use the word in its widest sense—is a magic mirror which shows us the facts about us reflected in it as no telescope or microscope could show them to us. Let a person of experience look into this, and experience then becomes culture. For in that magic mirror we see our life surrounded with issues viewless to the common eye. We see it compassed about with chariots of fire and with horses of fire. Then we know the real aspect of our joys and sorrows. We see the lineaments, we look into the eyes of thoughts, and desires, and associations, which had been before unseen and scarcely suspected presences—dim swarms clustering around our every action. Then, how all kinds of objects and of feelings begin to cling together in our minds! A single sense or a single memory is touched, and a thrill runs through countless others. The smell of autumn woods, the colour of dying fern, may turn by a subtle transubstantiation into pleasures and faces that will never come again — a red sunset and a windy sea-shore into a last farewell, and the regret of a lifetime.'

Laurence had chosen these illustrations of his quite at random;

but in the last he was fortunate in a way which he never dreamt of. Lady Ambrose had been engaged before her marriage to a young penniless Guardsman, whom she threw over for Sir George and his million of money; and her last meeting with her lover had taken place at a little Sussex watering-place, on a windy September evening.

'Ah,' she exclaimed with an abrupt emotion in her voice, 'I know what you mean now. Why, there have been poems, at one time or another of one's life, that one could hardly bear to hear repeated. Byron's song, "When we two parted;" it's very silly of me, but still there was a time, just because it was connected with something—I really——'

Lady Ambrose suddenly grew conscious that she was showing more feeling than she thought at all becoming. She blushed, she stammered a little, and then, making a rush at another topic, 'But what is Mr. Rose,' she exclaimed, 'saying about the Clock-tower and the Thames Embankment?'

'I was merely thinking,' said Mr. Rose, who had been murmuring to himself at intervals for some time, 'of a delicious walk I took last week, by the river side, between Charing Cross and Westminster. The great clock struck the chimes of midnight; a cool wind blew; and there went streaming on the wide wild waters, with long vistas of reflected lights wavering and quivering in them; and I roamed about for hours, hoping I might see some unfortunate cast herself from the Bridge of Sighs. It was a night, I thought, well in harmony with despair. Fancy,' exclaimed Mr. Rose, 'the infinity of emotions which the sad sudden splash in the dark river would awaken in one's mind—and all due to that one poem of Hood's!'

'Yes,' said Laurence, not having listened to Mr. Rose, who spoke, indeed, somewhat low, 'Yes,' he said, continuing the same train of thought he had left off with, and looking first at Lady Ambrose and then at Miss Merton, 'is it not poetry that does all this for the world? I use poetry in its widest sense, and include in it all imaginative literature, and other art as well. Is it not the poet that gives our existence all its deepest colours, or enables us to give them to it ourselves? Is it not—if I may quote a translation that I made myself—

Is't not the harmony that from his bosom springs,
And back into itself the whole world brings?
When Nature round her spindle, cold and strong,
Winds on and on the endless threads of things;
When all existences, a tuneless throng,
Make music as with jangling strings,
⌊Whose life-breath makes the flux of blind creation

Move to a rhythmic music of his own ?
Who calls each single thing to the common consecration,
When rapturously it trembles into tone ?
Who sets our wild moods and the storms in tune ?
Our sad moods, and the still eve's crimson glow ?
Who showers down all the loveliest flowers of June,
Where she, the heart's beloved, will go ?
Who, of a few green leaves in silly twine,
Makes toil's immortal guerdon art's reward,
Raises the mortal, draws down the divine ?
The power of man incarnate in the bard.

'And so,' said Laurence, 'if it is to the bard that we owe all these fine things, we need not fear to admit that the best society draws much of its choicest nourishment from poetry ; and all the books that I saw in my mind's eye in our Utopian drawing-room were meant for signs not of how much its inhabitants were given to reading, but of the variety of ways in which they have thought of life, and consequently of the exquisite delicacy with which they are able to appreciate it. I myself,' said Laurence, 'am devoted to literature as literature, to poetry as poetry. I value it, not only because it makes me appreciate the originals of the things it deals with, but for itself. I often like the description of a sunset better than I like a sunset ; I don't care two straws about Liberty, but my mind is often set all aglow by a good ode to her. I delight in, I can talk over, I can brood over, the form of a stanza, the music of a line, the turn of a phrase, the flavour of an epithet. Few things give me such pleasure, for the moment, as an apt quotation from Horace or Shakespeare. But this, I admit, is a hobby —a private hobby—this distinct literary taste, just as a taste for blue china is, and must certainly not be confused with culture in its deeper and wider sense.'

'Ah,' said Mr. Rose earnestly, 'don't despise this merely literary culture, as you call it, or the pleasure it is to have at command a beautiful quotation. As I have been lying on the bank here, this afternoon, and looking up into the trees, and watching the blue sky glancing between the leaves of them—as I have been listening to the hum of the insects, or looking out with half-shut eyes towards the soft floating sea across the green rustling shrubs, and the red roses, fragments of poetry have been murmuring in my memory like a swarm of bees, and have been carrying my fancy hither and thither in all manner of swift luxurious ways. The 'spreading favour,' for instance, of these trees that we sit under, brought just now into my mind those magical words of Virgil's—

Oh qui me gelidis in vallibus Haemi
Sistat et ingenti ramorum protegat umbrâ !

What a picture there! What a thrill it sent all through me, like
a rush of enchanted wind! In another moment the verse that
goes just before, also came to me—

> Virginibus bacchata Lacaenis
> Taygeta——

and into the delicious scene now around me—this beautiful
modern garden, mixed instantly visions of Greek mountains, and
rugged summits, and choirs of Laconian maidens maddened with
a divine enthusiasm, and with fair white vesture wildly floating.
Again, another line from the same poem, from the same passage,
touched my memory, and changed, in a moment, the whole complexion of my feelings—

> Felix qui potuit rerum cognoscere causas.

Think of that! The spirit is whirled away in a moment of time,
and set amongst quite new images, quite other sources of excitement. But again, in another moment, the splash of the fountain
caught my ear, and awoke, I scarce know how, the memory of
some lines in one of Petrarch's Epistles—

> Soporifero clausam qui murmure vallem
> Implet inexhausto descendens alveus amne——

and my imagination, on the wings of the verses, was borne away
floating towards Vaucluse. Think, then, within the space of five
minutes, how many thoughts and sensations, composite and
crowded, can, by the agency of mere literature, enrich the mind, and
make life intenser.'

'And I—' said Laurence, smiling, 'do you see that far-away
sail out on the horizon line?—well, I caught myself murmuring
over a scrap of Milton, only two minutes ago—

> As when afar at sea a fleet descried
> Hangs in the clouds, by equinoctial gales
> Close sailing from Bengala.

Why I could go on capping verses with you the whole afternoon,
if we had nothing else to do. But, besides this, a knowledge of
books as books has got another use. How it enriches conversation,
by enabling us to talk by hints and allusions, and to convey so
many more meanings than our actual words express. I came
across an exquisite instance of this the other day, in a book of
anecdotes about the poet Rogers, which shows how a familiarity
with the events even of Greek fiction may give a brilliance to
fashionable talk in the nineteenth century. One evening at Miss
Lydia White's—she was a Tory, and well known then in society—
a guest who was a Whig, said *à propos* of the depressed state of

his own party at the time, " There is nothing left for us but to sacrifice a Tory virgin." " Yes," said Miss Lydia White, " I believe there's nothing the Whigs wouldn't do *to raise the wind*." But yet after all this is not the important thing, and I hope Lady Ambrose will forgive us for having talked so long about it.'

'And so one *must* read a great deal, after all, to be really cultivated,' said Lady Ambrose in a disappointed tone. ' You've made culture seem such a nice thing, that I really feel quite ashamed to think how seldom now I look at a line of poetry.'

' Don't be afraid,' said Leslie ; ' to keep a society cultivated, a good deal of reading must be done by many. But with women, if they have had any serious experience, I have often been startled to find how far a very little poetry will go.'

' I expect,' said Miss Merton, ' that we are naturally more introspective than men, and so, in what concerns ourselves, a very little will make us cultivated ; although we don't certainly get so easily as men that indifferent way of looking on life as a whole, which I suppose is what you call the dramatic spirit, and which people praise so in Shakespeare. But as to what Mr. Leslie says, I have so often myself noticed the same thing in girls—especially at times when they are passing into womanhood, without having made much of a success of youth. I remember one poor friend of mine, whose whole life seemed to become clear through just one line of Tennyson's—

My life has crept so long on a broken wing.'

' And I,' said Leslie, ' often think of some one I used to know at Baden, who spent half her time at the tables, who was stared at for her beauty by everyone, and was certainly not a woman who gave much of her time to reading. She was very wretched with her husband, and her name was far from being above the reach of gossip. Talking one day to her in a hard and flippant way—a tone of talk which she affected to like—I alluded by some chance to Francesca di Rimini in Dante ; and I shall never forget the tone in which she exclaimed, " Poor Francesca!"—its passion and its pathos. I was surprised that she had even looked into Dante : but she had ; and that one passage had lit up her whole life for her—that one picture of the two lovers " going for ever on the accursed air." '

' How nice of you, Mr. Leslie,' said Mrs. Sinclair, ' to remember my poor verses ! '

' Let us consider, too,' said Laurence, ' that poetry does not only enable us to appreciate what we have already experienced, but it puts us in the way of getting new experiences. This was Wordsworth's special claim for poetry, that it widened our sympathies—widened them in some new direction—that it was ever giving us, in fact, not new quotations, but new culture.'

' And just consider for a moment,' said Leslie, ' the wonderful effect of even this partial, this Wordsworthian culture. Consider the effect of it on a common worldly woman, who without it would be nothing but a social hack, living, as far as her interests went, a wretched hand-to-mouth existence of thin distraction, or eager anxious scheming for herself or her daughters. Cultivate her, I say, just in this one direction—give her but this one fragment of culture, a love of Nature—and all the mean landscape of her mind will be lit up with a sudden beauty, as this beam of ideal sunshine breaks across it—"the light that never was on sea or land." I don't say that such a woman will become better for this, but she will become more interesting. In a girl, however pretty, what is there to interest a man if he reads nothing in her face from night to night but that she is getting daily more worn and jaded in the search for a rich husband ? Or even, to go a step higher, take the unthinking, uncultivated flirt, so common in every class of society—what is there in her that a man will not soon discover to be insipid and wearying ? '

' Surely,' remonstrated Mrs. Sinclair softly, 'that rather depends on what she is like. I must stand up for my sex.'

' But give her,' Leslie went on, ' one genuine, one disinterested taste, and all is changed. If I had an audience about me of young ladies, whom it was not too late to advise—girls entering on the world, determined to run the worldly course, and to satisfy all the expectations of the most excellent and lowest-minded of chaperons, I would say this to them :—I have no doubt you are all ignorant ; of course you are all vain. That to make a brilliant match is your great object, you all avow. That you have a real delight—some of you—in a certain sort of not very admirable flirting, is your most genuine point. I know all this (I should say), and I can't help it ; nor do I ask you to try to alter one of these points for the better. But this I do ask you to do. Try to cultivate one true, genuine taste. Study Wordsworth, or some parts of Shelley ; open out your sympathies, by their aid, in just one direction. Learn to love the sea, and the woods, and the wild flowers, with all their infinite changes of scent, and colour, and sound—the purple moor, the brown mountain stream, the rolling mists, the wild smell of the heather. Let these things grow to " haunt you like a passion," learn in this way the art of

desiring
More in this world than any understand.

You'll perhaps find it a little dull at first ; but go on, and don't be disheartened; and then—by-and-by—by-and-by, go and look in the looking-glass, and study your own face. Hasn't some new look, child, come into your eyes, and given them an expression—a something that they wanted before? Smile. Hasn't your smile some strange meaning in it that it never used to have? You are a little more melancholy, perhaps. But no matter. The melancholy is worth its cost. You are now a mystery. Men can't see through you at a glance as they did; and so, as Sterne says, "you have their curiosity on your side," and that alone—even that will have increased your value tenfold in the marriage-market.'

'Well, Mr. Leslie,' said Lady Ambrose with severe gravity, ' if that's the way you'd talk to young ladies, I should be very careful you never spoke to any that I had anything to do with.'

'It is a common notion,' went on Leslie, passing by the rebuke, ' that the men who really understand life and the art of living are the men who merely drive four-in-hand, or dance, or run away with their friends' wives, and who never read at all. But no mistake can be greater. It is really the men of culture who are the true masters of life—to whom all exercise or distraction, mental or bodily, moral or immoral, yields the finer—the keener—pleasures; the men whose company and conversation, on the top of a drag or in a ball-room, will make that of their illiterate brothers, in the judgment of men as well as of women, seem vapid, and dull, and tasteless.'

Lady Ambrose much disapproved of the tone of this speech; but all the same, in some mysterious way, it increased her appreciation of culture, and she felt that she thoroughly agreed with Laurence, when he said, by way of summing up—

'And so now, I think, we see what culture is. We see that, much as it depends on books, life is really the great thing that it has to do with. It fits us to discern and choose, or at least to long for, the best in every way that the world, in its present state, is capable of giving or suggesting to us. The question now is, what do we, as people of culture in this last quarter of the nineteenth century, most long for or try to attain?—what sort of lives, pleasures, virtues, happinesses? Let us consider these; and our whole Utopia will shape itself out of what is implied in them.'

Mr. Luke and Lord Allen both here began to speak at the same moment; but Mr. Luke, with the lofty courtesy of an elder, insisted that Lord Allen should—so Mr. Luke put it—' let them hear first what he had to say.'

What Lord Allen had to say shocked Lady Ambrose terribly. It was simply this, and he said it rather bluntly, and as if he had the matter really at heart: that for his part, as far as he knew himself, he didn't care for culture at all.

'What I should want in a Utopia,' he went on, 'would be something definite for the people to do, each in his own walk of life. What I should want would be some honest, definite, straightforward, religious belief that we might all live by, and that would connect what we did and went through here with something more important elsewhere. Without this, to start with,' he said, half sadly and half coldly, 'all life seems to me a mockery.'

'And are you quite sure,' said Laurence, with a slight sigh, 'that it is not a mockery?'

Lady Ambrose stared at Laurence. Miss Merton, who was sitting by him, also turned her eyes upon him, full of a pained interest.

'Don't say that,' she said to him, in a low tone; 'I know you don't mean it.'

Laurence, who had been sitting a little above her on the bank, moved quietly down, and placed himself at her side.

'You make me feel ashamed of myself,' he said to her, 'when you speak like this.'

There was something in his manner which a little embarrassed Miss Merton. She looked down, and pulled for a moment at the grass; and then, not having quite command of her voice, she answered him in a tone rather louder than she intended.

'Well,' she said, 'and don't you think that some definite faith or other is needed by the world?'

She looked again into Laurence's eyes; but Laurence made no answer.

There were two reasons for his silence—one internal, which cannot be very definitely described; the other external, which can be. This last reason was the fact that, scarcely was Miss Merton's question out of her mouth, when it was answered vehemently, and in the affirmative, by some one else. This was the last person in the company from whom such an answer could have been expected. It was Mr. Saunders.

'Yes, I think so—I think so,' he exclaimed, having shaken off his sleep with a suddenness that surprised everybody. 'I entirely agree with Miss Merton.'

'The deuce you do!' cried Mr. Luke, facing round to contemplate Mr. Saunders.

'Yes,' said Mr. Saunders, 'I entirely agree with Miss Merton and Lord Allen. What they have just said,' he continued, 'was, in fact, just what I was going to say some time since, when I called out "Stop." I wanted to point out to you then—and I may as well do it now—how utterly futile it was to try to construct a Utopia, and not to give it, before all things, one single creed—one Catholic absolute creed. And here, as far as I can judge, are you—wittingly or un-wittingly—including in your state all the worst evils we are now trying to get rid of—doubt, and private judgment, and so forth—and even the miserable paganism that still lingers on among us.'

Everyone stared at Mr. Saunders, everyone except Mr. Luke, who simply smiled at the sky, and said, with an air of sup-pressed pleasantry, 'I had imagined that our young friend's motto was *freedom*.'

Mr. Saunders was nettled at this beyond description. With a vindictive quickness he fixed his eyes upon Mr. Luke.

'Sight is free,' he said, uttering his words very slowly, as if each one were a dagger in itself, and could give Mr. Luke a separate smart; 'sight is free,' he said, 'and yet the sight of all healthy men, I conceive, is in agreement. It differs, I admit, when our eyes are dim with tears of hysterical feeling; or when we are drunk; or when we are fighting—in this last case, Mr. Luke, I am told we are often visited with illuminations of a truly celestial radiance—but it is surely not such exceptional vision as this that you praise as free. And it is just the same,' said Mr. Saunders triumphantly, and getting self-complacent again as he went on, 'with the mind. The minds of men will have never been so free as on that day when they shall first all agree. And agree they will,' he said, slapping his knee with his hand, 'and that before fifty years are over. That agreement is the great event we are now working our way towards. On that it is that the new birth of humanity depends. Surely, then,' he added, with a supercilious persuasiveness, 'any Utopia—any anticipation of the future—must be simply so much nonsense—forgive the plain word—if it be not based upon this— if it do not get rid of all our present doubt, private judgment, and paganism.'

'Paganism!' repeated Laurence.

'Why, I thought Mr. Saunders was a pagan himself,' said Lady Ambrose.

(To be continued.)

From Dreams to Waking.

BY E. LYNN LINTON.

CHAPTER VIII.
WITHOUT FALTERING.

'INDEED, Venny, it was not my fault. It has all come about I cannot tell how; but believe me, dear, it was not my fault!'

These were the first words that Graziella spoke when the two girls had returned home, and Venetia had gone as usual into the Creole's room to bid her good-night and see that all was arranged to her satisfaction. And she said them with the most excellent imitation of truth imaginable. One of those perfect make-believes who deceive even themselves, for the moment she did really think, as she said, that it had not been her fault, and that she had not known how it had all come about; certainly not by her own desire and still less by her own endeavour. It was the temporary blindness of the false, when, frightened at what they have done, they seek to quiet conscience and set themselves straight with those whom they have wronged.

'It was not my fault,' she repeated, burying her face in Venetia's lap and shedding some half forced, half nervous tears.

Venetia laid her hand lightly on the pretty head of the girl who had been for two long years her little queen and cherished idol, and whom even now she could not accuse of intentional ill-doing.

'Don't cry, dear,' she said quietly; 'I ought to have known that it would have come to this. He could not help loving you, Gracie—who could?'

'But it was very wrong, and he ought not,' said Graziella with pretty vehemence. 'If he had not cared for me first, and showed it so much, I never should for him. But, Venny,' lifting up her eyes imploringly, 'you yourself know how charming he is, and that no woman in the world could possibly resist him if he chose to make himself beloved!'

'How can I blame you, then?' said poor Venetia. 'It is no more your fault for loving him than it is his for loving you.'

'How good you are! how generous!' cried Graziella with a curious mixture of shame and pretence: shame in that she had acted so unworthily toward one so true and brave, one so much her superior—pretence in that this kind of unselfishness was a height of morality to which she in her jealous exclusiveness could neither rise nor yet wish to rise; neither understand nor yet wholly respect. This latter feeling became eventually the strongest, so that after a moment she thought to herself: 'All the same, Venny could not have cared so very much about him, else she would not have given him up so easily.'

'Generous!' said Venetia hopelessly. 'He has taken himself from me and given himself to you. I have only to accept what I cannot help.'

'I wish I had never come!' cried Graziella petulantly. 'If it had not been for that horrid scarlet-fever everything would have gone right, Venny, and you would perhaps have been married before the summer was out.'

'Don't!' said Venetia with a sharp cry.

She covered her face for a moment, then lifted it again and spoke as quietly as before.

'And which is best,' she said; 'that he has seen and loved you before instead of after? What would have become of me, Gracie, if it had been after?'

'Oh! a married man!' cried Graziella with becoming repudiation.

'If I could not keep him now I should not have kept him then,' Venetia answered wearily; 'or I should have kept him against his will; and I would rather he were happy without me than unhappy with me.'

'You are an angel,' murmured Graziella.

She did not know what else to say. It seemed so strange to her that Venetia should be sitting there with her hand in hers, her voice as gentle, her pale face as kind as ever, when she knew in her own heart that she had plotted against her happiness and stolen her lover from her by intentional wiles and charms displayed for the purpose. If such a thing had happened to her, Graziella, she felt that she would have killed the woman who had supplanted her; she would have sprung at her throat and strangled her, not have sat there holding her hand, caressing her head, and speaking in quiet, gentle tones, more sorrowful than angry—indeed not angry at all. And that Venetia should take her heart-break so patiently seemed to her the most wonderful part of all the strange little drama of love and infidelity, of faith and treachery, that had been playing of late.

She was glad, however, that all had been got over so well. She thought Venetia very silly to be so fond of her ; very mean-spirited to let her lover go so easily ; but it was a comfort not to have had a scene. And when the first interview between them both and Ernest had been gone through, and she had been formally recognized as his deliberate choice and her friend's successful rival, then there would be nothing to fear, and things would go smoothly. So she reasoned in the tangled jungle of thoughts and motives which made up her mind ; and her reasoning justified her action throughout.

It is not always that the largest amount of womanly strength lies with those who make the greatest display. Those muscular creatures with swinging step and resonant voice who look fit to lead an army, are sometimes as soft as wax when touched by mental sorrows and difficulties ; while essentially womanly women have a reserve force which carries them bravely through the darkest hours. As now with Venetia. Her strength was in her unselfishness and her love. She was one of those who love beyond self ; whose first thought is for others ; whose main desire is the happiness of the beloved. But though she was too unselfish to grieve in the headlong way of women who think only of their own misfortunes, and though she was determined to do her best to sympathize with the joy that was built up on her own despair, yet she could neither prevent nor conceal her suffering. She paled and drooped under her sorrow as if her life had been suddenly weakened ; and when she came downstairs the next morning she looked like one who has just come out of a deadly illness. Still, she held on her way without faltering. She loved both Ernest and Graziella better than herself ; and she had beside that pride of reticence which belongs to the gentler kind of women, and which makes them forbear to complain under suffering.

Nothing in her manner could have told the keenest observer that she had cause against Graziella when the two girls met over the breakfast table, and exchanged kisses and sweet greetings as usual. Only her face was deadly white, even to her lips ; her blue eyes were purpled and heavy, swollen and sad ; and instead of the graceful but elastic curves which had been one of her distinguishing charms, her figure seemed shrunk and as if bent under a heavy weight. Even Aunt Honoria could not fail to see the change which twelve hours had worked in her niece, and cried out in a tone of personal injury—

‘ Good gracious, child ! what on earth is the matter with you this morning ? What have you been doing to yourself ? Your complexion is horrid, and you look anyhow.’

'Yes, Venny, dear, you look as if you had a bad headache,' said Graziella tenderly.

'I have,' Venetia answered without affectation; and heartache, too, she might have added.

'Then do, for goodness' sake, child, get something to take it away,' said Aunt Honoria; 'some red lavender or something. It is quite dreadful to see you look such an object.'

'I shall be better after breakfast, auntie,' said Venetia in the same quiet, simple, uninterested way as before—as if she had been speaking of something that did not concern herself at all.

'Then get your breakfast,' said Aunt Honoria peevishly. 'I cannot bear to see you look so washed out and dreadful.'

Breakfast, though useful enough as a reviver in some cases, cannot do much for a girl whose lover has proved faithless and her best friend treacherous; and when Venetia had finished her tea and toast she was just as white and broken as before. But as she did not cry, Graziella was not so very much disturbed; and as she insisted that nothing was really amiss with her, Aunt Honoria subsided into silence. So she was left to herself; which was what she wanted.

Thus the early morning hours passed—Venetia apparently reading that crabbed bit of Jean Paul which she took as her soul's comfort, but forgetting to turn the pages and not seeing the words; while Graziella, with a show of doing modern point, alternately watched her friend and wondered what she was thinking of, or looked at her watch and wished that Ernest would come, both to get it over and rescue her from this appalling dulness. And, sure enough, exactly at twelve o'clock Ernest arrived to-day just the same as on any other day. He too wanted to get it over. If he could he would willingly have avoided the ordeal altogether; but we all have to face the consequences of our own acts, and the fate which we ourselves fashion is our Frankenstein and our master.

It was a bad quarter of an hour for the young man—nearly as bad as that when Amy's mother brought him her poor daughter's last letter, the letter written two days before her death, when she sent him back the lock of hair which he had given her; the rose which he had kissed and put into her hand, whispering 'My soul is with you now;' the little amaranth which he had also kissed and given her, saying 'An emblem of my love'—sending back all these cherished treasures of her fatal hope, and with them 'the love that she carried with her to the grave,' and the pardon that she breathed beyond it. But the bad quarters must be lived through all the same as the good ones, and Ernest had to live through his.

As he came into the room, nerved to meet his accusing angel, his face made up to a mask of false innocence and ignorance of evil alike, he found only his enchantress ; and the reprieve came upon him with almost as great a sense of relief as if he had been going to suffer torture and was suddenly respited. Was it lingering tenderness or conscience which made Ernest say rapidly, after his first embrace, ' How does she take it ? '

Graziella, keen and jealous, understood it as the first, if, wise and crafty, she did not choose to show what she thought. A shade came over her face—subtle, undefinable—but all the same, a shade. She took her hands from Ernest's arm, where she had clasped them in a pretty abandonment of loving pleasure, and said with a forced laugh—

' Admirably ! Your Venetia is not of the kind to break her heart for you or anyone else. Girls with milk-and-water in their veins never do.'

' I am glad she takes it so quietly,' Ernest answered with as much mortification as relief. ' Though I never gave her any real cause—never did more than pay her the ordinary attentions which all men pay to pretty girls before they have seen *the* one '—lovingly, yet, with an air of helpless virtue unjustly assailed—' I was afraid that the poor little thing was fond of me.'

' So was I,' said Graziella. ' But you see we need not have frightened ourselves. She was no fonder of you than you were of her,' suddenly lifting her eyes and looking full at the young man kneeling by her side—his favourite attitude of worship.

' I have never been really fond of anyone before you, my beautiful child-queen, my pearl of the Antilles ! ' cried Ernest enthusiastically. ' All the rest was only the prologue, the preface, the shadow. This is the real thing, and this only ! '

' I am afraid however that your shadows were very like the substance,' said Graziella prettily ; and Ernest, kissing her hands, answered quickly—

' I have never loved before now. Will you not believe me— do you not believe me, my darling ? '

' It is too pleasant not to believe,' said Graziella, laying her cheeks on his forehead while she clasped her hands again on his arm, when the litany of lovers' prayers and praises began again, and time lost itself in the old, old follies that never weary and never change.

If Ernest and Graziella both felt that it ' had to be got over,' so did Venetia. She knew that she had committed the most fatal mistake possible to a woman—let her lover see his power before he has established his right—given frank possession before formal demand. And now she had to hark back on her mistake and do that most difficult thing of all—meet as a mere friend pledged to another the man who knew that she loved him, and not to let her love be seen—the man who had been her lover in the silent confessions between them, when all had been understood and nothing spoken. Yes, he had been her lover. Unsaid though it was, the truth between them was indestructible if to the world she had no 'case.' For though he had made love to her he had not made her an offer; and, until the final self-committing word is said, no woman should suffer her soul to stray. It had all been vague, unpunctuated but understood; and it was this very vagueness of form, coupled with that terrible clearness of understanding, which made the present moment so difficult.

But it had to be done; and when the luncheon bell rang Venetia came down from her room to face her ordeal, and greet as the acknowledged lover of her dearest friend the man who up to nine o'clock last evening had been her own.

Just as she was crossing the hall, Colonel Camperdown rode up to the door, which stood open. With an indescribable feeling of support, as if she were now under the guardianship of a brother, she went up to him quickly and held out her hands eagerly.

'I am so glad you have come!' she cried with a girlish kind of fervour.

For the first time since last night her eyes filled with tears. He was her friend, the only person who really understood her; the one who had been with her in the moment of her supreme anguish, the one from whom she had no secrets—poor, honest, clumsy Charley not counting. But his presence unnerved her even to tears, for many a loving soul, strong enough when left alone in its anguish, breaks down into the weakness of self-pity in the presence of a sympathizer.

'Have you recovered from your fatigue, Miss Greville?' asked Harold, quite in a natural matter-of-fact tone; but his eyes were not as quiet as his voice.

'Yes; thanks. I am better—quite well,' said Venetia, scarcely knowing what she did say, but repeating again, 'I am so glad that you have come!' After a moment she gathered her thoughts together so far as to add, 'You will stay to luncheon, will you not?'

He took in the whole situation.

'Yes,' he answered, 'I will stay if you ask me.'

'Of course I do! of course!' was her eager reply.

And the servant, standing there, made his own comments; which were not friendly to his young mistress; and wondered if after all, good as [she looked, his young lady was no better than some others, and would be a fly-by-night all the same as those others —one down and another come on—if she had her head. His thoughts however were nothing to the action of the present moment, which was that Venetia and Colonel Camperdown should go into the drawing-room where Ernest and Graziella were sitting on the sofa in the unmistakable attitude of engaged lovers, and not show —he, his disgust; she, her despair—but should greet these two traitors with the hypocritical decorum exacted by good breeding from wrath and sorrow alike.

'I hope that you have recovered from your indisposition, Miss Greville?' said Ernest affectedly.

For all the *savoir-faire* belonging to him by right as a man of the world greatly experienced, he felt himself horribly out of place and as diffident as a schoolboy. The presence of Colonel Camperdown made it all so much more awkward, he thought to himself peevishly. But he acted well, and thoughts are not always visible on the face.

Venetia trembled. It was *his* voice that she heard; *his* eyes that were looking into hers—hers, which until now had always met his with such glad and loving confidence; *his* hand in which her own lay clasped. It was the man whom she had placed as a god in the temple of her heart, and who, still dreaming as she was, not yet awake to his true nature, was even now her god—with face averted. Her life was all in ruins; but he himself, the beautiful and divine destroyer, was the same as ever and showing no change, no difference, save in his attitude to her. It was only she who had suffered; his fascination and Graziella's charm remained as before. How vague and unreal it all was! Was this really life, or was it a dream of the night that looked like day and truth?

'You are better now, Venetia, are you not?' said Graziella in her sweet, caressing voice, watching her with those burning eyes which so strangely belied the soft voice, the gentle manner.

'Yes,' said Venetia with an effort. Then, at a long interval, followed, 'Thank you,' as if it had been an independent sentence and said in a voice that was not her own.

'I am glad of that,' said Ernest with admirable compassionateness and sweet, seductive sympathy.

Venetia turned to the window to hide the sharp and sudden pain which made her wince; and Colonel Camperdown, looking at her, comforted his soul, so far as he could, by a manner to Ernest that bordered on insult. Horse-whipping is ruffianly, duelling out of date, but how ardently he longed to have his hands on the throat of the man who found his life's noblest ambition satisfied by making a succession of pretty girls in love with him, that he might say to his intimate friends, 'Ah, poor little thing, she would have given ten years of her life if I would have married her!'

When however the spasm had passed, and Venetia understood what was going on about her, she came back to the group with a face controlled to an almost statuesque calmness; and with the tender craftiness of love spoke to Ernest with a cheerful kind of indifference that cost her more pain than all the rest. But she must not let Colonel Camperdown think that he was to blame. It was she herself; she had been precipitate, unwise, self-deceiving— he had not been false; and her friend, as she had begun to call him, her friend, Harold Camperdown, must understand this at once and not make her lover bear the weight of an unjust condemnation. She must carry her burden so bravely that none should see where it pressed; accept her part without faltering, so that none should blame her lover or her friend. If she died under the strain of conceal- ment the world should know nothing; and though the relative position of each to the other was changed, the terms of the Holy Alliance should appear to be as of old.

Grains of gold to be thrown into the eyes that were watching her so eagerly! Would they blind them?

Those grains cast now by the dear, unselfish, loving hands did not blind Harold Camperdown. He read the girl's heart and meaning, and let her see that he did; for when he shook hands with her and bade her good-by in the garden, he said in rather a husky voice—

'Miss Greville, I have often heard of angels, but I have never seen one till now. I thank God that I have known you.'

On his side Ernest thought—

'She is pluckier than I gave her credit for. Poor little woman, how desperately she loves me! Nothing but love could make her take it so sweetly. Ah, she is a dear, good girl!—I do not know a better, but—she was not destined!'

Graziella's thoughts went back to the forked road at which they had stood from the beginning.

'How can she take it so quietly? Either she did not love him, or she hopes to win him back by her patience: I must watch and see which.'

If rarely, yet it does sometimes come to pass that the innocence of the dove comes to the same thing in the end as the wisdom of the serpent—that unselfishness has the same result as worldly cleverness and astute calculation. Had Venetia been guided by the craftiest old veteran who had ever made wise walking among social ploughshares her chief study, she could not have been better counselled than now by the purity, the loyalty of her own heart. She stopped the mouth of gossip. That was the first thing to do; and unwittingly she did it. For who could take, the part of one who made it evident to all that she had no part to take, but had cast in her lot with the rest? How constitute himself a champion when no cause was proclaimed and no defender summoned? People might say that she looked ill; but what of that? Girls often look ill, yet others do not make it cause of general quarrel, or think it necessary to take sides as to the reason why. Who could possibly say that it was because of Ernest Pierrepoint's engagement to Graziella, when she, Venetia, accepted that engagement so quietly, spoke of it so frankly, expressed her belief in its perfect fitness with so much ease, and when all three were as inseparable and apparently as close friends as before? The world began to think that it had deceived itself, and that there had never been anything warmer than mere friendship between Miss Greville and Mr. Pierrepoint. It had been his flirting manner and her ingenuous simplicity; but he had not meant and she had not taken. So by reason of that generous protection given to her false friends, the talk died out, and her burden, carried without faltering, freed them from theirs.

There were two persons however whom her gentle heroism did not mislead—Harold Camperdown and Charley Mossman. Both knew what Ernest had done, and one of the two, something of what she had suffered. And both in consequence did their best to make life unpleasant to the young man, and to let him feel that if he had gathered a rose unlawfully it was one plentifully beset with thorns. For, as Charley said—

'How it has all come about I cannot for the life of me make out! But Miss Greville does not tell lies, and she told me distinctly that she was engaged. There is only one way out of it, so far as I can see—my old friend, Ernest, is a scoundrel!'

To which Colonel Camperdown replied emphatically, as chorus—

'Thorough!'

CHAPTER IX.

MADE FOR EACH OTHER.

'MADE for each other,' as they were, alike in many characteristics, and sympathetic if chiefly in the least admirable of their qualities, Graziella and Ernest for the first days of their engagement led that life of blind happiness which comes in the early time of confessed love. No cloud veiled the glory of their sky, no presage of coming evil shadowed the brilliancy of the present; it was all excitement, intoxication, delight; and even Ernest, in spite of his wide experience, was so much swept away as to think that this was really true at last, and that he had skirted by so many dangerous possibilities to be saved by a good providence for perfection in the end. 'Made for each other;' that was just it; and in face of such prearranged fitness where could there have been place for Venetia, and how could he repent?

All the same, if he neither regretted nor felt remorse he had a great deal of brotherly affection for the 'poor little thing,' as he used to call his former Beatrice when he spoke of her to Graziella. He was always glad to give her a few nice little words of kindness when he could, out of general sight and hearing; and to make her feel that he regarded her as a sister—but his dearest sister; as a friend—but his most trusted, his best beloved friend. He tried to slip into the new arrangement as if there had never been any other kind of relationship between them; but if he was clever, Venetia was sincere, and sincerity is generally a difficult quality to manage.

For all her gentleness, all her sweetness, and that kind of tender submissiveness which goes with the best sort of womanly love, Venetia had too much self-respect to let herself be led into doubtful action—too much loyalty to Graziella, who had had none for her, to come within her boundaries. When, by chance, she found herself alone with Ernest, and he began his prose-poems on the charms of friendship between men and women, and the exquisite delight which her sweet friendship gave to him, infusing into his theme the meaning and the manner of love, but love that for some other weightier reason had had to die in its original form and had now risen again in its new character, Venetia used to shrink as if touched by hot iron, and leave the room in a very tempest of grief and doubt, of bewilderment and despair. What did it all mean? Had something miscarried, and might things have been different? Was he, as well as herself, the creature of circumstance rather than the creator of his own fate?

But this feeling by degrees wore off, and she began to see that what he really wanted was to hold her while giving nothing of himself in return, to be engaged to the one and loved by the other. And the greatest pain in all this chapter of pain was in these early glimpses into the hidden truth of things, these partial forebodings that the golden idol of her dreams had feet of coarser clay than belong to most.

The two girls were one day sitting in the garden, when Ernest came as usual. As the accepted lover of Graziella, pending the arrival of the letter from her father in Cuba, to annul or to ratify the engagement, he was every day at Oak-tree House; and it was a question whether this frequent intercourse was for the happiness of any of them. Ernest and Graziella themselves were best when under control; and to Venetia, the slow process of awaking to the true nature of the man whom she had loved with so much sincerity, however salutary, could scarcely be called happiness. But whether to the good or ill of the triad, this frequent intercourse was of the accepted order of things, and had to be endured.

This day, when Ernest came and found the girls in the garden, he found also Colonel Camperdown, where he was often to be met now, sitting quite at home on a stool at Venetia's feet, holding in his hands a skein of silk which she was winding. His face was turned up to her smiling, hers bent down to him also smiling, as she pulled at a knot with her long fair fingers, and passed the winder in and out the tangled strands. Graziella was looking on yawning. Since her engagement to Mr. Pierrepoint the Colonel had become to her as if carved out of stone, and she had left off by now trying to make him flesh and blood.

The knowledge that he had lost Venetia, though by his own deliberate choice, and for compensation, and the fear that Harold would profit by his ' lapsed legacy,' was the bitter drop in Ernest's present cup of sweets. As he came up to the little group, his pale face white and his dark eyes aflame, even Graziella's exquisite beauty and charming coquetry failed to move him. For the moment he felt that he would have given up her and all the world to have Venetia to himself again. But he smiled and talked with admirable propriety, and was careful not to betray himself. It was only that his face was pale and his eyes aflame, and the smile about his mouth pinched and forced.

' Your work is an apt emblem of human life, Miss Greville,' he said after a short pause, during which he had apparently watched the progress of the disentanglement as a puzzle of which the solution interested him—Graziella watching him.

' Yes,' said Venetia gently.

She remembered the time when his vapoury disquisitions were utterances of wisdom and beauty combined, and she dreaded the stirring of the depths.

' An emblem of human life,' he repeated with half a sigh. ' The smooth running of the silken strands all at once interrupted by some cruel complication which nothing but patience and dexterity, and let me add confidence in your ultimate success, can undo.'

'Yes,' said Venetia again, with a deep blush.

'For my part,' put in Graziella carelessly, 'I could never have the patience that Venny has. I would cut the knot at once, not spend the best part of the day in undoing it. When it is undone the silk is spoilt,' she added, lifting up her eyes to Ernest s face with an odd kind of look.

'Do you think so?' he said tenderly.

He wanted her to understand that his affair with Venetia—if indeed that could be called an affair at all which was simply the infatuation of a girl for a young man who has never done more than pay her a few ordinary civilities—had been the knot which had been overcome by her and through her; to Venetia it was this entanglement with Graziella that he secretly counselled her to traverse with patience, dexterity, and hope.

'What do you think, Colonel Camperdown?' asked Graziella suddenly.

'I?' he answered with unmistakable disdain. 'Nothing. Sentimentalities and mock philosophy have no charm for me, and, thank Heaven, are not in my way.'

'A soldier's trade is not one of delicate thought or poetic insight, I know,' said Ernest superbly. 'You must forgive me, Camperdown. I forgot the speciality of my audience when I spoke '—with a superior smile.

'A soldier's trade, as you call it,' answered Harold, with a look that seemed to measure the younger man from head to foot, and to find him wanting when measured, 'is generally one of straightforwardness and truth—of manliness and honour. We leave your delicate thought and poetic insight to the men who have none of these things.'

'Yes, a city delivered up to pillage, villages set in flames, spies and ambushes—these are the proofs of your four virtues,' laughed Ernest, as if it was all a good joke that was passing between them. 'What were they? truth, honour, manliness—ah yes, and straightforwardness—straightforwardness!' He laughed again.

'You find the word difficult to pronounce, Mr. Pierrepoint?' said Harold viciously.

'With its present adjuncts? Well, yes,' was his answer.

'You are right,' flamed Harold. 'Its present adjuncts must make it, I should say, impossible for you to pronounce. Miss Greville,' he said, suddenly turning to Venetia as if he dared not trust himself longer with the man whom he so much despised, 'now that you have conquered your little difficulty, will you mind singing me that song I like so much—"Grant but my prayer?"'

He rose and held out his hand in a manner that scarcely

admitted of a refusal, it seemed to take consent so much for granted.

‘ If you like,’ stammered Venetia, rising too.

‘ And you ? ’ said Ernest, bending down to Graziella.

She let her pretty eyes droop.

‘ Oh ! ’ she half whispered, playing with her fan, ‘ I would rather stay here. But don’t let me keep you if you would prefer to go with them,’ she added sweetly. ‘ I have a headache and do not want to be in the house.’

‘ As if I could prefer to go with them ! ’ said Ernest, Venetia and the Colonel being well out of hearing. ‘ As if I would not rather be with you than with anyone in the world, my little queen !—with you rather than in heaven, you being indeed my heaven ! ’

She smiled.

‘ All the same, I don’t think you like to see that long man make love to Venetia,’ she said prettily.

He kissed her hand, and looked at her with his well-worn expression of worship.

‘ With this in mine, have I thought or care for anyone else ? ’ he asked.

‘ Am I expected to answer ?—Yes,’ was her reply.

He dropped her hand with a wounded air.

‘ Et tu, Brute ! are you too of the tribe of the doubters ? ’ he said with half-playful sorrow. ‘ I had believed better things of you, my queen ! ’

‘ I am of the tribe of those who keep their eyes open, and who know that two and two make four,’ said Graziella with a charming smile and a fiery glance.

‘ And those open eyes—those beautiful eyes that I should like to close with a kiss—what do they see ? ’ asked Ernest caressingly, but with just the faintest shade of mockery in his accent.

‘ What ? ’ blazed out Graziella passionately ; ‘ that you have not given up Venetia, and that you are still trying to keep her in love with you. Don’t talk nonsense to me, Ernest ! As if I did not know you ! ’

‘ Graziella, is that you ? ’ he said, rising with a deeply-wounded air.

‘ Yes, it is me ! ’ the Creole answered, with more passion than good grammar. ‘ And just because it is me I speak the truth. Don’t think that I am like that poor, spiritless Venetia who dares not call her soul her own before you, and who was so stupidly in love with you that you could make her believe anything you liked —that black was white if you chose to try. I love you very much in my way'—here she began to show signs of weakness—'very much indeed, Ernest. For your sake I have been a very naughty girl to the best friend I have, and the dearest darling that ever lived,' wiping her eyes; 'but for all that I cannot see you go on like this and put up with it.'

'Go on like what, Graziella? My angel! what ideas have you in that sweet head?' remonstrated Ernest.

'Well, you *know* that you are trying to keep Venny with one hand, while you are playing on me with the other,' cried Graziella. 'And I cannot bear it, Ernest. I cannot and I will not. It must be one thing or the other. You must either give up flirting with Venetia or being engaged to me. That is only fair. I don't flirt with anyone else, and you ought not!'

On which she turned her pretty little round shoulder to her lover, and began to sob hysterically.

'Graziella, I would rather shoot myself than see this,' cried Ernest in an agitated voice.

'You had better shoot me than go on so,' sobbed Graziella. 'If you like Venetia the best, say so—but don't try to keep us both.'

'Graziella!' was all that Ernest could say, for indeed he was too utterly amazed at her clearness of vision and confused by this sudden accusation to know what else to say. After a moment's stupor he took her hand and led her into the shrubbery, where they were out of sight of the house and where no one could see or hear him. And there, having recovered himself, he comforted her handsomely; protesting that he did not care more for Venetia than he did for Miss Honoria Marris; that he had never loved her, never thought of her otherwise than any man would naturally think of a nice kind of girl who was pleasant to talk to and fairly intelligent; that he had never given her cause to think that he did; and that he had never loved in his life before—never, until he saw his queen, his pearl, his fairy-like Graziella, his exquisite and most dainty siren. Would she not believe him? he asked, as the burden in between these strophes of love, kissing her dainty little hand and worshipping her as he knew so well how.

No; at first she would not believe him, and went on sobbing as if she were really suffering, really breaking her heart for loving doubt. It was so pleasant to be petted and made love to! —she did not care to shorten her enjoyment by giving in too soon; and she wanted moreover to understand the extent of her power. Besides, she was really jealous; though she was not in sorrow, she was suffering so far as jealousy went; and to this extent her display was not all acting.

After a time however she let herself be slowly calmed down—

slowly convinced to all appearances that Venetia was nothing to her lover, and never had been ; and that she was everything, and would be always as she had been from the beginning. In reality she was as incredulous and unconvinced as ever ; but she knew when to give way ; and as her vanity was fed, her jealousy soothed, and her love for Ernest satisfied for the moment, she had no reason for not granting the smiles which he said it would break his heart were she to withhold.

But from this time the halcyon days of their love were over. As it so often happens, one little blow breaks through the surface smoothness so that the harm done is never repaired, and the old state of things can never be restored. That blow had now been given, and things went between them as it might be expected they would. With every outburst of jealousy from Graziella the habit of jealousy grew stronger, the outbursts easier, and were with more difficulty soothed away ; with every fresh demand for stricter exclusiveness and more complete absorption, the chain between them shortened, till Ernest more than once regretted the sweet placidity, the trustful worship of his Beatrice—set aside for the disturbing charms of this enchanting little volcano beneath a garden of roses and fire-flies.

It was her volcanic nature however and the imperiousness of her selfishness over-mastering his, that kept him steady. They were perhaps the only things that could. It was a question with him, as well as with some other men, of master or slave. He must dominate entirely or be entirely subdued ; he could not live side by side with a woman as an equal ; and Graziella had cleverly seen this characteristic from the beginning, and as cleverly profited by her insight. She had determined that he should not be her master—hence that he should be her slave; and she fulfilled her determination to the letter. If his traditional soul remained his own, certainly his eyes, his time, his speech, his attention were not ; and she made him understand this, and that he was hers and no other person's, and especially not Venetia's. Her indeed she watched with unappeasable suspicion ; though her watching never brought her an inch of foothold against the loyalty of the friend whom she had supplanted. And though, when she was not in the room, Ernest still went on with his prose-poems on friendship, and still tried to make Venetia understand that she was as dear to him as ever—only, for some cause never rightly explained, she had been left and the other taken—yet in her presence she had established so much influence as to make him cool almost to ill-breeding to the 'poor little thing' who had loved him without cause and whom he had never tried to win—never !

His varying manner created, little vain as Venetia was, a certain feeling of revulsion as a woman, that was not unwholesome as a styptic; and when she remembered all that had been and endured all that was, with interludes of prose-poems on friendship and subtle arts of love-making when Graziella was not in sight or hearing, she scarcely knew which she despised most—her past self or his present personality; with whom she was most indignant— with him that he should dare to offer or with herself that she should be made the object of secret attentions as degrading to her to receive as to him to offer. The consequence of it all was, that she grew colder and colder to Ernest, he in return more anxious to keep what he had lost; that Graziella, who had eyes which nothing could blind, saw through the whole position clearly, and while as charming to Ernest as ever when not in a state of open mutiny and revolt, considered how she should best revenge herself; and that Venetia, for mere protection if not for liking, grew more and more intimate with Colonel Camperdown and his sister, and more and more averse from private moments with Ernest Pierrepoint.

Still they came sometimes. They came this afternoon when the three were on the way to the river-side, and Venetia had kept behind to give the lovers the conventional *tête-à-tête*. But Graziella, who was in a bad humour, had walked on in front; and Ernest, with a sudden show of politeness, had waited for Venetia.

'I so seldom see you for a moment alone now!' he said in a low voice, as they walked down the garden drive. 'You, who were once my comfort—my guardian angel!' He sighed. 'And I who need so much comfort now!'

He sighed again. Life was very dreary to him. He wished Venetia to understand this, and to console him.

'I am sorry to hear you say this,' she answered; 'I should have thought you had more need of congratulation than comfort.'

'You can say that sincerely?' He looked into her eyes yearningly—his own so handsome, tender—speaking as if wishing to read her very soul.

'I am generally sincere in what I say,' answered Venetia gravely; 'why should you doubt me?'

'I should have thought you saw more clearly,' he said with meaning. 'I thought our souls were more in unison than I find they are.'

Again he sighed; those handsome, speaking eyes searching her face.

Venetia blushed to the roots of her hair. For all a woman's good resolutions, for all the discovery of the sordid truth, the romance lying round the first love never quite goes; and just for the instant Ernest's voice and eyes and manner made the old chord vibrate with the old dear harmonies.

' I am sorry ' was all she said, her face full of tenderness ; and Graziella turned round just at the inopportune moment.

How strangely different everything was this grey and cloudy afternoon from what it had been on that exquisite evening when they had rowed to St. Herbert's Isle, and poor Venetia's golden idol had given way about the feet, and had sunk into the sand for ever ! Yet they were the same boatful that had pulled up the stream, singing part-songs and dreaming dreams—the one to the world, the other for themselves. Again Venetia sat in the stern and steered ; and again Graziella nestled like a tropical bird on her shawls and cushions, and stole glances from under her broad white eyelids and from beneath her long curved lashes. But the glances were not all for Ernest to-night, and blue-eyed Charley had his share. She had given up Colonel Camperdown by now, as we know, having found him impenetrable and impracticable ; but honest Charley, Venetia's faithful dog and so generously beloved by Emily, Graziella thought might prove a more facile instrument of chastisement when Ernest went wrong, and at all events he would be a handsome pendant to her first conquest.

Yes, the world was right ; Mr. Pierrepoint and Miss Despues were eminently ' made for each other.'

It was not to be St. Herbert's Isle to-night, but Friar's Point, farther up the river, where there was a bog, a steep climb, a rough path, and a waterfall. The waterfall was one of the show-places in the neighbourhood ; but it was a difficult passage for those not to the manner born, and pretty little dainty persons, like Graziella, with pretty little dainty feet lightly shod, required a great deal of help everywhere.

Graziella had still those two faces on her mind when she turned round at the inopportune moment—Ernest's yearning, tender, suffused ; Venetia's tender and suffused too. She saw that something of a confidential nature had been said ; and she disallowed things of a confidential nature to pass between them. And having these two faces on her mind, she had asked Charley Mossman to help her out of the boat and through the first roughnesses, and was now some distance in advance of the rest, close at his heels in the middle of the bog.

Presently she gave a short scream. The step that she had to make between two tussocks of reeds was rather wide, and she stood on the point helplessly, and screamed in the prettiest little way possible.

Charley, over the footwide gulf, looked infinitely disturbed.

'Oh! I never can do it, Mr. Mossman!' and her voice and look were of that helpless and confiding kind which, when they belong to a fascinating little person with a waist that you can span, and maddening eyes, appeal irresistibly to broad-shouldered men able to carry heavy weights and endure Herculean fatigue.

'It is only a jump,' cried Charley reassuringly, holding out his large, strong hand.

'But I cannot jump!' said Graziella, sweetly impotent.

'Oh, yes; try! It is nothing, I assure you!' said Charley.

'I shall fall in!' she answered, still helpless and despairing.

'I promise you not,' he returned earnestly.

'I shall! I know I shall!' said Graziella; and by this time the rest of the party came up, wondering what the difficulty was. Ernest was behind—the last of all. He had a woman's horror of muddy boots, and a cat's of wet feet; so he picked his way carefully among the tussocks, and avoided those treacherous stretches of yellow moss, reddened with sundew, as if he had been a young lady shod for a ball. Hence he was of no use to the girls, and was not at hand to help Graziella.

'What is it?' asked Colonel Camperdown, who was attending to Venetia and his sister Emily. It was as natural that he should attend to Venetia now as once it had been natural that Ernest Pierrepoint should; and she was happier with him than with anyone else. He was her 'brother;' and brothers are so dear to the sisters—who are not their mothers' daughters!

'Miss Despues is afraid of the jump,' said Charley, who thought her none the less lovely for her timidity.

'It is nothing,' said Colonel Camperdown shortly.

'Oh, yes it is—I can never do it!' said Graziella.

'Indeed, Gracie dear, it is nothing!' echoed Venetia; and to give colour to her assertion she made the little jump lightly, and crossed without even a hand to help her.

'Oh, but you are so big and strong!' pouted Graziella, as if Venetia had been a six-foot grenadier. 'I cannot do half the rough things that you do!'

'I am not much bigger than you, and I can do it!' said Emily Backhouse with unmitigated disdain, as she took her brother's hand and followed Venetia cleanly.

'Yes, but you have been born and brought up here, and I have not,' said Graziella. 'Things come easier to girls who have been used to scramble about such places all their lives than they do to poor little me. I have not been used to bogs in my beautiful country!' as if Emily had been the typical bog-trotter, and had lived on tussocks of rushes and jumping spans of yellow moss all her life. 'Oh!' as Ernest came up, 'I am so sorry to make all this fuss, but I cannot get across this place!'

'It is a nasty place,' said Ernest sympathetically. In his own distaste for this uncouth kind of work he quite understood her despair.

'But what is to be done?' said Charley.

'Some one must carry me,' said Graziella, holding out her arms as a child might. With the most enchanting simplicity, the most bewitching ingenuousness, she looked up into Charley's face. 'You, Mr. Mossman,' she said; 'you are the strongest, and I am not very heavy.'

Venetia opened her eyes, and Emily said beneath her breath, 'Little wretch!' Colonel Camperdown laughed, not pleasantly, and turning to Ernest said contemptuously—

'And you stand by and see that, Mr. Pierrepoint?' shrugging his shoulders.

But Ernest laughed back as gaily and unconcernedly, in appearance, as if he had had no part in the matter at all, and answered—

'Why not? You strong fellows are the natural porters of the race; now a sack of coals, and now a pretty woman—what does it matter?'

Charley, his fair face flushed like a girl's, and his heart beating more than he would have cared to own, cut the conversation short by taking Graziella in his arms and carrying her over half a dozen such places without stopping; she leaning back as in an arm-chair, with her pretty little hands clasped round his neck—to steady herself.

When she was set down on the dry land once more, and had laughed and looked and lisped her thanks, she waited for Ernest to come up.

'What a pity it is that you are not as strong as that good Mr. Mossman!' she said in the sweetest voice that she had—and she had more voices than one. 'It was so funny being carried like that!' but, looking into his face, 'it would have been so nice if it had been you instead of that great, clumsy fellow!'

'Oh! for the matter of that, I dare say he did quite as well as I or anyone else!' said Ernest with false good-humour.

She pouted.

'Do you judge me by yourself?' she asked. 'Would it have been as pleasant to you to have carried anyone else as me?'

'That depends,' said Ernest.

'Venetia, I suppose?'

'Yes, Venetia would not be a disagreeable burden to any man,' answered Ernest, flicking off some dust from his coat-sleeve.

'You had better go to her, then—I dare say she will not tell you to go away, unless she likes Colonel Camperdown better,' said Graziella with dangerous sweetness; and, without another word, she turned back and joined herself to Charley Mossman and Emily Backhouse—poor Emily!—throwing out so many lines of fascination that the poor fellow, soft as he was in certain directions, grew confused, and wondered what on earth it all meant, and did it really mean that—? It was the kind of thing to make such a man as he lose his head; and this was what Graziella had counted on.

But she had not counted on Colonel Camperdown, who was not the kind of man to lose his. And he kept Charley pretty straight for the moment, if he a little hurt his pride, by half a dozen words which rubbed off some of the gilt and tore down a few of the cobwebs.

'You will not be taken in by that little witch, will you, Mossman?' he said over their cigars that night. 'She is playing a game, Heaven only knows what, and you are marked out as the victim.'

'I cannot think her bad,' said poor Charley ruefully.

'Miss Greville did not think that fellow bad, nor see her friend's treachery, which was patent to everyone else,' he answered. 'However, it is no business of mine, but I should be sorry to see you in a mess.'

'Oh! I can take care of myself!' said Charley a little crossly; and Harold changed the conversation.

This happened just about the time when Graziella and Ernest, in the midst of a tremendous quarrel, for the first time in their affair appealed to Venetia as the judge between them; and when she for the first time in her life paltered with the truth and did not say what she thought; which was—that Graziella had been decidedly in the wrong about Charley, and that Ernest had been just as much to blame about herself.

(To be continued.)

Cupid's Alley.

A MORALITY.

BY AUSTIN DOBSON.

It runs (so saith my Chronicler)
  Across a smoky City ;—
A Babel filled with whirr and stir,
  Huge, gloomy, black and gritty ;
Dark-louring looks the hill-side near,
  Dark-yawning looks the valley,—
But here 'tis always green and clear,
  And this—is 'Cupid's Alley.'

And, from an Arbour green herein,
  Set somewhere towards the middle,
An ancient Fiddler, gray and thin,
  Scrapes on an ancient fiddle ;
Alert he seems, but aged enow
  To punt the Stygian galley ;—
With wisp of forelock on his brow
  He plays—in 'Cupid's Alley.'

All day he plays,—a single tune !—
  But by the oddest chances,
Gavotte, or Brawl, or Rigadoon,
  It suits all kinds of dances ;
My Lord may walk a *pas de Cour*
  To Jenny's *pas de Châlet* ;—
You need not e'en have danced before
  To dance—in 'Cupid's Alley !'

And here, for ages yet untold,
  Long, long before my ditty,
Came rich and poor, and young and old,
  From out the crowded City ;
And still to-day they come, they go,
  And just as fancies tally,
They foot it quick, they foot it slow,
  All day—in 'Cupid's Alley.'

Strange dance !   'Tis free to Rank and Rags :
  Here no distinction matters,
Here Riches shakes its money-bags
  And Poverty its tatters ;

Church, Army, Navy, Physic, Law ;—
 Maid, Mistress, Master, Valet ;
Long locks, gray hairs, bald heads, and a',—
 They bob—in ' Cupid's Alley.'

Strange pairs ! To laughing, fresh Fifteen
 Here capers Prudence thrifty ;
Here Prodigal leads down the green
 A blushing Maid of fifty ;
To some it seems a serious thing,
 To some mere shilly-shally ;
And some e'en danse without the ring
 (Ah me !)—in ' Cupid's Alley.'

And sometimes one to one will dance,
 And think of one behind her ;
And one by one will stand, perchance,
 Yet look all ways to find her ;
Some seek a partner with a sigh,
 Some win him with a sally ;
And some they know not how nor why,
 Strange fate !—of ' Cupid's Alley.'

And some will dance an age or so
 Who came for half a minute ;
And some, who like the game, will go
 Before they well begin it ;
And some will vow they're ' danced to death,'
 Who (somehow) always rally ;
Strange cures are wrought (mine author saith),
 Strange cures !—in ' Cupid's Alley.'

It may be one will dance to-day,
 And dance no more to-morrow ;
It may be one will steal away
 And nurse a life-long sorrow ;
What then ? The rest advance, evade,
 Unite, dispart, and dally,
Re-set, coquet, and gallopade,
 Not less—in ' Cupid's Alley.'

For till that City's factories vast
 And shuddering beams shall crumble ;—
And till that Fiddler lean at last
 From off his seat shall tumble ;—
Till then (the Civic records say)
 This quaint, fantastic *ballet*
Of Go and Stay, of Yea and Nay,
 Must last—in ' Cupid's Alley.'

Tasbrook's Testimonial.

BY JAMES PAYN.

WHEN a man had been at an English public office for forty years, his friends, and especially his juniors in the same department, used to think it was nearly time he should retire. But now-a-days we move a good deal quicker. A measure was brought in and carried by a truly Liberal Government that all clerks of a certain standing might leave their situations before the time arrived for superannuation, each receiving a certain *bonus*, that varied, of course, with his length of service, and which was, in fact, the discount value of his future pension. It was impudently said that this scheme was devised to get rid of ' the Queen's Hard Bargains,' as they were termed—the indolent, the incapable, and generally those who never do a stroke of work they are not compelled to do, and who leave the office as the clock strikes five, though they are by no means so punctual in arriving at the proper hour in the morning.

This scandal, I, Thomas Tasbrook, hurl back with indignation in the teeth of those who utter it; for, though I had been but six years a clerk in the Wax and Wafer Office, I had done my duty during that period in a manner with which my conscience is perfectly satisfied. It is true that I never hurried myself about anything, for does not the poet tell us that ' Raw Haste ' is ' half-sister to Delay ; ' and, if I was sometimes a little late in the morning, I thought about the work to be done as I drove leisurely down to the office in a cab, and arrived there, as it were, with my judgment matured. It was said that I spent more time than was usual over the newspapers, which is an accusation that I frankly admit ; but that again, I maintain, was to the advantage of the public service. Every clerk reads one paper, to improve his mind, and to see what the world is saying about the Government he has the honour to serve ; but to confine oneself to a single journal is to narrow the intellect, and incapacitate it from taking larger views of things. The charge always brought against the Wax and Wafer Office was that ' it wanted Grasp ; ' and I endeavoured to supply that deficiency by acquiring the most varied information, to be applied, of course, when opportunity offered, for the benefit of my employers. I have an uncle in Japan (from whom I have no expectations whatever, and of whom I may therefore express myself quite freely) who makes a positive fool of himself over the ' Times ' newspaper. When a file of them arrives, he reads one at a time, every morning at breakfast, with the idea of persuading himself that he is still in England. His last paper is finished when the next mail comes in ; so that he flatters himself that he gets his news fresh and fresh, instead of being a month behind everybody else in the place. He believes in the ' Times ' in a manner that is only attributed to Englishmen in a farce. He cured a horse of jibbing by reading the whole sheet of it from first to last upon his back, and not allowing him to move ; so that he has now only to rustle a bit of paper, and off the poor creature goes at a hand-gallop, for fear he should be in for another ' reading.' But, of course, the same result would have been effected by any other journal, if it was only big enough For my own part, I used to patronise *all* the papers at the office, and never paid one so ill a compliment as to leave a leading article or even a police report unfinished, just because some contractor or other commonplace individual happened to wish to see me on business.

' Learn to labour and to *wait*,' says Longfellow; and, of course, what is good for one to learn oneself is good to teach others. Then, again, I used to be accused of playing practical jokes with the speaking-tubes in the office ; but ' all work and no play,' it must be remembered, ' makes Jack a dull boy,' and the opportunities to give absurd orders in one's chief's voice, when he happened to be out of the room, or to throw water down the pipe when we *knew* our friend's mouth was at the other end of it, were sometimes irresistible. There were exceptional temptations, too, connected with the conveyance of parcels from top to bottom of the establishment by the medium of an endless chain ; and it is true that once, when a poor woman called with her baby about some School Board case, I did put the baby in the basket, and sent him up to the Comptroller-General instead of certain official returns; but, after all, that was but once and away, and the amusing experiment was never repeated.

Many clerks used to waste their time, and, what was worse, that of the Government, by going out to lunch between one and two—a practice against which I always set my face on principle. I used always to have a good wholesome lunch sent up to me in my own room, where it was understood that privacy was established for the full hour ; and if I chose to take a cigar afterwards to assist digestion, I don't see even now, and in spite of the censure passed upon me by the authorities, that there was anything but good in the practice. Smoke kills the moth, which, as everybody knows, is the bane of our public departments, and is generally allowed to be a remedy against infection—by no means a superfluous precaution to persons who are necessarily brought into constant connection with strangers. If I have ever been found asleep during business hours, it was with the hope of being invigorated by that refreshment for more strenuous exertions : it is what may happen to anybody after meals, and in warm weather; and I may add that there is such an expression as ' always wide awake,' which, whatever compliment it may imply as regards the intellect, is by no means a tribute to a man's merits with respect to moral feeling. No: taking the whole six years, during which I filled a not wholly irresponsible office in the Civil Service of my country, I think I did—well, as much as everybody who knew me could fairly expect of me : and how few of us can say more ! There was nothing brilliant—nothing flashy—in the performance of my duties; but I may say that I hit the golden mean. Now Crammer, who lived in the next apartment, took too much out of himself; he was the first to come in the morning (as I understood) and the last (as I was told, for I never saw him do it) to go away at night. He went at his work, as it was graphically described by a contractor of my acquaintance, ' like a navvy at a barrow,' and what was worse than all, and disgraceful in a servant of the Crown, he took his work home with him. If such conduct as this had been followed by others, the whole office would have been demoralised, and the establishment might have been reduced by three-fourths; and even as it was, some of the authorities used to say, ' Look at Mr. Crammer; see how *he* puts his shoulders to the wheel,' in a way that persons conscious of shortcoming would have pronounced offensively personal.

For my part, I did look at him with a good deal of pity. The wheel they spoke of seemed to be too heavy for him to push, and even to be going over him with crushing effect. He grew thinner and thinner everywhere except his head, which swelled and swelled like that of an infant with hydrocephalus. He was one of those fungoid growths (if I may be allowed the expression) fostered by the system of competitive examinations, and altogether unwholesome. Still Crammer and I were on very good terms, and when there was an overplus of work in my particular department I was always ready to gratify him by permitting him to share it. I thought little enough about the matter at the time ; but, as things have turned out, I am thankful that I was able to do the poor fellow these little kindnesses. However, to my story: I took the

Government ' composition,' as it was called, and retired from the
Wax and Wafer Office, if not exactly upon my laurels, on a genteel
competence. I had never pretended to deserve so well of my
country as to have a statue erected to me, but I could lay my hand
upon my heart, and say I had done my duty—within all reasonable
limits; I had not so exhausted myself in her service that I was
unfit for any other calling, and I now proceeded to enter my new
one—that of a man of leisure—with considerable energy. Having
formed this moderate estimate of my own virtues, you may imagine
my astonishment on receiving, about a fortnight after I had given
up my appointment, the following communication from my late
fellow-clerks :—

' DEAR TASBROOK,—We cannot permit your brief but distinguished career among us to come to a close, without expressing to
you our sense of the loss that has befallen, not only ourselves, but
the public service, in your withdrawal from the Wax and Wafer
Office. It is a void which we honestly feel can never be filled up
by your equal.'

Here I felt ' a man's rare tears,' as the poet calls them, coming
very near my eyes, and laid down the letter to recover myself.
The terms in which the recognition of my poor services had been
expressed were really very agreeable—' a void not to be filled up
by my equal.' This seemed to be almost too happy an expression
for Crammer ; and yet the ' Memorial,' if I may call it so, was in
Crammer's handwriting, and bore his autograph at the head of the
long list of signatures. I was touched by this fact ; for, to say
truth, I should have thought Crammer would have been the very
last to have appreciated my humble exertions, I do not say as they
deserved, but at the very high figure at which my late companions
were obviously disposed to rate them. I had almost thought, on more
than one occasion, that Crammer entertained the erroneous idea
that I might have worked a little harder without putting myself
to much inconvenience. It was now evident, however, that I
had done him wrong.

' There has been much discussion amongst us,' he went on,
' as to the form which the expression of our united admiration
of you, dear Tasbrook, ought to take. Some thought that a Testimonial on vellum, handsomely illuminated, would be an appropriate offering, and one which your descendants could hand down
from generation to generation in testimony of the diligence and
business abilities of their progenitor ; but then it was urged that
since at present you were a bachelor, this would appear too like
dictation. We felt that, however near might be our relations with

you, we had no right to advise you to take a wife, especially as we knew of no particular lady who would ensure your happiness.'

Here I ventured to think Crammer a little obscure. He, of course, did not mean to imply that no lady who was 'particular' would suit me, and yet the sentence would have borne such an interpretation. However, a man may be good at a *précis*, and yet be unable to compose a complimentary memorial : his intentions were evidently of the most admirable kind.

'Then, again, it was proposed that you should be presented with a service of plate, the principal piece of which might bear some suitable inscription—" To Thomas Tasbrook, Esquire, in testimony of nearly six years' honourable service in the Wax and Wafer Office, during which he acquired the esteem of his superiors, the affection of his equals, and the respect of his subordinates." '

This fairly overcame me. I was conscious (as I have said) of having done my duty ; but this unanimous approval of all classes of my fellow-labourers in the Government vineyard went to my very heart. The mode in which they had contrived to conceal their feelings throughout what, to say truth, had seemed to me a somewhat protracted connection with them, was itself a most striking circumstance. The head of my department had even reprimanded me on one or two occasions ; and, though my pretty frequent quarrels with my fellow-clerks might be now considered to have been only 'the renewals of love,' there had been some rather serious ones. I had playfully dropped little Jones, for example, over the banisters down three flights of stairs, and yet here was Jones's name standing second in the list of those who were wishing to do me honour. His hand was not a bold one—in fact, it was a running hand, and significant of his pusillanimous disposition ; but I did not think of that now. I only reflected, 'Here is Jones, notwithstanding the limp in his leg consequent upon that drop-fall, forgetting and forgiving everything, and swelling this tribute of good feeling towards his ancient foe.' I was sorry, however, they had not decided on the plate, which is an article that always comes in handy. I thought the reasons against the service of plate, to say the least of it, inadequate. It might be very true that I was 'not one to prize a gift for its money value ;' but I confess that I should have experienced some satisfaction if my humble services had, so to speak, been reflected if only in a silver salver. Having no man-servant, it would have been a pleasing occupation to me on wet days to have kept up the brilliancy of such a testimonial with wash-leather. However, it was not for me to dictate to my generous admirers. What they had determined upon was a Testimonial dinner. If Tuesday, the 15th instant, would suit me to receive this tribute of respect, that was the date which had been appointed for its presentation.

I wrote back to Crammer by return of post to express my gratitude for the honour in prospect for me, and to beg him to convey the same to his brother signataries ; and from that moment to the 15th instant I gave myself wholly up to composition. I had not been accustomed to public speaking, and it had certainly never entered into my mind that I should have to acknowledge a compliment of so exceptional a nature. The consequence was that I passed rather a nervous time, including some sleepless nights. And when I had composed my speech, of course I had to commit it to memory. I was not going to make so bad a return for the kindness of my friends of the Wax and Wafer Office as to address them extemporaneously. I should as soon have thought of playing them a tune upon the piano, without previous acquaintance with that instrument. This speech was so much upon my mind— though I often forgot what I wished to remember in it—that nothing else had much chance of troubling me ; else I did think it odd that Crammer and ' the committee,' as he called them, should have selected so obscure a locality, for what I may be allowed to call so signal a celebration, as the ' Viper's Head ' in the City. ' St. James's Hall ' and the ' Criterion ' are well-known restaurants, and expressly adapted for such public manifestations of good feeling ; but of the ' Viper's Head ' I, for my part, had never heard. Crammer himself thought it necessary to apologise for the selection of such a spot, but assured me that it was ' snug ' and ' cleanly.' I confess I thought these adjectives inappropriate as recommendations for his choice ; but it was not for me to object to the arrangements. ' There will be no reporters present,' said Crammer ; which was also a disappointment to me, for by this time I had composed a really admirable speech, and worthy, I flattered myself, of an extensive audience. Moreover, I should have liked to have sent a few printed copies here and there, to quarters where my professional career had been hitherto unappreciated or misunderstood. For there were people I knew in the world who would have expressed their surprise that Thomas Tasbrook should have received any public testimonial for his services to the State, and with whom I should have wished to put myself right. They had had the ill-nature to observe that ' I was conceited enough for anything ; ' forgetting that there is a certain consciousness of merit which begets an agreeable confidence in a man, and without which, I may perhaps be allowed to add, greatness is rarely found. My modest nature had no doubt been a little puffed up by the honour that was about to be conferred

upon me, but I submit that a little exaltation was but natural.
To have a public dinner given one (even at the ' Viper's Head ')
by four-and-twenty members of the public service, with a man
like Peter Crammer acting as their hon. sec., would have been
a matter for congratulation to any man. I felt that such a
tribute would only have been accorded to true worth.

It is not too much to say that on the morning of that eventful
15th instant I felt as tall without my boots as I usually did with
them, and that I walked down to the City at the appointed hour
like one who treads on air. There was in reality but very little
to tread upon, for the day had been the hottest we had had that
summer, and the streets were all glare and dust. Still I thought
I would walk ; partly from humility of mind, and partly because
my impatience had caused me to set out too early. It was not
without difficulty that I discovered the ' Viper's Head,' which was
an indifferent coffee-house up an alley which I should have hesitated to enter alone had it not been broad daylight. But I
recalled to my remembrance that some of the most famous places
of refreshment in London, such as ' Dolly's ' and the ' Cock,' are
by no means magnificent to look at, and comforted myself with
the notion that the ' Viper ' might bear some precious jewel in its
' Head ' in the way of wines or cookery.

The ground-floor apartment, into which you entered straight
from the street, was not only an eating-room but a kitchen ; one
of those old-fashioned places with a sanded floor where you sit and
see your chop cooked before your eyes—a prospect which, however
charming in winter time to a hungry man, is not attractive in
July with the thermometer at 86 in the shade.

' Good Heavens ! ' observed I to the nearest waiter ; ' one
doesn't dine here, does one ? '

' Well, sir ; yes, sir ; the upper room is reserved to-day for the
Tasbrook Testimonial Banquet.'

It was with a feeling better imagined than described that I
modestly observed, ' I am Mr. Tasbrook ; ' when he immediately
ushered me up a winding stair to the Banquet Hall.

This apartment was similar to the one below, except that
there was no kitchen in it, and that the floor was boarded instead
of sanded. From end to end of it ran a long table laid for five-
and-twenty persons, with a profusion of red and blue glasses, looking very quaint if not absolutely tasteful.

' That is Mr. Crammer's fancy, sir,' remarked the waiter, observing the direction of my glance ; ' he is an old customer, and so
we strive to please him as much as we can.'

'I should not have thought him very difficult to please,' said I; 'he is not a particular sort of gentleman.'

'Well, he's not so much particular, as peculiar. If you have not seen him lately——'

Here he stopped; for at that moment Crammer himself entered the room with an eager air, accompanied by a stranger.

'My dear fellow,' cried he, 'I am afraid I am behind time.'

'Nay,' said I, returning his hearty greeting; 'it is I, I think, who am too early, since the rest of our company,' it seems, have not yet arrived.'

'Ah! just so; they haven't come, have they? Permit me to introduce you to Scrivener, my friend and amanuensis.'

I was so overcome by the idea of Crammer keeping an amanuensis, that for the moment I could only think of that, instead of giving my attention to the gentleman himself; for Crammer wrote one of those beautiful hands that you only see on the first pages of copy-books and in the windows of law-stationers, and had about as much need of a copyist as his Holiness the Pope of a private chaplain. Moreover, when I came to consider him, Mr. Scrivener didn't look like an amanuensis; tall and strong, muscular and well-fed, he gave me rather the idea of a publican taking a holiday, than a person connected in ever so indirect a way with letters. The next instant, Crammer favoured me with a wink of intense significance—and all the more so since I had never seen him wink before—which gave me somehow to understand that the stranger was a reporter for the press, notwithstanding the assurance I had had that none such would be present. It was rather hard to spring upon me such a mine as that; but, as it happened, I had got my speech well by heart, and was rather pleased than otherwise; only I wondered greatly what paper he reported for, and came to the conclusion that it must be the 'Morning Advertiser,' which is the licensed victuallers' organ.

It was now a quarter of an hour past the appointed time, and I began to feel a little fatigued at my friends' delay; if ever people should be punctual, it was surely on an occasion like the present, when modest worth was about to be recognised. I had got so far in my indignant reflections, when they were cut shoit by a peal of laughter from Crammer: it was not a pleasant laugh; but, as I had never heard him laugh before, I set down its failure in the way of harmony to a first attempt.

'What is the joke, my dear sir?' inquired I.

'Well, the joke is, that here is the table laid for twenty-five persons, and only three are come, one of whom, my amanuensis, Mr. Scrivener (here he again introduced us), was not invited.'

' But I suppose they *will* come ? ' observed I, rather nettled by this inopportune pleasantry.

' I don't know, I'm sure,' replied he, coolly ; ' I only know that I am not going to wait for them. Sit down here, Tasbrook, guest of the evening, on my left, and let us drink, boys, drink, and the cannikin clink ! '

I then perceived, of course, that the poor fellow had been drinking already ; doubtless the responsibility of ordering the entertainment and making all the necessary preparations for so important a matter, had driven him to take a little stimulant. Under the influence of liquor he had, perhaps, made some mistake in his communication to me as to the hour for the dinner ; for it was to the last degree unlikely that three-and-twenty clerks in the Wax and Wafer Office should sign such a memorial as I had received, and then omit to keep their own appointment.

' Indeed,' said I, ' I think we had better wait for our friends a little longer.'

' Do you, now?   That astonishes me in a person of your business habits and punctuality.   The man in the whole office who may be said to be the model of what a Civil Service official should be : so diligent, so accurate, so conscientious '—and then he burst out into that laugh again, which I have already described as so objectionable—' Come, sir, sit down, and let us begin.'

Here the amanuensis bent down and whispered in my astonished ear, ' You had best sit down and humour him, sir ; it's always——'

' Waiter ! Bring me a carving-knife ! ' cried Crammer, excitedly.

' No, no, none of that,' exclaimed the amanuensis, with sudden authority; ' spoons and fish-knives only, if *you* please.'

Then I began to grasp the situation ; Crammer was as mad as a March hare, and this 'was his keeper. The poor fellow had lost his wits—which was a warning to everybody—through an exaggerated attention to business.

As a matter of fact, however, as I subsequently discovered, he was at present under surveillance only. He had had an attack of brain fever, and, of course, was invalided so far as the office was concerned ; but his mind had still run on office work and had formed the idea (and not a wholly unnatural one) of presenting me with a testimonial. He had shown, as I have described, great method in his madness, and exhibited his usual skill in imitating the handwriting of all his brother clerks ; so there was no such wonder why I should have been deceived. I could never understand why some people said, 'You must have been mad, yourself, Tasbrook, to have believed in such an absurdity.' I see no absurdity in the thing at all, and yet I believe I possess some sense of humour.

The worst of the joke, if I must call it so, was that I had to sit through the whole feast—the keeper whispered the poor man would be 'dangerous' if I didn't; and though fear is, I hope, unknown to me, I did not wish to increase his malady by irritation. We had only soup and fish, and toast-and-water in the red and blue glasses, but it was a very tedious business nevertheless. When it was over Crammer got up and made a speech, upon 'the interesting ceremonial we had just witnessed,' to an imaginary audience, and then sat down, drumming on the table with his spoon, as if impatient for my oration in reply.

At first, I peremptorily refused to speak; but, upon the amanuensis representing that the poor man would perhaps be driven to deeds of violence, I did actually repeat the speech that I had prepared for the occasion. It was a painful task that of rehearsing a noble oration—intended, I may say, for the world at large—to a madman, his keeper, and the head waiter of the 'Viper's Head,' but I got through with it somehow. When I spoke of 'the barren years of toil,' from which I had never hoped to reap 'this glorious crop of eulogy and appreciation,' Crammer broke out into laughter that I cannot stigmatise as otherwise than fiendish. As I had here expected loud applause, and had framed the next sentence upon that supposition, the incident was especially embarrassing. In fact, if I had not been supported by the consciousness that I was humouring the invalid, and perhaps conducing to his cure, I think I should have experienced throughout some degree of humiliation. As a public acknowledgment of my services to the State, the banquet was, I confess, not entirely satisfactory; but as for its being 'ridiculous,' the 'mere whim of a madman,' &c. &c., I can only say I differ from those who have expressed themselves to that effect, and who would probably make fun out of Shakespeare himself. I cannot but think that something complimentary on a large scale was intended for me, until poor Crammer spoilt it by his interference. I am told that to this hour, 'in the long nights of winter, when the kid (or, at least, the Welsh rarebit) burns on the spit,' the clerks of the Wax and Wafer Office still talk of the 'Tasbrook Testimonial;' and, perhaps, some day or another, the thing may yet assume a definite and less questionable shape.

Joshua Haggard's Daughter.

BY THE AUTHOR OF 'LADY AUDLEY'S SECRET.'

CHAPTER XXXI.

THE FACE IN OSWALD'S SKETCH-BOOK.

THAT idea of his brother's suicide took no strong hold upon Arnold after his conversation with Naomi; but he could not put the possibility out of his mind altogether. That his brother had suffered some disappointment—that a cloud of some kind had darkened his life—he was ready to believe. Oswald's latest letter had betrayed a mind ill at ease; that sudden determination to leave his country, while independence was still a new thing for him, and with every advantage in life that could make a young man happy, argued the existence of some deep-rooted sorrow, a misery that made familiar scenes hateful, and exile a welcome means of escape from the haunting memories that follow a fatal passion.

But, having resolved upon exile, could Oswald have been so weak or so wicked as to seek the darker and more desperate Lethe of the suicide? Arnold argued that his brother was too good and brave a man to contemplate, much less to commit, such a crime. But then Arnold had not read Werther, the apotheosis of suicide.

He went back to the Grange, after his interview with Naomi, more than ever at sea as to his brother's fate, more than ever resolved to unravel the mystery. His first act was to make an enquiry which had some bearing upon the suicide question. Instead of entering the Grange by the hall door, he went under the old stone archway that led into the quadrangle, from which the kitchens and stables alike opened, being tolerably certain of finding Nicholas the butler sunning himself on the solid old bench beside the kitchen door.

There sat the old man, bareheaded, basking in the spring sunshine. It did not last very long, the sunshine of these April afternoons; but while it lasted there was warmth and a balmy sweetness in the air, and a yellow light that made all things lovely. The wallflowers blended their rich red and gold with the cool greys and purples of the old stone archway, the dark brown shadows on stable doors and deep-set windows, the vermilion lights upon the tiled roofs. The stonecrop on the gables, the sage-green house-leeks nestling round the disused chimney-stacks, the fleecy clouds sailing high in a bright blue sky, were all beautiful to contemplate, but such familiar objects to the drowsy eye of old Nicholas, stretching out his feeble legs in the warmth, as he stretched them towards the kitchen hearth indoors, that he was scarcely conscious of their existence. If he had an idea at all about the old quadrangle, it was that all ' they ' wallflowers, and houseleek, and stonecrop, and rubbish ought to be swept away, and the whole place renovated with a coat of clean whitewash.

He was puffing slowly at his afternoon pipe when Arnold came up; but at the sight of his master he rose and did obeisance.

' Sit down, Nicholas, and go on with your pipe,' said the sailor, in a friendly voice ; ' I want a little quiet talk with you.'

The butler obeyed, and Arnold seated himself on the bench by his side, and took out a short German pipe, which he carried in his pocket, and began to smoke. It was in the days when a German pipe was a mark of a traveller, when for a gentleman to smoke a pipe of any kind implied a republican turn of mind.

Captain Pentreath looked round the quadrangle. There was no one within earshot. The stable boy was throwing a pail of water at Herne's hind legs at the farthest end of the yard—a liberty which the animal bore with the resignation engendered of custom. Two fantail pigeons were puffing out their chests and spreading out their fans on the deep red tiles yonder ; and a most vagabond collection of poultry was disporting itself on a golden mountain of straw in a distant corner—a mountain which would have made the old Squire wild with agony had he seen such a wasteful expenditure of litter; but Herne's bed now-a-days was a Sybarite's couch, Arnold having taken his brother's horse under his own especial protection.

' You remember the day my brother went away the last time, Nicholas; the day you got his trunks taken down to the coach office ? '

' Yes, Captain ; as well as if it was yesterday.'

' Did you see him just before he left the house ? '

' Yes ; he called me into the hall as he was going out to give me his last orders about they trunks.'

' Do you know if he carried pistols ? There was a pair used to hang over the mantelpiece in his bedroom. I've noticed the mark of them on the wall where the panelling has changed colour. Do you know if he took them with him ? '

' Yes, Captain. I saw the butt-end of a pistol poking out of his breast pocket. He wore a frock coat buttoned up tight, and there was just the end of the pistol showing. They was pretty little pistols, as small as tyes, and he was uncommon proud of 'em. They'd belonged to his great uncle, the Colonel, you see ; and was furrin made. " You beant going to carry they pistols, be ye, Squire?" said I, for I thought it was dangersome. But he said he wanted to take the pistols away with him, and he'd forgot to pack 'em in his box. " And perhaps it's as well," he says ; " for it beant wise to go on a coach journey without fire-arms;" and I says, " Lawks, master Oswald," for I forgets myself sometimes with un, and thinks he's still a bye, " you aint afeard o' highwaymen in these days, be ye, with the Reform Bill a comin' to make things pleasant to everybody ? " But he on'y larfed, and shuk his head, and went out without another wurred.'

' With a pair of pistols in his breast-pocket,' thought Arnold, much disturbed by this information, for it seemed to jump with Joshua Haggard's idea of self-slaughter. He asked no further questions of old Nicholas, but went slowly to his own room—the large airy bedchamber, with windows facing seaward, which had been Oswald's—and sat down at his brother's writing-table, to meditate upon the mystery that veiled the absentee's fate.

That there was a mystery of some kind, Oswald was fully assured. It was now high time that somebody in England should have heard from the wanderer. The brothers had corresponded more or less regularly in all the years of their separation, and Oswald had always been the best correspondent. The landsman had made excuses for the rover when Arnold's letters were in arrear, and had written by every mail, so that Captain Pentreath often found a packet of letters waiting for him when his ship came into port, full of pleasant gossip about the old home which he dearly loved, although he loved the sea better. That Oswald should be away nearly a year, living, and in his right mind, and in all that time make no communication with his brother, seemed improbable to the verge of impossibility.

' Where did he go when he left the Grange that August day ?' pondered Arnold. ' Some one must have seen him; some one must know something about him. The woman he loved—for whose sake he jilted that noble girl— she could give me the clue to the mystery, perhaps, if I only knew where to find her.'

Who was she ? Who was the object of that fatal passion which had darkened Oswald's life just when it seemed happiest ? Arnold wondered exceedingly. Some one his brother had known in London, perhaps ; for it could hardly be anyone at Combhollow without everyone in the place knowing all about it; and the people who talked to Arnold about his brother were clearly quite in the dark as to the reason of his falling away from his allegiance to Naomi. No, it could be no one at home, or he would have heard of it at the street corners; and yet it was evident to him that Joshua Haggard knew more about the circumstances of Oswald's sin or folly than he cared to tell. He had known enough to feel justified in breaking off his daughter's engagement—a strong measure, assuredly, where Naomi had so much to gain by the intended marriage. How had Oswald's conduct in London reached the Methodist minister's knowledge? That was puzzling. But even the remotest village has generally some channel of communication with the great city—some curious rustic, who has a brother or cousin living within sound of Bow Bells, and is occasionally gratified by his city friend with a dish of scandal. No latest rumour, or darkest insinuation about courts or princes, so interesting to Mr. Chawbacon as the news of his brother parishioner's doings ' up in London.'

There stood Oswald's two big trunks in the deep recess by the chimney, one on the top of the other, just as they had been placed when the coach brought them back from Exeter. Might not one of these hold the clue to their owner's intentions when he left his home? Arnold had his sea-going tool chest close at hand. He had a good deal of mechanical skill, and had always rigged up his own cabin, with the book-shelves and three-cornered brackets, and small conveniences that give a comfortable and civilised air to an apartment which, to the landsman's eye, looks like an exaggerated rabbit-hutch.

Arnold had picked the lock of the topmost trunk before he had time to reason upon his idea. It was an old leather-covered trunk of his father's; black with age, and iron-clamped at the corners, and so heavy in itself that it was a matter of comparative indifference to the person who carried it whether it was full or empty. Arnold lifted the lid with a curiously nervous feeling, as if some sudden and appalling revelation were lurking immediately beneath it.

This uppermost trunk contained Oswald's modest collection of books—the well-thumbed Shakespeare and Byron, the queer little duodecimo Tom Jones, and Joseph Andrews; Arnold took them up one by one, and looked at them tenderly. He too was a worshipper of that poetic star so lately set, and carried ' Childe Harold ' and ' Don Juan ' in his sea-chest, and had sat dreaming over their pages many a night, with no other light to read by than the broad tropical moon; he too was a lover of Shakespeare and of Fielding. He turned over the leaves of that

battered old Byron meditatively, and it seemed to him that
the volume opened at the saddest passages, as if the reader had
dwelt with morbid fondness upon the complainings of a kindred
despair.

Below the books there was an old leather writing-desk, and
below that nothing but clothes and boots, packed with a careless
roughness, which indicated haste or pre-occupation of mind on the
part of the packer. In all the contents Arnold saw nothing that
tended to his enlightenment, and he began to replace the things,
putting them in carefully, with an orderly closeness of arrangement which reduced their bulk considerably.

He put in the books one by one, and had nearly finished his
task, when his attention was caught by a shabby little volume
without any title on the back, which had hitherto escaped his
notice. It was bound in red morocco, and had grown dingy from
much usage.

Arnold opened the book. It was a manuscript book, containing
entries in Oswald's penmanship, alternated with pencil sketches,
and here and there a few verses, with much interlineation and
alteration, to denote the throes of composition.

'This must tell me something,' thought the sailor.

The pencil revealed the tastes of the owner of the little volume.
The first pages were full of marine sketches, pencil dottings of
familiar bits of coast. They brought back the memory of Arnold's
boyhood—those old days when his chief delight was to get on board
one of the fishermen's boats, and to be out at sea from dawn to sunset, or—better still—from sunset to sunrise. He had offended his
father many a time by these unauthorised excursions, and his final
offence had been an absence of three days and nights at the
beginning of the pilchard season. He had come home and begged
pardon for his wrong-doing, but the Squire, who had suffered some
pangs of paternal anxiety for the first time in his life, resented
this trifling with his finer feelings, and gave the truant a ferocious
flogging. Whereupon the sea-loving scapegrace made up his bundle,
and set out after dark to walk to Bristol.

It was fifteen years since he had seen these picturesque bits
of coast, Clovelly and Hartland Point, and the remoter glories of
Bude and Tintagel. Yes, every angle of cliff, every jagged
rock, brought back the fervour and freshness of his boyhood, the
days when his love of the sea was a worship, and not a merely professional ardour.

There was the 'Dolphin,' pitching and rolling in heavy seas,
or mirrored in summer lakes of sultry calm. There were a good many
attempts at versification in this earlier part of the book, all

savouring of Byron—addresses to ' My Barque,' invocations to storm and ocean, all unfinished.

Here, about midway in the volume, comes a woman's face— Naomi Haggard. Yes, although the likeness is by no means perfect, there is no mistaking the noble brow, the dark deep eyes, with their look of thought; the masses of dark hair. This face was repeated many times: the heavy eyelids drooping, the full eyes lifted, in profile, three quarter, full front; and now the poetic effusions took a bolder flight, and it was no longer the sea, but his mistress, the lover apostrophised. ' To N.' the verses were sometimes headed, or ' Midnight after leaving N.' First love rang the changes in tenderest gushes of sentiment. All the old platitudes, the stock comparisons were brought out, and the conventional Pegasus was duly exercised. He was not a winged horse to soar over the topmost pinnacle of Parnassus, but a quiet cob rather, warranted easy to ride and drive, a steed that took his rider over familiar ground at a gentle trot, and never showed the slightest inclination to bolt with him.

The middle of the book was entirely filled with sketches of Naomi, and verses to Naomi, and here and there a faint murmur against Naomi's coldness jotted down in prose. Then came a change: Naomi disappeared altogether; there were no more poetic efforts, but page after page closely written—a journal, evidently, kept from day to day. The earliest date was in the March of the previous year.

And now appeared a face which was unknown to Arnold; a girlish face, in a Puritan cap, delicately traced, as if the lightest touch of the draughtsman's pencil had not been fine enough to mark the ethereal character of his subject. Sweet face—now grave, now pensive, now touched with a vague melancholy, now with deepest sadness in the tender uplifted eyes —eyes that seemed to pity and deplore.

' This is the woman he loved,' thought Arnold. He turned to the diary, and read a page at random. It was dated April 12, ten days before the Squire's death.

' She is here still. It is a new life which I lead while she is near me. Nothing can come of it but sorrow and parting, yet the lightest sound of her footstep thrills me with joy, an accidental touch from her little hand sets all my pulses throbbing. I cannot be unhappy in her presence—yet despair sweeps over my soul ever and anon, like a cloud across a sunlit landscape. My loved one, my dearest, why did we not meet sooner, or why meet at all? Two lives are sacrificed to a caprice of destiny—a cruel, hard, and inexplicable Fatality, which rolls on like an iron wheel, and grinds men's hearts into the dust. I am almost an unbeliever when I think how Nature meant my sweet love for me, and me for her, and how Fate has come between and sundered us!'

'Poor Naomi! How true and good she is! How noble, single-minded, frank, unsuspecting. There shall be no more reviling of destiny. I will struggle with this wicked passion—struggle and conquer—or if I fail, end all!'

'Or if I fail, end all,' Arnold repeated, musingly.

'Yes, my Naomi, I will remember the days when you were all the world to me—when I had no sweeter hope than a placid life spent in your company, when that calm friendship and reverent admiration which I felt for you seemed to me all that is best and noblest in love. For the sake of those days I will conquer myself and be true to you; and if there can be no more happiness for me, there shall at least be peace and quiet days, and a conscience at ease. Perhaps, after all, those things constitute real happiness, and this fever-dream of passion is but a mock beatitude, like the wild brief joys of delirium, the flashes of unreasoning delight that fire the maniac's brain for a moment, to leave him lost in deepest gloom. Oh no, I do *not* believe that passion means happiness, any more than storm or lightning mean fine weather. Both are grand, both are beautiful; and they leave ruin and death behind them.'

'When honour ceases to be my guide, let me perish.'

'Death hovers near us, and our thoughts are full of sadness. A few days, a few hours may bring the inevitable end. Where she is, there is always sunshine. Her presence soothes me like tenderest music—like the songs my mother sang beside my cradle! 'God help me, for my heart is breaking!'

Arnold read on for an hour. The journal continued in the same strain, with much repetition of motive—going over the same ground very often, as the writer argued with himself, and made good resolves, which were evidently broken as soon as made. It was the old story of a fatal, unconquerable passion. Sometimes the sorrow deepened to despair, and Arnold read with a sinking of the heart, feeling that a man who could write thus might not be very far from the suicide's state of mind.

The name of the object of such an unhappy love was not once written, and there was a general vagueness in the journal which left Arnold considerably in the dark. He only knew that

the woman his brother loved had been one who lived near him—
with whom he was almost daily associated—some one belonging to
Combhollow. Who could she be? Arnold was very sure that he
had never seen the original of those delicate pencillings in his brother's
book. Oswald's likenesses of Naomi were good enough to prove that
there must be some degree of likeness in the other portraits—unless,
indeed, these were not portraits, only the semblance of some airy
nothing that lived but in the draughtsman's fancy.

No, the same face appeared too often not to be real. The
face and the confession of a fatal love came too near each other
in the book for Arnold to doubt that the sketches were faithful
portraits.

' I have been to the parish church every Sunday since I came
home, and I have seen no face that bears the faintest resemblance ˉ
to this,' thought Arnold, sorely perplexed.

Naomi could perchance have enlightened him. Naomi must
have known to whom her lover's heart had gone forth when she
lost him ; but it would have been direst cruelty to ask Naomi such
a question.

' And if I knew all, would it tell me my brother's fate ? ' Arnold
wondered, sorrowfully ; for since he had seen Oswald's diary it seemed
to him that self-destruction was no improbable end for the writer.

' When a man once gets out of the right line, who can tell how
far he may stray ? ' thought the sailor.

CHAPTER XXXII.

REPUDIATED.

CAPTAIN PENTREATH went back to London on business of his own.
He had to wind up his affairs with the shipowners who had employed him from the beginning of his career ; and this was no easy
matter, for the owners had rarely had so good a captain, and were
disinclined to lose him. Arnold had made up his mind that his
place was on shore for some time to come. His brother had left
him the stewardship of his estate, and he meant to be faithful to
that trust till Oswald came back to claim his own, if it pleased
God to bring him safely back by-and-by—a result for which Arnold
most fervently prayed. The neglect into which all things had fallen
appealed strongly to the Captain's love of order; there was a
pleasure for him in making crooked things straight. He assumed
the command at Combhollow with as much decision as if he had
been on board ship ; and people obeyed him as well as his sailors
had done; and it is to be remarked that the most popular com-
mander is the captain who is best obeyed.

Business kept him in London some time; but when he went back to Combhollow he was a free man, and his career as land steward lay before him—till Oswald's return. Hope had argued the question with fear, until Arnold had taught himself to believe that the idea of Oswald's suicide was a morbid delusion of Joshua Haggard's, and that, sooner or later, the welcome letter would come from some remote spot of earth, to say that the young Squire had forgotten his griefs, and was happy, and homeward bound.

It was May when Captain Pentreath returned to the Grange, in this more hopeful state of mind. The Exeter coach came in to Combhollow at five o'clock in the afternoon, and after a hasty dinner Arnold went straight to the minister's house. He had made no friendships in his native place, and it seemed to him that Naomi Haggard was the nearest and dearest to him in his home. Had Oswald remained true, she would have been his sister. He felt all a brother's tenderness for her already.

'She shall be my sister,' he told himself; 'my friend and counsellor. Both our lives have been made lonely.'

Mr. Haggard's family had just finished tea when Arnold was ushered into the parlour. Sally had been carrying out the tea-board when she heard his knock, and had been so flurried by such an unusual circumstance as to be scarcely able to deposit her burden on the kitchen table without loss or damage. When she opened the door and saw Captain Pentreath, she gave utterance to one of those suppressed screams with which she always greeted his likeness to his brother. 'It was like seeing the young Squire come back again, broader chested, and nobler looking,' she told Jim, with whom she was on more confidential terms than with any other member of the household. Aunt Judith had gone back to the shop; Naomi sat reading by the open window; Joshua was in his armchair, his head thrown back upon the cushion, his eyes half closed. He was resting himself after one of those pilgrimages over hill and dale which had of late sorely exhausted him. His whole life was much more exhausting than it had been, the candle was being burned more fiercely. Traces of fatigue showed plainly in the sharpened lines of his face, in the pallor of his skin, and the shadows about his eyes.

There was no one else in the room.

Joshua Haggard opened his eyes and started up. He looked at Arnold curiously for a moment or so, as if he scarcely knew him—like a man not quite released from the thraldom of a dream.

'I'm afraid I've disturbed you in a comfortable nap, Mr. Haggard,' said Arnold.

'No, I was hardly asleep—only resting.'

' You look as if you had much need of rest.'

' Do I ? ' asked the minister, musingly. ' Well, the scabbard must wear out in time, I suppose. It matters little, if the sword is only bright till the last.'

' You don't ask me if I have found out anything about my brother in London,' said Arnold.

' Because I don't expect to hear that you have. I have told you my opinion,' replied Joshua, gloomily.

' It is an opinion which I will never entertain until it is forced upon me by positive proof. My watchword is, Hope—yes, Naomi, hope,' he added, turning to Joshua's daughter, who was looking at him gravely, with no answering ray of hope in her sad eyes.

He held out his hand to her, and they shook hands warmly, like brother and sister. Joshua sank back into his chair, and took up an open volume from the table, and resumed his reading, as if to indicate that he had no more to say to his visitor.

This reception was so cold as to be scarcely civil ; but Arnold was not going to take offence easily. He wanted to know more of Naomi. In his mind she was the only person who could thoroughly sympathise with him in his longing for the absent, or in his grief for the lost. She alone in Combhollow had fondly loved his brother. -

He began to talk of indifferent subjects, trying to infuse a little cheerfulness into the conversation ; but there was a leaden gloom in the atmosphere of the minister's parlour which Arnold had no power to brighten. Naomi listened and replied with grave attention.

She was gentle and friendly, but he could not win a smile from her. She seemed weighed down by an unconquerable melancholy.

' Do they ever smile, I wonder ? ' thought Arnold. ' Or has the household always this funereal air ? Is it grief for my absent brother that makes her so sad ? I should have given her credit for strength of mind to surmount such a grief, or at least to hide it. And the parson—well ! I suppose that gloomy cast of countenance is simply professional.'

Despite Naomi's lack of cheerfulness, Captain Pentreath was interested in her. That melancholy look lent a poetic air to her beauty. He felt that she was a woman of deepest feelings, one who would love but once and love for ever. Even Oswald's inconstancy had not weakened her affection. He would have given much to be alone with her again for a little while, to have talked freely with her, heart to heart. He felt as if he could have spoken about his brother, and his brother's errors, without wounding her. But that figure of the minister sitting between him and the light, oppressed him like a waking nightmare. There came an awkward silence presently, and Arnold felt he had no more to say, and must needs take his leave.

He had just risen to depart when the door opened, and a girl with fair hair, pale face, and Puritan cap came into the room.

At sight of him she gave a faint cry and put her hand to her heart, and then, with a great effort of self-restraint, made him a grave courtesy, and crossed the room to an empty chair near Joshua.

' My God !' cried Arnold, turning very pale.

The sudden apparition wrung the exclamation from him before he had time to summon up his self-command. This was the face he had seen in his brother's journal. This was Joshua's young wife, of whose girlish beauty he had heard people talk, but whom he had never seen till this moment, for she had been ailing of late, and had kept much in her own room. And this was Oswald's fatal love—a love so wildly foolish, so deeply dishonourable, that it might well work the ruin of him who harboured it.

Joshua looked up as the door opened, and heard Cynthia's cry and Arnold's ejaculation, and saw the pale, startled look of one, the utter amazement of the other.

' He will be like his brother, perhaps,' he thought gloomily, and an angry shadow stole over his dark face. He looked at his wife as she seated herself quietly near him. She was very white, and her lips trembled. This sudden appearance of Oswald Pentreath's brother affected her as if she had seen a ghost.

Arnold took a hurried leave of the minister and his daughter, made a grave bow to Cynthia, and was gone. He could not have conversed calmly after the revelation which had surprised and shocked him. It was an awful thing to know that his brother had been guilty enough to fix his affections here.

Did Joshua know or suspect the truth ? Yes, Arnold thought, he did suspect, and this suspicion was the cause of his coldness about Oswald, and that gloomy tone which suggested animosity.

Having discovered the fatal siren who had beguiled his brother from the paths of peace, Arnold's next desire was to be able to question her about his brother's fate. Who so likely to be in the secret of Oswald's intentions at the time he left Combhollow, as the woman he loved ? Doubtless he had contrived to see her during his ast brief residence at the Grange, and he had told her what he meant to do with his life.

The difficulty was for Arnold to obtain an interview with Joshua's wife without doing harm of some kind. Joshua was unfriendly and repellant in his manner, very ready to suspect evils no doubt, of anyone bearing the name of Pentreath. Arnold had also to consider Naomi's feelings. It was just possible that she was ignorant of her stepmother's part in the tragedy of her life.

Accident brought about a meeting which could have been only contrived with difficulty. Arnold had been out for a long rambling ride on Herne on the third day after his return to the Grange, and coming slowly homeward in the afternoon sunshine, he overtock Cynthia Haggard walking alone in one of the green lanes just outside Combhollow. She was walking very slowly, with bent head and listless step, like one whose thoughts are far away from the scenes that surround her.

The full western sunlight shone through the young oak leaves, the hawthorns were fleecy masses of white blossom, and filled the air with perfume, the sea glittered above the waving line of the hedge, and through the deep cleft in the rich red bank the little town of Combhollow showed its tiled roofs, and many gables, its mellow thatches, and cool gray slates, and shining ochre walls that seemed made of sunlight.

Arnold slipped quietly from his horse and put the bridle over his arm. Herne, having been as fiendish in behaviour as in name during the first half of his day's work, was now in a calm and philosophic mood, and cropped the young ferns contently.

'Mrs. Haggard, may I have a few words with you?' Arnold asked, gently.

Cynthia had looked up startled at the sound of the horse's hoofs. She dropped a curtsey, and answered nervously—

'If you please, sir.'

'You wonder what I can have to say to you, perhaps?'

'Yes, sir.'

'And yet you must know that my mind is full of anxiety about my brother.'

Her cheek crimsoned, and then paled.

'I am—we are all anxious,' she said. 'It is so strange that he has not written to you. He was not likely to write to anyone else—but to you, his brother, of whom he was so fond.'

'You have heard him talk about me, then?' enquired Arnold.

'Very often. He looked forward so anxiously to your return.'

'Would to God I had come sooner! I might have kept him at home, perhaps. Come, Mrs. Haggard, be candid with me. This mystery about my brother is making me very wretched. Cannot you help me? You may know something, perhaps, which no one else knows—something which might enlighten me as to his intentions when he left home. For Heaven's sake, be truthful with me. Do not be afraid to trust me. I know the trouble that made my brother leave his country. A diary of his fell into my hands a little while ago, with the story of his unhappy love written in it. I know that it was for your sake he became an exile. I implore you to tell me all you can that may help me to discover his fate.'

Cynthia trembled, and grew deadly pale, yet looked at her questioner steadily. There was innocence in the look, Arnold thought. This was no guilty wife—but, not the less, a most unhappy woman.

' I know that he was going to America,' answered Cynthia, 'and I know no more than that.'

' Did you see him on that last day ? '

' I did. But pray do not tell Naomi or anyone else. No one knows of our meeting. It was a secret. He wished to say good-bye to me before he went.'

' Were you the last person who saw him ? '

' I think so. When he left me, he was going to the coach.'

' Are you sure he meant to go by the coach ? '

' He told me so.'

Arnold's countenance fell. This gave a darker aspect to the affair.

' What time in the day did you see him ? '

' About four o'clock in the afternoon.'

' And where did you meet ? '

' Will you promise to tell no one ? '

' Yes, I promise.'

' On Matcherly Common, by the old shaft.'

' I know the place. We have played there many a time when we were children. Are you sure that no one knew of your meeting ? '

' Quite sure.'

' And that no one met you, or watched you, that afternoon ? '

' I saw no one. I do not believe that anyone saw me.'

' My brother told you he meant to leave by the coach ; yet he did not leave by it. You saw him at four o'clock that last afternoon, and I cannot hear of anyone who saw him after that hour. It is strange—alarming even—is it not ? '

' Very strange. But I trust in God that he is safe ; though we do not know where he is.'

' That's an easy way of putting it,' said Arnold, with a shade of bitterness.

' No one can be more sorry for him than I am,' answered Cynthia, with a sudden sob. ' It is my sin to be so sorry.'

' Poor child ! Forgive me for speaking harshly. I fancy sometimes that everyone except myself is indifferent to my brother's

fate. Your husband thinks he committed suicide; but I can't and
won't believe that. You don't believe it, do you?' he asked, turning upon her quickly.

'Oh, no, no, no,' she cried, with a startled look, full of pain, as
if the idea were new to her. 'He would never do that. He would
never be so wild—so guilty—as to shoot himself, like Werther.'

'Who is Werther?'

'A man in a book your brother read to us; but it was a real
person, who was very unhappy, and who shot himself. He did
not seem to know that suicide was a sin. But I cannot believe
that Oswald would be so rash. Oh, no, no, God forbid that he
should be tempted to such a dreadful deed. I cannot think it.
He was very calm when we bade each other good-bye. He blessed
me, and promised to take more heed of serious things in days to
come than he had done in days past.'

'And there was no wildness in his manner? He did not talk
like a desperate man?'

'No, indeed.'

'I thank you for having been truthful and frank. It is a sad
story. Would to God that he had been constant and faithful to
that noble girl, your stepdaughter!'

He could not spare her this implied reproach. His brother's
fate seemed ever so much darker to him after what he had just
heard; and for all this sorrow and uncertainty, the fair young
creature standing by his side was in some measure to blame. Even
that last secret meeting might have been in some wise the turning-point of his destiny.

'Had you been in the habit of meeting my brother secretly?'
he asked presently. 'Had you met him often before that day?'

'Never in my life before,' answered Cynthia, with an indignant
look; 'I should not have gone then, even though he made my
going a last favour, if I had not had a purpose in seeing him. I
thought I might win him back to Naomi. I knew he had once
loved her dearly; and I thought perhaps it needed but a few words
to awaken the old love in his heart.'

'And do you think you were the best preacher to preach that
sermon?' asked Arnold. 'Well, you acted for the best, I dare say;
and again I thank you for your candour. But I am no nearer
the secret of my brother's fate than I was an hour ago. Good-
bye!'

He raised his hat and left her with a somewhat formal salutation, not offering her his hand. There was resentment in his
heart against this fair-faced wife who had spoiled Naomi's life and
his own. He led Herne to the end of the lane, and there

...her house is the way to hell, going down to the chambers of death. Yea, will her feet go down to death; her steps take hold on hell. Away with you, this devil!"

His arm was raised to strike but she fell on her knees and the

mounted him, and trotted quickly home, the sagacious animal scenting the oats and clover in his now luxurious stable.

Cynthia walked slowly on, crying a little in a languid, helpless way, like one who was accustomed to solitude and tears. The sharp sound of Herne's hoofs died away in the distance. A lark was singing loud and shrill in the high blue sky, and there was a drowsy bee among the hawthorns, but all the rest of Nature was silent. Suddenly there broke upon that summer stillness a loud rustling of boughs, and a man sprang through a gap in the hedge and confronted her.

She looked up full of sudden fear, expecting to see some unknown ruffian bent on robbery or murder, but the dark and angry face looking into hers was the face of her husband.

'Joshua! How you frightened me!'

'No doubt. Women who meet their lovers in secret are easily startled.'

'My lover! Joshua! Are you mad? I have been talking to Captain Pentreath, who overtook me by chance a little while ago.'

'By chance! Do you think I am going to believe that story? Woman, I know you too well. Satan set you in my path for my undoing—to the peril and loss of my soul; for my ruin and destruction here and hereafter. Fool, fool, fool!'—this with a cry of anguish, striking his forehead with his clenched fists. 'I ought to have known it was a snare: the fair strange face under the burning summer sky—the gipsy waif—homeless—nameless—a stranger to Christ and salvation—spawn of Beelzebub, why did I not recognise you?'

'Joshua, for pity's sake—I am your true wife—I have honoured and obeyed you——'

'Honoured! Was it to honour me you lured that young man to his doom? Was it for my honour you met him and kissed him? Yes—I saw him holding you in his arms under God's all-seeing eye, clasping you to his breast, as I held you that accursed night when I thought myself the happiest among men, because I had won you for my own. Won you! Oh, thou incarnate falsehood! fair as an angel to the eye, foul as sin to the heart that knows thee. And having tempted one brother to death and doom eternal, you are spreading your nets for the other. You would have him, too. You are like her that waiteth at the street corner, "in the twilight, in the evening, in the black and dark night. Her house is the way to hell, going down to the chambers of death. Yea, verily, her feet go down to death; her steps take hold on hell." Away with you, fair devil!'

His arm was raised to strike, but she fell on her knees, and thus

'I WILL SEE YOUR FALSE FACE NO MORE.'

by a happy chance escaped the degrading blow, and saved her husband that last shame.

'Joshua, what madness has seized you? I never wronged you willingly, as God knows. If I did do you wrong, it is because human nature is weak, and God does not always stand by us. He lets us stand alone a little while in order to show us how weak we are without Him—how soon we stumble and fall when that heavenly hand is withdrawn. Yes, husband, I have been a sinner. God hid His face for a time. Oswald loved me, and I loved him, and forgot my wickedness in the sweetness of being beloved by him. It was like a dream. But when he spoke of his love my heart awakened, and I was your true wife. I have said no word to him —never, from first to last—that I dare not repeat to you, or that I am ashamed to remember. I am your true wife, and honour and revere you now as I did that first day, when you took me to the only decent home I had ever known. Have I forgotten what I owe you, Joshua? Oh, no, no, no. I am not so base, nor so ungrateful.'

'Your speech is like your face,' said Joshua, with set teeth; 'passing fair— passing fair. But I know you, pretty one! Yes; look up, eyes, blue as God's summer sky—look up in sad, innocent wonder. A lie—a lie; nothing but a lie. Satan has made you so: he painted your cheeks, and limned your smile, and every delicate feature, that you might lure good men to death and hell. Can he work without his instruments, do you think? He does not walk this earth in palpable shape, lest we should know him and avoid him. But he puts on such a pretty garb as yours, and counts his worshippers by the score. Every priestess such as you brings a crowd to his altar. But I have done with you. I have rent the net. I will have no further dealings with you. I will see your false face no more!'

'Joshua, have pity!'

'"Can a man take fire in his bosom and not be burned?"'

'Joshua!'

'"He that doeth it destroyeth his own soul. A wound and dishonour shall he get; and his reproach shall not be wiped away."'

'Joshua, can you believe that there was any harm—any wrong against you—in my meeting with Captain Pentreath just now?' cried Cynthia, still at her husband's feet, looking up at him in an agony of supplication, trying to grasp those strong, cruel hands that thrust her from him.

'I know that you are false to the core. I know that Satan made you to lead me down to the pit. What do I know about you and Captain Pentreath? Very little. I was just in time for the fag end of your interview. I came across the field, and saw you through a break in the hedge. You were standing in close converse with him just as you were with his brother——'

'Ah!' cried Cynthia, startled, 'you were there that day—you saw us. You said so just now.'

'The kisses were over, I dare say,' continued Joshua, too much beside himself to heed this interruption. 'The kisses were done with before I came. He heard my step, perhaps, and so left you with a stately salutation, as if you were strangers parting. Hypocrites, liars both—children of the accursed. But I have done with you. I turn my face away from Satan and his witchcraft, and I will make my peace with God before I die. Go back—go back to your tents—to the children of Baal. Go back to your juggleries and mummeries, and leave me to repent of my folly—to put on sackcloth and ashes—to go up alone among the hills—like Elijah in the mountains, to wait for the advent of my God.'

'Joshua, for mercy's sake be calm—speak to me quietly that I may know what you really mean. I have no wish but to obey you. If you say that I am to go away from you—to go back and be a servant, and work for my daily bread as I did before I was your wife—I shall go and make no complaint. But I am your true and obedient wife all the same. Do not doubt that. I will obey you when you are cruel, just as I obeyed you when you were kind—and I shall never murmur.'

'Fair of speech, and fair of face,' muttered Joshua. 'Yes, Lucifer, her master, was beautiful as the morning star.'

'Do you mean to turn me out of doors, Joshua? Do you mean that your home is to be mine no longer?'

'I do. You have brought misery and shame into my house. You have poisoned my cup, turned my daily bread to ashes. I would fain be rid of you for ever. I cannot serve God while you are near me. Satan is too strong for me while he works in such a guise.'

'And you wish us to part,' she said deliberately, 'for ever?'

'Yes. I love my imperishable soul better than that viler human heart which cleaves to you. In heaven there is neither marrying nor giving in marriage. In heaven I shall forget the anguish of an unsatisfied love.'

'Joshua, I am your servant to obey you in this as in all things. You have but to say you wish me gone and I shall go. When you cease to pity God will forgive and take pity on me, because He does not make our burdens too heavy for us. Do you remember that night in the pine wood, Joshua? when you took me to your heart and told me that I was precious in your sight? I said then that I was not good enough to be your wife, that it would be happiness for me to be your servant, and wait upon you and work for you, and gather words of wisdom from your lips. But you would have it otherwise. I was wiser in this, you see, for now you are weary of me, and want to send me away. Let it be so, then ; I will forget that I am your wife and remember only that I am your servant, and bound to obey in all things. I am your servant, and you have dismissed me. I can go back to Penmoyle and work for my living, far away, where I shall not disgrace you. Good-bye, sir.'

She took his hand and kissed it, still on her knees. He shuddered at the contact of those rosebud lips, but never looked at her. His eyes were fixed on the distant sea-line, wide-open eyes gazing blankly at the blue bright light.

'Am I really to go, Joshua?' Cynthia asked meekly, after a brief silence in which the hum of insects, the sharp whirring sound of the grasshopper, filled the air.

He passed his hand across his brow wearily.

'Get thee behind me, Satan. Yes, go, go, go. I can never scale the walls of God's eternal city while this weight of earthly passion cleaves to me. Go far out of my reach lest I should slay you—and think of your dead lover, and repent your sin.'

'What, he *is* dead, then—and you know it?' she exclaimed with a bitter cry.

'Yes,' answered Joshua, flinging her away from him into the dust, 'go and weep and howl for him. It was your sin that slew him!'

She lay for a little while where he had thrown her on the sun-baked grass of the bank, amongst the ferns and wild flowers, not quite unconscious, but with a brain in which strange and familiar images whirled wildly as in a demon dance. Then came a few moments in which all was blank, moments of blessed repose, and then she staggered to her feet and looked about her. The lane was empty. Joshua had said his last word and was gone.

She stood looking round her in the westering sunshine, pondering what she ought to do. Not for an instant did she contemplate rebellion against her husband's decree. He had bidden her to leave him, and she would go away, meekly, uncomplainingly, as Hagar went out into the wilderness.

'Ah me,' she said to herself piteously, comparing herself with Hagar, 'I have no Ishmael to be my comfort and hope.'

It never occurred to her to go back to her husband's house, and claim the place which was hers by right, and which no act of hers had forfeited. She did not even contemplate going back to claim her own—the clothes and books, and small possessions, dear to womanhood, which she had acquired since her marriage. Empty-handed and penniless as when Joshua found her sitting by the water-pool on the distant Cornish waste, she left the scene of her brief and hapless married life. She had neither purse nor scrip, not so much as a few shillings to help her on her way. But she turned her pale face steadily to the west and set out to walk to Penmoyle. In all this wide world she had no other friends than the spinster sisters whom she could turn to for a refuge in her desolation, and even from them she could not feel quite sure of a kind reception. They had offered her their friendship, telling her, on the day she left them, to appeal to them in any hour of need. But how would they receive her when she told them that Joshua had cast her off, they who reverenced Joshua as a saint and prophet?

To them she must needs turn in her distress, having no other earthly haven. She had served them faithfully in the past, and had won their favour, and she was willing to serve them in the future for her daily bread and nightly shelter, and the privilege of worshipping her God in the faith Joshua had taught her. She thought of the white-haired old minister, with his gentle, old-world manners, and his ready kindness. She remembered how his praise had thrilled her at the thought that Joshua would hear of her well-doing and be glad. And now all was over. Joshua hated her. Joshua spurned her as a vile and guilty creature. No man's praise, no woman's favour, could ever lift her up in his esteem any more. She was degraded and cast off for ever.

Well, she could be a servant again, and toil for her bread, and serve her God in patience so long as life's burden was laid upon her. It seemed to her that the road along which she had to carry her burden was not interminable. A little way off there came a region of mist and cloud, entering which she would be at peace, and would lay down her load, and rest her weary head upon the sweetest pillow, and let her tired eyelids close amidst a divine sunshine, light as of the resurrection morning, when the glad sunbeams danced upon the hill-tops.

It was a long way from Combhollow to that little village high up among the rolling Cornish tors. Cynthia could not calculate the number of miles, but she had an idea that Penmoyle was very far away—many days' journey at the rate at which she could walk, which was slow, for her cough and low fever had left her weak.

'Luckily, I know how to sleep under a hay-stack, and I am not ashamed to beg my bread when I see a kind face at a cottage-door,' she said to herself.

She had her silver watch and chain, which she thought she might sell in one of the towns she had to pass through—and there was the gold keeper above her wedding-ring; this too she might dispose of, if hard pressed by want; but if people were kind she could get on without money; so little would serve to keep body and soul together.

So she set out on her journey, a new Hagar, but with no sweet child companion to make the desert blossom like the rose.

CHAPTER XXXIII.

WHAT THE COWBOY COULD TELL.

AFTER his interview with Cynthia Haggard, Captain Pentreath reasoned himself into an easier state of mind about his missing brother. His sanguine nature leaned towards the brighter view of the question. Oswald had been calm and resigned when he parted with the object of his fatal love; he had gone away to begin a new life, had cast off the fetters of passion, and gone forth a free man.

'I shall hear from him in due time. All will be well,' said Arnold.

Having made up his mind deliberately to go on hoping—and indeed entertaining the conviction that the riddle of his brother's destiny would be solved in time—Arnold Pentreath considered it his duty to inspire Naomi with the same hopeful view. It afflicted him to see her pale, sad face, to watch her slow, listless movements. It became his most ardent desire to cheer and console her.

With this end he went very often to the minister's house, and sat in the quiet old parlour where Oswald had spent so many hours of his life, and talked to Naomi while she sewed. There was no one to object to his visits. Aunt Judith was in the shop; Joshua was away, no one knew whither. It was his habit now to come home wearied at night-fall, save on those evenings when he had class-meetings, or Bible meetings, or some kind of service in his chapel.

Cynthia was gone, and Joshua had accounted briefly for her absence by stating that she had gone to see her friends at Penmoyle.

'You had better send her trunk on by the coach,' said Joshua to Naomi.

'But why did she go so suddenly, father?' Naomi asked, puzzled by this disruption of the household.

'Because it was her whim to go, and it was not my pleasure to say her nay,'

' Has she gone by the coach ? '

' I suppose so.'

' And when is she to come back ? '

' When I please to bid her come.'

Naomi sighed, and obeyed her father's order. Alas, for this change which made her father a person to be obeyed with fear and trembling, rather than with faith and love ! Naomi had not forgiven Cynthia for all the misery she had wrought ; but this sudden disappearance of her father's wife oppressed her with a sense of injustice and wrong done by Joshua. With what cruelty had he driven that meek and sorrowful offender away from him ? His daughter had noted his conduct to his wife, and had seen his harshness, his coldness, his growing aversion—the chilling mask which passionate love puts on when jealousy gnaws the heart.

Cynthia was gone, and Naomi's life was now quite lonely. She was glad of Arnold's visit, and took some comfort from his hopeful talk about the absent master of the Grange.

' He will come back to his home and to you, Naomi,' said the Captain ; ' come back a new man, and an honest one, proud to redeem his faith.'

' Were he to come back to-morrow I should give him a sister's loving welcome,' answered Naomi, ' but never more than a sister's love. He has broken my heart once—I won't let him break it again.'

' But if he were honestly repentant and sincere, Naomi ? '

' He might believe himself sincere. I could not trust him with my peace. Do not think that I am angry with him. I am only sorry that he should ever have been so mistaken as to believe in the reality of his love for me. He never knew what love meant till he gave his heart where it should not have been given.'

' Well, Naomi, perhaps you are wise. The vessel that fails to answer to her helm in the hour of danger is hardly a ship to be trusted. Then we will think of Oswald as an absent brother only— and look forward hopefully to his return.'

' God knows I try to hope for it,' said Naomi, with a sigh.

' Why should he not be really your brother—brother in fact as well as in name ? ' pleaded Arnold, taking her unresisting hands. ' Make him your brother, Naomi, by making me your husband. We have not known each other very long, but our mutual sorrow has brought us nearer together than years of common acquaintance could have done. I have looked into your heart, Naomi, and I know its worth. Let me take my brother's place, dear ; I shall never wander ; my love shall know no change. It is founded on a rock—for it was my esteem for your noble nature which first taught me to love you.'

Naomi withdrew her hands from his, and stood up, looking at him seriously with eyes full of tears.

'Never again let this be spoken of between us, Arnold,' she said. 'It can never be.'

'Why not?'

'There is a reason which you must never know.'

'But I am not to be satisfied like that, Naomi. There is no reason that I can recognise—unless you say you do not love me—can never teach yourself to love me.'

'I will say that, then—I can never love you!'

'And your eyes are brimming with tears, and your lips tremble as you say the words. It is not true, Naomi; it is a lie, a lie against the might of love. You love me as I love you, and we were meant for each other, and for happiness. Why should you or I be miserable all our lives because a foolish young man has run away from felicity? Naomi, dearest love, make my life happy.'

'You are good, and I honour you—like him, and my heart yearns towards you,' answered the girl falteringly—for it seemed to her at this moment as if the picture of a new life were suddenly unfolded before her eyes, and the vision was marvellously bright; 'but I can never be more than your friend and sister.'

'I see. You love the truant still. Did I not say so?'

'His memory is very dear to me.'

Arnold said no more. Those eloquent eyes, those tremulous lips, had told him he was beloved, and yet this love was denied him. What was he to think? He was hardly inclined to despair, or to accept this answer of Naomi's as final. She had some mistaken notion of fidelity to a departed love doubtless; she would sacrifice a lover in the present—a real and living love—for the sake of that inconstant lover in the past.

'Patience,' thought Arnold, 'I shall be able to talk her out of her folly sooner or later.'

Meanwhile he was content to be accepted on the friendly and brotherly footing. He contrived to see Naomi very often. He found his way even into the Wilderness, that burial-ground of dead joys and bitter memories. He met her in all her walks. It was difficult for her not to think that her lost lover had come back to her with a nobler mind and larger ideas. Here she found no languid indolence—no placid unconcern for the welfare of others, so long as summer skies were blue, and one could lie at ease under the beeches reading Byron. Arnold was full of care for the labourers on his patrimonial estate, full of sympathy and kindness for the struggling tenant farmers and their industrious wives ; for the young men who desired a little more enlightenment and education than their fathers had deemed needful for the fulness of life's measure. With Arnold benevolent deeds were not castles in the air, Utopian schemes to be set on foot in some convenient hour of the future, but duties to be done at once, now while it was yet day.

Arnold was glad of so intelligent a sympathiser with his cares as steward of his brother's fortune. Naomi was always ready to help him with counsel and experience. She had visited among the labouring poor, and knew their needs and shortcomings—knew where disease found them weakest—how fever crept into their dwellings.

' I can't think what I should do without you,' said Arnold ; and it was a new happiness to Naomi to feel that she had been useful. Life at home was so empty and barren, her duties mechanically performed, her service unrecognised. The change in her father had made the very atmosphere of home gloomy and oppressive.

Cynthia had been away nearly a month, and there had been no tidings of her. This seemed strange to all the household, but as Joshua expressed neither wonder nor anxiety, it was supposed that his wife's absence was understood and approved by him.

' Poor weak-minded mortal ! ' sighed Aunt Judith, after discussing the question with her niece at their lonely tea-table ; ' the first time I saw that pink and white piece of prettiness step across the threshold I knew what he was laying up for himself. A man of his years can't set his heart upon a wax doll without paying the penalty ; above all when it's a doll that has neither parents, nor a good stock of house linen, nor decent bringing up. *I* knew what was coming,' cried Aunt Judith, with a laugh of exultant irony, ' and my only wonder is that things haven't turned out much worse.'

' Poor thing ! ' sighed Naomi, thinking with some touch of compunction of the pale, sad face from which she had averted her eyes so coldly of late. ' Do you think father sent her away ? '

' If he did he'd have done no more than was right,' said Aunt Judith. ' And if he'd done it when I first tried to open his eyes about her he'd have shown himself a wiser man. But whether she got tired of her life here and went off of her own free will, or whether your father sent her, matters very little to us. She's gone,' concluded the spinster decisively, ' and I hope it's not un-christianlike to wish she may never come back.'

Having put the idea of his brother's suicide out of his mind
Arnold had not attached any dark meaning to his interview with
Cynthia. Her statement seemed to him natural and credible, and
rather calculated to reassure than to alarm. Oswald had been
calm and resigned. He had stated his intention of going to a new
world to begin a new life. What ground was there for supposing
that a man in this frame of mind had been so false to manhood as
to take his own life? Arnold sent to an Exeter bookseller for
the 'Sorrows of Werther,' and read the story carefully; but not
being of so sentimental a turn as his brother, and not being in
love with another man's wife, he had found the reading rather a
laborious business, and Werther a weak-minded youth with a fatal
habit of prosing about his own emotions.

'God forbid that my brother should ever follow the example
of such a booby,' said Arnold, when he had seen Werther laid in
his unconsecrated grave, in the memorable blue coat and yellow
waistcoat, with Charlotte's pink breast-knot in his pocket; 'I should
have as much contempt for his want of sense as regret for his want
of religion.'

Arnold had not yet gone to look at the spot where Oswald had
parted from Mrs. Haggard. He remembered the scene well
enough in days gone by; the lonely common with its hillocks
and hollows and marshy spots over which the swift-winged plover
skimmed lightly, vanishing with a shrill cry into blue distance.
The scene was so familiar to him that it had no special significance; it never struck him that just that one spot of all others,
that little bit of sunburnt common by the abandoned mine, might
be fatal, that here yawned a natural grave, ready for the end of a
tragedy.

He went up to an old farm-house one afternoon to settle a
question of roofing and thatching which had been for some time
in discussion. It was the last house on the way to Matcherly
Common, a house that stood on the edge of the wood, or almost
in the wood. The latticed casements looked down a beechen
glade. It was a place of silence and soft cool shadows, a welcome
retreat on a summer's day like this on which Arnold rode over to
settle matters with Farmer Weston about his granary roofs.

Herne had been made happy in a spacious stable where the
good old white waggon-horses dozed over their hay and clover, and
where the thud of a ponderous tail whisked round for the slaughter of
a forest fly, and the slow munching of fodder, were the only sounds
that broke the slumberous stillness. Captain Pentreath had
made his inspection of the premises, and was drinking a glass of
Mrs. Weston's famous perry before departing, when the farmer

mentioned a subject which always found Arnold an attentive listener.

'You haven't heerd anything of your brother, I suppose, Captain?'

'Not a line. But I don't despair of getting news of him before long. He's not been gone a twelvemonth yet, you see, Mr. Weston, and a year is a short time when a man has to cross the sea. He may have changed his mind about America, and gone to New South Wales, and that's half a year's voyage to begin with.'

'That's where the convicks go, ain't it, Captain? The young Squire 'ud never go theer, surely.'

'There's no knowing how far a man may go when he's once made up his mind to turn rover,' said Arnold cheerily.

'Ah,' sighed the farmer, 'this here world of ours be a strange 'un; there's things in it that puzzles my poor old wits, a'most as much as that theer thatch catchin' fire the identical day arter I refused Aunt Nancy the faggit.'

There was a lurking significance in this remark that caught Arnold's attention.

'You have heard something about my brother!' he cried. 'You can tell me something; for God's sake, keep nothing from me; it is a matter of life or death.'

'The by's a truth-spoken by,' said the farmer, 'or I shouldn't ha' listened to un.'

'What boy?'

'It isn't because a by earns his bit o' mate minding cows that he hasn't got a soul to be saved,' continued the farmer, as deliberately as if pursuing a philosophical argument; 'and I can't say as ever I found out this here lad in a lie.'

'Will you tell me what you mean, how this bears upon my brother?' cried Arnold, breathless with impatience.

'My wife and me have sat under Mr. Haggard for the last ten years. He was the first to tell us our souls were in danger, and he's gone on warning of us ever since. 'Tain't likely I'm going to speak agen him.'

'Speak plainly at any rate,' exclaimed Arnold, 'if you mean anything. And from your manner it's clear you mean something. What has this boy of yours to do with my brother's fate?'

'It ain't what he has to do, but what he can tell. It was a hot summer day, you may remember, that day as the young Squire was last seen at Combhollow—harvest time, and regular harvest weather. This lad o' mine, Tim, was out in the forest mindin' cows. But perhaps you'd sooner hear it from the lad's own lips?' suggested the farmer.

' I don't care how I hear it, so long as I hear it quickly ! '

' Well, I'll call the by ; he's close handy, diggin' taties.'

' Let's go to him,' said Arnold, taking up his whip and gloves. The farmer wished to bring the boy to the parlour, as a mode of proceeding more consistent with the respect due to his landlord ; but the Captain was too eager to endure ceremony. He hurried to the straggling old kitchen-garden at the back of the house, where ancient espaliers which had long outgrown their sustaining framework spread wide their arms against the blue June sky.

Here, digging up the smooth golden-skinned potatoes, they found the farmer's cowboy, a frank-looking blue-eyed lad, over whose sun-burnt forehead trickled the dew of toil.

' Now, lookye here, Tim,' said the farmer ; ' I want 'ee to tell the Captain what it was you saw and heerd that day in Matcherly wood, when th' young Squire passed 'ee by.'

The boy wiped his forehead upon his shirt sleeve, shifted his spade from one hand to the other, and after some moments of obvious embarrassment found a voice.

' I were mindin' cattle in the forest, you see, sir, and theer were one cow wi' a white face ; she were a new un that master had boughten' at Barnstaple last market-day, and she were strange, poor thing, and strayed away ever so far up towards the common ; and I was goin' arter her, when who should I see but the minister on afore me, goin' right up to the common.'

' Do you mean Mr. Haggard ? '

' Surely. And he went on ahead o' me, till he come right out o' the wood, just wheer the old shaft be, and he looked about un a bit, when he got clear o' the trees, and then went into the engine house. I watched a bit, wonderin' what he were up to, and then I see un standin' just inside the doorway, where there's a lot o⌐ fallen stones and rubbish, and tansy growin' as tall as young trees, and he stood there lookin' out, yet keeping of himself hidden like as if he were watchin' for somebody. And just then I catched sight o' the white-faced cow, ever so far across the common, and I ran after her.'

' Strange, warn't it ? ' said the farmer ; ' but there's more to tell.'

' I cotched the old cow, and I was taking of her back to the wood, when I comes right up agen the young Squire. I was a bit scared at seein' he, for I'd heerd tell as he were away from Combhollow. He didn't take no notice o' me, but went on, swingin' his stick round, and singin' to hisself, soft-like. Well, I thowt no more about un, and I was here and theer with they cows, and they would stray up towards the common ; though there warn't much but tansy for they to eat up theer ; and I were up close to the common about an hour afterwards, when I heerd a shot fired, and then another, so close together they might 'a been one a'most.'

A white blankness spread itself over Arnold's face—the vacant horror of despair. It was some moments before he could speak.

'You ran to see what those shots meant?' he cried.

'I couldn't tell wheer they come from, not for sartain; but I thowt it was somewheer near the old shaft, and I went up theer arter a bit, but theer was nowt to be seen, and no one about. I went into the engine house, but the minister was gone.'

'Why has this been kept from me?' asked Arnold. 'Why, in Heaven's name, didn't you let me know this sooner, Mr. Weston? You know how anxious I have been about my brother.'

'I only heerd of it t'other day, when I overheerd Timothy talkin' to our Prudence, the dairy maid. He was tellin' her about the shot.'

'Don't you think it was your duty to have told your master, boy?' asked Arnold.

'I didn't think it was any harm. It might ha' been some one firing at a rabbit or a gull. There's plenty o' say-gulls flies across Matcherly Common.'

'You saw no more, you heard no more?'

'No, there was nowt arter that. It were milkin' time and I had to take the cows home.'

'Now look here, Weston,' said Captain Pentreath, taking the farmer aside. 'Those shots may mean nothing, or they may mean a great deal. I know my brother was up yonder, by the old shaft, that August day. I know he had an enemy, and was watched, and followed. I have no evidence that he was ever seen alive after that day. Till to-day I've hugged myself with the hope that he is living in some distant country, and that I shall hear of him in due time. I begin to think that hope is a delusion, and that he never left this neighbourhood. If he has been murdered, it is my business to bring his murderer to the gallows. But I must first find his murdered body. Will you help me? You've plenty of farm labourers in your service. Will you help me to search Matcherly Common, and the mine below it?'

(To be continued.)

LONDON : PRINTED BY
SPOTTISWOODE AND CO., NEW-STREET SQUARE
AND PARLIAMENT STREET

DR. ROOKE'S ANTI-LANCET.

All who wish to preserve health, and thus prolong life, should read Dr. Rooke's "Anti-Lancet, or Handy Guide to Domestic Medicine," which can be had GRATIS from any Chemist, or POST FREE from Dr. Rooke, Scarborough.

Concerning this book, which contains 168 pages, the late eminent author, Sheridan Knowles, observed:—" *It will be an incalculable boon to every person who can read and think.*"

CROSBY'S BALSAMIC COUGH ELIXIR

Is specially recommended by several eminent Physicians, and by Dr. ROOKE, Scarborough, Author of the "ANTI-LANCET."

It has been used with the most signal success for Asthma, Bronchitis, Consumption, Coughs, Influenza, Consumptive Night Sweats, Spitting of Blood, Shortness of Breath, and all Affections of the Throat and Chest.

Sold in bottles at 1s. 9d., 4s. 6d., and 11s. each, by all respectable Chemists, and Wholesale by JAMES M. CROSBY, Chemist, Scarborough.

☞ Invalids should read Crosby's Prize Treatise on "Diseases of the Lungs and Air-Vessels," a copy of which can be had GRATIS of all Chemists.

MAYFAIR SHERRY

36s per doz.

C. WARD & SON
CHAPEL ST WEST MAYFAIR.
LONDON.

36s per doz.

MAYFAIR SHERRY

SWANBILL CORSETS.
(REGISTERED.)

SWANBILL CORSET (Registered). 14 bis, B.—A full deep Corset, especially for ladies inclined to *embonpoint*. The Swanbill is most effective in reducing the figure, and keeping the form flat, so as to enable ladies to wear the fashionable *vêtements* of the day; busk 13½ inches long. Price 14s. 6d. Finest quality, 21s. Scarlet, 15s. 6d.

SWANBILL CORSET (Registered). 51 bis, —Hand-made. Perfect in shape, and producing—even in indifferent figures—that graceful *contour* which is the distinguishing feature of the present style of dress; busk 13 inches long. Price 31s. 6d.
Send Size of Waist with P.O. Order to prevent delay and inconvenience.

Mrs. ADDLEY BOURNE, Ladies' Outfitter, &c.,
97 PICCADILLY (opposite St. James's Church); & 76 RUE ST. LAZARE, PARIS.

MORSON'S PREPARATIONS OF PEPSINE.
HIGHLY RECOMMENDED BY THE MEDICAL PROFESSION.

See Name on Label

INDIGESTION!

SOLD IN Bottles, as Wine, at 3s., 5s., & 9s. Lozenges, 2s. 6d. & 4s. 6d. Globules, 2s., 3s. 6d. & 8s. 6d. And Powder, in 1-ounce Bottles, at 3s. each. By all Chemists, and the Manufacturers T. MORSON & SON, Southampton Row, Russell Square, London.

CHEAP POCKET HANDKERCHIEFS.

The *Queen* recommends all ladies who require cheap Irish cambric pocket-handkerchiefs to try Messrs. ROBINSON and CLEAVER, 30 CASTLE PLACE, BELFAST, IRELAND, who sell these goods at wholesale prices, and being in the town where they are manufactured can frequently supply job lots of ladies', gentlemen's, and children's handkerchiefs, slightly soiled or imperfect, but all pure linen, from 3s. per dozen. Their ladies' fine cambric hem-stitched handkerchiefs at half-a-guinea per dozen, and their gentlemen's Irish linen cambric handkerchiefs with either fancy or tape border, at 3/11d. per dozen, are the best value we have seen. Samples post free.—See *Queen* of March 13th, 1875.

N.B.—IRISH LINEN SHEETINGS AT LOWEST WHOLESALE PRICES.

TOTTENHAM COURT
Illustrated Catalogue

CARPETS—FURNITURE—BEDDI

£5. 5s. SILK COSTUMES

Bodice Made. Silk Recommended for Wear.

Plates of Styles and Patterns of Silk Free on Application.

JAMES SPENCE & CO.
76, 77, 78, & 79
ST. PAUL'S CHURCHYARD.

John Heath
PENS

BIRMINGHAM.

SIGNAL VICTORY AT YORKSHIRE EXHIBITION.
Awarded the only Medal. All Comers beaten.

TAYLOR'S
PATENT SEWING MACHINES
ARE THE BEST FOR
DRESSMAKERS AND FAMILIES,

being simple to learn, easy to
work, quiet in action, not liable
to get out of order. Intending
purchasers, if unable to obtain
Taylor's Patent Sewing Machines from local agents, are
respectfully requested to send
for a prospectus to
97 CHEAPSIDE, LONDON, E.C.

Rook

Possess the follow-
ing advantages :—

1st.—Great Strength.
2nd.—Exceeding Beauty
of Tint.
3rd.—Great ———
and.
4th.—It cannot ——
injure the ——

Patronised by the ———

To be had of all ———

CADBUR

The reason why so many are unable to take Cocoa is, that the ———
commonly sold are mixed with Starch, under the plea of rendering ———
soluble; while really making them thick, heavy, and indigestible. ———
may be readily detected, for if Cocoa thickens in the cup ———
starch. Cadbury's Cocoa Essence is genuine, it is the ———
the strength of these Cocoas, and ———

HW 28JS F

FEB 8 1964

NOV - 15 1969

MAR   1968 H

1663363

CANCELLED

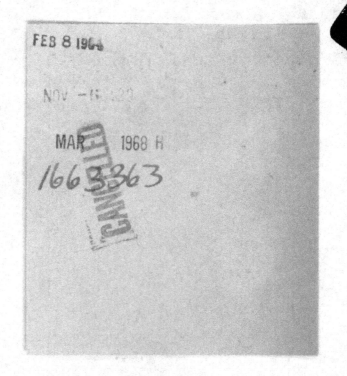

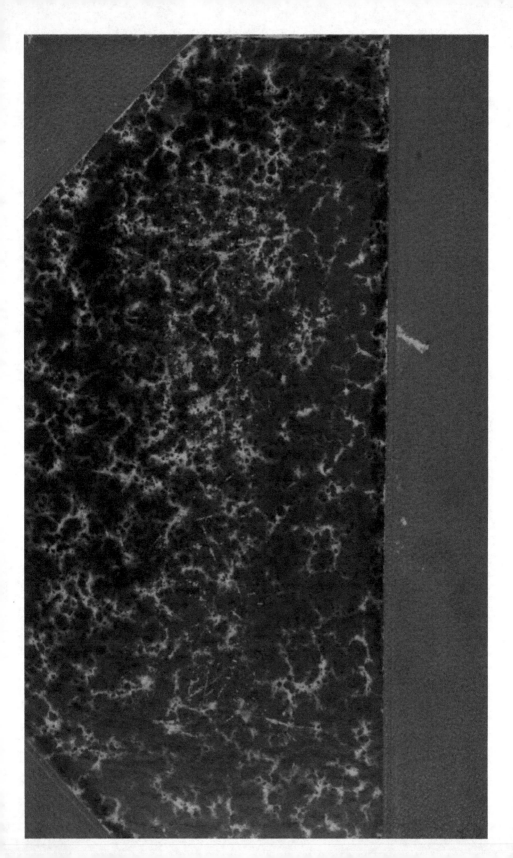

Check Out More Titles From HardPress Classics Series In this collection we are offering thousands of classic and hard to find books. This series spans a vast array of subjects — so you are bound to find something of interest to enjoy reading and learning about.

Subjects:
Architecture
Art
Biography & Autobiography
Body, Mind &Spirit
Children & Young Adult
Dramas
Education
Fiction
History
Language Arts & Disciplines
Law
Literary Collections
Music
Poetry
Psychology
Science
...and many more.

Visit us at www.hardpress.net

Im The Story

personalised classic books

"Beautiful gift.. lovely finish.
My Niece loves it, so precious!"

Helen R Brumfieldon

★★★★★

UNIQUE
GIFT

FOR KIDS, PARTNERS
AND FRIENDS

Timeless books such as:

Kids

Alice in Wonderland • The Jungle Book • The Wonderful Wizard of Oz
Peter and Wendy • Robin Hood • The Prince and The Pauper
The Railway Children • Treasure Island • A Christmas Carol

Adults

Romeo and Juliet • Dracula

Highly
Customizable

Change
Books Title

Replace
Characters Names
with yours

Upload
Photo for
inside page

Add
Inscriptions

Visit
Im The Story .com
and order yours today!

CPSIA information can be obtained
at www.ICGtesting.com
Printed in the USA
BVHW040620130819
555626BV00023B/750/P